John Murray

Handbook for Travellers in Ireland

John Murray

Handbook for Travellers in Ireland

ISBN/EAN: 9783337247713

Printed in Europe, USA, Canada, Australia, Japan

Cover: Foto ©Lupo / pixelio.de

More available books at **www.hansebooks.com**

HANDBOOK FOR TRAVELLERS

IN

IRELAND.

WITH TRAVELLING MAPS.

SECOND EDITION REVISED.

LONDON:
JOHN MURRAY, ALBEMARLE STREET.
1866.

LONDON: PRINTED BY W. CLOWES AND SONS, STAMFORD STREET,
AND CHARING CROSS.

PREFACE.

The Editor has endeavoured by personal visits and research to make this Handbook as trustworthy as possible. He takes ⸺ opportunity of offering his thanks to his many friends in ⸺ ⸺land for the help, co-operation, and hospitality so kindly ⸺orded him during the progress of the work. He would also ⸺commend the proprietors of Hotels, with a few exceptions, to offer more inducements to the tourist by an improved organisation of their establishments, particularly in the matter of cleanliness.

He will feel obliged for any reliable corrections, alterations, or additions, and requests that they may be sent to him, to the care of the Publisher, 50, Albemarle Street, London.

The TRAVELLING MAP OF IRELAND, in two sheets, attached to this work, has been most carefully compiled by Mr. Stanford; and it is hoped will be found more complete and useful for its purpose *than any* other, on the score of clearness and correctness.

An elaborate *Plan of Killarney*, on a large scale, will be found at the end of the Introduction.

Although the following extract from a leader in the *Times* did not give rise to the *Handbook for Ireland*, which was nearly printed at the time it appeared, it furnishes at least a justification for such a guide-book, in pointing out how great attractions for travellers and visitors Ireland possesses, and how little they have hitherto been explored.

Extract from the 'Times,' *Feb.* 29, 1864.

"There is nothing in these isles more beautiful and more picturesque than the south and west of Ireland. They who know the fairest portions of Europe still find in Ireland that which they have seen nowhere else, and which has charms all its own. One might suppose the island just risen from the sea, and newly beamed on by the skies—as if sea and land were there first parting, and the spirit of light and order beginning its work; such is the infinite confusion of surge and beach, bay, headland, river, lake, grass; of land and sea, sunshine in showers, and rainbow over all. Thackeray doubted, and any one may doubt, whether there is in all the earth a grander view than that over Westport to Clew Bay. But the whole coast west and south, indeed all round the island, has beauties that many a travelled Englishman has not the least conception of. The time will come when the annual stream of tourists will lead the way, and when wealthy Englishmen, one after another, in rapid succession, will seize the fairest spots, and fix here their summer quarters. They will not be practically further from London than the many seats of our nobility in the North-Midland counties were thirty years ago. Eighteen hours will even now take the Londoner to the Atlantic shore, and twenty will soon carry him to the furthest promontory of the island. There are those who will not welcome such a change upon the spirit of that scene; but if we see in the beauty of Ireland even a surer heritage than in hidden mine or fertile soil, why may we not hope that it will again cover her land with pleasant homes, and a busy, contented, and increasing people, such as we see in many other regions with nothing but their beauty and salubrity to recommend them?"

May, 1866.

INTRODUCTION. ix

ROUTES.

⁎ The names of places are printed in *italics* only in those routes where the *places* are described.

ROUTE	PAGE
1. Holyhead to *Kingstown* and Dublin	2
2. Dublin to *Drogheda* and Dundalk	19
3. *Dundalk* to Belfast . . .	30
4. Newry to Belfast, through Rostrevor and *Downpatrick* .	38
5. *Belfast* to Donaghadee . . .	47
6. Dundalk to *Enniskillen* and Sligo	54
7. Enniskillen to *Derry*, by *Omagh*	61
8. *Sligo* to Strabane, through Ballyshannon and Donegal .	70
9. Enniskillen to *Pettigoe*, Donegal, and *Killybegs*	80
10. Strabane to *Letterkenny*, *Gweedore*, *Dunglow*, *Ardard*, and Killybegs	85
11. Londonderry to Gweedore, through *Dunfanaghy* . . .	93
12. Londonderry to Belfast, by the Northern Counties Railway .	99
13. Coleraine to Belfast, by Portrush, the *Giants' Causeway*, and *Ballycastle*	106
14. Dublin to *Mullingar*, Athlone, Ballinasloe, and Galway . .	119
15. *Edenderry* and Enfield to Drogheda, through *Trim* and Navan	129
16. Drogheda to *Navan*, *Kells*, and Cavan, by Rail	142
17. Mullingar to Portadown, through *Cavan* and *Armagh*	147
18. Mullingar to Sligo, through *Longford*, *Carrick-on-Shannon*, and *Boyle*.	152
19. Athlone to *Roscommon*, *Castlereagh*, *Ballina*, and *Belmullet*	159
20. *Galway* to Clifden, through Oughterard and *Ballynahinch*	164
21. Galway to *Ballinrobe* and Westport	180
22. *Clifden* to *Leenane*, *Westport*, and Sligo	187
23. Dublin to Wexford, through *Wicklow*, *Arklow*, and *Enniscorthy*	199
24. Dublin to *Rathdrum* and Arklow.—Tour through *Wicklow*	207
25. Dublin to Cork, by Gt. Southern and Western Railway .	219
26. Dublin to Carlow, *Kilkenny*, and Waterford, by Rail . .	239
27. Kilkenny to Athenry, through Parsonstown and *Loughrea* .	251
28. Wexford to Cork, through *Waterford*, *Dungarvan*, and *Youghal*	254
29. Youghal to Cahir, through Lismore and *Fermoy* . . .	266
30. Limerick to Waterford . . .	271
31. Mallow to *Killarney* and Tralee. THE LAKE OF KILLARNEY .	277
32. Limerick to *Tralee*	295
33. *Limerick* to Boyle, through *Ennis* and *Tuam*	306
34. The Shannon, from *Athlone* to Limerick	317
35. Killarney to *Valentia* and *Kenmare*	324
36. Cork to *Kenmare*, viâ *Bandon*, *Bantry*, and *Glengarriff* . .	331
37. *Cork* to Bantry, viâ *Macroom* .	339

INDEX 349

INTRODUCTION.

		PAGE
I.	Physical Geography	ix
II.	Geology	xxiv
III.	Points of Interest for the Geologist and Botanist	xxxiii
IV.	Industrial Resources	xxxiv
V.	Travelling View	xl
VI.	Antiquities	xlvi
VII.	Places of Interest	lviii
VIII.	Skeleton Routes	lxiv
IX.	Glossary of Irish Words	lxix

I. Physical Geography.

Ireland is one of the most singular countries as to physical composition; for whereas the usual arrangement of mountains is more or less in the interior, in this case it is the reverse, the ranges for the most part constituting a belt or rim all around the seaboard edge, leaving the basin of the interior comparatively level. It must not, however, be inferred that there are no considerable heights in the interior, but merely that the general law is stated which seems to prevail over the country. It will be advisable to take the four great divisions of Ulster, Leinster, Connaught, and Munster, and describe them *seriatim*.

1. *Ulster.*—In the county of Down is some of the finest scenery in Ireland. Its S. boundary is the Bay of Carlingford and the Newry River, a considerable portion of the district being occupied with the ranges of the *Mourne Mountains*, which, commencing to the W. of Newry and Rathfriland, speedily attain a great height in the neighbourhood of Rostrevor, Newcastle, and Bryansford. Slieve Donard and Slieve Bingian are the two most lofty eminences, although there are a great number of peaks very little inferior in height. The rivers which take their rise here vary according to their positions. Those on the precipitous or seaward side are rapid and insignificant, such as the Shimna, which runs through Tollymore Park, and falls into the sea at Newcastle, and the Causeway Water at Greencastle. But the high table-lands on the N. and N.E. give birth to the Clanrye, which runs past Newry; and the Bann, one of the finest and most economically important rivers in the country. Its upper

course is past Hilltown and Banbridge to Portadown, where it falls into the waters of Lough Neagh, the lower section belonging entirely to another district. The next range to the N. is in the neighbourhood of Ballynahinch, extending S. from thence towards Castlewellan. Slieve Croob is the highest point. From its S.E. flanks rise the Quoil, which empties itself, after a short career, near Downpatrick; and a few minor streams flowing in or near Dundrum. From the northern face of Slieve Croob issues the Lagan, which, after a roundabout course past Dromore, Moira, and Lisburn, finally discharges itself into Belfast Lough, at Belfast. The district between Down and the Strangford Lough, although bleak and elevated, has no hills worth mentioning; neither has the peninsula of Ards, which extends from Portaferry to Donaghadee. There is a line of rather striking hills extending from Belfast to Newtown Ards, to the N. of the rly.; and of these, Scrabo and Carngaven are features in the landscape, more from their isolation than intrinsic height. The district between Newry, Portadown, and Lisburn consists of undulating ground, frequently rising to a considerably elevated tableland; but from Moira to Lisburn, to the W. of the rly., a chain of hills runs N., with little interruption, past Belfast, Carrickfergus, and Larne, where they gradually subside. Divis and Cave Hill, overlooking Belfast and Duncrue, near Carrickfergus, are the principal heights, gradually declining on the W. towards Lough Neagh, but on the E. offering very steep elevations seawards. The interruption at Larne is, however, only for the breadth of a single valley, for on the N. and N.W. the mountains rise still more suddenly and steeply, forming the lofty range of chalk that extends past Glenarm to Cushendall and Ballycastle, and is only bounded W. and S. by the rly. to Ballymena and Coleraine, and on the E. by the picturesque terrace-road from Glenarm to Ballycastle. This long range is in its turn subdivided into groups by small river valleys, having a general direction towards the great basin of Lough Neagh, which drains the whole of this district, the streams that flow into the sea being little more than cataracts, from the sudden escarpments that the ranges present on this side.

Between Larne and Glenarm are Agnew's Hill, 1558 ft., and Lough Duff, 1262 ft., the group to the N. of Glenarm being separated by the Glenarm brook on the N.E., and the Braid river, a tributary of the Main, on the S.W. Overlooking Cushendall and Waterfoot are Slieveanc, 1782 ft., and Trostan, 1817 ft., on whose western slopes rises the Main, a very considerable stream, that drains the district of Ballymena, and joins Lough Neagh at Randalstown, being separated on the W. from the valley of the Bann by a long, though not lofty, range of high ground. To the N. of these is the Slieveanorra range, which contributes the Glendun stream to the sea at Cushendun, and the Bush, that flows in the opposite direction towards Bushmills; and from this point the hills begin to diminish in elevation, the principal one being Knocklayd, 1695 ft., in the neighbourhood of Ballycastle, although the whole country between this and Coleraine consists of high table-land, with magnificent escarped cliffs along the coast from Fairhead to the Giants'

Causeway and Portrush, where the great river-valley of the Bann forms a marked line of demarcation. In fact, to speak broadly, we may look upon the Bann, from its rise near Hilltown, in the Mourne Mountains, to its termination at Coleraine, as the physical boundary of the N.E. portion of Ireland. The next great mountain district may be defined as lying between the Bann and the Foyle, and bounded on the S. by the rly. from Omagh to Dungannon. A study of the map of Ireland will show that the arrangement of this important group is in the shape of two sides of a square, with rounded corners, connected with lesser ranges both within and outside the square. The principal chain commences between the valley of the Bann and the Roe, at the sea-shore; so close, indeed, that the Londonderry and Coleraine rly. is tunnelled through them. The hills of M'Gilligan, Benyevenagh, Keady, and Donald Hill, overlooking Newtown Limavaddy, are all extremely interesting, both from their marked contour and their geological formation; they follow the valley of the Roe, attaining at Benbradagh, near Dungiven, the height of 1500 ft. Between Dungiven and Draperstown, near the source of the Roe, this lofty chain suddenly changes its direction to run E. and W. The southern chain is grouped together under the name of the Sperrin Mountains, which run with little interruption as far as the Foyle, at Strabane, and have a fine southern escarpment; while on the N. the decline is much more gradual, and several important rivers, such as the Roe and the Faughan, have their watershed. The Sperrin Mountains rise to considerable heights, as Muinard, 2061 ft.; Sawel, 2240 ft.; and Straw Mountains, 2088 ft. The district inside the square, between the rly. and the sea, is principally undulating table-land, occasionally rising into hills of 1000 ft. in height; while between Derry and Dungiven, a defined range fills up the space between the Faughan and the Roe. To the S. of the Sperrin Mountains, which may be regarded as a great backbone, we have parallel ridges, varying in height from 1000 ft. to 1500 ft., an arrangement which is repeated, though with decreasing influence, almost as far S. as Enniskillen; and it will be noticed that the farther we get S., the directions of the ranges have a tendency to run from S.W. to N.E. From Newtown Stewart a range runs parallel with the Sperrins nearly to Draperstown, being separated there by the valley of the Glenelly. Munterlony, 1456 ft., is the principal height. This is separated on the S. by the Owenkillen, from the group which runs from Omagh to Maghrafelt, and terminates near that town in Slieve Gallion, 1730 ft. Between Omagh and Enniskillen is a large tract of bleak elevated ground, gradually culminating in a long irregular range from Enniskillen to Ballygawley and Dungannon. To this again succeeds a much lower chain, running from Lisnaskea to Clogher; and to the S. of this there is nothing to speak of, as the high grounds subside into the bogs and levels of Cavan. As might be expected, the watersheds of the various rivers follow the parallel course of these mountains. Running N. from Omagh to the sea we have the great draining-river of the Strule, which, with its confluents the Derg and the Finn, becomes first of all the Mourne, and ultimately the Foyle; and it is into this basin that the following cross streams flow, viz. the Glenelly and the Owenkillen at Newtown Stewart, and the Camowen at Omagh. A fresh basin is provided, however, when we cross the high grounds near Enniskillen, for the rivers will be observed to flow in a more southerly direction to Lough Erne, which, like Lough Neagh, acts as the receptacle for an enormous district. From the eastern end of the ranges just mentioned the direction of the rivers is towards the latter lake, which receives the Moyola, the Torrent, and the Blackwater, the latter an important stream, rising near Clogher, and flowing thence past Aughnacloy, Caledon, Blackwatertown, and Moy. Before we cross the Foyle into the mountainous regions of Donegal, we must mention a detached group in the county of Armagh, which may be said to be in some degree connected with the Mourne Mountains. It commences a little to the S.E. of Monaghan, and runs past Newtown Hamilton to Newry, the rly. between Dundalk and Newry being carried through the group, and leaving the picturesque summit of Slieve Gullion a little to the l. To the rt. of the line it evidently forms a continuation of the Carlingford Mountains, although, geographically speaking, they are in the division of Leinster. To the N. of Derry lies the district of Innishowen, isolated from its being bounded on either side by Lough Foyle and Lough Swilly. The mountains appear to have been grouped very much according to the outline of the peninsula, Slieve Snaght, 2019 ft., forming a lofty central point, round which the subordinate heights are grouped, such as Squire's Cairn, 1058 ft., near Moville, on the E.; Raghthmore, 1657 ft., on the W.; and Scalp, 1589 ft., to the S.

It is difficult to divide the next great mountain-ranges of the Donegal highlands, which, in fact, comprise the remainder of Ulster, extending from Letterkenny and Lough Swilly all the way to the Atlantic on the W., and to Ballyshannon, with the river Erne, on the S. If a line is drawn between Ardara and Lifford, roughly following the course of the Finn, it will be perceived that the mountains to the N. are all singularly arranged in parallel directions from N.E. to S.W. Outliers of these ranges are noticed in the neighbourhood of Letterkenny rising at Cark and Gregory Hill, between which is the valley of the Swilly, to 1205 ft. and 1111 ft. To the N. of the latter are the valley of the Lannan, flowing N.E., and the Glendowan ranges, which, commencing at Lough Salt Mount, 1546 ft., separate the parallel basins of Garton and Derryveagh Loughs. Although the summits of the Glendowan Mountains in themselves are not lofty, they have a fine appearance from the abruptness with which they descend into the Glenveagh valley, from the N. of which issues the Owencarrow, which falls into the sea at Sheephaven; and from the S. the Gweebarra, a fine salmon river, that joins the Atlantic at Doochary Bridge, after a magnificent highland course through the Glen Laheen.

Immediately on the W. side of Glenveagh are the Derryveagh Mountains, a magnificent range, which, rising gradually from Glen, have their culminating points in Dooish, 2147 ft.; Slieve Snaght, 2240 ft.; and Crockaratarive, 1627 ft. These are separated by a broad mountain glen only from the still more noble groups of Muckish, 2197 ft.; Aghla, 1916 ft.; and Arrigal, 2466 ft., at once the highest and most beautiful mountain in the N.W. of Ireland. A deep pass, entering the vale and lakes of Dunlewy, separates Arrigal from Slieve Suaght, forming one of the grandest though least known views in all Ireland; and from this point the mountains gradually decline, as they border the valley of the Clady to Gweedore. Nevertheless, the district to the N. of this is still elevated and hilly, and at the headlands of the Bloody Foreland and Horn Head, rises to 1038 ft. and 835 ft. The next valley to the S. of the Gweebarra is that of the Finn, which rises in the chain of mountains between Glenties and Stranorlar, near the source of the Owenea; but while the Finn runs to the E., to join the Mourne at Lifford, the latter river has a shorter course to the W., falling into Loughros More Bay at Ardara. Knocklawer, Aghla, Scraigs, and Shuraghy, are amongst the principal heights in the Finn valley, which emerges into the open country at Stranorlar. To the S. of this valley the hills appear to take a rather different direction from E. to W., occupying the whole area between Stranorlar, Ardara, and Donegal, and extending thence through the promontory of Killybegs and Glen. Between Stranorlar and Donegal are the Barnesmore Hills, 1491 ft. through which is carried the road known as Barnesmore Gap, and from whence the range travels westward without any intermission, under the various names of Bluestack, 2219 ft. (at the foot of which is Lough Eask); Knockroe, 2211 ft.; Binbane, 1493 ft.; Mulmosog, Crownarard, and Slieve League, 1972 ft., with its magnificent mural precipices. The streams issuing from these mountains are of necessity short and rapid, and include the Eask, flowing in at Donegal; the Eanymore, Corker, Ballydoo, Oily, and Glen Rivers, all having their embouchures in Donegal Bay. Between Donegal and Ballyshannon the country is monotonous and bleak, though a little to the E. the chain just mentioned continues, with gradually lessening heights, to the neighbourhood of Lough Derg and Pettigoe, extending eastward from thence to Omagh, and brought up on the S. by the basin of Lough Erne. Between Ballyshannon on the N. and the lakes of Melvin and Macnean on the S., the ground rises again to a considerable height; that on the E. terminates in very picturesque escarpments overlooking Lough Erne, and extending nearly to near Enniskillen; and on the S. shore of Lough Melvin we enter

2. *The Division of Connaught.*—The district between Bundoran and Sligo is marked by a very characteristic range of limestone hills, which follow pretty much the contour of the coast, towards which it sweeps down in a fine line of escarpment. The salient points are Truskmore, Benbulben, and King's Mountain. They do not, however, run quite as far as Sligo, but when over Drumcliff Bay suddenly turn round to the E., and continue their course to Manor Hamilton and Lough Macnean. At Belmore Mount, overlooking Enniskillen, they make another sudden turn to the N., to join the high grounds of Church Hill, that run parallel with the W. shore of Lough Erne, and thus form altogether an irregular block of mountains, diversified with many tarns

and lovely streams, particularly in the neighbourhood of Manor Hamilton and Lurgan Boy, where the river Bonet emerges from the picturesque valley of Glenade, in its course southwards to Lough Gill.

To the S. of the road leading from Manor Hamilton to Enniskillen the chain of limestone hills suddenly recommences with still more bold and romantic outlines, and occupies the district between Manor Hamilton and Lough Allen under the name of the Lackagh Hills. The principal escarpments of the chain are to the S.W. of Enniskillen, overhanging Florence Court and Swanlinbar, where they trend to the S.W., to die out gradually in the neighbourhood of Drumshambo and Carrick on Shannon. This portion of the range is particularly famous for containing the source of the mighty Shannon, that issues from a singular cavern or "pot" in Legmonshena. There are also many other features characteristic of the carboniferous formation. The drainage of the largest portion of this block of mountain is provided for by Lough Allen, which may be said to be more or less surrounded by it, particularly on the N. and E. sides; the ranges on the W., although practically part of the same system, being known as the Bralieve Mountains, which rise to the height of nearly 1400 feet (Cashel and Carrow). Notwithstanding the large area of the basin of Lough Allen, few rivers of any size enter it, save the Shannon and the Arigna, a fact which may be accounted for by the proximity of the mountains to the lake. Returning northwards to Sligo, we find it occupying an advantageous position at the mouth of the basin of Lough Gill, which on the N. side is bounded by the outliers of the limestone ranges before mentioned; and on the S. by the abrupt eminences of Slieve Slish and Slieve Daene. A most prominent feature in Sligo landscape is the truncated cone of Knocknarea, which occupies an isolated position overlooking Ballysadare Bay.

The next great batch of Connaught Mountains may be defined by a diagonal line drawn from Ballysadare to Foxford, Castlebar, and Westport, and includes all the barren and wild district of Erris, Tyrawley, and Burrishoole. The ranges of the Ox Mountains and Slieve Gamph extend from Ballysadare to the neighbourhood of Foxford, where they are rather suddenly brought up by Loughs Conn and Cullin. Their direction is from N.E. to S.W., and they attain a height of 1778 ft. at Knockalongy overlooking Screen, although their average is not more than 1200 ft. As they slope steeply towards the coast on the N., the rivers given off on that side are insignificant, the Easky, which runs past Dromore, being the only one worth mention; but from the S.E. flanks issue the Owenmore, which has a northern course past Collooney and Ballysadare; and the Moy, which for several miles flows in the opposite direction, but turns sharp round to the N. near Foxford, and becomes a tidal river at Ballina. From Killala Bay to Belmullet extends a long series of high bleak tableland (having an average of 700 ft.) through the centre of the district running N. and S., forming a sort of lofty ridge or backbone, which commences at Maumakcogh with an elevation of 1243 ft., and rapidly increases as it merges into the Nephin Beg range, a magnificent series of mountains overlooking Blacksod Bay, with the island of Achill on the W., and Clew Bay with the opposite cone of Croagh Patrick on the S. The principal heights are Slieve Car, 2369 ft.; Nephin Beg, 2065 ft.; and Cusheamcarragh, 2343 ft.; which give several small rivers flowing through the wild district of Ballycroy into Blacksod Bay. This range is continued westward into the peninsula of Curraun (which indeed it altogether fills with the hill of Knockletteragh), and into the island of Achill, that contains some of the finest mountain-cliff scenery in the W. of Ireland; such as the rugged mass of Slievemore, the precipices of Croghan, and the cliffs of Minnaun. Between Nephin Beg and Loughs Conn and Cullin, there is the still more lofty mountain of Nephin, 2646 ft., the rounded summit of which is visible for an enormous extent of country: and running S.W. from it towards Newport, are the hills of Berreen-corragh, and Buckoogh, not very much inferior in height. Notwithstanding the large scale of these mountains, very few streams, and these but of small size, issue from them; some to drain into Lough Conn; and some, as the Newport river, into Clew Bay. To the S. of Nephin is the parallel range of the Croaghmoyle Mountains, 1290 ft., intervening between it and Castlebar.

The next great group may be said to extend from Clew Bay to Galway Bay, and includes the principal portion of what is commonly known as Connemara; the boundary on the E. side being the river Ayle, that runs from Castlebar into Lough Mask, and thence becomes the subterranean Cong River, which connects the latter with Lough Corrib.

For simplifying the arrangement, this group may be subdivided into the northern group, occupying the peninsula of Murrisk, and bounded on the S. by the inlet of the Killaries and the Errive River. The whole of the peninsula is occupied by a mass of mountain which does not appear to have any definite name. The N. is principally marked by the wonderful cone of Croagh Patrick, 2510 ft., which flings out its shoulders E. and W.; while in the S., rising directly up from the Killaries, are the towering heights of Muilrea, 2688 ft., Benbury, 2610 ft., and Bengorm, 2303 ft.; from whence a lofty line of hills follows the N. side of the valley of the Errive almost all the way to Westport. Between the Errive and Lough Mask is the range of the Partry Mountains, somewhat monotonous in their outline, which, as they approach their southern termination, become amalgamated with the great mountain system of the Joyce country, that occupies the northern portion of the peninsula, bounded respectively by the Killaries and Galway Bay.

Between the Killaries and the foot of Lough Mask, are Farrennamore, 2239 ft., and Bengoriff, 2039 ft.; and further S., partly separating Lough Mask from Lough Corrib, are the ranges of Benlevy and Lugnabricka, at the foot of which flows the Bealnabrack, separating them from the Mamturk Mountains, and entering the arm of Lough Corrib at Maume. This latter range, of which Shanfolagh, 2045 ft., is the highest point, occupies the area between the valley of the Bealnabrack and the high road from Oughterarde and Clifden, and forms one of the most beautiful series of panoramas in that route, especially at the junction of the cross valley of the Derryclare and Inagh Lakes. These last separate the Mamturk Mountains from the Twelve Pins, which may be considered as the centre of the mountain district of Connemara. Bunnabeola, of which Benbaun, 2395 ft., is the loftiest summit, is a series of 12 singular peaks rising close to one another, and throwing out a number of secondary ranges that extend for a considerable distance; yet, taking the Twelve Pins as a whole, we find a distinct line of demarcation that contributes to give an air of independence and centralization to this magnificent group. On the N. it is bounded by the Gap and Lake of Kylemore; on the S. by the Lake of Ballynahinch; and on the E. by Loughs Inagh and Derryclare, at the foot of which is the singular little hill of Lissoughter, forming as it were the key to this cross-valley.

The remainder of the peninsula of which Clifden is the chief town consists of high rocky ground, relieved by some considerable hills on the seaward side, viz.: Rinvyle, between Ballinakill and the Killaries; Urrisbeg, overlooking Roundstone on the S., with Cashel and Lettershanna, between Ballynahinch and the sea. The district between the high road to Oughterard and Galway and the sea, consisting of Connemara Proper and Iar Connaught, is nothing but a succession of lofty table-lands as dreary and as little known as any portion of Ireland. E. Connaught is comparatively free from mountain ranges, though it is by no means level like the plains of Westmeath; but consists of rocky and poor ground, averaging from 100 ft. to 500 ft. in height. The range called Kesh Corrin, 1183 ft., and Carrowkeel, extends along the W. bank of Lough Arrow, and is there united with the Curlew Hills, over which the road to Boyle is carried; it is, however, merely a continuation westward of the Fermanagh Mountains and the Bralieve Hills near Lough Allen. A range of rather high ground is also found extending from Claremorris to Castlereagh and Elphin; and a second runs from Tuam eastward, crossing the Suck to Roscommon, between which place and Longford it rises at Slieve Baun to nearly 1000 ft. The only other remaining mountains worth mention in Connaught are to the S. of Loughrea, where a considerable block, called the Slieve Baughta, occupies the interval between Gort and the western shores of Lough Derg, extending from Portumna and Woodford to Scariff, at which point it crosses the boundary, and enters the co. Clare.

3. *Munster*.—South of Galway rise the curious bare limestone hills of the Burren country, terminating in Black Head, and reaching a height of about 1000 ft. These slope southwards to Liscannor and Miltown Malbay, between which place and Ennis is the domical mountain of Slieve Callane, 1282 ft. To the E. of these hills is a low tract with lakes running from Ennis to Gort; and eastward of that again rise the Slieve Boughta Hills, the greater portion of which have been mentioned as running into Galway alongside Lough Derg. The interval between these two groups is watered by the Fergus, which, rising near Kilfenora, flows past Castle Clare into the Shannon by a wide estuary.

Between Broadford and Killaloe rises the range of the Slieve Bernagh, separated from the Arra Mountains by the long, narrow channel of the southern portion of Lough Derg and the Shannon. Craig Mountain, 1729 ft. above Killaloe, is, next to Glennagalliagh, 1746, the highest point of the Slieve Bernagh, which is continued to the S.W. nearly to Six Mile Bridge, and separated by a narrow valley from the Cratloe Hills that rise immediately N. of Limerick. Divided from the Arra Hills by the valley of the Kilmastullagh River are the Silvermine Mountains, which are themselves cut off by another valley called Glen Collos from Mount Keeper (2278 ft.), visible for an enormous extent of country. The Slieve Phelim Mountains, a portion of the same group, are conspicuous features as the traveller passes along Limerick and Waterford Rly., and keep company with him the whole distance to Limerick Junction, stretching away to the N., and occupying a very large area between Nenagh, Tipperary, and Cashel. The greater number of the rivers that rise amidst these heights are insignificant, and fall, after more or less meandering, into the Shannon; though the eastern slopes, which overlook Thurles and Holycross, send down tributaries to the Suir, which rises N. of the Devil's Bit Mountain, and runs through Tipperary, and the borders of Cork, Waterford, and Kilkenny, into the harbour of Waterford.

The only hills that remain to be mentioned in the county Clare consist of a series of irregular groups of no great height that run parallel with the Shannon towards Kilrush and Kilkee.

The next district may be bounded by the Shannon on the N., the Tralee and Killarney Rly. on the S., and the Great Southern and Western on the E. Although strictly a mountainous district, there are no lofty ranges in it; it rather consists of extensive tablelands, extremely wild and desolate, and not of a character that affords much attraction to the tourist. These tablelands appear to culminate in the centre, and are known by the different names of the Stack, Clanruddery, Mullaghareirk, and Use Mountains, which, with their extensive connections, fill up the whole area between Tarbert and Newcastle on the N., Listowel on the W., Charleville on the E., Tralee and Kanturk on the S. As might be expected from the large amount of country covered by these hills, a number of rivers take their rise: the Deel and the Maigue flowing into the Shannon; the Geale and the Feale direct into the Atlantic; the Maine, which forms the estuary of Castlemaine Harbour; the Blackwater, with its tributaries the Owentanglin, the Owendale and the Allow, flowing eastward to Mallow and Youghal.

The peninsula of Dingle, lying to the W. of Tralee, is nothing but a broad ridge of lofty mountains, which descend so abruptly to the sea as to leave very little level ground. Nearest to Tralee are the Slievmish Mountains, of which Cahirconree and Bautregarm are the chief points; and close upon them, separated only by a mountain valley, are the ranges of Benoskee and Connor Hill, which further W. rise into the magnificent mountain-peaks of Brandon (3127 ft.), one of the giants of the West. The extreme point of the peninsula is marked by Mount

Eagle, though it is probable that the high ground once extended considerably farther out, as evidenced by the cliffs of the Blasket Islands.

It is difficult to divide the next district, which includes the loftiest mountains in Ireland and the exquisite beauties of Killarney—the cynosure of all Irish tourists. The minuter features of the Killarney Hills have been described in Rte. 31, so that it will be unnecessary to recapitulate any but the broad distinctive characteristics. To the S. of the rly. between Mallow and Millstreet are the Bochra Mountains, which give off streams N. and S. to the Blackwater and the Lee respectively. Having passed Millstreet, we have the very marked ranges of Cahirbarna (2239 ft.), and the Paps (2268 ft.), separated from Croghane by the valley of the Flesk. Then comes Mangarton, with its magnificent subordinate cliff scenery of Glen-na-Coppul and Lough Guitane, together with Torc Mtn., at the base of which reposes Killarney, the most exquisite of British lakes. Divided only by the Long Reach and the basin of the Upper Lake, are the Toomies, Glena, the Purple Mountain, M'Gillicuddy's Reeks, and Carrantuohill, the most lofty point in all Ireland, offering in their river-gullies and precipices some of the finest scenery in the whole island. As the coast is neared towards Cahirciveen the ranges gradually lessen in height and grandeur, although scenery very little inferior to that of the Reeks is found in the mountains that overhang Lough Carra. These ranges with their intervening valleys occupy the whole promontory between the bays of Dingle and Kenmare, S. of which latter is another mountainous promontory which stretches from the hills that surround Glen Flesk to Bearhaven.

Once the tourist in his travel from Millstreet has crossed the watershed of the Blackwater, he descends into the valley of the Flesk, which rises in the Derrynasaggart Mountains, and cuts itself a way between the ranges of Croghan and the Paps, to fall into the lake near the town of Killarney. With the exception of the Laune, the main outlet of the lake into Castlemaine Harbour, the rivers both on the N. and S. of the peninsula are short and rapid, such as the Anagarry, the Carra, and the Ferta or Valentia rivers on the N., with the Inny, Coomeragh, Blackwater, and the Roughty on the S. The latter stream rises within a short distance of the Flesk on the western slopes of the Derrynasaggart Mountains, while from the S. and E. of the same group rise the Lee and the Sullane, flowing in an entirely opposite direction.

Between Kenmare and Bantry the traveller crosses the other range of mountains forming the backbone of the promontories of Bantry and Bear. They extend in a S.W. direction to the very end of the coast, under the names of the Caha and the Slieve Miskish Mountains, and attain a considerable height, rising at Hungry Hill to 2251 ft. The same range is continued to the N.E. of Glengarriff, and gives birth to the Ouvane and the Gomboola—affording in its rocky fastnesses the magnificent scenery of the Pass of Keimaneigh and the cliffs of Gougane Barra. But from this point eastward the picturesque element is on the decline, and the lofty escarpments give place to the long shoulders of the Sheehy and Clara Hills that bound the valley of the Lee on the

S., and that of the Bandon on the N. To the S. of Bantry is the district of West Carberry, which is hilly, though not very lofty, the principal ranges extending in narrow ridges through the promontory of Dunmanus, where in the neighbourhood of Skull they are 1339 ft. in height (Mount Gabriel). The same high ground is continued eastward to the N. of Skibbereen and Clonakilty, until it dies out in the neighbourhood of the Kinsale river.

East Munster may be roughly described as that portion of the country to the E. of the Great Southern and Western Rly., and, although containing some very fine chains of mountains, it has not that systematically hilly character which we have observed to prevail in the West.

Immediately to the S. of Tipperary is the Galty range, extending from Charleville to Cahir. On the northern side the ridge of Slievenamuck is thrown out like an outwork, and is separated by the Glen of Aherlow from the main group, which rises to the height of 3000 ft. in sudden and grand sweeps. The finest scenery is on the southern face overlooking Mitchelstown and the valley of the Funcheon, and containing the celebrated caves (Rte. 29). On the eastern or Cahir side, the Galty Mtns. approach the town pretty closely, but towards the W. they give off gradually diminishing shoulders, which, under the name of the Ballyhoura Hills, are conspicuous in the neighbourhood of Buttevant and Doneraile, and give birth to the Awbeg or Mulla (Rte. 25).

To the S. of Mitchelstown, and separated from the Galty range by the broad elevated valley of the Funcheon, are the Kilworth and Knockmealedown Hills (2598 ft.), a noble chain that forms the northern boundary of the Blackwater Valley, and constitutes the principal features of the landscape during the sail from Youghal to Cappoquin. To the E. of Cappoquin the hills begin to decline, but speedily rise again to form the range of the Monavullagh and Commeragh Mountains (2478 ft.), the loftiest and most striking ranges in the county of Waterford. They differ from the foregoing mountains in having their escarpments all directed eastward instead of to the south.

The streams that flow to the N., such as the Nier, drain into the Suir; but those to the S. fall direct into the sea—viz., the Colligan at Dungarvan, the Tay at Stradbally, and the Mahon at Bonmahon. To the S. of the Blackwater, and, in fact, between Fermoy, Rathcormack, and Cork, there is nothing but a succession of high table-lands, occasionally rising into eminences of 1000 ft., and, in the case of the Nagles Mountains, between Fermoy and Rathcormack, to 1406 ft. This range gives rise to the Bride, a tributary to the Blackwater.

The only remaining mountain in Munster is Slievnaman, a rounded boss of 2364 ft. in height, that rises in singular isolation to the N. of Clonmel and Carrick.

4. The surface of *Leinster* may be designated as the great grazing-ground of Ireland, and is not nearly so occupied by mountains as that of the other three divisions.

Commencing on the N., we have (1) the Carlingford ranges, that occupy the promontory between Dundalk and Warrenpoint, and may really be said to belong to the Mourne district, together with the mountainous ground through which the rly. to Newry passes. The greater part of North Leinster consists of undulating series of hills and plains, although towards the boundaries of Ulster the former predominate. There is a great deal of wild, uncultivated ground to the N. of Virginia and Lough Ramor, rising in the neighbourhood of Bailieborough to 1116 ft., the highest point in the district. This arrangement prevails as far as Lough Sheelin and the rly. from Mullingar to Cavan, on the rt. of which isolated groups rise to 1050 ft. Southwards towards Mullingar, with the exception of the picturesque hills on Lough Dereveragh, the grazing-plains of Westmeath predominate, and, interrupted only by an occasional hillock, such as Croghan, Edenderry, Hill of Ward, Tara, and others, stretch into the counties of Kildare on the S.E., and to the banks of the Shannon on the W. A few miles from Kildare are the low ranges of the Dunmurry Hills, conspicuous simply from their isolation in the plain, and from the singular indentation called the Chair of Kildare. This range, however, is the commencement of long ridges of high ground, which run nearly N. and S., though with a slight westward tendency, for very many miles, even to the borders of the counties of Tipperary and Kilkenny. There are three of these parallel ridges, each of them forming the boundaries of a great river-valley. To the W. are the Slieve-Bloom Mountains, between Maryborough and Parsonstown — a fine chain, rising to upwards of 1700 ft., and showing a very steep face to the S.E. Towards Roscrea they decline in height, but rise again to the S. near Templemore, this continuation being remarkable for the Devil's Bit (1583 ft.), which is visible for a very great distance, and is an unmistakable landmark. A few miles to the N. of it, and just 2 miles N. of the source of the Suir, rises the Nore, which first flows northward, but soon takes a wide sweep, and turns to the S.E., uniting with the Barrow near New Ross, and both flowing S. into Waterford harbour.

The second range, about 1000 ft. high, extends from Monasterevan to Castlecomer and Kilkenny, and forms the boundary of the valley of the Barrow, which rises on the N. slopes of the Slieve-Bloom Hills, and takes a similar course and curve, although on a much larger scale than the Nore. It is the lower portion of this range that forms the coal-basin of Castlecomer, the flat table summits of which are well seen by the traveller by rail from Carlow to Bagnalstown.

The northern course of the Barrow is through comparatively level country, stretching eastward for some distance until brought up by the outliers of the Wicklow Mountains in the neighbourhood of Baltinglass and Dunlavin; but in the course of the river S. towards Borris and Inistiogue, high grounds close in on each side, those on the E. forming one of the loftiest ranges in Leinster. This chain commences to the N. of Newtown Barry, and runs almost as far as New Ross in an abrupt series of heights, viz., Mount Leinster (2610 ft.), Blackstairs (2409 ft.), and White Mount (1259 ft.), immediately opposite which, on the W. bank of the Barrow, is Brandon Hill (1694 ft.).

On the E. side of the Mount Leinster range is the parallel valley of the Slaney, a river not much inferior in length and volume to the Nore or Barrow, and which rises on the skirts of Lugnaquilla, turning to the S. near Baltinglass, and thence flowing tolerably direct past Enniscorthy to Wexford. The picturesque district known as the Wicklow Mountains is after all the great feature of Leinster. Commencing so near to Dublin that its southern suburbs are almost on the slopes of the hills, they occupy a large oval area extending from the metropolis to Arklow on the E., and to Blessington and Baltinglass on the W. The Dublin and Carlow rly. pretty well defines this western outline, for, although at a tolerable distance from the mountains, it rarely loses sight of them. The Wicklow Mountains have not the same parallel arrangement of the other Irish ranges, and to this fact they probably owe a large amount of their wild and romantic features. Beginning near Dublin with Tallaght, the Three Rocks, and Tibradden, they gradually rise in height, up to the lofty eminences of Kippure, 2473 ft.; Djouce, 2384 ft.; and War Hill, which gives birth to the Liffey; while close to the line of coast are the Killiney Hills, with the isolated peaks of the Sugarloaves. To the S. of Kippure the country becomes wilder and more elevated, until it reaches its culminating point in Lugnaquilla, 3039 ft., one of the loftiest mountains in Ireland; and from thence rapidly declines as far as Tinnahely. Although there is much picturesque scenery on the W. slopes of the Wicklow Hills, particularly near Blessington, yet the E. district is more particularly rich in scenery, and more sought after by tourists; and especially the valleys of the Avoca, the Vartrey, and the Dargle, which have a short but exquisitely romantic career before they make their exit into the sea. Between Arklow and Wexford the country is generally low, with a few isolated hills here and there, and to the S. of Wexford, with the exception of the Forth Mountains, there is very little to relieve the comparative monotony of the views.

It need scarcely be added that, in this brief summary of the mountain physiognomy of Ireland, only the most important chains and groups have been mentioned, as it would take too much time, and would be also useless, to make mention of all the smaller hills, which, as far as they are interesting to the tourist, will be found described in the separate routes. The following is a tabular list of the principal heights:—

		Feet.
Carrantuohill	Kerry	3414
Caher	,,	3200
Brandon	,,	3127
Lugnaquilla	Wicklow	3039
Galtymore	Tipperary	3015
Slieve Donard	Down	2796
Cahirconree	Kerry	2796
Mangerton	,,	2756
Bautregaum	,,	2713
Muilrea	Mayo	2688
Nephin	,,	2646
Benbury	,,	2610
Mt. Leinster	Wexford	2610
Knockmealedown	Waterford	2598

		Feet.
Coomacarra	Kerry	2542
Croagh Patrick	Mayo	2510
Kippure	Wicklow	2473
Commeragh	Waterford	2478
Arrigal	Donegal	2466
Slieve Bingian	Down	2449
Toomies	Kerry	2413
Black Stairs	Wexford	2411
Benbaun (12 Pins)	Galway	2395
Douce	Wicklow	2384
Slieve Car	Mayo	2369
War Hill	Wicklow	2250
Slieve Naman	Tipperary	2364
Cushcamcarragh	Mayo	2343
Bencor (12 Pins)	Galway	2336
Black Rocks	Wicklow	2296
Berreencorragh	Mayo	2295
Paps	Kerry	2268
Keeper	Tipperary	2278
Hungry Hill	Kerry	2251
Cahirbarna	,,	2239
Sawel	Tyrone	2240
Slieve Snaght (Dunkerry)	Donegal	2240
Bengorm	Mayo	2303
Bluestack	Donegal	2219
Lugnabricka	Mayo	2193
Croghan	,,	2192
Muckish	Donegal	2197
Cuilcagh	Fermanagh	2188
Dooish	Donegal	2147
Truskmore	Sligo	2113
Straw Mt.	Tyrone	2068
Muinard		2061
Croghan Kinshela	Wicklow	2060
Bengoriff	Mayo	2039
Slieve Snaght	Donegal	2019
Nephin Beg	Mayo	2065
Shanfolagh	Galway	2045
Slieve League	Donegal	1972
Aghla (Finn Valley)	,,	1953
Carlingford	Louth	1935
Slieve Gullion	Armagh	1893
Aghla	Donegal	1916
Trostran	Antrim	1817
Mothers' Mt. (Sl. Phelim)	Tipperary	1783
Slieve Bloom		1783
Slieveanie	Antrim	1782
Slieve Gamph	Sligo	1778
Slieve Croob	Down	1753
Glenagalliagh	Clare	1746
Craig Mtn.	,,	1729
Slieve Gallion	Derry	1730
Benbulben	Sligo	1722

Introd.   1. *Physical Geography.*   xxiii

			Feet.
Knockletteragh	Mayo		1715
Knocklayd	Antrim		1695
Ox Mnts.	Sligo		1685
Raghthmore	Donegal		1617
Sugarloaf	Wicklow		1659
Brandon Hill	Kilkenny		1644
Crockerraterive	Donegal		1627
Devil's Bit	Tipperary		1583
Divis	Antrim		1567
Agnew's Hill	"		1558
King's Mtn.	Sligo		1527
Benbradagh	Derry		1536
Binbane	Donegal		1493
Bralieve Mtn.	Roscommon		1450
Munterlony	Donegal		1456
Sernig's	"		1406
Nagles	Waterford		1406
Mt. Gabriel	Cork		1339
Croaghmoyle Mtns.	Mayo		1290
Slieve Callane	Clare		1282
Benyevenagh	Derry		1260
White Mtn.	Wexford		1259
Mammakeogh	Mayo		1243
Bochra	Cork		1209
Kesh Corran	Leitrim		1183
Cave Hill	Down		1168
Loughanleagh	Cavan		1116
Keady	Derry		1101
Knocknarea	Sligo		1088
Bloody Foreland	Donegal		1018

Before quitting the subject of superficial features, a brief mention should be made of the hydrography of Ireland; a subject of peculiar importance to a country which has such vast water power at disposal, and which is running to waste in seven cases out of ten. From its position in the Atlantic, Ireland is naturally subject to much rain; although, speaking strictly, there is not so very much more actual rainfall than in England, but a great increase of damp, a fact to which the extraordinarily rapid growth and bright hue of vegetation is owing. The average quantity of rainfall is about 36 inches. The following statistics (from Sir R. Kane) show the main arteries of drainage from the interior of the country:—

	Sq. miles.		Sq. miles.
Shannon has a total basin of	4544	Blackwater and Boyne	1086
Barrow, Nore, and Suir	3400	Liffey, Dodder, and Tolka	568
Slaney	815	Erne	1585
Avonmore	200	Foyle	1476
Avoca	281	Bann	1266
Blackwater	1214	Blackwater (Armagh)	526
Lee	735	Lagan	227
Bandon	228	Roughty	475
Galway River	1374	Inny and Maine	511
Moy	1033	Feale and Geale	479

It has been calculated that, taking the average elevation of the country to be 387 ft., there is "distributed over the surface of Ireland a water-power capable of acting night and day, without interruption, from the beginning to the end of the year, amounting to 1,248,849 horse-power." One of the most singular features in Ireland are the Lakes, which in many cases assume the size and importance of inland seas. The larger ones, which would seem to be of such inestimable value with regard to inland navigation, are nevertheless practically useless from their shallow and rocky beds. As an example we may cite the chain of lakes between Galway and Ballina, viz. : Loughs Corrib, Mask, Cullen, and Conn, through which it was fondly hoped that a navigable line might be made, so as to save a large amount of dangerous westerly coasting. Lough Erne contains in the upper lake an area of 9278 acres, and in the lower lake of 28,000 acres, and is mainly fed by the river of the same name. As it extends for upwards of 40 m., a good deal of accommodation might be afforded at a comparatively small outlay between the towns and villages on its banks; although an outlet to the sea is completely prevented by the rapids at Belleek and Ballyshannon.

Lough Neagh has a shore line of 66 m. in circumference, and an area of 98,255 acres. It is fed by the Upper Bann, Maine, Blackwater, and Six-mile Water, and has its outlet only by the Lower Bann. The only feature of interest lies in the river Bann, which is almost a solitary example of extensive natural advantages being turned to good account for economical purposes. Loughs Allen, Rea, and Derg should better be spoken of as broad estuaries of the Shannon, which in its latter half is really made useful for the purposes of navigation. Lough Corrib, which occupies a large portion of the co. of Galway, has been of late years turned to some account in that way, and a considerable trade developed as far as Cong and Headford. Had the unfortunate ship-canal ever come to anything, there is no knowing how much the interior of Mayo would have been benefited, and perhaps the hindrances of shallow beds overcome, and thus the Moy and Galway rivers united. The Lakes of Killarney can only be viewed with the eye of an artist or an angler, and not with any commercial intentions; were any such ever entertained, it is doubtful whether the popular indignation of those dependent on the tourist district would even allow them to be tried. In the smaller lakes, such as Loughs Gill, Ennell, Owell, Gowna, Dereveragh, Arrow, Gur, Cooter, Glendalough, Carra, &c., the fisherman and tourist are the most interested, as they are not sufficiently important to class amongst the industrial resources of Ireland.

II. Geology.

Taking into consideration the extensive area of the map of Ireland, we may feel somewhat surprised at the comparative sameness and regularity of the strata. The great central plain previously alluded to is in fact composed for the most part of carboniferous limestone surrounded on all sides by elevated ground belonging to the older rocks. The more recent formations of the Cainozoic and Mesozoic periods are but scantily represented.

1. The former or Tertiary group consist of clays of the Pleistocene era, and are usually found on somewhat elevated positions bordering the coast. The localities where they have been noticed are on the shores of Belfast Lough, a good example being visible near the Belfast Waterworks; also along the S. E. margin of Lough Neagh, between Washing Bay in the co. of Tyrone and Sandy Bay in the co. of Antrim, occupying a district of 10 m. in breadth, and consisting of alternations of clay with sand and irregular beds of lignite. Tertiary clays (probably Pleistocene) are met with in the co. of Derry, forming isolated patches on either side the valley of the Roe, extending westward as far as Muff, and southward to Dungiven. The shells which characterise these beds consist of Turritella terebra, Cyprica islandica, and Nucula oblonga. Elevated beds of the Pleistocene era have been noticed along the E. coast as far as Wexford. The Basaltic plateau of Antrim, consisting of many flows of lava (basalt often columnar) and stratified beds of ash with lignites, &c., is certainly tertiary, probably miocene, like the leaf-beds of Mull.

2. Cretaceous or chalk formation is exclusively limited to the N.E. of Ireland, commencing near Lurgan and running in a narrow fringe or belt round the coast as far as Portrush, and for the most part underlying the igneous district of which Antrim and a large portion of Derry are composed.

From Portrush the chalk runs S. to the W. coast of Lough Neagh, though occasionally interrupted by patches of limestone and yellow sandstone. On the N. coast especially, the intimate connection of the chalk, trap, and basalt is well seen; for instance, at Ballycastle, where they are in contact on the sea-shore W. of the harbour; at Ballintoy, where ochreous trap may be observed immersed in the chalk; on the Portrush strand, "where a deep hollow is observed at the top of the chalk, entirely filled by the massive overlying trap." At the White Rocks, lumps of basalt may be observed isolated in the chalk. "Whether the basalt in the crevices of the cliffs flowed in from above, or was erupted from below, cannot be determined; taking it, however, in connexion with the isolated and imbedded lumps of very hard basalt, it appears probable that some of the eruptions took place prior to the induration of the chalk; that the chalky paste was then gradually indurated, and afterwards pierced by later eruptions."—*Portlock*.

The junction of the basalt and chalk can be well studied on the road from Portrush to Dunluce; the basalt, which is amorphous, being seen to rest on the drift flints, which in their turn repose on the eroded surface of the chalk proper. Between Ballintoy and Bengore Head, a valley opens to the sea at White Park Bay, in which the lias strata underlying the chalk are disclosed, containing ammonites and gryphites. The same rocks are visible again at the Portrush peninsula, where they are observed to be divided by interposed masses of greenstone, and in fact assume the appearance of igneous rock; but the presence of typical fossils proves that this apparent flint slate of Portrush and the Skerries is lias-shale, indurated by the action of trap in a state of fusion.

Westward, in the neighbourhood of Down Hill and M'Gilligan, the chalk is still observable at the base of the basalt cliffs, and soon trends to the S., dipping at a small angle to the S.E. Underlying the chalk from M'Gilligan to Dungiven, a small strip of Triassic or New Red sandstone is visible; and in some of the deep valleys between Benyevenagh and Keady the geologist can obtain a good section of chalk, greensand, and new red, the whole capped by basalt. Passing upwards from the sandstone, grey indurated marls are met with forming a link between the new red and oolite; and these contain teeth and scales of the following fishes:—Saurichthys apicalis, Gyrolepis Albertii, G. tenuistriatus, Acrodus minimus; all fossils typical of the Rhætic beds. E. of Ballycastle the chalk reappears together with the beds of lias underneath; as far as Red Bay forms a magnificent line of escarpment round by Garron Point, Carnlough, Glenarm, Larne, and Carrickfergus; and is next seen capped by basalt at Cave Hill and Divis, near Belfast. The lias beds are well exposed at Larne, and the new red forms splendid cliffs at Waterfoot. It is also seen accompanying the chalk to the W. of Lough Neagh, in the neighbourhood of Dungannon.

3. The Coal-beds of Ireland are neither of the extent nor of the practical value that they fortunately possess in Great Britain. We may divide them into

A. The Kilkenny and Castlecomer coal-field, an irregularly oval basin running S.W. from Carlow nearly to Cashel, that may be roughly described as occupying the high grounds between the Nore and the Barrow, an elevated table-land "constituting a true mineral basin, in which the strata incline from the edge towards the centre." The following is the general section of the coal-measure series of this district:—

	Ft.	In.		Ft.	In.
Uppermost beds, about	12	0	Intermediate beds	180	0
Peacock coal	1	10	Foot coal	1	6
Intermediate beds	45	0	Intermediate beds	300	0
Stony coal	9	0	Gale Hill coal	0	6
Intermediate beds	21	0	Flagstone series	650	0
Three ft., or Old Colliery coal	3	0	Black shale series	500	0

See *Geol. Surv. Maps and Explan.*, 136, 137.

As coal-mining has not reached a very advanced stage in Ireland, the only beds hitherto worked have been the three uppermost, as lying nearest the surface, the coal produced therefrom being anthracite or smokeless coal, which contains about 96 per cent. of carbon, and is only adapted to certain uses, such as malting. The Nore separates the Slieve Ardagh and Tipperary coal-fields from that of Castlecomer; the Slieve Ardagh collieries, near Killenaule, being some of the best in the country.—(*Geol. Surv. Maps and Expl.*, 146, 155, 156.) The beds in the southern part of the basin, which is sometimes called the Tipperary coal-field, dip at a much steeper angle, and "lie in deep troughs, from which arises a peculiar mode of working, the shaft being sunk in the centre of the trough, and the coal wrought by working upwards on both sides of it."—*Kane.*

B. The Munster coal-field, although extensive in area, is unimportant in results. It occupies the hilly districts in the counties of Clare, Limerick, Cork, and Kerry, embracing all the country between Kilfenora on the N. and Killarney on the S., and bounded inland by a line from Kilfenora through Ennis, Foynes, Newcastle, Charleville, and Kanturk. But with a small exception the whole of this great area shows merely shales, often cleaved into slates, and gritstones, often making good flagstones, the only practicable coal being in Clare, where there are thin beds of culm, from which, however, one colliery-owner clears his 4000*l.* a year. This exception is in the barony of Duhallow, in the neighbourhood of Kanturk and Millstreet. Here are six veins of anthracite coal, three of which, known as the Bulk-vein, Rock-vein, and Sweet-vein, are of tolerable thickness and have been pretty extensively worked. "The coals of the Munster field lie in a series of troughs, the hills usually striking from E. to W., and the strata dipping on either side, N. and S., at considerable angles, often perpendicular."—*Kane.* The coal rocks in Clare are of an estimated thickness of 3350 ft., and consist of

	Ft.	In.
Alternating grits, flags, and shale, with occasional seams of coals	350	0
Limestone band (a good horizon mark)	0	3
Grits, flags, and shale, with thin beds of coal	2000	0
Grits and flags, about	850	0
Dark shales, highly fossiliferous	150	0

They have yielded numbers of plant-stems, together with Aviculopecten papyraceus, Posidonomya, and Goniatites. The grits which are quarried near Kilrush and Kilkee are covered in the most complicated manner by the tracks of marine animals.

On the Kerry side of the Shannon there is about the same thickness of grits and shales, together with three seams of coal, viz.: Hard-seam, Coal Hill vein, and Rock Lodge vein, which have been worked to the S. of Glyn and Foynes. Many characteristic coal-plants and shells are to be found at Foynes Island.

Between Ardagh, Newcastle, and Abbeyfeale, there are some thin beds of coal which have been partially worked. The equivalent of the Munster coal-field will be found in those beds of coal and grit, known in South Wales as Rosser veins.—See *Survey Maps and Expl.*, 131, 132, 140, 141, 142, 144.

C. The Roscommon and Leitrim coal-field differs from the preceding in yielding bituminous coal instead of anthracite. It is generally known as the Arigna basin, and occupies the hill district on either side Lough Allen, exhibiting the crops of three veins.

To the W. of Lough Allen is the valley of the Arigna river, flowing between the two hills of Kilronan, 1081 ft., and Altagowlan, 1377 ft. At the base of the former are the Arigna Iron-works, which were established in 1788 with every prospect of working the coal and ironstone of this district to advantage. After a career of 25 years the concern failed, not from any want of material or inability to produce good iron, but simply from getting into the hands of a parcel of dishonest jobbers, who made the undertaking so notorious, that the very name of Arigna became a sufficient terror to everybody who was tempted to try his luck in mining enterprise.

The three veins of coal, two of which are to be found cropping out at a considerable height of the mountains, are—the Upper Seam, only 8 or 9 in., and only observable at the summit of Slieve ni-Aran (Iron Mountain) on the E. of Lough Allen; the Top coal, 2 ft. 6 in.; the Crow coal, 1 ft. to 3 ft. The coals in the Kilronan Mountain have been principally worked to supply the Arigna Iron-works, from which a tramroad was carried to the townland of Aghabehy. Both in Kilronan and Altagowlan Mountains the beds are much disturbed by faults; in the former " being traversed by at least six faults radiating from the centre of the hill."—*Du Noyer.*

The wonderful results of denudation may be instructively studied here.

" In truth, there is no reason why, at one period of our geological history, the great mass of the bituminous coal-bearing strata occurring in England should not have extended over what is now Ireland; but, strange to say, while this store of inestimable wealth was being preserved in England, and covered by the New Red sandstone, and probably Tertiary rocks, the adjoining portion of the earth's crust was being gradually raised from beneath the sea, and well nigh effectually denuded of its carbonaceous covering."—*Du Noyer.*

D. The Tyrone coal-field supplies bituminous coals. It is considerably disturbed and contorted, and differs from the preceding coal-basins by being partly covered over by New Red or Triassic rocks. It has been subdivided into the Coal Island and Annahone districts, the former containing an area of about 7000 acres, and six workable beds of coal :—

	Ft.	in.	ft.		Ft.	in.	ft.
Annagher	8	0 to	10	Balteboy	0	9 to	3
Yard	2	0 „	3	Derry	4	6 „	5
Braghaveel	4	9 „	5	Gortnaskea	2	0 „	6

—thus presenting the extraordinary thickness of 22 to 32 ft. of solid coal in a depth of 120 fathoms.

The Annahone basin is very small; is bounded on the N. by the carboniferous limestone, and is overlaid on the S. by the new red. There are three beds of workable coal in it.

E. The Ballycastle field is the most singular in its geological position and association with the basalts of the Causeway and Fairhead. In fact, it is altogether covered over by a layer of columnar greenstone;

and were it not for the escarped precipice facing the sea, the coal would probably never have been discovered. There were six beds of coal at Murlough Bay, of which four were bituminous and two anthracite; the coal is now worked out, the only value of the field being now in the ironstone. As the basalt is found lying amongst the coal, a better locality could not be found for investigating how far the production of anthracite is influenced by the proximity of the igneous action; in other words, whether the change is chemical or mechanical. Interesting questions might also be raised as to the age of this coal-basin. The Ballycastle colliery has an additional claim to notice as being the earliest coals known and worked in Ireland, for, it is said, when the colliers were pursuing operations in 1770, they broke into an ancient gallery containing primitive and rude mining implements.

4. The Carboniferous Limestone may be said to comprise half Ireland. Indeed, with a few exceptional patches, the whole of the great central plain is composed of it; and the tourist may journey across the island from Dublin to Galway, Mallow, or Killarney, without touching any other formation. In parts of the carboniferous formation of Ireland a peculiar series is interposed, which is wanting in Great Britain, and necessitates its division into three series—Upper, Middle or Calp, and Lower Limestone. i. We find the former constituting high and romantic ranges in the neighbourhood of the coal-fields, viz.: to the N. of Dungannon and Coal Island, in the magnificent ranges that run from Sligo to Enniskillen and Swanlinbar, and in fact completely encircle the Roscommon coal-field. A large area also commences at Clare-Galway to the N. of Galway, and extends, according to Sir Richard Griffiths's map, in an unbroken surface to Ennis and the Shannon, bordering on the E. the Clare field, and thence continuing southward to form a narrow belt around the S. Munster field. A similar though broader belt is to be found in Kilkenny and Tipperary surrounding the sandstones and grits of the Castlecomer and Kilkenny basins.

ii. The Calp or Middle Limestone is usually an impure earthy or argillaceous limestone, generally black or very dark grey, frequently containing beds of black limestone, separated by partings of black shale. Although fossils are scarce, when compared with those found in the Upper and Lower series, they are of the same typical character, comprising Flustra, Cyathocrinus, Avicula, Posidonia, Leptœna, Orthoceras, &c.

iii. The Lower Limestone forms the bulk of the central plain of Ireland, spreading to the feet of the hills of old red sandstone and other inferior rocks, or running up the valleys between them. The Lower Limestone is generally a good grey limestone, like that of Derbyshire and other parts of England and Wales.

iv. Beneath the limestones there are almost always found some beds of black shale, as in S. Wales, with their flaggy limestones in the upper part, and their grits and sandstones below. These may be called the Lower Limestone shales. They thicken out in co. Cork, and pass into the carboniferous slate of that district.

b 2

5. Lying below the limestone shales is a great thickness of rock, respecting which a considerable amount of discussion has prevailed amongst Irish and English geologists. By the former it is generally claimed as the upper old red, but from the predominance of yellow or white sandstone is usually known (and is coloured by Sir R. Griffith) as the yellow sandstone group, and divided by him into the subordinate groups of carboniferous slate and yellow sandstone proper. "The boundary between the upper old red and the rocks below is a perfectly arbitrary one, since they graduate quite insensibly into each other."— *Geological Survey.* For convenience sake, therefore, it is as well to describe them with the old red, which occupies a large area in the S. of Ireland that may be roughly described as extending from the southern side of the Blackwater to the coast, occasionally interrupted by a valley of limestone, such as the Lee near Cork. N. of the Blackwater it extends to Clonmel (valley of the Suir), and forms the noble range of the Galty Mts. near Tipperary. N. of the Suir, near Slievenaman, we find it again running N.E. as far as Goresbridge, and crossing the valley of the Nore between Thomastown and Inistiogue. In central Ireland it is observed in patches to the W. of Lough Derg, forming the Slieve Boughta Mountains, and from Killaloe running N.E. to Roscrea and Maryborough, surrounding a patch of upper Silurian rocks in its course. In the S.W. districts it is largely developed in the Dingle promontory, the Reeks, and Caha Mountains, and fringing the promontories of Kenmare and Bantry. In the Slieve Mish Mountains at Bautregaum, near Tralee, " the lowest beds seen are red sandstones obliquely laminated, and about 200 or 300 ft. in thickness. Above them is a conglomerate consisting of rounded pebbles, of quartz, jasper, and limestone, cemented together in a base of red sand. Above the conglomerate are more red sandstones and red slates, with occasional calcareous beds or limestones which pass upwards into the beds of the Upper Old Red."— *Geological Survey.*

The Old Red is of great thickness in the Dingle and Cahirciveen formations, for on the S. side of the Black Glen (Killarney) a section is obtained through part of the Glengarriff grits and purple beds which form the lowest series, of upwards of 5000 ft., and Mr. O'Kelly determines one section to the W. of the Blackwater of 8000 ft. These Glengarriff grits and Dingle beds are in all probability the equivalents of the Corn and Brownstones of Breconshire and Herefordshire. The fossils of the Old Red in Ireland are scanty, but peculiar, such as the *Anodon Jukesii*, a freshwater mussel, and the *Cyclopteris Hibernica*—a magnificent fern, a specimen of which in full fructification was discovered near Waterford, and at Killamery, to the E. of Slievenaman.

6. The Upper Silurians are mainly confined to the S.W. district of Kerry, commencing on the S. side of the Blackwater between Millstreet and Mallow, and occupying the greater part of the promontories of Bearhaven and Iveragh, with the western half of the Dingle promontory. These beds are the representatives of the Wenlock and Ludlow beds of Shropshire. On the shores of Lough Mask are strata which Professor

Melville considers to be the equivalents of the May Hill deposits—the base of the Silurians passing upwards into the Wenlock beds. This district between Lough Mask and the coast contains some unusual Silurian fossils, viz. Portlockia sublœvis, Asaphus marginatus, Harpes megalops, &c.

The Lower Silurians are more scattered. They occupy the district from the base of the Commeragh Mountains to Waterford, yielding Ampyx nasutus, Phacops Jamesii, Asterias, Favosites, &c. They then cross the estuary, and cover most of the county of Wexford, running northward as far as Wicklow, where the Cambrian rocks show themselves between Killoughter and Bray. The Lower Silurians are also found on the slopes of the Galty Mts., in a detached portion to the E. of Slievenaman ; and in the centre of Ireland rise from underneath the Old Red in the Slieveboughty, Arra, Keeper, and Silvermine Mountains, extending from the W. coast of Lough Derg to near Thurles and Templemore. We find them again on the E. of the Southern and Western Railway, running from Baltinglass to within a few miles of Dublin, and only separated from the Wicklow Silurians by an extensive district of granite, which commences at the sea-coast in Dublin Bay, and stretches without intermission almost to New Ross.

In the N. of Ireland a very wide district of Lower Silurian prevails, commencing a little to the N. of Longford, from whence it runs N.E. past Cavan, Armagh, Hillsborough, to Donaghadee—its southern boundary being a line drawn through Granard, Virginia, Kells, and Drogheda. The only interruptions in all this long range are in the strata of lower limestone running southward from Carrickmacross, and the granite patches of the Mourne Mountains.

The Cambrian rocks of Ireland are almost devoid of fossils, with the exception of some obscure traces of Fucoids, some well-marked Annelid burrows, and the zoophytes found at Bray and elsewhere, known as the Oldhamia antiqua and radiata.

7. Seven-tenths of the N. of Ireland is composed of metamorphic or igneous rocks. In Donegal we have large districts of granitic and metamorphic schists composing the Derryveagh and Errigal Mountains, interspersed with quartz-rocks and mica-slates. This last is occasionally talcose, or passes into shining slates, and embraces the southern portion of Donegal, including the peninsula of Glen and fully one-half of the county of Derry. The remaining half (except what is occupied by the coal and limestone), together with Antrim, is composed of tabular trap overlying the chalk, associated with basalt (p. xxv). With the exception of the granite masses of the Mourne and the Slieve Gullion range, followed by the quartz Cambrian rocks and greenstones of Howth and Lambay, we have nothing but isolated traps until we reach the granites of Killiney, which extend S.W. through Wicklow nearly as far as New Ross. There are also several isolated trap and granite rocks scattered through Wexford.

The S. W. of Ireland, otherwise so intricate in its geological arrangement, is mercifully free from the complications of igneous rocks, the nearest point where they are found being between Limerick and Tipperary. A good example is seen in the basaltic columns of Linfield (Rte. 30). There are also some detached traps in the central limestone plain, as at Croghan near Edenderry.

In the W. of Ireland (Connemara) they are in great force. Granite extends from Galway to Roundstone, and mica-slate with quartz-rocks occupies the remainder of the country as far as the Silurians of Lough Mask. Mica-slate is seen on the S. coast of Clew Bay, and also forms the greater portion of Ballycroy and Achill.

The mountainous district of Erris is principally quartz, which abruptly displaces the yellow sandstones and limestones that extend hence to Sligo.

8. One of the most remarkable features in the geology of the central plain of Ireland is the drift which may be so frequently observed occupying the slopes of the valleys, and taking the form of long straight ridges. They may be studied by the traveller from Dundalk to Newbliss, from Dublin to Galway, and from Mallow to Killarney and Killorglin. "The drifts of Ireland are divided by some geologists into—1st, Clay Drift; 2nd, Great Drift; 3rd, Escar Drift. The last is supposed to be the effect of eddies, as the land approached the surface. Much of Ireland has evidently been submerged long after the Boulder drift epoch; and the rounded hills of the Escar Drift, being to a certain extent stratified quartz, must have been deposited by currents of water, and not by glaciers or floating bergs."

A few words should be said of the botany of Ireland, not merely on account of its peculiarity, but because that peculiarity bears in a considerable degree on the early geology of the country. The flora of Ireland, especially in the W. and S.W., is of an Andalusian or Iberian type, according to the nomenclature of the late Professor Forbes, who believed that a great continent, which connected Spain and Ireland, was formed by the upheaval of the Miocene Tertiaries, and that this tract bore the peculiar fauna and flora which are still met with in the Azores, Madeira, Spain, and Ireland. For instance, the Trichomanes radicans, found at Killarney, is only found elsewhere in the north of Africa, Madeira, the West Indies, and Western Spain. The Arbutus, indigenous to Killarney, is found indigenous only in N. W. Spain. The Saxifrage, or London Pride, of which there are six species, is confined to Ireland and the Spanish Mediterranean shores. The heaths, again—Erica Mackayana, Mediterranea, and Daboccia, all typical heaths—are of Andalusian kindred. "One of the orchis tribe, Spiranthes gemmifera, grows upon the coast of the county of Cork, and many botanists are of opinion that this plant is not to be found in any other portion of the world. However, more recent observations tend to establish a relationship between it and another species abundant in Western Europe."— *St. James's Magazine.* All these facts, whether altogether tenable or not, are unusually interesting, as throwing light on the early condition of a large country by means of a science which is not generally sufficiently studied with a view to collateral results.

Introd. III. *Points of Interest for Geologist and Botanist.* xxxiii

The geologist should on no account omit paying a visit to the Museum of Irish Industry in Stephen's Green before he commences his explorations in the country, as, in addition to the specimens of rocks and fossils that he will find there, he will be able to obtain the necessary information from the officers of the Survey, who are ever ready to advise. He should also get the small geological map of Sir R. Griffiths, which is reduced from his large one, and only costs a few shillings. The pamphlets of the Survey, called 'Explanations of the Maps,' are the best guides that can be taken for those districts which are described in them, and the sheets of the map of the Geological Survey, which are published separately, should be purchased for any district to be closely examined. They can be obtained at the Museum, or at Hodges and Smith's in Grafton-street.

III. POINTS of INTEREST for the GEOLOGIST.

Pleistocene beds on the W. shore of Belfast Lough, near Belfast.
Ditto at Youghal. Submerged forest at low water.
Escars between Dundalk and Newbliss.
Ditto Clonmacnoise.
Drift at the base of Mangerton and in the Killarney valley.
Moraines and glacier strata in Gap of Dunloe.
White Rocks of Portrush.
Junction of chalk and basalt at Dunluce.
Basalts of Giant's Causeway and Fairhead.
Altered lias of Portrush.
Muschelkalk strata near Belfast.
Cave Hill quarries in chalk and basalt.
Ditto in valleys between Benyevenagh and Keady (New Red fishes).
Annahone and Coal Island collieries.
Billion colliery, Castlecomer. Bellinurus found here.
Foynes Island. Coal - plants and shells.
Ballycastle collieries at Murlough Bay. Coal with and under the basalt.
Mitchelstown, caves in lower carboniferous limestone.
Hills overlooking Florence Court. Upper carboniferous limestone. Pentremites found here.
Lough Shinny, near Rush. Posidonia with both valves found in carboniferous shales.
Hook Point, Wexford. Lower carboniferous limestone. Crinoids in remarkable preservation.
Marble Arch, Cuilcagh, Enniskillen.
Cork. Lower carboniferous limestone. Good Cephalopoda and Gasteropoda.
Carboniferous sandstones at Kilkee. Tracks of marine animals.
Upper limestones of Galway and Lough Corrib. Pigeon-hole at Cong.
Knocknarea, Sligo. Upper limestone.
Lough Neagh. Lignites.
Lisbellaw near Enniskillen. Silurian conglomerates.
Muckross. Yellow sandstone.
Section at Bantry Bay from Glengarriff grits to carb. slates.
Glengarriff grits and Purple beds, Gap of Dunloe and the Reeks.
Flanks of Slieve Mish, Tralee. Yellow sandstone.
Upper Silurians, Lough Mask; Passage from May Hill beds into Wenlock.
Ferritor's Cove, Dingle. Good Upper Silurian fossils.
Chair of Kildare. Lower Silurians.
Kilnaleck, near Lough Sheelin. Anthracite coal in Lower Silurians.
Courtown, co. Wexford. Lower Silurians.

Tramore, Waterford. Lower Silurians; Bala beds.
Bray. Cambrian rocks. Oldhamia radiata and antiqua.
Howth and Ireland's Eye. Ditto.
Killiney. The shore of the bay, at low water, shows veins of granite

traversing mica schist with layers of Staurolite, &c.
Granites of Donegal.
Tabular traps of M'Gilligan and Kendy.
Killamery, near Clonmel. Yellow sandstone. Cyclopteris Hibernica.

For the BOTANIST.

Killarney, Torc, Carrantuóghal.
Portmarnock.
Benyevenagh.
M'Gilligan.
Urrisbeg (Roundstone). Erica Mackayana and Mediterranea.
Pass of Keimaneigh (London Pride).
Cave Hill, Belfast.
Connor Mt. } Dingle, Sibthorpia
Brandon Mt. } Europæa.
Coast near Dundrum.
Slieve Donard range.
Dungiven, Valley of the Roe.
Hungry Hill, Glengarriff.
Devenish Island.

Dargle and Powerscourt.
Muckish and Donegal hills.
Lough Gartan, Donegal.
Narrow Water Castle, Newry.
Slieve Bán, Rostrevor.
Colin Glen, Belfast.
Lough Bray }
Glencree   }
Benbulben, Sligo.
Lough Easke, Donegal.
Grey Abbey, Down.
Valley of the Lee, Cork. Pinguicula grandiflora.
Muilrea Mt. Erica Mediterr.
Burren Mt. Dryas octopetala.

IV. INDUSTRIAL RESOURCES.

1.—*The Flax-plant.*

Of all the articles of commerce yielded by Ireland, flax may be said to be the most valuable, if not the staple trade; and although the flax-producing and linen-making area does not comprise more than a third of Ireland, the numbers of those engaged in the trade, together with its social features, at once stamp it as the manufacture *par excellence* of the country. Although linen is mentioned in early times, it was not till the 17th cent. that it became an article of much importance, a great deal of encouragement having been given by Lord Strafford, the then Lord Lieutenant, and many improvements introduced by Louis Crommelin, a French refugee, who settled at Lisburne. Since his day it has considerably increased, though not to the extent that might be supposed, the number of acres that were sown in 1861 being only 147,866.

The flax-plant (Linum usitatissimum) requires a dry, loamy soil, which is considered by some to be much impoverished by the crop. This is, however, a mistake; for it has been proved, that, if not grown oftener than once in 10 years on the same soil, it is not of an exhaustive nature.

The average yield is from 30 to 35 stones per acre, and the average profit from 4*l.* to 5*l.*, though it has been known under favourable circumstances to have reached as much as 14*l.*

The flax-seed is sown about April, at the rate of about two bushels to an English acre, and at a depth of an inch below the surface, which is then gently harrowed and rolled, great care being taken that the weeds be removed before the plant becomes too high.

The conditions of sowing depend on whether the farmer wishes for seed or superiority of fibre. "When seed is the principal object, the crop is sown thinly; when fibre, on the contrary, as thickly as can with safety be allowed, for the purpose of drawing up long thin stems, and gaining thereby a fine quality of fibre."—*Charley*. The pulling of the stems should be done in fine weather, the next operation consisting in passing the tops of the plants through a sort of iron comb, called a "rippler," the object of which is to remove the flax bolls which are full of seed. The stems, bound in sheaves, are then taken to be soaked in streams of water for from 10 to 14 days, during which period a process of fermentation goes on, dissolving out of the stem a quantity of nitrogen and inorganic material. They are then removed and spread lightly over a grass-field to dry. The traveller in Ulster during the steeping and drying season is not likely to forget it, unless he is gifted with a nose insensible to odours, for the whole country seems to be impregnated with the pungent and filthy smell.

After being taken up from the grass, the fibre is separated from the woody portion by an operation termed "scutching," in some districts done by hand, and in others by machinery, consisting of "a horizontal shaft with wooden blades attached, revolving and acting on the flax vertically." In 1852 there were 956 scutching-mills at work in the country, some by water, others by steam. The flax being now cleaned is ready for market, and is taken by the grower to the various towns where flax-markets are held, such as Derry, Strabane, Armagh, Tanderagee, Monaghan, &c., where it comes into competition with Belgian and other foreign productions. The next process is spinning, the first operation being rough sorting, according to the different yarns required; and secondly, "hockling," in which the fibre is still further combed and cleaned by the aid of machinery, which is now the agent until the linen is finished. The flax is then "drawn" for the purpose of having all the fibres equalised, and is then transferred to the spinning-jennies. The spinning is carried on principally at Belfast, although by no means confined to that city; there are in the whole of Ireland upwards of 82 spinning-mills, containing nearly 700,000 spindles. The various localities are noted for different productions; for instance—Lisburn, for damasks; Lurgan, for cambrics and lawns; Armagh, for heavy linens; Ballymena, for light ones; Keady, for brown and coloured goods, &c. The exports from Belfast in 1861 amounted to 65,000,000 yards of linen, and 13,200,000 lbs. of linen yarn and thread. We must not forget in connection with flax the important trade of sewed muslins, which gives occupation to nearly half-a-million people; or the manufacture of starch from wheat, which is largely carried on at Belfast, 10 firms employing yearly 30,000 quarters of wheat. A vigorous effort is now being made to extend the flax culture to the S. and W. of Ireland, and so far seems encouraging. Munster has now between 3000 and 4000 acres under cultivation, while Kilkenny county alone possesses over 2000. In Connaught, too, notwithstanding the discontinuance of the government grant that formerly existed, the crop has become very popular, and is likely to be more so as the people become sensible of its value.

2.—Agriculture.

Although a dissertation on farming scarcely comes within the province of a Handbook, a few statistics may not be uninteresting; for, apart from the interest necessarily excited by the prosperity or ill-success of Ireland as a social topic, the traveller cannot fail to have noticed the extraordinary conditions of surface which are characteristic of the greater part of the country. From inquiries made in 1862, it appears that the quantity of land under tillage, and the number of live stock, had considerably decreased; there being, in 1862, 2,552,223 acres under cereal crops, showing a decrease of 73,734 acres from the year before. There was a decrease of nearly the same extent in green crops, and what is rather more serious, a decrease of more than 116,000 acres under potatoes. As a consequence, there has been a diminution in live stock in all save the matter of pigs. But, though there appeared a decrease as compared with one year's produce, there was a vast increase if we take an average of the last 20 years; the reason being "that the agriculture of Ireland as a whole is greatly advanced. Examples of management have been extensively multiplied in all districts; in some localities the farming shows universal improvement in the adoption of alternate husbandry and stall-feeding, in draining and building, and the management of manurei and tillage processes; while in other parts of the country no perceptble progress has been made." An enormous amount of good has been effected by the working of the Encumbered Estates Court, which has disposed of lands to the amount of nearly 24,000,000*l*., and established a Parliamentary title over nearly 3,500,000 acres. As a consequence, a large amount of capital has been introduced into the country, bringing in its wake all the modern improvements of scientific farming. Of course in such an extensive area, embracing so many geological formations and soils, every variety of agriculture is to be seen.

In Cork co. the great feature consists in dairies, from which no less than 200,000 cwts. of salt-butter are annually sold in Cork market. Thus in this county grazing lands predominate, although there is a fair proportion of tillage. The district principally consists of old red sandstone, with friable sandy loams, rented at from 18s. to 30s. per acre, and in the limestone valleys at 40s. There are several model farms in the vicinity of Cork, amongst which may be mentioned that of Mr. St. John Jefferies, at Blarney, who farms 2500 acres; and the Duke of Devonshire's model farm at Lismore.

The land in co. Kerry is not nearly so rich, most farms having bog or mountain land in connexion, the value being estimated by the "collop," equal to the maintenance of one cow; so that a farm contains so many collops, according to its size and qualities. The wild mountains maintain a good many sheep and cattle, of which the far-famed Kerry cow is a peculiar feature; though, in consequence of the fancy prices given by Englishmen, the true Kerry breed is very scarce. In the lands which border the Lakes of Killarney a good deal of fine wheat is grown.

There is productive grass and tillage land in co. Limerick, particularly along the banks of the Shannon, where the alluvial land called "carcass" is of extraordinarily rich quality, and yields $3\frac{1}{2}$ tons to the acre, without flooding or manure. The best farming will be found on Lord Dunraven's estate at Adare, and in the neighbourhood of Rathkeale.

Tipperary possesses grazing-lands of high quality and fertility, and supports a large class of graziers and dairymen. No county can show more improvement than Galway, which supports a great number of sheep and cattle, and has, particularly in the E. districts, some very fine farms, such as that of Mr. Pollock, near Ballinasloe (Rte. 14). In the neighbourhood of Clifden, too, a considerable amount of improvement and reclamation of barren lands has taken place.

Mayo embraces a quantity of small farms, "exhibiting the same sloth, waste, and poverty that characterised them generations ago." The Earl of Lucan is the great landholder in this county, and cultivates one of the best estates in Ireland at Castlebar.

Roscommon is a producer of sheep and horned stock, which thrive well on the rich grazing-lands produced by the overflowings of the Suck and the Shannon. From hence, right through the centre of Ireland, including Westmeath and Meath, we find the principal grazing district, by far the greatest number and the best sort of stock fattening in these pastures. Westmeath contains also a certain amount of tillage as well as grazing farms. Cavan is a butter country, with much grass depastured by cattle, but few sheep; but to the N. we enter quite a different character of land, Tyrone being principally plough-land and lea under grazing or hay. The neat English appearance of the farm-steadings is a great contrast to the slovenly look of those in the W. "Both Tyrone and Derry display minute farming of good corn-land, unadapted for permanent pasture, by an industrious, thrifty population, mainly dependent upon flax, oats, and potatoes, and prospering and improving under the security of tenure obtained by peculiar Ulster tenant-right."

The flax-crop, the particulars of which are detailed in p. xxx, is a staple produce in Derry, Tyrone, Antrim, and Down, and exercises a peculiar and characteristic influence over the husbandry of the districts. In the wilds of Donegal a vast amount of reformation is needed amongst the thinly-scattered and poor population, though a great improvement has already been effected by the labours of Lord George Hill in his Gweedore estate (Rte. 10).

Along the E. coast we find that Kildare is about the best-farmed county, and Waterford the worst; the former containing fine tillage land, with large, well-kept farms; and the latter presenting wretched small-farm husbandry, "with half-starved oat-crops, and lazy-bed potatoes; yet with localities exhibiting great advance, where good landlords and considerate agents are assisting in building and draining, and generally instructing the tenants in better modes of farming."

"The tenure of landed property varies considerably. Formerly the custom prevailed of granting leases, either in perpetuity, for 999 years, or for lives renewable for ever, with or without renewal fine. Hence some of the owners of very large estates receive a very small share of the actual profits. The leases commonly granted at present are for 61, 31, or 21 years, with very frequently a life or lives. Estates are of every extent, from a very small quantity to 50,000 acres, and every holder who has under-tenants assumes the grade and bearings of a gentleman. Hence the class of respectable yeomen is scarcely known. The cottier system, by which the occupying tenant receives a patch of land, in part or whole payment of wages, and that of rundale, in which a large tract is held by a number of individuals in common, are still prevalent in places."—*Thom's 'Directory.'*

3.—*Minerals.*

A. *Coal.*—The geology of the Irish coal-fields has been explained in p. xxvi, and it only now remains to give their statistical produce. According to the last Mining Records, the following is the number of collieries, of which about one-third were not working:—

Ballycastle coal-basin 2	Munster (Slieve Ardagh) .. 15
Tyrone ,, ... 3	,, (Kanturk) 2
Leitrim ,, ... 7	,, (Limerick) 7
Castlecomer and Carlow .. 33	

The total produce of the coal-fields was 120,630 tons, of which 80,420 tons were anthracite. Coal-mining is, however, carried on in too desultory a manner to be considered as a national branch of commerce as it is in Great Britain, from which country, consequently, nine-tenths of the whole supply is brought.

B. Although *Turf* cannot be called a mineral, yet its general substitution for the purposes of coal entitles it to consideration amongst the industrial resources of Ireland. Indeed, no tourist can help being struck with the vast amount of turf which he sees either being cut or stacked for drying in the inland counties, or with the universal topic of conversation with respect to the turf-crop, the success or ill-success of which brings comfort or tribulation to hundreds and thousands of poor families. Various attempts have been made to dry and compress peat, so as to utilise it instead of coal, and a company is working at Ballymena with that object. The late Lord Willoughby d'Eresby and Mr. Charles Williams paid much attention to the subject, and the latter brought several plans into operation; one of which was, to dry the turf and then impregnate it with tar, by which it was rendered incapable of absorbing more moisture, and made more calorific. Another plan was to break up the fibre of the fresh-cut turf, and then subject it to strong hydraulic pressure, by which the water was driven out. This compressed peat costs only about 5s. per ton, and moreover makes a very fine coke, the density of which is greater than that of wood charcoal.

C. *Iron.*—Although iron-ore in some shape or other is plentiful in Ireland, iron-making is, with one exception, not carried on at all; a fact partly owing to the difficulty of obtaining the necessary fuel for smelting purposes, and partly to the disrepute brought on iron-making undertakings by the affairs of the Arigna Company (p. xxviii), which gave a complete check to the development of the trade. The brown hydrated oxide occurs in abundance in the Tyrone coal-field, together with clay ironstone in the Connaught and Leinster fields; in the former being so abundant (at Arigna) as to have given the name of Slieve-ni-arान (Iron Mountain) to one of the hills.

In the western districts of Achill and Donegal a large quantity of bog-iron ore is raised and shipped for Liverpool. It is valuable from its easy fusibility, and its adaptation to fine castings.

In 1858, 1000 tons of spathose and hydrate oxide, and 2000 tons of blackband from the Belfast district, were imported.

D. *Lead* is extensively diffused in Ireland, though principally worked in the granite districts of Dublin and Wicklow, "the veins crossing in an oblique direction the junction of the granite with the mica slate." The Lugganure vein is the finest in the district, having been traced for 900 fathoms, and being usually 5 ft. wide, yielding about 4 tons of galena to the cubic fathom. The Lugganure and Glendalough mines yielded, in 1858, 1495 tons of lead-ore and 2828 of silver-ore.

The principal mines in Ireland are at Newtownards, co. Down, the College mines in Armagh, and some mines in Waterford; the total produce of ore being 2298 tons, yielding 1407 of lead. The Mining Company of Ireland have large smelting-works at Ballycorus, near Bray.

E. The *Copper*-mines have been divided by Sir Robert Kane into three groups:—

1. The Wicklow group, which comprises the works at Ballymurtagh, Tigroney, Cronebane, and Connoree (Rte. 24).

2. The Waterford group embraces the mines at Knockmahon. Here the copper-lodes consist of quartz, and produce native copper, sulphuret, black oxide, and grey copper-ore.

3. The Cork and Kerry group contains the Audley, Roaring Water, Skull, Ballydehob, and the Allihies mines near Berehaven.

The ores of nearly all these mines find their way to the Swansea smelting-houses, and yielded, in 1857, 8000 tons of ore, producing 916 tons of copper, of the value of 98,500*l.*

F. In addition to these staple articles of commerce, there are a few others which are only locally important; such as the salt-mines at Duncrue, near Belfast; the gold deposits of Wicklow, at Croghan-Kinshela (p. 214); and the working and quarrying of the different rocks, such as granite, carboniferous limestone, steatite (in Achill), &c.

G. A very valuable industrial resource has of late years been developed in the fisheries of Ireland, which are now being carried on in a systematic manner, the result of private enterprise, assisted by the salutary legislation which has within the last few years happily come into fashion. It is a curious fact, that during the great famine in the west, although salmon and other fish was in abundance, and to be had for the catching, scarce one of the starving peasantry would touch it. Perhaps, if it had been more difficult to obtain, it would have been more valuable. Galway is indebted to Mr. Ashcroft for the perseverance with which he has bred young salmon, and formed a salmon-walk between Loughs Mask and Corrib. The same may be said of the late Mr. Cooper of Markree, who placed salmon-ladders at Ballysadare, and thus created an extremely valuable fishery. The fisheries on the Moy at Ballina, on the Erne at Ballyshannon, on the Gweebarra at Doocharry Bridge, on the Bann at Coleraine, and on the Shannon at Killaloe, are, it is to be hoped, but beginnings of a profitable and economical trade.

V. Travelling View.

The first thing for the intending traveller in Ireland is to make up his mind by what route he shall enter the island. He has plenty of choice from which to select, according to his locality in the sister country, his love or horror of the sea-passage, and other circumstances.

The routes by sea are as follows:—

1. From Holyhead to Kingstown twice every day by the mail steamers, *Connaught*, *Ulster*, *Leinster*, and *Munster*—four of the most splendid and serviceable boats in any country. This is the route patronised by ninety-nine out of a hundred tourists and travellers, from its speed, comfort, punctuality, and short sea-passage. The distance is only 66 m., which is almost invariably performed in four hours.

2. From Holyhead to Dublin direct is a slower though rather more economical way of proceeding. The time occupied is about six hours, as the steamers are more calculated for carrying cargoes than for running at a high speed.

3. From Liverpool to Dublin the distance is 137 m., and the duration of passage 12 hours. This route cannot be recommended, except to the traveller who has plenty of time on his hands.

4. From Stranraer (Portpatrick) to Larne is a convenient and easy passage for those who live in the North of England and want to get to the North of Ireland. The sea-passage is only 2 hours, though the sail up the respective lochs occupies ¾ of an hour more.* From Larne a rly. recently opened conveys the traveller to Belfast. The shortest steamer route, viz. from Portpatrick to Donaghadee, was abolished when the mail station at that port was closed. It will, however, be no doubt re-established, now that there is direct rly. communication from Belfast.

5. From Fleetwood to Belfast is a favourite route for northern tourists, and is in connection with the Midland Rly. The distance between the two ports is 120 m., taking 12 hours in its performance.

---

* This passage has been temporarily suspended in consequence of the traffic being insufficient.

6. From Whitehaven to Belfast, the sea-passage is only 9 hours, but there is not the same amount of travelling accommodation as there is by the Fleetwood route.

7. From Milford Haven to Waterford a mail steamer sails daily, in connection with the Great Western and South Wales Rlys. It is a fine passage of about 10 hours, though one requiring smooth water for the enjoyment of it.

8. From Bristol to Cork, Waterford, and Wexford, calling at Tenby and Swansea. Length of passage, 18 hours.

9. From Newport and Cardiff to Cork. These last two routes are principally for heavy traffic, although large numbers of passengers avail themselves of the steamers from Bristol, which are well-found, good sailing boats.

Through fares are in every case provided for by the London and North-Western, Great Western, and Midland Rlys., which provide for the passengers by the Holyhead, Milford, and Morecamb steamers respectively. But the tourist during the summer months should by all means provide himself with a "tourist's ticket," which is available for one month, and is issued by the London and North-Western and Great Western Companies, enabling the traveller to break his journey at all the principal places worth seeing, where he may stay as long as he likes, provided he returns within the time specified. This enables him to see a certain district with great economy and precision, though, of course, it will not be of much use in a prolonged tour. The tariff of prices, times, and arrangement of transits, can always be found in the current 'Bradshaws,' without which, together with a 'Falconer's Irish Railway Guide,' the tourist should never travel. The London and North-Western tourist's ticket entitles the holder to stop at Chester, Bangor, Holyhead, and Dublin, as long as he likes, provided he returns within the month. Fares from Euston to the Lakes of Killarney are 115s. 1st class, 95s. 2nd class, viâ Holyhead. For the Giant's Causeway, 63s. and 50s., viâ Fleetwood; 90s. and 70s. viâ Larne. For Lough Erne, 96s. and 76s., viâ Fleetwood; 115s. and 95s. viâ Larne. Tourists from Dublin only can obtain supplemental tickets for the north, or Killarney, at the offices of the different rlys.

Ireland is becoming well supplied with railways, which have already effected incalculable good, and, as they increase, are likely to effect still more, by bringing fresh capital into the country, by cheapening the carriage of all marketable and agricultural produce, and by opening up what were formerly wild and unfrequented districts, to the approaches of civilisation—breaking down the barriers of prejudice and ignorance, and bringing the inhabitants of the two sister isles into closer intercourse, to which even the narrow-minded rancour fostered by party bigots must yield in course of time. The lines at present running through the country are :—

1. The Great Southern and Western, from Dublin to Cork, a distance of 166 miles, embracing in its system branches to Carlow, Athlone, Parsonstown, Nenagh, Tralee, and Fermoy. In addition this company

subsidises and works the lines of the Irish South-Eastern from Carlow to Kilkenny and Ballywilliam; also the direct Cork and Limerick, from Charleville to Limerick.

2. The Midland Great Western is next in length and importance, connecting Dublin with Galway, and intersecting Ireland right through the centre. Its branches are to Cavan, Sligo, Clara, Tuam, and Westport; the last named, which starts from Athlone, belongs to the Northern and Western Company, although worked by the Midland; while partly working with it, though governed by a different company, is (3) the Dublin and Meath Railway, branching off from Clonsilla and running to Navan and Kells.

4. The Irish North-Eastern runs from Dundalk to Enniskillen, and from thence to Londonderry. The branches are generally short and unimportant, viz. to Cootehill, Cavan (*viâ* Clones), Fintona, Stranorlar (*viâ* the Finn Valley), and from Omagh to Dungannon, where it meets a branch of

5. The Ulster line, which mainly connects Belfast with Portadown, sending off divergences from thence to Armagh, Monaghan, and Clones, as well as to Dungannon and Banbridge.

6. The Dublin and Drogheda rly. connects those two towns, and gives off a branch to Howth, and one to Navan, Kells, and Oldcastle.

7. Between Drogheda and Portadown is the Dublin and Belfast Junction, which thus completes the link between those two cities. It has only one short branch to Banbridge.

8. From Belfast northward is the Northern Counties, which runs partly along the coast to Londonderry, giving off branches to Carrickfergus, Randalstown, Newtownlimavaddy, and Portrush. Working in connection with the Carrickfergus branch is (9) a short line to Larne, from whence a steamer plies to Stranraer.

10. From Derry also runs the Lough Swilly line to Buncrana, by which the tourist can visit Rathmelton and the district on the shores of the Lough.

11. The Belfast and County Down provides for the traffic to Donaghadee and Downpatrick, with short subsidiary lines to Ballynahinch, Hollywood, and Bangor.

12. While in this district we must not forget to mention the line from Newry to Armagh, and (13) the little Warrenpoint and Newry Railway.

14. The Dublin and Wicklow lines have two rlys. out of Dublin—one from Harcourt-street to Bray direct, the other by the coast through Kingstown and Killarney; the main rly. running from Bray to Wicklow and Enniscorthy, from whence an extension is being made to Wexford. A short branch runs from Wooden Bridge to Shillelagh.

15. The Waterford and Limerick Co. accommodates these two cities, crossing the Southern and Western at Limerick Junction; and the same directorate provides for the management of (16) the Waterford and Kilkenny, (17) Limerick and Ennis, (18) Limerick and Foynes, and (19) Limerick, Killaloe, and Nenagh lines.

20. The little Tramore Railway carries the citizens of Waterford to their bathing-machines.

A line has just been opened from Cork to Macroom, passing through Ballincollig.

The only remaining ones are (21) the Cork and Youghal, with a branch to Queenstown; (22) Cork and Passage, a suburban short railway of 3 miles; and (23) the Cork and Bandon lines, the latter sending off a branch to Kinsale.

In addition to these a large number are projected, some of which will probably be "faits accomplis," while the greater part will fall into oblivion.

There are some features in which Irish differ from English rlys.; of which the most striking are the enormous distances between the stations, and (in the W. and S.) the comparatively thin population all around, which makes the traveller who is accustomed to the crowded traffic and numerous stations of the English lines wonder what there can be in the country to support a rly. There is also an absence of mineral trains, which are the great support of manufacturing district lines. It must, however, be remarked that the lines in Ireland are made much cheaper than in England from the decreased value of the land, added to which the general rate of travelling is very much slower, and the number of trains less.

The inland navigation scarcely affects the tourist one way or another, but it would not be right to pass it over altogether on that account.

1. The Royal Canal connects the Shannon with the Irish Channel, and is 93 m. in length, starting from Dublin, and ending at Termon-Barry on the Shannon. The summit-level is 322 ft. above the sea, and it is fed from Lough Owel, near Mullingar. A branch is sent off from Killashee to Longford.

2. The Grand Canal also starts from Dublin, and runs to the Shannon at Shannon Harbour, sending off branches to Ballinasloe, Naas, Athy, Portarlington, and Kilbeggan, the total length being 160 m.*

3. The Ulster Canal connects Lough Neagh by the Blackwater with Upper Lough Erne, passing by Monaghan and Clones.

4. Communicating with the Grand Canal at Athy is the Barrow Navigation, running past Carlow, Bagenalstown, and Borris, to the sea at Ross.

5. The Boyne Navigation extends from Drogheda to Slane by the river, and thence to Navan by canal.

6. The Newry Canal commences at Fathom, below Newry, and ends at Portadown, where it joins the Bann, and so to Lough Neagh.

7. The Tyrone Navigation connects Lough Neagh by the Blackwater with Coal Island, near Dungannon.

8. The Lagan Canal accommodates Belfast and Lisburn, and affords a waterway to Lough Neagh.

9. The Shannon is navigable from Lough Allen to Limerick, a distance of 143 m.; a portion of which, between Killaloe and Athlone, is suitable for and is partly employed in the use of steamers. It is to be regretted, however, that such an interesting route is not better patronized by the tourist.

10. The Lough Corrib is now well supplied with appliances, as a steamer plies daily between Galway and Cong.

---

* For an account of the passage-boat on this line in former days, the tourist should consult 'Jack Hinton.'

11. A steamer also plies on Lough Erne between Enniskillen and Belleek.

Where the rail has not yet penetrated, the land is well supplied with coaches or public cars, the times and seasons of which will be found in the monthly Rly. Guide. The Irish car is such a peculiar and characteristic institution that it will not be amiss to give a brief sketch of the author of the system, Mr. Charles Bianconi, of Longfield, near Cashel. A native of Milan, he arrived in Ireland about 1800, and set up in Clonmel as a picture-dealer. He was early struck with the want of accommodation that existed between the various towns of the district, and brooded over the idea until, having saved some money, he determined to try and supply some of the deficiency by starting his first car in 1815 between Clonmel and Cahir. The foresight and the pluck evinced in this proceeding was wonderful in those days, when locomotion was not the necessity that it is now, and has long ere this reaped its just reward. Although meeting with many reverses, and—what is worse in the trial of a new scheme—with much indifference, people gradually began to make use of this solitary conveyance, until its owner was encouraged to run others to Limerick and Thurles. Since then the system has taken deep root, and, until the spread of railways, was the grand artery of communication over all the length and breadth of the land. A few years ago, before the engine had knocked some of the road conveyances off, Mr. Bianconi had in his establishment upwards of 45 double cars, travelling over 3600 miles daily. It is satisfactory to relate that his perseverance and spirit has been rewarded as it deserved, and that he is still looked upon, in the character of a country gentleman, as one of Ireland's greatest benefactors.

The greater number of the roads are serviced by cars instead of coaches, and there is no doubt but that the long car is better suited to the country than the coach. Its advantages are that it holds a great many, in addition to a fabulous quantity of luggage that is deposited in the well; moreover, accidents can rarely happen on account of the even balance afforded by the passengers; and should such occur, the traveller, unless he be blind or halt, can at once reach the ground with a very moderate amount of risk. Its disadvantages are, that there are no inside places for bad weather or delicate passengers. The following hints are worth attending to previous to a journey on a car. Ascertain which way the wind is blowing, if the weather is cold or likely to be bad, and choose your side accordingly, as the tourist will find it no slight comfort to hear the rain beating on the other side while the well and the luggage shelter him. Aprons are provided in the car; at the same time, a private waterproof apron is a great convenience; added to which, the traveller should obtain a strap by which he may buckle himself to the seat during night journeys, and thus go safely to sleep without fear of being jerked forward. For seeing the view, the driver's box is, of course, the "post of vantage," but it is not comfortable, and cannot be recommended for a long journey. In conclusion, a good word should be said for the drivers of the Bianconi cars, who are, with scarcely an exception, steady, obliging, and civil men, and pleasant companions to boot. Indeed, it may be acknowledged with truth, that the traveller in Ireland, as a general rule, meets with ready and cheerful civility; and, for the comfort of those who sit at home and read the accounts of those unfortunate agrarian outrages, that it is a most rare occurrence to hear of any stranger being molested in any way —a fact which seems to arise more from the native politeness of the Irish character than from love of the Saxon. Over cross-roads and in districts as yet unaccommodated with public conveyances, the traveller will seldom have difficulty in obtaining a one-horse car. Posting is much cheaper in Ireland than in England, cars being rarely more than 6*d.* a mile for one person, and 8*d.* for two, although in some tourists' districts the car-owners have raised their tariff rather higher. In addition to this, there are no turnpikes to be paid—all the roads being kept (and very well kept, too) by a county fund. Before engaging the car, particular inquiries should be made as to the distance, and whether it is computed by Irish or English miles, as in some districts they charge for English, while in the W. and N.W. the distances are Irish. In a long journey it makes a considerable difference, for 4 English statute miles go to 3 Irish ones. All the distances in the Handbook are given in English miles, as it is easy to calculate the difference, and, moreover, there is a growing tendency to assimilate them to the English measure, which will, no doubt, soon pervade the entire country.

A few hints may be useful to the tourist. Never give to beggars. Whenever the car or coach stops, swarms of impudent mendicants rise up as if by magic, and try which can excel the other in noisy whining and falsehoods. To give to these is simply wrong, for they are mostly beggars by choice, and not from necessity. If work were offered to them, they would in all probability refuse it—preferring to lead a life of disgusting idleness to honest labour. The tourist may well wonder to what defect in the social laws, or to what misplaced soft-heartedness in the hearts of the civic rulers, these intolerable nuisances owe their continuance.

Be careful how you engage yourself in any discussion or opinion on party, and particularly religious, subjects. The traveller will soon find out for himself that party spirit attains a pitch which is unknown in England; that extreme statements are in many districts the rule and not the exception; and that a dispassionate and unprejudiced ventilation of a national subject is not always to be obtained.

The social features of Ireland are unfortunately so mixed up with political ones, that the tourist had better make his own observations on them, and keep them to himself. He will find much to admire, especially in the hospitality and warm-heartedness which seem to be every Irishman's birthright. He will also find some things to condemn; but he cannot fail to return home interested in Ireland's social progress, and with an earnest hope that she will some day thoroughly and truly feel the real love that England has for her, and that the Celt will come in time to consider that "repale from the Sassenach" would be the worst thing that could happen to him.

VI.—ANTIQUITIES.

In the matter of antiquarian remains, Ireland is a Tadmor or a Nineveh, for throughout the length and breadth of the land, ruins of some sort or other are scattered in melancholy profusion, and scarce a barony or parish but has its castle, abbey, church, round tower, or, may be, still more primitive and early remains.

Under these circumstances, the traveller must not be surprised at meeting a considerable resemblance to each other in the different ruins, remembering that each marks an era when a particular style of building was prevalent.

Irish antiquities cannot be divided better than has been done by Mr. Wakeman, in his excellent little Handbook (the only fault of which is its brevity), viz.: Pagan, Early Christian, and Anglo-Irish remains.

I. PAGAN may be subdivided into—
1. *Religious—*
    *a. Sepulchral—*such as Cromlechs, Caves, Mounds, and Cairns.
    *b. Memorial—*Pillars, Steles, Inscribed Stones.
2. *Military—*Raths, Forts, &c.

a. The *Cromlech,* about which there has been much discussion with reference to its use, would appear to have been used as a sepulchral monument in the dark ages antecedent to the Christian era; since frequent discoveries, made at different times, strongly militated against the formerly received opinion that they were used for sacrificial purposes. A singular feature in the cromlechs, and one which seems to have been generally overlooked, is their usual position, overlooking or very near to the sea; cromlechs in the interior of the country being comparatively uncommon. The same peculiarity is noticeable in the cromlechs of North and South Wales. In Ireland there are some fine specimens, though few that have not suffered from the hand of time or still more from ruthless destruction. Amongst these may be mentioned the cromlechs of Mount Venus, Howth, and Shanganagh, near Dublin; Broadstone, near Ballymena; Kilclooney, near Narin, co. Donegal; the cromlechs on island Magee and co. Antrim, and at Knockeen, co. Waterford.

Tumuli.—Monuments of this class abound in Ireland, from the simple cairn, which is common, to the rare and magnificent barrow, on which every species of barbarous ornamentation was lavished. The line of tumuli running from Drogheda to Slane, of which Newgrange and Dowth are the principal, are in themselves worth a pilgrimage to see, and cannot fail to strike the beholder with astonishment at the wonderful skill with which the interior is constructed, and with the ingenuity and taste of the carving on the stones. The Pagan Irish looked upon the sepulture of their kings and heroes as the most important and venerable rite. They appear to have interred the body in both a horizontal and perpendicular position, or else to have performed incremation. "The small square stone grave, or kistvaen, containing a single cinerary urn, placed beneath the surface of the soil and so frequently exposed by the spade; the collection of urns, apparently marking the site of an ancient cemetery, possibly that of a battlefield; the grassy mound and the massive cromlech breaking the level outline of the landscape; the large stone circle, or the oblong enclosure, popularly termed 'a giant's grave;' the huge temple-like barrow, with its enveloping mound of stones or earth (the Western type of the true Oriental pyramid); the simple, rude pillar-stone; the Ogham-inscribed monolith or the sculptured cross; the wayside monument; the horizontal gravestone; the stone coffin; the modern vault or stately mausoleum; the carved recumbent figure in the decorated abbey, as well as the modern tablet in the modern church, all afford abundant examples of the use of stone materials in sepulchral and funeral rites, and evince the piety and reverence with which the dead were regarded in Ireland from the very earliest time."—*Wilde's Catalogue of R. I. A.* Of cinerary urns, for the purpose of holding the ashes of the dead, beautiful examples are to be seen in the Academy Museum in Dublin, ornamented with most cunning workmanship. The usual position of these urns, when discovered, has been in small kists or churches. The tumulus, or mausoleum, like that at Newgrange, is of a different order of sepulture, and consists of a large cavern, which contained one or more sarcophagi, and were probably also the receptacles of treasure. The Danes were evidently of this opinion, as we read of their having broken open the grave of Gobhan's wife at Drochat-atha, now Drogheda, A.D. 862. Stone circles and avenues are not uncommon, and are sometimes found connected with sepulchral mounds, and at others apparently isolated. In the first case, they were evidently used for marking with greater effect the sacred enclosure, as is the case at Newgrange, where the circle surrounds the tumulus; in the latter case, however, it is probable that they were used to consecrate some spot to which unusual reverence was due from religious or judicial associations: such as the Giant's Ring and the Kempe Stones; circles and raths in Hazlewood demesne, co. Sligo; Beltany Hill, near Raphoe; Slieve na Griddle, near Downpatrick. An example of a burying-ground on a large scale will be found at Rathcroghan, in co. Roscommon, one of the cemeteries celebrated equally with those of the Boyne district. Detached and isolated graves, popularly spoken of as giant's "beds," are far from uncommon: examples may be found at Lough Gur.

b. Memorial.—Pillars were used from the earliest times to mark the place of interment or to commemorate some deed. In these cases they were known as steles; but when they were used, as in Wales, for the purpose of boundary or division, they were called "maen-hir," long stones. They were more generally plain, though sometimes inscribed with the name of the person to whose memory it was erected. Of this class are the famous Ogham stones, the elucidation of which has been a favourite study with antiquaries.

"The Ogham alphabet consists of lines or groups of lines, variously arranged with reference to a single stave-line or to an edge of the substance on which they are traced. The spectator looking at an upright Ogham monument will, in general, observe groups of incised strokes of four different kinds:—1. Groups of lines to the left ; 2. Others to the right ; 3. Other longer strokes, crossing it obliquely ; and 4. Small notches upon the edge itself. The inscriptions, in general, begin from the bottom, and are read upwards from left to right. Almost all those which have been deciphered present merely a proper name, with its patronymic, both in the genitive case. The monuments appear for the most part to have been sepulchral in the first instance. But there is reason to suppose that they were used to indicate the proprietorship of land ; either standing as boundary stones, or buried in crypts as evidences to be referred to in cases of dispute arising. By far the greater number discovered in Ireland have been found in Cork and Kerry graves."

2. *Defensive and Social.*—The ancient Irish lived after a very nomadic fashion ; in the summer retiring to their "booleys," or summer habitations, with their flocks and herds, and in winter returning to their entrenched villages and forts. Their houses were either of wood, wattles, clay, or stone, and in this latter case were termed cashels, or cabins, which, however, signifies properly the collection or enclosure of dwellings, the houses themselves being designated as cloghans. The best localities for examining these remains are in West Connaught (Arran Islands) and co. Kerry, particularly in the Dingle promontory. Nor should we omit the singular stockaded islands called Crannoges, which were always found in districts where clusters of lakes were grouped together. From their difficulty of access, they were more likely places to which the owner might take his plunder in security than regular habitations. Examples may be seen in the Museum of the Royal Irish Academy.

The number of raths or fortified villages that still remain, notwithstanding the thousands that must have been swept away as the improvements of agriculture extended over the country is something incredible, as may be easily seen by inspecting the Ordnance map, in which the locality of each is carefully preserved. They were always a mound made of earth and surrounded by a breastwork, and in many cases by a ditch as well. They varied in extent from a few perches to more than an acre, according to the number and rank of the inhabitants. Some of the larger raths were celebrated in the early annals of Irish history, and were used for the accommodation of chieftains and even of royal personages. Among this latter class are the Hills of Tara, Tailtean, and Tlachtgha, in Meath ; Grianan of Aileach, in Donegal ; Emania, or Fort Navan, near Armagh, &c. " Of the number of raths that we have examined, we have not in one instance known the mound to contain a chamber : but when the work consisted merely of a circular enclosure, excavations of a beehive form, lined with uncemented stones, and connected by passages sufficiently large to admit a man, are not unfrequently found. These chambers were probably used as places of temporary retreat, or as storehouses for corn, &c.; the want of any ventilation, save that derived from the narrow external entrance, rendering them unfit for the continued habitation of man."—*Wakeman.* Specimens of these subterranean chambers are to be found at Clady, on the Boyne, and near Navan. The dun or cathair was a more ambitious and a purely military work, built of uncemented stones, and varying much in the complexity and amount of defensive walls. The locale of these works is in the west and south-west of Ireland, where they may be seen in wonderful preservation: for example, Dunængus and Dunconnor, in the Isle of Arran. "To each of these forts, called raths, lisses, duns, cabins, or cahirs, were attached names which with some modifications have descended to modern times, such as Dunængus, Dundermott, Dunmore, Dungannon, Dunboyne, Dunlavin, Dundealgan (now Dundalk); Lismore and Listowel; Rathcormack, Rathcore, Rathcroghan, Rathowen; Cahir, Cahir-conlick, &c. Many of these forts give names to townlands, which, with other topographical appellations, have been transmitted to us for at least 2000 years."—*Catal. of Acad. Mus.,* by Sir W. Wilde.

As the most perfect example of a fort in Ireland, and probably in the known world, we must recommend the tourist to visit the Staigue Fort in co. Kerry (Rte. 35), a model of which is to be found in the Academy.

II.—*Early Christian* remains may be divided into Oratories, Round Towers, Churches, and Crosses.

1. The *Oratories,* or "duintheach," were originally built of wood, in contradistinction to the church or "daimhliag," a house of stone. But although wood appears to have been the original material out of which they were built, they were subsequently made of stone, and from their small size and peculiar features are among the most characteristic of early Irish remains. The average measurement was about 15 feet in length by 10 in breadth; and many were built without cement. They were evidently for the private devotions of the founders, whose cells and tombs are so frequently observed in the immediate neighbourhood. The most singular of these are in the west and south-west of Ireland, and are generally in sequestered and sometimes almost inaccessible spots. Examples are found in St. Senan's, at Scattery Island; on Bishop's Island, near Kilkee; on High Island, off Connemara coast; the very singular and beautiful oratory of St. Gallerus, near Dingle; oratory of St. Finan Cam, on Church Island, Lough Currane. A striking peculiarity in many of these buildings is the use of the domed roof, formed by the gradual approximation of stones laid horizontally, and closed at the top by a single stone. Dr. Petrie is inclined to refer to the class of "duintheach" the larger buildings, which combined the oratory and the dwelling, and which are styled "houses" or "dormitories," and usually possess an apartment or croft between the stone roof and the carved roof of the oratory. Of such are the dormitories of St. Declan, at Ardmore; St. Molaise's House on Devenish;

St. Colomb's House at Kells; St. Kevin's at Glendalough; St. Flannan's at Killaloe.

2. *Round Towers* have been deeply and fully discussed and illustrated in Dr. Petrie's admirable work 'On the Origin and Uses of the Round Towers of Ireland,' a work with which every traveller in Ireland should provide himself, and of which the writer of this Handbook has largely made use. It will suffice now to give a very brief outline of what the towers were considered by different antiquaries to have been, and what they are, with every appearance of probability, proved not to have been.

a. They were supposed to have been erected by the Danes: a theory originally brought forward by John Lynch, the author of 'Cambrensis Eversus,' and followed by Walsh, Molyneux, and Sedgwick.

b. Their Phœnician, Persian, or Indo-Scythian origin, was advocated warmly by General Vallancey, who considered them to have been fire-temples,—places from which to proclaim the Druidic festivals, gnomons, or astronomical observatories, Phallic emblems, or Buddhist temples. These opinions, embracing what is called the Pagan doctrine of the Round Towers, were afterwards followed by O'Brien, Lanigan, Miss Beaufort, and Mr. Windele.

The Christian origin and uses were successively declared to be—

a. Anchorite towers, in imitation of the pillar of St. Simon Stylites: an opinion broached by Dean Richards, and followed by Harris, Milner, and King.

b. Penitential prisons: a theory advocated by Dr. South.

The opinions which Dr. Petrie has so ably argued out, and which are now generally received, are that the round towers were designed for the double purpose of belfries and castles : for, if they had been erected for belfries only, there would have been no necessity for making the doorways so small or so high from the ground; and if they had been intended for castles only, they need not have been so slender or so high. The following is the summary of his results. With respect to belfries :—

1. It is most certain that the Irish ecclesiastics had from a very early period, in connexion with their cathedral and abbey churches, campanilia, or detached belfries, called in the Irish annals and other ancient authorities by the term "cloicteach" (cloıȝceaċ).

2. It is equally certain that in all parts of Ireland where the Irish language is yet retained, these towers are designated by the same term, except in a few districts, where they are called by the synonymous term "clogar" (cloȝáṙ), or by the term "cuiltheach" (cuılȝceac), which is only a corrupted form of "cloictheach" by a transposition of letters very usual in modern Irish words.

3. It is also certain that no other building, either round or square, suited to the purpose of a belfry, has ever been found in connexion with any church of an age anterior to the 12th century, with the single exception of the square belfry attached to a church on Inis Clothran, or Clovin, an island in Lough Ree, and which seems to be of earlier date.

4. Lastly, it is certain that this use is assigned to them by the uniform tradition of the whole people of Ireland, and that they are appropriated to this use in many parts of the country even to this day.

Their intended use for castles as well as belfries must be inferred—

1. From some of the peculiarities found almost invariably in their construction, and particularly in their small doorways placed at so great a height from the ground : an obvious mode of securing safety which is very common in ancient castles.

2. Many of the remaining doorways of the towers exhibit abundant evidences of their having been provided with double doors.

3. An examination of our ancient literature tends strongly to the conclusion that the Irish people so generally recognised this use of the round towers as a primary one, that they very rarely applied to a tower erected for defence any other term but that of cloictheach or belfry.

4. It may be clearly inferred from several records in the Irish annals that the towers were used for the purposes of safety and defence.

Although history gives the foundation of a round tower in the 6th century, Dr. Petrie shows that the majority of them were erected about the 9th and 10th centuries ; and there is no doubt that, owing to the destructive ravages of the Danes, the reconstruction of many towers was rendered necessary, and that they consequently show various styles of masonry and differences of materials, according to the times and circumstances of their restoration. To some towers, as the Great Tower of Clonmachnois, he ascribes a date of the 12th century.

It is needless, in this place, to give a description of the towers, as in every locality where they are found the peculiar points of each are given in detail.

3. *Early Churches* of Ireland were usually, if not always, built of stone and lime cement, and were invariably of small size, rarely exceeding 80 feet, and usually not more than 60 feet. The only exception was in the Cathedral church of Armagh, which was 140 feet in length. In form they are a simple quadrangle, in larger churches extending to a second oblong which forms the chancel. The peculiar features are the doorways and windows, the sides of which almost always incline, and are framed with a certain amount of Cyclopean masonry. The doorways are crowned by a horizontal lintel, or headed with a semi-circular arch, which is sometimes cut out of a single stone. The roofs, where they remain, are of exceedingly high pitch.

"In short these ancient temples are just such humble, unadorned structures, as we might expect them to have been ; but even if they were found to exhibit less of that expression of congruity and fitness, and more of that humbleness so characteristic of a religion not made for the rich but for the poor and lowly, that mind is but little to be envied which could look with apathy on the remains of national structures so venerable for their antiquity."

The Churches of later date are extremely interesting in their architectural features, arising from the proof that anterior to the 11th cent., the Irish not only built decorated chs., but used a style of decoration which was generally supposed to be characteristic of the Norman period. We see in the ornamentation of the Round Tower of Kildare—the tower at Timahoe—the chs. at Rahin—some of the chs. at Glendalough—the ch. of Killeshin—Teampull Fingain at Clonmacnoise—the ch. at Inishcaltbra—the ch. at Freshford—the stone-roofed ch. at Cashel—some of the most exquisite sculpturing in the moulding of the doorways, the capitals of the arches, the reredos, &c. "Chevron and other decorations, which in England are supposed to indicate the Norman period, are commonly found; but they are generally simple lines cut upon the face and soffit of the arch. Pediments now appear; and the various mouldings and other details of doorways become rich and striking, and in some respect bear considerable analogy to true Norman work. The capitals frequently represent human heads, the hair of which is interlaced with snakelike animals."—*Wakeman.*

4. *Crosses* exhibit every degree of diversity from the rude cross without any ornament whatever—save, perhaps, that the upper part of the shaft is cut in the form of a circle from which the arms and top extend—to the elaborately sculptured crosses of the dates between the 9th and 12th cent. Many of them are valuable for two reasons; the extreme beauty of the sculptures, and because they give an accurate representation of the costumes, ecclesiastical and military, of the Irish during th-9th and 10th cent., as in the case of the magnificent crosses of Monasterboice and Clonmacnoise. Inscribed flagstones were numerous, but have become to a great degree destroyed and defaced in the lapse of time. They generally consist of a plain cross rudely marked on the stone, together with the name of the person whom it is intended to memorialise. It is also worth notice that the priests were usually buried with their face towards the congregation.

5. *Anglo-Norman Remains* date from the time of the invasion by the English, who may have brought into the country their own styles of architecture, which became transplanted and acclimatised. "Certain it is that the close of the 12th and the beginning of the 13th cent. witnessed a great change in the style of architecture as applied to ecclesiastical edifices in Ireland; but that this change was in consequence of the invasion, or that the Pointed style was borrowed from or introduced into Ireland by the English, has not been ascertained." As might be expected, a great similarity exists in the plans of nearly all the abbeys in Ireland, which are generally cruciform, with aisles, transepts, nave, and chancel, and a slender tower rising from the intersection. Of the same date, and erected under the same circumstances, are the greater portion of the Irish castles, which vary from the single keep-tower of the predatory chieftain to the defensive fortresses of Tuam and Roscommon, or the modernised castles of Malahide and Kilkenny. Of walls and gateways a good many remains are left, and from the style of their building and the history of the place, we know that they occupy the same date as the castles. Athlone, Drogheda, Londonderry, Clonmel, Wexford, all furnish good examples. The traveller is referred to the following Compendium of remains that are described in the Handbook.

Introd. VI. *Antiquities.* liii

"At no period of their history were the people of Ireland either so settled or prosperous as to be enabled to undertake the erection of any great ecclesiastical buildings such as are found everywhere in Great Britain, from Kirkwall to Cornwall. The cathedral of Dublin must always have been a second-class edifice for a metropolitan church, and those of Cashel and Kildare are neither so large nor so richly ornamented as many English parish churches. The same is true with regard to the monasteries: they are generally small, though rich in detail. Some of them still retain their cloisters, which in all instances have so foreign an aspect as to be quite startling."—*Fergusson.*

TABLE OF THE MOST INTERESTING ANTIQUARIAN REMAINS.
The Figures refer to the Routes.

Cromlechs.
12. Broadstone.
4. Finn's Finger Stone.
23. Glendruid.
2. Howth.
10. Kilclooney near Naran.
23. Kilternan.
18. Lough Gara.
25. Lough Gur.
1. Phœnix Park.
23. Shankill.
33. Slieve Callane.

Circles, Stones, &c.
10. Beltany near Raphoe.
36. Clonakilty.
4. Clough More.
37. Dripsey (Ogham).
31. Dunloe Cave (Ogham).
32. Gallerus Pillar Stone.
5. Giant's Ring.
5. Kempe Stones.
32. Kilmakedar.
3. Kilnasaggart.
25. Lough Gur.
4. Slieve na Griddle.
32. Temple Geall.

Tumuli (Sepulchral).
2. Barnageera.
15. Dowth.
2. Drogheda.
15. Knowth.
15. Newgrange.

Oratories, Cashels, &c.
20. St. Benans.

32. Bishop's Island.
16. St. Columb's, Kells.
28. St. Declan's, Ardmore.
37. St. Finbar, Gougane Barra.
32. Gallerus, Smerwick.
22. High Island.
24. St. Kevin's, Glendalough.
32. Temple Geall.

Raths and Mounds (with or without underground Passages).
3. Cairn Bane.
3. Cairn Cochy.
15. Clady.
3. Crown Bridge.
5. Donaghadee.
4. Downpatrick.
3. Druibh Mor.
17. Emania.
3. Faughart Hill.
7. Grianan of Aileach.
23. Kilfinane.
29. Lismore.
26. Moat of Ardscull.
17. Moat of Granard.
26. Mullaghmast.
4. Slieve Croob.
15. Tara.
16. Tailtean.
17. Tomb of Nial Caille.

Forts, Duns, &c.
35. Ballycarbry.
35. Caherdaniel.
20. Dubh Cahir.
20. Dubh Cathair.
20. Dun Ængus.

c 2

20. Dun Connor.
25. Dun Ailline.
20. Dun Onaght.
3. Lisnagade (and Dane's Cast).
25. Lough Gur.
35. Miltown.
10. Naran.
20. Oghill.
35. Staigue.
35. Templenakill.

Churches.
17. Abbeylara.
18. Asselyn.
31. Aghadoe.
21. Annaghdown.
28. Ardmore.
12. Banagher.
15. St. Bernards.
37. Carrigaline.
15. Cannistown.
13. Carrickfergus.
34. Clonmacnoise.
30. Clonmel.
15. Donaghmore.
16. Donaghpatrick.
2. St. Doulough's.
33. Dysert.
6. Enniskillen.
18. St. Fechan's, Fore.
2. St. Fintan's.
27. Freshford.
3. St. Flannan's, Killaloe.
24. Glendalough.
3. Glynn.
20. Galway (St. Nicholas).
34. Iniscalthra.
37. Iniscurra.
31. Inisfallen.
6. Iniskeen.
21. Inismaan.
2. Kilbarrock.
15. Kilcarn.
33. Kilfenora.
26. Killeshin.
24. Killiney.
33. Killone.
33. Kilmacduagl.
32. Kilternan.
36. Kinsale.
20. St. Macdara.
2. Monasterboice.
2. St. Nessan.

25. Oughterarde.
16. Rathmore.
32. Rattoo.
27. Roscrea.
27. Seir Kyran.
8. Sligo.
20. Teampul Brecain.
20. Teampul Chiarain.
20. Teampul Mic Duach.
20. Teampul Patrick.

Abbeys, Monasteries, and Cathedrals.
32. Ardfert.
28. Ardmore.
25. Ardpatrick.
17. Armagh.
32. Adare.
    Trinitarian Abbey.
    Augustinian.
    Franciscan.
32. Askeaton.
14. Athenry.
30. Athassel.
21. Ballintober.
18. Ballymote.
15. Ballybogan.
29. Ballynatray.
15. Bective.
13. Bonamargey.
18. Boyle.
22. Burrishoole.
25. Buttevant.
4. Carlingford.
25. Cashel.
    Hore Abbey.
    Dominican.
26. Castle Dermot.
33. Clare.
28. Clare.
21. Claregalway.
28. Clonmines.
21. Cong.
25. Gt. Conell.
33. Corcumroe.
37. Cork (St. Finbar).
19. Deerane.
7. Derry.
6. Devenish.
    Donegal.
1. Dublin.
    Christ Ch.
    St. Patrick's.

VI. Antiquities.

16. Duleek.
28. Dunbrody.
28. Dungarvan.
12. Dungiven.
4. Downpatrick.
2. Drogheda.
    St. Mary D'Urso.
    Dominican.
3. Dundalk.
33. Ennis.
23. Ferns.
18. Fore.
29. Glanworth.
24. Glendalough.
5. Grey.
25. Holycross.
2. Howth.
4. Inch.
26. Jerpoint.
14. Kilconnell.
37. Kilcrea.
25. Kildare.
19. Killala.
34. Killaloe.
25. Kilmallock.
    Dominican Priory.
17. Kilmore.
11. Killydonnell.
10. Kilmacrenan.
26. Kilkenny.
    St. Canice.
    Black Abbey.
    Dominican.
    St. John's.
33. Knockmoy.
33. Limerick.
27. Loughrea.
3. Louth.
32. Manister.
2. Mellifont.
25. Moor.
19. Moyne.
32. Mungret.
30. Muckross.
18. Multifarnham.
22. Murrisk.
15. Newtown Trim.
34. Portumna.
33. Quin.
25. Rahin.
32. Rathkeale.
29. Rhincrew.
28. Rosbercon.

36. Roscarbery.
19. Roscommon.
19. Roserk.
21. Ross.
4. Saul.
15. Slane.
    St. Erc's Hermitage.
8. Sligo.
36. Timoleague.
28. Tintern.
20. Toombeola.
15. Trim.
    Dominican.
33. Tuam.
23. Wexford.
    Selsker.
28. Youghal.
    Dominican Friars.

Round Towers.

31. Aghadoe.
25. Ardpatrick.
20. Ardkyne.
13. Armoy.
12. Antrim.
21. Aughagower.
28. Ardmore.
22. Balla.
17. Belturbet.
25. Cashel.
26. Castle Dermot.
6. Clones.
1. Clondalkin.
34. Clonmacnoise.
37. Cloyne.
6. Devenish.
15. Donaghmore.
2. Dromiskin.
8. Drumcliff.
5. Drumbo.
32. Dysert.
33. Dysert O'Dea.
24. Glendalough.
34. Iniscalthra.
32. Iniscattery.
6. Iniskeen.
25. Kilcullen.
25. Kildare.
26. Kilkenny.
19. Killala.
33. Kilmacduagh.
26. Kilree.

36. Kinneith.
2. Lusk.
2. Monasterboice.
25. Oughterarde.
12. Ram's Island.
32. Rattoo.
27. Roscrea.
27. Seir Keyran.
2. Swords.
14. Taghadoe.
25. Timahoe.
3. Trummery.
26. Tulloherin.

Wells and Baptisteries.

28. Ardmore.
2. St. Doulough.
2. Mellifont.

Castles.

32. Adare.
37. Aghamarta.
20. Ard.
2. Ardee.
30. Ardfinnan.
4. Ardglass.
20. Ardkyne.
22. Ardnaglass.
32. Askeaton.
16. Athcarne.
2. Athclare.
14. Athenry.
14. Athlone.
15. Athlumney.
26. Athy.
4. Audley.
20. Aughnanure.
2. Baldangan.
18. Ballinafad.
18. Ballymote.
36. Ballinacarrig.
33. Ballyportry.
2. Balrothery.
37. Ballinacollig.
36. Baltimore.
7. Benburb.
25. Blarney.
32. Bruree.
33. Bunratty.
32. Carrig-a-Gunnell.
33. Clare Castle.
36. Cor.
36. Castle Donovan.

37. Castle Masters.
15. Carbery.
15. Castle Dexter.
14. Castle Knock.
13. Carrickfergus.
37. Carrigadrohid.
30. Cahir.
26. Carlow.
22. Clare Island.
21. Claregalway.
4. Carlingford.
3. Castletown.
1. Dublin.
4. Dundrum.
31. Dromaneen.
31. Drishane.
25. Dunamase.
22. Doon.
13. Dunseverick.
11. Doe Castle.
15. Donore.
36. Domdaniel.
1. Drimnagh.
23. Enniscorthy.
23. Ferns.
29. Glanworth.
4. Greencastle.
2. Howth.
3. Hillsborough.
20. Hag's Castle.
21. Hen's Castle.
31. Kanturk.
4. Kilclief.
4. Killyleagh
26. Kilkenny.
23. Kildare.
8. Kilbarron.
15. Kinnafad.
33. Limerick.
29. Lismore.
26. Leighlin.
25. Liscarroll.
25. Lea.
2. Lusk.
21. Lough Mask.
33. Liscannor.
16. Liscarton.
6. Monea.
9. M'Swyne's.
14. Maynooth.
15. Mylerstown.
37. Monkstown.
21. Moyne.

Intro.I.   VI. *Antiquities.*   lvii

2. Malahide.
4. Narrowwater.
32. Newcastle.
13. Olderfleet.
14. Oranmore.
30. Oola.
19. Rindown.
19. Roscommon.
22. Rinvyle.
31. Ross.
27. Roscrea.
26. Rheban.
16. Rathaldron.
32. Shanes.
15. Scurloughstown.
29. Strancally.
21. Shrule.
2. Swords.
2. Termonfeckin.
29. Temple Michael.
25. Thurles.
15. Trim.
15. Ticroghan.
6. Tully.
9. Termon M'Grath.

Bridges.

26. Cromaboo, Athy.
36. Cromwell's Bridge.
35. Castlemaine.
26. Inistiogue.
14. Leixlip.
14. Newbridge.
33. Thomond Bridge, Limerick.

Crosses.

25. Cashel.
26. Castle Dermot.
1. Clondalkin.
21. Cong.
7. Carndonagh.
6. Clones.
34. Clonmacnoise.
7. Donaghmore.
8. Drumcliff.
24. Fassaroe.
1. Finglas.
9. Glen.

16. Kells.
25. Kilcullen.
33. Kilfenora.
2. Monasterboice.
16. Nevinstown.
27. Roscrea.
33. Tuam.
17. Tynan.

Walls.

13. Carrickfergus.
7. Derry.
2. Drogheda.
30. Fethard.
18. Fore.
20. Galway.
25. Kilmallock.
23. Wexford.

Gates.

26. Athy.
    Preston's Gate.
13. Carrickfergus.
2. Drogheda.
    Butter Gate.
    St. Lawrence Gate.
30. Fethard.
18. Jamestown.
25. Kilmallock.
27. New Ross.
14. St. Wolstan's.

Mansions.

25. Ardmayle.
36. Coppinger's Court.
7. Castle Caulfield.
8. Duncarbry.
8. Donegal Castle.
20. Galway.
    Lynch's House.
    Lombard Street House.
    Joyce's House.
26. Inchmore.
25. Loughmore.
    Kilmallock.
6. Manor Hamilton.
28. Youghal.
    Sir W. Raleigh.

VII. PLACES OF INTEREST.

Dublin.—Carlisle Bridge. Four Courts. Custom House. South Wall. Bank. Exchange. Trinity College. Castle and Chapel. Christ Church. St. Patrick's. Royal Dublin Society's Museum. Royal Irish Academy. Museum of Irish Industry. St. Andrew's ch. St. Andrew's Cath. chapel. Phœnix Park. Zoological Gardens. Hibernian School. Kilmainham Hospital. Clondalkin Round Tower. Glasnevin Cemetery. Botanic Gardens. Dunsink Observatory. Castle Knock. Clontarf Castle. Bull Wall at Dollymount. Drimnagh Castle. Mount Anville.

Kingstown.—Harbour. Monkstown Castle. Bullock Castle. Dalkey Island. Killiney Hill and Quarries. Killiney ch.

Howth.—View from Hill. Cromlech. Baily Lighthouse. St. Fintan's ch. Castle and Abbey. St. Doulough's Church and Well. Ireland's Eye. St. Nessan's ch. Killbarrock ch.

Malahide.—Castle. Swords Castle and Round Tower. Lusk Round Tower. Baldangan Castle. Balrothery ch.

Balbriggan.—Skerries.

Drogheda.—Walls. West Gate. St. Lawrence's Gate. St. Mary's Abbey. Magdalene steeple. Rly. viaduct. Mound of the Tomb of Gobhan's wife. Mellifont Abbey. Monasterboice Round Tower, Church, and Crosses. Battlefield of the Boyne. Donore ch. Newgrange Tumulus. Dowth Tumulus. St. Bernard's ch. Athcarne Castle. Duleek Abbey. Maiden Tower.

Castle Bellingham.—Ardee Castle. Miltown Castle.

Dundalk.—Ch. R. C. chapel. Friary. Louth Abbey. Ravensdale. Iniskeen Church and Round Tower.

Newry.—Crown Bridge Rath. Narrow Water Castle. Cairn Bane. Cairn Cochy.

Warrenpoint.—Drive to Rostrevor. Omeath. Carlingford Castle. Abbey. Tower.

Rostrevor.—Kilbroney ch. Ascent of Slieve Bân. Cloughmore. Finn's Fingerstone. Greencastle. The Woodhouse.

Kilkeel.—

Newcastle.—Maggy's Leap. Armor's Hole. Donard Lodge. Ascent of Slieve Donard. Tollymore Park. Bryansford. Dundrum Castle.

Banbridge.—Danes Cast. Lisnagade Fort. Tanderagee Castle.

Portadown.—

Lurgan.—Waringstown.

Moira.—Trumery Church and Round Tower.

Lisburn.—Ch. Hillsborough Castle. Dromore Cathedral. Druibh Mor.

Ardglass.—New Works. Horn, Choud, and Jordan's Castles. Ardtole. Kilclief Castle.

Strangford.—Audley Castle.

Downpatrick.—Cathedral. Slieve na Griddle. Saul and Inch Abbeys. Wells of Strucl. Rath.

Ballynahinch.—Wells. Montalto. Slieve Croob. Killyleagh Castle.

Portaferry.—View from Blackbank. Castle.

Newtownards.—Courthouse. Mount Stewart. Grey Abbey.

Comber.—Ogilvie Monument. Carngaver Hills.

Donaghadee.—Harbour. Rath.

Bangor.—Castle.

Belfast.—Docks. Harbour. Flax-mills. Commercial Buildings. Ulster

Introd.   VII. *Places of Interest.*   lix

Bank. Queen's College. Cave Hill. Divis. Drumbo Church and Round Tower. Giant's Ring. Kempe Stones at Dundonald. Holywood.
  Carrickfergus.—Castle. Walls. Gates. Ch. Duncrue Salt-mines.
  Larne.—Olderfleet Castle. Glyn ch. Magheramorne Landslip. Cromlech in Island Magee. The Gobbins Cliffs at Carncastle.
  Glenarm.—Castle. Ch. Deerpark.
  Carnlough.—Cliff scenery. Garron Tower. Clough-na-stookan.
  Cushendall.—Waterfoot. Red Bay. Glendun.
  Cushendun.—Caves.
  Ballycastle—Fairhead. Coal Workings at Murlough Bay. Bonamargy Abbey. Rathlin Island. Cliffs at Doon. Bruce's Castle. Knocklayd. Armoy Round Tower. Gobhan Saer's Castle.
  Ballintoy.—Carrick a rede. Dunseverick.
  Giant's Causeway.—Bengore Head. Pleaskin. Dunseverick Castle. Kenbane Castle. Caves. The Organ.
  Portrush.—Dunluce Castle. White Rocks. Portstewart.
  Coleraine.—Salmon Leap. Mount Sandel.
  Dunloy.—Broadstone.
  Randalstown.—Shane's Castle.
  Antrim.—Castle. Round Tower. Ram's Island and Round Tower. Lough Neagh.
  Newton Limavaddy.—Ascent of Keady. Dungiven Abbey and Castle. Valley of the Roe. Banagher ch. McGilligan. Cliff scenery. Down Hill.
  Derry.—Walker's Pillar. Cathedral. Walls. Corporation House. Harbour. Bridge. Grianan of Aileach.
  Buncrana.—Dunaff Head. Malin Head.
  Moville.—Carndonagh Cross. Inishowen Head. Greencastle.
  Rathmelton.—Killydonnell Abbey. Fort Stewart. Rathmelton Priory. Lamb Head. Moross Castle. Fanad Head. Letterkenny. Kilmacrenan Abbey. Rock of Doone. Lough Salt. Gartan Lough. Milford. Glenveagh.
  Gweedore.—Dunlewy. Arrigal. Bunbeg.
  Dunfanaghy.—Horn Head. McSwyne's Gun. Ard's Castle. Doe Castle. Rosapenna Sands. Falcarragh. Ascent of Muckish.
  Dunglow.—Anagarry. Rutland Isle. Tholla Bristha. Doocharry Bridge.
  Glenties.—Naran. Early Remains. Kilclooney Cromlech.
  Ardara.—Glen Gleask. Scenery at Loughros.
  Glen.—Glen Head. St. Columb's Bed. Tormore. Malinmore.
  Carrick.—Ascent of Slieve Liagh. Bunglass. Corrigan Head. Kilcar.
  Killybegs.—Ch. Schools. Fintragh. Inver ch. McSwyne's Castle.
  Donegal.—Castle. Abbey. Lough Easke. Gap of Barnesmore. Finn Valley.
  Lifford.—Bridges over the Mourne and Finn.
  Raphoe.—Cathedral. Beltany Circle.
  Ballinira. Pullens.
  Ballyshannon.—Salmon Leap. Kilbarron Castle. Belleek. Rapids of the Erne. Garrison. Lough Melvin.
  Bundoran.—Duncarbry Castle. Coast scenery. Lough Melvin. Kinlough. Glenade Valley.
  Sligo.—Abbey. Ch. Lough Gill. Hazlewood. Dromahaire. Crevelea Abbey. Knocknarea Hill and Glen. Ballysadare Falls. Markree Castle. Glencar. Lissadill. Raghly Pigeon Hole. Drumcliff Round Tower and Crosses. Ascent of Benbulben.

VII. *Places of Interest.*

Manor Hamilton.—Castle. Glenade Valley. Lough Macnean.
Enniskillen.—Ch. Lough Erne. Devenish Island, Abbey, and Round Tower. Cole Column. Portora School. Lisgoole. Coole Castle. Crum Castle. Ely Lodge. Tully Castle. Monea Castle. Florence Court. Swanlinbar. Marble Arch. Cuilcagh. Source of the Shannon.
Pettigoe.—Termon McGrath Castle. Lough Derg.
Clogher.—Cathedral. Cascade in Lumford Glen.
Omagh.—Donaghmore Cross. Castle Caulfield.
Dungannon.—Moy. Charlemont Castle. Benburb Castle.
Newton Stewart.—Baron's Court. Ascent of Bessy Bell.
Lisnaskea.—Crum Castle. Upper Lough Erne.
Clones.—Ch. Round Tower. Cross.
Monaghan.—Tynan Cross.
Castle Blayney.—Lough Muckna.
Armagh.—Cathedral. Observatory. Library. Palace. Emania. R. C. Cathedral.
Keady.—Linen Manufactory.
Cavan.—Kilmore Cathedral. Lord Farnham's Grounds.
Belturbet.—Round Tower. Upper Lough Erne.
Granard.—Moat. Abbey Lara ch. Lough Gowna.
Virginia.—Lough Ramor.
Kells.—Round Tower. St. Columb's House. Crosses. Headfort House. Pillar on Lloyd Hill. Hill of Tailtean.
Navan.—Liscarton Castle. Donaghpatrick ch. Rathaldron. Nevinstown Cross. Rathmore ch. Castle Dexter. Donaghmore Church and Round Tower. Dunmoe Castle. Chambers at Clady. Athlumney Castle. Cannistown ch. Kilcarn ch.; Font.
Slane.—Abbey. Hermitage of St. Erc. Castle. Brugh na Boinne.
Trim.—Castle. Dominican Friary. Abbey of St. Peter and Paul. Yellow Steeple. Wellington Monument. Newtown Trim Abbey. Bective Abbey. Hill of Tara. Dangan Castle. Trubley Castle. Scurloughstown Castle. Donore Castle.
Hill of Down.—Clonard Church and Font. Ticroghan Castle. Ballybogan Abbey. Croghan Hill. Kinnafad Castle.
Edenderry.—Castle. Ch. Monasteroris ch. Castle Carbery. Source of the Boyne. Mylerstown Castle. Carrick Castle.
Maynooth.—Castle. Colleges. Carton. Taghadoe Round Tower. Clongowes College.
Leixlip.—Bridge. Salmon Leap. Celbridge Castle. Newbridge. St. Wulstan's (Gateways). Castletown House. Woodlands. Strawberry Beds.
Mullingar.—Lough Ennel. Lough Owel. Multifarnham Abbey. Wilson's Hospital. Lough Dereveragh. Knockeyen. Fore Church and Walls. Edgeworthstown House and Church.
Longford.—R. C. Cathedral.
Dromod.—The Shannon.
Carrick on Shannon.—Rockingham House. Lough Key.
Boyle.— Abbey. Curlew Hills. Ballinafad Castle. Lough Arrow. Kesh Corran Hills. Ballymote Abbey and Castle.
Athlone.—Fortifications. Rly. Bridge. Castle. Chs. Clonmacnoise. Round Tower. Chs. Castle. Inscribed Stones. Esker Ridges. Lough Ree. Hare Island. Rindown Castle.
Roscommon.—Castle. Abbey. Deerane Abbey.

VII. *Places of Interest.*

Ballinasloe.—Garbally Park. Battlefield of Aughrim. Lismany Model Farm. Kilconnell Abbey.

Athenry.—Abbey. Castle. Abbey Knockmoy. Loughrea Abbey. Oranmore Castle.

Galway.—Walls. Bastions. St. Nicholas ch. Docks. Joyce's and Lynch's Mansions. House in Lombard Street. Ancient Houses. College. Claddagh. Menloe Castle. Lough Corrib. Clare-Galway Castle and Abbey.

Aran Island.—Arkyne Castle and Round Tower. The Chs. of Teampall Breenin. T. Benan. T. Mic Duach. Forts of Dun Ængus, Dun Onaght, Dubh Cahir, Dubh Cathair, and Oghill. Limestone Cliffs. Lighthouse.

Oughterarde.—Waterfall. Aughnanure Castle. Hag's Castle.

Clifden.—Castle. Ardbear. Waterfall. Erislannin. Slyne Head. Roundstone. Urrisbeg. Ballynahinch. Toombeola Abbey. Recess. Ascent of Lissoughter. Twelve Pins. Derryclare and Inagh Lakes. Ballynakill Harbour. Letterfrack. Streamstown. Doon Castle.

Kylemore.—Rinvyle Castle. Twelve Pins. Derryclare and Inagh Lakes. Lough Fee. Maamturk Mountains.

Leenane.—Salrock. Errive. Delphi. Lough Doo. Ascent of Muilrea. Killaries.

Cong.—Ruins on Inch a Goill. Abbey. Pigeon Hole. Horse's Discovery. Canal. Cross. Maume. Hen's Castle. Benlevy. Lough Mask Castle.

Ballinrobe.—Inishmaan ch. Scenery of Lough Mask. Hollymount. Shrule Castle.

Headford.—Annaghdown ch. Clydagh. Moyne Castle. Ross Abbey. Headford House. Knocknaa Hill.

Tuam.—Cathedral Doorway. Cross.

Westport.—Harbour. Ch. Lord Sligo's Domain. Murrisk Abbey. Croagh Patrick. Drive to Louisburg. Aughagower Round Tower. The Source of the Ayle. Ballintober Abbey.

Newport.—Burrishoole Abbey. Carrigahooly Castle. Clare Island Castle and Abbey.

Achill.—Kildaunet Castle. Settlement. Ascent of Slieve More and Croghan. Keem. Dooega. Achill Beg.

Castlebar.—Lord Lucan's Farm. Pontoon.

Ballina.—Nephin Mt. R. C. ch. Ruins of Abbey. Roserk and Moyne Abbeys. Killaloe Church and Round Tower. Coast Scenery from Bealderig to Benwee Head, Belmullet, and Erris. The Stags.

Bray. Cromlechs at Glendruid and Kilternan. Kilternan ch. Ballycorus Smelting Works. Bray Head. Kilruddery. Hollybrook. Valley of Diamonds. Dargle. Powerscourt and Waterfall. Glencree. Kippure Mountain. Lough Bray. Enniskerry. Fassaroe Cross. St. Valery. Ascent of the Sugar Loaf.

Newtown Mount Kennedy.—Glen of the Downs. Bellevue.

Ashford.—Vartry River. Devil's Glen. Waterworks.

Rathdrum.—Valley of the Annamoe. Claragh. Vale of Avoca.

Glendalough.—Military Road. Round Tower. Our Lady's ch. St. Kevin's House. Gateway. Cathedral. The Monastery. Trinity ch. Reefert ch. Pollanass Waterfall. St. Kevin's Bed. Lakes. Luggannasau Lead Mines. Glenmalure. Ascent of Lugnaquilla.

Roundwood.—Vartry Scenery. Water-works. Lough Dan. Luggelaw. Sally Gap. Source of the Liffey.

VII. *Places of Interest.*

Wooden Bridge.—Copper Mines at Ballymurtagh. Croghan Kinshela. Shelton Abbey. Aughrim Bridge. Tinnahely.
Wicklow.—Castle. Ch. Cliffs at Wicklow Head.
Arklow.—Shelton Abbey.
Gorey.—Courtown House.
Ferns.—Cathedral. Monastery. Castle.
Newtown Barry.—Valley of the Slaney. Ascent of Mount Leinster.
Enniscorthy.—Castle. Vinegar Hill. Ch. Scenery of the Slaney.
Wexford.—Ruins of Selsker ch. Walls. St. Peter's ch. R. C. College. Bridge.
Straffan.—Lyons Castle. Oughterarde Church and Round Tower.
Sallins.—Clane Abbey. Clongowes College.
Naas.—Rath. Jigginstown House. Blessington. Pollaphuca Waterfall. Scenery of Mountains. Kilcullen Old Town. Round Tower. Cross. Dun Ailline.
Newbridge.—Gt. Conall Abbey. Curragh of Kildare.
Kildare.—Round Tower. Abbey. Castle. Chair of Kildare.
Monasterevan.—Moore Abbey. Ch.
Portarlington.—Spire Hill. Emo. Lea Castle. Ballybrittas.
Tullamore.—Earl of Charleville's Park. Rahin ch. Phillipstown.
Maryborough.—Lunatic Asylum. Dunamase Rock. Timahoe Round Tower.
Athy.—Castle. Woodstock Castle. Preston's Gate. Cromaboo Bridge. Rheban Castle. Moat of Ardscull. Rath of Mullaghmast. Kilkea Castle. Castle Dermot Round Tower. Abbey. Crosses.
Carlow.—Castle. Ch. R. C. Cathedral. College. Killeshin ch. Collieries near Castle Comer.
Leighlin Bridge.—Black Castle.
Kilkenny.—Castle. Bridges. St. Canice's Cathedral and Round Tower. St. John's ch. Black Abbey. Franciscan Monastery. R. C. Cathedral. College. Cave of Dunmore. Inchmore Castle. Freshford ch.
Templemore.—Priory. Devil's Bit. Loughmore Castle.
Thurles.—R. C. Cathedral. Castle. Holy Cross Abbey.
Cashel.—Rock. Cathedral. Cross. Cormac's Chapel. Round Tower. Hore Abbey. Dominican Priory. Ardmayle Castle.
Tipperary.—Galty Mountains. Athassel Abbey.
Knocklong.—Castle. Moor Abbey. Hospital.
Kilmallock.—Walls. Gates. Old Mansions. Ch. Dominican Priory. Lough Gur. Forts. Cromlech. Desmond Castle. Carrig-na-Nahin.
Ardpatrick.—Rath of Kilfinane. Round Tower. Monastery.
Buttevant.—Castle. Franciscan Abbey. Scenery of the Awbeg. Kilcolman Castle. Doneraile Castle. Liscarroll Castle.
Mallow.—Scenery of the Blackwater. Abbey Morne. Dromaneen Castle.
Cork.—Blarney Castle. Scenery of the Lee. St. Finbar's. Court House. Harbour. Bridges. The Cove. Queenstown. Spike Island. Passage. Carrigaline ch. Cloyne Round Tower. Aghada. Blackrock Castle. Matthew Tower.
Thomastown.—Bridge. Altar in R. C. Chapel. Dominican Abbey. Jerpoint Abbey. Inistiogue. Bridge. Ch. Woodstock. Scenery of the Nore.
New Ross.—River Scenery. Bridge. Gate. Ch. Rosbercon Abbey. Mountgarrett Castle. Dunbrody Abbey. Duncannon. Hook Point. Clonmines Abbey. Tintern Abbey.

VII. Places of Interest.

Waterford.—Cathedral. Bridge. Reginald's Tower. Quay. Scenery of the Suir to Passage. Tramore. Dunmore.
Kilmacthomas.—Bonmahon Copper Mines. L. Coumshingawn.
Dungarvan —Abbey Side. Castle. Bridge. Valley of the Colligan.
Youghal.—Collegiate church. Dominican Abbey Ruins. Sir Walter Raleigh's House. Wooden Bridge. Rock Scenery in the Bay. Ardmore Round Tower. Ch. Cathedral and Well of St. Declan. Rhincrew. Strancally Castle. Ballynatray Abbey. Dromana. Scenery of the Blackwater. Cappoquin. Mount Melleray Monastery. Killeagh. Grounds of Ahadoe.
Lismore.—Castle. Rath.
Fermoy. — Barracks. River Scenery. Macollop Castle. Glanworth Castle and Abbey Ruins. Castletown Roche ch. Castle Widenham. Glen of the Araglin.
Mitchelstown.—Castle. College. Caves.
Carrick on Suir.—Coolnamuck. Scenery of the Suir. Bridge at Fiddown.
Clonmel.—Ch. Walls. Gates. Scenery of Suir. Ascent of Slieve Naman. Fethard. Walls and Gates. Valley of the Suir.
Cahir.—Castle. Cahir House and Grounds. Caves of Mitchelstown. Ardfinan Bridge and Castle.
Limerick Junction.—Ballykisteen. Oola Castle.
Pallas.—Basaltic Columns at Linfield.
Limerick.—Thomond Bridge. Wellesley Bridge. Cathedral. Castle. Treaty Stone. Quay. R. C. Chapel. Barrington's Hospital.
Killaloe.—Cathedral. St. Flannan's House. Rapids at Castleconnell. Scenery of the Shannon. Lough Derg. Scariff. Iniscalthra Round Tower. Ch. Ruins.
Woodford.—Scenery of Lough Derg and Slieve Boughta Mountains.
Portumna.—Abbey Ruins. Loragh Abbey.
Banagher.—Bridge. Meelick Abbey. Clonfert.
Gort.—Church and Round Tower of Kilmacduagh. Lough Cooter House and Lake.
Ennis.—Franciscan Monastery Ruins. Clare Abbey. Killone Abbey. Slieve Callane. Miltown Malbay. Ennistymon. Liscannor Castle. Cliffs of Mohir. Black Head.
Kilfenora.—Ch. Crosses. Inchiquin Castle. Ballyportry Castle. Dysert Church and Round Tower.
Clare Castle.—Bridge. Castle.
Quin.—Abbey.
Cratloe.—Castles. Bunratty Castle.
Mungret.—Abbey Ruins. Carrig-a-Gunnel Castle.
Croome.—Dysart Church and Round Tower. Manister Abbey. Bruree Castle.
Adare.—Lord Dunraven's Seat. Trinitarian Abbey. Augustinian Abbey. Franciscan Abbey. Desmond Castle.
Rathkeale.—Priory. Newcastle Castle.
Askeaton.—Waterfall on the Deel. Ch. Franciscan Abbey. Castle of the Desmonds.
Foynes.—Estuary of the Shannon. Glin Castle. Shanid Castle.
Kilrush.—Iniscattery Round Tower. Oratory of St. Senanus.
Kilkee.—Cliff and Coast Scenery. Natural Bridge. Bishop's Island. Early Remains. Dermot and Graine's Rock. Puffing Hole.
Listowell.—Castle. Ballybunnion Caves. Rattoo Round Tower.

Tralee.—Blennerville. Mountain Scenery in Dingle Promontory. Brandon Mountain. Dingle. Smerwick. Oratory of Gallerus. Kilmalkedar Pillar Stone. Templegeal. Ardfert Abbey. Ballyheigue.
Castlemaine.—Bridge. Forts.
Killarney.—Lake Scenery. Ross Castle. Inisfallen. O'Sullivan's Cascade. Glena. Dinish Island. Old Weir Bridge. Long Range. Eagle's Nest. Lord Brandon's Cottage. Upper Lake. Cave of Dunloe. Gap of Dunloe. Cummeenduff. Ascent of Carrantuohill. Aghadoe Church and Round Tower. R. C. ch. Cloghreen. Muckross Abbey. Torc Waterfall. Mangerton. Police Barrack. Looscaunagh Lough. Galway's Bridge. Lough Guitane. Glen na coppul. Valley of the Flesk. Paps. Millstreet. Drishane Castle. Kanturk Castle.
Killorglin.—Miltown. Kilcoleman Abbey. Lough Carra. Glenbehay. Mountain Scenery. Terrace Road to Cahirciveen.
Cahirciveen.—Ballycarbery Castle and Fort. Valentia Island. Slate Works and Quarries. Knight of Kerry's House.
Waterville.—Lough Curraun. Early Ecclesiastical Remains on Church Island. Ballinskellig Bay. Dowlas Head. Skellig's Rocks. Derrynane Abbey. Forts at Templenakilla (earthen), Cahirdaniel, and Staigue (stone).
Kenmare.—Bridge over the Blackwater. Dromore Castle. Suspension Bridge. Road to Killarney.
Glengarriff.—Castle. Scenery of the Bay. Cromwell's Bridge. Adrigoole Waterfall. Hungry Hill.
Castletown Bearhaven.—Defences. Mines at Allahies.
Bantry.—Scenery of Bay. Falls of the Mealagh. Pass of Keimaneigh. Gougane Barra. Oratory of St. Finbar. Inchigeelah. Castle Masters.
Skull.—Copper Mines at Ballydehob. Bay of Roaring Water. Crookhaven.
Skibbereen.—Coast Scenery at Baltimore. Lough Hyne. Leap Ravine.
Clonakilty.—Stone Circle. Fortresses on the Coast. Roscarberry Cathedral. Templefaughtna. Timoleague Abbey.
Dunmanway.—Ballyna-carrig Castle.
Bandon.—Ch. Castle Bernard. Inishannon. Domdaniel Castle. Castle Cor.
Kinsale.—Ch. Harbour. Forts. Old Head of Kinsale.
Macroom.—Carrigaphooca Castle. Dundareirke Castle. Mashanaglass Castle. Macroom Castle. Carrigadrohid Castle.
Ballincollig.—Powder-mills. Ovens. Kilcrea Abbey. Dripsey. Ogham Stone. Inishcarra ch. Scenery of the Lea at Inishcarra and Ardrum. Carrigrohane Castle.

VIII. SKELETON ROUTES.

I. A MONTH'S TOUR IN THE NORTH.

1. Dublin to Howth, St. Doulough's, Malahide, and Lusk; sleep at Drogheda.
2. See Drogheda. Excursion to Mellifont and Monasterboice, and Duleek.
3. Rail to Navan, returning by road to Drogheda; see Slane, Newgrange, Battlefield of the Boyne, and Dowth.
4. Rail to Dundalk, Clones, Enniskillen; see Devenish.

Introd.   VIII. *Skeleton Routes.*   lxv

5. Florence Court. Cuilcagh. Marble Arch. If time in evening, row up the lake to Lisgoole.
6. To Sligo: see Abbey and Knocknarea.
7. Lough Gill. Dromahaire. Hazlewood.
8. To Bundoran and Ballyshannon. Ballintra. The Pullens. Sleep at Donegal.
9. See Castle and Abbey. To Killybegs and Carrick.
10. Ascend Slieve League; see Glen Coast.
11. Glengeask. Ardara. Get on to Glenties (very poor accommodation).
12. To Doocharry Bridge, Dunglow, and Gweedore.
13. Ascend Arrigal. Dunlewy. To Dunfanaghy.
14. Horn Head. Doe Castle. Glen. Lough Salt. Rathmullan.
15. To Rathmelton. Kilmacrenan. Letterkenny.
16. To Strabane. Derry; see Derry.
17. M'Gilligan. Newtown Limavaddy. Dungiven. Portrush.
18. To Dunluce and Causeway. Sleep there.
19. To Ballintoy. Carrick-a-rede. Ballycastle. Fairhead.
20. To Cushendall; see Caves. Glenarm. Larne. Olderfleet Castle.
21. Cliff Scenery in Island Magee; see Carrickfergus. To Belfast.
22. Belfast. Drumbo. Giant's Ring.
23. Excursion to Cave Hill, Antrim, Lough Neagh.
24. Excursion to Downpatrick, Saul, Inch, &c.
25. To Armagh; in afternoon to Dungannon.
26. By rail to Banbridge. Drive to Briansford.
27. Ascend Slieve Donard. Newcastle.
28. To Rostrevor. Warrenpoint.
29. Carlingford. Evening by rail to Dublin.
30. Excursion to Trim and Bective.

II. A TOUR THROUGH CONNAUGHT.

1. Dublin to Mullingar. Multifarnham. Lough Ennell.
2. Athlone. Lough Rea.
3. Clonmacnois; in evening to Ballinasloe.
4. Ballinasloe. Galbally. Kilconnell. Athenry.
5. Athenry Ruins. Abbey Knockmoy. Tuam.
6. Tuam to Headford. Ross Abbey. Claregalway. Galway.
7. Galway.
8. Lough Corrib to Cong, Pigeon Hole, &c.
9. Excursion to Maume. Hen's Castle. Inchagoill. Return to Galway.
10. To Oughterarde and Recess. Ascend Lissoughter.
11. To Roundstown. Urrisbeg. Clifden.
12. See Clifden. Afternoon to Kylemore.
13. Ascend Twelve Pins.
14. Lough Fee. Salrock. Leenane.
15. Killaries. Delphi. Lough Doo. Ascend Muilrea.
16. To Westport. Clew Bay, &c. Aughagower.
17. Murrisk. Ascend Croagh Patrick.
18. To Achill. Sleep at the Settlement.
19. Ascend Croghan. Visit Keem, Dooega, &c.
20. Return; see Burrishoole. Newport to Castlebar.

21. Excursion to Balla and Ballintober. The Ayle.
22. To Ballina by Pontoon and Foxford.
23. Roserk. Moyne. Killala. Ballycastle.
24. Along the coast to Belmullet.
25. Return by Crossmolina to Ballina; on to Sligo.
26. See Abbey. Town. Lough Gill.
27. Knocknarea. Glencar.
28. Boyle Abbey. Carrick. Longford. Dublin.

III. A TOUR OF SIX WEEKS THOUGH THE SOUTH.

1. Dublin to Kildare. Athy. Timahoe. Maryborough.
2. By rail to Roscrea. Parsonstown. Thurles.
3. Holy Cross. Cashel.
4. To Limerick : see the city.
5. Killaloe. Castle Connell. Scariff. Iniscalthra.
6. Excursion to Bunratty. Quin. Clare Castle. Ennis.
7. Carrigagunnell. Adare. Rathkeale.
8. Askeaton. Shanagolden. Foynes; and by steamer to Kilkee.
9. Kilkee.
10. Return to Tarbert. Listowell by Ballybunnion Caves. Tralee.
11. Excursion to Dingle.
12. Visit early remains at Smerwick. Return to Tralee. Evening to Killarney.
13. Lower Lake. O'Sullivan's Cascade. Innisfallen. Ross, &c.
14. Aghadoe. Gap of Dunloe. Cummeenduff.
15. Ascend Mangerton. Muckross. Torc.
16. Ascend Carrantuohill.
17. Cahirciveen. Isle of Valentia.
18. To Waterville. Lough Curraun.
19. To Kenmare, Staigue Fort, &c.
20. To Glengarriff.
21. To Castletown Bearhaven. Adragoole Waterfall.
22. By water (if weather permit) to Bantry. Gougane Barra. Macroom.
23. To Cork.
24. See Cork. Afternoon to Blarney.
25. Kinsale. Bandon.
26. Queenstown. Cloyne Round Tower. Youghal.
27. Up the Blackwater to Lismore and Fermoy.
28. Mallow. Buttevant. Kilmallock. Sleep at Limerick Junction or Tipperary.
29. Athassel Abbey. Cahir.
30. Caves. Mitchelstown Castle. Ardfinane. Clonmel.
31. Clonmel. Ascend Slieve Naman, or visit Fethard.
32. Carrick. Coolnamuck. Waterford.
33. Excursion to Jerpoint. Thomastown.
34. Kilkenny.
35. Return to Inistiogue. By water to Ross. Tramore to Waterford.
36. Steamer to Duncannon. Dunbrody.
37. Duncannon through Clonmines to Wexford.
38. Enniscorthy. Arklow. Sleep at Wooden Bridge.
39. Vale of Avoca. Rathdown. Wicklow. Ashford.

40. Devil's Glen. Annamoe. 7 Churches.
41. Vale of Glenmalure. Roundwood. Lough Dan.
42. Luggelaw. Sally Gap. Glencrea. Enniskerry.
43. Powerscourt. Waterfall. Douce Mountain. Dargle.
44. Scalp. Cromlechs. Killiney. Kingstown.

IV. A WEEK'S TOUR IN WICKLOW.

1. Dublin to Bray. Bray Head or Sugarloaf. Kilruddery. Glen of the Down.
2. Delgany. Killoughter. Ashford. Devil's Glen.
3. Wicklow. Rathdrum. Wooden Bridge. Shelton.
4. To Rathdrum. 7 Churches.
5. Glenmalure. Ascend Lugnaquilla.
6. Round Wood. Lough Dan. Pollaphuca.
7. Luggelaw. Glencree. Lough Bray. Enniskerry.
8. Dargle. Powerscourt. Bray. Scalp.

V. A FORTNIGHT IN KERRY.

1. Dublin to Mallow. Mallow to Kanturk and Millstreet.
2. Ascend Paps. Descend Valley of Flesk to Killarney.
3. The Lake, &c.
4. Mangerton. Lough Guitane. Muckross.
5. Aghadoe. Dunloe.
6. Carrantuohill.
7. To Tralee and Ventry.
8. Ascend Brandon. Sleep at Dingle.
9. By water to Valentia (if weather permit).
10. To Waterville.
11. Sneem. Kenmare.
12. Glengarriff. Bantry.
13. Pass of Keimaneigh. Inchigeelah. Macroom.
14. To Cork.

VI. A WEEK'S TOUR IN CLARE.

1. Dublin to Limerick.
2. Limerick to Kilrush. Iniscattery.
3. Kilrush to Loop Head and up the coast to Kilkee.
4. Kilkee to Miltown Malbay.
5. Excursion to Slieve Callane and Ennis.
6. To Ennistymon. Liscannor.
7. Cliffs of Moher. Kilfenora. Corrofin. Ennis.
8. (Ennis to Killaloe. Up the Shannon to Athlone).

VII. A WEEK ON THE BOYNE AND BLACKWATER.

1. Dublin to Enfield. Carberry and Edenderry.
2. Clonard. Trim.
3. Trim. Bective. Hill of Tara.
4. Trim to Athboy and Kells. Oldcastle. Virginia.

5. By the Blackwater to Navan.
6. Navan to Slane and Drogheda.
7. Drogheda. Mellifont. Monasterboice.

VIII. A FORTNIGHT IN DONEGAL AND DERRY.

1. Dublin to Enniskillen.
2. Pettigoe. Lough Derg. Donegal.
3. Donegal. Killybegs. Carrick.
4. Ascend Slieve League. Glen.
5. Glengeask. Ardara.
6. Ardara to Gweedore.
7. Ascend Arrigal. Dunlewy. Dunfanaghy.
8. Horn Head. Lough Salt. Letterkenny.
9. Lough Gartan. Milford. Rathmullan.
10. Rathmullan. Rathmelton. Grianan of Aileach. Derry.
11. See Derry. Afternoon to Buncrana.
12. Moville. Inishowen. Return to Derry.
13. M'Gilligan. Dungiven. Coleraine. Portrush.
14. Causeway. Dunluce. Portrush to Belfast by rail.

IX. A WEEK IN DUBLIN.

1, 2. Devote the first 2 days to the immediate city.
3. Howth. Malahide. Swords. Clontarf.
4. Phœnix. Glasnevin. Dunsink. Lucan.
5. Clondalkin. Drimnagh. Celbridge.
6. Rathmines. Rathfarnham. Kilternan. Shanganagh. Glendruid. Scalp. Bray.
7. Kilruddery. Bray Head. Killiney. Kingstown. Monkstown.

X. A MONTH IN THE SOUTH,

commencing at Waterford (from Milford).

1. Waterford. Thomastown. Inishtiogue. Jerpoint.
2. Kilkenny.
3. Clonmel. Cahir.
4. Mitchelstown. Caves. Castle. Glanworth. Fermoy.
5. Lismore. Cappoquin. Steamer to Youghal.
6. Ardmore. Youghal. By rail to Cork.
7. Cork. Blarney.
8. By water to Queenstown. Cloyne. Aghadoe. Carrigaline. Drive to Kinsale.
9. Old Head of Kinsale. Bandon River. Bandon.
10. Clonakilty. Roscarbery. Timoleague. Skibbereen.
11. Baltimore. Ballydehob. Mines. Bantry.
12. By water to Castletown-Bearhaven. Allihies Mines.
13. Adragoole. Glengarriff.
14. Excursion to Pass of Keimaneigh and Inchigeelah.
15. To Kenmare and Killarney.
16. Lake, &c.

Introd.   IX. *Glossary of Irish Words.*   lxix

17. Dunloe.
18. Mangerton.
19. To Sneem and Waterville.
20. To Valentia.
21. Cross over to Dingle or Ventry.
22. Ascend Brandon—visit early remains—into Tralee.
23. To Ardfert, Listowell, Ballybunnion and Tarbert.
24. To Kilkee.
25. Return to Limerick.
26. Killaloe. Castle Connell and Scariff.
27. Adare. Askeaton—by direct line to Charleville and Kilmallock.
28. Excursion to Lough Gur, Athassel, Tipperary.
29. Cashel. Holycross.
30. To Dublin.

IX.—GLOSSARY OF IRISH WORDS, USUALLY FOUND IN THE CONSTRUCTION OF NAMES OF PLACES.

Achadh	Field.	Cloch	Bell or clock.
Acha	Mound.	Cloig-theach	Steeple.
Abhan	River.	Cluain	A plain between two woods — hence a retreat.
Ag'h	Battle.		
Ail	Stone.		
Aileach	Stone-horse.	Cua	Good.
Aill	Course, also a steep precipice.	Cnoc	Hill.
		Coimh	The inflexion of comh—equal.
Aird	Coast or quarter.		
Airde	Height.	Coinne	Woman.
Ath	Ford.	Coll	Head.
All	Rocky cliff.	Comh	Equal, or partner.
Alluigh	Wild.	Crioch	Country.
Anmber	Great.	Crubh	Hand.
Aoi	Country.	Cruadh	Hard.
Baile	Town.	Cuan	Bay.
Ball	Place.	Da	Good.
Bealach	Highway.	Daimh	House.
Beanna	Top. [wells.	Dairbhre	Oak.
Birra	Abounding in	Dinn	Hill.
Brac	Arm.	Dis	Two.
Bràn	Black.	Domnach	Church.
Brug	Fortified house or palace.	Drochad	Bridge.
		Drom	Back part.
Caircnic	Rock.	Dun	Fortress.
Caiseal or Cashel	A stone fort.	Dubh	Black.
Caislean	Castle.	Easai	Cataract.
Carn	Heap of stones.	Feadh	Wood.
Cahir or Cathair	Stone fort.	Fear	Man.
Cead	100.	Fcoran	Mountain valley.
Ce'all, Cill	Church.	Fronn	Small.
Ceann	Head.	Garbh	Rough.
Cia'r	Black.	Geal	White.
Clochan	Causeway.	Gort	Field.

IX. *Glossary of Irish Words.*

Grian	Bottom of a sea	O'ir	Golden.
Iach	Salmon. [or lake.	Ramhad	Road.
Iar	Black. [west.	Rath	An earthen fort.
	Also back, the	Ral	Plain.
Inis	Island.	Righ	King.
Leacht	Grave.	Rinn	Point.
Leabhhar	Book.	Ruadh	Red.
Leath	Half.	Sean	Old, ancient.
Lia	Stream or flood.	Siol	Tribe.
——	Great stone.	Sliabh	} Mountain.
Loe	A place.	Slieve	
Mam	Mother.	Sneacht	Snow.
Ma'm	Hand or foot.	Soib	Hand.
Meall	Hill.	Suil	Eye.
Mile	1000.	Sul	Sun.
Mòr	Great.	Ta'n	Counting.
Magh	Plain.	Tlacht	Earth.
Neall	Cloud.	Tur	Tower.
Oil	Rock.	Uisg	Water.

LAKES OF KILLARNEY, AND THEIR NEIGHBOURHOOD.

HANDBOOK
FOR
IRELAND.

ROUTES.

⁎ The names of places are printed in *italics* only in those routes where the *places* are described.

ROUTE	PAGE
1. Holyhead to *Kingstown* and *Dublin*	2
2. Dublin to *Drogheda* and *Dundalk*	19
3. *Dundalk* to Belfast	30
4. Newry to Belfast, through *Rostrevor* and *Downpatrick*	38
5. Belfast to *Donaghadee*	47
6. Dundalk to *Enniskillen* and *Sligo*	54
7. Enniskillen to *Derry*, by *Omagh*	61
8. *Sligo* to Strabane, through *Ballyshannon* and *Donegal*	70
9. Enniskillen to *Pettigoe*, Donegal, and *Killybegs*	80
10. Strabane to *Letterkenny*, *Gweedore*, *Dunglow*, *Ardara*, and *Killybegs*	85
11. Londonderry to Gweedore, through *Dunfanaghy*	93
12. Londonderry to Belfast, by the Northern Counties Railway	99
13. Coleraine to Belfast, by *Portrush*, the *Giants' Causeway*, and *Ballycastle*	106
14. Dublin to *Mullingar*, *Athlone*, *Ballinasloe*, and *Galway*	119
15. *Edenderry* and Enfield to Drogheda, through *Trim* and *Navan*	129
16. Drogheda to *Navan*, *Kells*, and *Cavan*, by Rail	142
17. Mullingar to Portadown, through *Cavan* and *Armagh*	147
18. Mullingar to Sligo, through *Longford*, *Carrick-on-Shannon*, and *Boyle*	152
19. Athlone to *Roscommon*, *Castlereagh*, *Ballina*, and *Belmullet*	159
20. Galway to Clifden, through *Oughterard* and *Ballynahinch*	164
21. Galway to *Ballinrobe* and Westport	180
22. *Clifden* to *Leenane*, *Westport*, and *Sligo*	187
23. Dublin to Wexford, through *Wicklow*, *Arklow*, and *Enniscorthy*	199
24. Dublin to *Rathdrum* and Arklow.—Tour through *Wicklow*	207
25. Dublin to Cork, by the Great Southern and Western Railway	219
26. Dublin to Carlow, *Kilkenny* and Waterford, by Rail	239
27. Kilkenny to Athenry, through *Parsonstown* and *Loughrea*	251
28. Wexford to Cork, through *Waterford*, *Dungarvan*, and *Youghal*	254
29. Youghal to Cahir, through *Lismore* and *Fermoy*	266
30. Limerick to Waterford	271
31. Mallow to *Killarney* and Tralee.—The Lake of Killarney	277
32. Limerick to *Tralee*	295
33. *Limerick* to Boyle, through *Ennis* and *Tuam*	306
34. The Shannon, from *Athlone* to Limerick	317
35. Killarney to *Valentia* and *Kenmare*	324
36. Cork to Kenmare, *via Bandon*, *Bantry*, and *Glengarriff*	331
37. *Cork* to Bantry, *via Macroom*	339

[*Ireland.*]   B

ROUTE 1.

FROM HOLYHEAD TO KINGSTOWN AND DUBLIN.

Few routes of travel, even in these days of speed and comfort, can show such palpable improvement as that between Holyhead and Kingstown. Instead of the old sailing packet-boat, that made its crossing subject to wind and weather, the tourist is conveyed by magnificent steamers, each of 2000 tons and 700 horse-power, which perform the distance of 66 m. in 4 hours, with most undeviating regularity — the punctuality that is kept, even in stormy weather, being something marvellous. The tourist will wonder less at it perhaps when he knows that, by the terms of the contract with the Post Office authorities, a fine is enforced of 34s. for every minute behind time, except in cases of fog. The Leinster, Ulster, Munster, and Connaught are four of the most comfortable and splendid steamers to be found in any mail-service; they are also the speediest, the measured mile by which all steam-vessels are tested having been traversed by them at the rate of 18 knots or 20 m. an hour; and the accommodations for landing, particularly on the Dublin side, are so perfect that the traveller has nothing to do but step from one carriage into the steamer, and out again into another on the opposite side. Two packets leave Holyhead (*Hotel:* Royal) during the 24 hours, the total distance from London to Dublin of 330 m. being performed in about 10 hours by the express trains and steamers. It may not be amiss to advise the traveller by the night-mail to secure his sleeping-berth directly he puts his foot on board. As the vessel emerges from the harbour, it glides past the noble breakwater, and the quarries from whence the stone for the works is obtained; then past the Holy Head, with its telegraph-station, and the Stack Rock, with its lighthouse. The first 20 m. of the passage is generally rougher than the remainder, owing to the prevalence of strong currents in the Race of Holyhead. In due course of time the distant hills of the Emerald Isle loom in the far west, disclosing, as the steamer approaches near enough, a magnificent panorama of the whole coast from Balbriggan to Wicklow, with its glorious groups of mountains catching the rays of the rising or setting sun, as the case may be. Nearer still, the populous line of coast between Bray and Dublin appears as though occupied by continuous chains of villas. To the l. is the distant Lambay Island, with Ireland's Eye, and nearer home the Hill of Howth, with the Baily Lighthouse. Some 8 m. from Kingstown vessels pass the Kish Light, placed there to designate a long chain of bank which runs down the coast from Howth. The tourist has scarce time sufficient to drink in the exquisite views of the Bay of Dublin, ere the steamer enters the capacious harbour of

Kingstown (*Hotels:* Royal, Anglesey Arms — both excellent), bearing somewhat the same relation to Dublin that Clifton does to Bristol — a pleasant marine neighbour, where much of the fashion of Dublin migrates for fresh air and sea-bathing, and many of the wealthier citizens reside. Most of this portion dates from 1821, when George IV. embarked here, and gave permission to change the name from Dunleary to Kingstown. This fact has been commemorated in an ugly obelisk of granite surmounted by a crown.

The Harbour, towards which Parliament advanced 505,000*l.*, is a fine work, the first stone of which was laid by Lord Whitworth, the Lord Lieutenant, in 1817. It embraces an area of 251 acres, and is surrounded by piers to the extent of 8450 ft.; these terminate towards the sea by an inclined plane, so as to make the thickness of the base 310 ft. At the pier-head, where there is 24 ft. of water at the lowest spring, is a lighthouse showing a revolving light. From the S. pier runs out a long covered quay, called the Carlisle Landing Quay. This is laid down with rails, to allow the mail-packets to exchange passengers at once with the railway carriages, so that little or no time is lost in the transference. The whole of these massive works were built with granite from the neighbouring quarries of Killiney (Rte. 24). Immediately fronting the entrance to the harbour are the St. George's Club-house, the Royal Irish Club-house, and the Railway Stat., which, with the fine open space around them, contribute very much to the handsome and bright look of the place. This space is the rendezvous of the military bands, which in the season play twice a week, and, together with the Pier, forms a constant promenade for the gay folks of Kingstown, who generally muster in large numbers about the time of the arrival and departure of the 7 o'clock evening packet. This is apparently the great event of the day.

The town itself is straggling, most of the houses fronting the sea being of a superior class to those at the back, after the fashion of watering-places. But the chief beauty of Kingstown is in the neighbouring scenery, particularly towards the S., where a short trip by rail, or a very moderate walk, will enable the tourist to climb the steeps of Killiney Hill, the antiquary to visit Killiney ch. and a number of minor objects, and the geologist to hammer away at the granite quarries (Rte. 24). But the traveller who has to make the tour of Ireland will not have much time to spare, so he must enter the train *en route* for Dublin, 6 m. distant. This line, which is now incorporated with and worked by the Dublin and Wicklow Company, was opened first in 1834, and extended from Kingstown to Bray in 1854. To show the convenience that it is to the public, it is sufficient to mention that, in 1860, 2,200,000 passengers were conveyed by it. Although the speed is not great, and the stoppages are numerous, yet the Kingstown line is pleasant, comfortable, and well managed — indeed, the scenery in itself would indemnify the traveller for a good deal of discomfort. The line runs for the whole distance along the curve of Dublin Bay, so as to produce a constant succession of charming views, while inland are numerous terraces and villas, and now and then a wooded park, with occasional peeps of the Dublin Mountains in the background. The stations on the line are at Salthill, Blackrock, Booterstown, Foxrock, and Sandymount — all of them accommodating a large suburban population.

From *Salthill*, where Parry's is a remarkably excellent hotel, and the Lovegrove's of Dublin, the tourist may visit Monkstown ch., a singularly incongruous building — "an edifice *sui generis;* outside it looks somewhat of a mule between the Gothic and Saracenic; the steeple is surmounted by a cross, but the summits have something of a crescent." In the adjoining grounds are ruins of old Monkstown Castle, one of several defensive establishments built to protect the vessels which lay in Dublin Sound, owing to the shallowness of the Liffey navigation. The remainder of the neighbourhood can be better visited from

Dublin (Pop. 254,513), which the tourist enters at the terminus in Westland Row.

The *City of Dublin*, the metropolis

of Ireland, is situated on the shore of Dublin Bay, and in the basin of the Liffey, which, flowing from W. to E., divides the city into two equal parts. In addition to this river, two or three minor streams water it, viz., the Tolka, which accompanies the Midland Great Western Rly. on the N., and flows into the bay above the N. Wall; the Dodder, which rises in the Dublin Mountains, and, skirting the southern suburbs, joins the Liffey close to its mouth at Ringsend. Probably no city in the world has such a magnificent neighbourhood as Dublin—particularly on the S., where it abounds in mountain-scenery of a high order, approaching the city sufficiently near to form an appreciable background in many of the street-views. Before commencing anything like a detailed survey of the city, it will be as well to give a general outline of the arrangements of the streets, so that the tourist may be *au fait* as to the leading thoroughfares. The "watery highway" of the Liffey is a great landmark which can never be mistaken, as it divides the city into the northern and southern portions. A great thoroughfare, running N. and S., intersects the Liffey at rt. angles, consisting of Rutland-square, Sackville-street, Carlisle-bridge, Westmoreland-street, Grafton-street, and Stephen's-green. As almost all the public buildings are within a radius of 5 minutes' walk from one or other of these thoroughfares, the tourist need not fear losing his way to any great extent.

Hotels. — Dublin is largely supplied with hotels, though, considering it as the metropolis, there are not so many first-class establishments as might be expected. It will suffice to enumerate a few. On the N. side are, in Sackville-street, the Bilton, a family hotel, very good; the Gresham, good; Imperial, tolerable; Prince of Wales, commercial, but good and clean. On the S. side, in Dawson-street: Morrison's, first-class; Macken's, comfortable, and much frequented by military men and bachelors; the Hibernian, very good. In Stephen's Green, the Shelburne (family). In College Green, Jury's, commercial (a good table-d'hôte here). There are, of course, numbers of others of every grade, from the hotel to the coffee-house, but the above will include everything necessary.

Street Conveyances. — Omnibuses traverse special routes at stated times, forming a pleasant way of visiting the suburbs. The various routes will be found in the official Railway Guide; but, wherever their destination, they almost invariably depart from Nelson's Pillar in Sackville-street. Cabs and cars are legion— the former are after the London fashion, but the cars, with their respective Jarveys, are exclusively Dublin. To see the city, a car must be taken—the fares being but 6*d.* for what is called a set-down, viz., a drive to and from any place within the Corporation bounds, special bargains to be made for stoppages or hiring by time. As a rule, the Dublin carmen are civil and obliging —considerably more so than their *confrères* in London.

In describing Dublin in detail, we should begin by its main artery, the *Liffey*, which, rising in the mountains of Wicklow, near Sally Gap, takes a circuitous course by Blessington, Kilcullen, and Newbridge, from whence it flows nearly due E. through Leixlip, with its salmon-leap (Rte. 14), the Strawberry-beds near Chapel-Izod, and past the Phœnix-park, where it may be said to enter the city. A little before reaching the Wellington Testimonial, it is crossed by (1) the *Sarah-bridge* (after Sarah Countess of Westmoreland, who laid the first stone). It has one fine elliptic arch, 104 ft. in diameter, and is 7 ft. wider than the Rialto at Venice. Close to the terminus of the Great Southern and Western Rly. is (2) the King's-bridge, built in commemoration of George IV.'s visit to Ireland in 1821. This also is a single arch of 100 ft. span, with abutments of granite, and cost 13,000*l*., collected by public subscription. Passing on l. the Royal Barracks, it reaches (3) Barrack-bridge, which replaced one of wood, known as the Bloody-bridge, and consists of 4 semicircular arches. The name of the Bloody-bridge originated from a battle "between the Duke of Lancaster and the Irish under their King Art O'Cavanagh, in which the English were defeated with such slaughter that the river ran red with blood for 3 days." (4) The Queen's-bridge, built in 1768, has 3 arches, and is 140 ft. in length. Arran-bridge, which preceded it, was swept away by a flood. A very ancient structure stood where is now the (5) Whitworth-bridge, built during the rule of Lord Whitworth, Viceroy in 1816. It was formerly called, at different times, Old, Dublin, and Ormond Bridge, and was rebuilt, after a fall, in 1427, by the Dominicans, "for the convenience of their school at Usher's Island. This bridge, like the Arran, was swept away by the flood in 1812. In sinking for the foundation of Whitworth-bridge, it was discovered that the foundation of the Old Bridge rested upon the ruins of another still more ancient, which is supposed to have been constructed in King John's reign."—*Currey.* It may be mentioned that Church-street and Bridge-street, the streets on either side, are two of the oldest in Dublin.

Passing l. the Four Courts is (6) Richmond-bridge, of 3 arches of Portland stone, and with an iron balustrade. The heads on the keystones of the arches represent on one side Peace, Hibernia, and Commerce; on the other, Plenty, the Liffey, and Industry. The space on the N. between the Whitworth and Richmond Bridges is almost entirely occupied by the magnificent front of the Four Courts, forming one of the finest views in Dublin.

(7) Essex-bridge was rebuilt in 1755, during the Viceroyalty of the Earl of Essex. It is a fine bridge of 5 arches, fashioned after the model of Old Westminster Bridge. The vista at the S. end of Parliament-street is formed by the colonnade of the Exchange.

(8) The Wellington, more commonly known as the Metal-bridge, is a light iron bridge of one arch. A toll is exacted here.

(9) The bridge *par excellence* of Dublin is Carlisle, nearly in the centre of the city, which the inhabitants of Eblana consider, and not without reason, as the point from whence the finest view of the public buildings and the river can be obtained. It connects the two leading thoroughfares of Sackville-street and Westmoreland-street. The view on the N. embraces the former, with the Nelson Pillar and the General Post-office; on the W. the numerous bridges, the Four Courts, and the towers of Christ Ch. and St. Patrick; and on the E. the docks crowded with shipping, the quays, and the Custom House. The bridge itself consists of 3 arches surmounted by a balustrade, and is 210 ft. in length. From hence, the Liffey, bearing numbers of ships on her bosom, flows past the quays and the noble custom-house to the sea. The long line of quays on the N., from whence most of the steamers start, is called the North Wall, and at the end of it is a fixed light. The South Wall begins at Ringsend, near the mouth of the Dodder, and was erected for the purpose of guarding the harbour against the encroachments of the South Bull Sands. It is really an astonishing work, consisting of large blocks of granite cramped together, and running out into the Bay of Dublin for nearly 3½ m. Half way is the Pigeon House Fort and Arsenal, together

with a basin which was much in request prior to the formation of Kingstown. At the very end of the wall is the Poolbeg Lighthouse, bearing a fixed light.

To guard the harbour against the sands of the North Bull, another work, called the Bull Wall, was erected. It runs from the coast near Dollymount in a S.E. direction to within a few hundred yards of the lighthouse. "The commerce of the port of Dublin had increased so much towards the close of the last century that the accommodation afforded in the river for shipping was found insufficient, and Parliament consequently granted 45,000*l*. for forming docks on each side of it. The docks communicating with the Grand Canal on the S. side were opened in 1796, and St. George's, the latest of the Custom House docks, in 1821. These latter cover an area of 8 acres, have 16 ft. depth of water, and 1200 yards of quayage, and are capable of accommodating 40,000 tons of shipping, surrounded by stores which will hold 8000 casks of sugar and tobacco, and 20,000 chests of tea, with cellarage for 12,000 pipes of wine."—*Thom*. The duties raised in the port in 1859 amounted to 1,066,252*l*.

The other water highways of Dublin are the Royal Canal, a branch of which enters the city alongside of the Midland Great Western Rly., while the main channel follows the course of the Circular-road, and falls into the Liffey at the North Wall. The Grand Canal makes a corresponding ellipsis on the S. side, and falls in at Ringsend with the Dodder. At its mouth are the Grand Canal Docks, which are well seen from the Kingstown Rly.

Dublin possesses 5 rly. stats. :—

1. The terminus of the Kingstown line at Westland Row offers nothing of interest, either in architecture or arrangement.

2. The Bray and Wicklow Stat. in Harcourt Str. is a plain, but massive Doric building, approached by a broad flight of steps and a colonnade.

3. The Great Southern and Western Stat. at Kingsbridge has a fine, though rather florid Corinthian front, flanked on each side by wings surmounted by clock-towers. These 3 last are all in the S. quarter of the city.

4. The Midland Great Western at Broadstone is a heavy building, of a mixture of Grecian and Egyptian styles, which, together with the sad-coloured limestone, gives it a sombre appearance.

5. The Drogheda terminus in Amiens St. decidedly carries off the palm for architectural beauty, with its light and graceful Italian façade.

Most of the public buildings are situated within a short distance of each other. In fact, with a few exceptions, there is scarce 10 minutes' walk between any of them; and this circumstance contributes to the noble street views, for which the city is so famous. Occupying the angles of Westmoreland and Dame Strs., and forming one of the sides of College Green, is

The Bank of Ireland, which possesses an additional interest from its having been the old Parliament House. It was purchased from the Government for 40,000*l*., after the Act of Union, by the Bank of Ireland Company. The whole of it was built, though at three separate intervals, during the last cent., at a cost of nearly 100,000*l*. Externally it consists of a magnificent Ionic front and colonnades, the centre occupying three sides of a receding square. The principal porch is supported by 4 Ionic pillars, and is surmounted by a pediment with the Royal arms, and a statue of Hibernia, with Fidelity and Commerce on each side, the last 2 having been modelled by Flaxman. The open colonnade extends round the square to the wings, and is flanked on each side by a lofty entrance arch. This main front, which was the earliest portion of the building, and said to have been the design of Cassels, is connected with the E. and W. faces by a circular screen wall, with projecting columns and niches in the intervals. The E. front, looking down College Green, was a subsequent addition, and, by some inconsistency, possesses a Corinthian porch of 6 columns. Over the tympanum is a statue of Fortitude. The W. front is the latest of all, and has an Ionic portico. Adjoining this side, which is in Foster Place, is a guard-room, approached by an archway with Ionic columns. Internally the visitor should see the principal Hall, or Cash Office, forming the old Court of Requests, which is entered through the main portico. It is a handsome room, decorated in the same classical style as the exterior.

The old House of Lords is not particularly striking. In the recess where the throne used to be, is a statue by Bacon, of George III., in his Parliamentary robes. Of more interest are 2 large tapestries of the Siege of Derry and the Battle of the Boyne.

By making special application to the Secretary, an order can be obtained to see the operations for printing the notes, the machinery for which is most ingenious.

The General Post Office is an extensive building on the W. of Sackville St., and was built for 50,000*l.* in 1815. In the centre is a portico, also of Ionic character, with 6 fluted pillars and a pediment with the Royal arms. Notwithstanding the balustrade and cornice round the exterior, the front has a bald appearance.

The Custom House is on Eden Quay, not far from Carlisle Bridge. Externally it is the finest building in Dublin, possessing 4 decorated faces, of which the S., facing the river, is, of course, the principal. This front has a centre Doric portico, with a sculpture in the tympanum of the Union of England and Ireland. They are represented as seated on a shell, while Neptune is driving away Famine and Despair. From the portico extend wings, the basement portion of which is occupied by open arcades, while the summit is finished off by an entablature and cornice.

Flanking each end of these wings are 2 "pavilions," above which are the arms of Ireland. The other fronts are in the same style, but plainer, and the carrying round of the open arcades gives a very light and graceful effect. The interior is occupied by 2 courts and a central pile of building, from which springs a fine dome, crowned by a monster statue of Hope. The Custom House possesses what very few London buildings can boast, viz., an open space all round, so as to allow it to be seen to advantage.

When all the different Boards of Customs were consolidated into a general department in London, this building was well nigh emptied, but is now used as offices for the Poor-Law Commissioners, Board of Public Works, and Inland Revenue.

The Exchange is in Cork Hill, at the top of Dame St., and commands from its portico a long avenue of streets, looking down Parliament St., Essex Bridge, and Capel St. It is of the Corinthian order, and is a square building of 3 fronts. The N. or principal face has a portico of 6 columns. The entablature, which is highly decorated, is continued round the 3 sides, as is also an elaborate balustrade on the summit, except where interrupted by the pediment of the N. portico. In the centre is a door, though so low that it is scarcely visible. Owing to the rapid incline of the street, the end of the terrace at the W. is on a level with it, but on the E. is considerably higher.

The interior is singularly arranged in the form of a circle within the square, and contains statues of George III.; Dr. Lucas, some time M.P. for Dublin; Grattan; and O'Connell.

The *Commercial Buildings* and Stock Exchange are in Dame St., but do not offer anything very special.

The *Four Courts* is a splendid and extensive pile, occupying the whole area of King's Inn Quay, between the Richmond and Whitworth Bridges. It was built at an expense of 200,000*l*. at the end of the last cent., a portion being the work of Mr. Cooley, the architect of the Royal Exchange; but after his death the remainder was finished by Mr. Gandon. It consists of a centre, flanked on each side by squares recessed back from the front, the continuity of which, however, is preserved by arcades of rusticated masonry.

The principal front is entered under a portico of 6 Corinthian columns, having on the apex of the pediment a statue of Moses in the middle, with Justice and Mercy on each side. This leads into the central division, which externally is a square block of buildings, surmounted by a circular lantern and dome. Internally the square is occupied by the 4 Courts of Chancery, Queen's Bench, Common Pleas, and Exchequer, each of which occupies one of the angles, leaving the centre of the dome free, to form a noble hall, which in term time is the high 'change of lawyers. The panels over the entrances to the Courts exhibit:—1. William the Conqueror instituting Courts of Justice; 2. King John signing the Magna Charta; 3. Henry II. granting the first charter to the Dublin inhabitants; 4. James I. abolishing the Brehon Laws. Between the windows of the dome are allegorical statues of Punishment, Eloquence, Mercy, Prudence, Law, Wisdom, Justice, and Liberty. Besides these 4 principal Courts the wings and other portions of the building contain several minor courts and offices, which are almost entirely consolidated in this single locality. There is, however, another law establishment at the

King's Inn, fronting the Constitution Hill, and nearly opposite to, though on a much lower level than, the Great Western stat. Dublin did not possess an Inn of Court until the time of Edward I., in whose reign Collet's Inn was established; this was succeeded by Preston's Inn, but both were in course of time pulled down, obliging the societies to migrate elsewhere. Towards the close of the last cent. the present building was raised. It consists of a centre, crowned by an octangular cupola, and flanked by 2 wings of 2 stories, surmounted by a pediment. In this establishment are held the Consistorial, Probate, and Prerogative Courts.

The Castle is situated on high ground at the top of Dame-st., adjoining the Royal Exchange. Architecturally speaking, there is little to admire in either of the 2 courts round which the buildings are grouped. Entering by the principal gateway from Cork Hill is the upper quadrangle, containing the Viceregal apartments (on the S. side), and the offices of the Chief Secretary for Ireland and officers of the Household. Between the 2 entrances on the N. side the façade is surmounted by a cupola, from the top of which a flag is hoisted on State days.

The principal objects in the State apartments are the Presence Chamber and St. Patrick's Hall or Ball-room, which contains a ceiling painted with the following subjects:—St. Patrick converting the Irish; Henry II. receiving the submission of the Irish chiefs; and (in the centre) George III., supported by Liberty and Justice.

In the lower court are offices of the Treasury, Registry, Auditor-General, &c.; and on the S. side the Round Tower and the Chapel.

The former building was erected in place of one more ancient, known as the Birmingham Tower, which was occasionally used as a State prison. It is also called the Wardrobe Tower, from the fact of the Royal robes, &c., being kept in it; but is now almost entirely occupied with the offices and staff of the Records, which include in their valuable deposits the pedigrees of the nobility of Ireland since Henry VIII.; records of grants of arms; plea-rolls of all the Courts from 1246 to 1625; records of the Parliament; references to all grants of manors, lands, titles, fairs, markets, &c.

The Chapel is a single aisle, without nave or transept, and is altogether built of Irish limestone, in a style of late Gothic. Externally notice the decorations of heads, which are over 90 in number, including all the sovereigns of Britain; and over the N. door the rather singular juxtaposition of the busts of St. Peter and Dean Swift.

It is lighted by 6 pointed windows on each side and a fine stained glass E. window: subject, Christ before Pilate. The present building replaced an older one in 1814, at a cost of 42,000*l.*

The erection of Dublin Castle at the commencement of the 13th cent. is ascribed to Meyler Fitzhenry, natural son to Henry II.; and the completion of it to Henry de Lowndes, Archbishop of Dublin in 1223. It was then built for and held as a fortress, and was defended by a single curtain wall and several flanking towers, surrounded by a deep moat. In the reign of Elizabeth it was appropriated as the residence of the Viceroys, which honourable duty it has ever since fulfilled, at least officially, as it is only on State occasions that the Lord-Lieutenant makes his appearance here. The Castle may be said to be the locale of the Irish Government, as from hence all the orders of the Chief Secretary are issued, together with the direction of affairs, military, and police. The courts are seen to best advantage in the forenoon, when the guard is changed to the pleasant accompaniment of a full band. The great excitement takes place, however, during the season, when the Viceroy gives his levées, to which all Dublin (that is eligible) makes a point of going.

At the bottom of Dame St., and forming a grand point of junction for Dame, Grafton, and Westmoreland Sts., is

Trinity College, the cradle of much learning and wit, and the Alma Mater of as long a roll of names honourable in science and literature as any seat of learning in the world can boast. The principal front is a Corinthian façade, facing College Green; while the main premises, occupying altogether an area of 30 acres, run back a considerable distance, occupying the interval between Nassau and Brunswick Sts. The interior is divided into several quadrangles. The first, or Parliament Square, contains the chapel, marked externally by a colonnade of Corinthian pillars; on the S. side the theatre for examinations, in which are portraits of benefactors and one of Elizabeth, the foundress of the University; also a monument to Provost Baldwin, 1758, who bequeathed 80,000*l.*; the refectory, or dining-hall, in which are portraits of Henry Flood; Chief Justice Downs; Grattan; Frederic Prince of Wales; Cox, Archbishop of Cashel; Provost Baldwin, &c.

The *Library*, in Library Square, is a fine building, 270 ft. long, also of Corinthian order. The interior is conveniently fitted up for the purpose of reading, and contains 10,600 volumes, together with many rare curiosities, such as the Egyptian hieroglyphics collected by Salt the traveller. Connected with this room is one in which is deposited the Fagel Library, so called from its having been the property of a family of that name in Holland. The *sanctum sanctorum*, however, is the

Manuscript-room, in which are Archbishop Usher's collection, Vallancy's Irish MSS., Johnston's Icelandic MSS., and Overbury's MSS. of Persia. Of Irish MSS. "the collection in Trinity College consists of over 140 vols., several of them on vellum, dating from the early part of the 12th, down to the middle of the last cent. There are also beautiful copies of the Gospels known as the Books of Kells and Durrow; and Dimma's Book, attributable to the 6th and 7th cents. The Saltair of St. Ricemarch, Bishop of St. David's in the 11th cent., contains also an exquisite copy of the Roman Martyrology, and a very ancient Hieronymian version of the Gospels, the history of which is unknown, but which is evidently an Irish MS. of not later than the 9th cent.; also the Evangelistarium of St. Malins, Bishop of Ferns in the 7th cent., with its ancient box, and numerous Ossianic poems relating to the Fenian heroes, some of very great antiquity."—*Prof. O'Currey.*

The Museum, over the entrance gateway, contains a number of interesting though miscellaneous articles, and amongst them the harp of Brian Boroimhe, whose son Donogh presented it to the Pope in 1023. In his turn he gave it to Henry VIII., who passed it over to the first Earl of Clanricarde, and from him through several hands, until it finally rested here.

Besides the squares described, there are Park Square and Botany Bay Square, principally for the accommodation of students. On the N. side of the former is the Printing House, entered by a Doric portico.

To the S. of the Library is the Fellows' Garden, with the Magnetic Observatory, the first of the kind ever established. The Transactions of the British Association embody most of the scientific observations that have been carried on here by Prof. Lloyd and the Irish astronomers.

Adjoining these gardens is a pleasant park for the use of the students, well planted and laid out, and looking on to Nassau St. At the W. end, facing Grafton St., is the Provost's House. The University dates from 1591, when Archbishop Usher procured from Elizabeth a charter and "mortmain licence for the site of the dissolved monastery of All Saints." The constitution of the Corporation at present consists of a provost, 7 senior fellows, 28 junior fellows, and 70 scholars, and the average number of students is about 1500.

The Roman Catholic University is situated on the W. side of Stephen's Green. It is quite modern, having been only established in 1854. Dublin does not possess many public statues or monuments. The principal one is

Nelson's Pillar, occupying a conspicuous position in the centre of Sackville Street. It is a Doric column, 134 ft. in height, the summit of which is crowned by the statue of Nelson leaning against the capstan of a ship. It is worth ascending for the sake of the panorama of the city.

The Wellington Testimonial is described at p. 14.

In College Green is a bronze equestrian statue of William III., on a marble pedestal,—the object of vehement adoration and hatred in years gone by, when it was the custom to decorate it with orange ribbons, as the usual prelude to a party fight. Fortunately the strong arm of the law has stepped in to control those passions which could not be guided by moderation and common sense.

In front of the Mansion House in Dawson Street is an equestrian statue of George I. In Stephen's Green there is one of George II.; and George III. is placed in the Bank of Ireland and the Royal Exchange. A memorial to the late Sir Philip Crampton has been placed at the top of Brunswick Street; and one to Goldsmith, by Foley, in Trinity College.

The *Royal Dublin Society* holds its meetings in Kildare Street, formerly the residence of the Duke of Leinster, the grounds extending as far back as the N. side of Merrion Square. It boasts the honour of being the oldest Society in the kingdom, for it was incorporated in 1750, and has been in the enjoyment of Parliamentary grants for more than 90 years. The visitor can see the library (which contains 30,000 vols.) daily, on introduction by a member; and the Natural History Museum on Mondays, Wednesdays, and Fridays, free—on the remaining days on payment of 6d.

The *Royal Irish Academy* should be seen by every student of Irish history and antiquities. Visitors are admitted on Wednesdays, Thursdays, and Fridays, on a member's introduction. The Museum contains a complete and classified series of early remains of all kinds that have hitherto been found in Ireland, for the admirable arrangement of which not only the Academy, but every antiquary owes a debt of gratitude to Sir W. Wilde, who has devoted an immense amount of time and knowledge in rendering the Museum not so much a collection of odds and ends, as an exposition of the social features of the country from the earliest times to the present. The catalogue written by him is more a history of Irish Antiquities than a mere catalogue.

The visitor should pay particular attention to the department of celts, arrow-heads, and flint implements; also some exquisitely beautiful earthen mortuary urns, the work of which will bear the most minute inspection. Amongst the collection of gold ornaments is the Cross of Cong (Rte. 21), "made at Roscommon by native Irishmen about 1123, and containing what was supposed to be a piece of the true Cross, as inscriptions in Irish and Latin in the Irish character upon two of its sides distinctly record. The ornaments generally consist of tracery and grotesque animals, fancifully combined, and similar in character to the decorations found upon crosses of stone of the same period. A large crystal, through which a portion of the wood which the cross was formed to enshrine is visible, is set in the centre, at the intersection."—*Wilde.*

The *Museum of Irish Industry* is well worth a visit. It is on the E. side of Stephen's Green, and contains a series of geological, mineralogical, and chemical specimens, to exhibit the economic resources of Ireland. It is also the head-quarters of the Geological Survey, and no geologist, about to visit the interior of the country, should leave Dublin without consulting the officers of the Survey, who are at all times most ready and anxious to furnish information. Admission is free.

The *Irish National Gallery*, on N. side of Leinster Lawn, opened 1864, is devoted to collections of works of the Fine Arts, the lower story to sculpture, the upper to paintings. The cost has been defrayed by Parliamentary grants to the amount of 21,000*l.*, and 5000*l.* from the Dargan Fund. On the opposite side of the Square is the Museum of Natural History. The bronze statue of Mr. William Dargan stands on the site of the Great Exhibition building of 1853, inaugurated by his munificence.

In addition to the Libraries of the University, Irish Academy, and Dublin Society, there is a public one known as

Marsh's or *St. Patrick's Library*, open to everybody, and situated close to St. Patrick's Cathedral. It contains about 18,000 vols., and amongst them the whole of the collection of Stillingfleet, Bishop of Worcester, which was purchased and placed there by Archbishop Marsh in 1694.

The *Cathedral of Christ Church* is situated a little to the S. of the river, and to the W. of the Castle, in an unprepossessing neighbourhood. It is said to have been built in 1038 by Sitric, son of Amlave, King of the Ostmen of Dublin; and lest there should be any jealousy between the two cathedrals, an agreement was made that Christ Church should have the precedence as being the elder, but that the Archbishops should be buried alternately in the one and the other. As it at present stands, since the restoration in 1833, it is a venerable cruciform ch., consisting of nave, transepts, and choir, with a rather low tower rising from the intersection. The principal entrance is in the S. transept, through a fine Norman doorway. The nave, which is 103 ft. in length, has a northern aisle. The S. wall fell down in 1562, and was replaced by the present one, the erection of which is commemorated by a stone inserted in the wall.

The northern aisle is separated from the nave by a row of beautiful E. Eng. arches springing from piers of clustered columns, and displaying chevron mouldings; and said to be the most ancient portion of the cathedral. Unfortunately their bases are buried under the pavement. "The capitals are particularly graceful and elegant. They are composed of the usual E. Eng. stiff-leaved foliage, enclosing heads of bishops and female saints. The mode in which the slender shafts between the larger ones are made to hold the foliage that springs from them is singularly beautiful." The nave contains the following monuments: to Sir Samuel Auchmuty; Thomas Prior, 1751, the friend of Bishop Berkeley; Lord Bowes, Chancellor of Ireland, 1767; Bishop of Meath, 1733; and Lord Lifford, High Chancellor, 1789. The most interesting one is that of Strongbow and his wife Eva, with the following inscription above it:—

"This : avneyent : monvment : of : Rychard : Strangbowe : called : Comes : Strangvlensis : Lord : of : Chepsto : and : ogny : the : fyrst : and : principall : invader : of : Irland : 1169 : qvl : obiit : 1177 : the : monvment : was : broken : by : the : fall : of : the : roff : and : bodye : of : Crystes : chvrche : in : An : 1562 : and : set : up : agayn : at : the : chargys : of : the : Right : Honorable : Sr : Henrii : Sidney : Knyght : of : the : Noble : Order : L. : President : Watles : L. : Deputy : of : Irland : 1570."*

The N. transept is remarkable for its fine Norm. windows, which were restored in 1833, when the whole of the transept from the height of the doorway was rebuilt. The choir is separated from the nave by a screen, on which is the organ. The interior is rendered heavy by the ceiling being intersected with quadrangular mouldings, with bosses at the intersections. The objects worthy of notice in it are an altar composed of green scagliola, and the monuments of the Earl of Kildare and Francis Agard, 1577. The musical service in Christ Church is particularly good, and is held in high estimation by the citizens, who always attend in great numbers.

Its younger sister, the Cathedral of *St. Patrick*, is situated more to the S., between Stephen's Green and the district known as the Liberties. It is a fine cruciform ch. with a low tower surmounted by a granite spire rising from the N.W. angle, and is a good example of the Early Pointed style. The spire, however, is an addition of the last cent. "The body of the ch. consists of a nave with aisles; a N. and S. transept, each with a western aisle; a choir with two aisles of great length, in comparison with the nave; and a Lady-chapel. The aisles of the choir are carried out beyond the E. end as far as half the length of the Lady chapel, which, on the exterior, appears almost detached, as it is so much lower than the choir. The latter is supported by flying buttresses over the aisles, one of which at each angle is very remarkable

* Notwithstanding this inscription, the armorial bearings seem to throw discredit on the fact of the tomb being that of Strongbow.

for the period at which it was erected, being carried diagonally, the usual mode being to have them at right angles to the sides and end." The expense of the restoration has been entirely defrayed by the princely munificence of one man, A. Guinness, Esq., who has devoted an enormous sum of money to this noble work. It is to be regretted, however, that some of the faults of the old building have been perpetuated in the new one. "Copying has been carried on with the most praiseworthy care, but unfortunately the bad has been copied with the same care as the good; and to prove that this censure is not unmerited, the N.E. angle will show that E. Eng. pinnacles, which have in late times been restored with Perp. panelling, are retained as genuine in the new restoration."

The nave is separated from the side aisles by 8 pointed arches with octagonal piers. The transepts, also, have aisles separated by 3 arches. The W. (Perp.) window was presented to the Cathedral by Dr. Dawson, the late Dean.

The choir is 90 ft. long, and is a fine example of Early Pointed architecture. "It was formerly roofed with stone flags of an azure colour, and inlaid with stars of gold; but the weight of the roof being too great for the support underneath, it was removed, and discovered traces of 100 windows."—*Currey.* It contains the throne of the Archbishop, and the prebendal stalls and throne of the Knights of St. Patrick, over each one being the helmet, sword, and banner of the order.

There is a good triforium, and the arches in the S. transept should be particularly noticed. The choir is separated from the Lady Chapel by a pointed arch with deeply recessed mouldings and clustered columns.

St. Patrick's contains on the whole a larger and more interesting selection of monuments than Christ Church. The principal are those of Archbishop Smith, 1771; Bishop Marsh, the founder of the library; the Earl of Cavan, 1778; Mrs. Hester Johnson, otherwise 'Stella,' the friend of Swift. There is also one of the Dean himself, with an epitaph, the bitterness of which sufficiently reveals the author:—

"Ubi sæva indignatio ulterius cor lacerare nequit."

In the choir is one of those immense and massive monuments in which the family of the Earls of Cork seemed to delight, and which contains a large number of figures, remarkable for the freshness of the colouring. In the upper part is Dean Weston; and beneath him, Sir Geoffrey Fenton and his wife. Still lower are the Earl and Countess of Cork, with 4 sons kneeling by them, and at the bottom are their 6 daughters, together with a child, supposed to be Sir Robert Boyle. Opposite this gigantic tomb is a slab in memory of Duke Schomberg, with an epitaph by Swift, which gave mortal offence to George I., who declared that "the Dean of St. Patrick's had put it there out of malice in order to stir up a quarrel between himself and the King of Prussia, who had married Schomberg's granddaughter."

The remaining monuments of note are those of Sir E. Fytton, Lord President of Connaught, and, in the N. transept) of the 18th Royal Irish, representing the death of Col. Tomlinson at Chappoo, and the storming the Pagoda at Rangoon. A portion of the S. transept was formerly known as the Chapel of St. Paul or the Old Chapter House, and is said to have been the prison of the Inquisition. In it should be noticed the steps and enamelled tiles leading up to the altar. The approaches to St. Patrick, which are very bad, and no wonder, considering that it is situated in one of the worst parts of the city, are about to be much improved.

In front of the S. transept a statue (by Foley) to Mr. Guinness is to be placed, and one to Dean Swift is also in contemplation.

The organ is fine-toned, and was originally built for a church in Vigo.

Amongst the most noticeable of the Dublin churches are the following:—

On the S. side—*St. Audoen's*, between Christ Church and the Corn Market. Here are some good specimens of Early Pointed architecture, although in ruins; the only portion of the ch. that is used being the N. aisle of the ancient building, which consisted originally of a double aisle, separated by 6 octagonal columns, supporting pointed arches. The choir and side aisle were built by Lord Portlester, who also erected a tomb with the recumbent figures of a knight and his lady. This ch. is the burial-place of Dr. Parry, Bishop of Killaloe; Sir Matthew Terrell, 1649; and the Molyneux family; and contains several monuments of wood.

St. Werberg's, near the Castle, has a mixed front and several stories of the Corinthian and Ionic orders. In the interior are monuments of ecclesiastics and knights; and in the vaults lie the remains of Lord Edward Fitzgerald, who died of wounds received during his arrest in 1798. This ch., like its sister in Bristol, is dedicated to St. Werberg, daughter of Wulherus, King of Mercia.

St. Andrew's, between Grafton and Dame Streets, is now being rebuilt, and will be, when finished, a beautiful building. The old ch., which was burnt down, was an imitation of Sta. Maria di Rotonda at Rome, and was generally called the Round Church.

On the N. side of the Liffey are *St. Michan's*, near the Four Courts, the vaults of which were celebrated for the extraordinary powers of preservation of the bodies within it. In some cases the corpses of people who had been buried for 30 years were found to be perfectly free from decay,

a circumstance in all probability attributable to the extreme dryness of the vaults, and the ability of the stones to resist moisture. In the interior of the ch. is a monument to Dr. Lucas, M.P. for Dublin, whose statue is in the City Hall.

In the very N. of the city near Mountjoy Square, is *St. George's*, which has a lofty tower, steeple, and portico, erected in 1802 from designs by Johnston, at a cost of 90,000*l.*

The remaining chs. do not present any very particular objects of interest. They are St. Michael and St. John's, St. Kevin's, and St. Peter's, all in the neighbourhood of Christ Church and St. Patrick's; St. Ann's, in Dawson Street (where Mrs. Hemans and Cæsar Otway are buried, and where the musical service is well done), St. Bride's, St. Mary's, St. Stephen's (in Upper Mount Street) St.Catherine's, St. James's, St. Paul's, St. Luke's, and St. Mark's.

Of the Roman Catholic Chapels, the tourist should see the Metropolitan Chapel in Marlborough-st. (a little to the E. of Sackville-st.), which has a Doric front with a hexastyle portico raised on a platform, and a pediment ornamented with figures of the Virgin, St. Patrick, and St. Lawrence O'Toole. The interior has a nave and aisles, and a beautiful white marble altar.

St. Andrew's, near the Westland Row Terminus, is worth visiting for the sake of a fine group representing the Transfiguration, the work of Hogan, one of the greatest sculptors that Ireland ever produced.

The Chapel of St. Saviour's, in Dominick-st., has one of the most elaborately decorated fronts in the whole city, and a particularly elegant rose window. A new chapel, in good taste, has recently been built at Phibsborough in the N. of the city.

The *Phœnix Park* is the Utopia of every citizen of Dublin, who believes that there is nothing in the world like it; it is in truth an adjunct of which any city might be proud, containing an area of 1759 acres, of which 1300 are open to the public. The principal objects in it are the Wellington Testimonial near the S.E. gate, a massive obelisk, on a pedestal of granite, on the 4 sides of which are panels and inscriptions commemorative of all the victories gained by the Duke during his long career. The total height of the obelisk is 205 ft., and the cost of it was 20,000*l*. From the knoll on which this memorial is placed, as also from the Magazine Fort a little to the E., some of the finest views of Dublin are to be obtained.

In the N.E. portion of the park are the *Zoological Gardens*, which contain a tolerable collection, together with the Lodge, which is the principal residence of the Lord Lieutenant, the houses of the Chief and Under Secretary, and the Constabulary Barracks. Near to the W. are the Mountjoy Barracks, and on the S. side is the Hibernian Military School, where 400 boys, sons of soldiers, are educated.

The western extremity extends as far as Castleknock, and the Strawberry Beds on the N. bank of the Liffey. No tourist should quit Dublin without taking a drive round the Park.

The Rotunda, at the top of Sackville-st., is a fine series of public rooms, used for concerts and meetings. Externally, however, it is eclipsed by the superior architecture of the Lying-in Hospital, which has a Doric façade fronting towards Great Britain St., and flanked on each side by Tuscan colonnades terminated by porticoes. It is a matter of regret that such a splendid line of building was not placed a little more to the E., where it would have terminated the vista of Sackville-st. Such was the original intention, had not the founder, Dr. Moore, quarrelled with Lord Mountjoy, who was the owner of the ground.

Kilmainham Hospital, a little to the S.W. of Kingsbridge, is built on the site of the old priory of Kilmainham, an establishment of Knights Templars, in 1174, and was turned into an asylum for invalid soldiers in 1690. It consists of a quadrangle encircling a court, said to have been built from designs by Sir Christopher Wren. The visitor will see in the dining-hall a collection of portraits of celebrities of the 17th and 18th cents. The altar-screen in the chapel is of Irish oak, carved by Grinling Gibbons.

The handsome building for the Great Irish Exhibition of 1865 includes a Winter-Garden, filled with beautiful plants. It was built at the principal cost of Mr. Guinness.

The remaining institutions of Dublin are the Royal College of Surgeons on the E. side of Stephen's Green (the Anatomical Museum of which is well worth seeing), Stevens' Hospital, City Hospital, Sir Patrick Dunn's, Simpson's, Mercer's, Swift's Hospitals, Richmond Lunatic Asylum, and many others of lesser note; indeed, few cities are so well provided with institutions and societies for charitable purposes of all sorts. The antiquary will perhaps be disappointed in the modern aspect of Dublin, and in the few old buildings that remain. Indeed, with the exception of the ancient Archiepiscopal Palace in Kevin-st., now used as a police barrack, there are no houses left prior to the commencement of the last cent. The Liberties will however furnish many specimens of the time of Queen Anne, particularly in Rainsford-st. They were once the abode of the rank and fashion of the period, but at present the population that inhabit them are not of the choicest description, and the tourist may possibly obtain from them more notice than may be agreeable. Sufficient has now been mentioned to point out the leading and most interesting features of the city, and it only remains to direct the visitor to the things most worth seeing in the suburbs:—

1. Kingstown by rail has been already described (p. 2). Trains run every ¼ hour through the day.

2. To Clonskea, Sandford, and Ranelagh, there are omnibuses from Nelson's Pillar. The route is through Westmoreland St., College Green, rt. Bank, l. Trinity College, Grafton St., Stephen's Green, Harcourt St., and Charlemont St., at the end of which the Grand Canal is crossed.

2½ m. Donnybrook, on the N. bank of the Dodder, is celebrated for its fair, which with its noisy mirth and pugnacity has become known throughout all the civilised world as the arena for breaking heads:—

"An Irishman all in his glory was there,
With his sprig of shillelagh and shamrock so green."

It is now fortunately abolished, for, though the humours of Donnybrook were many, they were far counterbalanced by the riot and misery that the fair occasioned. Continuing S. this road leads to Stillorgan, passing a great many villas and residences, amongst which that of Mount Merrion, belonging to the late Lord Herbert of Lea, is conspicuous on rt.

3. To Rathfarnham, the greater portion of the distance is traversed by omnibus every ¼ of an hour from Sackville-st.

2 m Rathmines is a very populous and respectable suburb, although it formerly had an infamous notoriety for the slaughter of the early English colonists of Dublin by the Irish of Wicklow. The route followed is the same as in the last up to the end of Harcourt St., where there is a divergence to the rt., the Rathmines road crossing the canal near the Portobello Barracks.

At 3 m. Round Town, a road to rt. is given off to Blessington and Naas, while that to Rathfarnham runs S., passing rt. Terenure House and crossing the Dodder.

3¾ m. Rathfarnham. Here is the College of St. Columba, for the education of students for the Protestant ministry. The castle was formerly the seat of the Loftus family, but now of Lord Justice Blackburne. The grounds are pretty, and worth driving through. If the tourist wishes to ascertain what romantic scenery exists near Dublin, he may follow up the Dodder to its source in Glanasmole, or the Valley of the Thrush, a river which Wordsworth was accustomed to say was not much inferior to the Duddon. Southward the road leaves to l. the Loretto Convent, and continues through Willbrook to Bray, passing l. Marley (D. La Touche, Esq.), then on rt. Mount Venus with its cromlech, and so through the Scalp (Rte. 24).

4. To Lucan, through Chapel Izod and Palmerstown, the road runs past the Royal Hospital of Kilmainham, and crosses the Great Southern and Western Rly. at Inchicore. Chapel Izod is supposed to have obtained its name from La Belle Isode, a daughter of one of the Irish kings who possessed a chapel here. The lands that formerly belonged to the Knights Templars of Kilmainham, came into the possession of the Knights of Jerusalem until the dissolution of the monasteries, when they were purchased by the Crown, and taken to enclose the Phœnix Park, which, though on the opposite side of the river, is in this parish. A little further on is Palmerstown, which gives the title to the family of Temple. Adjoining the village are Palmerstown House and St. Lawrence House, both on the S. bank of the Liffey.

9 m. Lucan (Rte. 14).

5. To Clondalkin, by road either from Kilmainham, turning off from the Lucan road at Inchicore, or by a more southerly course near the village of Crumlin. 3½ m. on rt. is the well-preserved castle of Drimnagh, a remarkably perfect bawn

and fosse. It was considered a place of great strength during the rebellion of 1641.

6½ m. Clondalkin, a pretty village and station on the Great Southern and Western Rly., is famous for its round tower, the construction of which Dr. Petrie likens to that of Bronllys Castle in Breconshire. Clondalkin is remarkable for its projecting base nearly 13 ft. in height, and composed of solid masonry. "The apertures are all quadrangular, the jambs of the doorway inclining as in those of the oldest churches." The total height is 84 ft.

The abbot St. Mochna, who lived in the 7th cent., was the founder of the see of Cluain Dolcain, an ecclesiastical establishment of great importance. Nothing is now left to mark it but the tower, and a granite cross in the chyard. The tourist can return to Dublin by rail.

6. The road to Blanchardstown is on the N. bank of the river, immediately opposite the preceding and skirting the whole length of the Phœnix. It then passes the gate of Knockmaroon, and through the village of Castleknock to Blanchardstown 6 m. (Rte. 14).

7. Glasnevin Glaseen-even, "the pleasant little field") is a very pretty northern suburb; the way to it running past the Midland Great Western Stat. at Broadstone and then through Phibsborough. It next crosses the Liffey branch of the Royal Canal, leaving on l. the Prospect Cemetery, where, amongst many other celebrities, the remains of John Philpot Curran lie buried. A very ugly and conspicuous Round Tower has been erected to the memory of O'Connell.

Glasnevin is famous for its botanical gardens, which are upwards of 30 acres in extent, and contain a fine collection of exotic plants. The visitor should endeavour to see the ferns in the possession of the curator, especially the Trichomanes radicans, the fern peculiar to Killarney. The demesne now occupied by the gardens originally belonged to Tickell the poet, who resided here; indeed, this was a favourite neighbourhood amongst the littérateurs of those days, for it boasted the residences of Addison, Swift, Delany, Steele, and Parnell.

To the l. is the Observatory of Dunsink in connection with Trinity College, where the Professor of Astronomy has a residence. The tourist should visit it for the sake of the glorious view obtainable from the elevated knoll on which the building is placed.

On the opposite bank of the Tolka is Glasnevin House, the seat of Hon. G. Lindsay.

The village of Finglas, where there is an ancient cross, is not only celebrated for its early origin, which is believed to date very nearly from the time of St. Patrick, but in later times was the scene of May sports, which attracted all the world, and were probably the relics of the Pagan "feriæ."

8. A mail car goes every morning to Swords (Rte. 2), passing the village of Santry, and Santry House, the seat of Sir Charles Domville, Bart.

9. To Howth and Malahide by rail, Rte. 2.

10. To Clontarf and Dollymount omnibuses run every half hour from Sackville-st. The road first crosses the Liffey branch of the Royal Canal, and then the Tolka by Annesley Bridge, leaving to the l. the Convent, with Drumcondra Ch. and Castle (Lord J. Butler). The chief attractions of Clontarf (anc. Cluain-tarbh) are Marino, the seat of the Earl of Charlemont, and Clontarf Castle (J. E. Vernon, Esq.), a beautiful mansion of "mixed Elizabethan and castellated styles." Here was fought the great battle of Clontarf on Good Friday, 1014, between the Danes under Sitric, and the Irish under their king Brian Boroimhe, who received

his death wound on this occasion, together with 11,000 of the flower of his army. The Irish, notwithstanding their loss, were triumphant, and the decline of the Danish power may be dated from this action, although it was not immediately extinguished. At Dollymount a visit can be paid to the Bull wall and pier, which protects the harbour of Dublin from the sands of the N. Bull (p. 6).

Conveyances from Dublin :— In addition to the local services established for the use of the city, railways radiate to all quarters of the compass : 1. To Drogheda, Dundalk, Newry, and Belfast, by the Dublin and Drogheda line in Amiens St.; 2. To Mullingar, Cavan, Longford, Athlone, Roscommon, Castlebar, Sligo, Westport, Ballinasloe, and Galway, by the Midland Great Western (Broadstone) ; 3. To Kingstown, Bray, and Wicklow, from Westland Row and Harcourt St.; 4. Kildare, Tullamore, Maryborough, Kilkenny, Waterford, Mallow, Killarney, Tralee, Limerick, Cork, by the Great Southern and Western (Kingsbridge). Coaches and cars to Ashtown, Baltinglass, Blessington, Wexford, and Enniskerry. By steamers to Holyhead daily ; to Kingston 5 times a day ; Belfast weekly ; Falmouth, Plymouth, Portsmouth, and London, bi-weekly ; Belfast and Glasgow 3 times a week ; Liverpool daily ; Whitehaven bi-weekly ; Wexford weekly ; Bristol weekly ; Silloth weekly.

A brief notice of the history of Dublin may not be uninteresting, although to give it in detail would be to write the history of Ireland. The name of Eblana is occasionally given it, because a city of this name is mentioned as existing in the same latitude by Ptolemy ; but with more probability it acquired its appellation from Duibh-linne, the Blackwater ; " in fact, so called from a lady named Dubh, who had been formerly drowned there. The Danish or English name Dublin is a mere modification of Dubhlinn, but the native Irish have always called, and still do call the city Ath Cliath, or Bailé Atha Cliath, the Ford of Hurdles, or the Town of the Ford of Hurdles."— *O'Currey.* In the time of St. Patrick, the Danes, or Ostmen, were well established as merchants, as we hear of his celebrating mass in one of the vaults of the cathedral built by them for storehouses. In the 9th cent., however, they entered as conquerors, and from this date the annals of Dublin present very stormy details of wars and fights between the Ostmen and the native Irish. But the power of the Danes in Ireland received its great overthrow at the battle of Clontarf (p. 17), although they still kept possession of the city and founded Christian churches in the reign of Sitricus, 1038.

In the same cent. Godred, King of Man, overran Dublin, and for some years exercised his sway. But on his death we find the city in the hands of native Irish rulers until the invasion of Wexford by the English in 1169, who under Strongbow occupied it with the ostensible view of assisting MacMurrough, King of Leinster, against his enemy Roderic O'Connor.

The principal subsequent events were—the arrival of Henry II., who granted a charter to the inhabitants ; the erection of the castle by King John ; the attack and partial destruction of Dublin by Edward Bruce in 1315; the rebellion of Lord Thomas Fitzgerald, commonly called Silken Thomas, during the reign of Henry VIII.; the landing of Cromwell in 1649 ; and the insurrection of Robert Emmett in 1803. The intervals between these dates, especially up to the 17th cent., were characterised by repeated outbreaks and attacks made by native Irish, who presumed on the weakness of the government.

ROUTE 2.

FROM DUBLIN TO DROGHEDA AND DUNDALK.

The Dublin and Drogheda Rly. (opened in 1849) is the first link in the great northern chain that connects Dublin with Belfast, and is, so far, of importance, although the length of the whole line, including the branches to Howth and Oldcastle, is not more than 71 m. Starting from the stat. in Amiens-street, a very graceful building with an Italian façade, the rly. is carried through the N.E. part of the city on a viaduct, crossing the Royal Canal by a fine iron lattice beam bridge of 140 ft. span, and soon emerging on the sands of Clontarf Bay, which are traversed by an embankment 30 ft. high. On l. is a granite bridge of 3 arches, known as the *Annesley Bridge*, over the Tolka river, which here empties itself into the bay. From the embankment a very charming panoramic view is gained on every side, embracing the city with its forest of masts and chimneys, and the whole coast as far as Kingstown, backed up by the Dublin and Wicklow Mountains, while inland are numerous villas and handsome seats. On l. is the gateway of the mansion of *Marino*, the seat of the Earl of Charlemont; and rt. is the pleasant suburb of *Clontarf*, with Clontarf Castle (J. E. Vernon, Esq.), and many other residences; but as there is a regular communication by omnibus from this place and Dollymount to the city, it is described in the environs of Dublin (Rte. 1).

At 1¾ m. the line crosses the Howth turnpike-road, having on l. Mount Temple and Donnycarney House, and soon enters the deep Killester cutting in the black calp limestone, through which it is carried for 1½ m. to Raheny. On l. of the rly. is *Killester* ruined ch. and abbey, the latter the seat of D. Nugent, Esq. *Artane* (T. Alley, Esq.), ¼ m. l., was the scene of a cruel murder perpetrated in 1533 on John Allen, Archbishop of Dublin, and one of Wolsey's protégés, when flying from the resentment of Lord Thomas Fitzgerald. "It is universally supposed that Fitzgerald, moved with compassion, and intending only to have the prelate imprisoned, cried out to the people in Irish, 'Take away the clown,' but the attendants, wilfully misconstruing his words, beat out the bishop's brains." On rt., close to the line, is *Furry Park* (T. Bushe, Esq.), formerly the seat of the Earl of Shannon.

3¾ m. *Raheny* Stat., or more properly Rathcny, from its situation near an ancient rath, still to be traced. In the neighbourhood are Raheny Park (T. Gresham, Esq.), and Sybil Hill (J. Barlow, Esq.). From hence the line passes through an undulating country, occasionally affording pleasant peeps of coast scenery.

4¾ m. Junction Stat. [From this point the rly. to Howth turns off to rt. On the shore are the remains of *Kilbarrock Ch.*, once the votive chapel for all mariners of the bay of Dublin. It contains some roundheaded and pointed arches. In the 13th cent. the manor was held by the tenure of presenting a pair of furred gloves to the king.

6¾ m. Baldoyle Stat. From the bridge, crossing the line, there is a very lovely view of the promontory of Howth, with the rocky island of Ireland's Eye a little to the N.

On rt. is *Sutton*, famous for its bed of oysters. Large quantities of dolomite or magnesian limestone have been quarried from the rocks in this vicinity.

8¼ m. *Howth*. *Hotel*: Royal. The hill of Howth, so dear to all the inhabitants of Dublin, is "an elevated promontory connected with the mainland by a sandy isthmus, and forming the northern entrance of Dublin Bay, over which it is elevated 560 ft. above low-water mark." The town, which is on the N. side, consists of one street running along the edge of the cliff, and overlooking the *Harbour*, 52 acres in extent, and enclosed by 2 fine piers. Owing to the difficulties of the undertaking, the cost was very great (no less than 300,000*l.*), a large portion of which might have been saved by the choice of a more judicious spot. It once enjoyed the advantages of being the point of arrival and departure for the English packets, but since the selection of Kingstown the trade of Howth has become very small, and chiefly confined to coasters; indeed, vessels of any magnitude cannot enter, and even small ones find the anchorage too hard for them. There is a fixed lighthouse at the entrance of the harbour. The ch., or *abbey*, is situated on a precipitous bank above the sea, and is surrounded by a strong embattled wall. It is of the date of the 13th cent., and is a single-bodied building, the nave separated from the aisle by 6 pointed arches, the 4 most westerly of which spring from rude quadrangular piers. The W. front is entered by a round-headed doorway, and surmounted by a bell-turret of 2 stages. "The porch in connection with the northern doorway is a very unusual feature in Irish churches, a fact not easily to be accounted for, as they appear to have been common in England during every age of Gothic architecture." — *Wakeman.* Howth Ch. was founded in the 13th cent. by a member of the family of St. Lawrence, who held the manorial estates of Howth, and whose original name was Tristram. It is related of Sir Armoricus Tristram that, being about to encounter the Danes at Clontarf, he made a vow to St. Lawrence, the patron saint of the day, that he would take his name as a surname if successful. The tomb of Christopher, 20th Lord Howth (1580), stands in the nave, near the E. gable. It is an altar-tomb, containing recumbent figures of a knight and lady, the former with his feet resting on a dog. On the sides are the armorial bearings of the St. Lawrences and Plunkets. The *Castle* (the seat of Lord Howth) is on the W. side of the town, and is a long and irregular battlemented building, flanked by square towers. The hall contains a collection of weapons, and amongst them the 2-handed sword said to have been wielded by Sir Armoricus on the occasion of the battle of Clontarf. See *ante.* There is also a painting representing the abduction of young Lord Howth by Grace O'Malley, in the time of Elizabeth. Having landed at Howth, she requested the hospitality of its lord, which was refused, the family being at dinner with the doors shut. She therefore seized the son and heir and carried him off to her castle of Carrigahooly, where she detained him until she had extracted a promise from Lord Howth that the gates of his castle should be always thrown open during meals. In the upper apartments is the bed used by William III. on his visit to Ireland. The whole of the peninsula of Howth has been in the hands of the present family ever since their earliest arrival from England in the 13th cent. The walk through the grounds leading up to the hills is very charming.

An excursion of 2 m. across the hills will bring the tourist to the Baily Lighthouse, one of the most prominent objects that greet the English traveller by night or day as he approaches the bay of Dublin. It is finely situated on a peninsulated perpendicular rock, 110 ft. above high-water mark, and in form is a frustrated cone, exhibiting a fixed white light. In an adjoining room a telescope is kept "by means of which the shoals which obstruct the entrance to the bay may be observed, viz. the Great Kish, the Bennett, and Burford Banks, which are links of the chain extending along the Wicklow and Wexford coasts, and known as the Irish Grounds." It was erected in 1814, the light that previously existed on the summit of the hill being uncertain on account of the mists which so often shrouded the head. An ancient stone fortress formerly occupied the site of the Baily Lighthouse, from whence the name (Ballium) was probably derived; and it is believed that these remains, which are still faintly visible, indicated the residence of Criomthan Nia-nair, who reigned over Ireland about the year 90; and whose sepulchral cairn crowns the summit of Sliath Martin. The whole of the coast scenery on the S. of Howth Head is very fine, particularly at the so-called "Lion's Head," and the Needles or Candlesticks, some bold isolated rocks, a little to the W. of the Baily. Indeed it would be difficult to overrate the beauty of the views from any part of the hill, but more particularly towards the S., extending over the magnificent sweep of Dublin Bay and the Wicklow Mountains. On the eastern side of *Ben Howth*, which rises in the centre of the promontory to the height of 560 ft., is *St. Fintan's Ch.*, a remarkably small building of the date of the 13th cent. Internally it measures only 16½ ft. by 7 ft. 8 in., and is lighted by 5 windows of various forms, deeply splayed in the interior. There is a lancet doorway in the W. gable, which is surmounted by a disproportionate bell-turret. A little distance off is the well of St. Fintan. Between this ch. and Howth Castle is a large dismounted *cromlech*, once formed of 10 supporters, and covered by a quartz block, 8 ft. in depth and about 18 ft. square. There are 2 *Hotels* on the peninsula besides the one in Howth, viz. Byron's, near Sutton, and the Baily, near the lighthouse. As regards geological position, the coast of Howth affords clear sections of Cambrian rocks, principally quartz, separated from each other by bands of greenish-grey slate dipping to the S.W. At a point called the Cliffs, on the S. coast, is a large green hornblendic dyke; while the formation of the Needles is of quartz rock resting on porphyritic greenstone. At the extreme end of the Nose of Howth, on the N.E., Dr. Kinahan found Oldhamia antiqua. The hills in the centre of the district, such as Ben Howth, Loughoreen, Dang Hill (on which is the old lighthouse), are also formed of thick beds of quartz. "Taking Howth as a whole, it presents hardly a feature in common with the Cambrian rocks of Wicklow or Wexford, with the exception of some of the quartz rock masses, and the occurrence of green grits and slates at some points. Whether Cambrian or Silurian, it seems to occupy a horizon distinct from any rocks hitherto examined on the eastern coast."—*Geological Survey.* Towards the N. and W., from the harbour of Howth to the S. part of the southern shore, the carboniferous rocks (lower limestone) are visible. Erica cinerea and Asplenium maximum have their habitat here.] 1 m. to the N. of Howth is the small island of *Ireland's Eye*, a wedge-shaped mass of quartz rock resting on contorted Cambrian grits, forming a good natural breakwater for the harbour. It contains the ruins of an ancient chapel founded in the 6th cent. by St. Nessan, which was famous for possessing a copy of the 4 Gospels, called the "Garland of Howth," and of great sanctity. Not many years ago the island obtained a less enviable notoriety from a terrible murder committed there, known as the Kirwan tragedy.

From the Howth Junction the

line continues northward, having on l. Grange House ; and crosses the Mayne river to 6¾ m. *Portmarnock*, a small village close to the shore, which is of so smooth a character as to have obtained the name of the Velvet Strand. The botanist will find here Ammi majus, Alyssum minimum, Equisetum variegatum, Carex extensa, Schœnus nigricans.

The singular ch. of *St. Doulough*, 1 m. l., has puzzled antiquaries from the incongruity of its style, uniting the high stone roof of very early Irish date, with the pointed features of the 13th cent. It is an oblong ch., 48 ft. in length, from the centre of which rises a low square tower with graduated battlements. "A projection on the S. wall of the tower contains a passage leading from the upper part of the building to an exceedingly small chamber, in the eastern wall of which are 2 windows, one commanding the only entrance to the ch., the other an altar in an apartment or chapel between the tower and the W. gable."—*Wakeman.* At the E. is a 2-light pointed window, while another of the same date, but with cinquefoil heads, occupies a singular position near the base of the S. side of the tower. "The vaults of the lower apartments form the floor of a croft, occupying uninterruptedly the whole length of the building. The roof is double, of an extremely high pitch, and between the 2 is a small dimly-lighted chamber." The ch. is now undergoing a process of restoration, which it sadly needed. The *Well*, outside the chyard, is covered in by an octagon-shaped, stone-roofed building, and has a circular interior, formerly decorated with religious paintings. Close by are a stone cross, and a subterranean bath known as St. Catherine's Pond. 7¼ m. l., in the grounds of Grange, are the remains of an ancient fort. Still more on the l., conspicuous by a windmill on its summit, is the *hill of Feltrim*, in the mansion-house of which James II. passed a night on his flight from the Boyne. Passing Hazelbrook (A. Norman, Esq.), Beechwood House (R. Trumbull, Esq.), and Broomfield, beyond which on the shore are remains of a castle known as Roebuck or Rob's Wall, the line arrives at

9 m. *Malahide* (*Hotel*: Royal, good), a somewhat dull bathing-place, frequented by the inhabitants of Dublin, and situated at the mouth of a considerable estuary, called Meadow Water. The chief attraction to visitors is the *Castle of Malahide*, the ancient baronial seat and residence of Lord Talbot of Malahide, whose family has been seated here for more than 700 years. The visitor is admitted on presenting a card, to be obtained at the hotel. The castle was founded by Richard Talbot, who received a grant of the lordship in the reign of Henry II., and is still an interesting building, though modern alterations and additions have been made, not altogether in the best taste. As it at present stands, it is an ivy-covered building, flanked on each side by a slender drum tower, with Irish stepped battlements. The one at the S.E. angle is very modern. The principal features of interest in the interior are, an oak panelled room, with an elaborately carved chimney-piece, representing the Conception; respecting which the following legend is told. In 1653 the castle was inhabited by Miles Corbet the regicide for 7 years, during which time the figure of the Virgin Mary took miraculous flight, never appearing again until the unholy tenant had fled. The dining-hall, a fine lofty room, contains the original oak roof and gallery, with many family portraits, amongst which are Charles I. and Henrietta Maria by Vandyke, James II. and Ann Hyde (Sir P. Lely), Queen Anne (Sir G. Kneller), and one of Lord Tyrconnel,

Lord Lieutenant of Ireland in James II.'s time. There is also a painting in 3 compartments by Albert Durer, which belonged to Mary Queen of Scots, and was purchased by Charles II. for 2000*l.*, as well as others by Canaletti, Cuyp, Vandyke, &c. The library contains the documents of a grant made by Edward IV. to the Talbots.

Adjoining the house is the ruined abbey, a single-aisled building, of nave and chancel, divided by a good arch, and lighted by trefoil windows on the S., and a perpendicular window on the W. There is also a 2-light window under the little belfry, ornamented with crocketed ogee canopies. Inside is the altar-tomb of Maud Plunkett, the heroine of Griffin's ballad of the 'Bridal of Malahide,' whose husband fell in a fray immediately after the celebration of his marriage, thus making her maid, wife, and widow, in one day, though she afterwards lived to marry her 3rd husband, Sir Richard Talbot :—

> "But oh, for the maiden
> Who mourns for that chief
> With heart overladen
> And rending with grief!
> She sinks on the meadow
> In one morning tide,
> A wife and a widow,
> A maid and a bride."

The tomb is surmounted by her recumbent effigy in the costume of the 15th cent. It is a pity that the weeds and underwood are allowed to grow in such profusion within the precincts of the ruins.

[3 m. to l. of Malahide is the village of Swords, remarkable for its ch., round tower, and castle. It was formerly a place of some importance, a ch. having been founded here in 512 by St. Columb, which was subsequently made the seat of a bishopric, under the jurisdiction of St. Finian. The round tower is 73 ft. in height, and very perfect, even to the conical cap on the summit. It has a lower quadrangular doorway 3 ft. above the level of the ground, with a 2nd aperture of nearly the same shape, 20 ft. above the ground. The castle, or the archiepiscopal residence, consists of long ranges of embattled walls flanked by square towers. It is said to have been destroyed, together with the town, no less than 4 times by the Danes. Adjoining the round tower is a ch. of the 14th cent., to which is appended a modern excrescence forming the body of the building. In the neighbourhood of Swords are Brackenstown House, the seat of R. Manders, Esq., in whose grounds is a large rath ; and Balheary House (H. Baker, Esq.)]. The line now crosses the estuary for 1¼ m. by means of a considerable embankment, divided in the centre by a timber viaduct set on piles. There is a fine view from it over Malahide, Lambay Island, and the promontory of Portraine.

11¼ m. To the l. of *Donabate* Stat., are the remains of the square castle of Donabate, "the high fortress of the bay," also Newbridge House, the seat of the family of Cobbe, in whose demesne are the ivy-covered ruins of Landestown Castle : also on l. is Turvey House, the estate of Lord Trimleston. On rt., overlooking the shore, is *Portraine*, the castellated seat of J. Evans, Esq. Close to the sea is a modern round tower, erected to the memory of a former member of the family by his widow.

3 m. off the coast is *Lambay Island*, the Limnius of Pliny, the cliffs of which, rising to the height of 418 ft., form a beautiful feature in the scenery. Geologically speaking, it consists of a mass of dark porphyry, overlaid at Kiln and Scotch Points (the S.E. and N.E. respectively) by grey Silurian limestone and grey slates. Both Kiln Point and the shore at Portraine are capital fields for Silurian fossils, especially in the matter of trilobites and gasteropods. "There is a

curious old polygon building evidently constructed for defending the place, which its battlements and spikeholes command in every direction: it has been built entirely on arches without timber."—*D'Alton.* The cliffs of Lambay were the scene of the wreck of the iron steam-vessel 'Taylour.' The lands of Portraine, in which barony Lambay is included, were formerly given by Sitric, the Danish King of Dublin, for the endowment of a Christian ch.

14 m. *Rush* and *Lusk* Stat. Rush is a small maritime village on the rt., possessing no feature of interest; but the visitor should by all means see the round tower of· Lusk 1 m. l. An abbey was founded in the 5th cent. by St. Macculind, who is supposed to have been buried here. The chief peculiarity of the ch. is its square embattled steeple, probably of the latter time of E. E., supported on 3 sides by slender round towers, with Irish stepped battlements. The further side is flanked by a round tower of undoubted antiquity, measuring 7½ ft. diameter at its base, though deprived of its conical apex. The body of the ch. consists of 2 aisles, divided by a range of blocked pointed arches, and contains a richly-decorated monument to Sir Christopher Barnewell and wife (16th cent.), "by whom he had issue 5 sons and 15 daithers." Underneath the tower is a crypt in which the founder was buried, and this crypt, "being termed in Irish 'lupea,' is supposed to have given name to the locality."—*D'Alton.* In the black carboniferous shales of Lough Shinny, in which copper has been worked, may be found the fossil called "Posidonomya Becheri."

15 m. rt. is *Kenure Park*, once the residence of the Duke of Ormond, and now of Sir Roger Palmer.

16 m. l., on an eminence, are the ruins of *Baldangan Castle*, "the town of the fortification." Some square towers and walls are all now left of this once fine fortress, which formerly belonged to the De Berminghams, from whom it passed to the Lords of Howth, and subsequently held out in 1641 for the confederates of the Pale, against the Parliamentary army. Portions of a ch. are also visible. Passing rt. Hacketstown (J. Johnston, Esq.), and l. 1 m. Milverton House (G. Woods, Esq.), the traveller arrives at 18 m. *Skerries*, a thriving little fishing harbour anciently called Holmpatrick, from a tradition that St. Patrick once landed here. The islands of the Skerries lie a short distance out. They are 3 in number—Red Island, Colt, and St. Patrick's; beyond which is the Rock o' Bill. Connected at low water with the mainland is Sherrick's Island, on which there is a martello tower. There is a lighthouse on one of the Skerries islands showing a red revolving light.

At Barnageera, 19 m., the antiquary may see a couple of sepulchral tumuli, which in 1840 were opened, yielding a coffin and bones. On l. are Ardgillan, the castellated residence of Col. Taylour, M.P., and Hampton Hall (G. A. Hamilton, Esq.).

About 1 m. l. is *Balrothery*, the ch. of which possesses a peculiarity similar to Lusk in having a round tower flanking one of the angles of the steeple. As the line runs close along the coast, fine views are obtained in a northerly direction of the head of Clogher, above which, in clear weather, the Mourne Mountains rise in noble ranges.

22 m. *Balbriggan* (*Hotel :* Hamilton Arms), a town of about 2250 Inhab., associated with hosiery and stockings in particular, in which it still carries on an important trade. It owes its prosperity almost entirely to the family of Hamilton of Hampton, and particularly to Baron Hamilton, who in 1780, with the help of the Irish Parliament, established cotton-works, and built a pier 420 ft. in length;

subsequently to which an inner dock was constructed almost at the sole expense of another member of the same family. The harbour is lighted by a fixed light.

The rly. is carried across the harbour by a viaduct of 11 arches of 30 ft. span.

24 m. *Gormanstown.* On l. is Gormanstown Castle, the finely wooded seat of Viscount Gormanstown, in whose possession it has been since the time of Edward III. It is a large rectangular pile of building flanked by slender round towers, and is not remarkable for much architectural taste. The wooded glen of the Delvin river, which here separates the counties Dublin and Meath, offers a pretty contrast to the somewhat bleak coast-lands through which the line has hitherto been passing. On rt. is the headland of *Knocknaccean,* "the hill of dead men's heads," in which excavations made by Mr. Hamilton revealed a chamber containing a vast number of calcined bones. Respecting these a tradition existed that a large body of giants, of Irish and Danish birth, overthrew an army of invaders who landed at this spot in the 5th cent. 26 m. rt. is Morney House (late Capt. Pepper).

27 m. *Layton* Stat., from whence on l. a tumulus is visible on the bank of the Nanny, a considerable stream, crossed by a viaduct 300 ft. long. On the S. bank is *Ballygarth,* the castellated seat of the Peppers, who have inhabited it from the time of Charles II. Further up the river are the village of Julianstown and *Darlistown Castle,* the residence of Sir Thomas Ross.

29 m. rt. is *Betaghstown,* commonly called Bettystown, which is rising into repute as a bathing-place with the inhabitants of Drogheda, from whence omnibuses run several times a day. The Maiden Tower is a lonely tower on the coast, named after Queen Elizabeth. It is situated in the district of Mornington, which gave a title to the Wellesley family. Close by is a solid mass of masonry, known as the Finger. "They were evidently landmarks erected before lighthouses were employed in this country."

32 m. *Drogheda,* pronounced *Droyda* (*Hotel:* Simcox's Imperial), an ancient city (Urbs Pontana of the Romans' with a strong fish-like smell, and altogether so dirty and uncomfortable, and with such miserable accommodation, that the tourist will not feel inclined to linger in the town any more than is necessary for him to view the many objects of interest in the neighbourhood. (Pop. 14,740,. It is finely situated on the Boyne, the bulk of the town being on the N. bank of the river, which runs in a deep valley, affording the traveller fine views from any of the surrounding high grounds. Indeed, that from the station is perhaps as good as any other, and presents Drogheda under the most favourable circumstances, viz. those of distance. But this favourable impression is soon dispelled on entering the narrow and crowded streets, especially if it happen to be market or fair day. Apart from antiquities, the most striking part of the town is the harbour, which at the lower end is crossed by an extremely graceful railway viaduct, which in size and proportions ranks 2nd to none in the kingdom. On the S. side, and extending over the largest half of the river, it consists of 12 arches of 60 ft. span, between which and 3 similar arches on the N. side, the communication is maintained by a lattice bridge of 3 beams, each 550 ft. in length, and 90 ft. above the level of high water, sufficient to allow vessels of any size to pass underneath. The *Harbour,* which is formed "by the outfall of the Boyne, assisted by the ebb from a considerable tide basin below the town," has been at different times much improved, greatly to the benefit of the

trade, which has increased so rapidly as to place Drogheda high amongst Irish ports. "About 80 years since the shipping interest from this town gave employment to but a solitary vessel, the 'Mary Anne,' whose ladings, insurances, departures, and returns, were at the time a source of reiterated excitement to the merchants."—*D'Alton.* At the present time Drogheda possesses more than 50 vessels with a tonnage of 4376, and employs 9 steam-vessels trading to Liverpool and other ports. Great numbers of cattle are shipped, besides butter, oats, &c., in enormous quantities; in addition to which, an extensive trade is carried on in linen, cotton, salt, distilling, and tanning, not forgetting the Drogheda ale, about the pleasantest thing in the town. At one time the manufacture of table-linen was so large, that 10,000*l.* was the average expenditure on market-days.

The *Walls* of Drogheda, some portions of which still remain, were about 1½ m. in circumference, and were entered by 10 gates, 5 on the N. or Meath side of the town, and 5 on the S. or Louth side; of these the only ones remaining are a portion of the *West* or *Butter Gate*, an octangular tower, defended by long narrow loopholes, and entered by a circular arched passage strengthened by a portcullis, and *St. Lawrence's Gate,* one of the most perfect specimens in the kingdom. It consists of 2 lofty circular towers of 4 stories, between which is a retiring wall pierced like the towers with loopholes. "It is probable that the latter was anciently, upon the town side, divided into stages by platforms of timber extending from tower to tower, otherwise the loopholes could not have been used by the defenders of the gate."—*Wakeman.*

The ruins of the *Abbey of St. Mary D'Urso,* situated between West Gate and the Boyne, are small, and consist of a central tower with a fine pointed arch, spanning a dirty thoroughfare called the Abbey Lane. It was once an important and extensive building of 150 ft. in length, and is believed to have been founded by St. Patrick, and to have been the temporary residence of St. Columb in the 6th cent., subsequently to which it was occupied by Augustinian friars.

The *Dominican,* or Abbey of Preaching Friars, is conspicuous in the N. portion of the town from its sole remaining feature, the Magdalene steeple, a lofty tower of 2 stories springing from a noble pointed arch. It is lighted by 2 pointed windows on each side, and contains 2 upper apartments. In the E. battlement is a breach made by Cromwell's cannon. This religious house, which was once cruciform, was founded in 1224 by an archbishop of Armagh, and was the place where Richard II. in 1394 received the submission of O'Neill, Prince of Ulster, and his subordinate chieftains. Unfortunately for the archæologist, these ruins stand in the midst of a most wretched collection of hovels.

On the N. or Meath side, the only other building worth notice is the *Tholsil,* an important-looking building surmounted by a cupola. Close to it the Boyne is spanned by an inconvenient *Bridge,* "on one side of which may be still seen the wicker Corragh, with its horse-skin covering, the same in design and execution perhaps as floated there 1000 years ago; and on the other we find the latest invented and most improved screw steamer."—*Wilde.* On the S. side are the ch. of St. Mary, formerly devoted to the use of the Carmelites; the poor-house, a really handsome building for the accommodation of 1000 inmates; and a martello fort, commanding the whole of the town from a mount which was formerly the grave of the wife of Gobhan the smith, and which is recorded to have been robbed by the Danes of its contents in the 9th cent. Behind the poor-house is the mound from whence Cromwell, in his attack on the town. "made the breach assaultable, and, by the help of God, stormed it." A handsome addition has been made to Drogheda, in the shape of a fine hall, called the Whitworth Hall, presented to the town by Mr. Whitworth, the member for the borough.

The early name of Drogheda was Drochat-Atha—the Bridge of the Ford—afterwards Anglicised into Tredagh. The principal events in the history of its annals, which up to the time of Cromwell are traceable with remarkable regularity, are the holding of several parliaments, one of which, known as the Poynings Parliament, and held in 1493, provided for the dependence of the Irish legislative assembly upon that of England. It was frequently the rendezvous of the armies that were sent against the rebellious inhabitants of Ulster, and in 1641 held out successfully against Sir Phelim O'Neill under Sir Henry Tichborne and Lord Moore; and again for a time in 1649 under Sir Arthur Ashton against Cromwell, who at last took the town by storm, accompanied by circumstances of great ferocity, "so that, except some few, who during the time of the assault escaped at the other end of the town, there was not an officer, soldier, or religious person belonging to that garrison left alive."—*Clarendon.* James II. sojourned here previous to the battle of the Boyne, the events of which are described in p. 141.

Conveyances.—By rail to Dublin, Belfast: also to Navan and Oldcastle; by steam to Liverpool; mail-car to Virginia.

Distances.—Dublin, 33 m.: Belfast, 81; Liverpool, 133; Duleek, 4½; Betaghstown, 5; Mellifont Abbey, 5; Monasterboice, 6; Oldbridge, 2½; Newgrange, 7; Hill of Dowth, 5; Dunleer, 10; Slane, 8.

Excursions.—
1. Oldbridge and the Boyne (Rte. 15).
2. Mellifont and Monasterboice.
3. Newgrange and Dowth (Rte. 15).
4. Duleek and Athcarne (Rte. 16).

[The tourist will of course visit the abbey of *Mellifont*, the first Cistercian Abbey ever founded in Ireland. It owes its establishment to Donough O'Carroll, Prince of Oirgiallach, in 1142, who was influenced by the request of St. Malachy the Archbishop of Armagh. At the time of its consecration in 1157, a very important synod was held here, attended by the primate, 17 bishops, and 4 or 5 kings. At the introduction of the English power into the Pale, the abbey (which was an offshoot of that of Clairvaux in Normandy) was taken under the special protection of Henry II., who granted a charter, afterwards confirmed by John. Towards the end of the 16th cent. the last abbot retired, and Mellifont then became the residence of Sir Edward Moore, in whose time it underwent a siege during the Rebellion. At the time of the dissolution it contained 140 monks, besides lay brothers and servitors. The ruins are pleasantly situated on the steep banks of the Mattock, which here divides the counties of Meath and Louth. On a projection of rock near the river is the gateway, a massive square tower, carried up on one side to a considerable height. Admittance was gained by a circular arch, through which now runs a mill-stream. The baptistery is a singular octagon building, of which only 5 sides remain. Each face is entered by a semicircular door with good pillars and mouldings; and above the crown of the arches externally runs a string-course. Although the roof is gone, the corbels in the interior show the points from which the arches sprang to support it. "The effect of the colour from the red bricks introduced into the architraves is very pleasing, and they constitute a feature in Irish architecture pronounced by Dr. Petrie to be almost unique."—*D'Alton.* On the top, according to Archdall, was a reservoir for water, which was conveyed by pipes to the different offices. Close by, and apparently of later date, is *St. Bernard's Chapel,* consisting of a crypt and an upper chamber, the basement floor being considerably lower than the surface ground outside. The crypt has a beautifully groined roof, and arches springing from clustered columns, having capitals elaborately carved in foliage. The centre columns are carried down to the ground, but the others stop short at a basement running round at a little height from the floor. It is lighted by an eastern and 2 side windows, of Decorated style, with good mullions, though but little of the tracery, which resembles Flamboyant, remains. This chapel was formerly entered by a pointed doorway, that, to judge from plates given by Wright in 'Louthiana,' and the 'Irish Penny Journal,' 1832, was most elaborate in its ornamentation. Near the baptistery are remains of dungeons in which Dervorgoil, "whose abduction by Dermod Mac Morrough, king of Leinster, led to the introduction into Ireland of the English under Strongbow," is said to have closed her career.

About 2 m. to the N.E. of Mellifont, and 6 from Drogheda, are the venerable ruins of *Monasterboice,* consisting of 2 churches, a round tower, and 3 of the finest crosses in Ireland. The churches are of different dates: the oldest, which is probably anterior to the tower, measures 45 ft. in length, and formerly consisted of aisle and choir, separated by a round arch, which at present terminates the building, as the choir has disappeared. The doorway is in the centre of the vast gable, and has a rude horizontal head. The 2nd ch.,

adjoining the tower, is considerably smaller, and is of the date of the 13th cent.

The *Round Tower,* the great feature of Monasterboice, is considered by Dr. Petrie to be about the date of the 9th cent. It is 17 yards in circumference at the base, gradually diminishing to the summit, which is 90 ft. in height, and is broken off, presenting at a distance somewhat of the aspect of a huge steel pen. The most noticeable point about it is the door, standing 6 ft. from the ground, the head formed of 2 stones laid horizontally one above the other. "A band extends round the head and down the sides of the doorway, but terminates on a level with the sill, or rather turns off at a right angle, passing horizontally for a distance of 8 inches, from which point it ascends, and running upwards round the doorway head gives the appearance of a double band."—*Wakeman.* Above the doorway is a small pointed window, but all the others are square-headed. Of the 3 *Crosses,* 2 are considered to be the finest specimens of the kind in Ireland. The largest one is 27 ft. high, and is composed of 3 stones, viz., the shaft, the cross (the arms of which are bound together by a ring), and the top piece. The shaft is divided into 7 compartments, all of which were filled with elaborate sculpture, more or less weathered and worn. In the 2nd from the bottom are 5 figures, of which one is presenting a book, while a bird rests on his head. In the 3rd, 4th, 5th, and 6th are the Apostles. The body of the cross is filled with a representation of the Crucifixion. The circle by which the arms of the cross are connected are enriched with elaborate ornament, conspicuous for its cable moulding. The 2nd cross is even more distinct, but is not nearly so large, being only 15 ft. high. There are 3 main compartments in the western face of the shaft, each of which is filled with 3 figures habited in the ecclesiastical or military dress of the period, viz. the 9th or 10th cent. "The history which these sculptures are intended to commemorate evidently commences in the lowest entablature, where an ecclesiastic in a long cloak fastened with a brooch stands between 2 figures, either soldiers or robbers, armed with long Danish swords. In the compartment over this, the same personages are represented as students, each with a book, but the soldiers have assumed the ecclesiastical garb, although they retain the moustache. In the top division the figures are again repeated, all in long flowing dresses; the central one —then perhaps aged or at the point of death—is represented giving his staff to one and his book to the other of his former assailants."—*Catalogue of Irish Acad.* The centre piece on the eastern face represents our Saviour sitting in judgment, while below it are the Adoration of the Wise Men, the Temptation, and Expulsion in the 5th and lowest division, besides 1 or 2 compartments that are obscure. From an inscription on the lowest part of the shaft, which runs " A prayer for Muiredach, by whom was made this cross," we learn the name of the builder. From the Irish Annals it appears there were 2 Muiredachs, one who died in 844, and the other in 924, to the latter of whom Dr. Petrie inclines, as it is known that he was a man of great wealth and distinction, and therefore more likely to have erected such a work of art. To Cromwell is ascribed the crime of breaking the 3rd cross, which is very imperfect, the head and part of the shaft only remaining uninjured. Besides these crosses there is a monumental stone inscribed in Irish, " A prayer for Ruarcan." " The crosses of Monasterboice may be regarded not only as memorials of the piety and munificence of a people whom ignorance and prejudice have too often sneered at as barbarous, but also as the finest works of sculptured art of their period now existing."—*Wakeman.* This religious establishment was founded about the end of the 5th cent. by St. Buithe, the son of Bronnagh, from whom it derived its name. Buithe, the founder, was buried himself here in 521, and subsequently to this period the abbey was visited by St. Columb. With the exception of the destruction of the belfry by fire in 1097, the annals of this house are not marked by any events of importance.]

The Dublin and Belfast Junction line now conveys the traveller northward. This line, opened in 1852, completes the railway chain from Dublin to Belfast, by uniting with the Ulster Rly. at Portadown, 56 m. distant. After crossing the Boyne Viaduct, a smaller one is entered upon at Newfoundwell Bridge, built in a style to harmonise with the walls of Drogheda. On rt. 1½ m. is Beaulieu House (R. Montgomery, Esq.), pleasantly situated just at the mouth of the Boyne. The family of Montgomery have inherited this estate from Sir Henry Tichborne, Governor of Drogheda in 1641.

From hence to Dundalk the line passes through a prettily cultivated country, though not so rich in archæological remains as the district to the W. of Drogheda. The tourist frequently obtains charming views of the Mourne Mountains and the hilly country between Dundalk and Newry.

35¼ m. rt. 2 m. is the village of *Termonfeckin,* in former times the residence of the Abps. of Armagh, the last of whom was Abp. Ussher, who died in 1612. It was also the residence of R. C. Arbp. Plunket, who was executed for treason. There are remains of the ancient castle. The name of Termon means " sanctuary,"—the sanctuary of St.

Fechan—it being the habit for a certain portion of land, answering to our glebe, and called "Termon land," to be set apart for the use of the clergy attached to the foundation.

37¼ m. rt. is Black Hall (G. Pentland, Esq.), and some 2 m. to the E. the village and headland of Clogher, a very prominent object in all the coast views.

40½ m. rt. is *Barmeath*, the seat of Lord Bellew; soon after which the traveller arrives at 42 m. rt. *Dunleer*, a small town situated in the valley of the White River. By a singular charter given by Charles II., the inhabitants had the privilege of electing a sovereign of their own, which however has not been exercised since 1811. Atheiare Castle, a little to the S. is a good specimen of the fortified manor-house, one end being defended by a massive battlemented tower.

[From Dunleer it is 5 m. S.W. to the hill of Collon, 744 ft., on the slope of which is Temple, the beautifully wooded demesne of Viscount Massareene and Ferrard.]

[About midway between Dunleer and Castle Bellingham, 6 m. l., is *Ardee*, a town of about 2700 Inhab., situated, as its name implies, on the river Dee. It was of great importance in ancient times, chiefly through the exertions of Roger de Pippart, an English settler, who built a strong castle, now used as a gaol. It is a quadrangular building with a high roof; the E. and W. fronts are defended by projecting towers rising above the rest of the building. There is also another castellated building in the town, which is inhabited, and the residence of W. Hatch, Esq., to whose family it was granted by Cromwell. Scarce any traces are left of the Augustinian Friary and of the Carmelite Friary, which was burnt by Edward Bruce, as was indeed the whole of Ardee by O'Neill in 1538.

In later times it was occupied by James II.'s troops after leaving Dundalk, and also by William's army, who advanced direct from hence to the Boyne.]

44 m. rt. Charleville (— Dease, Esq.), and a little beyond Drumcar (J. M'Clintock, Esq.) and Greenmount. At 47 m. the line crosses the river Glyde, a stream rising in 3 waterheads, under the name of the Lagan, in the counties Monaghan, Meath, and Louth, and arrives at *Castlebellingham*, a neat little town, famous for its ale, on the rt. of the line, flourishing under the proprietorship of Sir Arthur Bellingham, whose residence is adjoining.

49 m. rt. *Dromiskin*, in addition to a pretty ch., contains the lower portion of a round tower, which has been recapped and now serves as a belfry. On l. 2 m. are Branganstown House (Rev. A. Garston) and Darver Castle (Mrs. Booth); not far from which is *Miltown Castle*, a square fortress "defended by round towers 45 ft. high, surmounted by tall graduated battlements. Near the summit of a rising ground ¼ m. distant is an arched subterraneous vault, supposed to have communicated with the castle."

50 m. The line now crosses another river, the Fane, which, rising in Monaghan, skirts the county of Louth, and, passing through a pretty valley, falls into the sea at Dundalk Bay, close to the village of Lurgan Green, and near the grounds of Clermont Park (Lord Clermont).

54 m. Dundalk. Rte. 3.

ROUTE 3.

FROM DUNDALK TO BELFAST.

Dundalk (anc. Dun-dealgan) (*Hotel*: Arthur's) is a large, prosperous town (Pop. 10,428), interesting more in its commercial relations than in its antiquarian features, though it played no unimportant part in the early history of the country, having been the head-quarters of Bruce in 1315, who here proclaimed himself king, keeping his position for a whole year. It was afterwards granted to the powerful family of the De Verdons, who founded a Franciscan monastery in the reign of Henry III. Charters were granted by that king, as also by Richard II. and Henry IV., who allowed the inhabitants to surround their town by walls.

Dundalk is built on marshy ground on the S. bank of the estuary of the Castleton river, as it falls into the bay of Dundalk, which extends for about 7 m. across from the Moat of Cooley to Dunany Point. The entrance to the harbour was obstructed by a very dangerous shoal of sunken rocks, until Sir John M'Neill, the good genius of the neighbourhood, removed them, and by so doing gave immense impetus to the trade of the port. An extensive business is done here in flax, leather, and corn, besides which there are large distilleries and breweries, the amount of customs duties for 1859 being upwards of 31,000l.

The town itself will not detain the visitor long. He should see the ch., which stands a little back from the main street, and has a singular wooden steeple sheathed with copper. The R. C. chapel, one of the handsomest in Ireland, was erected by Mr. Duff, from designs after King's College chapel, Cambridge. There are also courthouse, gaol, guildhall, and the usual collection of municipal buildings. The town has the advantage of a fine park, as well as the neighbourhood of the grounds of Lord Roden at Dundalk House, which are free to visitors. To the E. are the ruins of the Franciscan Friary, consisting mainly of a high square tower. "This building is said to have been very large and beautiful, and the E. window, according to Ware, was particularly admired." After the dissolution it was granted by Henry VIII. to James Brandon at a rent of 6d. per annum.

"On the plains of Ballynahatna are the remains of a Druidical temple, partly enclosed by a curious rampart, on the outside of which is a circle of upright stones."—*Lewis*.

Conveyances.—By rail to Dublin, Belfast, and Enniskillen. Steamer to Liverpool.

Distances.— Drogheda, 22¼ m.; Portadown, 33½; Newry, 15; Enniskillen, 62; Castle Blayney, 18; Louth, 5½; Castle Bellingham, 7.

[Louth (anc. Baile-Lughmhaigh) was formerly the seat of a celebrated ecclesiastical establishment founded by St. Patrick, where 100 bishops and 300 presbyters received their education. The ruins of the abbey, which occupy the site of the original monastery, are rather extensive, and contain some good traceried windows. In the modern ch. on the hill above is a monument to the late rector, Dr. Little, with the punning epitaph "Multum in parvo." There are several interesting traces of ancient earthworks in this parish, particularly in the glebe-land at Castlering near the village, where the foundations of an hexagonal mural fort may be examined.]

Leaving the Dundalk Stat., the line passes on l. Lisnawully House (P. Byrne, Esq.), and further on 2 m. *Castletown House*, the seat of J. Eastwood, Esq. Adjoining the mansion is the old quadrangular castle, with slender square towers at the angles.

3 m. is the hill of *Faughart*, "an ancient fort, consisting of an artificial mound, 60 ft. in height, surrounded by a deep trench with a counterscarp. The whole area of the summit is circumscribed by the foundations of an octagonal building, but whether it was a tower or not is difficult to

determine. Mr. Wright conjectures that it may have been a funeral monument, and in later times a beacon or fort to defend the frontier of the Pale."—*Wakeman*. Here it was that Edward Bruce lost his crown and his life in an encounter with a picked body of troops under De Bermingham and Verdon in 1316. 2 m. to the E. of Faughart is a cromlech remarkable for the size of the rock supported, and the smallness of the points of support of the 3 stones on which it rests. Close to it is the giant's grave, an arrangement of stones, with a large one overlapping them at one end. On the rt. of the rly. are several seats— Bellurgan (Capt. Tipping), on the southern face of Trumpet Hill, Ballymascanlon House (F. J. Foster, Esq.), Mount Pleasant (Sir John M'Neill), Carrick Bridge House, and Claret Rock.

4 m. To rt. of *Mount Pleasant* Stat. the beautiful *Ravensdale* opens out, emerging from the southern slopes of the Mourne mountains. The river Flurry runs through it to Ravensdale Park, the residence of Lord Clermont. It is magnificently situated at the foot of Clermont Cairn, which rises bluffly to the height of 1674 ft. In the lower portion of the glen is Annaverna (late Mrs. M'Clelland). The scenery has been gradually changing, from the undulating and pastoral country near Dundalk and Castle Bellingham, to higher and less cultivated grounds. We are now at the southern base of a very remarkable group of mountains which shut off Ulster from the county of Louth, and which contain in their ranges scenery of a very high order. The Mourne mountains extend from Slieve Gullion, the highest westerly point, to Slieve Donard overlooking Dundrum bay, near Downpatrick, and occupy northwards a very considerable portion of Co. Down, the outlying groups indeed reaching to within sight of Belfast.

The tourist who can afford the time to explore these hills at length, making his head-quarters at Newry or Rostrevor, will not regret his stay.

6 m. l. at *Moyry Castle*, a single quadrangular tower, the line crosses the Carrickbroad river, and enters the co. of Armagh. This is the locale of the famous Moyry Pass, where in 1595 a severe action took place between the Elizabethan troops under Sir Wm. Russell and those of O'Neill, who for 5 or 6 years subsequently held this defile against every attempt on the part of the English to dislodge him. He was, however, compelled to retire in 1600 before Lord Mountjoy, who in his turn was a few days afterwards intercepted by O'Neill in Ravensdale, when the Lord Deputy was severely wounded, and the English compelled to retreat to Dundalk, leaving the northern districts in the hands of the Irish. Passing l. under the base of the Forkhill mountains, the line leaves on rt. 7 m. the village of Jonesborough, burnt by the rebels in 1798 : near it is the singular pillar stone of Kilnasaggart, on the face of which is an inscription and a wheel-cross below it. We now enter a wild hilly region, little inhabited, and still less cultivated.

On l. the granitic head of Slieve Gullion rises abruptly to the height of 1893 ft., being the most westerly point of the Mourne range. At the summit is a cairn, containing a chamber underneath, supposed to have been the burial-place of Cualgne, son of Breogan, an early chieftain, who fell in battle on the plain beneath. The locale of this mountain has been the subject of a poem, believed to have been written by Ossian, in which he makes Fingal his principal hero. The mountains in this parish (Killeary) were formerly infested by bands of robbers, of whom the famous Redmond O'Hanlon was the chief. At the base of Slieve Gullion is Killeary Castle, the Elizabethan residence of J. Foxall, Esq.

9 m. rt. near the village of *Meigh* the line has reached its highest elevation, and enters a deep cutting through the Wellington Hill, emerging at the base of the Newry mountains. A magnificent view now opens out to the traveller, who would willingly delay his rapid progress for a few minutes to feast upon it. On his rt. the whole of the vale and town of Newry lie at his feet, together with Carlingford Bay and the villages of Warrenpoint and Rostrevor, the whole backed up by the lofty ranges of Mourne, and forming altogether a panorama not to be surpassed.

15 m. Newry Stat. As the town is some little distance off, it will be more convenient to the traveller to proceed as far as 18 m. Goragh Wood Stat., from whence a short line (a section of the Newry and Armagh Rly.), runs directly into the heart of the town. In its passage between the 2 stations the main line is carried over the ravine of *Craigmore* by a remarkably fine viaduct 2000 ft. in length and 110 high, formed by a series of 18 arches of 50 ft. span. From Goragh Wood it is about 2¼ m. of steep gradient to *Newry*

Rte. 4 *Hotels*: Victoria; Newry Arms; Downshire Arms, a rapidly increasing business town, much changed since the days when Swift wrote of it—

"High church, low steeple,
Dirty streets, and proud people."

From its singularly beautiful position, and its proximity to a picturesque coast, Newry has attracted both the commercial and the tourist sections of the community, advantages which the inhabitants have had the good sense not to abuse by exorbitant charges. Taking the whole district from the town to the end of Carlingford Bay, there are few places in the kingdom where the lover of scenery can spend his time with such economy. It is situated in a broad vale, expanding towards the N.W., contracting on the S.E., and bounded by high hills on each side—on the W. by the Newry mountains (1385 ft.), and Slieve Gullion, and on the E. by the wooded shoulders of the more lofty Mourne range, which are seen overtopping them. Through the centre of the vale runs the river Clanrye, eclipsed to a considerable extent by the more important Newry Canal, which here empties itself into the sea, though the port of Newry may be properly said to be at Warrenpoint, 6 m. distant, and connected by a rly. (Rte. 4). The place itself is clean and well laid out, is remarkably free from the disagreeable suburbs of Irish towns, and has a pleasant air of bustle and business about it. Four stone bridges cross the tidal river which separates the Cos. Down and Armagh, and 4 others span the canal; of these the Ballybot Bridge is a handsome granite arch of 90 ft. span. The churches are all modern or modernized buildings, although St. Patrick's is said to have been the first professedly Protestant ch. ever erected in Ireland, and still possesses a part of the tower, with the arms of the founder, Sir Nicholas Bagnall, 1578. The R. C. cathedral in Hill-street has a good Perp. exterior. There are scarce any traces whatever of the abbey of Newry, founded in 1157 for Cistercian monks by Maurice M'Loughlin, king of Ireland. The charter of this foundation is still in existence, and was enlarged by Hugh De Lacy in 1237. Within its precincts 2 yew-trees were planted by St. Patrick, from whence the town derived the name of Na yur or the yew-trees, afterwards corrupted into Newries. Respecting this tree we find the following extract from the Annals of the Four Masters:—" 1262. The monastery of the monks of

Newry was burnt, and also the yew-tree which St. Patrick himself had planted." The Bagnalls (the same who built St. Patrick's ch.) possessed a castle formed out of a portion of the buildings of this abbey and built on its site, which was granted them by a patent of James I. This family long possessed the surrounding manors of Newry, Mourne, and Carlingford, which afterwards descended to the Anglesea and Kilmorey titles. At the northern entrance is a granite obelisk erected in memory of a Mr. Trevor Corry. The town carries on a busy export and import trade, possessing good quays and warehouses. The port might be made the safest in Ireland at a very moderate cost. "The lough is navigable for 6 m. by vessels of the greatest burden at all times, and the port admits vessels of 1000 tons to Warrenpoint, where the larger vessels remain, but those drawing 15 ft. water can go up by the Ship Canal to the Albert Basin, a distance of 5 m. from the sea. Barges ply by the Newry Canal Navigation to Lough Neagh 32 m. inland. The income of the port amounts to 6000*l.* per annum, arising from canal dues on tonnage, 1*s.* per ton inwards, and 1*d.* outwards." — *Thom's Directory.* The port contained in 1859 110 vessels of 6300 tonnage. (Pop. 12,188.)

The antiquary should visit the rath at Crown Bridge. It is surrounded by a ditch 600 ft. in circumference, and has on the W. side a singular platform also surrounded by a fosse, the use of which is not very apparent.

Conveyances.—Steamer to Liverpool and Glasgow. Rail to Dundalk, Belfast, Armagh, and Warrenpoint. Car to Downpatrick, to which a rlwy. is in progress; car to Kilkeel.

Distances.—Dundalk, 15 m.; Portadown, 18½; Banbridge, 17; Hilltown, 9; Warrenpoint, 6; Rostrevor, 8½; Carlingford, 12; Omeath, 7½; Greenore, 15½; Kilkeel, 18; Newcastle, 30; Narrowwater, 4; Dundrum, 29;

Downpatrick, by coast road, 61; Castlewellan, 18.

Excursions.—
1. Warrenpoint and Rostrevor (Rte. 4).
2. Hilltown.

[From Newry the pedestrian should walk to Warrenpoint, and thence make his way round the coast to Downpatrick and even to Donaghadee, by which route he will constantly have opportunities of exploring the magnificent mountain scenery of the Mourne Mts. (Rte. 4).]

Proceeding from Goragh Wood is 19 m. l. *Mount Norris*, a small village marking the position of a fort built in the reign of Elizabeth to guard one of the many passes near Newry. It gives the title of baron to the Annesley family.

20 m. on rt., near the canal, is the tumulus of Cairn Bane, "which has a deep sloping bank outside the central mound, enclosed with upright stones, and which is about 200 yards in circumference, covering above a rood of ground. Within the glacis or slope, the base of the Temple gradually rises towards the mound, which is 160 yards in circumference, and is completely girt with long and ponderous stones set upon it and joined together. On the N.W. is the entrance, and on the opposite side is the altar, the slab of which is very ponderous, resting upon 3 upright stones, each 10 ft. long."—*Coote's Armagh.*

A little further N. is Drumbanagher, the residence of Col. Maxwell Close, built in Italian style, and situated in beautiful grounds.

On rt. of the line is Drumantine House (A. C. Innes, Esq.).

The *Newry Canal* keeps close fellowship with the rly. all the way from Newry to Portadown, near which place it enters the bed of the Bann, and thus flows into Lough Neagh. It was originally made with the intention of exporting large quantities of coal from the Dungannon district, and supplying Dublin, but unfortunately, the quality of the article not being sufficiently liked, the canal is used for importing coals to the very districts which should have furnished them. It was commenced in 1730, and opened in 1741, at a cost of 896,000*l.*, the average of the annual tolls being between 4000*l.* and 5000*l.*

23 m. *Poyntz Pass*, so called from Sir Toby Poyntz, who defended the pass against Hugh O'Neill's Irish troops. There is a neat little town here, with an hotel. The antiquary should stop for the purpose of examining the *Dane's Cast*, a sort of dyke, similar to that of Offa in Wales. It is called by the natives Glean-namuck-ddu, "the glen of the black pig," and was ascribed by them to enchantment. From Lisnagade (Capt. Trevor), near Scarva, it extended to the bay of Dundalk, having a depth of 12 to 20 ft., but, as in most of these early earthworks, the progress of agriculture and improvements have obliterated it in very many places. Passing Acton House (J. Alexander, Esq.) and Druminargal House, the tourist arrives at

26 m. *Scarva*, where William III.'s army held its rendezvous on arriving in Ireland. Here are several archæological remains of interest : viz. the ruins of Glenilesk Castle, built by Monck in the time of Cromwell ; and of a much earlier date, the cairn of *Caira Cochy*, an immense heap of stones 70 ft. high, which marks the spot of a prehistoric battle, A.D. 332, "between the 3 Collas, princes of Heremon's race, and Fergus Foglia, the last of the race of Ir. The battle, in which the latter was killed, lasted for 6 successive days." The parish of Aghaderg, meaning the battle of the cairn at the bloody ford, takes its name from this occurrence. In the grounds of Lisnagade House is the fort, from whence the Dane's Cast is supposed to commence. It is circular, with triple ramparts, the 3 moats or intrenchments being about 70 ft. in breadth.

[2½ m. rt. is the small town of *Loughbrickland*, in the street of which William III. is said to have sat on horseback for many hours, while his army passed before him in single file.]

From Scarva there is a junction line of 7 m. through the village of Laurencetown to *Banbridge* (*Hotel* : Downshire Arms) (Pop. 3800), a pleasant busy little place on the Bann, although of an entirely modern date. It is peculiar from the fact of the main street having been excavated in the centre, leaving a broad passage on each side for the purposes of traffic. Linen is the staple trade of Banbridge, as it is of every northern town which the tourist will visit in this route.

Distances.—Loughbrickland, 3 m. ; Dromore, 7 ; Lurgan, 9¼. A new line has been recently opened between Banbridge, Dromore, and Lisburn.

28 m. *Tanderagee* Stat., to the rt. of which is Gilford, another little linen town on the Bann, containing the extensive factory of Messrs. Dunbar, Dickson, and Co. Gilford Castle, close to the town, was formerly a seat of Sir W. Johnston, but is now used as an hospital.

About the same distance on the l. of the stat. is the well-to-do town of *Tanderagee*, to which very large quantities of flax are weekly brought to market. The summit of the hill is crowned by the *Castle*, a pretty Elizabethan mansion of the Duke of Manchester, originally built by the Count de Salis on the site of the fortress of Redmond O'Hanlon, the most renowned outlaw of Irish history, whose estates were confiscated in the reign of James I. From hence the line, crossing the Cusher river, follows the valley of the Bann, passing on l. Mullavilly House, rt. Moyallen (the residence of the Quaker family of Wakefield) and Carrick House (Col. Blacker) to

34 m. *Portadown* Stat. (Rte. 17), an important rly. centre, from whence radiate the Dublin and Belfast junction, the Ulster, the Clones, and the Dungannon lines. Portadown, from its position on the Bann, and its contiguity to Lough Neagh, has a large trade in linen and agricultural products. For the next 25 m. the traveller will pursue his journey on the Ulster Rly., which was opened to Belfast in 1848. The same Company, however, own the line to Monaghan and Clones (Rte. 17), as well as that to Dungannon and Omagh (Rte. 7). The features of the country from Portadown to Belfast are not marked by any romantic scenery, nor by objects of archæological interest, but are rather characterized by richly cultivated fields, prosperous linen towns and villages, and a general air of wellbeing which, supposing it was universal over the kingdom, would place Ireland in a very different position from that which she has hitherto borne. Crossing the Bann by a wooden viaduct of 5 arches, and leaving on l. the ch. of Drumcree, the line traverses a rather flat low district lying between the hills and the shores of Lough Neagh, which is only a couple of miles distant. Occasional glimpses of the lough are obtained near Lurgan; but as the visitor to Antrim will see it to much greater advantage, it will be described in Rte. 12. As this district is watered wholly by the Upper Bann, the tourist should be acquainted with the improvements made by the manufacturers to ensure themselves a constant and equable water-power, by constructing a reservoir at Lough Island Reavy, which embraces an area of 100 acres. The river rises in the northern face of Slieve Muck, in the Mourne range, and flows N.W. with a considerable fall past Hilltown to Banbridge and Gilford. Apart from its commercial value, it was long famous for its pearls, which, like those in the Conway river in N. Wales, are found in the shell of the muscle (*Unio atratus*), and which in the last century were so highly esteemed, especially those of rose colour, that they were sold for 20*l.* or 30*l.*

39 m. *Lurgan*, a populous flax town (7772), celebrated for its diapers, the numerous bleaching-greens in the vicinity betokening the prevailing occupation. There is little to see in it except the demesne of Lurgan Castle, the modern residence of Lord Lurgan, a handsome Elizabethan house, built of Scotch sandstone, and placed in a finely-wooded park.

[3 m. S.E. is Waringstown, a manufacturing village established by a merchant of the name of Waring in the time of Queen Anne. Hard by is an old manor-house, in which is preserved a tapestried chamber occupied by Duke Schomberg in his passage through the country.]

Passing rt. Grace Hall (C. Douglas, Esq.), is 44½ m. *Moira*, a prettily-placed town about 1 m. to the rt. of the stat. At this point we cross the Lagan Navigation or Ulster Canal, running from Lough Neagh by Moira and Lisburn to Belfast, a distance of 28 m., with a summit level of 120 ft., and affording a cheap and convenient water carriage to the busy manufacturing villages on its course. Several pleasant seats are congregated near Moira, viz., Moira Wood, belonging to the Earls of Moira, Broommount (— Gordon, Esq.), Friar's Hill, Drumbane House, and *Trumery House*; where once stood a very beautiful round tower 60 ft. in height, which, however, has unfortunately fallen. Adjoining it is the gable of the old ch., containing a high pointed arched window. Between Moira and Lisburn the line passes l. the ch. of Magheragall, and rt. the Maze, a common on which the Hillsborough races are held.

52 m. *Lisburn* (*Hotel:* Hertford

Arms', a populous town of between 7000 and 8000 Inhab., all engaged in the staple trade, particularly in the manufacture of damasks. The tourist who is interested in it should visit the factory of the Coulsons, one of the largest damask makers in Ireland. The creation of the place may be ascribed to the Conway family, to whom Charles I. granted a patent, and who erected a castle here. The ch., which is conspicuous from its handsome octagonal spire, is the cathedral ch. of the diocese of Dromore, and contains a monument to the pious Jeremy Taylor, Bishop of Down and Connor in 1667; also to Lieut. Dobbs, who fell in an action against Paul Jones, the privateer, as he was returning from a raid on the Scotch coast. In the ch.-yard are the gravestones of several Huguenots who settled here and introduced the finer branches of the linen manufacture. Lisburn and Lurgan suffered severely in the war of 1641, having been both burnt to the ground. Adjoining the town are the castle gardens, which are at all times open to the townspeople by the liberality of the late Marquis of Hertford. In the centre of a triangular area is a handsome market-place, surmounted by a cupola.

Distances.—Hillsborough, 4 m.; Dromore, 8½, [which places may be visited by rail. The former is an English-looking little town on the side of a hill, containing a well-preserved fort, built by Sir Arthur Hill in the reign of Charles I., and still kept up as a hereditary garrison under the Marquis of Downshire, who enjoys the titles of Marshal of Ulster and Governor of the Royal Fortress of Hillsborough. William III. tenanted it for a night during his march through this part of Ireland, "while his army encamped on the Moor of Blaris 2 m. on the l. of the Lisburn road, which tract has ever since been exempt from paying tithe." It is a massive building defended by 4 quadrangular bastions, and entered by a good pointed arched gateway, above which are 3 pointed windows. This fort (now used as an armoury for the yeomanry) is placed in the centre of a fine park, the modern 'demesne of the Marquis of Downshire, who owns Hillsborough as well as several other towns, all of which are characterised by an unusual aspect of neatness and care. There is here a pretty Gothic ch. with spire 200 feet in height. It contains some stained glass, a sweet-toned organ, and a monument by Nollekens to Archdeacon Leslie. Crossing a somewhat hilly district we arrive at *Dromore*, from very early ages the seat of an abbey for Canons Regular, which afterwards became the cathedral for the Protestant diocese of Down, Connor, and Dromore. It fell into ruins, however, and the present ch. was built on its site by Bishop Jeremy Taylor, who, together with Dr. Percy, author of 'Reliques of Ancient English Poetry,' were the 2 most noteworthy prelates. Adjoining the town is the Palace, the grounds designed and planted by the latter bishop after the model of Shenstone's Leasowes. The scanty ruins of a castle and some earthworks are to be seen near the town, and in the grounds of Gill Hall, the residence of R. C. Brush, Esq. To the N.E. is the rath of Druib Mor, 200 feet in diameter at the base, and surrounded by a rampart and parapet. It is said that there was a covered way between it and the Lagan.]

From Lisburn the rly. is accompanied on l. by a chain of hills extending to Belfast, where they assume a considerable height, and add very much to the beauty of that city. They are in fact a range of chalk rocks capped by basaltic strata, which run southward as far as Lurgan, being the most southerly point in which chalk strata are observed in Ireland. In the neighbourhood of Lisburn the height is only 820 ft., but it soon increases to 1567 at Divis, and 1142 at Cave Hill overlooking Belfast.

54 m. l. the village of Lambeg, and Glenmore, the seat of J. Richardson, Esq. Crossing the river Derraghy, and passing the pretty factory village of Dunmurry, the tourist arrives at 60 m. the northern metropolis of

Belfast (*Hotels*: Donegal Arms; Imperial). (Rte. 5.)

ROUTE 4.

FROM **NEWRY** TO **BELFAST**, THROUGH **ROSTREVOR** AND **DOWNPATRICK**.

Newry (Rte. 3) is connected with Warrenpoint by a short rly., which leaves the town from stats. at Dublin Bridge and Edward St., and runs parallel with the Newry river, having on l. a pretty road garnished with woods.

At 4½ m. *Narrow Water* the estuary is suddenly contracted by the projection of a tongue of rock, occupied by the ruins of Narrow Water Castle (anc. Caisl-nisce), a singular square battlemented tower, which before the days of artillery was well situated for defensive purposes. The present fortress was built by the Duke of Ormonde in 1663 to replace an older one that had been destroyed in the previous wars. It has seen many vicissitudes; amongst others, serving as a kennel for hounds, and a salt-work. The botanist will find Sagina maritima near the ruins.

The woods overhanging the road on the l. are those of Narrow Water House (Roger Hall, Esq.), a charmingly situated residence, commanding grand views of the opposite mountains of Carlingford. The house is a mixture of styles, but the grounds are well worth a visit. At the entrance of the Clanrye, or Newry River, into Carlingford Bay, is

[6 m. *Warrenpoint*, the terminus of the rly., and the port of Newry (*Hotels*: Victoria; Crown). It is a pleasant little town, exhibiting at one end the characteristics of a seaport, and, at the other, of a bathing-place, though from the latter portion, which is washed by the waters of the Lough, there is such a view as falls to the lot of few watering-places in Great Britain. On the rt. are the large ranges of the Carlingford Mountains, amongst which the chief are Clermont Cairn 1674 ft., and Carlingford 1935 ft. At their foot nestles the village of Omeath nearly opposite Warrenpoint, and further down is Carlingford itself; while on the horizon are the lighthouses of Greenore Point and the Block House. On the l. the Mourne Mountains rise still higher and more abruptly. In a corner, under Slieve Bân, is Rostrevor, embowered in woods, the road to it skirting the coast amidst a succession of pretty residences. Below Rostrevor the Lough expands, but contracts again at Greencastle, from which point the open sea may be said to commence.

Warrenpoint is largely patronized by the inhabitants of Newry and the N.E. counties generally; and perhaps there is scarce any place which offers so many seaside advantages with so little of the expense or extortion peculiar to such towns.

Distances.—Newry, 6 m.; Carlingford, 6; Kilkeel, 12; Rostrevor, 2.

Excursions.—
1. Rostrevor and Slieve Bân.
2. Carlingford and Omeath.

Conveyances.—Rail to Newry.

Before quitting Warrenpoint the tourist should take a boat and cross over to Omeath (*Hotel*: O'Hagan's), a picturesque little spot at the foot of the mountains, and thence proceed to Carlingford. The road runs close to the sea, but little room being left for it by the hills which rise so abruptly. Soon the Two-mile River rushes down from the Omeath Mountain; and a little further on, the Golden River, after a rapid course from the rugged heights of Slieve Foy, falls into the sea.

6 m. *Carlingford* (*Inn:* Humphreys') was once a town of such importance that it is said to have possessed no less than 32 buildings in the shape of castles and abbeys, and of such antiquity that it claims the honour of being the landing place of St. Patrick in the 5th cent. The probable explanation of the former statement is, that in the warlike days of the Pale every house in Carlingford was built in the castellated form for the purposes of defence and protection. King John ordered a castle to be erected, which was accordingly done by De Courcey in 1210. The town quickly grew up around it, and played no inconsiderable part in the troublous history of the times. As evidence of the rank it took, Carlingford obtained charters from Edward II., Henry IV., Henry VII., Elizabeth, James I., and James II. It is charmingly situated in a little nook of the Lough, and commands glorious views of the Mourne Mountains, but has this disadvantage, that, owing to the height and position of the hills behind, it gets shorn of a large proportion of sunlight. The ruins consist—

1. Of King John's Castle, a rambling, massive fortress of the 13th cent., the situation of which is not the least curious thing about it. It is built upon a rock, somewhat the shape of a horseshoe, with the eastern side overlooking the sea. Here was the principal entrance, defended by a platform, the west or land side being protected by the mountain-pass. In the interior, in addition to the apartments, is a courtyard, round which ran a gallery, with recesses at the loopholes for the protection of the archers. The walls were of the thickness in some places of 11 ft.

2. Between the castle and the abbey is a square tower, the windows of which are curiously carved with serpents, grotesque heads, and other devices.

3. The Abbey, founded by Richard De Burgh, Earl of Ulster, in the 14th cent., for the Dominican order, combines in an unusual degree the military with the ecclesiastical character.

It consists of a nave and chancel, at the junction of which rises a square tower on pointed arches. At the W. end are two other towers or turrets connected by a battlement, and at the E. end is a pointed window, all the tracery and mullions having disappeared long ago.

In 1649 Lord Inchiquin, one of Cromwell's generals, occupied Carlingford, and, with the usual irreverence of those days, turned the abbey into a stable.

There is one more square tower, which probably belonged to the fortified houses of the Pale. On the roof is the King's Seat, "so called because the Lord Thomas of Lancaster, son of Henry IV., who landed in 1408 as Lord Lieutenant of Ireland, used often to sit upon a stone seat between the battlements to enjoy the prospect."

Though Carlingford is well situated for the purposes of trade, it has none, save in an article dear to gourmands—oysters. To every inhabitant of Dublin the name of Carlingford oysters is sacred, and deservedly so, as they are unquestionably the finest and most luscious kind to be obtained. "The oyster fishery is late, not commencing before the 1st Monday in November, and ending on the 1st Saturday in March. The beds extend from Greenore Point up to Narrow Water, and during the season 8 or 10 sail-boats, and nearly 100 row-boats, with 5 men in each, are engaged in dredging." Such is the reputation that "rale Carlingfords" have obtained, that 9-10ths of the supplies sold in the towns are Carlingfords only in name. Should the traveller be in the N.E. of Ireland during the oyster season, he should pay a visit to Warrenpoint for the purpose of identifying and tasting the true kind.

The pedestrian should not leave this beautiful neighbourhood without ascending Carlingford Mountain, the highest point of the lofty range that fills up this promontory of Louth. It commences at Fathom Hill, opposite Newry, and from that point abruptly rises to 1000 ft., attaining the maximum at Carlingford, 1935 ft., to the E. of which a deep glen runs up from the sea, dividing the range like a fork. The view, as may be easily imagined, is superb. Northward are the Mourne Mountains, Slieve Bân, and Slieve Donard, with their attendant groups. Eastward are the Slieve Gullion Hills and the undulating country between Dundalk, Castleblayney and Armagh. Southward is the bay of Dundalk with its headlands, from Cooley Point immediately underneath to Dunany Point and Clogher Head. The geological structure of the Carlingford mountains is trap, in various states of crystallization, from amorphous basalt to porphyrated and crystalline greenstone.

3 m. beyond Carlingford is Greenore Point, where it is in contemplation to erect a large dock for the accommodation of Newry shipping, the connection to be maintained by a rly.]

The drive from Warrenpoint to Rostrevor is hardly to be equalled for beauty, either of mountain or coast scenery. The road is lined with pretty seats, the most conspicuous being Moygannon (Major Hall), Bladenburgh, otherwise called Topsy-turvy (D. Ross, Esq.), Rosetta (S. Reid, Esq.), Carpenham (Mrs. Ford), Green Park (Hon. Mrs.Maude), and Drumsisk (H. Bowan, Esq.), near which last is a lofty granite obelisk to the memory of Gen. Ross, who, according to the inscription, was present at the affairs of Alexandria, Maida, Vittoria, Corunna, and the Pyrenees.

8 m. *Rostrevor* (*Hotel:* Sangster's), the sweetest little watering-place to be found in the 3 kingdoms: quiet, sheltered by mighty mountains and shady woods, it will equally suit the delicate invalid requiring sea air, the artist seeking materials for his taste, and the general visitor. The little town is placed between the embouchure of 2 rivers, and is flanked on one side by the Lodge, the residence of Col. Roxburgh. From the Woodhouse (the beautiful villa of S.Ramadge, Esq.), rather more than a mile from the town, the ascent is usually commenced of the Rostrevor Mountain, or Slieve Bân, which rises very steeply to the height of 1595 ft. About 2-3rds of the way up, on the top of a secondary hill, separated by a valley from Slieve Bân, is Cloughmore ("Cloech Mor," great stone, or Clocch Meor, finger stone), a singular boulder mass of granite, of about 30 tons. There is a legend attached to it that the giant Finn M'Comhal was challenged by Benandonner, a Scotch giant, which challenge being accepted, the pair confronted each other, the one on Carlingford, the other on Slieve Bân. Finn, by way of a preparatory training, flung Cloughmore at his antagonist across the Lough, who decamped in a fright. The walks in the neighbourhood of Rostrevor are numerous and varied, the Mourne Hills alone furnishing as much collar-work as is needed by any pedestrian.

Excursions.—
1. Warrenpoint.

2. Cloughmore and Slieve Bán.
3. Kilbroney and Hilltown.
4. Kilkeel and Greencastle.
[A picturesque road runs through a gap in the hills to
7 m. *Hilltown*, passing Kilbroney and its ruined ch., one of the simplest and earliest form, overshadowed by the branches of a fine old oak, which has grown out of the wall to a greath eight. Hilltown (*Hotel*, Devonshire Arms, very good) is a remarkably neat village under the care of the Marquess of Downshire, situated at the confluence of the 2 or 3 streamlets that form the Bann. About 2 m. on the Downpatrick road is a cromlech supported on 3 stones, locally known as Finn's Fingerstone.]

Passing on the rt. Ballyedmond (A. Stewart, Esq.), and crossing the Causeway Water, the tourist reaches 15 m. Mourne Park, the beautiful estate of the Earl of Kilmorey, the woods and grounds of which clothe the base of Knockchree (Hill of the Deer), 1013 ft., crowned on the summit with an observatory. Here the White Water is crossed, and a road on rt. leads to the sands into which it empties itself, near Greencastle Point. The fortress, which gives this name, is one of those square massive towers erected by the Anglo-Norman barons to protect their possessions, and prior to the days of ordnance it must have proved a sufficient guard for the entrance of Carlingford Lough, though now it would be overlooked from any one of the neighbouring heights. A square embattled tower flanks it at each corner. The second floor is on a level with the rock on which the castle is built, and is supported by arches. A direct road of 4½ m. runs from it to

Kilkeel (Inn: Kilmorey Arms; middling), a thriving townlet of some 1300 Inhab. Though placed on a fine strand, affording every accommodation for bathing, and not far from the foot of the Mourne Mountains, Kilkeel has not as yet assumed the position of a watering-place. Perhaps, however, in the estimation of many this may be an additional attraction. Near the town is the Abbey, the residence of T. Gibson Henry, Esq.

Conveyances.—Car to Newry; to Newcastle.

Distances.—Rostrevor, 10 m.; Newry, 18; Newcastle, 12; Dundrum, 17; Greencastle, 4½; Mourne Park, 3; Hilltown, 13.

From Kilkeel the road, crossing the Kilkeel River, speedily approaches to the coast, occupying the very limited strip of level ground between the mountains and the sea. At Annalong, near which is Glass Drummond, the seat of Mrs. Senior, another of these mountain streams is crossed, and again a 3rd at Bloody Bridge, above which Spence's Mountain and Crossone 1777 ft. rise abruptly to the l. "The road rises perpendicularly more than 100 ft. above the sea, from which it is separated by rocky precipices and shelving cliffs, indented with yawning caverns, so terrifically lashed by the tremendous waves as to impart to the coast a character of extraordinary sublimity." As we wind along the cliffs, the beautiful woods of Donard Lodge come in sight, and at the very foot of Slieve Donard itself the little town of

30 m. *Newcastle* (*Hotel*: Annesley Arms, good), where the tourist, especially if a pedestrian, should by all means halt for a short time, that he may ascend the mighty Donard.

Between Bloody Bridge and Newcastle are several spots marked by some natural curiosities, and consequently invested with a legend; such as Donard's Cave, Maggy's Leap, and Armer's Hole, which latter attained its notoriety from a foul murder committed by one Edward Armer on his father.

Newcastle must soon prove a

formidable rival to Rostrevor, as, in addition to the usual advantages for bathing, and more romantic scenery, it possesses a rather celebrated Spa; indeed, Dr. Knox calls it the Scarborough of Ireland. The Spa is situated about ¼ m. from the town on the hill-side and adjoining the beautiful grounds of Donard Lodge, through which, by the courtesy of the Earl of Annesley, the tourist is free to wander. There are various pleasant and picturesque spots in the neighbourhood of the Spa, such as the Hermit's Glen, the Rookery, the Waterfall, &c.

[It is a longer excursion to Bryansford (*Hotel*: Roden Arms, very good), a charming little village close to *Tollymore Park*, the seat of the Earl of Roden. The visitor will not easily tire of the beauties which meet him at every turn during his wanderings through the grounds. The river Shimna,—

"a brooklet gushing
From its rocky fountain near,
Down into the valley rushing,
So fresh and wondrous clear,"

—flows through the grounds in a series of cascades to fall into the sea at Newcastle, while the views of the ocean, the Isle of Man, and the overhanging mountains, are inexpressibly fine. From Tollymore it is a little over 3 m. to *Castlewellan*, another neat and flourishing little town, almost surrounded by pleasant demesnes. Of these the most important is Castlewellan House, also a seat of the Earl of Annesley, in the grounds of which is a considerable lake. Near the town are the extensive flax-spinning mills of the Messrs. Muirhead, the first place in Ireland where machinery was used for this purpose.

Distances.—Dundrum, 5 m.; Hilltown, 9½; Newcastle, 4½; Newry, 19.]

Slieve Donard, 2796 ft., is the highest point of the lofty Mourne range that stretches from Newry to Dundrum, at once the finest and most picturesque hills in the N. of Ireland, with the exception of the Donegal Mountains. The ascent may be made either from the Spa Well, or by following the course of the Glen River on the N. side. A precipitous escarpment that overhangs this stream is called the Eagle Rock. Magnificent indeed is the view which greets the pedestrian from the summit of Slieve Donard. To the W. is a vast expanse of ocean, relieved only by the blue hills of the Isle of Man, in which Snafell is plainly visible; while Newcastle, Annalong, and Dundrum lie snugly at the feet. To the N. are the rich and varied plains of the district known in former times as Lecale, embracing many a fruitful acre and many a prosperous town. To the W. and S.W. are minor satellites in the shape of the less lofty peaks of the Mournes; the principal of which are Slieve Commedagh, 2512 ft.; Slieve Bearnagh, 2394; Slieve Meel, 2257; the Cock and the Hen Mountains in the most northerly group; the Chimney Rock, 2152;—Slieve Bingian, 2449; Slieve Lamagan, 2306; Shanlieve, 2055; and the Eagle Mountain, 2084, more to the S. Over Rostrevor are Slieve Bân and Knockchree; while still further beyond Newry are the ranges of Slieve Gullion. Southwards we have the Carlingford Hills, the Hill of Howth, and in clear weather the faint ridges of the Wicklow Mountains. From its peculiar position and its huge height, Slieve Donard certainly offers one of the most extraordinary prospects in Great Britain.

The botanist will find on these hills Polypodium dryopteris, Lycopodium alpinum, Carex spicrostachya, Salix herbacea, Pinguicula Lusitanica, Melanopsis cambrica, &c. The geological composition of the Mourne Mountains is granite, yielding in some places good specimens of beryl, topaz, and emerald. "The principal place at which they may be obtained is the southern face of Slieve-na-Glogh or the Diamond Rock. Near the Chimney Rock beryls have been found in great numbers."—*Doyle.*

"A deep vale divides it from Slieve Guaven, or the Creeping Mountain, which stands to the S.W., and presents to the view a huge rock resembling at a distance an old fortification, very high, and detached, as it were, from the eastern side of the mountain."

Conveyances from Newcastle daily to Ballynahinch; daily to Downpatrick.

Distances.—Newry, 30 m.; Rostrevor, 22; Dundrum, 5; Annalong, 7; Kilkeel, 12; Castlewellan, 4½.

Excursions.—
1. Armer's Hole, Maggy's Leap, and Kilkeel.
2. Slieve Donard.
3. Tollymore and Briansford.
4. Dundrum and Ardglass.

The next point in our route is 35 m. *Dundrum*, a small bathing and fishing village, situated on the northerly sweep of Dundrum Bay, in which the Great Britain steam-ship went ashore soon after the commencement of her career. To the precipitous and rugged cliffs on which the road has been hitherto carried, succeed large tracts of sandhills and warrens, amidst which the village occupies no very pleasant situation. Lithospermum maritimum flourishes in this locality.

On an eminence overlooking the bay are the keep and a few outworks of the castle, generally reputed to have been built by De Courcey in the beginning of the 11th cent., and held by the Templars: it afterwards passed into the hands of the Magennises, a powerful clan who had many possessions in this part of Ireland. It was a strong fortress, and, "when in repair, often proved a good guard to this pass, and as often an offensive neighbour to the English planted in Lecale, according to the hands that possessed it."—*Harris.* Its principal features are a circular keep and tower, with a barbican and other outworks, which were dismantled by Cromwell.

Near the castle is a ruined mansion, of probably the 16th cent. Dundrum possesses a small pier built by the Marquess of Downshire, and an equally small trade: indeed the navigation hereabouts is not very safe, owing to a bar at the entrance of the river, and an ugly reef of rocks, known as Craigalea, and the Cow and Calf.

[The traveller who wishes to proceed at once to Downpatrick 8½ m., can do so by striking inland, passing Ardilia (Rev. W. Annesley), and Mount Panther (J. Allen, Esq.): the latter place acquired its singular name from a certain legend resembling that of St. George and the Dragon.

At the village of Clough there is only a single tower remaining of the castle, and in the neighbourhood is Seaforde village and House (Rev. W. Forde).]

Passing 37½ m. rt. Tyrella House (A. H. Montgomery, Esq.) and ch., the road again approaches near the coast, which further on juts out to the Promontory of St. John, the western boundary of Dundrum Bay. On the point is a Coast Guard Stat., and a Lighthouse showing an intermittent light.

The ch. of St. John's contains a singular font, in which there is no passage for the water to escape.

43 m. *Killough*, a fishing village, on the E. shore of the little bay of Killough, which runs up for some little distance, necessitating a considerable détour in the road. On the opposite shore is Coney Island, and ¾ m. further

Ardglass, which in the days of its glory was the principal port in all Ulster, and was thought of such great importance as to require the protection of no less than 5 castles. Although these palmy times are gone, Ardglass even yet enjoys a good deal of trade, from being the head-quarters of the northern herring fishery, in which something like 3000 fishermen are engaged. It is also an attractive bathing-place for the residents of Downpatrick.

The name of Ardglass (anc. Ardglaisi, "High Green," is derived from its position between two hills, the Ward of Ardglass on the W., and the Ward of Ardtole on the E., both useful landmarks to sailors. A large trading company obtained a grant from Henry IV. and settled here, and it is to them that with most probability must be ascribed the erection of the *New Works*, a very singular range of buildings overlooking the rocks of the bay. They are in length 250 ft., and are flanked by a square tower at each end, in addition to one in the centre, the intervening walls being entered by 15 arched doorways, between each of which is a square window. There were thus 18 rooms on the ground floor, with the same number in an upper story, and were evidently used as a fortified warehouse for merchants. "In 1789 Lord Charles Fitzgerald, son of the Duke of Leinster, who was then proprietor, caused that portion of the building between the central and western towers to be enlarged in the rear, and raised to the height of 3 stories in the castellated style; and from that time it has been called Ardglass Castle. It was formerly called Horn Castle, either from a great quantity of horns found on the spot, or from a high pillar which stood on its summit previously to being roofed."—*Lewis*. To the W. of this is the square tower of Choud or Cowd Castle. Overlooking the town on the N.W. is the ancient King's Castle, which has been incorporated with the handsome modern residence of Major Beauclerk, the proprietor of the town. Lastly, in the centre is Jordan's Castle, the only one which has any historical celebrity among the whole number. During the insurrection of the Earl of Tyrone, in the reign of Elizabeth, one Simon Jordan held this fortress successfully for 3 years, until he was relieved by the Lord Deputy Mountjoy. It is singular that, considering the former importance of Ardglass and the evident care bestowed on its defences, so little is known of its history or of the builders of these fortresses. Their age is probably that of the 15th cent. The only remaining curiosity in the neighbourhood is a cavern at the head of the creek of the Ardtole, about ½ m. from the town.

Distances. — Dundrum, 9 m.; Strangford, 9; Downpatrick, 7.

The road continues parallel with and at a short distance from the coast, which is rocky and precipitous. At 47 m. is Guns Island, connected with the mainland by a causeway, and at Killard Point, a little further on, commence the narrow straits that connect Strangford Lough with the sea.

50 m. *Kilclief*, a lofty square fortress of Anglo-Norm. character, and generally ascribed to De Courcey as the founder, although it subsequently came into the possession of the Bishops of Down, who occasionally used it as a residence. The bishops of those days were not as stainless in reputation as they are now, for we are informed that John Ross, who was made Bishop of Down in 1387, was "marked with almost every vice." The first story is vaulted, and the second has a carved chimney-piece. At the narrowest part of the straits is

53 m. *Strangford*, a fishing town, exactly opposite Portaferry (Rte. 5). Adjoining is Castleward, a beautiful estate of Viscount Bangor; and overlooking the town on the N. is the ruined keep of Audley Castle, one of

the 27 fortresses that were founded by De Courcey.

Distances.—Portaferry, ¼ m.; Downpatrick, 8; Ardglass, 9; Kilclief, 2¼.

The tourist now bids adieu to the wild sea-girt road which he has travelled for so many miles, and follows an inland route to

61 m. *Downpatrick* (*Hotel:* Denvir's). (Pop. 3840.) This ancient city is situated on the side of a hill, which, curving round like an amphitheatre, overlooks a plain through which the river Quoile winds its reedy way towards Lough Strangford. Approaching either by rail or road, the tourist has a good view of the cathedral, standing at the extreme W. of the town. There can be no doubt of its great age, as we hear of it even before St. Patrick's time as being the residence of the native kings of Ulidia and the Dunum of Ptolemy. St. Patrick did not arrive till 432, and then founded an abbey, the site of which was granted to him by Dichu, son of Trichem, lord of the soil, whom he had converted to Christianity. The sanctity in which this abbey was held may be inferred from the fact that St. Patrick was buried here, together with St. Bridget and St. Columb, 2 of Ireland's most holy saints, a circumstance commemorated by a distich of Sir John de Courcey in 1185, on the discovery of the graves—

"Hi tres in Duno tumulo tumulantur in uno;
Brigida, Patricius, atque Columba Pius."

This De Courcey had established himself in Down *ri et armis*, and maintained his position not only against the native princes, but even against the army of King John, whose allegiance he had shaken off to transfer it to Arthur of Brittany. He was, however, ultimately seized when performing his devotions in the cathedral, and made prisoner. The cathedral suffered much at different times, having been burnt down by Edward Bruce, and again by Lord Grey in 1538, for which act of profanity he was afterwards beheaded.

The town is well built, and divided into English, Irish, and Scotch quarters, the latter being an important element in the population of all the N.-eastern towns; there are also some handsome county buildings—such as the Court-house, Infirmary, and Gaol, the cost of this last being 63,000*l*. The cathedral is comparatively modern; the old building, burnt by Lord Grey, continued in ruins for 250 years, the ch. of Lisburn doing duty in the mean time as the cathedral. In 1790, however, the present Perp. building was raised, consisting of a nave, choir, and aisles, with clerestory, and a fine tower of 4 stages at the W. end. At the E. end are also 2 small castellated towers of 3 stages, surmounted by a parapet, and finished off with broach spires. There is an E. window of 12 compartments, and above it 3 ogee-headed niches which once contained the images of the saints so ruthlessly mutilated by Lord Grey. Under the window is a deeply recessed doorway, which is said to have belonged to the old cathedral. The aisles are separated from the nave by ranges of pointed arches, and the roof is groined and ornamented at the intersections with clustered foliage. From earliest times the Bishopric of Down has been joined to that of Connor, although one or two bishops caused them to be separated: they were, however, again united in the 15th cent., and are now incorporated with that of Dromore. Amongst the Protestant bishops, after the Reformation, was the pious Jeremy Taylor, who at the same time held the see of Dromore.

The visitor will not fail to enjoy the exquisite panorama of distant hills from the ch.-yard, in which the Mourne ranges are especially conspicuous.

It may be mentioned that a fine round tower once stood at the W. end, but was taken away, as fears were entertained lest it should fall and damage the cathedral.

The antiquary should visit the Rath of Downpatrick, not far from the gaol. It was formerly known as Rath Keltain, "the Fort of Celtain," and is the largest in the county, being 895 yards broad at the base and surrounded by 3 ramparts.

There is also a remarkable Druidical ring, with an avenue of stones running for 35 ft. in a N.E. direction, on the hill of Slieve-na-griddle, 3 m. to the E. On the way thither are the wells of *Struel* (Struile or Sluith-fuile, the Stream of Blood), whither on Midsummer-day crowd pilgrims from every quarter to try the efficacy of the waters in washing away their sins. It is one of the most celebrated resorts in all Ireland, and famous, or rather infamous, for the mingled scenes of credulity, impiety, and indecency which are allowed to be openly carried on. Having completed their weary pilgrimage on bare knees up Struel Hill, they resort to the wells. "These are 4 in number—the Body Well or Well of Sins, the Limb Well, the Eye Well, and the Well of Life. If they pay a fee, they can go into the first, in which they are accommodated with a place to undress; if not, they must go to the Limb Well, in which case they have to undress before the multitude, and repair in a state of nudity to the well, into which they plunge promiscuously. Having thus washed away their sins at the expense of their modesty, they repair to the Eye Well to wash away the impediments to their spiritual vision, after which they partake of the 'Waters of Life,' or, as some call it, the Well of Forgetfulness."—*Doyle.* The performances were usually closed with a series of religious (?) saturnalia, which, if the accounts of some writers be true, should have been long ago summarily stopped by the civil authorities.

2 m. N.E. are slight remains of the abbey of *Saul*, built in the 12th cent. by Malachi O'Morgan, Bishop of Down. It was formerly a cruciform ch., but the greater part of it has disappeared. About a mile to the W., on the shore of the estuary of the Quoile, stand the ruins of an embattled tower.

On the opposite side of the estuary are the ruins of the abbey of *Inch*, erected in the 12th cent. by John de Courcey, and supplied with monks from Furness, in Lancashire. Although originally a cruciform ch., little is left of it save the chancel, which is lighted by E. Eng. lancet windows of beautiful design. A primitive ch. of much earlier date still exists on the island, and is said to have been the predecessor of the present abbey. Over the S. door is a sculpture, representing a person praying to the Saviour on the Cross.

Conveyances from Downpatrick to Belfast by rail. Car daily to Newry and Newcastle.

Distances.—Newry, by the coast road, 61 m.; Dundrum, 8½; Strangford, 8; Ardglass, 7; Killough, 7½; Killyleagh, 6; Belfast, 27; Ballynahinch, by rail, 12½; Struel, 3; Saul, 2.

Excursions.—
1. Strangford and Kilclief.
2. Struel and Saul.
3. Ballynahinch.

Passing the village and stat. of Crossgar 5½ m., we arrive at a point from whence a short branch is given off to

[*Ballynahinch*, which of late years has attracted valetudinarians from its bracing air and the efficacy of its medicinal waters. There are 2 wells, the one containing lime, sulphuric, muriatic, and carbonic acids; and the other having, in addition, a small amount of protoxide of iron. They are strongly recommended by Dr. Knox in cases of hepatic affections, cutaneous diseases, and general debility. The Spa is tastefully planted and laid out in ornamental walks, and the accommodation cheap and good. Adjoining the town is Montalto, formerly the residence of the Earls of Moira, and now of D. Kerr, Esq., M.P. Ballynahinch is situated pleasantly enough in a vale at the foot of the Slieve Croob Mountains (1753 ft.), which lie between it and Castlewellan, and contain the sources of the river Lagan, that runs by Dromore to Belfast. On the side of Slieve Croob the antiquary will find a very large rath, 80 yards round at the base. Excursions may also be made to Hillsborough, 9 m.; Banbridge, 17 (Rte. 3 ; and Castlewellan, 12¼.]

. *Excursions.—*
1. Hillsborough and Dromore (Rte. 3).
2. Slieve Croob.
3. Killyleagh, a small town on the rt. of the rly., and beautifully situated on the shores of Lough Strangford. It is remarkable for being the birthplace of Sir Hans Sloan, the founder of the British Museum. The learned Dr. Hincks, so well known for his Egyptian and Assyrian researches, is the present rector of the parish. A very ancient castle, beautifully restored by the late Archibald Hamilton, and of which one of the towers certainly dates from the reign of King John, crowns the hill at the back of the town.

Continuing our course on the main line, we arrive at

11¼ m. *Saintfield*, a small but busy manufacturing town, where linens are made for the Belfast market. Here was fought the battle of Saintfield in 1789, a sharp and bloody engagement between the United Irishmen under Munroe, and the Yeomanry under Col. Stapleton. The latter retreated after losing 60 men, though the rebels are stated to have lost 360. Three days after this action Munroe advanced on Ballynahinch with an army of 7000, but here his good fortune deserted him. The Royal forces under Gen. Nugent had occupied the town, and, although the rebels fought with desperate gallantry, discipline prevailed, and they were routed with great slaughter, Munroe himself being captured and executed. The ill-success of this last movement completely crushed the rebellion.

19 m. Comber Stat., the point of junction with the Donaghadee line (Rte. 5). From hence it is 8 m. to Belfast.

ROUTE 5.

BELFAST TO DONAGHADEE.

Belfast (*Hotels*: Imperial, Royal, the best; Queen's, Albion, good; besides several others of a less expensive character) is the metropolis of N. Ireland, and indeed ranks next to Dublin in the whole kingdom for size and importance. It is a city of essentially modern growth and appearance, and as such will surprise and please the traveller who visits it after any lengthened experience of Irish towns, on account of its spacious and well-arranged streets and squares, its general cleanliness and good order, and the beautiful examples of decorative architecture displayed so largely in its public buildings. Belfast appears to owe these advantages in a great degree to the fact that it is presided over and inhabited by a race which unites the Scottish thrift and decorum with Irish impulsiveness and kindliness. A fort is known to have existed at "Benla-fearsad," the Mouth of the Ford, before the year 1178, but, with the exception of repeated incursions by the natives, it had but little history, and its importance as a port may be altogether dated from the time of James I., when the estates were granted to the Chichester family, and certain port monopolies were purchased from the Corporation of Carrickfergus. In the Parliamentary wars it was taken by Gen. Munroe, and changed hands four times in six years, a state of things which did not add to the increase of trade or population. (Pop. 120,544.)

The situation is well adapted for commercial as well as residential purposes, the town lying at the base of a lofty chain of hills that runs up from the S., and ends abruptly with the Cave Hill, a somewhat precipitous basaltic eminence rising to the height of 1158 ft. To the E. is the noble Belfast Lough, the head of which is marked by a singularly long bridge crossing the Lagan at its mouth. In consequence of the shelter afforded by these hills, the temperature is very mild, being only one degree below that of Torquay.

The communications of Belfast are many and regular : inland by 4 railways; seaward, by steamers innumerable, which keep up a daily intercourse with the principal English and Scotch ports.

The number of vessels that entered and cleared out from the port in 1859 was between 6000 and 7000, the annual value of its imports and exports being 9,000,000*l*., and the gross produce of the customs in the same years 376,000*l*. Linen is of course the staple trade, Belfast being the centre of all the manufacturing districts of Down, Antrim, and the northern counties. "A great source of employment for females has of late years sprung up in the north of Ireland in the working of patterns on muslin with the needle. This manufacture employs about 300,000 persons scattered throughout Ulster. About 40 firms are engaged in the trade, some being Irish houses, and others agents for Scotch firms; the gross value of the manufactured goods amounts to about 1,400,000*l*."—*Thom's Directory.*

The harbour is formed by the tidal channel of the Lagan, through which excavations were cut, with a depth of 23 ft. at high water. Both sides are lined with quays, 5000 and 3500 ft. respectively on the western and eastern sides. The Prince's and the Clarendon Docks afford every accommodation for foreign vessels loading or unloading, and there are graving-docks and slips for repairs.

The Lagan is crossed by 3 bridges, of which the Queen's (of 5 granite arches of 50 ft. span) is the most beautiful. It stands on the site of the Long Bridge, which was 840 ft. in length. The other 2 are the Albert and the Ormeau Bridges. The places of interest in the town are soon exhausted, as their chief beauty consists in the exteriors. The Commercial Buildings have a fine Ionic façade, and the Customhouse, which is well situated, is a freestone edifice, with a Corinthian front. The Banks, however, carry off the palm for decorative art, and the Ulster Bank in particular should be well studied for its elaborate details, particularly of the entablatures and cornices. The visitor should also inspect the interior, which is equally beautiful, though perhaps as a whole a little overdone.

The Queen's College, near the Botanic Gardens (well worth visiting), is a Tudor building, with a front 600 ft. in length, relieved by a graceful tower in the centre. Of very opposite style is the other educational institution of Belfast, the Presbyterian College.

The Belfast Museum, in College Square, has "its first story in imitation of the Choragic monument of Thrasyllus, with a portico which is an exact copy of that of the octagon tower of Andronicus at Athens; the upper portions are designed after the Temple of Minerva."

The churches are, generally speaking, of the classical order of architecture; the 2 best being the Parish Church, which has a lofty tower and cupola, and Christ Church, a Perp. building with an octagonal spire, an agreeable exception to the prevailing style. The portico of St. George's was originally a portion of the front of Ballyscallion House, a mansion erected by the eccentric Earl of Bristol, on the shores of Lough Neagh. On his death, it was purchased and presented to this ch. by Dr. Alexander, Bishop of Down. The visitor should also notice the Ulster Hall in Bedford Street, the Music Hall in May Street, and a very fine Institution, of the Tudor order, for the Deaf, Dumb, and Blind.

The flax-mills are perhaps the most interesting objects in the city, and the visitor should not omit seeing one of these establishments. That of Messrs. Mulholland is the largest, and will give a better idea than almost any other of the extent of the trade. The firm that owns this enormous factory was one of the first to start the linen-yarn manufacture in Belfast, and now employs directly and indirectly nearly 25,000 persons. The other principal factories are those of Craig and Co., which contain 321 looms; the Bedford Weaving Co.; Messrs. Hinds, Foster, Connor, and Co., &c. A sketch of the flax and linen trade will be found in Introduction (p. xxxiv.; but it may be mentioned here that in 1860 there were exported from Belfast upwards of 65,000,000 yards of linen, valued at about 2,000,000*l.* sterling, and at the same time yarns and threads to the amount of 3,000,000 lbs., valued at 764,000*l.* Nor is it only as a manufacturing centre that Belfast is pre-eminent; she is equally noted for the position gained by her inhabitants in literature and the arts, which are cultivated to an extent unknown in any other city in Ireland, save Dublin. The earliest edition of the Bible was printed here in 1704, and the third newspaper, as regards date, viz. the Belfast News-letter, began its existence in 1737. The communications by land and water are many and frequent. Three railways have their terminus here, viz., the Belfast and County Down to Donaghadee and Downpatrick; the Ulster to Portadown and Omagh; the Northern Counties to Coleraine: all of which throw out branch-lines in different parts of their course.

The following steamers also sail from the port: to Bristol weekly; Fleetwood daily; Annan 3 times a week; to Carlisle; to Dublin, Dumfries, Liverpool, Glasgow, Whitehaven, Morecambe, Waterford, Londonderry, London.

Distances.—Dublin, 113 m.; Drogheda, 81; Dundalk, 59; Derry, 94; Downpatrick, 27; Donaghadee, 22; Holywood, 5; Bangor, 12; Newtownards, 13½; Comber, 8; Lisburn, 7; Moira, 14; Hillsborough, 19; Antrim, 22; Carrickfergus, 9¼.

Excursions.—
1. Cave Hill and Divis.
2. Dundonald, Kempe Stones.
3. Drumbo.
4. Holywood.
5. Carrickfergus (Rte. 13).
6. Antrim (Rte. 12).

The tourist should not leave Belfast without paying a visit to *Cave Hill*, which overhangs the city, at a distance of about 2 m., and is interesting both in a geological and antiquarian point of view. It forms the northern termination of the chalk ranges that stretch from Lisburn and are capped with basalt; although, geologically, the same strata are seen to recommence to the N.W. of Carrickfergus, and to extend along the coast as far as the Giant's Causeway. "It consists of an overlying mass of tabular trap in a vast series of strata, which in some places exceed 900 ft. of thickness in the aggregate, resting upon a stratum of white chalk in a highly vitrified state, in which there is a large quantity of flint both in laminæ and nodules; the greensand underlies the chalks, beneath which the oolitic formation crops out, but of such a thickness that its series of beds of gray, white, and variegated gypseous marls have not yet been fully explored."—*Doyle.* In the perpendicular face of the rock are the 3 caves which have given its name to the hill; the 2 lowest being 21 and 10 ft. respectively in length, and the upper one considerably larger, though so placed as to be well-nigh inaccessible. The summit is crowned by an earthwork, known as the Fort of Mac Art, "from its having been one of the last strongholds of Brian Mac Art (O'Neill), who, with his sept, was exterminated by Deputy Mountjoy in the reign of Elizabeth." On one side it is protected by the precipice, and on the other by a deep ditch. Cave Hill is not the highest point of this range, being overtopped on the S. side by Divis, 1567 ft., and on the N. by Collinward, 1196, while at the back are the Wolf's Hill, 1210, and Squire's Hill, 1230. In the former hill are other caves in the chalk limestone, and at the base of the latter are several raths where implements of early warfare, such as celts, arrow heads, and hatchets were discovered. If the visitor be neither antiquary nor geologist, he will, nevertheless, be delighted with the view from any one of these heights, which embrace a panorama of great beauty. At the foot lies Belfast, with its churches, mills, and docks; the harbour, and the broad lough of Strangford; the hills of Down on the opposite side, sprinkled with many a smiling village; while afar in the distance are the dim outlines of the Ayrshire coast, and on a clear day the cliffs of the Isle of Man. To the W. is a broad expanse of Co. Antrim, in which Lough Neagh plays a conspicuous part, while the chalk hills in the neighbourhood of Coleraine and Derry fill up the background with grand effect. The following plants are found here and at Colin Glen: Asplenium ceterach, Aspidium lobatima, A. aculeatum, Equisetum variegatum, Festuca calamaria, Listera nidus avis, Orobanche rubra, Hieracium murorum, Circæa alpina, Adoxa moschatellinæ. On the return to the town, the remains of an intrenchment, thrown up by William III. in the grounds of Fort William close to the water's edge, may be visited; and near the Belfast water-works the geologist should notice an elevated deposit of marine shells of the tertiary (pliocene) era. On the E. bank of the Lagan, 1 m. from Belfast, is Ormeau, the seat of the Marquis of Donegal. For further particulars about Belfast the traveller may consult M'Comb's 'Guide,' a handy and useful little work.

[It is a pleasant excursion up the valley of the Lagan to the village of Newtown-breda, and thence to *Drumbo.* The former overlooks the Lagan, from the foot of the hill of *Castlereagh,* the site of the once famous palace of Con O'Neill. By an inquisition in the reign of Elizabeth it appears that Con O'Neill was the last of that sept, and was possessed of no less than 224 townlands, all freehold. Adjoining the village are a Grecian ch., built by Viscountess Middleton, and Belvoir Park, the seat of Sir R. Bateson, Bart. The ruins of the old parish ch. of Knock are in the S.E. portion of the district, and near it is a cromlech of 5 supporters, together with a rath.

The round tower at Drumbo is 35 ft. in height and 47 in circumference. Of this Petrie observes, "The oldest towers are obviously those constructed of spawled masonry and large hammered stones, and which present simple quadrangular and semicircular arched doorways with sloping jambs. The doorway of Drumbo is only about 4 ft. from the ground, which has been much raised by interments about it, so that there is no doubt but that its elevation was originally at least 8 or 10 ft." The foundations of the old ch., ascribed to St. Patrick, are visible to the S.E. of the town. A large quantity of bones and a portion of skeleton were found within this tower, which, when opened, presented all the appearances of vitrification. On the return from Drumbo the tourist should visit the *Giant's Ring*, one of the largest and most striking early remains existing in the kingdom. It is an extensive circle, about 580 ft. in diameter, embracing an area of 10 acres, and enclosed by a lofty mound, of which the thickness at the base is 80 ft. This will give some idea of what the height may have been when it was perfect, for even now, though greatly dilapidated, it is high enough to shut out the view of the country around. In the centre is the altar, 4 large blocks supporting the incumbent stone, while on the W. and S. are also other detached stones, though in the time when Harris wrote his 'History of County Down,' in 1744, the incumbent block is stated to have been supported by 2 ranges of pillars, 7 on each side. The protection, which this venerable remain so greatly needed, has been afforded to it by the late Viscount Dungannon, who built a strong wall all round.]

The visitor may return to Belfast from the Knock Stat. on the Belfast and County Down Rly., which conveys the traveller to Donaghadee and Downpatrick, 39 m. in length, including short branches to Holywood and Ballynahinch. The stat. is on the E. bank of the river.

[Directly on leaving the town, a branch skirts the shores of the lough to Sydenham and Holywood, 5 m., both pleasant marine suburbs, where the Belfast merchants love to dwell. Sydenham has within the last few years been extensively built over with villas, some of which occupy the site of an ancient burying-ground, said to have contained the tomb of Con O'Neill (see *ante*).

Holywood derives its name from a Franciscan Priory founded in 1200 by one Thomas Whyte, but is now known only as an agreeable bathing-place, for which its position on the shore of the lough offers many advantages. The Bishop of Down and Connor has a residence here, known as the Palace. The rly. is in course of extension to Bangor.

Distances.—Belfast, 5 m. ; Bangor, 7.]

Returning to the main line, the first stat. is 2¼ m. Knock, from whence the tourist may excurse to the Giant's Ring and Drumbo.

5 m. *Dundonald*. 1 m. to the E. is a relic of antiquity known as the *Kempe Stones*, an enormous mass of rock, weighing upwards of 40 tons, supported by 5 rude pillars. In appearance they resemble Druidical altars, "but their name, and that of the townland in which they are situated, as well as tradition, seem to assign to them a different origin, and to raise the probability that they were erected as a memorial to the dead. The Celtic name of the district was Baille-clough-togal, *i. e.* 'The Town of the Stone of the Strangers :' the townland is still called Greengraves."—*M'Comb.* In the summer of 1832 the head and horns of a moose-deer (now extinct) were found in an adjacent bog resting on marl.

8 m. *Comber*, the junction from whence the line to Downpatrick diverges (Rte. 4), is a neat thriving town, chiefly dependent on the linen trade. The ch. is built on the site of an ancient abbey, founded

in 1201, the monks of which were furnished from Whitland, or Alba-Lauda, in Caermarthenshire. It contains monuments to the memory of persons who fell in the battle of Saintfield, 1798 (p. 47), and in the market-square is a monumental obelisk to Sir R. Gillespie, a native of this town, who fell in Java.

The rly. to Donaghadee now turns round the base of Scrabo Mount, and soon comes in sight of the craggy hill of Carngaver 720 ft., which is capped by a tower erected in memory of Charles William Marquis of Londonderry, the landlord and owner of all this property. On the rt. is Strangford Lough, an inlet of which flows to within ¼ m. of Comber.

13½ m. *Newtownards* (*Hotel:* Londonderry Arms), or Newtown of the Ards, the latter being the distinguishing name of the promontory lying between Lough Strangford and the sea, formerly designated "Altitudo Ultorum juxta Mare Orientale." It is a large and well-built town, possessing the advantages of a careful supervision by the Londonderry family, whose seat Mount Stewart, to the S.E., between Newtown and Grey Abbey, is a fine classic building, beautifully situated in a wooded demesne on the shores of Strangford Lough. Newtownards, though now a bustling linen town, was formerly noted for having been the centre of a large number of religious establishments, the ruins of many of which are still in existence. The Court-house, which possesses a good doorway, was originally the old ch., built by Sir Hugh Montgomery, to whom James I., after the forfeiture of Con O'Neill's estates, granted the whole of the district. The town contains a handsome octagonal cross, built to replace the one destroyed by the insurgents. Newtownards is well situated at the foot of the Scrabo hills, where limestone and lead-ore are obtained, and at the head of the lough of Strangford, an arm of the sea about 14 m. in length and 4 to 5 wide. The channel of Portaferry, however, which communicates with the sea, is so very narrow, that the lough looks almost like a freshwater lake — an appearance to which the number of small islands contributes; and this same cause makes it nearly useless for navigation purposes (Pop. 9543).

Conveyances. — Rail to Belfast and Donaghadee. Car to Cloghy.

Distances. — Grey Abbey, 7 m.; Mount Stewart, 5; Bangor, 5; Donaghadee, 9½; Comber, 5¼.

Excursions.—
1. Scrabo.
2. Grey Abbey and Mt. Stewart.

[This is the nearest spot from whence to visit Grey Abbey, the road to which skirts the N.E. shore of Strangford Lough, and passes 5 m. the Grecian mansion of Mount Stewart, the seat of the Londonderry family. The house is built of Scrabo stone, and the interior is floored with bog fir found on the estates. The grounds are well wooded, and laid out with taste, and contain a classic temple, copied from the "Temple of the Winds."

7 m. *Grey Abbey*, a small town, which took its rise from the foundation of an abbey in the 12th cent. for Cistercian monks, by Afric, wife of John De Courcey, and daughter of Godred, King of Man. The ruins of this E. Eng. abbey are in remarkably good preservation, probably owing to the fact that it was used as a parish ch. as late as 1778. The choir contains some lancet windows on the N. wall, and a noble E. window of 3 lights, upwards of 20 ft. in height; also 2 recumbent figures. A tower, now fallen, rose from the centre of the ch., and was supported by very graceful and lofty arches. The abbey was destroyed in the rebellion of Tyrone, "ruinated in Tirowen's rebellion," but was subsequently rebuilt by the Montgomery family (see *ante*), whose seat of Rose-

mount adjoins the ruins, which still serve as their mausoleum. From its picturesque situation on the lough and the beauty of the ruins, Grey Abbey is a favourite excursion with the citizens of Belfast. Anchusa sempervirens and Andromeda polyfolia grow here. Pursuing the road southward, the tourist reaches

10½ m. *Kircubbin*, a small town, the inhabitants of which are chiefly occupied in the manufacture of straw bonnets. The little bay, on the shore of which it is situated, rejoices in the name of the Bloody Burn.

15 m. rt. *Ardkeen*, once the chief residence of the Bishops of Down, once possessed a monastery, of which slight traces still exist.

17½ m. *Portaferry* (Hotel : Nugent Arms), the most southerly town in the peninsula of Ards. "It owes its origin to a castle built by the Savage family, who came into this part of the country with John de Courcy shortly after the arrival of the English, and, the place being well secured and garrisoned by that powerful family, its situation on the strait made it a port of great importance in all the subsequent wars, during which neither it nor the neighbouring district of the southern Ards ever fell into the hands of the Irish."—*Lewis*. The visitor should ascend the hill of Blackbank to the N. of the town, from which he will obtain a very fine view of the whole of the Strangford Lough, or Lough Coyne, as it is also called. Portaferry is a neat, thriving little town, carrying on a coasting trade with Scotland and Liverpool. It contains the crumbling remains of the castle of the Savages, which once protected and fostered the village. It now enjoys the more favourable protection of a good resident landlord, J. Nugent, Esq., whose residence, Portaferry House, is near the town. The channel that separates the town from the opposite one of Strangford is about 5 m. in length and ¼ in breadth. "There is a violent tide through the channel in and out of Strangford Lough, and it makes a heavy swell when running against the wind, but it is not dangerous to persons acquainted with the passage."—*Fraser*. The tourist can cross the ferry to Strangford, and thence to Downpatrick (Rte. 4), or else return by the coast to Donaghadee through Cloghy and Ballyhalbert. Burial Island off the shore at this point is the most eastern land in Ireland. From Ballywalter, near which is Springvale House (A. Mulholland, Esq.), it is 7½ m. of a rocky coast-road to Donaghadee.]

Donaghadee (Hotels : Arthur's; Commercial), apart from its claims to admiration as a fine bathing-place and marine residence, derives much importance from the fact of its being the nearest port to Scotland, the distance to Portpatrick being only 22 m. As the rly. in the sister island is now completed from Carlisle to Portpatrick, it is not unlikely that ere long a fast steamer will be placed on the station, and that this short passage will be much patronised by all northern Irish tourists, who are haunted by the dread of the terrible 4 hours between Holyhead and Kingstown. Indeed, so near is the Scottish coast, that not only the outlines of the hills but even the houses can be distinctly seen in clear weather. This is also the crossing point of the Magnetic Telegraph. The harbour is good, and was improved at a cost of 145,000*l*. Vessels drawing 16 ft. of water can enter at any time of the tide. The piers are built of Anglesea marble, as is also the lighthouse, which shows a fixed red light. The only relic of antiquity in the town is an enormous rath 70 ft. high, of which advantage has been taken to erect a powder-magazine on the summit. The view from it is beautiful, embracing the sweep of the bay and town, and a long extent of Scotch coast. (Pop. 2671.)

Distances.—Grey Abbey, 9 m.; Newtownards, 8½; Groomsport, 4; Bangor, 5½, to which the shore-road may be taken, although there is a shorter and better one across country.

Excursions.—
1. Bangor.
2. Grey Abbey.

A little to the N. of Donaghadee the coast trends to the W., and forms the entrance to Belfast Lough. Some distance out at sea are Copeland Island (of considerable size), Mew and Lighthouse Islands; on the latter is a fixed light.

The fishing village of Groomsport is the locale of the disembarkment of the advanced guard of William III.'s army under Schomberg. Adjoining is Groomsport House (the Elizabethan seat of R. P. Maxwell, Esq.).

Bangor (*Hotel:* Royal), as its name implies ("Beann chair," White Church), was in former days the seat of an abbey of regular canons, founded by St. Comgall in 555, and of a school so famous for its learning, that Alfred resorted to it for professors when he restored the university of Oxford. Like most of this district, it formed a portion of O'Neill's confiscated property, and was transferred by James I. to the family of Hamilton, afterwards Viscount Clandeboye. Only a very minute fragment is left of the abbey. The town is principally dependent on muslin sewing and embroidering, and a large amount of work is annually sent to England in the shape of fine embroideries for ladies' attire. The modern mansion, the seat of the Ward family, is an Elizabethan building near the town, and in close proximity to the site of the old castle.

Distances.—Newtownards, 5 m.; Holywood, 7½; Donaghadee, 5½; Groomsport, 2.

Steamers ply daily to Belfast.

2 m. on the road leading from Bangor to Holywood is Clandeboye, the seat of Lord Dufferin. The house was originally erected in the reign of James I.; but subsequent alterations have obliterated its ancient character. At the southern extremity of the demesne rises a hill, crowned by a tower built for the purpose of enshrining some beautiful verses written by Lady Dufferin to her son. The structure has received the name of Helen's Tower, and has been still further dignified by a poetical inscription from the hand of Alfred Tennyson. A small private chapel in the park contains some ancient architectural fragments built into its inner walls, and an hieroglyphic cartouche of Tirhakah, the contemporary of Hezekiah, Isaiah, and Sennacherib. From the western side of the demesne an avenue leads to the seashore, distant about 3 m.

At Cultra, more than halfway between Holywood and Bangor, the geologist will observe some singular beds of dolomite, considered by Sir R. Griffith on lithological grounds to represent the Permian system of Ireland.

ROUTE 6.

FROM **DUNDALK** TO **ENNISKILLEN** AND **SLIGO.**

The Dundalk and Enniskillen Rly. was opened in 1852, and, taken *per se*, is 62 m. in length; but as this company have also leased the Enniskillen and Londonderry line, the two are the same for all practical purposes, and are now worked under the name of the Irish North-Western. Through carriages run from Dundalk to Derry, thus saving a great deal of time between Dublin and Derry, in comparison with the route to Belfast. The rly. cannot be said to run through a pretty country in general, although some portions, especially near Enniskillen, are very charming. Quitting the Dundalk Stat., there is nothing of interest until *Inniskeen* Stat. 7 m. is reached. On l. are ruins (of no great extent or architectural beauties) of the abbey of Inniskeen: and here we may remark that the Irish tourist must not expect to find in every abbey ruin anything more than the remains of a simple parish ch., generally consisting of a nave and choir, with probably a belfry. They were built in a rude age, as the nucleus of a monastic establishment which most frequently had to provide for their personal defence as well as religious duties. Inniskeen presents, however, an additional attraction in the shape of the stump of a round tower and a stone cross.

Conveyances.—A daily car to *Carrickmacross* (*Inn:* Shirley Arms), [a little town prettily situated on high rocky ground of the lower limestone series, which is here surrounded by upper Silurian rocks, principally gray or purple slates alternating with quartzite, and occasionally with conglomerate or fossiliferous limestone. In the neighbourhood are Lisinisk and Lough Fea House (E. P. Shirley, Esq.. The district to the S. of Carrickmacross becomes wild and hilly, rising to a considerable height at Loughanleagh (1116 ft.), between Bailiborough and Kingscourt.

Conveyances.—Car to Inniskeen; car to Bailiborough, through Kingscourt.

Distances.—Inniskeen, 7½ m.; Virginia, 22; Kingscourt, 7; Bailiborough, 14; Ardee, 14.]

From Inniskeen the line is carried up the little valley of the Fane through Silurian cuttings, in the intervals of which the traveller gains distant views on the N. of the Slieve Gullion group between Dundalk and Newry.

12 m. *Culloville*, 2½ m. rt. of which is the village of Crossmaglen.

The country becomes more diversified and prettier at *Castle Blayney* (*Inn:* King's Arms), named after Sir E. Blayney, governor of Monaghan in the reign of James I., who gave him land on condition of his erecting a fort between Newry and Monaghan. It is a pretty English-looking town on the borders of the well-planted lake of Muckna, which is still further embellished by the grounds of Castle Blayney, the residence of T. H. Hope, Esq.

Distances.—Armagh, 17½ m.; Keady, 10.

21½ m. *Ballybay*, like Castle Blayney, owes its prosperity to the linen trade. Beyond being placed in a very pretty country, it does not contain much of interest. "The approach to the town opens upon a picturesque district. To the E. are seen, at the distance of 20 m., the blue summits of the lofty Slieve Gullion, with the town about a quarter of a mile beneath, apparently embosomed in hills, and situated on the margin of a lake 1 m. in diameter."

[From hence a branch line has been formed to 9 m. *Cootehill*, passing 5 m. *Rockcorry*.

Cootehill (*Hotel:* M'Cabe's), on the borders of Cavan co., a pleasant well-built town, on the banks of the river of the same name, which connects it by a chain of navigable lakes with Ballybay. There are some fine estates near the town: *Bellamont Forest*, the former residence of the Earl of Bellamont, and now possessed by Mrs. Coote; *Dartrey* (Lord Cremorne), the great place of this district, with a very fine modern mansion situated in an extensive and finely wooded domain; and *Ashfield* (Col. Clements). (Pop. 1994.)

Conveyance.—Car to Monaghan.

Distances.—Ballybay, 9 m.; Ballyhaise, 11; Stradone, 10.

The road continues to Ballyhaise, passing Tullyvin House (J. Bromley, Esq.), and 4½ m. *Rakenny*, where in an old fort a large gold fibula was found in an iron pot. 11 m. Ballyhaise (Rte. 17).]

34 m. *Newbliss*, a neat village, close to which is Newbliss House (A. Kerr, Esq.).

39 m. *Clones* (Rte. 17) (*Inn*: Dacre Arms), an ancient and not over clean little town, though it is placed on a hill high enough to secure all the advantages of drainage. It has derived its name from Cluain Inis, "the Island of Retreat," from having been formerly surrounded by water. It was also a celebrated ecclesiastical locality, and the seat of a bishopric, St. Tigernach, the first bishop, having died here of the plague in 550. The abbey was burnt in 1395, and again rebuilt and finally dissolved in Henry VIII.'s time. The tourist should stop at Clones to visit the ruins, though they are but small. They are situated at the foot of the hill on the S. side of the town, together with the round tower, which is peculiarly rough and irregular on the outside, but of smooth limestone within. The masonry is rude, and the top is wanting. At the summit of the hill is the market-place, adorned with a handsome ch. and the cross of Clones, in very fair preservation, though the sculpture on the shaft is somewhat indistinct. The arms of the cross are connected by circular portions, similar to that at Tynan near Armagh (Rte. 17). (Pop. 2390.)

Conveyance.—Car to Monaghan.

Distances.—Cavan, 15 m.; Belturbet, 11½; Monaghan, 11.

A rly. is here given off to Cavan en route for Mullingar, as also one to join the Ulster line at Monaghan.

44 m. At *Newtown Butler*, a bridge crosses a small tributary to Lough Erne. This village was the scene of a very decisive action in 1689. "About 1 m. from Newtown Butler the Irish faced about and made a stand. They were driven up on a hill, at the foot of which lay a deep bog. A narrow paved causeway which ran across the bog was the only road by which the cavalry of the Enniskilleners could advance. Macarthy placed his cannon in such a way as to sweep this causeway. Wolseley ordered his infantry to the attack. They struggled through the bog, made their way to firm ground, and rushed on to the guns. The Irish cannoneers stood gallantly to their pieces till they were cut down to a man. The Irish dragoons, who had run away in the morning, were smitten with another panic, and without striking a blow galloped from the field."—*Macaulay*. In this affray the Irish lost above 2000 men, while the loss of the Enniskilleners was only 20.

Portions of the beautiful reaches of Lough Erne every now and then become visible, although on no point from the rly. is the lake seen to any extent. In the distance to the S.W. the blue limestone ranges of Leitrim, in which the Shannon takes its rise, form very fine features in the landscape.

[2½ m. l. on the banks of Lough Erne is *Crom Castle*, the charming residence of the Earl of Erne, situated at the bend of a wooded promontory overlooking the windings of the upper lake. It is a castellated building, placed in very picturesque grounds, which also enclose the ruins of the old castle of Crom, in 1689 "the frontier garrison of the Protestants of Fermanagh." It was besieged by Mountcashel, a circumstance that induced the battle of Newtown Butler, in consequence of his being obliged to retire from Crom to meet Wolseley.]

51 m. *Lisnaskea* Stat. (*Hotel*: Erne Arms), a neat town with well-built schools, ch., market-house, &c. The town and neighbourhood owe

much to the resident landlord, the Earl of Erne. Near Lisnaskea is Clifton Lodge (Major Archdall).

54 m. *Maguire's Bridge*, another townlet situated on the Colebrooke river, which flows into Lough Erne near here. 3 m. N. is the village of Brookeborough, and further N. Colebrooke, a fine park and mansion belonging to Sir Victor Brooke, Bart. To the l. of Maguire's Bridge is Lough Erne, studded with islands, on the largest of which is Belleisle, the residence of J. Porter, Esq.

Soon after passing 57½ m. *Lisbellaw*, the rly. skirts the demesne of Castle Coole, and arrives at

62 m. *Enniskillen* (anc. Inisceithlean' (*Hotels*: Imperial, tolerable; White Hart', the stat. being placed at the most disadvantageous point from whence to see the town. Enniskillen is one of the prettiest places in Ireland, a circumstance to which, together with its stirring Protestant associations, it owes its principal attractions, for it is destitute of any archæological objects of interest. From almost every point it has a peculiarly beautiful appearance, being entirely watergirt by Lough Erne, or, to speak correctly, by the river which unites the upper and lower lake; from the level of which the houses rise symmetrically, the apex being formed by the graceful spire of the ch. It consists of one long street of well-built and well-ordered houses, and is remarkably free from those abominably dirty cabins which disgrace the entrances of Ireland's best towns. The streets are broad and clean, the shops good and well filled, and a general air of prosperity and business pervades the whole place. In the reign of James I. Enniskillen was merely a stronghold of the Maguires, chieftains of Fermanagh; but its great celebrity is subsequent to that period, when in 1689, not content with fortifying their town against the soldiers of Tyrconnel, the gallant Enniskilleners actually pursued their invaders, who made a precipitate retreat, without stopping till they reached Cavan. The actions at Belturbet and Newtown Butler were still more telling and decisive affairs in the brief campaign. On a wooded hill overlooking the town above the stat. is a lofty pillar to commemorate the heroic deeds of Sir Lowry Cole of Peninsular fame. The view from the hill is very beautiful, though the trees are allowed to grow too densely around the column. At either end of the town is a fort, and there are also extensive barracks occupying the site of the castle, a portion of which still exists close to the W. bridge. From its position on the lake, a considerable trade is carried on by water between Enniskillen and Belleek at the western extremity of Lough Erne; and if any communication existed between this latter place and Ballyshannon, it would at once open the way to a very extensive inland trade. With the towns on the lower lakes, as Belturbet, &c., there is at present little or none, probably owing to the very serpentine course of the river. 1 m. from the town is the magnificent demesne and mansion of *Castle Coole*, the seat of the Earl of Belmore. It is a large Grecian house, built by the elder Wyatt of Portland stone, and is very prettily situated. To see the neighbourhood of Enniskillen to advantage the tourist should discard terra firma and take to the lake, for which purpose good boats may be had at the W. bridge. *Lough Erne* is one of the largest and most beautiful of Irish lakes. It boasts little mountain scenery or craggy shores, but is, save at one locality, for the most part sylvan in character, and indeed, for combinations of wood and water is probably unequalled. The river Erne, which feeds it, rises in Lough Gowna, about 3 m. N. of Granard (Rte. 17), and runs due N. until it expands into Lough

Oughter, from whence it emerges with broader proportions, passing Butler's Bridge and Belturbet. At or near Crum it is generally called Lough Erne, though in fact it is nothing more than a very broad river, fringed with innumerable bays, and studded with islands, many of them of considerable size. The upper lake is at its broadest opposite Lisnaskea, and from this point soon narrows to assume the river character again. There are several pretty residences in this portion of its course, such as Crum, Belleisle, Belonia, and Lisgoole Abbey (W. C. Jones, Esq.)—an abbey only in name, as there are no traces of ch. architecture about it; nevertheless the row from Enniskillen hither will amply repay the lover of river scenery. The reach from the town to the lower lake is about 1 m. in length, and passes on l. *Portora*, a very beautifully situated school, built in 1777 to accommodate the scholars of the Royal School, founded in 1626 by Charles I. The channel of the river at this point has been considerably deepened; and at the entrance into the lake stand on l. the ruins of a small fortress consisting of some circular towers. About 2 m. from Enniskillen, on the rt. of the lake, lies the island of *Devenish* (anc. Daim-inish), with its melancholy-looking ruins, viz. an abbey, portions of a 2nd ch., and a round tower, the most perfect in the whole country. The lower ruins close to the tower are very scanty, possessing only one or two round-headed windows deeply splayed inwardly. The round tower is 70 ft. high, and remarkable for the extraordinary fineness and regularity of the masonry up to the very apex. Looking N.E. are 3 windows, the lower one round, the middle triangular, and the uppermost square-headed. As usual there is no entrance, but 3 rude steps have been made in the stones to the lower window, which is about 12 ft. from the ground.

In addition to being remarkably well preserved, it has the unusual decoration of a cornice or band immediately under the conical apex, of very rich design, and with a well-sculptured head in the centre of each side. A little higher up the hill are the ruins of the abbey, consisting of the tower and the N. wall of the choir, in which is a good pointed doorway deeply moulded and crocketed. The intersecting arches are similar to those of Sligo, though scarcely so lofty. A spiral staircase leads to a chamber in the tower, and in the floor are holes for the bellropes. Beyond Devenish, although this is generally the limit for a rowing excursion, the lake gradually expands as far as Church Hill, at which point it assumes the character of an inland sea, being 5 m. broad; "stretching from Enniskillen to Rosscor House, a distance of 20 m., its greatest breadth 5 m., and its least 2 m. It contains nearly 28,000 statute acres, and embraces 109 islets, many of them small and of trifling importance, others, and not a few, varying from 10 to 150 acres, while Boa Island, near the northern extremity of the lake, contains 1300 statute acres."—*Fraser.*

Conveyances from Enniskillen.—Daily to Ballyshannon and Bundoran; daily to Donegal; daily to Monaghan; daily to Pettigoe; daily to Sligo by Manor Hamilton; daily to Omagh.

Distances.—Sligo, 39 m.; Donegal, 34; Belcoo, 11½; Manor Hamilton, 25; Clones, 23; Ballyshannon, 27; Ely Lodge, 4½; Devenish Island, 2; Pettigoe, 19; Kesh, 14; Florence Court, 7; Swanlinbar, 12; Crum Castle, 22, by water; Derry, 60; Dundalk, 62.

Excursions.—
1. Devenish Island.
2. Ballyshannon and Belleek.
3. Florence Court and Swanlinbar.
4. Belcoo and Marble Arch.
5. Crum Castle.
6. Lisgoole by water.

[The tourist who wishes to proceed at once to Bundoran will take the Ballyshannon road, which is traversed by 2 or 3 cars daily, and is ere long destined to possess the advantages of a rly. It keeps close to the western shore of Lough Erne for nearly the whole distance to Belleek, affording views that for soft beauty are almost equal to the foot of Windermere.

4½ m. rt. is the entrance to *Ely Lodge*, the lovely seat of the Marchioness of Ely, upon an island connected by a bridge with the mainland. The grounds are exquisite, and the house contains some good paintings. The ground on the l. of the road begins to assume a more broken and rugged aspect, and near the village of Church Hill rises into lofty escarpments of blue mountain limestone some 1000 ft. above the level of the sea. The ruins of Tully Castle are close to the lake; it was a fortified mansion, built by the Humes, a branch of the Scotch family of Polwarth, who settled in Fermanagh in the reign of Elizabeth. It was the scene of a frightful massacre in the rebellion of 1641, when Lady Hume, her family, and all the inmates of the house, amounting to 60, were slain by Rory, brother of Lord Maguire, who had induced them to surrender, under promise of a free pass to Enniskillen. A similar tower exists at Monea, a few m. to the S.E. The lake is here at its broadest; the depth at many places is great, and its general level about 119 ft., which shows at once the very great descent that the Erne has to accomplish in the 5 m. between Belleek and Ballyshannon. The opposite shore of the lake is rather low and wooded in comparison with the crags of Church Hill. A road Rte. 9 runs along its bank to Pettigo and Donegal; it is fringed with fine residences, some of which are visible from the Ballyshannon road — such as Riversdale (Major Archdall), Rockfield (Capt. Irvine), Castle Archdall (Capt. Archdall, M.P.). On the northern bank a little beyond Church Hill are Castle Caldwell (J. C. Bloomfield, Esq.), and the Elizabethan mansion of Maghramena (J. Johnstone, Esq.). The lake soon narrows again, and reassumes its river character at *Belleek*, a small village prettily situated on the rt., containing a disused fort, and a large china manufactory, which gives employment to a good many hands. A little distance from the village is Cliff, the residence of T. Conolly, Esq., M.P., the owner of the soil around Ballyshannon, and probably one of the largest landholders in Ireland.]

[From Belleek a road runs S. 4½ m. to the village of *Garrison*, situated in a half-reclaimed wild district on the eastern shore of Lough Melvin. It is occasionally frequented by anglers, who will find a public-house in which to put up.]

The course of the Erne from Belleek is marked by an extraordinary series of rapids, which the tourist may observe at different points, though he cannot skirt the banks of the river all the way down to Ballyshannon. "From Belleek the angler will be enabled to fish Loch Erne, which contains some of the finest trout in the world, running from 2 to 20 lbs. weight. These trout, up to 6 and 7 lbs. weight, take the fly well. The lough abounds also in pike, perch, and bream, of which cartloads may be taken in some spots. Flies can be had in Ballyshannon."— *Angler's Register.*

Passing 25 m. rt. Cauldan, the castellated mansion of T. Tredennick, Esq., the tourist arrives at 27 m. Ballyshannon *(Hotels:* Coburn's; Erne) (Rte. 8.]

[It is a very beautiful excursion to Swanlinbar 12 m., where the magnificent limestone scenery is seen to great advantage. 4 m. l. are Skea House (C. Hassard, Esq.), and Fairwood Park, followed by the exquisitely-situated grounds of *Florence Court*, the residence of the Earl of Enniskillen. The house, which is worthy of the surrounding scenery, was built by Lord Mount Florence in 1771, and is in form "a centre connected by wings of handsome arcades adorned with an entablature and low balustrade, the whole façade being 300 ft. in length." In the interior are some good paintings by Rembrandt, Poussin, Rubens (Jephtha's Vow) Sir P. Lely, &c.; and a geological museum which has an European reputation. As regards the carboniferous formation, and particularly the fishes of the coal period, the name of Lord Enniskillen stands deservedly high in scientific circles. There is also a splendid skeleton of the Megaceros Hibernicus, or the Irish elk. The park extends for a long distance on the slopes of the hills, and affords views remarkable for their extent and variety, as well as some very fine timber, in which an avenue of the silver fir should be particularly noticed, as well as the parent plant of the Irish or Florence Court yew. At the rear of the house and grounds is a long continuous escarpment of mountain limestone hills, which extend from Swanlinbar, past Manor Hamilton, to near Lough Gill, and are remarkable for the strange freaks of nature which abound in them, as indeed is the case more or less in all carboniferous regions. The principal of these heights are—Benaghlan, just above Florence Court; Cratty, 1212 ft. over Swanlinbar; Cuilcagh, 2188; Benbrack, 1648; and Lachagh, 1448. "The Calp limestone of this district extends from Lough Erne to Bundoran; and in Belmore near Enniskillen, and Ben Aghlan near Florence Court, it is surmounted by 600 ft. of upper carboniferous limestone. The calp in this district is highly fossiliferous, and full of encrinital heads and stems, with large and perfect productions. In the limestone of Ben Aghlan is the rare Pentremitis ovalis; and the Hymenophyllum Tunbridgense fern grows upon the summit of the hill."—*Geologist.*

12 m. *Swanlinbar*, a neat town, which formerly had a considerable reputation as a Spa, placed in a valley between the Slieve Russell chain on the E., the principal height of which is Legavreagra, 1279 ft., and the Slieveanieran range on the W. The little river Claddagh flows through the town. It rises in a fine gorge between Cuilcagh and Cratty, and has a subterranean course of 3 m., through caverns abounding in stalactites. The tourist should by all means ascend Cuilcagh, and thence make his way westward to a spot called Legmonshena, or the Source of the Shannon, 7 m. from Swanlinbar and 3 from the Black Lion at Belcoo. "The source or spring is of a circular form, about 50 ft. in diameter, called the Shannon Pot. It boils up in the centre, and a continued stream flows from it about 8 ft. wide and 2 ft. deep in the driest weather, running about 4 m. an hour. There are numerous caverns and cliffs on the top and sides of Cuilcagh which receive the rain-water; and from the circumstance of no stream descending this side of the mountain, it is probable that the drainage, combined with subterranean springs, here find an outlet. After winding its way through the valley, it falls into Lough Allen, about 9 m. S., having in this short course swelled to a considerable river from 50 to 60 yds. wide, varying in depth from 5 to 10 ft."—*W. S.* The summit of the Cuilcagh is associated with the early history of the district, "it having been the spot where the Maguires invested their chiefs with the supreme command over Fermanagh."—*Lewis.*

On the northern escarpment, looking over Lough Macnean, is another singular limestone curiosity, known as the Marble Arch, which is simply a subterranean cavern, with the roof fallen in.]

From Enniskillen a coach starts to Sligo daily, passing through a richly-wooded and luxuriant country. The traveller will also notice the formal manner in which part of the road is planted with elms and poplars, giving it the appearance of an approach to a Flemish town. Crossing the Sillees river, is Lisbofin House (T. Irwin, Esq.), beautifully situated under the towering limestone hill of Belmore, 1312 ft., beneath which the road is carried for several miles. On the opposite side are the strongly marked limestone ridges above Florence Court, while the valley between is filled up with the lower reach of Lough Macnean, forming altogether most exquisite landscapes. At 73½ m. the river, which connects the 2 lakes, is crossed to *Belcoo*, a particularly neat-looking hamlet, from which the tourist may pay a visit to the Marble Arch, which is within 3 m. distance. The upper Lough Macnean, about 5 m. in length, and embracing a considerable area, now comes in view, and sufficiently occupies the attention, although it certainly is not as romantic a lake as the lower reach. The northern shore is well planted with timber belonging to the estate of Glenfarn (the property of I. A. Tottenham, Esq.

At the hamlet of *Red Lion*, several roads branch off southward into the wild and hilly districts of Leitrim. The geologist or pedestrian will find plenty to occupy him in this neighbourhood. Legmonshena, the source of the Shannon, is about 3 m. distant. We now follow the course of the Glenfarn, a mountain stream that falls into Lough Macnean, the road becoming rather dreary and uninteresting, as it passes through a broadish mountain valley, bounded on l. by the Lackagh range 1448 ft., and on rt. by Mullaghatire 1275. Leaving on l. Lakefield (— Rutherford, Esq.) and Hollymount (S. Armstrong, Esq.), the tourist reaches

87 m. *Manor Hamilton* (*Inn:* Robinson's), a small town, situated in a high valley, surrounded by ranges of limestone hills on every side. On the N. is the continuation of that noble range which is terminated seaward by Benbulben (Rte. 8), and extends all the way to Lough Macnean, or indeed to Enniskillen. The charming valley of the Bonet, runs up to Glenade under the heights of Crockavallin 1408 ft., Saddle Hill 1245, and Doey 1511. (Rte. 8.) The town itself need not detain the tourist long, as he can soon inspect the ivy-covered block of buildings which formed the baronial mansion of Sir Frederick Hamilton. It is a good example of the 17th cent., although the details are very plain. The road now crosses the Bonet, leaving to the rt. the village of Lurganboy, which, as far as situation goes, has the superiority over Manor Hamilton. Two roads here branch off on rt.: 1. to Glenade 5 m.; 2. to Glencar, which, if time is no object, should be taken by the tourist, so as to visit the lake and waterfall. The road to Sligo turns to the l. underneath Benbo, 1365 ft., and continues through the same romantic formation until the high grounds above Lough Gill are reached. High as they are, however, not a single glimpse of this beautiful lough is obtained from the coach-road.

101 m. Sligo (*Hotels:* Imperial; Victoria) (Rte. 8).

ROUTE 7.

FROM ENNISKILLEN TO DERRY, BY OMAGH.

The whole of this route is performed by rail, a continuation of the Dundalk and Enniskillen line, which has been merged into the same undertaking, although originally made under separate companies. The greater portion runs through an uninteresting country, consisting of high lands, with a good deal of bleak hill and moor. The latter half is the most picturesque, particularly when we reach the valley of the Foyle and its tributaries. Lough Erne, which is skirted by the line, is barely visible, high banks intervening.

6 m. *Ballinamallard*, on the river of the same name.

8½ m. Lowtherstown Road. The station is 3½ m. distant from the town, which lies to the l.

10 m. *Trillick*, a thriving village seated at the foot of the range of the Brocker Mountains, which, commencing at Lisbellaw, near Enniskillen, run N.E. at an average height of 1000 ft., and form a marked watershed for rivers running N. to the Foyle and S. to Lough Erne.

17 m. l. Dromore, which suffered much at the hands of the insurgents in 1641. St. Patrick is said to have founded here a monastery for the first female who received the veil at his hands.

20 m., connected by a short branch line, is *Fintona*, placed on the Fintona Water, and having a "manufacture of linen and spades." The town dates from the reign of James I. Close by are Ecclesville (C. Eccles, Esq.) and Derrybard (S. Vesey, Esq.).

[9 m. to the S., on the opposite side of the Brocker range, is *Five-mile Town*, also founded temp. James I. by Sir William Stewart, who built the castle of Aghentine, of which slight remains still exist.

9 m. E. of Fintona is *Clogher*, the Regia of Ptolemy, and the seat of the most ancient bishopric in Ireland, originally founded by St. Patrick. It derived its name, "Clogh-or," from a "stone of gold" said to have emitted oracular sayings. It was also the royal residence of the ancient princes of Ergallia, traces of which in the shape of earthworks are still extant within the grounds of the episcopal palace, a handsome mansion, within a park of 500 acres. The first Protestant bishop, Miles Magragh by name, did not take office until the reign of Elizabeth; and amongst succeeding prelates was Bishop Tennison, a great benefactor to the ch., who, together with Bishop Sterne, nearly rebuilt the cathedral in the last cent. It is a plain cruciform building with a tower rising from the W. front. The visitor after having inspected the ch. should go and see a pretty cascade at Lumford Glen, a little way from the town.

Conveyances.— Car to Five-mile Town and Glasslough (Rte. 17), through Aughnacloy, a small town prettily placed on the Blackwater.

Distances.—Five-mile Town, 7 m.; Aughnacloy, 9½; Glasslough, 18; Fintona, 9.]

From Fintona the rail still ascends through bleak and cold hills to

26 m. *Omagh* (*Hotels:* Abercorn Arms; White Hart), the county-town of Tyrone, a flourishing place of some 3600 Inhab., situated at the junction of the Drumragh river with the Camowen, their united waters falling into the Foyle. The castle of Omy played an important part in the wars of 1498, when it was rased to the ground; and again in 1641, when Sir Phelim O'Neil took possession of it. The town contains little to detain the tourist, save the usual county structures—a courthouse with a good Doric front, a gaol, a barrack, and a church with a lofty spire, which looks very well from the rly. In the neighbourhood are Lisanelly (R. White, Esq.) and Creevenagh (Hon. A. Stewart).

Conveyances.—Rail to Enniskillen, Derry, and Dungannon. Car to Monaghan Road, through Ballygawley.

[An important cross communication has been lately made by the Ulster Rly. Company, by the extension of their line to Omagh from Portadown and Dungannon. It follows up the course of the Camowen to 7½ m. *Beragh*, a decayed village at the foot of Shantauny, 1035 ft., which on its southern face descends in a bold sweep, overlooking the little town of *Ballygawley*. Here are some walls of the castle built by Sir Gerard Lowther in the 17th cent.

1¼ m. from the town is Ballygawley House, the seat of Sir John Stewart. Crossing the Cloghfin river, a branch of the Camowen, we arrive at 9 m. *Six-mile Cross.*

13 m. *Carrickmore*, or Termon Rock, so called from the elevation on which it is built. Adjoining it are the ruins of the old ch., a small E. Dec. building.

The highest portion of the line is reached at 18 m. *Pomeroy*, the hills on each side of which rise to about 900 ft. The demesne of Pomeroy House (R. Lowry, Esq.) was formerly celebrated for its timber, some of the oaks having measured 29 ft. in circumference.

24 m. Donaghmore. Of the important monastic buildings that once existed here, all that remains is a beautiful inscribed cross about 16 ft. high, which, having been mutilated and thrown down in 1641, was subsequently re-erected. The Rev. George Walker of Derry celebrity was vicar of this parish. At Castle Caulfield, rt. 2 m., there is a ruined mansion of the Charlemonts, most picturesquely situated on a limestone rock. It is a fine example of domestic architecture of the time of James I., who granted this property to Sir John Caulfield, afterwards Lord Charlemont. It was quaintly described by Pynnar in his Survey as the fairest house he had seen. Parkanaur is the seat of J. Y. Burges, Esq.

Crossing the Torrent river, we arrive at

27 m. *Dungannon* (*Hotels*: Ranfurly Arms; Imperial), celebrated in early days for having been the chief residence of the O'Neils, who, being in constant rebellion against the English government, involved the town in a never-ending series of assault and siege which lasted until the close of the 17th cent. The independence of the Irish parliament was declared here in 1782 by the delegates from the corps of the Ulster Volunteers. An abbey was founded by the O'Neils, and castles were built at different times by them and their successors the Chichesters, but all traces of them have disappeared, and Dungannon now presents the features of a busy manufacturing town, for which its position—about 3 m. from Lough Neagh, and in the centre of the Tyrone coalbasin—well qualifies it. The principal buildings are the ch., which has an octagonal spire, and a grammar-school and college founded by Charles I., and the object of special care from Primate Robinson, who erected the present buildings on lands given by him. On Kneekmany Hill, which lies to the S.W., is a circle, with singular tracings on some of the stones. (Pop. 4000.)

The coal-field of Tyrone is interesting to the geologist from the various and speedy succession of rocks occurring in so limited a space, and its commercial importance in the industrial economy of Ireland. The coal-seams rest on the limestone of Dungannon, and many of the hills and high grounds are covered over with triassic or new red sandstone beds for a considerable distance. The basin is divided into two portions:—1. The Coal Island district to the N.E. of Dungannon, which is about 6 m. in length by 2 in breadth, and contains 7000 acres. Within a depth of 120 fathoms, 6 beds of good workable coal are found, of the aggregate thickness of 22 to 32 ft.—a remarkable instance of so many seams being found close together at so short a depth (See Introd.) 2. The Annahone district is only 1 m. long, embracing 320 acres, and affording 8 or 9 workable seams. "Notwithstanding the smallness of the basin, its strata are so much contorted and disturbed as to cause great irregularity in the workings by change of level and the occasional disappearance of the bed. But, with all these drawbacks, this basin merits particular attention. The coal is excellent, burning rapidly with flame, and evolving great heat; it is not difficult to raise, and its quantity is such as to be capable of diffusing the blessings of industrial prosperity over an extensive area."—*Kane.* The principal collieries are at Annahone, Coal Island, and Drumglass.

In the neighbourhood of Dungannon are Springfield (J. Irwin, Esq.) and Northland House, the seat of Lord Ranfurley.

Conveyances.—Rail to Omagh and Portadown; car to Cookstown.

Distances.—Moy, 5½ m.; Blackwatertown, 8; Coal Island, 4½; Stewartstown, 7; Cookstown, 11; Armagh, 13.

Passing 31 m. Trew Stat., the line crosses the Blackwater, a considerable stream, which receives at Moy the waters of the Ulster canal connecting Lough Erne near Belturbet with Lough Neagh.

[3 m. on rt. is *Moy*, a small town on the Blackwater, built by Lord Charlemont on the pattern of Marengo in Italy; on the opposite bank of the river is Charlemont—both of them places of importance in the days of Elizabeth. The latter was disgraced in 1641 by the treacherous murder of Lord Caulfield, the governor of Charlemont, by Sir Phelim O'Neil, who had been hospitably invited to supper. The castle, now a depôt of the Ordnance department, "is still of great strength, fortified with bastions, a dry ditch, a scarp, and counterscarp; and there are 2 ravelins, one in front, the other in rear of the works, surrounded by a glacis which runs along the side of the Blackwater." In the neighbourhood are Roxborough, the seat of Lord Charlemont, and Church Hill (Sir W. Verner, Bart.).

2½ m. to the S., between the river and the Ulster Canal, is *Blackwatertown*, a large village doing a good deal of business in the way of coals and timber. Like Charlemont, it played an important part in the Tyrone rebellion temp. Queen Elizabeth. 5 m. Armagh (Rte. 17.) A little higher up the river is the Castle of Benburb, on a lofty escarpment above the water, which surrounds it on two sides. Here O'Neill defeated the English army after a desperate battle in 1646. It does not present any interesting architectural features.]

35 m. *Anaghmore*, from whence the line runs in view of the S. end of Lough Neagh to 41 m. Portadown (Rte. 3.)]

28 m. at Fairy Water Bridge the main line crosses the Fairy Water close to its junction with the Strule, and keeps parallel with the latter river, occasionally crossing it, to

35 m. *Newtown Stewart* (*Hotel*: Abercorn Arms). Here the Shrule river joins the Owenkillow, which rises in the lofty chain of the Munterlony Mountains, and flows from E. to W. These hills, with the still higher ranges of the Sperrin Mountains, run E. as far as Maghera, and then turn round to the N. into the neighbourhood of Coleraine. Their southern faces are extremely steep, and the general altitude is not less than 2000 ft.—the highest point, Sawel, being 2246. The town of Newtown Stewart is finely situated on the side of a hill known by the pretty name of Bessy Bell (1386 ft.), the counterpart of which (though not so lofty) is the eminence of Mary Gray, on the rt. of the rly. The town is pleasant and

pretty, and is rendered attractive by the close proximity of Baron's Court, the princely estate of the Marquis of Abercorn, in which hill, wood, and water afford many beautiful landscapes. James II. spent a night in Newtown Stewart, and in return for the hospitality received ordered the castle to be dismantled and the town to be burnt—a blow which it was long in recovering. Like most northern Irish towns, linen-weaving affords plenty of employment. There are remains of some forts which commanded the bridges on the Mourne and Strule at Moyle.

6 m. E. are the village of Gortin, and Beltrim Castle (Major Hamiltor, romantically placed in the valley of the Owenkillew, between the hills of Slievemore (1262 ft.) and Curraghchosaly (1372).

10 m. l. on the Derg is Castle Derg, through which the traveller can make a short cut to Stranorlar and Donegal (Rte. 8).

Conveyances.—Rail to Enniskillen and Derry.

Distances.—Strabane, 11 m.; Omagh, 9; Castle Derg, 10.

38½ m. the Derg flows into the Mourne, and on rt. the Sperrin Mountains are very conspicuous features in the landscape. The latter river is crossed at 40 m. Victoria Bridge Stat.

41½ m. Sion Mills; soon after which the tourist arrives in sight of,

46 m., the busy and not over-clean town of Strabane *Hotel*: Abercorn Arms, Rte. 8, situated, like Newtown Stewart, at the junction of 2 rivers—the Mourne and the Finn. Each of them is crossed by remarkably long bridges, and from this point the Mourne takes the name of the Foyle. The course of these rivers is marked by a considerable expanse of alluvial land, which in wet weather is generally flooded—a state of things to which the Finn in particular is very liable. Strabane contains very little to detain the visitor, who will speedily find out from his olfactory senses that the inhabitants are principally dependent on flax. This is, however, only offensive in the autumn, when the plant is being steeped and dried in all the fields of the neighbourhood. Strabane once possessed a castle built by the Marquis of Abercorn in the time of James I., but it has disappeared, and has given place to a warehouse. The town has some claims to be called a port, as it is connected by a short canal with the navigable portion of the Foyle (Pop. 4911).

Conveyances.—Rail to Derry and Enniskillen; rail to Stranorlar; car to Sligo daily; car to Letterkenny; car to Ballybofey, through Castlefinn.

Distances.—Derry, 15 m.; Lifford, 1; Newtown Stewart, 11; Castle Finn, 6; Urney, 3; Raphoe, 7; Letterkenny, 16½; Rathmelton, 23; Manor Cunningham, 12; Stranorlar, 13.

The line now pursues the even tenor of its way along the alluvial valley of the Foyle, which soon swells out into a stately stream. 48 m. Porthall (J. Clarke, Esq.).

Before arriving at 53 m. St. Johnstown Stat., we pass on l. a square tower, all that is left of the Castle of Montgavlin, in which James II. held his court till the termination of the siege of Derry.

57 m. *Carrigans.* The Foyle here loses the character of a river, and becomes an estuary, increasing in width until we arrive at

61 m. the time-honoured city of *Derry* or *Londonderry* (Rte. 12) (*Hotels*: Imperial, good; Foyle).

Its situation is picturesque in the extreme, the great bulk of the town being on a hill, 119 ft. high, overlooking the l. bank of the Foyle, which is here 1068 ft. wide, and is crossed by a long rly. bridge. It expands at the Rosses, a little below the town, to a width of 1¼ m. The geology of the hills on either side of the river consists " of primary schistose rocks, spreading over the whole of the parish of Templemore (in which the city is situated), with the exception of a considerable detritic patch at Culmore, to the N.E., which probably conceals a part of the new red sandstone. Associated with these are occasional beds of granular ilimestone and greenstone."— *Geol. Survey.* Previous to the reign of Elizabeth the history of Derry (in Irish ꝺoiꞅe, the place of oaks) presents nothing remarkable, and is chiefly occupied with affairs ecclesiastical, it having been one of the monasteries of St. Columb, the abbot of which, Flahertach O'Brolchain, was made first bishop of Derry in 1158. The last Roman Catholic bishop died in 1601, up to which time the city " may be regarded as being in the hands of the native Irish, and governed by their chiefs, with at best but an occasional acknowledgment of British power." But all previous historical events are thrown into the shade by the great siege of Londonderry in 1689, when King James's Irish army, under Rosen and Edward Hamilton, laid close siege to the city for 105 days, and tried their best, by the horrors of assault, famine, and pestilence, to reduce the courage of the brave Protestant defenders. The governor on this occasion was the treacherous Lundy, who made many attempts to give up the city into the enemy's hands, and only succeeded in evading the rage of the garrison by escaping in the guise of a porter. The command was then taken by the Rev. George Walker, rector of Donaghmore, whose apostolic fervour and simple bravery will be the theme of admiration as long as religious liberty endures. The blockade was at length put an end to on the 26th of July, when the *Mountjoy*, a merchantman of Kirke's fleet, filled with stores, gallantly broke through the barrier placed across the Foyle, and relieved the starving garrison. " Five generations have passed away, and still the wall of Londonderry is to the Protestants of Ulster what the trophy of Marathon was to the Athenians. A lofty pillar, rising from a bastion which bore during many weeks the heaviest fire of the enemy, is seen far up and down the Foyle. On the summit is the statue of Walker, such as when, in the last and most tender emergency, his eloquence roused the fainting courage of his brethren. In one hand he grasps a Bible; the other, pointing down the river, seems to direct the eyes of his famished audience to the English topmasts in the distant bay. Such a monument was well deserved; yet it was scarcely needed; for, in truth, the whole city is to this day a monument of the great deliverance. The wall is carefully preserved, nor would any plea of health or convenience be held by the inhabitants sufficient to justify the demolition of that sacred enclosure which, in the evil time, gave shelter to their race and their religion. The summit of the ramparts forms a pleasant walk. The bastions have been turned into little gardens. Here and there among the shrubs and flowers may be seen the old culverins which scattered bricks cased with lead among the Irish ranks. One antique gun, the gift of the Fishmongers of London, was distinguished during the 105 memorable days by the loudness of its report, and still bears the name of 'Roaring Meg.' The cathedral is filled with relics and trophies. In the vestibule is a huge shell, one of many hundreds of shells which were thrown into the city. Over the altar are still seen the French flagstaves taken by the garrison in a desperate sally; the white ensigns of the house of Bourbon have long been dust, but their place has been supplied by new banners, the work of the fairest hands of Ulster. The-

anniversary of the day on which the gates were closed, and the anniversary of the day on which the siege was raised, have been down to our own time celebrated by salutes, processions, banquets, and sermons. Lundy has been executed in effigy, and the sword said by tradition to be that of Monmouth has on great occasions been carried in triumph."
—*Macaulay's Hist. of England.*

The principal objects of interest in Londonderry are the walls and the cathedral. The original English town, erected by Sir Henry Docwra, was burned by Sir Cahir O'Doherty in 1608, and the present town may therefore be considered to have derived its origin from the Londoners' plantation, which was the immediate result of that catastrophe. The present walls were built about 1609, at a cost of 8357*l.*, and were known during the siege as the Double Bastion, on which the gallows were erected for the threatened purpose of hanging the prisoners; the Royal Bastion, "from the advancing of the red flags upon it, in defiance of the enemie;" Hangman's Bastion; Gunners' Bastion; Cowards' Bastion,— "it lyeing most out of danger, it's said it never wanted company good store;" Water Bastion; and Ferry Bastion. Some of these are still in existence (though others, together with the external dry ditch, have been removed in process of time), and contain many of the guns, given by various Companies. The gates are 6: Bishop's Gate, erected to the memory of William III.; Shipquay Gate; Butchers' Gate; Ferryquay Gate; New Gate; and Castle Gate.

The cathedral stands on a lofty eminence overlooking the whole of the town, and is a beautiful Perp. building. It has been only lately restored. It consists of a central and 2 side aisles, separated on either side by 6 pointed arches with octagonal piers, and lighted by Perp. windows. The erection of the ch. in 1633 is commemorated in a tablet which runs as follows :—

ANO DO CAR REGIS
1633.
If . stones . cvld . speake .
Then . London's . prayse . shovld . sovnde .
Who . bvilte . this . chvrch .
And . cittie . from . the . grovnde .

Inserted into the top of this tablet is a smaller one with the inscription :—

" In templo verus Deus est
Vereque clemens."

Amongst other curiosities are a bomb-shell fired into the town during the siege, as well as the poles of the flags captured from the enemy. There are also a couple of 17th cent. tablets and monuments to the memory of Bishop Knox, and of Capt. Boyd of the *Ajax*, who perished in the storm at Kingstown in 1860, while attempting to rescue others.

The visitor should on no account forget to mount the top of the tower, which commands a noble panorama, embracing the city with the walls, Walker's Monument, the Bishop's Palace and Garden, the Gaol, the Lunatic Asylum, the Docks, the noble expanse of the Foyle, backed up by the distant outlines of the hills of Inishowen, while, looking up the river, are the woods and grounds of Prehen, the seat of the family of Knox. The other buildings worth notice are the Corporation Hall, in the middle of the Diamond or principal square; the Court House, the Ionic façade of which is modelled after the temple of Erechtheus at Athens; the Gaol, which is most complete, and designed on the circular plan, with a panoptic gallery; and the new Bridge, which serves both for the Northern Counties Rly. and a public road. It has superseded the old timber bridge, which was in its day a great curiosity. "Its length was 1068 ft., and its breadth 40: being laid on oak-piles, the pieces of which were 16 ft. asunder, and were bound together by 13 strong pieces equally divided and transversely bolted. As both the water and the gas were brought across the bridge, they had to be separated whenever it was open for the passage of barges." The whole of this singular structure was put up by Lemuel Cox, a Boston American, at an expense of 16,000l. (Pop. 20,875.)

From the port of Londonderry a large colonial and coasting trade is carried on. It is, moreover, a calling-station for the North American steamers from Liverpool, all the important telegrams being forwarded from Derry direct to London. The tonnage of the port increased in the four years from 1848 to 1852 from 147,212 to 215,409; and if the long-entertained project is ever brought to bear of uniting Lough Foyle with Lough Swilly by a ship canal it will tend very much to place Derry in the foremost rank of Irish ports.

No antiquary should leave Derry without paying a visit to the *Grianan of Aileach*, an early remain situated on the summit of a hill 800 ft. high, about 5 m. from Derry, in the county of Donegal, and overlooking Lough Swilly. It consists of 3 extensive concentric ramparts formed of earth mixed with uncemented stones, and enclosing in the centre a cashel. This is a circular wall, enclosing an area of 77 ft. in diameter, not quite perpendicular, but having a curved slope, like Staigue Fort in Kerry. On each side of the entrance gateway are galleries within the thickness of the wall, extending in length to one-half of its entire circuit, though not communicating with the gateway, but having entrances from the area at their northern and southern extremities. In the centre of the area of the cashel are remains of a small oblong building—probably of a chapel—supposed to be of more recent erection than the other portion of the remains. Although, from the etymology of the word, some writers have considered the Grianan of Aileach to have been a Temple of the Sun, it is more probable " that it was the palace of the northern Irish kings from the earliest age of historic tradition down to the commencement of the 12th centy." There is a fine view from the Grianan, of Loughs Foyle and Swilly, backed up by the Donegal mountains.

The other antiquity is St. Columb's stone, on the Greencastle-road, 1 m. from the town. This is a mass of gneiss, exhibiting the rude impress of 2 feet, and was one of the inauguration stones of the ancient chiefs of this district.

Conveyances.—Rail to Enniskillen and Belfast; rail to Buncrana; car daily to Dungiven; daily to Letterkenny; daily to Malin; daily to Moville; to Rathmelton 4 days a week.

Distances. — Letterkenny, 20 m.; Grianan, 5; Moville, 19; Buncrana, 13½; Rathmelton, 14½; Manor Cunningham, 14; Culmore, 5; Portrush, 26; Coleraine, 33; Strabane, 15.

Excursions.—
1. Grianan Aileach.
2. Moville.
3. Buncrana.
4. Down Hill.
5. Dungiven (Rte. 12).

[Derry is the starting-point for an excursion through the peninsula of Inishowen, famous for its poteen, and in more early and uncivilised times as being the stronghold of the descendants of Kinel Owen, a son of Nial of the Nine Hostages, who waged a constant and fierce war with the O'Dohertys, descendants of Connell Gulban. These latter, however, about the 15th cent., dispossessed the older residents. The tourist can proceed either by rail to Fahan and Buncrana, or by road, which, for the first mile or so, runs along the side of the Foyle, but turns off to the l. at Belmont (T. Macky, Esq.), in the grounds of which is the stone of St. Columb. It then passes in sight of Grianan Aileach Mountain, keeping it on l., and strikes upon Lough Swilly at Glen Collan (T. Norman, Esq.), opposite the island of Inch.

13½ m. *Buncrana* (*Hotel:* Commercial) is a pleasant and pretty little bathing-place, situated on the shores of Lough Swilly, between the embouchures of 2 rivers, the Mill and Crana, and at the base of the Meenkeeragh Hill, which rises on the E., and the Mouldy Mountain 1021 ft. on the S. It possesses some little trade arising from flax-spinning and the manufacture of chemical products, such as iodine, &c., and is also the head-quarters of the artillery for the district, embracing Loughs Foyle and Swilly. An old castle of the O'Dohertys is now incorporated with a modern building, and with its approaches and gardens is a picturesque object.

Distances.—Carndonagh, 12 m.; Rathmelton by water, 4½; Derry, 13½.

Conveyances.—By rail to Derry.

It is a pretty minor excursion to the Fort and Head of Dunree 7 m., the road thither running at the base of Aghaweel Hill 1106 ft., and passing Lin-fort and the ruin of Ross Castle.

Dunree Head is the termination of the Urris Hills, a group occupying the N.-western district of the Inishowen peninsula, and forming a portion of the great central chain of Slieve Snaght. The road terminates here, but the pedestrian can make a scramble of it to Dunass Head, the eastern guardian of the entrance to Lough Swilly. It is worthy of observation that the Urris Hills were evidently a continuation of the Glenalla Mountains on the opposite coast prior to the irruption of the sea which now forms Lough Swilly.

The scenery of the coast is wild and rocky, and the hills rise with considerable abruptness from the shore. The road from Buncrana to Carndonagh follows up the valley of the Owen Crana for some distance, giving off at Carroghill Bridge a branch road to the villages of Dunally and Ballyliffin on the N. coast. It then passes a tarn known as Mintiagh's Lough, and strikes into the heart of the mountains between Slieve Snaght ("Hill of Snow"), 2019 ft., on the rt., and the Urris Hills on the l.

25½ m. *Carndonagh*, is a neat little town, which principally supplies the commissariat of the Inishowen district. There is, however, but little to see, save across opposite the ch.-yard. From hence it is 19 m. by the direct road to Londonderry, and 3 m. to the village of Malin, which is situated at the head of the estuary of Trawbreaga Bay, an extensive sandy pill, that joins Lough Swilly, past the dreary dunes of Dough Isle. At its embouchure are Glashedy Island and the 15 Rocks, together with Carrickabraby Castle, another of the O'Dohertys' ruined fortalices. Adjoining Malin is Malin Hall (J. Hawby, Esq.), said to be the most northerly residence in Ireland.

8½ m. N.E. of the village is Malin Head, one of the famous northerly promontories that are so conspicuous to passengers by the Montreal steamers. It is of no great height, but the coast is exceedingly fine, and a scramble along the cliffs from the Five Fingers to the Head will amply repay the lover of stern rock scenery. On the head is a lighthouse and coastguard station, and a little way off shore is the group of the Garvan Hills. Another light is exhibited on the island of Inishtrahull, some 6 m. to the N.E., a precaution very necessary along this stormy coast. Between Malin and Glengard Heads the cliffs are very magnificent, being upwards of 800 ft. in height, and resembling those of Moher in Co. Clare, though not presenting the same sheer wall of precipice. From the village of Malin a road of 4 m. runs to Culdaff, where the river of the same name runs into the sea. Culdaff House is the seat of G. Young, Esq.

From hence it is 9½ m. to Moville (*Hotel*: Commercial), a watering-place which the citizens of Derry love to frequent in the summer. A pretty place it is, for, in addition to the sheltering ridges of the Squire's Cairn and Craignamaddy at the back, it commands the fine outlines of Benyevenagh and Keady, beyond Newtown Limavaddy, and is moreover enlivened by the constant stream of shipping entering and leaving the port. It is a favourite excursion to Inishowen Head 6 m., passing about half way the old fortress of the O'Dohertys at Greencastle, together with the modern fort that commands the entry of the Lough and M'Gilligan Point.

Conveyances. — A steamer plies from Derry during the summer months. Car to Derry daily.

Distances.—Derry, 18 m.; Culdaff, 9½; Inishowen, 6; Greencastle, 3.

The road from Moville to Derry keeps nearly the whole distance close to the shores of the Lough, passing 8 m. the village of Carrowkeel, where the Cabry river is crossed, and a road to Carndonagh given off. At this point the estuary of the Foyle is at its broadest.

13 m., adjoining the village of Muff, is Kilderry, the seat of G. Hart, Esq. Here the Buncrana road runs in, passing, between Muff and Bunfort, Miltown House, and skirting the base of the picturesque Scalp Mountain, 1589 ft. Soon after leaving Muff the traveller sights the Fort of Culmore, and guesses, from the number of pretty villas that border the road and shore, that he is approaching Derry.]

ROUTE 8.

FROM **SLIGO** TO **STRABANE**, THROUGH **BALLYSHANNON** AND **DONEGAL**.

Sligo (Rte. 6) (*Hotels:* Imperial and Victoria, the latter the best) is an important seaport town of some 10,700 Inhab., in close neighbourhood to scenery such as falls to the lot of very few business towns. The tourist in search of the picturesque cannot do better than take up his quarters here for a time. It is remarkably well situated in the centre of a richly-wooded plain, encircled on all sides, save that of the sea, by lofty mountains, the ascent of which commences from 3 to 4 m. of the town, while on one side of it is a lake almost equal in beauty to any in Ireland, and on the other a wide and sheltered bay. The connexion between the two is maintained by the broad river Garogue, issuing from Lough Gill, and emptying itself, after a course of nearly 3 m., into Sligo Bay. It is crossed by 2 bridges joining the parish of St. John (in which is the greater portion of the town) with that of Calry on the N. bank. The *Port*, in which a good deal of business is carried on, was considerably improved by the formation of the Ballast Bank Quay, 2250 ft. long, where vessels drawing 13 ft. water can moor, while those of larger draught can anchor safely in the pool. The approaches to the port are admirably lighted by 2 fixed lights on a small rock called Oyster Island, on which is also a beacon known as the Metal Man, and a 3rd placed further out on the Black Rock. The town itself, although containing several important buildings, cannot be admired for its general arrangement, or for the cleanliness of its streets, though it must be allowed that they are better kept than in many larger cities. The antiquities are few, notwithstanding the importance that Sligo (anc. Sligeach) attained as early as 1242 by the residence of Maurice Fitzgerald, Earl of Kildare, who founded a castle and abbey. Both were subsequently destroyed, first by O'Donell in 1270, and again by MacWilliam Burgh, after being rebuilt by the Earl of Ulster; of the former there are no traces. Sligo was also the scene of a siege in 1641, when it was taken and garrisoned for a time by the Parliamentary army under Sir Charles Coote.

The ruins of the *Abbey* are just behind the Imperial Hotel. The ch., which Fitzgerald first founded, was destroyed by fire in 1414, and "for its restoration Pope John XXII. granted indulgences to all who should visit it and contribute towards the expense of rebuilding it."—*Lewis*. It consists of a nave and choir with central tower of 2 stages, supported at the intersection by lofty pointed arches. The choir is lighted on the S. by 5 delicate early pointed windows, and at the E. by an exquisitely traceried 4-light window. It contains an altar with 9 compartments of good carving; also a mural monument 1623 to one of the O'Connors, on which he is represented with his wife kneeling. On N. of the choir a low pointed arch leads to a rude room connected with the graveyard. Notice the groined roof underneath the tower, and the small arches which are formed between the spring and the apex of the intersecting ones. In the nave only 3 arches of the S. wall are standing, with octangular piers. There is another altar-tomb here, of beautiful design, 1616. On the N. of the nave are the cloisters very perfect on 3 sides, in each of which are 18 beautifully-worked arches about 4 ft. in height. The visitor should study the pillars, which vary much in design, one of them having a head cut on the inside of the arch. These cloisters, as in most of the Irish examples, differ from the cloisters of our English cathedrals in their small dimensions, and in the fact that the interior passage is filled with gravestones, suggesting that they were intended more for burial purposes than for a promenade or ambulacrum.

The *Ch. of St. John* is a cruciform Perp. ch., with a massive tower at the W. end. The parapet carried all round it gives a singular effect. The only other building in the town worth notice is the Lunatic Asylum.

Conveyances.—Rly. to Boyle, Carrick, Longford, and Mullingar. Car daily to Westport through Ballina and Castlebar; daily to Ballyshannon, Donegal, and Strabane; daily to Manor Hamilton and Enniskillen; daily to Tobercurry.

Distances.—Boyle, 23½ m.; Carrick, 33; Ballinafad, 19½; Longford, 54½; Ballysadare, 5; Markree, 8½; Collooney, 6½; Ballina, 37; Dromore, 21; Lough Gill, by water, 2½; Dromahaire, 11; Hazelwood, 3; Manor Hamilton, 14; Enniskillen, 39; Glen, 4½; Ballyshannon, 25½; Drumcliff, 5; Knocknarea, 5; Benbulben, 8; Cliffoney, 14.

Excursions.—

1. To the hill and glen of Knocknarea.
2. Lough Gill.
3. Ballysadare and Markree (Rte. 18).
4. Benbulben.
5. Glencar.

[1. To *Knocknarea*, 5 m., a singular truncated hill of carboniferous limestone which occupies the greater portion of the promontory between Sligo Bay and Ballysadare Bay, and which, from its extraordinary form and abrupt escarpments, is a great feature in all Sligo and Donegal views. A road runs round the whole of the base of it, making the circuit about 11 m., passing on the N. side *Cummeen House*, the seat of the Ormsby family. Winding round Knocknarea, the tourist overlooks

Calleenamore (J. Barrett, Esq.), and soon arrives at the

Glen of Knocknarea. This is an example of disrupted strata so common in limestone districts, and is as romantic as can well be conceived. It consists of a deep chasm, ¾ m. long and 30 ft. broad, bounded on each side by vertical cliffs about 40 ft. in height, and overgrown and overshadowed in every direction with trees and trailing underwood. A walk runs through the defile, at the entrance of which is a charming little cottage ornée, embedded in flowers, and commanding a splendid prospect over Ballysadare Bay. Regaining the road, the tourist can easily ascend Knocknarea, although it is steep and sometimes slippery. The summit, on which is an enormous cairn visible far and wide, commands a magnificent panoramic view, embracing on the N. the Donegal Mountains with the scarred precipices of Slieve League and the promontory of Malin Head. Further E. the visitor traces the gap of Barnesmore beyond Donegal. Eastwards are the limestone ranges of Benbulben, Truskmore, and the Manor Hamilton hills, with the wooded banks of Lough Gill and the Slish Mountains nearer home. S. are the Curlew Mountains, and more westward the numerous ranges which intervene between Sligo and Ballina, overtopped in clear weather by the conical heights of Nephin and Croagh Patrick at Westport. Due W. the eye traces a long line of coast of Erris as far as the Stags of Broadhaven; while just underneath one's feet is a perfect map of Sligo, with the bay, islands, and lighthouses, and the long sandy peninsula of Elsinore. On the southern side is Ballysadare, with its numerous estuaries: on the furthest shore the woods of Carrowmore (the residence of Richard Olpherts, Esq.); on the northern bank of the estuary is Seafield (W. Phibbs, Esq.). Knocknarea forms the northern escarpment of that large tract of lower limestone that extends from Galway through Mayo and Sligo, and the geologist will find in its shales many characteristic fossils, and especially corals. He may return to Sligo by a more southerly road, passing l. Rathcarrick (Mrs. Walker), and rt. Cloverhill (W. Chalmers, Esq.) The antiquary may visit the ch. of Killuspugbrone, built by St. Patrick for Bishop Bronus in the 5th cent. It has a semicircular-headed doorway, placed in the S. wall, and not in the W., according to the usual custom.]

[2. The visitor will of course make an excursion to Lough Gill, which is considered by many, though on a small scale, to be almost equal to Killarney. A little steamer plies every 2nd day to the head of the lake, returning on the next. This is the best way of seeing it; but if the steamer does not suit, a row-boat may be engaged above the bridge. The 2½ m. of the river that intervenes between the town and the lake is lined by a succession of lawns and beautiful woods. Close to the town on the N. bank is the Glebe House, succeeded by the noble demesne of *Hazelwood* (Right Hon. John Wynne, M.P.), one of the finest and most charming estates in Ireland. The domain, which is remarkable for the richness and variety of its wood, extends for several miles on both sides of the river and lake, and includes, besides Hazelwood proper, the estates of Percy Mount, the former residence of Sir Richard Gethin, and Hollywell (formerly Hon. Rev. J. Butler) on the northern shore. The mansion of Hazelwood is situated on a tongue of land between the river and the lake. The great ornament of this estate is the remarkably fine timber, on which Mr. Wynne has expended many years of careful culture. He has introduced, amongst others, the yew and the arbutus, which flourish in great abundance, increasing the similarity

Route 8.—Lough Gill—Dromahaire.

of the foliage to that of Killarney. Within the deer-park the antiquary will find a stone enclosure called Leacht Con Mic Ruis, "the stone of Con, the son of Rush." The central space is 50 ft. long by 25 wide, and is connected by an avenue with 2 smaller enclosures. Within a circuit of 3 m. no less than 30 raths are to be found, and "in the townland of Carrowmore there still exist 60 circles and cromlechs, the largest collection of monuments of this kind in the British Islands, and probably, with the exception of Carnac, the most remarkable in the world."—*Petrie*. Lough Gill is about 5 m. in length by 1½ broad, and is situated in a basin surrounded on all sides by hills, those on the S. being rugged and precipitous. This range consists of Slieve Dacane 900 ft.) and Slish Mountain 967, having a gneissic character, passing into granite, whose dark rocks contrast admirably with the foliage of the lake shores.

There are several islands, many of them planted by Mr. Wynne. The largest of them are Cottage Island at the entrance, and Church Island in the centre; the latter contains some slight ruins. Both localities are the chosen resort of picnic parties from Sligo, who are particularly favoured in having such a lovely rendezvous. For those who prefer driving, the lake may be seen to great advantage by a road on the S. side, carried along the side of Cairns Mountain (which should be ascended by every visitor to Sligo, as it is near the town, of easy access, and commands magnificent views). It then passes Cairnsfoot Peter O'Connor, Esq.), Abbeyview — Phillips, Esq.), and Cleveragh Capt. Martin), adjoining the Hazelwood domain, and soon descends to the shores of the lake, running through a very romantic glen between Slieve Dacane and Slish Mountain to Ballintogher. "From a small rock rising out of the wood which adorns the shores of Lough Gill, and which is about a mile E. of the new Ballintogher entrance to Hazelwood, perhaps the best view is obtained. The rock is just that height which exhibits the limited area of the lake, its shores and little islands, to most advantage."—*Fraser*.

10 m. *Dromahaire*, a small town on the rt. bank of the Bonet river, which, rising in the hills near Manor Hamilton, drains all that part of the country and falls into Lough Gill. There are several remains here that will interest the antiquary. The old Hall, the property of G. Lane Fox, Esq., occupies the site of a castle of the O'Rourkes, chiefs of this district. The former building, however, was made use of in 1626 by Sir William Villiers to erect a baronial mansion under a patent from the Duke of Buckingham, by which he was granted 11,500 acres of land in Dromahaire. It has been considerably modernised, but contains some traces of its old importance. On the opposite side of the river, close to Friarstown (J. Johnstone, Esq.), are remains of the abbey of Crevelen, founded for Franciscans by Margaret, wife of O'Rourke, in 1508, and dissolved in James I.'s reign. O'Rourke's tomb, with his effigy, is still visible, together "with some curious figures over the graves of the Morroughs, Cornins, and others." Besides these remains there are also a ruined ch. on the hill-side, the foundation of which is attributed to St. Patrick, and a castle nearer the lake, known as Harrison's Castle.

Distances.—Sligo, 10 m.; Manor Hamilton, 9¼; Drumkeeran, 8¼.

The tourist should return to Sligo on the N. side of the lake, passing 3½ m. from Dromahaire the ruins of Newton-Gore, the manorial estate of Sir Robert Gore Booth, Bart. From hence the road keeps at the back of Hollywell and Hazelwood to Sligo 6 m. The whole of this circuit will be about 20 m. It

[*Ireland.*]

may be mentioned, for the benefit of the angler, that the fishing in the lough is excellent, but application for permission must be made to the owner.]

A car leaves Bianconi's coach-office daily for Donegal and Strabane. The road runs past the harbour, and soon rises into somewhat high ground, as it cuts across the neck of the Elsinore promontory. 1 m. rt. is Mount Shannon (F. M. Olpherts, Esq.), and a little further on rt. 1 m. are Doonally House (R. C. Parke, Esq.), and Willowbrook, a residence of W. O. Gore, Esq., M.P. The whole of the road from Sligo to Cliffony and Bundoran is carried between the sea and a long range of mountains, which, from their sudden rise from the plain, their fine escarpments, and their plateau-like summits, are marked features in the landscape. The general arrangement of these hills is that of an amphitheatre of which the northern point is Benbulben (1722 ft.), succeeded by King's Mountain (1527), Truskmore (2113), Keelogyboy (1430). To the S. of them are the basin of Lough Gill, with the plain and town of Sligo.

These limestone ranges offer good finds to the botanist, viz. Aspidium lonchitis, Asplenium viride, Poa alpina, Oxyria reniformis, Saxifraga vigoides, Arenaria ciliata, Draba incana, Melanopsis Cambrica, &c.

5 m. rt. is the pretty little ch. of *Drumcliff* (anc. Druim-chliabh), standing on the bank of the river of the same name, which here enters Drumcliff Bay. A monastery founded by St. Columb existed here in 590, and was made into a bishopric, afterwards, however, transferred to Elphin. The traces of its former greatness are now limited to two beautiful sculptured crosses in the ch.-yard, and the broken base of a round tower on the opposite side of the road and adjoining the glebe.

[A road on l. keeps along the N. side of Drumcliff Bay through the village of Carney to 4 m. *Lissadell*, the seat of Sir Robert Gore Booth, Bart., M.P., who has been most successful in demonstrating how much can be done to improve and beautify a coast so exposed to the fury of the Atlantic and devastated by sand-heaps as this is. If the pedestrian can afford the time, he will be interested in this wild promontory, and will be repaid by an excursion round it, rejoining the high road at Grange.

On the shore, close to Lissadell, are the scanty ruins of Dunfort Castle, while those of Ardtermon are about 1 m. further on, close to the miserable fishing village of *Raghly*. There is here, near the shore, a singular open basin called the Pigeon-holes, into which the tide rushes with great force through subterranean channels, and, as might be expected, under strong westerly winds, exhibits extraordinary effects.

The district to the N. of this is completely overrun with sand, and doubtless many a dwelling and perhaps buildings of more importance, as the churches at Perranzabuloe in Cornwall, have been buried here. As it is, there are sufficient ruins of churches and castles to make it a Tadmor in the wilderness.]

[6 m. a road on rt. branches off to Manor Hamilton 15 m. (Rte. 6) through the vale of

Glencar, one of the most beautiful and romantic spots in the whole country. It traverses a narrow defile, following the course of the Drumcliff river between the King's Mountain and some equally lofty mountains on the S. At 4 m. the source of the river is reached at Glencar Lough, a lovely sheet of water lying at the very base of the mountains. Here is a fine waterfall 300 ft. in height, the water of which, the visitor may chance to be told in Sligo, runs *up* hill, a state of things explained by the curious fact "that when the wind blows strongly from the S. the water is prevented from descending." Glencar is a justly favourite excursion from Sligo, from whence a new road has been made. The road beyond Glencar Lough continues through an equally fine valley past the little ch. of Killasnet to Manor Hamilton.]

At 10 m. *Grange* the corner of Benbulben is rounded, and the mountains gradually retreat further inland towards Lough Melvin.

The traveller will notice, some little way off the coast, the island of *Inishmurray*, famous for its potheen, and containing a very ancient monastery enclosed in a circular stone fort. The ch. was dedicated to St. Molaise or Molash, of the date of the 6th cent. It is built with a cement of lime: but the residences of the monks were constructed without any knowledge of the arch, with dome roof, and without any cement. In the interior is a wooden image of the saint. From Grange a singularly straight road runs for miles along the high ground overlooking the coast to

Cliffony 14 m., where the tourist interested in social improvements may inspect those made by Lord Palmerston in his estates. Indeed, it must be evident to everybody, whether interested or not, that the cottages, gardens, fields, fences, and inhabitants, are under a different treatment from those of other and less fortunate places, for there is an aspect of cleanliness and general comfort which at once strikes the English traveller. The view on the l. embraces a large extent of dreary sand-hills, but improves a little further N. at the promontory of *Mullaghmore*, overlooking the sheltered little community and harbour of *Classylaun*, which, together with a store, has been formed by Lord Palmerston, who caused to be planted a vast extent of Ammophila arundinacea, by which the soft ground was cemented, and could offer resistance to the driving sand.

At 17½ m. the Duff river is crossed at Bunduff Bridge, from which point the road hugs the coast pretty close, as it trends in a N.E. direction. The view opens out very finely over Bundoran and the bay of Donegal, backed up in the N. by the coast-line and mountains between Donegal and Killybegs.

19¾ m. a little beyond the village of Tullaghan, the Drowes river issuing from Lough Melvin is crossed, and the county of Donegal entered. On l., between road and sea, are remains of the castle of Duncarbry, built by Isabel MacClancy in the reign of Elizabeth. The frequent aspect of neat roadside cottages, together with now and then a more ambitious style of house, betokens the approach to

21½ m. *Bundoran* (*Hotels*: Hamilton's and Gallagher's), the great N.W. bathing-place, to which the rank and fashion of Ireland have been of late resorting. It is certainly beautifully situated on a bold portion of the coast of Donegal Bay, but, like many other watering-places, it lacks vegetation and shelter, the hills, although fine objects as a landscape, being too far off to be available for near resort. The opposite coast affords views of St. John's Point and Lighthouse, Inver and Killybegs Bays, terminated in the extreme distance by the cliffs of Teelin Head and Slieve League. Bundoran is the favourite resort of the Enniskillen people, who, together with visitors from the other side of the kingdom, frequent it in large numbers. The tourist will notice the envelope stuck up in the windows, as a notification that lodgings are to be let. The action of the sea has worn the cliffs into numerous grotesque forms, an example of which may be seen in "the Fairy Bridge, a single arch 24 ft. in span, having a causeway of half that breadth perfectly formed and detached from all architectural encumbrances."—*Wright*.

Conveyances.—Daily to Sligo; daily to Donegal; daily (3 times) to Ballyshannon and Enniskillen.

Distances.—Ballyshannon, 4 m.; Sligo, 21½; Enniskillen, 31; Donegal, 17½; Kinlough, 2½; Lough Melvin, 4; Glenade, 9½; Manor Hamilton, 15.

Excursions.—
1. Kinlough and Lough Melvin.
2. Ballyshannon.

[It is a very beautiful drive to Manor Hamilton through Kinlough. The Drowes is crossed at Lennox's Bridge.

2½ m. *Kinlough* (anc. Cean-lacka), prettily situated at the western extremity of Lough Melvin, contains a spring impregnated with sulphuretted hydrogen. There are some nice residences in the neighbourhood—Kinlough House (J. Johnston, Esq.), Brook Hill, and, on the southern bank of Lough Melvin, Mount Prospect, the residence of Mr. Conolly, M.P., the owner of Bundoran.

Lough Melvin is a very considerable sheet of water 7½ m. in length; but though the southern banks are extremely striking, it generally attracts the angler more than the general tourist. The former will find accommodation at an inn at the little village of *Garrison* on the W. side of the lake, and he can obtain permission to fish from Mr. Johnston of Kinlough House. There is good salmon until the middle of May, after which grilse comes in; also splendid trout-fishing, especially of the sort named gillaroo. There are several islands of no great size, one close to the S. shore containing the remains of the castle of Rossclogher, "and on the eastern shore are the ruins of the ancient ch. of Rossinver, supposed to have been that of the nunnery of Doiremell, founded by St. Tigernach for his mother St. Mella."—*Lewis*. From Kinlough the road is carried up a splendid ravine, similar to the one at Glencar (p. 74), the hills on each side rising in sudden escarpments to the height of 1500 ft. At the top of the water-level is

10 m. *Lough Glenade*, a small lake buried in the heart of the mountains, on the E. bank of which is Glenade House (C. T. Cullen, Esq.). From this lake issues the Bonet river, which flows into Lough Gill at Dromahaire (p. 73).

15½ m. Manor Hamilton (Rte. 6). The tourist should, however, before arriving here, turn off to the rt. to see the village of *Lurganboy*, which is situated in the middle of the most romantic scenery.]

From Bundoran the road is tame and surrounded by sandbanks. On l. is the ruined ch. of *Inishmacsaint*, which, as the name implies, was at one time situated on an island previous to the drifting of the sand.

25½ m. *Ballyshannon* (anc. Athseanaigh) (Rte. 6) (*Hotels*: Coburn's, Erne; both poor), famous for its salmon-leap, presents from a distance an infinitely pleasanter appearance than a nearer inspection warrants. Its situation is almost fine, on a steep hill overlooking the broad and rushing stream of the Erne, but the streets are dirty and mean, especially in the lower part of the town. The castle of Ballyshannon, of which scarce any traces remain, was the scene of a disastrous defeat of the English under Sir Conyers Clifford in 1597. They had besieged O'Donell, who was shut up here, for 5 days; but the garrison having made a desperate sally, they retreated in haste, and lost a great portion of their force in an unsuccessful attempt to cross the Erne. The 2 portions of the town, the lower one of which is called the Port, are connected by a bridge of 16 arches, a few hundred yards above the celebrated Falls, where an enormous body of water is preci-

Route 8.—Ballyshannon—Ballintra.

pitated over a cliff some 30 ft. high and 10 above high water, with a noise that is perfectly deafening. This is the scene of the salmon-leap. "The salmon that drop down in August and September return again up the same river in the months of spring, and this can only be accomplished by an ascent of the fall at Ballyshannon. Traps are laid in different parts of the fall, with funnel-shaped entrances, into which the salmon swim, and are preserved until required for the market; intervals are also left between the traps, through which the fish reach the top of the fall by a spring of at least 14 ft. in height, though it is at low water that the scene of leaping is displayed with the greatest activity."—*Wright*. The fishery is very valuable, and is rented by Dr. Sheil, to whom application must be made for leave to fish. Anglers are, however, so numerous, that it is not always possible for the proprietor to grant permission. The antiquary will find, in the parish of Kilbarron, in which the N. part of Ballyshannon is situated, no less than 14 Danish raths, and between 3 and 4 m. to the N.W. the ruins of *Kilbarron Castle*, an ancient fortress of the O'Clerys, renowned in their day for their skill in science, poetry, and history. Of this family was Father Michael O'Clery, the leader of the illustrious quartett of the Four Masters. It stands on a precipitous rock at the very edge of the coast. A little to the N. of this is Coolmore, frequented as a bathing-place. On the return (about ½ m. from the town), visit the site and a portion of wall of the abbey founded in 1179 by Roderic le Canavan, Prince of Tirconnel.

A considerable trade is carried on at Ballyshannon, and many improvements were made by Col. Conolly, the owner of the soil, although the existence of a dangerous bar at the mouth of the river acts injuriously to commerce. Pop. 3197.

Conveyances.—Donegal daily, also to Sligo; twice a day to Enniskillen and Bundoran.

Distances.— Sligo, 25¼ m.; Bundoran, 4; Donegal, 13½; Ballintra, 6½; Belleek, 4½; Enniskillen, 27; Pettigoe, 17; Manor Hamilton, 19; Garrison, 9.

Excursions.—

1. To Belleek and Rapids (Rte. 6).
2. Ballintra and the Pullins.

The route from Ballyshannon to Donegal is through a dreary uninteresting country. 28½ m. l. Cavan Garden, the seat of T. J. Atkinson, Esq.

32 m. is the village of *Ballintra*, in the neighbourhood of which the mountain limestone is very largely developed. Near it is Brown Hall (J. Hamilton, Esq.), through the grounds of which the Ballintra river flows in a very singular manner. The locality is called the Pullins. "It is formed by the course of a mountain torrent which runs nearly a mile through a most picturesque ravine shaded by a mass of deep wood. A solid bed of limestone seems to have been cleft from 30 to 40 ft. in depth, and in this narrow fissure, often turning at a very acute angle, the river foams along, frequently disappearing in caves, when its course passes under the rock for a considerable space.

"It seemed some mountain rent and riven
 A channel for the stream had given,
 So high the cliffs of limestone grey
 Hung beetling o'er the torrent's way."
                                        Rokeby.

After a course again of ½ m. through a meadow, the river reassumes its wild character, but with increased magnificence. It suddenly descends about 60 ft. in a deep chasm, the rocks actually meeting overhead, while a precipitous wall bounds it on either side; it then emerges under a perfect natural bridge, and, turning suddenly, a vista appears opening upon the sea in the distance, and on either side a perpendicular rock extends in a straight line to Ballintra, the river occupying the entire space between these walls."—*Hall.*

34½ m. Coxtown (J. Hamilton, Esq.), and a little further on the village of *Laghy*, to the l. of which are Belle Isle (A. H. Foster, Esq.), and, on an island at the entrance of Donegal Bay, St. Ernan's, the seat of John Hamilton, Esq.

39 m. *Donegal* (Dun na Gall) (Rte. 9) (*Hotel*: Dillon's), a small county town of about 1550 Inhab., is prettily situated at the mouth of the Esk and the head of the bay of Donegal. The numerous shoals and difficulties of approach have however interfered sadly with its position as a port, the business done here being very small. The principal object of interest is the ruined castle of the O'Donells. "Tyrconnel is the Celtic name of Donegal; meaning the Land of Connel, who was son to Nial of the 9 Hostages, a monarch of Ireland of ancient fame, from whom descended the O'Donells of Donegal. James I. conferred in 1602 the title of Earl of Tyrconnel and Baron Donegal on Roderick O'Donell, one of this race; but it was lost to the family from the want of male issue."—*Dublin Univ. Mag.* In 1587 O'Donell held his castle in defiance against the English government, who, not having sufficient force to send against him, captured him by stratagem. A vessel was sent to the coast laden with wine, the effects of which were too powerful for the chief, who had rashly accepted the hospitalities of the captain. He was bound, when drunk, and carried to Dublin Castle, from which, however, he eventually escaped. The castle of Donegal is a beautiful Elizabethan building, combining defensive with domestic purposes, and consists of a tall gabled tower with 2 bartizan turrets, of which only one is perfect. It is more than probable that it was rebuilt by Sir Basil Brooke, to whom a grant was made in 1610. The principal apartment is lighted by a very fine mullioned window, and contains a grand sculptured chimney-piece with the arms of Brooke and Leicester, below which may be noticed the ballflower. Beneath this hall is a lower room with a rudely vaulted roof, the stones placed edgeways. In the other portion of the castle are a fine roundheaded window-arch and a pointed doorway. The situation overlooking the Esk is very charming, and the castle, together with the old-fashioned garden—

"—— A garden wild,
Where mix'd jonquils and gowans grow,
And roses 'midst rank clover blow"—

make up a lovely picture. It now belongs to the Earl of Arran.

The *Abbey*, founded for Franciscan friars in 1474 by Hugh Roe, son of O'Donell, occupies a rocky position by the river-side. There is enough left to show that it was a large cruciform church, with probably a central tower. It has the remains of a good Dec. E. window, and also one in the S. transept. On the N. of the ch. are the cloisters, of which 7 arches remain on the E. and 6 on the N. They were of the same height and character as those of Sligo (p. 71). In this abbey were compiled the famous 'Annals of Donegal,' better known under the title of the 'Annals of the Four Masters,' of whom Father O'Clery, of Kilbarron, was the chief.

The object of this compilation was to detail the history of Ireland up to the time in which they lived, including all local events, such as the years of foundations and destructions of churches and castles, the obituaries of remarkable persons, the inaugurations of kings, the battles of chiefs, the contests of clans, &c. "A book, consisting of 1100 quarto pages, beginning with the year of the world 2242, and ending with the year of our Lord's incarnation 1616, thus covering the immense space of 4500 years of a nation's history, must be dry and meagre of details in some, if not in all, parts of it. And although the learned compilers had at their disposal, or within their reach, an immense mass of historic details, still the circumstances under which they wrote were so unfavourable, that they appear to have exercised a sound discretion, and one consistent with the economy of time and of their resources, when they left the details of our very early history in the safe keeping of such ancient original records as from remote ages preserved them, and collected as much as they could make room for of the events of more modern times, and particularly of the eventful times in which they lived themselves."— *Prof. O'Curry*.

The Protestant ch. is in the principal square, and has a pretty spire and a hideous body. A Dissenting congregation have lately erected a chapel, which might possibly be admired, had the builder not committed the unpardonable error of blocking up the best view of the old castle.

Conveyances.—To Sligo daily; to Strabane daily; to Killybegs daily.

Distances.—Sligo, 39 m.; Ballintra, 7; Ballyshannon, 13½; Stranorlar, 17; Strabane, 30; Barnesmore Gap, 7; Lough Easke, 4½; Killybegs, 17; Inver, 7½; Mount Charles, 4; Carrick, 24; Ardara, 17½; Dunkaneely, 11; Glenties, 15.

Excursions.—
1. Lough Easke.
2. Ballintra.

From Donegal the road now leaves the coast, turning inland and following up the valley of the Esk. The mountains now assume a very beautiful appearance, as the road allows a full view of the ranges to the l., principally consisting of the Croghgorm or Blue Stack Mountains 2219 ft.. Knockroe 2202, Croaghnageer (1793, all of which are a continuation of the chain which commences at Slieve League and Ardara. Immediately opposite is the formidable Gap of Barnesmore, and happy is the traveller who gets through it on a fine day without the usual accompaniment of wind and rain, or "smirr" as it is termed in Donegal. A most exquisite landscape opens out on the l., in which the blue waters of Lough Easke fill up the basin at the foot of the hills; and on its banks are the woods and groves of Lough Easke House, the beautiful seat of T. Brooke, Esq.; also the demesne of Ardnamona (G. C. Wray, Esq.). On an island near the S. bank are the ruins of O'Donell's tower, said to have been used by chiefs of that clan as a place of confinement. Polypodium phegopteris and Asplenium viride grow near the waterfall at the lake.

Soon after quitting the neighbourhood of the Lough Easke, the road crosses the Loweymore river and enters the *Gap of Barnesmore*, a narrow mountain pass, on either of which rises abruptly Barnesmore (1491 ft.), and Crough Conellagh (1724). When the day is fine and clear, the drive up to the watershed is very fine, and on looking back the traveller obtains an extensive view over Donegal and the bay; but if the day is wet, the sooner he gets out of the pass the better. Very near the summit, 538 ft. above the sea, a spot is pointed out where a man was hung in chains, not many years ago, for a murder committed at this place.

50 m. rt. *Lough Mourne*, a small sheet of water, as sad and melancholy as its name. At one end are slight traces of a castle, "in which it is supposed the Huguenot historian Rapin compiled his history."—*Black*. [A little before arriving at the lake a road on rt. is given off, following the course of the Mourne Beg river to Castle Derg, 15 m. (Rte. 7.)]

From Lough Mourne the road rapidly descends, following the stream of the Burn Daurnett. The views are extensive, but they are by no means equal to those that the traveller has left behind, as the character of the country is pastoral and flax producing, while the hills are much lower and monotonous in outline.

56 m. *Ballybofey*, a considerable village, adjoining the still larger one of *Stranorlar* (*Inn*: Miller's), the river Finn, which here first makes its appearance, intervening. The only building of interest is a very handsome Roman Catholic ch. lately built. Close to the town are the woods of Drumboe Castle (Sir S. Hayes), and a little further S. of the town Tyrcallen (Marquis of Conyngham), Summer Hill (James Johnston, Esq.), and Meenglass, the seat of Viscount Lifford. [Some very pretty scenery is to be met with by following the Finn up its stream on the N. bank to Fintown, or on the S. bank to Glenties (Rte. 10). 4 m. on S. bank is Glenmore, the residence of W. M. Style, Esq., and 7 m. on N. bank is Cloghan Lodge, that of Sir T. C. Style, to whose praiseworthy exertions the improvement, both social and moral, of a very large portion of country is due. An enormous amount of wild and useless land was reclaimed, a ch. built, industrial schools founded, and the whole condition of the peasantry ameliorated. There is a pretty waterfall on the Finn, which is here crossed by a bridge connecting the two roads.

The road now enters the hills, and the river assumes the character of a Highland stream, till the traveller reaches 17 m. Fintown, a small village, beautifully situated on the banks of Lough Finn, and under the steep cliffs of Aghla (1953 ft.), and Scraigs (1410). Some lead-mines, likely to be productive, have been opened here. From hence a road falls into the Dunglow and Glenties road (Rte. 10).]

Stranorlar is connected with Strabane by the Finn Valley Rly., opened in 1863, which boasts the merit of being the cheapest rly. in Ireland, as it only cost 5000*l*. a mile.

60 m. *Killygordon*, a pleasant village, also on the banks of the Finn, contains nothing to detain the tourist. About 1 m. rt. is a house where the Duke of Berwick is said to have passed the night in his northern campaign 1689.

2 m. rt. are Mounthall (W. Young, Esq.), and Monellan House (— Delap, Esq.). Further on are *Donaghmore Ch.* and *House*, the latter the glebe-house and residence of the Irving family, the patrons of the living. 63½ m. *Castle Finn* was anciently a possession of the O'Donells, from whose hands it passed in the reign of Elizabeth. The Finn here becomes navigable for vessels of small burden.

Distances.—Raphoe (p. 86), 6 m.; Castle Derg, 7.

At the village of Clady 65½ m. the Finn is crossed, as the road on the l. bank keeps on to Lifford. Passing the demesne of Urney (A. F. Knox, Esq.), the traveller soon reaches 69 m. *Strabane* (Rte. 7) (*Hotel*: Sim's Abercorn Arms).

ROUTE 9.

FROM **ENNISKILLEN** TO **PETTIGOE** **DONEGAL,** AND **KILLYBEGS.**

This route to Donegal by the E. bank of Lough Erne, is not usually followed by travellers, who for the most part go by Ballyshannon. It is, however, a beautiful drive to Pettigoe, particularly if the tourist keeps the road alongside of the lake, and not the car-road through Lowtherstown. For a short distance it runs close to the railway, diverging at a small pool called the Race-

Route 9.—Pettigoe—Lough Derg.

course Lake, and approaching Lough Erne at 4 m. Trony ch. On the rt. of the road is the mound of Mossfield Fort. Before reaching the ch. a road turns off on rt. to Lowtherstown. At 5 m. the Bellanamallard stream is crossed near its mouth. On rt. is Riversdale (Major Archdall), and further on are the demesnes of Rossfad (H. Richardson, Esq.). The views from this road are much finer than can be obtained from the Ballyshannon road, as it embraces all the cliff and hill scenery on the W. shore. The estates too on this side are fine and beautifully wooded, particularly those of Castle Archdall (Capt. Archdall, M.P.) and Rockfield (Capt. Irvine).

At 11 m. *Lisnacarrick*, a road comes in from Lowtherstown or Stromertown, 2½ m. distant. Close to it is *Necarn Castle* (H. M. D'Arcy Irvine, Esq.).

15 m. *Kesh*, a small place on the river of the same name, containing nothing whatever to interest the traveller. The country now begins to get wilder, an extensive and dreary range of hills stretching from Omagh on the E. into the neighbourhood of Donegal. The Kesh river rises about 10 m to the N.E. in the hills of Dooish, 1110 ft. Passing rt. Clonelly House F. W. Barton, Esq.), soon after which the tourist arrives at

20 m. *Pettigoe* (*Inn*: Hamilton's), on the river Termon, and very near the north bank of Lough Erne, opposite the long and narrow Boa Island.

Pettigoe is in the parish of Templecarne, near the glebe-house of which are the ruins of Termon Magrath, a strong keep with circular towers at the angles, said to have been the residence of Myler Magrath, the first Protestant Bp. of Clogher; it was battered by Ireton in the Parliamentary war. The prefix of Termon signifies sanctuary—" in former times the founder of a ch. being obliged, prior to its consecration by the bishop, to endow it with certain properties for the maintenance of the clergy connected with the establishment. To these lands, which were denominated Erenach or Termon lands, various privileges were annexed; they were exempt from all lay charges, and became sanctuaries, and were in some respects equivalent to our glebe-lands." Waterfoot is the seat of H. W. Barton, Esq. Notwithstanding the seeming insignificance of Pettigoe, it is the rendezvous of half the devotees in Ireland, who at certain seasons throng the place on their way to *Lough Derg*, which lies about 4½ m. to the N., in as wild and forbidding a mountain region as can well be imagined. "It is said that no road is constructed here, lest the devotions of the pilgrims should be interrupted by the presence of too many heretics. Nothing can be more desolate than the landscape around Loch Derg. Barren heathy hills surround it on every side, possessing neither form nor elevation to give the slightest interest to the scene." —*Inglis*. The lake itself is 6 m. long and 4 broad, and contains several rocky islands, the largest of them, the Station Island, being the scene of the annual visit of 10,000 unfortunate people, who journey hither from all parts of Ireland, and even the Continent, to undergo penance in St. Patrick's purgatory. From the 1st of June to the 15th of August is the time prescribed for their religious ceremonies, and the number of visitors at this period varies from 10,000 to 15,000. A ferry-boat, for the charge of 6d. a head, conveys the devotees to the Station Island, which is about half a mile from the shore. Even this spot of ground is only a few yds. across, and is covered with modern buildings, including chapels and accommodation for penitents. "In the vicinity of the chapels are a number of circular stone walls, from 1 to 2 ft. in height, called the Seven Saints' Peni-

E 3

tential Beds; and around these, on the hard and pointed rocks, the penitents pass upon their bare knees, repeating a certain form of prayer at each."—*Holy Wells of Ireland*. It would be foreign to a Handbook to describe the details of the ceremonies, accounts of which can be obtained in other works on Ireland. The geologist will notice the change from the limestones of Lough Erne to the extensive region of mica slates, which from this point embraces nearly the whole of the N.W. portion of the kingdom. The very vegetation in the neighbourhood of Lough Derg attests the change, and cannot fail to strike the intelligent observer.

From Pettigoe a wild mountain road passes under the base of Knockadrin 752 ft., and Oughtnadrin 1057 ft., falling into the Ballyshannon road at Laghy village, from whence it is 3½ m. to Donegal (Rte. 8). *Hotel*: Dillon's. A car leaves Donegal every morning for Killybegs, distance 23 m. From the bridge over the Easke the tourist obtains the best view of Donegal Castle, and the road then crosses the head of the bay, affording very pretty coast scenes overlooking Doorin and St. John's Promontories.

40 m. *Mountcharles*, a large village, built on the side of a steep hill. Facing the sea is the Hall, a property belonging to the Marquis of Conyngham, but generally occupied by his agent. Arrived at the top of the hill, it will be seen that the road cuts off the neck of Doorin Promontory, and descends a long hill to *Inver*, 49 m., which is conspicuous for a considerable distance from its pretty ch. spire embosomed in woods. Notwithstanding the tediousness of these hilly roads, the tourist will rarely find the time hang heavy, for the views of the Donegal mountains are superb. To his rt. he has the ranges of Blue Stack, Silver Hill, Benbane, and Mulmosog, extending from Barnesmore Gap on the E. to Ardara on the W.; while, in front of him is the mighty mass of Crownarad beyond Killybegs, and (seen from some points) the distant precipices of Slieve Liagh or League.

At Inver the Eanybeg river is crossed in its course from Silver Hill to the sea. In the woods to the rt. is *Bonyglen*, used as a fishing-lodge. The road again ascends and cuts off the St. John's Point, a singular narrow stretch of land that runs out to sea for some distance, and is terminated at the extremity by a fixed lighthouse.

53 m. *Dunkineely*, a decayed-looking village of one street, from which the traveller will be not loth to emerge. A little further on are the ch. and glebe-house of Killaghtee, overlooking the strand of M'Swyne's Bay. This district was formerly possessed by the M'Swynes, a very powerful sept, whose castle, a square massive tower, still exists close to the sea. There is a pretty bit of landscape at Bruckless, where the river Corker flows past a miniature pier, mill, and mansion embosomed in trees. Crossing the next high ground, we descend upon the most charming of land-locked bays, on one side of which, completely sheltered from storms, is

59 m. *Killybegs* (anc. Cealhabeaga) (Rte. 10), a clean pleasant little seaport, which, without any pretensions to the dignity of a watering-place, will, as far as situation goes, well repay a visit. (*Hotels*: Coane's and Rogers'; both comfortable.) The tide comes up to the doors of the houses, although the harbour is a complete refuge from its being so sheltered. At the entrance to the bay is a lighthouse, and on the western shore are the wooded grounds and residence of the incumbent (Rev. W. Lodge), together with the remnants (very slight) of a castle and of a ch., overgrown with

brushwood, and not possessing any remarkable features. The visitor should inspect the schools built by Mr. Murray, which are as well ordered as they are of pretty and tasteful design.

Conveyances. — Car to Donegal daily.

Distances.—Donegal, 23 m.; Inver, 10; Dunkaneely, 6; Ardara, 10; Glenties, 16; Fintragh, 2; Kilcar, 6¼; Carrick, 9; Slieve League, 12; Glen, 16½; Malinmore, 17.

Excursions.—
1. Kilcar.
2. Carrick and Slieve League.
3. Ardara.

The tourist should now take a car as there is no further public conveyance to explore the district beyond Killybegs, which, as far as scenery goes, is equal to anything in Ireland, and deserves to be thoroughly well known.

The next descent brings us down to 6 m. Fintragh Bay, overhung by the block of mountain known as Crownarard, 1619 ft. Fintragh House is the residence of R. Hamilton, Esq. The sea-views are very extensive as we journey along the elevated road, embracing the whole coast from the sandhills of Bundoran to Sligo, and the districts of Erris and Tyrawley. The limestone ranges of Benbulben and Truskmore are particularly conspicuous.

65¼ m. *Kilcar*, a romantic village on the slope of a hill, at the foot of which is the ch., and a brawling mountain torrent, forming altogether a charming picture. As the road ascends the steep hills again, the geologist will notice the heaps of bog iron-ore, which is largely extracted from this locality and taken to Teelin to be shipped, from whence it goes to Belfast and Liverpool. The percentage of iron is not very great, but from its fusibility it is particularly adapted to fine castings.

Again descending a wild moorland region, is 68 m. *Carrick*, another highland village, situated on the bank of the Teelin river, and at the foot of the gigantic mass of Slieve Liagh or League, which rises to 1972 ft., and has a very prominent and peculiar edge. The tourist should make Carrick his head-quarters at the pleasant little hotel, built by Mr. Conolly, M.P., where he will find great cleanliness and civility, with peculiar advantages for exploring a district teeming with coast and mountain beauty.

Distances.—Killybegs, 9 m.; Glen, 6; Ardara by Glengeask, 14; Slieve League, 2¼.

For the ascent of the latter mountain, the tourist had better take a guide, more for the purpose of saving time than because there is any danger; for the outlying ridges are so boggy and deceptive that a straight cut is especially to be guarded against. For about 1 m. the road follows the Glen or Teelin river, which like that at Killybegs speedily changes from a mountain torrent into a landlocked bay of great beauty. On the rt. bank is Roxborough, the residence of Rev. F. Labatt, the rector of Kilcar. There is a coastguard station at Teelin, the most likely place to obtain a boat, should it be required to row round any part of the coast. The guide should be told to bring the visitor first of all to Bunglas, "beautiful view," by which route he passes *Corrigan Head*, a fine promontory jutting suddenly out in splendid cliffs which are seen to great perfection by this path. From hence is visible one of the many martello towers which are placed in regular rotation round the coast. At Bunglas Point a view of singular magnificence bursts upon you—a view that of its kind is probably unequalled in the British Isles. The lofty mountain of Slieve League gives on the land side no promise of the magnificence that it presents from the sea, being in fact a mural precipice of nearly 2000 ft. in height, descending to the water's edge in one superb escarpment—

> "around
> Whose caverned base the whirlpools and the waves
> Bursting and eddying irresistibly,.
> Rage and resound for ever."
> *Shelley.*

And not only in its height is it so sublime, but in the glorious colours which are grouped in masses on its face. Stains of metals, green, amber, gold, yellow, white, red, and every variety of shade are observed, particularly when seen under a bright sun, contrasting in a wonderful manner with the dark blue waters beneath. In cloudy or stormy weather this peculiarity is to a certain degree lost, though other effects take its place and render it even more magnificent. This range of sea-cliff extends with little variation all the way to Malin, though at nothing like the same altitude. Having feasted the eyes well with the beauties of the precipices, the tourist should ascend, skirting the cliffs the whole way. Near the summit the escarpment and the land ascent approach so closely as to leave only a very precarious path, which is termed the One Man's Edge, and is looked on by the inhabitants of the neighbourhood in the same light as the Striding Edge of Helvellyn or the Bwlch-y-Maen of Snowdon. However, it cannot be considered so dangerous as these, because a fall on the land side, though unpleasant, would not entail destruction, though with a sharp sea-wind blowing it is no easy work to keep one's footing. At the very summit are the remains of ancient oratories. The view is wondrous fine. Southwards is the whole coast of Sligo and Mayo, from Benbulben to the Stags of Broadhaven: while further in the distance are faintly seen Nephin, near Ballina, and (it is also said) Croagh Patrick, at Westport. Northward is a perfect sea of Donegal mountains, reaching as far as Slieve Snaght and Arrigal, with all the intervening ranges near Ardara, Glenties, and Dunglow (Rte. 10). In the descent the path made for the use of tourists should be followed, passing down a deep cleft in the mountain, at the bottom of which reposes a small tarn.

A second excursion should be taken from Carrick to Ardara, to the magnificent glen of Geask, through which the road is carried across the highland moors to Ardara. It is, however, so abominably bad, that it is almost impassable, the writer of this notice having been obliged in many places to assist in carrying the car *vi et armis*, so that perhaps Glengeask will be more comfortably visited by proceeding from Killybegs to Ardara, and from thence making a special journey.

A 3rd visit should by all means be paid to Glen, a district which tourists should not fail to explore, instead of stopping short at Slieve League, as most are content to do. It is 6 m. from Carrick.

[At the 2nd m. a road turns off to the l. to *Malinmore*, where very comfortable accommodation can be obtained at a farmhouse kept by Miss Walker. The coast is very fine, although not on such a grand scale as at Glen, a little further on. There is a fixed lighthouse and coastguard station.]

After traversing the high moorground the road suddenly descends or breaks into the Glen Valley, a remote highland glen of great beauty, although impressed with a somewhat melancholy and sombre cast. A rather large population is scattered up and down the glen, at the bottom of which are the ch. and village of Glen Columbkill, or the Glen of St. Columb, for it was in this retired spot that the Saint Columb particularly loved to dwell. At a turn in the road the visitor will notice an ancient cross in fine preservation, which, together with the antiquarian as well as legendary lore of the district, has been carefully and zealously looked after by the Rev. V. Griffith, the incumbent. The remains which are accredited to St. Columb are the cross already alluded to, the house of the saint, his bed, and his well, close to which an enormous pile of stones attests the numbers of devout pilgrims. In the interior of the 4 walls, said to have been his bed, is a smooth stone, which according to tradition is said to have been placed by St. Columb (who was blind of one eye) on the sound one, that he might not oversleep himself. In consequence of this sacred use it is carried round the village with a view to exercising its miraculous powers of healing in cases of bad eyes. The well-marked path round the bed betokens the frequent pattern that is held here.

A very curious belief exists in Glen, viz., that it was for a considerable time the hiding-place of the Pretender, ere he could find his way out of Great Britain into another country. As has been shown by Mr. Griffith in the 'Dublin University Magazine,' the proofs of the story certainly give strong reason to believe in its truth. A headland is pointed out where the prince used to repair each day with his servant to scan the offing in search of ships. The mountains and cliffs abound in remarkable and fantastic shapes, and the tourist will be amply repaid by a ramble of about 2 m. over the hills to *Glen Head*, a precipice of 800 ft., which descends to the sea as sharp and clean as a knife. Impracticable as it seems, the peasants think nothing of being swung down to collect the few blades of sweet grass that grow in the crevices. On the headland above is one of the watch-towers that abound on this coast. As the cliffs trend to the east, they exhibit wonderful forms and positions, particularly at Tormore, where the rocks are pitched about as though the ancient giants had been playing with them. The geologist will observe the effects of sea action in a most marked manner; instead of returning to Glen, he should keep along the coast to Loughros Beg Bay, and so to Ardara (Rte. 10) (*Inn*: Mullany's, bad). The 20 m. from Teelin Bay to Loughros Bay is, as far as coast scenery goes, not to be excelled by any locality in Great Britain.

ROUTE 10.

FROM **STRABANE** TO **LETTERKENNY, GWEEDORE, DUNGLOW, ARDARA,** AND **KILLYBEGS.**

A mail-car leaves Strabane early in the morning for Letterkenny 16½ m., returning hence in the evening. Crossing the broad stream of the Foyle by a long and narrow bridge of 12 arches, the traveller enters the little town of *Lifford* (*Inn:* Erne), which, although the county town, is so small that it seems entirely made up of court-house and jail. Lifford was the scene of an obstinate battle in 1600, between the English garrison of Derry under Nial Garbh O'Donell and Hugh O'Donell, and, though now the quietest of villages, was an important market-town in the time of James I. From hence the road runs over a hilly open ground, pleasantly diversified with occasional views over Strabane and the valley of the Foyle, while the traveller sees ahead of him the blue peaks of the Derryveagh Mountains. 2 m. the river Deel is crossed [on either side of which a road l. is given off to *Raphoe* 5 m., passing through the village of Ballindrait, close to which are the woods of Cavanacor House (Col. Humphrey). Raphoe is a pleasantly-situated little town, once famous for being the seat of a bishopric, which was, however, united to that of Derry in 1835. A monastery established here by St. Columb was afterwards converted into a bishopric by St. Eunan in the 11th cent. From that time must be dated the commencement of the cathedral, a plain cruciform building, with a square tower of the last cent., which is also the date of the transepts added by Bishop Pooley in 1702. The ruined episcopal residence stands near the cathedral. At Beltany, on the summit of a hill 2 m. from Raphoe, is a stone circle 150 yds. in circumference, formed by 67 upright stones, on the E. side of which is an opening formed by 2 larger ones. "The name Beltany is supposed to be a corruption of Baal tinne, 'the fire of Baal,' intimating a spot where that deity was particularly worshipped in Ireland, and having the same etymology in Gaelic as the Beltani tree burned at Midsummer."—*Hall.* Raphoe is well placed at the foot of the great range of Donegal Mountains, as they begin to decline into the lowlands, and many fine views may be obtained in the neighbourhood from Mullafin 954 ft., and from the Herd's Seat, which rises over the village of Convoy. Some 7 or 8 m. higher up, the Deel takes its rise in Lough Deel, a small lake at the summit of the Cark Mountain 1205 ft.]. The traveller will soon discover that he is in the head-quarters of the flax country, especially if it happen to be in the latter end of August or beginning of September. All the little streams are dammed up for the purpose of soaking the flax, whilst the fields are strewn with regularly laid bundles, more pleasing to the eye than the nose, which is offended by a fresh burst of odour every 100 yards. (*Introd.*, p. xxxv.)

11½ m. a road on rt. branches off to the village of *Manor Cunningham*, and soon Lough Swilly comes into view. As it appears from its lower end, it is tame and bare, although the hills which loom in the distance give promise of better scenery.

16½ m. *Letterkenny* (*Hotel:* Hegarty's, very comfortable), a pleasant little town of one long street occupying the side of a hill and overlooking a large expanse of country. With the exception of the ch., on the summit of the hill, the poorhouse, and a new clock-tower, lately erected, Letterkenny itself contains nothing of interest, but it can be recommended as good head-quarters for those tourists who wish to explore the hill country. There are some nice residences in the neighbourhood, as Ballymacool (J. R. Boyd, Esq.), and Gortlee (Capt. Patterson).

Conveyances.—To Strabane daily. To Dunfanaghy daily. To Londonderry daily.

Distances.—Strabane, 16½ m.; Dunfanaghy, 22; Gweedore, 22; Dunglow, 30; Derryveagh, 17½; Kilmacrenan, 7½; Churchtown, 9; Rathmelton, 7; Raphoe, 8½; Doocharry Bridge, 22.

Excursions.—
1. Kilmacrenan.
2. Gartan Lough.

From Letterkenny the road traverses an open hilly country, diversified with distant views of hill, river, and lake. [At 20¼ m. a road on rt. is given off to Milford, 6½ m., passing 2½ m. rt. Ballyarr House, the seat of Lord George Hill, to whom the whole district which the traveller is about to visit is under deep obligations.

Crossing a small river at Drumman Bridge, the road runs parallel with *Lough Fern*, a sheet of water about 1¾ m. in length, on the E. side of which the ground rises to 500 ft. 6½ m. *Milford* (Rte. 11) is a small village, interesting only for its proximity to the beautiful scenery of Mulroy Bay.]

24 m. *Kilmacrenan* is very prettily situated in a mountain valley, through which the Lannan river rushes down in picturesque stream. As the road descends into the village, the tourist gets distant views on rt. of Lough Fern, and, considerably beyond it, the indented summits of the Glenalla Mountains, which intervene between it and Lough Swilly; on rt. are the ruins of Kilmacrenan Abbey, founded by St. Columb, consisting of a slender and rather graceful tower, lighted by pointed windows in the top stage, besides scanty remains of other buildings surrounded by an enclosure. The parish ch. is said to have been built on the site of a Franciscan priory, and has over the door the sculptured head of an abbot taken from the abbey.

Not far from the village is the *Rock of Doon*, "on which the O'Donells were always inaugurated by priests whom they regarded as descended from St. Columb."—*Lewis*.

Distances.—Dunfanaghy, 14½ m.; Letterkenny, 7½; Milford, 5; Rathmelton, 6½; Lough Salt, 5.

At the junction of the road to Dunfanaghy the road crosses the Lurgy river, and traverses a wild uninhabited district round which groups of rugged hills soon begin to close. Winding up a long and tedious hill, the traveller is well repaid by a delicious distant view of the blue waters of *Gartan Lough*, which, with its wooded banks, breaks on the eye with peculiar pleasure, after the brown and monotonous hill-sides.

[At 29½ m. a moorland road branches off to Gartan Lough and Church Hill, 4 m. What appears from the road to be one lake is really 2 sheets of water, the upper one, Lough Agibbon, being separated by a narrow neck of land from Lough Gartan, on the E. shore of which is Bellville, a seat of J. Stewart, Esq. Trollius Europæus flourishes on these lakes.

On the side of the upper lake is a ruined chapel, still used as the burial-place of the O'Donells. It was built on the spot where St. Columb is said to have been born in 521. His name was originally Crimthan, afterwards changed to Columb, from the simplicity of his disposition (Columba), a dove. "He was of royal extraction, being, by the paternal side, descended (through Conall Gulban) from Niall, while his mother Æthena was of an illustrious house of Leinster."

From hence the traveller can return by a different road to Letterkenny, 9 m., descending into the valley of the Swilly at Foxhall (J. Chambers, Esq.), passing afterwards the Glebe of Doon (Rev. Dr. Kingsmill, Rockhill (J. V. Stewart, Esq.), and Ballymacool (J. R. Boyd, Esq.), the last 2 demesnes lying on opposite banks of the river.]

The scenery from this point to Glenveagh resembles much of the Scottish Highlands—large extensive moors shut in on all sides by hills, some of them rising to a considerable height. For some distance it would appear that the way lies up a broad depression running N. and S., but a sudden turn of the road reveals the singular summit of Muckish 2197 ft., which, from its precipitous escarpment, seems higher than it really is. The traveller is now fairly amidst the mountain ranges, which, seen when the mist is rising, or the cloud shadows floating gently by, are charming, but which, when overtaken by Donegal "Smirr," he will scarcely appreciate, for there is not a wilder or bleaker road in Great Britain, or one so open to storms.

The geological composition of the mountains is granite, having a gneissic structure, the quartz lodes of which occasionally gleam with a brightness all the more dazzling from the contrast with the dark masses.

32 m. the Owencarrow river is crossed as it enters Lough Beagh or Veagh. A little further on there is a very charming glimpse of the lake, a long narrow piece of water entirely shut in by mountains, which, especially at the lower end, descend precipitously to the very brink. On the l. bank, looking downwards, are Altachoastia (1737 ft.), and Kinnaveagh (1270), and on the opposite side is Keamnacally (1220), a portion of the great range of the Derryveagh Mountains, the highest point of which is Dooish (2147). It would be well for the tourist to consult his map while journeying down this pass, in order that he may understand the physical arrangement of this part of Donegal. It appears that the country between Lough Swilly and the sea is traversed by several ranges of hills all running in nearly the same direction, viz. from N E. to S.W. Commencing near Lough Swilly, we have the Glenalla hills, which are separated by the valley of the Lannan from those which overlook and are parallel to Gartan Lough. Westward of this lake are the Glendowan Mountains, intervening between it and Glenveagh. Then come the Derryveagh Mountains just spoken of, divided by a considerable mountain valley from the Arrigal group, which abruptly slope towards the sea. There are, therefore, a succession of ranges, with more or less narrow glens between, all having the same definite arrangement—a feature which will enable the traveller to understand his whereabouts with great ease.

[A road turning off by the police-barracks runs down the glen along the bank of the lake to *Glenveagh*, the mountain residence of J. Adair, Esq., who allows free passage to the tourist over his property. Indeed, one of the most splendid excursions in Ireland is to be found in Glenveagh, passing through it to the Poisoned Glen. Noble cliffs, covered with brushwood, in which the golden eagle still build, rise from the water's edge to the height of 1200 ft., and with the thick growth of natural wood, make Glenveagh a formidable rival to the beauties even of Killarney. The scenery at the great waterfall of Astellion is particularly striking. If the excursionist does not wish to proceed to Gweedore by the Poisoned Glen, he may continue through the pass to Doocharry Bridge (p. 91), where he should previously order a car to meet him to take him either to Dunglow or Glenties, in whichever direction he was going. This precaution is necessary, as there is no inn or any accommodation at Doocharry Bridge. The distance from Owencarrow is 15 m.]. Quitting the valley of Glen Veagh, the road winds round the base of Kingarrow (1068 ft.), and turns to the l. to enter the last mountain valley. [A road straight on passes immediately under Muckish at the Gap, and runs to Cross-roads 7 m. (p. 98).] This is the valley of the Calabber, which joins the Owencarrow, and is singularly wild and desolate. On the rt. rises Muckish (the pig's back), remarkable for its peculiar shape and fine escarpment; next to it are Crocknalaragagh (1554 ft.), Aghla Beg (1860), and Aghla More (1916), while on l. is the Dooish range. The botanist will find on Muckish Saxifraga serratafolia and Melampyrum pratense. Peering loftily over the very end of the valley is the singular and beautiful summit of Arrigal (2466 ft.), with its glistening seams of quartz. As the traveller ascends towards the watershed, he gains charming peeps of Glen Lough in the foreground, with Mulroy Bay in the distance, while near the summit level the attention is arrested on the rt. by *Allan Lough*, a dark savage-looking tarn in a deep gap between Aghla More and Arrigal, both of which mountains slope down to its banks with great rapidity. At 37½ m. the watershed is gained, and a view opens up which is hardly to be surpassed in Great Britain. The road winds by the side of a very deep valley, through which the Owenwee runs. On the rt. is *Arrigal Mountain*, rising up with startling abruptness, and presenting from this side the regular cone that makes it so conspicuous among its brethren. Towards the summit, indeed, it preserves its conical shape so far as scarcely to allow room for a person to lie across it. On the l. is a grand amphitheatre of mountains, heaped together in irregular masses and terminating in the lofty, rounded head of Slievesnacht (the Hill of Snow, 2240 ft.). A deep "corrie," known by the name of the Poisoned Glen, runs up in a cul-de-sac into the very heart of the mountains, guarded by steep precipices, down which a small stream glances on its way to join the Devlin river just before it falls into Dunlewy Lake, which, together with Lough Nacung, forms a sheet of water 4 m. in length, filling up the valley in such a manner as to appear more like an arm of the sea than a freshwater lake. On the opposite bank of Lough Dunlewy is Dunlewy House (G. F. Brady, Esq., perched upon a knoll over the lake, and surrounded by woods. The situation is so exquisitely beautiful, that it is a pity that the intentions of the former proprietor, Mr. Russell, to rebuild the mansion, were not carried out, and a building more in character with the scenery substituted for the present one. At the head of the lake is a pretty ch., with glebe-house, schools, and other pleasant tokens of civilization. This charming route deserves to be more known, for there is scarcely any scenery in Ireland that surpasses it. From hence the road keeps rapidly down the side of Arrigal until it reaches the Clady river, the outlet of the lakes, and keeps along its bank to

45½ m. *Gweedore*, where the traveller will be surprised to find a comfortable and well-managed hotel, from whence he can make excursions through this picturesque district. The name of Lord George Hill, the proprietor of the estate, is so thoroughly identified with that of Gweedore, that it will not be amiss to detail a few facts concerning him. He first settled in this part of the country in 1838, purchasing 23,000 acres in the parish of Tullaghobegly, which he found in a state of distress and want so great that it became the subject of a parliamentary inquiry. Although there appeared to have been a considerable amount of exaggeration in the statements made, enough remained to show that famine, pestilence, and ignorance were lamentably prevalent. The prospects of the landlord were far from encouraging, on account of the sorry nature of the ground, the severity of the climate, the difficulty of collecting his rent, but, more than all, the extraordinary though miserable system of Rundale, which was universal through the district. By this arrangement a parcel of land was divided and subdivided into an incredible number of small holdings, in which the tenant very likely held his proportion or share in 30 or 40 different places, which had no fences or walls whatever to mark them. The utter confusion and hopelessness of each tenant being able to know his own land, much more to plant or look after it, may well be imagined. And not only to land was this system applied, but also to more portable property. "In an adjacent island, 3 men were concerned in one horse; but the poor brute was rendered useless, as the unfortunate foot of the supernumerary long remained unshod, none of them being willing to acknowledge its dependency, and accordingly it became quite lame. There were many rows on the subject; at length one of the 'Company' came to the mainland and called on a magistrate for advice, stating that the animal was entirely useless now; that he had not only kept up decently his one hoof at his own expense, but had shod this 4th foot twice to boot."—*Facts from Gweedore.* With much perseverance and many struggles, Lord George Hill gradually changed the face of things. Though not without meeting a fearful amount of prejudice and opposition, he overcame and altered the Rundale system, improved the land, built schools, a ch., and a large store at Bunbeg, made roads, established a post-office, and, what is perhaps of more importance to the tourist, an hotel, which is comfortable, well-managed, and reasonable. This is a capital place both for the fisherman and the general visitor; the latter should by all means make an excursion to *Arrigal*, taking a car to the foot of the mountain, which can be ascended in about 2 hrs. "Midway up there is an immense belt of broken stones, unrelieved by a vestige of vegetation. The mountain narrows towards the top to a mere rugged path of a few inches in width, with an awful abyss on either side." The view from the summit is magnificent, extending over a perfect sea of mountains, as far as Knocklayde, near Ballycastle, in the county Antrim, and Benbulben and Bengore near Sligo, while the whole coast for miles lies at one's feet. The fishing on the Clady and the freshwater loughs is very good. If tolerably late in the season he will get sea-trout and some salmon; "almost any flies will do, something with red or black hackle, and a mixture with hare's ear in it."

The geology of Donegal consists mainly of gneiss and mica-slate, traversed in a N.E. direction by an axis of granite, containing the mineral called oligoclase, whose occurrence in Great Britain has been lately noticed. The investigations of Prof. Haughton and Mr. Scott show a close relation between the granites of Norway and Donegal.

Distances.—Dunglow, 13 m.; Dunfanaghy, 17; Bunbeg, 4; Dunlewy, 4; Cross Roads, 10; Magheraclogher, 5.

Conveyances.—A mail-car daily to Dunfanaghy and Letterkenny.

Excursions.—
1. Arrigal.
2. Dunlewy and Slieve Snaght.
3. Bunbeg.

From Gweedore the road lies through a wild and desolate district, broken here and there by a few scattered hamlets with their little patches of green conspicuous in the grey mountain scenery. Inland the lofty ranges occasionally peer over the moorlands, while seaward the view is broken by numberless inlets and creeks, beyond which the breakers are seen dashing over the cliffs of the numerous islands that dot the coast in such profusion in this district, which is known as the Rosses. The principal of these islands, generally inhabited for a portion of the year only, are Inishfree, Owey, Gula, and Cruit.

At 48½ m. the *Gweedore river* is crossed at a spot where a combination of rock and waterfall offers charming scenery; and at 51½ m. is the creek of the *Anagarry stream*, enlivened by a police-barrack. On the coast at Mulladergh, near Anagarry, is a rock known as Spanish Rock, from the occurrence of a wreck of a Spanish vessel, supposed to have belonged to the Armada. Within the memory of inhabitants of the parish, a number of well-finished brass guns were fished up, but unfortunately got into the hands of some travelling tinkers, by whose advice they were speedily broken up and sold to themselves, of course at a fabulous profit.

[56 m. rt. a road branches off to Roshin Lodge, the residence of Mrs. Forster. Close off the coast is *Rutland Island*, where, during the Lord Lieutenancy of the Duke of Rutland in 1785, 40,000*l*. was expended in making a military station and general emporium for this part of the country. The sand has now almost entirely buried the costly enterprise in oblivion. At Burton Port, near Roshin, the Marquis of Conyngham, the proprietor of this estate, has built a large grain-store.

A conspicuous feature in this scenery is *Aran Island*, which must not be confounded with those of the same name off the coast of Galway. It is of considerable size, but contains nothing of interest, save some fine cliff and cave scenery.]

2 m. N. of Burton Port is the isolated ruin of Dunglow Castle, afterwards called Castle Port.

58 m. *Dunglow*, a dreary-looking village on the side of a hill which rises rather sharply from the water's side. The inn is very poor; but a car can be obtained. Between 3 and 4 m. S.W. of Dunglow is the headland of Crohy, which the tourist should visit; for, though it is no great height 800 ft., it affords an admirable and curious view over the district of Templecrone, with its numberless lakes and inlets. On the coast to the S.W. overlooking Gweebarra Bay is a singular landslip, called by the inhabitants "*Tholla Bristha*" (broken earth). "The rocks seem to have been shaken and shivered to pieces—in fact, macadamized on a prodigious scale, and present an awfully shattered appearance. The chasm varies in its dimensions, the greatest gash being 12 ft. wide above and upwards of 25 deep: at some places the edges accurately correspond and are serrated."—*Donegal Tourist*. There are also numerous caves and natural arches all round this bit of coast. In the open loughs near Dunglow are quantities of fine yellow trout rising up to 5 lbs. The best sport is found in the Meenmore Lough, 2 m. to the N.W., near the old barracks. There are also lots of wild fowl and seal shooting to be had. At *Lough Anure*, 4 m. N.E., there is work for the geologist. "The environs consist of mica slate with coarse granular dolomite: on one spot will be found basilar idiocrase and epidote crystallized in 6-sided prisms, with common garnet of a reddish-brown colour."—*Gicsecke*.

Distances.—Letterkenny, 58 m.; Doocharry Bridge, 8; Glenties, 18; Gweedore, 13.

For the next 7 or 8 m. the way lies through an untameably wild country, but with such constant and shifting panoramas of mountains that the attention is never fatigued. The ranges, at the base of which the road is carried, are those of the Crohy hills, with their numerous shoulders and outliers. Farther back are the Dunlewy Mountains, Slievesnacht, Crockatarrive, Arrigal, and, as we get further S., the Glendowan and Derryveagh chains. In fact, if the weather is fine—and it all depends on that—there is scarce such another mountain view in the kingdom. 67 m, at the brow of a steep hill, the traveller all at once looks over the deep glen of the Gweebarra river and up the Owenwee, until it is lost in the heights of the Glendowan Mountains. A road runs up the pass, through Derryveagh, and emerges at Glenveagh Bridge (p. 88). The view, as the tourist descends the zigzag road, is of a very high order, and assumes an additional charm in contrast with the dreary moor that he has been traversing. The Gweebarra is crossed at *Doocharry Bridge*, where there are a police-barrack and a fishing-station, but no inn, which is a pity, for the stages are long and fatiguing, and the scenery in the neighbourhood would be quite sufficient to attract visitors. The Gweebarra is a fine salmon fishery, and belongs to Mr. Daniel of Donegal. The distance from Doocharry to Glenveagh Bridge is 11 m. A road runs across the hills to join the Fintown road, but a new one keeping along the S. bank of the Gweebarra, which soon opens into a noble estuary, is easier and more generally followed. In about 3 m. it leaves the river and ascends the hills again, joining the Fintown and Donegal road at or near the 74th m. Near this point a short road from Dunglow falls in, but it is impracticable for cars, on account of the necessity of crossing the Gweebarra at Ballynacarrick Ferry. There is a fine view, looking back over Crohy headland and the country toward Dunglow, while an equally fine one opens forward over the ranges of hills that intervene between the traveller and Donegal. In front of him, although, from the turnings of the road, it is difficult to keep one's bearings, are Knockrawer (1475 ft.), Aghla (1953), and Scraigs (1406), at the foot of which lie the mountain lough of Finn and the village of *Fintown* (Rte. 8), in which district' some lead-mines are now being worked. From the junction of the 2 roads the distance to Fintown is 6 m., and to Stranorlar 22 m. The watershed has now been reached, and the road rapidly descends a broad mountain vale to

77 m. *Glenties* (*Inn*: Devitt's), a small town, the situation of which, at the numerous converging glens, is its best point. It has a grand-looking union-house, which adds much to the distant beauty of the place. Good fishing is to be obtained here either in the Shallogan river, down whose vale we have been descending, or the Owenea, which rises in Lough Ea, a tarn some 7 m. in the mountains to the W. It is preserved by Lord Mountcharles and Col. Whyte. "The angler in the latter river will have sport if he is on at the time of a spate, but, as it rises and falls very quickly, it would be hardly worth his while to go there on a chance."

Distances.— Ardara, 6 m.; Naran, 8½; Doocharry, 10; Dunglow by the ferry, 14; Killybegs, 14; Donegal, 18.

[If the tourist is not pressed for time, he may go on to Ardara by Naran, instead of by the direct road. For the first few miles the way lies at the foot of the hills, affording fine views of Gweebarra Bay. 8½ m. *Naran*, is a primitive little fishing-village, pleasantly situated opposite the island of *Inishkeel*, on which the antiquary will find a couple of ruined churches. The hills which rise just behind the village should be ascended for the sake of the magnificent view, particularly in the direction of Ardara, where the coast-scenery of the cliffs is of the highest order. The whole of the promontory between Naran and Ardara is worth exploring for the sake of the remains. On Dunmore Hill, a headland 1 m. to the W., there are 10 old forts. "It was probably the grand signal-station, so that a signal made there would alarm the rest." To the S. of Naran is *Lough Doon*, in which there is an island, containing the "Bawan," a round fort, a massive circular building, which occupies the whole of the area. In former years, before the lake was partially drained, it appeared as if it was actually built out of the water. Close by is *Lough Birroge*, on which is another similar remain. About 1 m. to the S.W. is *Kiltooris Lough*, on the banks of which is Eden House, the residence of G. Hamilton, Esq. A rather large island rises from the centre, on which are the scanty ruins of a castle belonging to the O'Boyles. From Naran to Ardara the distance is 7 m. About halfway at Kilclooney there is a cromlech.] The direct road from Glenties is carried over a more level country than we have hitherto been traversing. [At 79 m. l. a road is given off to Donegal, which falls into the Killybegs and Donegal route between Inver Bridge and Mountcharles (Rte. 9).] Directly afterwards it runs alongside of the Owentocker river, which rises amongst the heights of Binbane (1493 ft., and falls into an inlet of the sea close by

83 m. *Ardara* (pronounced with the accent on the last syllable)— *Hotel:* Mollaney's,—a stupid little town, with nothing whatever of interest save its extremely pretty situation, at the wooded base of steeply escarped hills. A pedestrian who is not particular about his accommodation will find it a very good starting-point from whence to explore the grand beauties of the coast round by Loughros, Tormore, and Glen (Rte. 9. From the peculiarity of the situation of Ardara all the roads is that lead out of it—viz. to Inver, Killybegs, and Carrick—are carried through so many gaps in the hills, the finest of them being that which goes through the pass of Glengeask, one of the wildest and steepest glens in the district, in which the highest point of the road (a very bad one) is about 1000 ft. Close to the town is Woodhill, the residence of Major Nesbitt.

Distances.—Carrick, 13 m.; Glen, 15 by road, but by coast about 17; Killybegs, 10; Inver, 10.

From Ardara the tourist traverses a wild mountain road, passing between the heights of Altnandewon (1652 ft.), and Mulmosog (1157). 87 m. l. is Mulmosog House. Soon afterwards the watershed is reached, and the road descends the valley of the Oily river to 93 m. Killybegs (Rte. 9). *Hotels:* Rogers's, Coane's; both comfortable.

ROUTE 11.

FROM **LONDONDERRY** TO **GWEEDORE**, THROUGH **DUNFANAGHY**.

The most direct route lies through Letterkenny, from whence a car starts for Dunfanaghy and Gweedore every morning; but as the finest scenery of this district principally lies on the coast, it will be better for the tourist to proceed to Rathmelton, to which there are 3 ways of going. 1. The road from Londonderry follows the l. bank of the Foyle, passing Foyle Hill, at which point it branches off to the rt., skirting a range of high ground, of which Greenan Hill is the most elevated point.

6 m. rt. are Portlough, a small tarn, with an island and a ruined tower, and Castle Forward (T. Ferguson, Esq.), situated at the corner of Blanket Nook, a pill given off by Lough Swilly, which is crossed by a ferry as it begins to narrow at Fort Stewart Ferry. On the opposite bank are the seats of Fort Stewart (Sir James Stewart, Bart.) and Shellfield (N. Stewart, Esq.).

13 m. Rathmelton (*Inns*: Brown's; Coyle's).

2. Should the traveller prefer going round all the way by the road, he will turn off to the l. at Newtown Cuningham, and follow the E. bank of the Swilly river to

12½ m. the village of Manor Cuningham.

18 m. Letterkenny (*Hotel*, Hegarty's, comfortable) will be found in Rte. 10.

The road from hence to Rathmelton is very pretty, passing l. Gordlee (T. Patterson, Esq.); rt. Barn Hill (Rev. J. Irwin), Castle Wray (Capt. Mansfield), and Castle Grove (G. Wood, Esq.).

Leaving on l. the Glebe House, the tourist reaches

26 m. Rathmelton. 3. By rail to Farland, from whence a steamer runs across to Rathmelton.] As the greater portion of the route from Letterkenny is over elevated ground, the traveller gets beautiful views of the hills in the neighbourhood of Inch and Buncrana, on the opposite side of the Lough. Rathmelton is prettily situated on the Lannan, a picturesque mountain stream that flows past Kilmacrenan into Lough Fern, emerging from it under the same name, only a few yards from its point of entrance. Like the Bann, it was at one time famous for its pearls.

The principal objects of interest near Rathmelton are the ivy-covered ruins of Fort Stewart, built at the commencement of the 17th cent.; the demesne of Fort Stewart (Sir J. Stewart, Bart.) facing the Ferry; and a little higher up, the ruins of Killydonnell Abbey, a Franciscan monastery, founded in the 16th cent. by an O'Donnell, and a chapel of ease to the ecclesiastical establishment of Kilmacrenan. By an inquisition made by James I., it was found that the revenues amounted to the magnificent sum of 3s. There is a legend about the bell of the Abbey of Killydonnell, to the effect that it was carried off by some marauders from Tyrone, who embarked on the Lough with the bell in their vessel. A storm arose, and the sacrilegious robbers were drowned; to commemorate which act of retributive justice, the bell is heard to ring once every 7 years at midnight. A legend with a similar finale is prevalent at Tintagel on the Cornish coast.

[From Rathmelton the tourist may proceed to Kilmacrenan, and there catch the car for Dunfanaghy, or proceed by Gartan Lough to Dunlewy. The road to Kilmacrenan is highly picturesque, and follows the rapid mountain stream of the Lannan, which is crossed at Tullyhall, near Claragh (Mrs. Watt) and Ballyarr, the seat of Lord George Hill (p. 86).]

Distances from Rathmelton.—Letterkenny, 8 m.; Derry, 13; Fort Stewart Ferry, 3; Rathmullan, 6½; Kilmacrenan, 6½; Milford, 4; Killydonnell, 4.

Excursions.—
1. Rathmullan.
2. Milford.
3. Kilmacrenan.

The road to Rathmullan runs alongside the estuary of the Lannan, and the W. shore of Lough Swilly, and about half-way crosses the embouchure of the Glenalla river that rises in the high grounds between the Lough and Mulroy Bay, and flows past Glenalla House (T. Hart, Esq.) and woods, which are very pretty features in the landscape. Further down are the woods of Hollymount, and

19½ m. the little town of *Rathmullan.* (*Inn*, Henderson's, good). "Close to it are the ruins of a priory of Carmelite friars, and a castle adjoining, formerly occupied by the M'Swyne Faugh, the possessor of Fanait. The eastern part, used as a ch. until a late period, exhibits considerable traces of pointed Gothic architecture. Over the E. window there still remains a figure of St. Patrick. The architecture of the remainder of the building is of the Elizabethan age, a great part of it having been rebuilt by Bishop Knox, of the diocese of Raphoe, in 1618, on obtaining possession of the manor of Rathmullan from Turlogh Oge M'Swyne."—*Lord G. Hill.* In the churchyard is a monument to the memory of the Hon. W. Pakenham, Captain of the 'Saldanha,' wrecked off this coast in 1811.

Rathmullan occupies a sheltered position at the foot of a range of hills that intervene between Lough Swilly and Mulroy Bay, of which the highest point is Crochanaffrin, 1137 ft. It is worth while making an excursion either up this hill or Croaghan, 1010 ft., which is nearer; for the extraordinary view over the inlets and indentations of this singular coast will put the traveller more in mind of Norwegian fiords than British scenery.

[Before leaving Rathmullan for Milford, the tourist who is fond of wild coast scenery should take the opportunity of exploring the peninsula of Fanet or Fanait, the ancient property of "the sept of the O'Breslans, descendants of Conaing, 3rd son of Conaill Gulban, son of Nial of the 9 hostages, who possessed Tir Connell." The O'Breslans, however, were succeeded by the M'Swynes, who established themselves and built several fortresses. Physically speaking, Fanet is intersected by 3 short ranges of hills running across the peninsula, viz., the Rathmullan range just mentioned; the Knockalla Hills, which attain a height of 1200 ft.; and a still more northerly group, about 800 ft.

A good road runs along the shore of Lough Swilly as far as Knockalla Battery, but as the Knockalla Hills here intervene, rising precipitously from the water, the traveller by car will be obliged to return and make a detour. Of course this does not apply to the pedestrian. This road is worth the drive, both for the sake of the rock scenery on the W., and the distant hills on the E. or Buncrana side, comprising the district of Inishowen. It passes Rathmullan House, the charming seat of T. Batt, Esq.; Fort Royal late Capt. Wray; and Kinnegar Strand; succeeding which there is some good rock scenery extending up to Lamb's Head Bay, and down thence to Knockalla Battery. Near Lamb's Head Bay, at a village called Drumhallagh, is a tolerably perfect "giant's bed," formed of large flat stones placed on their edge.

The cross-road to Fanait runs right across the peninsula to the shores of Mulroy Water, and keeps the E. bank of that beautiful estuary, skirting the base of the Knockalla Hills.

10 m. on the shore of one of the narrow inlets of Mulroy is the tower of Moross Castle, the most important of the fortresses of the M'Swynes. Near this point the main road again crosses the peninsula, between the 2 northerly ranges of hills, reappears on Lough Swilly at Ballymastocker Bay, the scene of the wreck of the 'Saldanha' in 1811, and from thence skirts the coast to Doagh, one of the most primitive native villages that it is possible to conceive. The coast scenery here is particularly fine, especially at the Seven Arches, a series of marine caves accessible by land. Near the Brown George Rock is a splendid natural arch, 80 ft. in height.

18 m. Fanad Head is the extreme westerly boundary of Lough Swilly, the entrance of which between the 2 heads, Fanad and Dunaff, is just 4 m. This dangerous coast is protected at this point by a lighthouse, 90 ft. above high water, consisting of 9 lamps, showing a deep red seawards, and a fixed white light towards the harbour. Should the tourist be a pedestrian, he should, instead of returning by the same road, work his way to the S.W., and cross one of the narrow inlets of Mulroy by a ferry between Leatbeg and Lower Town, and thus proceed either to Glen, through Carrickart, or Milford.]

7 m. Milford (Rte. 10), formerly known by the euphonious name of Ballynagolloglough, is most charmingly placed nearly equidistant from the head of Mulroy Bay and Lough Fern; the latter a fine sheet of water 4 m. in circumference, and fed by the Lannan. The scenery near Milford is well worth exploring, particularly on the Bunlin river, a small stream that flows through a romantic glen into Mulroy, forming in its course a fine waterfall, known as the Goland Loop.

Crossing Bunlin Bridge, the road to Carrickart skirts closely the W. shore of Mulroy, keeping on l. the group of hills that intervene near

Lough Glen and Sheephaven. But as the round is scarcely interesting enough to warrant it, the tourist should cut across by a mountain road, and join the route from Kilmacrenan.

Glen is a small village at the head of Glen Lough, a long narrow sheet of water running from N.E. to S.W., connected by a short stream, called the Lackagh river, with the Sheephaven, and drained by the Owen Carrow, which runs hence to Glenveagh (Rte. 10).

The student of physical geography cannot fail to be struck with the parallel directions of the great valleys of Donegal, together with their respective lakes and streams, almost all, without exception, from the N.E. to the S.W. It would seem as though some tremendous force, acting from the opposite direction, had been exerted simultaneously over the whole district, and had probably been the cause of the singular fiords which, it will be noticed, always have the same direction inland.

An excursion should be made from Glen to visit Lough Salt, 3 m. to the S., and on the road to Kilmacrenan —one of the most peculiar and romantic localities in the country. It is situated at the height of 1000 ft. above the sea, and at the foot of Lough Salt mountain, which rises perpendicularly on the E. to a height of 1546 ft. It is to this fact that it owes its name—Lough-agus-Alt, "the Lough and the Crag," being corrupted into Lough Salt. "Ascending the steep sides of the Kilmacrenan Mountain, we at length reached the top of the mountain, and suddenly turning the point of a cliff that jutted out and checked the road, we came abruptly into a hollow something like the crater of an extinct volcano, which was filled almost entirely by a lovely lake, on the rt. hand of which rose the high peak of the mountain— so bare, so serrated, so tempest-worn, so vexed at the storms of the Atlantic,

that, if matter could suffer, we might suppose that this lofty and precipitous peak presented the appearance of material endurance. Here were the brown heath, grey lichen, green fern, and red crow's-bill; and then, down the face of the cliff, from the top to the water's edge, the black, seared streak of a meteoric stone, which had shattered itself against the crest of the mountain, and rolled down in fiery fragments into the lake, was distinctly visible."— *C. Otway.*

The lake is of the great depth of 240 ft., and is said to be never frozen. There is another tarn, Lough Greenan, at a lower elevation on the W. side; and Lough Reclan, a still smaller one, on the N., giving off a streamlet that flows into Glen Lough. The view looking S. to Kilmacrenan, 4 m. distant, is pretty, but not to be compared to that extending on the N. over Glen Lough and Sheephaven, with its noble crags and the blue waters of the Atlantic; while to the W. the summits of the Donegal Alps are visible in the lofty crests of Muckish, Dooish, and Arrigal, with its cone-like top.

1½ m. the road crosses the Lackagh, and emerges on the sands which form the head of Sheephaven. To the N.E. they extend for a long distance under the name of the Campion and Rosapenna sands—the latter reaching to beyond Carrickart. Fifty years ago a beautiful residence built by Lord Boyne existed at Rosapenna, but it has long been as deeply overwhelmed by sand as the ch. of Perranzabuloe in Cornwall.

"A line of coast and country extends from the sea deep into the land, exhibiting one wide waste of red sand; for miles not a blade of grass, not a particle of bloom; but hills and dales, and undulating swells, smooth, solitary, desolate, reflecting the sun from their polished surface of one uniform hue. Fifty years ago this line of coast was as highly improved as the opposite shore of Ards, and contained the comfortable mansion of Lord Boyne, an old-fashioned manorial house and garden, with avenues and terraces, surrounded with walled parks. But now not a vestige of this is to be seen—one common mountain of sand covers all."—*Sketches in Ireland.* The cause of all this mischief appears to have been the carelessly permitting the rabbits to gnaw the roots of the tent grass (*Arundo arenaria*), which, when protected, serves as a sufficient guard against the incursion of the sand.

Beyond Rosapenna, at Downing's Bay, there is one of the finest views in Donegal, looking up and down Sheephaven, with the woods of Ards, and the tower of Doe Castle—backed up in the distance by the ponderous mass of Muckish.

Before arriving at Creeslough, the tourist should cross the Duntally, and visit Doe Castle, a singular stronghold of the M‘Swynes, which has been, to a certain extent, modernised and rendered habitable by the present owner. The prison will be found in the dairy, which contains the old gallows, with its beam fitted with notches. The building as it at present stands is surrounded by a bawn, upon which some small cannons are mounted. A little to the N., but separated by a prolongation of the marsh at the head of Sheephaven, is Ards House, A. Stewart, Esq., which, with its extensive mansion, beautiful woods, and adjacent farm, is one of the most desirable places in the N. of Ireland. The views, however, from this side the haven, are not so diversified or pleasant as they are from Rosapenna.

4 m. Creeslough is a poor little village situated on the N.E. slope of Muckish. "The Pig's Back" Rte. 10, which raises its truncated mass to a height of 2197 ft. Crossing the Faymore river, the road turns northwest, having on l. Sessiagh Lough,

and on rt. Marble Hill, the seat of G. Fitzgerald, Esq., which overlooks a pretty bay near the entrance of Sheephaven.

10 m. Dunfanaghy is a neat little town with a very fair hotel, whence the traveller can comfortably make his excursions to the scenery of Horn Head. On the way from Dunfanaghy a narrow channel is crossed, through which the tide rushes with great rapidity, to Horn Head House, the residence of Rev. C. Stewart.

1 m. to the W. in a direct line will be found M‘Swyne's Gun, concerning which marvellous fables are told. The coast here is very precipitous, and perforated with caverns, one of which, running in some distance, is connected with the surface above by a narrow orifice. Through this, in rough weather, the sea dashes, throwing up a volume of water, accompanied by a loud explosion or boom, said to have been heard as far as Derry! Such blow-holes are not uncommon on the coast of South Wales and Cornwall, although, of course, the effects differ in proportion to the scale of the phenomenon. A little to the N.E. of this spot is a circular castle. Horn Head is a projection in shape somewhat resembling a horn, bordered on one side by the inlet of Sheephaven, though on the other the coast trends away to the S. The cliffs are 800 ft. in height, and grandly precipitous. The view from the summit of the head is one of boundless Atlantic ocean, broken only on the N.W. by the islands of Inishbeg, Inishdooy, Inishbofin, and Tory; and on the N.E. by the different headlands of this rugged coast, viz., Melmore, Rinmore, Fanad, Dunaff, and Malin Heads, while on the E. is seen in the distance the little island of Inishtrahull. The cliffs in many places are higher and more romantic, but the view from Horn Head is one *per se*, and should not be omitted by the northern traveller in Ireland. The student of

[*Ireland.*] F

Natural History will find plenty of ornithological interest amongst the various sea-birds that frequent these cliffs, amongst which are the shell-drake (*Tadorna vulpanser*), the guillemot (*Uria troile*), the sea-parrot, the cormorant, the shag (*Phalocrocorax graculus*), the gannet, the stormy petrel, the speckled diver (*Colymbus glacialis*), and many others. The distance from Dunfanaghy to the signal tower is about 4 m.

Conveyances.—Car to Letterkenny and to Gweedore daily.

Distances. — Letterkenny, 24 m.; Kilmacrenan, 17 ; Milford, 18 ; Glen, 10 ; Rathmullan, 25 ; Doe Castle, 8 ; Ards, 6; Horn Head, 4; Cross Roads, 6¼; Gweedore, 22.

Excursions.—
1. Tory Island.
2. Horn Head.
3. Falcarragh and Muckish.
4. Doe and Ards.

[Should the tourist be adventurous enough to visit Tory Island (anc. Toirinis), which lies some miles from Horn Head, he should start on his expedition from Dunfanaghy. It is a bleak and desolate island, although containing some objects of interest; and if tradition is worth anything, was considered important enough to fight for in the early days, "when giants were in the land." The Book of Ballymote states that it was possessed by the Fomorians, a race of pirates and giants who inhabited Ireland 12 centuries before the Christian era. One of their number, named Conaing, erected a tower on the island, as is recorded in the Book of Leacan :—

"The Tower of the Island, the Island of the Tower,
The citadel of Conaing, the son of Fœbar."

It contains a portion of a round tower, called Clog-teach, "The Bell-House," and the remains of a ruined castle, together with a modern lighthouse, the only token of the civilised world on the island. The rock scenery of its coast is very fine and characteristic. "Some leagues out at sea, but seeming within your grasp, lay Tory Island, rising out of the deep like a castellated city, lofty towers, church spires, battlements, batteries, and bastions, apparently presented themselves, so strangely varied and so fantastically deceptive were its cliffs."— *Otway*. Porphyritic syenite appears to be the geological structure.

The tourist must be prepared for any emergencies in the matter of accommodation, and, in case of rough weather suddenly coming on, of unlimited detention on the island.]

5½ m. the road runs rather inland, and crosses the Ray river.

[6½ m., at the village of Cross Roads, or Falcarragh, a mountain-road through Muckish Gap joins the Dunlewy route. It follows the glen of the Ray, and skirts the base of Muckish.]

Adjoining Falcarragh is Ballyconnell House, the seat of Wybrants Olphert, Esq., in whose grounds is a stone of some local notoriety, called Clough-a-neely. In old Myrath ch.-yard is the cross of St. Columbkill, made of one piece of rock, said to have been brought by St. Columb from Muckish Mountain. Falcarragh is a good point from whence to ascend Muckish 2190 ft., which will well repay the trouble, though from its steeply escarped sides it is no easy work. "The geological structure consists of a very thin slaty mica, granular quartz, and silver white mica. At the height of 500 ft. is an extensive bed of white quartz sand in very minute grains, which has been exported to the glass-works of Dumbarton, being considered an excellent material."—*Giesecke*.

A little further on, the Tullaghobegly is crossed, as it descends from the Altan Lough, a savage tarn under the precipices of Arrigal (Rte. 10), the peak of which becomes a prominent object on the E.

From hence to Gweedore there is nothing to detain the tourist. The road runs over a desolate mountain-district, keeping on rt. the Bloody Foreland, the hill above which is upwards of 1000 ft. As the coast is again approached, the islands of Inishsirrer, Inishmeane, and Gola are conspicuous.

18½ m. Clady Bridge, or Bunbeg, where there are a store, a ch., and glebe-house, belonging to the Gweedore property.

22 m. Gweedore Hotel (Rte. 10).

ROUTE 12.

FROM LONDONDERRY TO BELFAST, BY THE NORTHERN COUNTIES RAILWAY.

The Northern Counties Rly. crosses the Foyle by the new bridge, and keeps close to the brink of the water for several miles, accompanied for some distance by the pretty villas of the Derry citizens.

5 m. *Culmore*. Here the Foyle narrows, previous to the sudden expansion known as Lough Foyle, which in several places is 7 m. in breadth. The fort of Culmore, a triangular tower on the l. of the rly., was built in the 16th cent. by the O'Dohertys, and afterwards kept up to secure the possessions of the English at Derry.

Crossing the estuary of the Faughan river, the line trends to the S.E., following the curve of the bay to

7 m. *Eglinton*. On rt. 2 m. are the villages of Muff, Foyle Park, and Templemoyle Agricultural School, occupying very pretty situations on the banks of the Muff Glen. There is a village of the same name on the opposite side of the lough, which must not be confounded with this one. On either side, the mountain scenery begins to assume larger dimensions; on the l. the hills of Inishowen loom in the distance; the highest point being Slieve Snaght 2019 ft. between Buncrana and Moville. On the rt. an important chain occupies the area between Derry and Dungiven, where it joins another and more marked group extending northwards between Newtown Limavaddy and Coleraine.

12¾ m. *Carrickhugh*: on rt. is Walworth Wood and House (Col. Sampson).

13¼ m. *Ballykelly*. This village is the property of the Fishmongers' Company, who in 1619 erected a large fortified mansion.

15 m. Newtown Junction, [leading to 2 m. rt. *Newtown Limavaddy* (*Inn*: Queen's Arms), which obtained its name from Lim-an-madadh, "Dog's Leap," a glen on the banks of which the O'Cahans, the first founders, erected a castle. Adjoining this a second was built, in 1608, by Sir Thomas Phillips, forming the nucleus of a village (Pop. 2732.. It is very beautifully situated in the valley of the Roe, and at the foot of a group of mountains, which are worth exploration by the geological tourist. (*Introd.* p. xxvi.) On the E. are Benyevenagh 1260 ft., and Keady Mountain 1101 ft., while to the S., Donald's Hill 1318, and Craiggore, are the most prominent. As far as the town of Newtown Limavaddy is concerned, there is little to detain the visitor, but the valley of the Roe may be followed up to Dungiven 9 m., and thence to Maghera or Draperstown, in which route the traveller will meet with some very peculiar and interesting scenery. In the immediate neighbourhood of the town

F 2

are Drenagh House (C. M'Causland, Esq.), Roe Park (Harvey Nicholson, Esq.), Streeve, Hermitage, &c. The Sperrin Hills run E. from Strabane to Draperstown; then turn rather abruptly to the N. to Coleraine, their course being marked by the towns of Maghera and Garvagh on the E., Dungiven and Newtown on the W. Between these 2 places, however, a minor chain runs in from Londonderry, interrupted only by the valley of the Roe.

Excursions.—
1. Dungiven.
2. Benyevenagh.
3. Keady.

Dungiven is in a charming situation at the confluence of the Roe with the 2 rivers Owen Nagh and Owen Beg, and at the foot of Benbradagh, which rises to the height of 1490 ft. directly to the E. of the town, and is cultivated nearly to its summit. To the S. are the Sperrin Mountains, the most lofty points of which are Sawel 2240 ft., and Mullaghancany 2070 ft. Dungiven contains ruins of the Skinners' Company's Castle, or fortified bawn, built in 1618, and also of an abbey, picturesquely placed on a rock 200 ft. above the Roe. It has a nave and chancel, the latter lighted by two lancet windows deeply splayed within, with a mitre on each side, the whole being surrounded by a blocked arch resting on corbels; there is also a square-headed window above. The nave is separated from the chancel by a good circular arch of apparently Trans. Norm., and has also in the N. side a circular-headed doorway. The church has a belfry at the S. angle of the W. front, which formerly exhibited the features of a round tower or cloictheach. Notice under an elaborate Dec. arch in the chancel the altar-tomb of Cooey-na-gall, a chief of the O'Cahans. It bears the effigy of a recumbent knight, and the sides are sculptured with armed figures. This abbey was founded in 1100 by the O'Cahans, and, having fallen to ruins, was restored with great solemnity by the Archbishop of Armagh. The clan of the O'Cahans held their territory under the O'Neills, "and, being of the greatest authority in these parts, had the honour of throwing the shoe over the head of O Neill when chosen, according to the barbarous ceremony then practised upon some high hill in the open air."—*Gibson.* Close to the town is Pellipar House (J. Ogilby, Esq.). The road to Draperstown runs over very elevated ground to the base of the White Mountain, in which is the source of the Roe, and then emerges through the romantic pass of Evishgore. The schist rocks in the neighbourhood of Dungiven are famous for their quartz crystals, called Dungiven diamonds, many of which are found of great size. The old ch. of Banagher, nearly 3 m. S.W. of the village, should be visited for the sake of its doorway, which is square-headed, and has inclined sides, somewhat resembling the one at Glendalough (Rte. 24). In the ch-yard is the tomb of St. Muiredach O'Heney, on which a curious relievo of the saint is depicted outside. Dr. Petrie considers it to date from the latter part of the 11th cent. "There is a custom in this neighbourhood which testifies the superstitious respect in which this monument is still held. In any horse-race, if a handful of the sand adjacent to the tomb be thrown upon the horse as it passes, it is thought that it will ensure success in the race."—*Doyle.* A similar early tomb is found at Bovevagh ch, between Dungiven and Newton. It is faced with sandstone, though it is minus the likeness of the saint.

Conveyances from Dungiven.—Car to Derry.

Distances.—Draperstown, 12 m.; N. Limavaddy, 9; Maghera, 13; Derry, 19.]

IRELAND. Route 12.—MacGilligan—Coleraine. 101

20 m. at Bellarena is a marine residence of Sir F. Heygate, Bart., at the mouth of the Roe and the foot of the mountain of Benyevenagh 1260 ft., "the face of which is encumbered by ponderous and shapeless masses, rising in successive stages to the base of the steep basaltic summit, and then breaking into pinnacles and precipitous cliffs. Standing on one of these and looking along the face of the mountain, the successive lines of rudely-formed hillocks, the basaltic face they present to the great mountain precipices, and the various beds of basalt and ochre which occur in earth, together with the isolated pinnacles which yet remain on some of them, explain the nature of these vast landslips and this magnificent under cliff."—*Portlock*. The geologist will perceive that the general composition of these masses of hill is chalk, capped by conglomerate and basalt, and resting on liassic or oolitic clays and shales. A little further on at *MacGilligan* the line approaches very closely to the escarped rocks, which contain numerous caves, attesting the long-continued and destructive action of the sea. Both this latter locality and Down Hill 26 m. are romantic in the extreme, and during the summer season attract large numbers of holiday-makers from Derry for the purposes of bathing and picnic celebrations. "A singular combination of picturesque beauty and grandeur presents itself at MacGilligan. Here the cliffs, everywhere striking, increase in altitude, and the pastoral banks which they cap are here much more varied by verdant knolls, sylvan dells, and terraced platforms. High on one of the latter, with several cottages, stands the ch. of MacGilligan, one of the most singularly and romantically situated of all our sacred edifices."—*Fraser*. Both Mac Gilligan and Benyevenagh are good botanizing fields, yielding amongst others—Botrychium lunaria, Ajuga alpina, Orobanche rubra, Hieracium murorum, H. Lawsoni, Dryas octopetala, Saxifraga oppositifolia, Arenaria verna, Draba incana, Ranunculus hirsutus. Looking across the estuary of the Foyle are the mountains forming the promontory of Inishowen Head. MacGilligan is interesting to scientific men, as being the base-line on which the Trigonometrical Survey of Ireland was laid down in 1826. At Down Hill the rly. pierces the chalk by a longish tunnel. The effects produced by the disruption of strata are even more peculiar than at MacGilligan, and show themselves in the form of isolated pinnacles and caves, the largest of which, called the Piper's Cave, is about 110 ft. in length. The geologist should also visit the Gap of Carnowry, "which terminates in a very beautiful fall, formed of successive cascades, where the ochreous conglomerate and basalt are seen in contact. The basalt penetrates as a vein into the conglomerate, and small fragments of flints are found in an amygdaloid, as at Ballycastle (Rte. 13.), indicating important chemical and mechanical changes."—*Portlock*. At Down Hill was the seat of Sir Hervey Bruce, built by the eccentric Earl of Bristol, and famous for its library and picture-galleries, which were unfortunately destroyed by fire, including the sculpture of Boy and Dolphin, by Michael Angelo.

The line now runs close to the Bann, which is crossed by a long and peculiarly light bridge at

33 m. *Coleraine*, pronounced Coole-raine anc. Cuil-rathaine) (*Hotel:* M'Grotty's) (Rte. 13., dates its importance from the reign of James I., who granted the whole of this district to the London Companies. They, however, did not trouble themselves much about its sanitary arrangements, if we are to believe the statement of Pynnar in 1618, "that part of the town is so dirty that no man

is able to go into it, especially what is called the market-place." Coleraine is now a clean, busy place, largely connected with the linen trade, and well situated on the Bann, which is crossed by a bridge connecting the suburb of Waterside with the main portions of the town (Pop. 5631). There are extensive salmon fisheries at the Crannagh, near the mouth of the river, and again higher up at the Cutty, where there is a fall of 13 ft., and consequently a salmon-leap. In former days Coleraine possessed a priory, monastery, and castle, all of which have disappeared, but on Mount Sandel, 1 m. S.E., there is a very large rath 200 ft. high, and surrounded by a dry fosse. It is mentioned in the 'Annals of the Four Masters' as having been built in 1197, and is supposed to have been the site of De Courcey's castle. In the immediate neighbourhood are Jackson Hall and Somerset (H. R. Richardson, Esq.), both of them situated on the banks of the river.

Though the Bann is here tidal, and Coleraine a seaport, there is at its mouth a bar, causing so much obstruction that the real harbour may be said to be at Portrush (Rte. 13).

Conveyances.—Rail to Derry, Portrush, and Belfast. Car to Bushmills; also to Kilrea.

Distances. — Portstewart, 3½ m.; Portrush, 6½; Ballymoney, 8; Mac Gilligan, 10; Newtown Limavaddy, 21; Bushmills, 8.

The rail now follows up the rt. bank of the Bann, quiting it at

41 m. *Ballymoney*, which is an industrious town extensively concerned in the sales of "Coleraines" and other linens, but does not possess much to interest the general tourist. Conveyances to Ballycastle, 17 m. distant (Rte. 13). At Dunloy, 49 m. the line is carried between 2 hills about 400 ft. respectively, and has on l. 3 m. Lissanoure Castle, the seat of G. Macartney, Esq. Some 3 m.

W. of Dunloy, in the picturesque mountain district known as the Craigs, is the interesting cromlech of the Broadstone, of which the incumbent stone is 10 ft. in length, and rests partially upon 2 supporters, the others having fallen. We then cross the watershed, and follow the Main river, a small stream flowing due S. into Lough Neagh, to

62 m. *Ballymena* (*Hotel:* Adare Arms), next to Coleraine the most important town in the district, which, since the introduction of the linen trade in 1733, has largely increased in population. It is said that the sale of brown linens alone averages 1,000,000*l.* yearly. It is a well-built and well-to-do town of some 8000 Inhab., situated on the Braid, which soon joins the Main.

About 1½ m. to the W. are Galgorm Castle, formerly a seat of the Earls of Mountcashel, and now of J. Young, Esq., and Grace Hill, a Moravian settlement, founded in 1746.

Conveyances.—Rly. to Belfast. Car to Kilrea.

Distances.—Maghera, 18 m.; Port Glenone, 9.

The line again runs side by side with the Main to

70 m. Cookstown Junction. [From hence a branch rly. runs W. to Cookstown, passing

3 m. *Randalstown*, a pleasant little business town on the Main, which is crossed by a bridge of 9 arches. It suffered considerable damage from the hands of the insurgents in 1798. The church is E. Eng., with an octagonal spire. The principal object of interest, however, is the beautiful demesne of *Shane's Castle* (late Viscount O'Neill), which stretches from the town to and along the shores of Lough Neagh for a distance of 3 m. The Main flows through the grounds, and is crossed by an ornamental bridge, connecting them with the Deer-park, which is of considerable extent. The former mansion was utterly destroyed by fire in 1816,

Route 12.—*Randalstown — Cookstown.*

when nothing was saved but the family papers. At present a portion of the stables has been converted into a residence, all that is left of the castle being some ruined towers and the fortified esplanade, upon which is a conservatory. The present representative of this once princely family, which claimed sovereignty over all the chiefs of Ulster — is the Rev. William O'Neill, who assumed the surname and arms by the will of the late Earl. The tourist can visit the tomb of one of the O'Neills, in the private burial-ground near the castle. The geologist will find traces of columnar basaltic formation at the back of the gardens.

From Randalstown the rly. sweeps along the northern bank of the lough, approaching it very closely at 11 m. Toome, where the Bann is crossed as it emerges from the lake, by a viaduct, as also by a bridge of 9 arches carrying the turnpike road. At Toome are the stables of a castle built by Lord Conway in the 17th cent. The river flows due N. for 1½ m., and then expands into a small sheet of water known as Lough Beg. As the Bann is the only river carrying away the waters of Lough Neagh, which is supplied by 10 or 12 streams, it is not a matter of much wonder that the surrounding shores are very subject to inundations, though they have been considerably checked by the operations of the Drainage Commissioners. This has been effected by lowering the Lough to its summer level, widening the lower basin, and forming a canal near the castle at Coleraine.

16 m. *Castle Dawson*, a small town possessed by the Dawson family since 1633, whose seat, Moyola Park, adjoins the town on the banks of the river of the same name. The eccentric Earl of Bristol erected an obelisk to commemorate the virtues of this family.

About 8 m. higher up the Moyola is *Maghera*, formerly a place of some antiquity, though now a quiet linen-bleaching little town, pleasantly situated at the base of the S.E. corner of the Sperrin mountains, which run hither from Strabane and turn suddenly to the N. to Coleraine. Carntogher 1521 ft., White Mountain 996, and Muinard 2064, are the principal heights. It is a fine mountain walk of 13 m. from Maghera to Dungiven (p. 100) through the pass of Glenshane. The old ch. contains over the W. door a rude sculpture of the Crucifixion, and in the ch.-yard is the tomb of Lenri, in whose grave, when opened some years since, a silver crucifix was found. The archaeologist will also find several good raths in the neighbourhood.

19 m. *Magharafelt* (*Hotel:* M'Fall's) is a linen town, belonging to the Salters' Company. The scenery on the W. is rather striking, the Slieve Gullion Mountains rising to the height of 1700 ft. A 2nd road leads from Magharafelt to Dungiven through Draperstown, near which is Derrynoyd R. Babington, Esq.).

25 m. *Moneymore* (*Inn:* Drapers' Arms), the property of the Drapers' Company, who have laid out large sums in the improvement of the place. Unfortunately, in the process the ancient castle was taken away to make room for a public-house, a circumstance to be regretted the more, as it is described by Pynnar as having been one of the most perfect in Ireland. Spring Hill is the residence of W. L. Conyngham, Esq.: the mansion is between 200 and 300 years old. The terminus of the branch line is reached at

30 m. *Cookstown* (*Hotel:* Imperial), a pretty, though singularly built place of one street, more than a mile in length. The pleasant aspect of the town is enhanced by the proximity of Killymoon, formerly the residence of the family of Stew-

art, the proprietors and founders of Cookstown. The house was built by Nash in the castellated style. At Derryloran the antiquary will find ruins of an old ch., and at Loughry, 2 m. to the S., a cromlech.

At Ardbo on the shores of Lough Neagh, about 6 m. from Cookstown, are the ruins (of very rude work) of the Abbey of St. Kieran; and close by stands a large sculptured cross, the figures of which are much weathered.'

Conveyances. — Car to Stewartstown, also to Dungannon.

Distances. — Dungannon, 10½ m.; Stewartstown, 6.]

From the Cookstown Junction the main line keeps in sight of the lough to

73 m. the county town of *Antrim* (anc. Auntruibh), situated on the banks of the Six Mile Water as it joins the waters of Lough Neagh (*Hotel:* Massareene Arms) (Pop. 2800). Historically, Antrim is known as the scene of a battle' in the reign of Edward III. between the English and native Irish, and again in 1798 of a fierce engagement between the insurgents, who had marched on the town simultaneously from Belfast, Carrickfergus, Ballymena, and Shane's Castle. So obstinate, however, was the defence, that they retreated with the loss of nearly 1000 men, though the victory was dearly gained by the death of Earl O'Neill. It is a well-built pleasant town, doing a considerable trade in linen and paper making. The principal building is the church, which has a good tower and an octagonal spire, but the suburbs possess far greater attractions than the town. Between the river and the lake is Antrim Castle, the seat of Lord Ferrard and Massareene. The present building dates from 1662, and is approached by a Tudor gateway, "the doors of which are cast iron, and are opened from a room overhead by means of machinery." The front of the house faces the gate, and is flanked by 2 square towers, each in their turn finished off by smaller round towers at the angles. It is decorated with the family arms, and medallions containing portraits of Charles I. and II The principal beauty of the place is in the gardens, which are very well laid out, and embellished with fishponds. Sir John Clotworthy, the founder of the castle, was granted a patent for building and repairing as many barks on the lake as were needed for the king's use. In connection with this singular right, a naval battle took place in 1642 between the Irish garrison at Charlemont and the amphibious garrison of Antrim, "but the rebels, being freshwater soldiers, were soon forced on shore, and the victors, pursuing their fortune, followed them to the fort and forced them to surrender it, and in this expedition 60 rebels were slain, and as many brought prisoners to Antrim."— *Sir R. Cox.*

About ¾ m. N.E. of the town, in the grounds of Steeple (G. J. Clarke, Esq.), is a very perfect round tower. It is 95 ft. high, and 53 ft. in circumference, and capped by a conical block, put up in lieu of the original, which was shattered by lightning. The door is between 9 and 10 ft. from the ground, facing the N., and is formed of single large stones for the lintels outside and inside. Between the 2 is fixed a large beam of oak. The whole of the doorway is constructed of blocks of coarse grained basalt, and is but 4 ft. 4 in. in height. It is also remarkable "for having a pierced cross within a circle, sculptured in relievo on the stone immediately over the lintel. Though the foundation of the church of Antrim is ascribed, perhaps erroneously, to St. Mochaoi, a contemporary of St. Patrick, the popular tradition of the country gives the erection of the town to the celebrated builder Gobhan Saer, who flourished in the 7th cent."— *Petrie.*

Conveyances from Antrim. — Rail to Belfast and Coleraine.

Distances. — Shane's Castle, 3 m.; Carrickfergus, 15¼; Belfast, 22; Randalstown, 5.

Excursions.
1. Ram Island.
2. Carrickfergus.

This would seem the proper place for a brief description of Lough Neagh (anc. Loch n'Eatharh, the largest lake in the British Isles, being 20 m. in length, 12 in breadth, 80 in circumference, and embracing an area of 98,255 acres. No less than 5 counties are washed by its waters, which form an important item in the physical geography and industrial resources of this part of Ulster. Although 10 rivers contribute to swell its basin, only one, the Bann, serves as an escape; to which circumstance may be attributed the inundations of the low shores, which frequently happened to such an extent before the drainage improvements that 30,000 acres were often flooded. The lake is about 45 ft. in the deep parts; though from the soundings of Lieut. Graves it appears to be 100 ft. in some places. The difference between winter and summer level averages about 6 ft. It contains char, and the species of trout known as gillaroo, also the pullan or fresh-water herring *Salmo lavaretus*. Perhaps the principal interest that attaches to Lough Neagh arises from its great size, as, from the absence of mountain scenery from its immediate neighbourhood, it lacks a very important feature common to lake districts. "In the white sand on the shore very hard and beautiful stones, known as Lough Neagh pebbles, are found; they are chiefly chalcedony, generally yellow, or varied with red, susceptible of a fine polish, and much valued for seals and necklaces." — *Lewis.* The waters of this lake had also the reputation of possessing petrifying properties, from trees having been found in this state at various times; but it has been considered by Gen. Portlock that they belong to the tertiary formations, from whence they have been washed out. " The clays and sands, with lignites, on Lough Neagh and Lough Beg, were of lacustrine origin, proving a former level of these lakes from 10 to 30 ft. higher than the present. The trunks and stems of trees found in the clay must either have been drifted and sunk into the soft mud, or have been silted up with mud after their destruction, which would imply a successive rise and fall of the lake." The legend of the buried city, which appertains to almost every large lake in the kingdom, is in full force on Lough Neagh, and has obtained a world-wide celebrity from its being the subject of one of Moore's favourite ballads :—

" On Lough Neagh's banks, as the fisherman strays,
When the clear cold eve's declining,
He sees the Round Towers of other days,
In the wave beneath him shining."

It is singular that such a large basin should contain so few islands, and none of any size. Ram Island should be visited, on account of the pretty cottage ornée of the late Earl O'Neill, and also for its round tower, which is not in such good preservation as the one at Antrim. It is almost 43 ft. high, and is lighted in the 2nd story by a square-headed window facing the S.E., and in the 3rd by one facing the N. It is said, but upon doubtful authority, that at low water in summer, a bank connects the island with Gartree Point, and that it presents all the appearance of a paved causeway.

From Antrim the rly. follows up the Six Mile Water (the Ollarbha of ancient Irish romance, passing on either side Ballycraigy House, Muckamore Abbey Maj. Thompson, and Upton Castle (Lord

Templeton), in the parish of Templepatrick, which is said to possess not a single Roman Catholic.

88 m. Carrickfergus Junction (Rte. 13.)

90 m. White Abbey, so called from a monastic establishment, founded in the 13th cent. An E.E. ruined chapel is all that remains.

Green Castle, a suburb of Belfast, takes its name from slight ruins of a fortress.

The whole of the line from the junction to the terminus runs close to Belfast Lough, and on the land side is lined with a succession of bleach-greens and the handsome residences of the Belfast merchants.

94½ m. Belfast (Rte. 5) (*Hotels*: Imperial; Royal; Queen's; Albion).

ROUTE 13.

FROM **COLERAINE** TO **BELFAST**, BY **PORTRUSH**, THE **GIANT'S CAUSEWAY**, AND **BALLYCASTLE**.

The tourist should make a point of following this route, which is known as the Great Coast Road, for it includes in one excursion a large proportion of the interest and beauty of the north of Ireland, whilst the scientific observer, and the geologist in particular, have unlimited opportunities of studying one of the most singular basaltic districts in Europe.

A short branch rly. runs from Coleraine to Portrush, passing 3½ m. l. the small watering-place of *Portstewart* (*Hotel*, Portstewart), situated so as to command fine views of the opposite promontory of Inishowen. A wooden castle, built by Mr. O'Hara, is happily placed on the cliffs, which here terminate on the W. of the great basaltic range, and contain veins of zeolite, ochre, and steatite. Adjoining the station is Cromore, the seat of the Cromie family.

6¼ m. *Portrush* (*Hotels*: Antrim Arms, one of the best and most comfortable hotels in Ireland; Coleman's) is a favourite spot, both from its attractions as a marine residence and its proximity to the Causeway. A peninsula of basalt runs out for ¾ of a mile, and on this the town is built, having a deep bay on either side, and opposite it the picturesque line of the Skerries, which forms a very fine natural breakwater, in itself a great means of shelter to the harbour of Portrush. The town is small though well built, and contains an obelisk in memory of Dr. Adam Clarke, to whose zealous efforts in the cause of religion the inhabitants of the district were much indebted.

The rock scenery, within five minutes' walk of the hotel, is rugged and picturesque, though the cliffs rise to no great height. On the S. side there are caverns in the white limestone of the chalk formation.

Both chalk and lias strata have undergone considerable metamorphic action from their juxta-position to the gneiss rocks, "as long gradations of changes from the silicious chert-like strata, replete with organic remains, to the highly crystalline rock, may be here distinctly traced." —*Portlock*. The indurated lias strata of Portrush are identical with those of McGilligan and Ballintoy. The fossil collector will find Ammonites (sp. intermedius and McDonnellii) Pecten, Lima pectinoides, Panopæa elongata, &c. (*Introd.*, p. xxi.)

Conveyances.—Rail to Coleraine; car to Bushmills; steamer weekly to Glasgow and Oban.

Distances.—Coleraine, 6¼ m.; Portstewart, 3; Bushmills, 6½; Giant's Causeway, 8½; Dunluce Castle, 3½; Ballintoy, 15½.

Excursions.—
1. Portstewart.
2. Dunluce and Causeway.

Keeping to the rt. of the strand of Portrush, the road soon gains a magnificent terrace elevation at a great height above the sea. The geologist should by all means walk to the Causeway, as he will thereby gain a more minute opportunity of investigation. The White Rocks occur between the strand at Portrush and Dunluce. "Entering from the strand an arch in the chalk and passing through it, a deep hollow is observed at the top of the chalk, which is entirely filled by the massive overlying trap."

Between the points mentioned the junction of the basalt with the chalk may be well studied. It is amorphous, and caps all the promontories along the coast : " the surface of the chalk on which the basalt rests being very uneven, and in some places excavated into wide and deep gullies, like the transverse sections of river-courses ; at others, it presents bluffs or pointing headlands, against which the basalt has flowed, and which it eventually completely overlays."—*Du Noyer.* A section on the Portrush strand shows —1. amorphous basalt ; 2. layers of drift-flints resting on the eroded surface of the chalk proper. The action of the sea has worn the cliffs into most singular and fantastic shapes and gullies, across one of which, the Priest's Hole, the road is carried.

10 m. l. overhanging a most precipitous cliff, are the picturesque towers and gables of *Dunluce Castle* ‹one. Douglas, which as far as situation goes is the most singular ruin in the north. It is built on a projecting rock, separated from the mainland by a deep chasm, which is bridged over by a single arch, 18 in. broad, the only approach to the castle, and one that is sufficiently dangerous and unprotected for a nervous visitor. Notwithstanding the great size of the castle, a nearer inspection is somewhat disappointing. The domestic apartments and offices appear to have been principally placed on the mainland, while the building on the rock is occupied by a small courtyard, a number of small apartments, and some round flanking towers overhanging the sea, into which it is said a portion of the castle really fell during a storm in 1639, when the Marchioness of Buckingham was residing here. By whom or when it was first erected is not known, but the site was occupied by a fortress of the M'Quillans, who possessed a large portion of this northern district, until it was taken from them by the M'Donnells (afterwards Earls of Antrim), the representative of whom was Sorley Boy, a celebrated character of those days. These possessors were in their turn ousted by Sir John Perrott, Lord Deputy, who occupied the castle by an English garrison. The rock on which it stands is basaltic (portions of the building itself showing the polygonal structure), and contains large caves underneath, said to communicate with the building. It should be mentioned, for the lovers of Irish pedigree, that Rory Oge M'Quillan could trace his family from their departure from Babylon 3000 years ago, whence they came to Scotland, and from their name of Chaldæans gave origin to the word Caledonian !

12½ m. Bushmills (*Hotel*, Imperial), a neat little town on the banks of the Bush, celebrated for its distillery and its salmon fishery, the latter being much in request among fishermen. Near the bridge in the bed of the river some curved basaltic columns are visible. Adjoining the town is Dundarave, the beautiful seat of Sir Edmund McNaghten, whose family was akin to the

McDonnells, Earls of Antrim, and came over to Ireland in the beginning of the 17th centy.

14½ m. The approach to the Causeway Hotel (tolerable) is self-evident from the numbers of guides and others who lie in wait for the unsuspecting traveller, and run by the side of his car, proffering their services or selling little boxes of fossils and minerals. As regards the former, the visitor had better avail himself of the knowledge of the head guide, Alexander Laverty by name, who is intelligent and strictly conscientious, being determined that nobody intrusted to his care shall depart without listening to his lecture on the formation of the Causeway. As to the fossils, it may not be amiss to mention that many of the specimens offered for sale were never obtained at the Causeway or even in the neighbourhood. At the hotel the visitor may obtain a tariff of prices for guides, boats, &c., by which he should strictly abide, and not allow any annoyance from the multitude of beggars, who, under pretence of showing some special curiosity, pester everybody for money. Should the day be calm enough, the first point is to see the caves which lie under the rocks a little to the N.W. of the hotel. The principal and most beautiful is Portcoon, into which a boat may be rowed for a long distance. It is 350 ft. in length and 45 ft. in height; and although there is an entrance landwards, the wonderful effects produced by the colouring of the peroxide of iron and the deep green of the water are to a great extent lost to the visitor who approaches it thus. The geologist should notice a fault running through the whole roof; and to the west of the cave a large whindyke. The same phenomenon of intrusion of trap may be seen at Dunkerry cave, which is 660 ft. long and 96 ft. high.

The 3rd cave, called Racksley, cannot be entered, on account of sunk rocks. After examining the caves the visitor is rowed eastward and landed on the Causeway; the first impression of which is frequently one of disappointment, arising perhaps from the overstrained accounts written at different times by older topographers. This feeling, however, speedily yields to astonishment when we take into consideration the immense scale on which all the phenomena exist, and more especially when we look minutely into the extraordinary arrangement of this pavement of nature. "The basalt which forms the columnar bed known as the 'Giant's Causeway' is quite a local deposit, measuring at the most 2600 ft. in width, or from E. to W., and appearing along the coast as a lenticular-shaped bed, thinning out at either side, and it occupies a flattened trough in the amorphous basalts which underlie the great ochre-bed of the Chimney Headland."—*Du Noyer*.

The columns on the E. slope to the E., others to the W., thus showing the direction of the longest axis of the lava flow.

It consists of three platforms, generally known as the Little, Middle, and Great Causeways, as they are approached from the W. In the Middle or Honeycomb Causeway, the principal curiosity is the Lady's Chair, a single hexagon pillar, surrounded by several others of taller proportions, so as to form a comfortable seat. Thence the Great Causeway is entered through the Giant's Gateway, a gap bounded on each side by basaltic columns. The beauty and order of arrangement of the pillars which form the pavement are the main attraction of the Great Causeway, and the guides take care to impress on the visitor the rarity of certain forms; that of 3-sided pillars there is but one, and of nonagons but 3 on the whole platform, while pentagons and hexagons are universal, and octagons, which they denominate the key-stone, are not so common. Each pillar will bear looking into, being not only distinct from its neighbours with which it is closely united, but, moreover, containing within itself an arrangement of small crystallizations radiating from a common centre. "The columns of this particular bed appear to radiate from a line of imaginary centres, which are coincident with the longest axis of the flow; the main circumference of these radiations being defined by the upper surface of the lava-bed, and hence the upright planes of columnar crystallization strike at right angles downwards from what must have been the primary cooling surface of the mass, that surface from the first having been slightly depressed in its centre."—*Du Noyer.* Having examined the forms of the columns and the various points of interest, such as the Giant's Loom, Well, Theatre, Pulpit, Bagpipes, &c., all of which the guides will take care to notice, let us take a comprehensive view of the cliffs, which, after all, form the chief grandeur of the scene. From W. to E., proceeding from the hotel, or, still better, from the Portheoon Cave headland, we have the Bay of Port-na-baw, Great Stoucan Point 271 ft., Weir Snoot 283, Ardsnoot 307 the latter overhanging the Causeway, the Bay of Portnoffer, the Organ Columns, Seagull Island, Portnoffer Point 327, the Chimney Head 320, Port-na-spania, Port-na-caillain, the Nursing Child, Plaiskin Head, Kenbane Head, Giant's Pulpit, Bengore Head. This list will enable the visitor to trace the various salient points of the whole coast. Standing on the Causeway, the attention is primarily attracted on the l. by the Chimney Headland, consisting of 2 thick beds of columnar basalt, a few isolated columns of which suggested the likeness to the chimney. These all rest upon the great ochre-bed, a very marked feature in the whole section, and below this again consist of possibly 4 deposits of amorphous basalt, each separated from the others by a thin layer of ochre. At Portnoffer Point to the W. of this, the same arrangement prevails, though the ochre-bed thins out and is nearer to the sea. The columnar beds above it now change their character, losing their parallelism of deposition, as well as distinct columnar structure; the ochre-bed disappears, a deposit of amorphous basalt takes its place, and a new series of pillars are seen below, called the Organ. The regularity and beauty of these pillars, which extend for about 200 ft., are particularly conspicuous, and may really be compared to the pipes of an organ without any violent stretch of imagination. The geologist must particularly notice the inclination of the Organ-bed to the W., and the dip of from 6 to 8 degrees; and supposing it could be traced all the way, it would eventually be found to be a continuation of the Giant's Causeway, proving the identity of these 2 beds.

On the cliffs to the S. of Portnoffer "the 2 columnar beds, which are so distinct at the summit of the Chimney Headland, are represented by not less than possibly 4 separate deposits of trap, the 2 lowest, which occupy the central position of the cliff, being rudely and massively columnar, and separated from each other by a layer of rather black shale." Overhanging the causeway is the Ard Snoot, to the W. of which is the Whindyke, 15 ft. thick. Proceeding W. to the hotel, it will be perceived that the ochre-bed is again visible by the pathway, overlaid by the same amorphous trap which rests on the Organ-bed. The whole of the coast, therefore, is a cutting, transverse to the longest axis of the lava flow. The tourist who wishes to go more at length into the geology of the district should consult a very able paper by Mr. Du

Noyer, in the 'Geologist,' vol. iii. No. 25, to which the writer of this notice is much indebted. The foregoing description embraces the principal and most curious features of the coast, but nevertheless no visitor should neglect to prolong his excursion to the E. of the Chimney, as the finest coast scenery in the north of Ireland occurs at Pleaskin. Between these two points is Port-na-Spania, so called from the cliffs having been battered by a Spanish vessel, under the impression that they were fortifications. From *Pleaskin*, which is 354 ft. in height, the tourist has a magnificent view eastward over Bengore and Fairhead. " The summit is covered with a thin grassy sod, under which lies the basaltic rock, having generally a hard surface somewhat cracked and shivered. At the depth of 10 to 12 ft. from the summit this rock begins to assume a columnar tendency and forms a range of massive pillars, standing perpendicular to the horizon, and presenting the appearance of a magnificent gallery or colonnade 60 ft. in length."—*Hamilton's Antrim*. The seat so often occupied by the author just quoted is still pointed out by the guides. The fantastic arrangements of the cliffs do not end with Pleaskin, but are continued in the Lion's Head, Kenbane Head, the Twins (two isolated rocks standing together), the Pulpit, the Ball Alley, and the Giants' Graves; beyond which the mighty headland of Bengore closes the range of excursions which more immediately belong to the Causeway district.

Distances from the Hotel.—Ballycastle, 12 m.; Bushmills, 2; Ballintoy, 7; Carrick-a-rede, 8; Dunluce, 5.

As there is no public conveyance from the Causeway, the traveller will have to take a car, if he follows the northern coast road, which cuts across the promontory to

17½ m. *Dunseverick* (Dun Sovarke or Sophairee—the fortress of Sophairee), where on an insulated rock stand the scanty ruins of a castle probably erected by the McQuillans, a family who arrived in Ireland among the earliest English adventurers. It afterwards came into possession of the O'Cahans or O'Hares, who settled in Antrim about the 13th centy. Very little is left, though the thickness of the walls (11 feet) attests its former strength. The views looking W. over Bengore Head are very fine, as also those over Fairhead to the E. The coast is worth exploring as far as Bengore, particularly at Portmoon and Portagoona, where there is a picturesque waterfall formed by the small river Fcigh. Soon after leaving Dunseverick the road falls into the high road from Portrush and winds along the strand of White Park Bay to

22 m. *Ballintoy*, a small village situated at the foot of the furzy hill of Lannimore, 672 ft. The lias rocks here seen are identical with those of Portrush and McGilligan. Lignite has also been occasionally worked here. The coast abounds in fine views, particularly to the N.E. where the cliffs of Rathlin Island are most conspicuous; and further in the horizon the Scotch coast in the neighbourhood of the Mull of Cantire is plainly visible. Close off shore is Sheep Island, and about 1 m. from the village is that of *Carrick-a-rede*, one of the most singular curiosities of the north, on account of the swinging bridge which connects the island with the mainland. The tourist who wishes for a closer inspection, or to cross over to the island, should get a boy to show him the way from Ballintoy, though a fine distant view is obtained from the road to Ballycastle.

Carrick-a-rede is an insulated rock, separated from the mainland by a chasm 60 ft. wide and more than 80 ft. deep. "At this place the salmon are intercepted in their retreat to the rivers. The fishing commences early in spring and continues till August; a rude bridge of ropes is thrown across, which remains during the season."—*Lewis*. This bridge, which is protected by a single rope rail, swings about in the most uncomfortable manner, oftentimes rendering it a dangerous feat in stormy weather, save to the natives, who cross it with the utmost indifference. The name is derived by Mr. Hamilton from "Carrig-a-ramhadh," the rock in the road, on account of the intercepting of the salmon.

From here the way lies over a hilly district, leaving to the l. 1 m. the headland of *Kenbane* (White Head), crowned with the shell of a castle of probably the same date as that of Dunseverick. Near it is a singular cave, known as Grace Staple's, the basaltic pillars of which are worth a visit.

26 m *Ballycastle* (*Hotel*: Antrim Arms, fair), a small uninteresting town, prettily placed at the foot of Knocklayd (Knoc-lade, Broad Mountain), which rises to the S. to the height of 1695 ft., and should be ascended for the sake of the fine view over the coast and Rathlin Island. A part of the town is situated about ½ m. from the rest, on the banks of the Glenshesk river, near its embouchure, and from its aspect it would seem as if an attempt had been made to create some business at Ballycastle, which at one time was rather noted for its collieries. But all is now dull and stagnant, and the town principally depends on the stream of visitors to the N. of Ireland. On the rt. bank of the river is the ruined abbey of *Bonamargy*, of which only the shell remains, with one or two good pointed windows.

The name *Bona*, or Bon-na-Margy, signifies the foot or mouth of the Margey, which is the former name of the small river which here joins the Glenshesk, and now becomes the Carey. The chapel is 100 ft. long. On the N. of the choir are the refectory and offices; and "the eastern porch was formerly ornamented with several well-executed bas-reliefs."—*McSkimmin*. The erection of Bonamargy is usually attributed to Sorley Boy or Somarle M'Donnell in the 14th centy., though some ascribe it to the M'Quillans; at all events it was selected by many of the English nobles as their last resting-place; among them by the 1st Earl of Antrim, whose continuance in this world must have had a great effect on the fortunes of the country, if we are to judge by an Irish inscription on his coffin :—

"At all times some calamity
 Befals the Irish once every seventh year;
 But now that the Marquis is departed
 It will happen every year."

The abbey is said to have been burnt down in a raid made by the Scottish islanders, though afterwards rebuilt by the clan of M'Cormick.

About 2 m. up the Glenshesk on l. bank is the site of a castle called after Gobhan Saer. It is a question whether it was erected by or a residence of Goblan, the architect who built the round tower of Antrim. A small ruin on the coast to the W. of Ballycastle completes the antiquarian curiosities. The geologist will be tempted to explore the cliffs towards Fairhead, which contain a large amount of coal strata, from which at one time 10,000 to 15,000 tons were raised annually, but owing to the estate falling into Chancery the workings were discontinued, though a considerable quantity of ironstone is still raised.

Cross Hill, on which the collieries are situated, is about 500 ft. high, and is composed of columnar basalt, resting on sandstone and clay slate, beneath which is the coal at an elevation of 200 ft. above the beach. The seam is penetrated by a large dyke of freestone, called Carrick Mawr. (*Introduction*, p. xxix.)

Conveyances. — To Ballymoney daily.

Excursions. —
1. Fairhead.
2. Cushendun.
3. Armoy.
4. Carrick-a-rede.
5. Rathlin.

Distances.—Ballintoy, 4 m.; Giant's Causeway, 11½; Fairhead, 5; Cushendun, 12; Cushendall, 17; Ballymoney, 17; Rathlin Island, 6; [which place is very seldom visited, though it is highly worth both the time and trouble. The weather is of course the main point on which the excursion hinges, as if stormy the sail or row across the Race of Sleuck-na-Massa, or the valley of the sea, is unpleasant, if not dangerous. At ebb tide the opposing waters form a very rough sea, which was anciently called the Caldron of Brecain, owing to the drowning of Brecain, son of Nial of the Nine Hostages, together with his fleet of 50 curraghs. *Rathlin*, Reachrainn, or Raghery Island, the Ricina of Ptolemy, is of considerable extent, of the shape of a finger bent at right angles (or, as Sir W. Petty quaintly describes it, of an "Irish stockinge, the toe of which pointeth to the main lande"), measuring from E. to W. about 4 m. Its singular position between Ireland and Scotland, its ancient remains, and its natural beauties, all combine to make it a very interesting visit. St. Columb founded a church here in the 6th centy., an honour which may be attributed to its position between Staffa and Ireland; but the same cause operated prejudicially when the Danes invaded the north, as the island had then to bear the first brunt of their savage assaults. Later on it was so repeatedly ravaged by the English and Scotch that in 1580 it was totally uninhabited. Rathlin is connected with the fortunes of Robert Bruce, who for a long period sought concealment in the castle which still bears his name, and in which the well-known episode of the spider and the web occurred. There is but one harbour in the island, viz. in Church Bay, and even this is untenable during westerly gales, to which it is freely exposed. Near the landing-place is the residence of the Rev. R. Gage, who, as proprietor of the island, lives amongst his people, and exercises patriarchal rule and influence. In this respect Rathlin was not always so fortunate, as at one time we read in the Ulster Visitation, "The isle of Raghline, possesste by the Earle of Antrym, has neither vicar nor curate, it not being able to mayntayne one." ¾ m. from the bay on the E. side is Bruce's Castle, or what is left of it—a small portion of wall, situated on a lofty precipice, nearly insulated from the mainland by a deep chasm. The chief beauty of Rathlin is the cliffs, which maintain a considerable elevation all round, the highest point being at Slieve-a-carn, 447 ft., on the N.W. coast, while there is scarce any part lower than 180 ft. The general structure of the rocks is chalk and basalt, the latter assuming, in some places, the same columnar aspect as on the opposite coast of Fairhead. At Doon Point, nearly 2 m. to the S. of Bruce's Castle, they are most peculiar, having a curved form, "as if they slid over while in a state of softness, and took the inclination necessary to their descent. At the base there is a small mole, composed of compact erect columns, forming a natural pier."—*Doyle.* There are also some singular caverns in the basalt to the S. of Church Bay; and at Runascariff the cliffs assume appearances similar to those at Doon. The island contains 3368 acres, of which about one-fourth is arable and pasture; the inhabitants are a simple quiet race, who chiefly gain their subsistence by fishing, gathering kelp, and growing barley, the last two of which are taken to Campbellton and Glasgow.]

[A second excursion should be

undertaken to Fairhead or Benmore (the Robogdium Promontorium of Ptolemy, whose magnificent escarpment is a striking feature in the drive from Ballintoy to Ballycastle, and forms a worthy finish to the basaltic wonders of the N. coast.

It is 639 ft. in height, of which 319 or nearly half is occupied by a mural precipice of enormous greenstone columns, many of them upwards of 30 ft. in width. From the base of these Brobdingnag piers, a buttress of debris runs at a sharp inclination down to the sea. A steep and broken path, called "Fhir Leith," or the Grey Man's Path, runs through a mighty chasm, across which a gigantic pillar has fallen; by following this the tourist will gain a good view of the columnar face of the promontory. The view from the summit is difficult to surpass for panoramic extent, embracing the island of Rathlin, a considerable portion of the Scotch coast, Islay, the Mull of Cantire, and in clear weather the Paps of Jura, while, to the W., the eye follows the coast to the Causeway, with the hills of Inishowen looming in the far distance. There are 3 small tarns on the headland, one of which, Lough Doo, is close to the cliff, and empties itself over it by a waterfall. The waters of the other 2, Lough-na-Fanna and Lough Fadden, also form a fall over Carrick Mawr, the whinstone dyke of the Ballycastle coal-field, which, it should be mentioned, reappears on the W. side of the headland at Murlough Bay. Even in this short distance, the effects of the disturbance to which the beds have been subject are very striking. There are at Murlough 6 beds of coal, the 1 uppermost of which are bituminous, while the lower ones are anthracitic. The history of these collieries, which have all been worked by adits in the sea-face of the cliff, would be interesting if known. That they were worked from a very early period is certain, for in 1770, when an English company had taken possession of them, the colliers employed discovered a long gallery, and chambers containing baskets, tools, and candles, the wicks of which were formed of rags; there were also barrows made of boulders of basalt, clearly proving the very early efforts that were made to get the coal. Mr. Hamilton also mentions that in the mortar of which Bruce's Castle in Rathlin Island was built, cinders of coal were found. The best way to visit this coast is to take a boat from Ballycastle, row round the head, and land at Murlough Bay, returning by foot along the coast.]

[The antiquarian may spend an interesting day in visiting *Armoy* anc. Airthear - maighe), 7 m. to the S.W., the road thither running at the foot of Knocklayd. In the ch.-yard is a round tower, 35 ft. high, by 46 round, with a circular doorway. A former rector surmounted it with a dome of wood and stone, and restored it to its original purpose of a Cloig-theagh, by keeping the ch. bell in it. From Armoy, a by-road may be taken into the lonely vale of the Glenshesk, which rises in the Sleive-an-Orra Mountain (1678 ft.), a portion of a lofty chain intervening between Ballycastle and Cushendall. On the l. bank of the river, 2 m. from Ballycastle, is the Castle of Gobhan Saer, the architect of Antrim Round Tower. It has, however, been proved by Dr. Reeves to have been an old chapel, "probably the Ecclesia de Druin Indict. of the Tripartite Life of St. Patrick." Large numbers of stone celts and weapons have been found in this neighbourhood from time to time, proving the struggles that have here taken place. On the summit of Knocklayd is a large cairn, said to have been erected to the memory of 3 Danish princesses. An inspection of the Abbey of Bonamargy (p. 111) will conclude a good day's work]

The road from Ballycastle follows

the vale of the Carey as far as the hamlet of (29 m.) Ballyvoy, where a branch is given off along the coast past Torr and Runabay Heads to Cushendun. For pedestrians who wish to obtain coast views, this route is very advantageous, and only about 1 m. longer. The car-road crosses the Carey, and strikes into the hills, passing along the base of Carneighancigh (1036 ft.).

The view from the top of the hill overlooking *Cushendun* (anc. Bun-athaine-Duine) is very charming, and embraces the little village with its pretty ch. and neat residences nestling by the sea-shore, and on the banks of the Glendun, a river of some volume rising in the Slieve-an-Orra hills, and flowing for its whole course between mountains of considerable height. About 2 m. from the village it is crossed by a lofty and exceedingly picturesque viaduct, which, as seen from a distance, completely spans the vale. Close to the sea-shore (where the tourist will find more caves) are the residences of Nicholas Crommelin and R. C. Dobbs, Esqrs.

Distance.—Cushendun from Cushendall, 5 m.; Ballycastle, 12.

43 m. *Cushendall* (a good Inn) is another pretty little town, placed close to the sea at the mouth of the Glenaan, amidst very lovely scenery. The Dall, a small stream from which the name is derived, also falls in here.

There are slight ruins of a castle on a mount hard by. The road now greatly improves in scenery, running close to the waterside, and affording magnificent coast views, in which the cliffs of Red Bay are well set off by the chalk strata of Garron Point.

The greater part of the district from Ballycastle to Cushendun, is composed of granitic rocks, occasionally interrupted by the coal-measures, and subsequently by the chalk. From the latter place, however, the Devonian, or old Red, make their appearance, and are exposed in magnificent sections all along the coast, particularly at the romantic village of *Glenariff*, or Waterfoot (44¼ m.), in which the road is actually carried under short tunnels of old Red. There are also several caves, which, as regards this series of rocks, are somewhat unusual, as they are generally found in the mountain limestone.

Red Bay is one of the most picturesque spots in the whole route. It is an irregular semicircle surrounded by cliffs; at one corner are the white houses of the village, situated just where the glen of the Glenariff opens up into the mountains, which are here of a considerable height. Immediately over the village are the escarpments of Lurigethan (1154 ft.), while Crochalough (1304), and *Trostran* (1817), the highest of the chain, close the view. The red sandstone now shortly disappears, giving place to the chalk cliffs, which have been blasted to form the magnificent terrace-road, executed by the perseverance and genius of Mr. Turnley.

Isolated columns of chalk stand fantastically by the side of the sea-shore, by the side of which the road runs closely, presenting sea views that are seldom surpassed. 48¼ m. at Clogh-a-stucan, one of the most peculiar of these columns, the road trends to the S., and passes *Garron Tower*, the castellated residence of the Marquis of Londonderry, who possesses in this and the neighbouring county of Derry very large estates. Close to Garron Point is the rock of *Drummail*, or Dunmaul, the summit of which is crowned by a fort, said by tradition to have been the locality where all the Irish rents were paid. From hence too the Danish ravagers took their departure. Continuing under the escarpments of Knockore (1179 ft.), which are every now and then interrupted by a lovely dell, we come to (51 m. rt.) *Drumnasole* (J. Turnley, Esq)., one of the most beautiful of the many beautiful localities in this district.

53 m. *Carnlough*, (a good Inn) a pretty and cheerful looking watering-place, has grown up under the fostering eyes of the Londonderry family, who erected a pier and tram-road for bringing the limestone from the quarries. It has the recommendations of lovely scenery, smooth beach, and general cleanliness. A small river falls into the sea here, rising in the hills of Collin Top 1426 ft.). About 4 m. to the rt. another wind of the coast-road brings the tourist in sight of the bay and valley of Glenarm, still more secluded than either Waterfoot or Carnlough. (*Hotel*: Antrim Arms, bad). Glenarm is a pretty little town of about 1000 Inhab., adorned with a graceful spired ch., and the baronial residence of the family of Macdonnell, Earls of Antrim. The latter stands in a wooded park, on the opposite side of the river to the town, and is entered by a tower on the N. side of the bridge. The castle itself is a modernized and singular mixture of towers, parapets, and pinnacles, though the exquisite situation and scenery are sufficient compensation for any architectural inconsistencies. The tourist should visit the terrace which overhangs the river, the walk down the glen to the sea, in the course of which are some charming waterfalls, and the Deer-park, which is hemmed in between the sea and a fine range of basaltic cliffs over 200 ft. high. Glenarm Castle has been inhabited by the Antrim family since 1750, their former residence having been at Ballymagarry, until its destruction by fire.

Distances.—Larne, 11½ m.; Cushendall, 13; Ballycastle, 30; Carnlough, 3.

Excursions.—
1. Carnlough and Garron.
2. Larne and Carncastle.

The old road is seen from the castle grounds to climb up a very steep hill. This was for long the only road to the place, but it was superseded in 1834 by the magnificent scheme of Mr. Bald, who, by blasting the chalk cliffs, and allowing the débris to serve as a bulwark against the sea, obtained room for a broad road, equal in every respect to the one completed by Mr. Turnley. The pedestrian, however, will do well to take the old road, which keeps high ground until about half way to Larne. Some miles out at sea, the two solitary Hulin or Maiden rocks are conspicuous, bearing a fixed lighthouse on each, 84 and 94 ft. respectively above high water.

63 m. at *Carncastle* is a very fine development of cliff scenery; on the rt. in the escarpments of Knock Dhu and Sallagh Braes, which are shaped like an amphitheatre, and on l. in Ballygalley Head, where the basaltic columns are again visible.

There are remains of a fort on an insulated rock between the road and the sea, and also of the Elizabethan manor-house of the Shaws: on rt. is Carncastle Lodge (J. Agnew, Esq.). The road now winds alongside of Drains Bay, and, passing through a basaltic tunnel known as Black Cave, arrives at

67½ m. *Larne* (anc. Lathama) (*Hotel*: King's Arms), a prettily placed town, which, though not offering many attractions in itself, is a convenient point from whence to explore Island Magee. From the security of its land-locked harbour a very considerable trade has been carried on here, particularly in the article of lime, which is extensively shipped at Magheramorne, about 4 m. to the S. A recently opened rly. connecting Larne with Carrickfergus will doubtless largely increase the prosperity of the port.

Between the town and the ferry the coast makes a singular curve, from its shape called Curran, a reaping-hook; and at the termination of the curve stands a square tower, which in former days was celebrated under the name of *Olderfleet Castle*. Henry III. granted the possession of this district to the Scotch family of Bissett, who built the fortress for the protection of their property, though it was subsequently forfeited on account of their participation in rebellion. The only historical event of importance connected with the castle is the landing of Bruce (1315), with an army of 6000 men, for the invasion of Ireland. Raphanus maritimus grows on the Curraun, near the salt-works.

Distances.—Carrickfergus, 14½ m. by rail; Glenarm, 11½; Magheramorne, 4; Glynn, 2.

Conveyances.—Car to Ballycastle; rail to Carrickfergus and Belfast; steamer daily to Stranraer.

Excursions.—
1. Magheramorne and Glynn.
2. Glenarm.
3. Island Magee.
4. Carrickfergus.

[1 m. from the town is a ferry (the rights of which were granted, together with the castle of Olderfleet, to the Chichester family in the 17th centy.) between the so-called Island Magee and the mainland. In reality it is only a narrow promontory about 5 m. in length and 2 in breadth, running parallel with and separating the mainland from the ocean. "The inhabitants are all of Scottish descent, and are still thoroughly Scotch in dialect, manners, and customs; they are a remarkably intelligent race; and it is worthy of notice, that out of a population of nearly 3000, no person living can recollect an instance of a native of this place being imprisoned for or convicted of any criminal offence."—*Hall.*

It was held by the singular tenure of a goshawk and a pair of gloves. On the E. coast the scenery is very fine, particularly at the *Gobbins*, a range of high cliffs, of basaltic character, and perforated by 7 caves. The W. coast is not remarkable for anything but its mud banks, particularly towards the S., where the shores of Lough Larne approximate.

The antiquarian will find near the landing-place a cromlech formed of six upright stones supporting a large flat slab nearly 6 ft. in length. Some years ago several gold ornaments, including a torque, were dug up near this cromlech. "There is an ancient Pagan remain called Carndoo, or locally 'The Abbey,' on the face of Ballybooley Hill (near Portmuck), consisting of several huge stones ranged in a circle."—*Doyle.* At Brown's Bay on the N. is a large rocking-stone, which was believed to tremble at the approach of a criminal. Good as was Island Magee as regards moral character, it had an unfortunate notoriety for witchcraft and superstition, the last trial which took place in Ireland being that of a native of this district, who was pilloried at Carrickfergus in 1711.]

Immediately after leaving Larne the road crosses the Larne Water, which rises about 4 m. S.E. at Ceaun Gubha, the "Hill of Grief." Here Tuathal Teachtmar was slain in battle, A.D. 106, by Mal MacRochraide, King of Ulster.

69½ m. at Glynn are the ruins of a ch., the nave possessing squareheaded windows of an earlier date than those of the chancel, which are pointed. The latter is evidently an addition. [From this village a road shorter by 2 m., but not so practicable, runs inland to Carrickfergus, rejoining the coast-road at Eden, and passing en route *Glenoe*, a very picturesque village in a deep glen, in which a waterfall adds to the beauty of the scene. A new ch. has been built in the vicinity by the exertions of the late Lord Dungannon.

Passing through the hamlet of Beltoy, we have on rt. Lough Mourne, the waters of which are said to cover a large town, which was thus overwhelmed at the request of a pilgrim who had been refused hospitality, and had cursed it at his departure.

8¼ m. Eden.] Between Glynn and Magheramorne House (C. M'Garel, Esq.), near which are the extensive lime-works before mentioned, the geologist will notice the effects of a large landslip which in 1834 carried away the coach-road. A narrow strip of lias runs alongside the lough and will yield a number of characteristic lias fossils to the collector— viz., Pentacrinites, Plagiostoma, Gryphæa, Ammonites, &c.

Nearly opposite the commencement of the Lough Larne are the village of *Ballycarry* (a station on the rly.) and the ruined ch. of Templecoran, note1 for being the cradle of the Presbyterian religion in Ireland, where the first congregation was established in 1613 by Rev. Edward Brice. The living of Kilroot was the first appointment obtained by Dean Swift, but was soon resigned by him, on account of its uncongenial solitude. Close to the high road is the dell of the Salt Hole, the scene of Sorley McDonnell's infamous ambuscade in 1597, when Sir John Chichester, governor of Carrickfergus, was captured, to finish his career by being executed at Glynn.

Red Hall is the seat of Rev. D. Bull.

76 m. near Slaughterford Bridge the road running through Island Magee falls in. About ¾ m. l. on the coast are the remains of the castle of the Chichesters, which thus protected the district on the S. as Olderfleet did on the N. 1 m. further up the coast is the promontory of Black Head, well worth visiting for its beautiful cliff scenery. Two isolated rocks, My Lord and My Lady, are especial attractions. At White Head the road suddenly approaches and as suddenly recedes from the coast, a fact of which the Magnetic Telegraph Company have taken advantage to put their wires in connection with Carrickfergus.

79 m. rt. are the demesnes of Bellahill (M. Dalway, Esq), Castle Dobbs (C. Dobbs, Esq.), and Orlands (J. Smyth, Esq.); and soon afterwards, passing the village of Eden, between which and Kilroot the botanist will find Orobanche rubra, Carex Buxbaumi, and Calamagrostis, we arrive at

82 m. the time-honoured port of *Carrickfergus* (anc. Carraic-Feargusa) (*Hotel:* Victoria, very poor) (Pop. 4028 . The town is mean and dirty, but its situation on the shores of the Belfast Lough, goes far to redeem these faults: added to which, its historic associations and its well-preserved remains will amply repay a day spent here. These remains are—
1. The Castle; 2. Walls; 3. Church.

The Castle is a magnificent specimen of an inhabited Anglo-Norman fortress, and was built by De Courcy in 1178, to protect his Ulster possessions. It changed hands, however, during the invasion of Bruce, who, having captured Olderfleet, occupied Carrickfergus after a long and spirited defence by the English garrison under Mandeville. After Bruce's fall, in the battle near Dundalk, the castle again reverted to the English, and, with a few occasional changes into Scotch or Irish possession during the troubled times of 1641, remained with them. Mention should also be made of the attack by the French, under Thurot, in 1760, though their success was but shortlived. The English squadron under Elliott overtook the French near the Isle of Man, and during the engagement that followed Thurot was killed. The castle occupies a strong position on a rock overlooking the Lough, and at high water is surrounded on 3 sides, the harbour occupying the area to the S. The entrance from the land side is through a fine gateway, flanked on either side by a tower, called a Half-moon. The visitor will notice the usual defensive appliances, such as portcullis, embrasures for fire-arms, and the apertures for pouring melted lead, &c., upon the assailants. Within the gates is the lower yard or ballium, containing guard-rooms and barracks; and to the S. again is the upper yard, from which rises the most conspicuous portion of the castle—the great donjon or keep, a huge square tower of 5 stories. "The largest room, called Fergus's Dining-room, was in the 3rd story, with some circular windows; it was 25 ft. high, 38 ft. broad, 40 ft. long; the ground story was bombproof, and within the keep was a draw-well 37 ft. deep, but now nearly choked up with rubbish."—*M'Skimmin's History of Carrickfergus*. The walls of the castle follow the sinuosities of the rock all round. Since 1843 it has been garrisoned for the crown by a detachment of artillery and pensioners, and has lately been refitted with guns of newer type and calibre. The visitor is allowed to inspect the whole, with the exception of the keep, part of which is used as a magazine.

The walls have to a great extent disappeared, but they may be traced on the W. side of the town, and partly on the N., where a round arched gateway still exists.

The ch., dedicated to St. Nicholas, is a cruciform building, surmounted by a broad spire with a balustrade round the base. Notice the singular Elizabethan style of the N. transept, with its gable ends. In the interior are some remarkable monuments, especially one to Lord Donegal, with 2 principal kneeling figures representing Sir Arthur Chichester, first Earl of Belfast, and his wife. Below is the effigy of Sir John Chichester, who was taken in the ambuscade at Salthole, and beheaded. It is said that "Sorley McDonnell, being in Carrickfergus, went to see the monuments in the ch., and, upon Sir John's effigy being pointed out, he said, 'How the deil cam he to get his head again? for I am sure I ance tak it frae him.'"

The transept is divided from the nave by 2 round-headed arches and round piers. The ch. is lighted by a 3-light window on N. of chancel, a stained-glass S. window, and 2 singular rose lights on either side of the organ. A subterranean passage now blocked up communicates with a Franciscan monastery, which formerly existed some way from the church.

A pleasant and useful custom exists of the bell ringing at 6 morning and evening, for the use of the workmen in the town, thus associating with the dignity of labour the practical remembrance of religion.

The geologist may pay a visit to the salt-mines at Duncrue, that lie to the W. of the town. They are situated in the triassic sandstone deposit, which borders the Belfast Lough all the way from White Head to Belfast.

Conveyances.—From Carrickfergus to Belfast, Antrim, and Larne, by rail.

Distances.—Belfast, 9½ m.; Antrim, 15½; Larne, 15½; Glenarm, 26.

Leaving on l. the ancient site of the Abbey of Woodburn, the traveller arrives at the Junction of the Antrim and Coleraine Rly., and is soon deposited at

91½ m. *Belfast* (Rte. 5).

ROUTE 14.

FROM DUBLIN TO MULLINGAR, ATHLONE, BALLINASLOE, AND GALWAY.

The whole of this route, 126 m., is performed by the Midland Great Western Rly., opened in 1852, one of the great trunk lines of Ireland, which cuts right across the country, dividing it as nearly as possible into 2 equal portions. It is the principal route to Connemara and the Western Highlands, and passes through such desolate tracts of land that the English tourist cannot be too thankful that he is travelling by the locomotive instead of an outside car. And yet the country is not altogether so bleak; for the first 25 miles or so it is characterised by wooded champaign country, watered by pretty streams, and dotted with farms and residences, while every now and then even in the worst portion a pretty bit of landscape breaks the monotony of the bog. The line starts from the Broad-stone Stat. in the northern part of the city. It is a large, though somewhat heavy building, of a mixture of Grecian and Egyptian style, which, however, impart an effect of massiveness and solidity. The interior arrangements are good, and the comfort of the traveller is attended to in a manner that might be well imitated by more than one rly. company in England. Close to the stat., and indeed running ddle by side with the line for 50 m., is the Royal Canal, also the property of the Midland Great Western Co. Proceeding from the offices of the stat. yard, the line passes through some of the pleasantest suburbs of Dublin, having on l. the Phoenix Park with its numerous objects of interest,

and on rt. the villages of Glasnevin, with its cemetery and botanical gardens, and Finglas, also the observatory of Dunsink, all of which are adjacent to the valley of the Tolka river. They have been described in Rte. 1. A fine background is afforded on the l. by the ranges of the Dublin and Wicklow mountains, which, however, after a few miles gradually trend to the S.

4½ m. *Blanchardstown* Stat. Here is a large religious house for nuns; and adjoining the village is Abbotstown, the residence of J. Hamilton, Esq., M.P.

[1 m. l., occupying the summit of Knockmaroon Hill, *Castleknock*, a small village, with the ruins of a fortress, formerly held by Hugh de Tyrrel against Edward Bruce in 1316. It was on this occasion captured, and again in 1642 by the Duke of Albemarle, "who slew in the assault 80 of its defenders, and subsequently hanged as many more." The worthy citizens of Dublin will doubtless find greater attractions in the strawberry-beds for which the valley of the Liffey is famous, and which extend for a considerable distance on the N. side of the river.]

7 m. *Clonsilla*, remarkable for a very deep canal cutting of 3 m. in length, through the calp or middle carboniferous limestone series. [From this station the line of the Dublin and Meath Co. branches off to Navan and Kells, passing through Dunboyne and Kilmessan, neither of them places of any interest.

20 m. *Bective*. The ruins of the Abbey are described in Rte. 15.

25 Navan.]

Between the rly. and the Liffey are the picturesque grounds of Woodlands, the well-planted demesne of Lord Arondly, and formerly the seat of the Earls of Carhampton. The house is said to contain a room in which King John passed a night.

9 m. *Lucan* Stat. The village of the same name, which gives the title

of Earl to the family of Bingham, is charmingly situated, about 1 m. to the l. on the S. bank of the Liffey, here crossed by a single-arched stone bridge of 100 ft. span, with iron balustrades. Lucan was celebrated for its spa, though fashion has long ago deserted it. "Its fame was derived from its sulphuretted hydrogen water, flowing from a bed of calp limestone, which contains pyrites." — *Knox.* The banks of the river are charmingly set off by ornamental parks and residences, amongst which are Lucan House (C. Colthurst, Esq.), Woodville House (Sir Hopton Scott), and St. Edmonsbury House (W. Berwick, Esq.). In the grounds of the former house, into which visitors are admitted, are the remains of the fortress of the Sarsfields, the ancestors of the Binghams.

[The tourist who may wish to return to town by a different route can go across from Lucan to the other stat. on the Great Southern and Western Rly. (Rte. 25), distant 1½ m. He may also proceed from the village to Leixlip, visit the salmon-leap, and rejoin the Midland line at Leixlip Stat.]

10 m. rt. (at which point the traveller enters Kildare county) are the partial remains of a curiously tall tower, known as *Confey Castle*, supposed to have been one of many that were erected by the early colonists to protect themselves from the attacks of the native Irish. When in preservation, it consisted of a massive square tower of 5 stages, with turrets at the N. and W. angles, and had a principal entrance under a semicircular archway.

11 m. *Leixlip* Stat. [¾ m. from which on l. is the ancient little town of Leixlip, situated at the confluence of the Rye Water with the Liffey, which is crossed by a stone bridge of 3 arches. Overlooking the wooded banks of the river is the modernized castle, flanked on the W. by a circular, and on the E. by a square tower, the building of which is attributed to Adam Fitz-Hereford, one of the earliest of Anglo-Norman settlers, and a follower of Strongbow. It is now the residence of C. P. Hoffman, Esq. The chief part of the property round Leixlip formerly belonged to the Earls of Kildare, from whom it passed into the Conolly family. A short distance up the stream is the famous salmonleap, where the Liffey tumbles over a broad though not high ledge of limestone rocks in a very picturesque cataract—a favourite resort of picnic-lovers from Dublin —

"For Leixlip is proud of its close shady bowers,
Its clear falling waters and murm'ring cascades,
Its groves of fine myrtle, its beds of sweet flowers,
Its lads so well dress'd, and its neat pretty maids."
O'Keefe.

The visitor must not found his hopes too strongly on seeing the salmon ascend the ledge "per saltum," as it is only at certain times and seasons that the operation is performed. The botanist will find Hieracium hirsutum growing near the Leap.

1 m. higher up the river is crossed at *Newbridge* by a very ancient bridge of 4 arches (the 2 middle ones being pointed), built in 1308 by John le Decer, then mayor of Dublin, and believed to be the oldest structure of the kind now existing in Ireland. On the rt. bank of the Liffey are the grounds of *St. Wulstans* (R. Cane, Esq.), containing some interesting Dec. gateways, the remains of the priory founded here by Adam Fitz-Hereford, at the beginning of the 13th cent., in honour of St. Wulstan, Bishop of Worcester, who had been just before canonized. On the opposite side of the stream is *Castletown House*, the seat of Thos. Conolly, Esq., M.P., whose ancestor, the Right Hon. William Conolly, was Speaker of the

House of Commons in the time of Queen Anne. The house is a fine though somewhat overgrown building, consisting of a centre connected with 2 wings by semicircular colonnades. By a favourite Irish fiction, it is supposed to contain a window for every day in the year, just as all the lakes are said to be furnished with 365 islands. The grounds contain some splendid cedar-trees.

3 m. from Leixlip is the pretty village of *Celbridge*, noted for being the residence of Miss Esther Vanhomrigh, the illfated Vanessa of Dean Swift. From hence the tourist can return to Dublin from Hazlehatch Stat. 1½ m. on the Great Southern line.]

Crossing the valley of the Rye Water, in company with an aqueduct 100 ft. in height for the accommodation of the canal, and skirting the woods of Carton on rt., the line reaches

15 m. *Maynooth* (*Hotel*: Leinster Arms, a small, tolerably built town, containing several interesting objects Pop. 1497). Conspicuous from the rly. is the massive tower of the castle, renowned for its strength and magnificence during its tenure by the powerful family of Kildare. It is said to have been built, or more probably reconstructed, in 1426 by John the 6th Earl, and remained in the possession of the Fitzgeralds until the reign of Henry VIII., when, in consequence of the rebellion of Lord Thomas Fitzgerald, better known as Silken Thomas, from his gorgeous accoutrements of silk, it was besieged by Sir William Brereton, to whom it was treacherously yielded by Christopher Parese, the foster-brother of the Geraldines. The traitor was, however, rightly served, for, after payment was made to him of the stipulated reward, "his head was chopped off." The ruins, which have been neatly kept in order by the Duke of Leinster, the owner of the soil, consist of a massive keep, with a considerable extent of outworks, strengthened at intervals by towers. The importance of the fortress at the time of its capture is thus quaintly described : " Greate and riche was the spoile—such store of beddes, so many goodly hangings, so riche a wardrob, such brave furniture, as truly it was accompted, for householde stuffe and utensils, one of the richest Earle his homes under the crowne of Englande."— *Holinshed.* Hard by is the College, which, from the political feelings called into play, has made Maynooth famous in modern Irish history. A college was founded here in 1513 by Gerald 8th Earl of Kildare, who appointed provost and vice-provost, and endowed it with lands round the tower of Taghadoe. It became, however, an institution for the education of Irishmen in 1795, in consequence of the suspension of the continental colleges from the continuance of the war. The former building was unsightly and inconvenient, being in fact a series of additions made at different times to a house built by Lord Leinster's butler; but all this has since been remedied by the beautiful designs of Pugin, consisting of an E. Eng. quadrangle, 340 by 300 ft. The college of Maynooth, ever since its foundation in 1795, has been maintained by grants, first from the Irish and afterwards from the Imperial Parliament, the annual vote from 1808 to 1813 being 8283*l*., afterwards raised to 8928*l*. By an act passed in the present reign, the college was permanently endowed for the maintenance and education of 500 students and of 20 senior scholars on the foundation by Lord Dunboyne, besides which 30,000*l*. was set apart for the erection of the necessary buildings. The course of study requires 8 years for its completion, and no student is admitted except he be intended for the Irish priesthood. Adjoining the college

[*Ireland.*] G

is the parish ch., possessing a very massive tower, and some Dec. windows.

Close to the town is the entrance gate to *Carton*, the seat of the Duke of Leinster, Ireland's only Duke. It is a handsome Grecian building, consisting of centre with wings, connected by corridors, and possessing in the interior a library and some choice pictures. The entrance is by a porch surmounted by a triangular pediment, in the tympanum of which are the arms of the family. The park is very extensive, and is more thoroughly English in the character of its timber and scenery than in almost any estate in Ireland. Landscape-gardening has been carried to a high pitch, and every point has been seized which could be made available for effect. The property of Carton formerly belonged to the Talbots, a younger branch of the Talbots of Malahide, and was purchased in 1738 by the 19th Earl of Kildare from a Mr. Ingoldsby. The mansion was designed by Cassels, a celebrated Dublin architect, who built the town houses of the Leinster and Waterford families, as well as the Lying-in Hospital.

The visitor to Carton by road from Leixlip need not return by the same gate, but may proceed direct to Maynooth.

[A few m. to the S. of Maynooth is the round tower of *Taghadoe*, remarkable for being of greater dimensions than is usual in such structures. The college of Maynooth was endowed with the lands round this tower.]

19½ m. *Kilcock*, a little town on the rt., need not detain the tourist, as it possesses nothing save a celebrity for provincial races.

A coach leaves *Fernslock* Stat., 21¼ m., every afternoon for Trim, 11 m. (Rte. 15).

25¼ m. l., very near the line, is *Cloncurry* ruined ch., and a singular mound, probably of a sepulchral character. The traveller will notice with regret that the pretty English scenery through which he has been hitherto passing has been gradually changing and giving place to melancholy and dreary bog, a portion of the bog of Allen, continuing for the greater portion of the way to Mullingar. The beautiful though distant ranges of the Dublin mountains have also nearly disappeared in the distance.

26½ *Enfield* (Rte. 15), a neatly kept little town, where the tourist who wishes to explore the archæological treasures of the Boyne will have to leave the rly.

Distances.— Edenderry, 11 m.; Trim, 11; Carbury, 7.

30½ m. *Moyvalley*, close to which is Ballina, the seat of Right Hon. More O'Ferrall, M.P.; and at 33 m. the line crosses the river Boyne, which, as far as picturesque features are concerned, will probably disappoint. In this early part of its course it is boggy and sluggish, a condition which the operations of the Draining Commissioners have not helped to remove, but have rather increased. About 2 m. to the l. the tower of Clonard ch. is visible (Rte. 15).

At 36 m. *Hill of Down* Stat., the traveller may have an opportunity of examining the ingenious manner in which Mr. Hemans, the engineer of the rly., overcame the difficulties which presented themselves. "In these bogs he has relied wholly on a careful and complete system of drainage, whereby the upper crust is so perfectly hardened and dried, that the rails and heavy trains are supported upon it by a light framework of timber." The Hill of Down itself is formed of drift gravel.

41 m. *Killucan* Stat. (*Hotel:* Moore's.) The town, a little to the rt., contains nothing of interest. In the neighbourhood are Riversdale (E. G. Briscoe, Esq.), Grangemore (J. Briscoe, Esq.), Hyde Park (G.

D'Arcy, Esq.', Huntingdon House (W. Gorman, Esq.', Clonlost (J. Nugent, Esq.', Lisnabin (G. Purdon, Esq.', Killynon (R. Reynell, Esq.). A good view is obtained from Knockshehan Hill (473 ft.).

The monotony of the bog now becomes more interrupted, and the country again assumes a cultivated and wooded appearance, till we arrive at the important inland town of,

50 m., *Mullingar Hotel*: Murray's) Rte. 18, one of the most extensive military depôts in Ireland Pop. 5426). The assizes and the usual county business for Westmeath are also carried on here. It is the centre of a large trade in butter, wool, frieze, and cattle, a horse-fair, which extends over several days, being held in November. Mullingar, both in the general appearance of its buildings and the absence of all archaeological features, would seem to be of modern times, although it was in reality one of the most ancient of palatinate towns, founded by the English settlers in Meath, and possessing a castle, a priory for canons of St. Augustine, and also one for Dominicans, of which buildings there are now no traces. It was the scene of an obstinate fight in 1330, when Lord Thomas Butler was attacked and slain by MacGeoghegan, and in later days it was garrisoned by Gen. Ginckel as the head-quarters of William III.'s army previous to the siege of Athlone. As a military station it still keeps its pre-eminence, for which its central position makes it particularly valuable. The country in the immediate neighbourhood is pretty and wooded, and is moreover well watered by very considerable lakes and their attendant streams, affording good sport to the fisherman: of these the principal are Lough Owel and Lough Dervaragh Rte. 18 to the N., and Lough Ennel some 2 m. to the S. Mullingar itself is on the Brosna, which, in English, signifies " a bundle of firewood;" and the whole district was formerly known as " The Country of the Waters."

The tourist should visit Multifarnham Abbey on the Longford Rly. (Rte. 18).

Conveyances.—Rail to Dublin, Athlone, Galway, Cavan, Longford, and Sligo. Cars to Ballymahon and Kilbeggan.

Distances.—Longford, 26 m.; Cavan, 36; Multifarnham, 7½; Dublin, 50; Athlone, 28; Ballymahon, 18; Kilbeggan, 14; Lough Owel, 2; Lough Ennel, 2.

Excursions.—
1. Lough Ennel.
2. Lough Owel and Multifarnham.

A pleasant excursion may be taken to the head of *Lough Ennel*, otherwise called Belvidere Lake, from the mansion and estate of the same name overlooking it. It is a pretty lake of about 5 m. in length, well wooded on one side, though not presenting any scenery to entitle it to higher praise. The fishing is good, and the trout run from 1 to 10 lbs., the best season being at the end of May and June, when the green drake is on the water. There are several residences on either bank: on the rt. are Lynnburry (J. Rutherford, Esq.', Bloomfield (Col. Caulfield), Belvidere (B. Marley, Esq.', a seat of the Earl of Lanesborough, in whose grounds is a large pseudo-ruin intended for a priory; Rochfort House, an untenanted mansion belonging to Sir Francis Hopkins, Bart., who, in consequence of an attempted assassination, suddenly abandoned it to reside elsewhere; Anneville House (Hon. H. Parnell), Dunboden Park (Mrs. Cooper, Gaybrook (R. Smyth, Esq.), Carrick (W. Featherstonehaugh, Esq.); while on the W. side are Lilliput House (— Hudson, Esq.), Middleton House (G. Boyd, Esq., Bellmount (A. Reilly, Esq., and Ladestown (J. Lyons, Esq.).

At 53¾ m. the canal, which has hitherto kept closely alongside the rly., leaves it at Ballina Bridge and turns off N. to Longford. With an occasional view over the low shores of Lough Ennel on l., the rly. now passes through a less attractive country to

58 m. *Castletown*, a small village on l. The whole of this district is abundantly dotted with raths, relieved every few miles by a single ruined tower, marking the residence of some native chief.

62 m. *Streamstown*, a little beyond which, on l., close to the line, is the ruined tower of Laragh. At this point is a junction with the Clara branch of the Great Southern and Western Railway.

67 m. l. is the newly-drained lakelet of *Ballinderry*, where the labourers employed on the rly. works in 1850 discovered large quantities of bones of animals, associated with ancient spears and weapons, together with some very primitive canoes cut out of a single tree.

88 m. *Moate*, a thriving little place, much frequented by Quakers, "taking its name from a moat or rath at the back of the town, in what was originally the territory of the McLoughlins, and which was called after Grace McLoughlin 'Grana oge,' or Grace's Moat." —*Lewis*. Close to the town are Monte Park (Lord Crofton) and Ballynagartry. Passing 73 m. l. Glynwood House, the seat of J. Longworth, Esq., the traveller soon perceives on l. the approaching junction line of the South-Western line, and, crossing the noble stream of the Shannon, enters

78 m. the city of *Athlone* (Hotel: Bergins', tolerably comfortable) (Rte. 25), which has played a more important part in the history of Ireland than any other town, with the exception perhaps of Londonderry (Pop. 6227. Although a settlement existed here, known by the name of "Ath-Luain," the ford of the moon, or, according to others, "Ath-Luan," the ford of the rapids, it was not until the reign of John that the castle was erected, and it became an important military station—so important, indeed, that when Henry III. granted the dominion of Ireland to Prince Edward, Athlone was expressly reserved. During the insurrection of 1641 the castle and town under Lord Ranelagh were closely besieged by the Connaught men for 22 weeks, until the garrison, reduced by famine and disease, was relieved by a convoy from the Dublin army; and it was taken a second time by the Parliamentary army under Sir C. Coote. It was, however, during James II.'s reign that Athlone was the scene of such stirring events. Col. Grace then held it successfully for that king for 8 days against William III.'s army under Gen. Douglas, who retired to make way for a more formidable opponent, Gen. De Ginckell, who occupied the eastern part of the town and commenced a cannonade lasting from the 20th to the 30th of June, 1691, during which time 12,000 cannon-balls and 600 shells were thrown on to the castle and the Roscommon side of the town. So brave a defence was offered by the Irish army under Gen. St. Ruth, that it was at last determined to storm the city by assault, and the final struggle took place at the ford of the Shannon, the narrow bridge over which had been well-nigh shattered during the cannonade. "It was 6 o'clock : a peal from the steeple of the ch. gave the signal. Prince George of Hesse Darmstadt, and a brave soldier named Hamilton, whose services were afterwards rewarded with the title of Lord Boyne, descended first into the river. Then the grenadiers lifted the Duke of Wurtemburg on their shoulders, and with a great shout plunged 20 abreast up to their cravats in water. The Irish, taken unprepared, fired one confused volley and fled, leaving their commander, Maxwell, a prisoner. The victory was complete. Planks were placed on the broken

arches of the bridge, and pontoons laid in the river, without any opposition on the part of the terrified garrison. With the loss of 12 men killed and about 30 wounded, the English had in a few minutes forced their way into Connaught."—*Macaulay.* St. Ruth removed his forces from hence to Aughrim, about 15 m. distant. The loss of Athlone is generally attributed to the overweening confidence of St. Ruth, who, intoxicated with success at the failure of the first attempt of the English army, "was roused from his slumbers just in time to learn the irremediable loss occasioned by his presumptuous folly."—*Taylor.* An amusing allusion is made to this in 'The Battle of Aughrim'—

"*St. Ruth.*—Dare all the force of England be so bold
I' attempt to storm so brave a town, when I
With all Hibernia's sons of war are nigh?
Return; and if the Britons dare pursue,
Tell them St. Ruth is near, and that will do.

"*Balm·n.*—Your aid would do much better than your name."

The only remaining history of the town is the destruction of a great portion, including the citadel, in 1697, from the explosion of the magazine during a thunder-storm. As seen from the rly. stat., it is divided into 2 portions by the Shannon, which here, a noble and stately stream, issues from Lough Rea in its southward course to Limerick. Although modern improvement has been busy, the greater part of the town, which is on the l. bank, is ill-built and confined; but the celebrated bridge, the scene of the contest, was pulled down a few years ago to make way for the present one, as handsome and well-planned as the former was inconvenient. It had been built in the reign of Elizabeth, and was only 12 ft. broad. The bridge is commanded by the castle, the massive round tower of which looks more ancient than it probably really is, as the whole building has been so altered and added to at different periods, that the only old portion is the keep, in the centre of the court, now used as a barrack. Like Mullingar, Athlone is a very important military station, and contains barracks (which line the road from the rly. stat.) for 1500 men, besides 15,000 stand of arms, with hospital, and all the necessary adjuncts to a garrison town, defended by forts and redoubts on the Connaught side of the town. The visitor will not fail to observe the singular but graceful railway bridge over which the Dublin line is carried across the Shannon, "being a construction on the bowstring and lattice principle. It is entirely of iron, supported by 12 cylindrical piers, and is 560 ft. in extreme length, including 2 spans over roads on either side of the river. It consists of 2 spans of 175, and 2 of 40 ft. each, the latter separated by a pier, formed by 4 cylinders, supporting a swivel, which admits of the navigation of the adjacent opens."—*Fraser.*

Athlone presents no archæological remains, with the exception of the castle, or portion of the town wall (of considerable height and thickness, and the doorway of the house in which Gen. Ginckell resided. The churches are all modern, although it formerly possessed 2 or 3 conventual establishments. The parish ch., close to the hotel, rejoices in 2 towers, one of which is isolated, and belonged to an earlier building.

Conveyances.—By rail to Dublin and Galway, to Roscommon and Castlebar, also by Great Southern Rly. to Portarlington en route for the S. A steamer every second day runs down the Shannon to Clonmacnoise and Killaloe (Rte. 34), whence there is rail to Limerick. Daily car to Longford through Ballymahon. Car to Parsonstown.

Distances.—Dublin, 78 m.; Mullingar, 28; Ballinasloe, 13; Lissoy, 8; Lough Rea, 2½; Roscommon, 18½;

Castlereagh, 33 ; Clonmacnoise, 8½ ; Banagher, 20 ; Killaloe, 59 ; Portumna, 32⅓.

Excursions.—
1. Lough Rea and Rindown.
2. Clonmacnoise.
3. Ballymahon.

[An excursion should be made to the foot of Lough Rea (anc. Ribh), one of those extraordinary though picturesque expansions of the Shannon which are so peculiar to this river, commencing about 2 m. above Athlone, and extending N. for several m. Although the character of the scenery is not hilly, yet the banks are in many parts richly wooded, as are also the numerous islands, some of them being of considerable size, and nearly all possessing some ecclesiastical ruins of ancient date. The principal are Incheleraun, Saints' Island, Inchturk, Inchmore, and *Hare Island*, the latter a perfect gem of woodland scenery, aided by art in the shape of a lodge belonging to Lord Castlemaine, who occasionally resides here.] [Another visit may be paid to Ballymahon 14 m., passing through the hamlet of Lissoy or Auburn. 3 m. at Ballykeeran the road crosses the Breensford river almost at its fall into one of the bays of Lough Rea. 1 m. rt. is Moydrum Castle, the beautiful mansion of Lord Castlemaine. Following the shore of Lough Killinure, a small expansion of Lough Rea, the road passes through 5 m. Glassan, where a branch on l. leads to the ferry to Hare Island. On rt. is Waterstown House (Hon. T. Harris-Temple). 8 m., the village of Lissoy or Auburn is supposed to have been delineated by the poet Goldsmith in his 'Deserted Village.' He is said to have been born in this spot, although a place called Pallas, near Ballymahon, also claims the honour. It is not so clear that Lissoy was in his mind when he wrote his celebrated poem; and although 'The Three Pigeons,' the apple-tree,

" The never-failing brook, the busy mill,
The decent church that topp'd the neighb'ring hill,"

have always been considered by enthusiasts as identical with the subjects of the poem, it is more probable " that everything in it is English, the feelings, incidents, descriptions, and allusions. Scenes of the poet's youth had doubtless risen in his memory as he wrote, mingling with and taking altered hue from later experiences."— *Forster's Life of Goldsmith.*

14 m. *Ballymahon*, a small town, prettily situated on the Inney, which runs under a bridge of 5 arches, and falls over ledges of rock, winding its way between wooded islands. In the neighbourhood are Newcastle (Hon. L. King-Harman), Castlecove (Captain Hussy), and Creenaghmore.]

From Athlone the line runs through a dreary and uninteresting country to

9½ m. *Ballinasloe* (anc. Bal-athana-sluigheadh) (*Hotel:* Railway), so well known through Great Britain for its enormous horse and cattle fairs (Pop. 3911). The town lies in a low position on the banks of the Suck river, which intersects and in fact divides Roscommon from Galway. On the eastern side are the Lunatic Asylum for Connaught, and the ruins of Ballinasloe Castle, which in the reign of Elizabeth was one of the strongest fortresses in Ireland. The outer walls only remain, and are incorporated with a modern residence. The great fair of the year, which, to English eyes, presents a scene of rare confusion, is held from the 5th to the 9th of October, partly in the neighbouring grounds of Garbally and partly in the town. In the park " the herds of the most extensive flockmasters of Connaught generally occupy the same localities from year to year; but there are sometimes stiff contests between them, in order to maintain their ground against intruders." The number of sheep sold at this fair in 1861 was 59,641, although in some former years as many as 97,000 have been disposed of. In 1862, however, the number of sales was considerably less. Adjoining the town is Garbally, the very beautiful park of Lord Clancarty, who liberally throws it open for the enjoyment of the townspeople. The house contains some good paintings.

Conveyances.— Car to Ballybrophy through Parsonstown and Roscrea.

Distances.— Parsonstown, 25¼ m.; Banagher, 18; Eyrecourt, 11½; Aughrim, 5; Kilconnell, 9.

Excursions.—
1. Garbally.
2. Kilconnell.
3. Aughrim.

[5 m. from Ballinasloe, on the road to Kilconnell, is the village of Aughrim, famous for the battle which took place on Anghrim Hill, about 1 m. to the S., on July 12th, 1691 just after the siege of Athlone), between the Irish army under Gen. St. Ruth and Sarsfield (Lord Lucan) and the English army under Ginckel and Talmarsh. The Irish position on Kilcommodon Hill (now capped by a modern ch., was very strong, but, notwithstanding this advantage and the superiority of numbers, the Irish were routed with a loss of 7000 men, besides their commander, St. Ruth, who was slain by a cannon-ball—

" Aughrim is no more, St. Ruth is dead,
And all his guards are from the battle fled;
As he rode down the hill he met his fall,
And died a victim to a cannon-ball."
Battle of Aughrim.

A spot by the ch. is still known as St. Ruth's flag. 4 m. to the S. is Lismany, the model farm of Mr. Pollok, well worth a visit from those who are interested in the social progress of Ireland. 450 people are kept constantly employed, and 700*l.* is paid monthly for wages.]

9 m. l. is the village of *Kilconnell* (anc. Cil-chonaill), which may be reached in 4 m. from Woodlawn Stat.: but as a car may not always be obtained, the safest plan will be to visit it from Ballinasloe. It is celebrated for its ruined abbey, founded in 1400 for Franciscan friars by William O'Kelly, on the site of an earlier ch. raised by St. Connall. " As picturesque a ruin as can be where there are neither hills, rocks, lake, nor river, and but a few distant trees: perhaps its ivy-mantled tower and roofless gables were better in keeping with the waste and desolation that presided over the place, destitute as it is of any modern improvement and decoration whatever."—*Otway*. It is a cruciform ch., consisting of nave, choir, and transept, with cloisters and domestic buildings, and a very graceful though slender tower of 2 stages rising from the intersection. The Dec. windows are remarkable for the beauty of their tracery, while the cloisters are one of the most perfect examples in Ireland. The area is small, only 48 ft. square, and is enclosed by pointed arches on each side, the columns of which are not carried down to the ground, but spring from a low wall. The whole effect is in fact " more like a cloister in Sicily or Spain than anything in these islands."— *Fergusson*. In the interior of the ch. are some monuments, and a tablet to the memory of some members of the Trimlestown family, " whoe, being transplanted into Conaght with others by orders of the vsvrper Cromwell, dyed at Moinivae, 1667." A pretty cross in the village has been restored by the Roman Catholic clergy.

101½ m. On l. of *Woodlawn* Stat. is Woodlawn House, the seat of Lord Ashtown. On a hill overlooking the station rt. is a castellated edifice, known as Trench's Monument, and used as a mausoleum for the Ashtown family. From hence the rly. runs over a miserable, bleak, and stony country to

113½ m. *Athenry* (with accent on last syllable) (*Hotel:* Railway) (Rte. 27), a miserable town, which, as far as ruined antiquities go, is a veritable Tadmor in the wilderness. It was thought by Sir James Ware to have been, with great probability, the chief town of the Auteri, whom Ptolemy places in this part of Ireland. At all events, it was of importance during the Anglo-Norman invasion, having been the first raised and the principal town of the De Burghs and Berminghams, whose fortress even now exists. Under the shelter of its defences many ecclesiastical establishments rose up, amongst which were a Dominican abbey founded in 1261, which became the favourite ch. and burial-place of the Earls of Ulster and all the chief Irish families; and a Franciscan priory, founded in 1464 by the Earl of Kildare. The importance of the town, however, decayed in 1577, when the 2 sons of the Earl of Clanricarde nearly destroyed it by fire, a proceeding which was again repeated (it having been rebuilt in the mean time) by the northern Irish in 1596. The castle consists of a massive quadrangular keep surrounded by outworks. It is of the usual square unornamented style, and lighted by a few eylet-holes. The walls of the town are in tolerable keeping, and retain a castellated gateway, the doorway of which presents some examples of interlacing work. The Dominican abbey is a cruciform church, of which the intersecting tower has disappeared. The E. window, of 4 lights, is of beautiful design. The whole of the ruins, together with the modern ch., are surrounded by as miserable a collection of hovels as can well be seen in any Irish town. In the neighbourhood of Athenry are Castle Lambert (W. Lambert, Esq.), Castle Ellen (W. P. Lambert, Esq.), and Moyode (R. B. Persse, Esq.).

Conveyances.—By rail to Dublin and Galway. By rail to Tuam. Coach to Westport. Car to Loughrea.

Distances.—Galway, 13 m.; Oranmore, 8; Loughrea, 11; Tuam, 16; Monivea, 7.

Passing on l. the square fortress of Derrydonnel, the traveller reaches

121 m. *Oranmore*, a village situated at the head of a creek which forms part of Galway Bay. Here is another square tower, built by the Earl of Clanricarde, who, on the breaking out of the war in 1641, "placed it under the command of Capt. Willoughby, who also held the fort at Galway, and surrendered both of them to the Catholic forces in 1643."—*Lewis*. From hence the rail runs through a dreary and stony district, though the monotony is soon relieved by exquisite views of the bay of Galway, which stretches out to the W. as far as the eye can see. Crossing an arm of the bay known as Lough Athaliah, on the N. shore of which are Merview (P. Joyce, Esq.) and Renmore (P. Lynch, Esq.), the tourist arrives at

126½ m. the ancient city of Galway (Rte. 20) (*Hotels:* Railway, comfortable; Black's; Kilroy's).

ROUTE 15.

FROM EDENDERRY AND ENFIELD TO DROGHEDA, THROUGH TRIM AND NAVAN.

Enfield (Rte. 14), a station, distant 26¼ m. from Dublin, on the Midland Great Western Rly., is the point from whence the traveller commences his excursion from the source of the Boyne to its mouth. A daily car runs from the stat. to Edenderry, 11 m., but it is better to be independent of this. At Edenderry another conveyance may be procured to proceed to Trim.

7 m. Carberry Castle occupies a conspicuous position on the summit of an isolated hill 471 ft., which, from the comparative level of the country round, commands very wide views.

The ruins of Carberry (anc. Cairbreva-ciardha) are extensive, although not all of the same date. The original castle was built by the De Berminghams, some of the earliest English settlers within the Pale, and suffered many rude attacks during the troubled times of the 15th cent., having been more than once demolished and burnt. From the De Berminghams it passed into the hands of the Colleys or Cowleys temp. 1518, the ancestors of the family of Wellesley, one Richard Colley having been created Lord Mornington in 1746. The general style of the building is that of a manorial castellated house of James I.'s time, embracing all the characteristic features of pointed gable, graceful chimneys, and mullioned windows, which are particularly good on the eastern side. Some of the chimneys have no less than 16 flues, and are beautifully moulded; but on a nearer inspection we perceive, from the character of the masonry, the massive walls, the deep stone-roofed donjons, the principal of which runs for 85 ft. underneath the great keep from S. to N., the manifest antiquity of the entire of the western end, and the general arrangement of the whole, that the present ruin consists of structures which would appear to be as old as the 12th cent."—*Sir W. Wilde.* On the summit of the hill are some ancient Pagan remains, and the ruined ch. of Temple Doath.

About 1¼ m. to the N. is the ruin of Mylerstown Castle, consisting of a lofty tower. This was also a fortress of the De Berminghams. The view from the summit of Carberry hill stretches over the counties of Meath, Westmeath, Carlow, Kildare, Dublin, King's, and Queen's; looking westward, the hills of Croghan, Edenderry, and Carrick rise conspicuous from the flats. S. are the ranges of Kildare, including the Chair; while, nearer home, the various castles and churches of Carberry, Mylerstown, Edenderry, Kinnafad, and Carrick are dotted about.

At the foot of the hill is Newberry Hall (F. Pilkington, Esq.).

11 m. *Edenderry* (Hotel: Nowlan's), a neat, well-to-do little town, under the care of the Marquess of Downshire, the owner of the soil. A statue in memory of the late Marquess occupies a conspicuous position near the ch. The castle of the Blundells picturesquely crowns the limestone hill that overhangs it. Although not near enough to be much benefited by the rly., it has the advantage of a branch from the Grand Canal. The geologist should visit the quarry in the lower limestone at Killan, a little to the S., which contains, in the lower portion, horizontal beds of black marble, and resting conformably on them crystalline limestones, jointed vertically, in such a way as to appear columnar.

Distances.—Enfield, 11 m.; Clonard, 6; Philipstown, 11½.

Conveyances.—Car daily to Enfield.

In the demesne is Trinity Well, the source of the river Boyne, 289 ft. above the sea. As might be expected from its varied course, and the historical incidents which everywhere mark it, the Boyne has been the subject of divers legends in its infancy, the basis of all which appears to be that it was so named after an Irish princess, Boan or Boinne, who was drowned in it. From hence it has a course more or less sluggish for about 70 m. to the sea at Drogheda, running generally from S.W. to N.E. Many parts are extremely beautiful, while all are more or less replete with ruins, Pagan remains, and scenes of historical interest. Probably no river in Ireland possesses so many celebrated towns and neighbourhoods:—

"Ecce Boan qui Trim celer influit, istius undas
Subdere se salsis Drogheda cernit aquis."
Necham, 1217.

Continuing on the road to Clonard, the tourist arrives at 11¼ m. the ruins of *Monasteroris,* a small ch. of the 14th cent. with a double belfry; also portions of a monastery with walls of great thickness, and, on an adjoining tumulus, of a square dovecot. This, too, was a foundation of the Berminghams, viz. Sir John, who was also Earl of Louth in 1325. Monasteroris is in Irish, Mainister Fcorais, which latter word, as Sir W. Wilde has pointed out, is the poetic translation of Pierce, the first of the Berminghams, a family well known by the Irish natives under the name of Clan-Feorais, or the Clan of Pierce. Close by is Monasteroris House (J. Hamilton, Esq.).

The monastery sustained a long siege by the Earl of Surrey, the Lord Lieutenant, who marched into the district of Offaly (as it was termed) against the O'Moores who had invaded the Pale.

13½ m. a road on rt. leads across the river to *Kinnafad* Castle, also founded by the Berminghams, who appear to have dotted the whole country with their strongholds. It is a large square tower, lighted by a few narrow windows, and more remarkable for its massive plainness than for any architectural features. It was doubtless erected to command the ford, for, in deepening the bed of the river from Kinnafad to Edenderry, numbers of weapons and celts, together with human remains, were discovered. They are now in the Museum of the Royal Irish Academy. The tourist should proceed by this road, as he will thus obtain the most interesting points on the Boyne.

15½ m. is the partly inhabited fortress of Grange Castle, near which the Boyne receives a considerable accession in the Yellow River, that flows in here from the W., separating Meath from King's County. About 1 m. to the rt. is Carrick Hill, rising 387 ft. with the same conspicuous outline as that of Carberry. Like Carberry too, it possesses the ruins of a castle, the chief court of the treacherous Baron Pierce de Bermingham. Here, "A.D. 1305, Murtagh O'Connor of Offalie, Mulmorrey his brother, and Calvagh O'Connor, with 29 of the choicest of their family, were treacherously killed by Pyers Bermyngham, within the castle of Carrickffeorus."—*Annals of Clonmacnoise.*

Of the castle there now remains only the S. wall of a high keep, and an adjoining ch. of the 13th or beginning of the 14th cent., with its E. and S. walls. Both the W. and E. gables have belfries. The hill of Carrick consists of mountain limestone, but on the summit is a large block of trap, similar to that of Croghan, from which place it was doubtless transported by means of local drift action. It bears the name of the Witches' Rock, and was originally thrown at one of the saints from

Croghan by an individual of that profession.

An indented flat stone, probably marking the site of a cell, is also called the Mule's Leap on the same legendary grounds. Stretching along the banks of the Boyne is the demesne of Rahin (Rev. Mr. Palmer).

18¼ m. close to the river side is *Ballybogan* Abbey, a very large cruciform ch. (of which the transepts have been destroyed, founded in the 12th cent. by Jordan Comin, for Augustinian canons. The priory was burned down in the 15th cent., and subsequently the lands and property fell into the hands of the Berminghams. The length of the ch. is 193 ft., but there are remarkably few architectural decorations about it. The W. gable is lighted by a long slender single window of E. Eng. date. In the N. wall of the choir are 3 trefoil-arched sedilia. At the junction of the 3 roads near the abbey is a picturesque holy well.

[From hence a road recrosses the Boyne en route for Kinnafad. The tourist may go to Clonard this way for the sake of visiting Tieroghan Castle; but the distance is greater, and he will probably have seen as many castles as he could wish before reaching Trim. It is worth recording, however, that when this stronghold was besieged by the Parliamentary forces under Col. Reynolds, the siege was about being raised, when it was discovered that the defenders were firing silver bullets, which was such an evident proof of their want of ammunition, that the opposing forces set to work again and soon reduced the fortress.

Crossing the river at Leinster Bridge, notice between the road and the river a mound where 150 Irishmen lie buried, part of a body of insurgents who laid siege in 1798 to the mansion belonging to Mr. Tyrrel, which he with 27 yeomen successfully held out for a whole day.]

22½ m. *Clonard* now presents very little for the inspection of the archæologist, but carries interest with it from its old associations, which extend back for the last 1000 years. Clonard or Cluain Ioraird ("The Retirement on the Western Height") was in early times the most famous bishopric in Meath, the first bishop being St. Finian (A.D. 520), one of the immediate successors of St. Patrick. It was also the centre of learning in Ireland, and, like Llantwit in S. Wales and Bardsey Island in N. Wales, was the seat of a world-famed college, which numbered 3000 students, including St. Kieran, St. Columb, and all the principal saints. Not only for its learning, but for its hospitality, was it celebrated, as visitors from Armorica and all parts of Europe were constantly journeying hither. The buildings formerly consisted of abbeys, chapels, cloictheachs or round towers, &c.; but of these absolutely no trace is left, though many of them existed at the beginning of this cent., and were described by Archdall in his 'Monasticon.' From the Annals we learn the misfortunes which attended Clonard: that in 1045 it was set on fire thrice in one week; that in 1136 it was sacked and plundered by the people of Brefney; and so on with various repetitions until it has become the wilderness it is. The only traces of archæological interest are a fragment of corbel over the door in the tower of the ch., and in the interior a singular font of grey marble, in shape an octagonal basin, the external panels of which are each divided into 2 compartments, and are ornamented with very curious figures and scriptural subjects, representing the Flight into Egypt, the Baptism in the Jordan, &c.

Near the ch. stands a singular tumulus or moat crowned by a spreading ash-tree. This was evidently sepulchral; but a little to the N.W. is a rath (military), very perfect, consisting "of an external fosse, encircling a raised ditch, within which we find a level platform, elevated somewhat above the surrounding plain, but not so high as the earthen circle which encloses it."—*Wilde.*

[From Clonard, the tourist who does not wish to extend his wanderings to Trim may rejoin the Midland Rly., at the Hill of Down Stat., 2 m. distant.]

27 m. Keeping on the l. bank of the Boyne and crossing a tributary stream, we arrive at Killyon (an old seat of the Magans), near which are the scanty remains of an ancient priory, and a little further on *Donore Castle*, a well-preserved square fortress (like a peel-tower) of the date of the Anglo-Norman invasion. The river is here crossed at Inchmore Bridge.

32 m. rt., near Doolistown House, the road again approaches the river, which has begun to improve very considerably in the character of its scenery.

35 m. l. Newhaggard House; and beyond, though on the opposite side of the stream, is *Trimlestown*, the ruined seat of Lord Trimleston. It dates from the 15th cent., and played a somewhat conspicuous part in the Parliamentary war, during which time it was garrisoned and fortified for 10 years.

36 m. *Trim* (anc. Ath-truim) (*Hotel:* Darling's) has been graphically described by Sir W. Wilde. "To see Trim aright, the tourist must approach it by the Blackbull-road from Dublin, when all the glorious ruins which crowd this historic locality, and which extend over a space of above a mile, burst suddenly upon him; the remains of St. John's Friary and castellated buildings at the bridge of Newtown—the stately abbey of St. Peter and St. Paul a little farther on, raising aloft its tall, light, and ivy-mantled windows—the neighbouring chapel, with its sculptured tombs and monumental tablets—the broad green lawns, through which the Boyne winds, between that and Trim—the grey massive towers of King's John Castle, with its outward walls and barbican, the gates and towers and bastion—the fosse, moat, and chapel—the sheepgate and portions of the town wall—and above all, the tall, commanding form of the Yellow Steeple, which seems the guardian genius of the surrounding ruins."

The Yellow Steeple is supposed to occupy the site of the original abbey of St. Mary, founded in 432 by St. Patrick; indeed Trim is believed to have been one of the oldest of the Irish sees. The present tower was erected in the Anglo-Norman period, and is a lofty building of 5 stages, 125 ft. in height. The W. wall and part of the N. and S. have been destroyed, according to some by the cannon of Cromwell, thus leaving the interior exposed to view. From its great height it was probably built as a signal and watch tower over the adjoining country. Amongst the ruined portions of the wall near the Yellow Steeple is a round-headed arch, known as the Sheepgate, which with the Watergate are the only remaining 2 entrances of the old town. The abbey of Trim was rich and powerful, and cultivated intimate relations with the Court of England.

N. of the town and without the old walls are scanty remains of the Black Friary of the Dominicans, founded in the 13th cent., by Geoffrey de Geneville, or de Joinville, Lord of Meath, as famous a crusader and military knight as he afterwards became a good ecclesiastic, of whom it was written—

" Ipse post militiæ bursum temporalis
Illustratus gratiâ doni spiritualis
Esse Xti cupiens miles specialis
In hoc domo monachus factus est claustralis."

Of the Grey Friary of Observantines no traces remain. The Castle of King John, who by the way had no connection with it save that of lodging there on a visit to Ireland, was originally founded by Hugh de Lacy in 1173, who then departed to England, leaving it in custody of Hugh Tyrrel.

Roderic O'Connor, King of Connaught, marched against the fortress to destroy it; but Tyrrel, finding himself too weak for defence, set it on fire and burnt it. The present building in extent surpasses anything in the country, and is believed to have been rebuilt by one Richard Pipard, although it is asserted by Camden that this individual lived previous to the grant of Meath being made to Lacy.

The ruins occupy an area of 2 acres, and consist of a lofty keep 80 ft. in height, and flanked by rectangular towers abutting from each side, so that it presents externally a figure of 20 sides. The outer wall is 486 yds. in length, and is strengthened by 10 circular towers at equal distances. By means of a moat which ran all round, the waters of the Boyne could be let in and thus completely isolate the castle. The barbican, portcullis, and drawbridge are still in remarkable preservation.

To describe in detail the numerous events of which Trim was the scene would be to write the history of mediæval Ireland; it will suffice to mention briefly that Richard Earl of Ulster held a gay court here in Edward II.'s reign—that Lord Gloucester and Henry of Lancaster, afterwards Henry IV., were imprisoned here by Richard II.—and that successive parliaments were held, at one of which a mint was established. And not only is Trim celebrated for its heroes of early times, but it can boast of being the abode at one time of the Duke of Wellington, who lived in a house in Dublingate-street, at the top of which a lofty pillar has been erected, crowned by his statue.

Trim possessed 2 other fortresses known as Nangle's Castle and Talbot's Castle, built by Sir John Talbot, the Lord Lieutenant of Ireland and the Scourge of France, in 1415. This latter building was converted into the Diocesan School where Wellington received his early education. The parish ch. is also an ancient edifice, and has a steeple erected in 1449 by Richard Duke of York.

In addition to these objects of interest are a few modern county buildings, of which the gaol, one of the most complete in the county, is worth an inspection. About 3 m. from the town on the Dublin road, and on both sides of the Boyne, which is crossed at the village of *Newton Trim*, are the extensive remains of the Abbey of St. Peter and St. Paul. On the N. bank are the cathedral remains, which exhibit some fine features in Transition-Norman. It was founded at the beginning of the 13th cent. by Simon Rochfort, the same ecclesiastic who removed the see of Clonard hither. " Broad strips of masonry, placed at a considerable distance apart, project from the walls of the ch. upon the exterior, a feature never found but in early work, and which is generally characteristic of the Norman period. Within, several chastely-formed decorated corbel-shafts remain, and support portions of the ribs by which the vaulted roof was sustained. The windows are of the lancet form, with piers between, and the mouldings which run round them are ornamented with beautifully designed bands. Sedilia of Norm. architecture may be seen in the wall, to the rt. of the space anciently occupied by the altar."—*Wakeman*. At the other end of the bridge are the ruins of the castle, a large rectangular keep with square towers at 2 of the angles, and a 2nd smaller tower lower down. There is a good 3-light window in a small chapel within the ruins, the whole of which taken together combine in a singular degree the religious and the military.

In a small ch. hard by are some remains of imposts, tombs, capitals, &c., recovered from the ruins, and placed here by the archæological care of Rev. Mr. Butler, vicar of Trim. There is also an altar-tomb bearing the recumbent figures of Sir Lucas Dillon and his wife, Chief Baron of the Exchequer in the reign of Elizabeth. On the sides are the arms of the Dillons, Baths, and Barnewalls. At the point where the Dublin road leaves the river is *Scurloughstown Castle*, a singular massive peel-tower, or rectangular keep with 2 round towers placed diagonally at the corners. It was called after its builder, William de Scarloug, an Aug.-Norm. settler in 1180, and in later times suffered somewhat at the hands of Cromwell, who, being challenged by the garrison, fired a cannon-ball which caused a crack in one of its sides.

Conveyances.—Rail to Dublin.

Distances.—Kells, 16 m.; Enfield, 10; Tara, 9; Dangan, 4; Bective, 5; Clonard, 14; Navan, 13½.

[In an excursion to Dangan Castle (4 m.). the tourist will pass 1½ m. *Laracor*, a quiet secluded little village associated with the name of Dean Swift, for it was once his residence. "Here also lived Stella and Mrs. Dingley, and here they sauntered through the quiet roads with Dr. Raymond, the vicar of Trim, and with the future author of Gulliver and the 'Drapier's Letters.'" The association is all that is left, as the dwelling of the witty divine has long ago crumbled to ruins.

4 m. *Dangan* was one of the seats of the Wellesley family, in which the late Duke of Wellington passed much of his early days, though he was not born here, as some biographers make out. There is little to interest in the present building, which consists of a keep, part of the old fortress, and attached to it a mansion in the Italian style. It is now almost a ruin, having fallen into the possession of a careless owner, who let the whole estate go to rack, a proceeding that was considerably hastened by a fire.]

38 m. Scurloughstown Castle (see ante); and 39 m. on the opposite side of the Boyne is Rathnally House (W. Thompson, Esq.), where the scenery of the river begins greatly to improve, and to assume a peculiarly English character. The banks rise to a considerable height, thus shutting out the river from the road.

40¼ m. l. *Trubley Castle* is a fortress of about the same importance as Scurloughstown, though very little is now left save the portion of a tower and a round pigeon-house. It is said that Cromwell slept a night here during his passage up the Boyne.

41 m. l. Close to Bective Bridge, on the l. bank, are the ruins of the noble abbey of Bective, one of the finest of the many noble remains of this district. Bective was founded for the Cistercian order in the 12th cent. by O'Melaghlin, King of Meath, who endowed it with 250 fat acres. Here was buried the body of Hugh de Lacy, treacherously murdered by a countryman while he was superintending the building of a new castle at Darrow. His head was taken to the ch. of St. Thomas in Dublin, which caused such umbrage to the monks of that establishment, that they appealed to the Pope, who decided that the abbey of Bective should give up the remainder of the corpse. Very little remains to show the whereabouts of the ch., the whole style of the abbey indicating a remarkable union of monastic with military arrangements. It is in good preservation, and enables us to trace the various apartments and halls. The general plan of the buildings is that of a quadrangle, with a strong battlemented tower, containing a vaulted hall, at the S.W. corner.

IRELAND. *Route 15.—Tara.* 135

In the centre are the cloisters, the E. Eng. arches of which are remarkably beautiful. They are cinquefoiled and supported on light clustered pillars. " The featherings are mostly plain, but several are ornamented with flowers or leaves, and upon one a hawk-like bird is sculptured. The bases, which are circular, rest upon square plinths, the angles of which are ornamented with a leaf, as it were, growing out of the base moulding."—*Wakeman.* From the splaying of the windows in the N. wall of the cloister, it might also have served as the S. wall of the ch.

The domestic portion of the monastery is on the E. side, and is remarkable for the great thickness of the walls, through which flues are carried up to be ended in tapering chimney-shafts. Much of this part of the building is of later date.

[About 5 m. to the rt. of Bective is a spot that should be visited by every Irish traveller, not for the sake of ruined castle or abbey, but for its old associations with all that was great and noble in Ireland's early history. The hill of Tara was for ages the centre of Ireland, the palace, the burial-place of her kings, and the sacred spot from which edicts were promulgated and justice dispensed; and yet nothing is left to mark this former metropolis but some grassy mounds and a few pillars. The 4th of the royal palaces "was that of Teamhair or Tarah, which originally belonged to the province of Leinster, where the states of the kingdom met in a parliamentary way, when several wise regulations were made for the better governing of the state." — *Comerford.* Indeed, so sacred was the locality considered, that not even a king could reside there who had any personal blemish. Accordingly we read in the Irish MS. entitled 'Seanchas na Relec' that Cormac, the Great King, held his court at Tara, until his eye was destroyed by Engus, when he was obliged to go and live at Cennannus or Kells. After the death of Dermot in the year 563, the hill was deserted in consequence of a curse pronounced against the king by St. Ruadan, and subsequently it was the scene of a decisive battle in which the power of the Danes in Meath was overthrown. The present remains consist of certain mounds or duns laid down in the Ordnance Map as Rath Riogh, Rath Laoghaire, Rath Grainne, and Rath Caelchu.

Of these the most important was Rath Riogh, of oval form, 850 ft. long, within the enclosure of which rises up a mound, known as the Forradh, and another called Teach Cormac, the House of Cormac. The Forradh is flattened at the top and surrounded by 2 lines of earth, with a ditch between. It is conspicuous from a single pillar stone, which has been suggested by Dr. Petrie with great probability to be no other than the celebrated Lia Fail, or Stone of Destiny, upon which for many ages the monarchs of Ireland were crowned, and which is generally supposed to have been removed from Ireland to Scotland for the coronation of Fergus Mac Eark, a prince of the blood-royal of Ireland, there having been a prophecy that, in whatever country this famous stone was preserved, a king of the Scotic race should reign. Teach Cormac is joined to the Forradh on the S.E., and is a double enclosure of about 140 ft. in diameter. On the N. of the Forradh is the Old Hall or Teach Miodhchuarta, consisting of 2 parallel lines of earth running N. and S., with 6 openings on each side denoting the ancient entrances. It was 360 ft. long by 40 ft., and was evidently intended for the accommodation of a large number at the same time. " The eating-hall had 12 stalls in each wing, tables and passages round them; 16 attendants on each side—8 to the astrologers, historians, and secretaries in the rere of the hall, and 2 to each table at the door—100 guests in all: 2 oxen, 2 sheep, and 2 hogs at each meal' were divided equally on each side."—*MSS*. Between the Rath Riogh and the Old Hall is a mound known as the King's Chair, and N. of the latter are the Raths Grainne and Caelchu. A road leading to the N. was the Slighe Fan na-Carbad, or Slope of the Chariots. The visitor to this ancient mausoleum of Ireland's glories will sympathize with the poet in his melancholy strain :—

> " No more to chiefs and ladies bright
> The harp of Tara swells,
> The chord alone that breaks at night
> Its tale of ruin tells."—*Moore*.

To go back to a yet more ancient period, the geologist will be interested to know that both the Hills of Tara and Skreen are composed of rocks of the coal-measure formation, which abound in Posidonomya.]

42 m. on a small strip of land, between the river and a tributary brooklet, are the ruins of Clady ch., remarkable for possessing a transept, a feature unusual in Irish early churches. In the S. chapel is a good E. Eng. window with cinquefoil arches. The brook is crossed by a singular bridge of 2 unequal arches, which are supposed by some antiquaries to be coeval with the ch. A discovery was made near the ch. of 2 subterranean chambers of beehive-shape, formed of rows of stones, each layer of which projects a little beyond the layer below. So far they are similar to the chambers at Newgrange (p. 139), but with this difference, that the dome in the latter springs from upright pillars and does not commence from the ground, as it does at Clady. The chambers are 9 ft. high, and are connected by a small passage about 9 ft. long. " There can be little doubt that they are to be referred to Pagan times, before the use of the arch or the advantage of mortar was known, and were probably employed by some of the very early people of this island as places of security, temporary habitations, and granaries."—*Wilde*. It is unfortunate, however, that the beehive houses have so fallen in that it is very difficult for a stranger to make them out. On the same side of the river is Beetive House, the residence of R. Bolton, Esq. Opposite is *Assey Castle*, a fortress resembling the numerous Boyne castles, being a square keep with circular towers at alternate angles. There are also some ecclesiastical ruins hard by. Following the course of the river are Ballinter House and Bridge (45 m.), with Dowdstown House, on the rt. bank; Ardsallagh House, the Elizabethan seat of the Duke of Bedford, on the l.; after which the tourist arrives at 47½ m. *Kilcarn*, from whence the road crosses to the l. bank to Navan.

Before crossing, he may diverge about ½ m. to the rt., to visit the ruined ch. of Kilcarn, which formerly contained one of the most perfect and beautiful fonts in the country. To prevent annihilation, the usual fate of every relic in Irish churches, it was buried, but afterwards dug up and placed in its present position in the Rom. Cath. chapel at Johnstone. The shaft is plain, but the basin is elaborately ornamented with a series of 12 niches, each containing a carved figure. Two of them indeed contain 2 figures, of which one compartment represents Christ blessing the Virgin Mary. In all the others are figures of the Apostles, carved with extraordinary delicacy, and the utmost attention to expression and costume. Each niche is surmounted by a small crocket.

[If the tourist prefers crossing the Boyne at Ballinter Bridge, he will pass near the ruins of Cannistown ch., a 13th cent. ch., with a remarkably good circular choir arch and E. window.]

About ¼ m. below Kilcarn Bridge is *Athlumney Castle*, a most picturesque fortress, or rather fortified mansion, of the 16th cent. At one end is an ivy-covered tower, adjoining the more modern mansion with its gables and mullioned windows. It is told of the former owner of this castle, Sir Launcelot Dowdall, that, rather than suffer the Prince of Orange to enter beneath his roof, as he had reason to suppose he would do, he himself set fire to his ancestral home.

49½ m. *Navan* (*Hotel:* Brady's) Rtes. 14, 16.

From hence the road skirts the beautiful grounds of Black Castle F. Rothwell, Esq. to 51 m. *Donaghmore*, remarkable for its church and round tower. In early times the great ch. of Domnachmor was celebrated for the veneration in which it was held, on account of the sanctity of St. Cassanus, a disciple of St. Patrick, who particularly confided this ch. to his care. The old building, however, has evidently given place to a later one of the 13th cent., erected by the Anglo-Norman settlers.

The round tower is similar in form to that at Kells (Rte. 16), and is considered by Dr. Petrie to be of the 10th cent. Its height is 100 ft., and the circumference at its base is 66 ft.; but the top has been of late years repaired, though not in a very accurate manner, for it has not the conical apex nor the upper windows so peculiar to Irish towers. "The doorway is remarkable for having a figure of our Saviour crucified, sculptured in relievo on its key-stone and the stone immediately above it. This doorway, which is placed at an elevation of 12 ft. from the base of the tower, measures 5 ft. 2 in. in height, and its inclined jambs are 2 ft. 3 in. asunder at the sill, and 2 ft. at the spring of the arch. It will be perceived that there is a human head carved on each side of the door, the one partly on the band and the other outside it."—*Petrie*. The fact of there being sculpture over the door has been used by some antiquaries as a proof that it was an after work, which would consequently throw the origin of the tower into Pagan times.

52 m. rt. on the bank of the river opposite Ardmulchan is the ruined fortress of *Dunmoe*, an Anglo-Norm. castle of about the 16th cent. It had its share of hard treatment in its time, and in 1641 held its ground so bravely against the Irish force sent against it that the assailants induced the commander, Captain Power, to surrender by means of a forged order from the Lords Justices. The river face is protected laterally by 2 circular towers, and it occupies a very fine position, probably overlooking an ancient ford.

53¼ m. l. Stackallan House, the seat of Viscount Boyne.

55 m. rt., nearly opposite the wooded eminences of Beauparc (Rte. 16), are the ruins of *Castle Dexter*, said to have been erected by one of the Flemings, the early lords of Slane, but supposed with greater probability to have been built by the D'Exeter family, a Connaught sept who were located in Meath. It is a rambling, ivy-covered ruin, beautifully situated, but not possessing any very remarkable features. A little higher up is Cruicetown Lock and the Fall of Stackallan, above which the river is crossed at Broadboyne Bridge. "The broad reach below the bridge has been supposed by some antiquaries to be in the vicinity of Brugh-na-Boinne, where the monarchs of Tara were interred of old; but we think that the evidence is in favour of the locality beyond Slane."—*Wilde*.

The traveller by road will notice nearly parallel with Castle Dexter the broken shaft of Baronstown Cross, the inscription on the sides showing that it was erected in 1590 by the Dowdall family.

57 m. Slane, in early days called Ferta-fear-feig (*Inn:* Dean's), a neat pretty town, in days gone by the residence and burial-place of

King Slanius, of whom it was said, "This Slanius is entombed at a hill in Meath, which of him is named Slane."

On a bank overlooking the river is Slane Castle, the modern residence of the Marquis of Conyngham, who had the honour of a visit here from King George IV. The archæological tourist will find more interest in the ruins of the ch. and monastery, so beautifully placed on the hill above the town, that is worth ascending for the sake of the view, which Sir W. Wilde justly considers to equal that from Richmond Hill, and which embraces the whole course of the Boyne from Trim to Drogheda, with the classic hills of Skreen and Tara, and the mounds that mark the burial-places of the kings. The best part of the abbey ruins is a noble tower, with a round-headed doorway on the western side, and a good Decorated Flamboyant window. The remains of the monastery are some little distance to the N.E. An abbey must have existed here for some time, as we read that in 948 the cloictheach or round tower of Slane was burned by the Danes, together with the crozier and the bells, "the best of bells." Previous to this time there was an establishment of Canons Regular, in which Dagobert King of France was educated. After being destroyed by the Danes the abbey gradually decayed, until it was restored by Sir Christopher Fleming in 1512. There are in the enclosure some singular gravestones, one of them formed of 2 headstones, shaped like the gable of a house. Sir W. Wilde considers it with great probability to be of greater antiquity than any Christian tomb in Ireland.

On the western brow of the hill, above the town, is a large circular rath, and on the same side of the river are the interesting ruins of the *Hermitage of St. Erc*, the 1st Bishop of Slane, consecrated by St. Patrick at the beginning of the 6th cent., whose piety was so great, that "his custom was to remain immersed in the Boinn up to his 2 armpits from morning till evening, having his Psalter before him on the strand, and constantly engaged in prayer." The building, which contains the tomb of the Earl of Drogheda, is of different dates, and the visitor will notice the fleur-de-lis and the rose ornaments on the inner pointed doorway. Also on the walk above, a stone, probably belonging to a tomb, on which 12 rather elaborate figures are sculptured.

On the opposite side of the river, close to Slane Bridge, are the ruins of the ch. and castle of Fennor, that need not detain the visitor.

Distances.—Drogheda, 8 m.; Navan, 7½.

The district on the l. bank of the Boyne, extending from within 1½ m. of Slane to the spot where the river Mattock joins the Boyne, was the *Brugh-na-Boinne*, the royal cemetery of the Fort of the Boyne, the great burying-ground of the kings of Tara, an account of which is given in an article of an Irish MS., entitled 'Senchas na Relec,' or History of the Cemeteries, translated by Dr. Petrie. From this it appears that Cormac king of Tara, having come to his death by the bone of a salmon sticking in his throat, desired his people not to bury him at Brugh (because it was a cemetery of idolaters), but at Ros-na-righ with his face to the E. His servants, however, came to the resolution to bury him at Brugh, but the Boyne swelled up three times, so that they could not come. A poet of West Connaught writes as follows:—

"The three cemeteries of Idolaters are,
The cemetery of Tailten, the select,
The cemetery of the ever-fair Cruachan,
And the cemetery of Brugh.
The host of great Meath are buried
In the middle of the lofty Brugh;
The great Ultonians used to bury
At Tailten with pomp."

In the area just mentioned "we find the remains of no less than 17 sepulchral barrows, some of these—the smaller ones—situated in the green pasture-lands which form the immediate valley of the Boyne, while the 3 of greatest magnitude, Dowth, Knowth, and Newgrange, are placed on the summit of the ridge which bounds the valley on the l. bank, making upwards of 20 in all, including the remains at Cloghalea and the great moat in which the fortress of Drogheda now stands (p. 26), and known in the annals as the mound of the grave of the wife of Gobhan."—*Wilde.*

Quitting the high road and turning to the rt., the tourist arrives at

61 m. the very remarkable tumulus of Newgrange, which, for the extraordinary size and elaborate ornamentation of its interior, is perhaps unsurpassed in Europe. This cairn, which is about 70 ft. in height, was surrounded by a circle of enormous upright stones, 10 being still visible, while it is said that a large upright stele stood upon the summit. Like the hill of Dowth, it is hollow in the interior, which is formed of large stones, the peculiarity of them being, that some are evidently brought from the bed of the Boyne, while others are basaltic, and others again must have been transported from the Mourne Mountains. The opening of the passage, first described by Edward Llwyd, the Welsh antiquary, in 1699, faces the S., and is remarkable for 2 very beautifully-carved stones, the lower one, below the entrance, being marked with spirals "like snakes encircled, but without heads," and the other, which projects above the entrance, being of a sort of diagonal pattern. The passage is 63 ft. long, and is formed of enormous upright stones, 22 on one side and 21 on the other; and having forced himself through it with some trouble, the visitor emerges into a lofty dome-roofed chamber, nearly circular, with 3 recesses leading out from it. The basement of this chamber is composed of a circle of 11 upright stones, above which is the dome, formed by large stones placed horizontally, the edge of each projecting somewhat more than the under one until the top is reached, and closed by a single big slab. Respecting this form of roofing, "Pocoke has observed a similar structure in the pyramid of Dushour, called by the Arab name of Elkebere-el-Barieh; and all the visitors to the Cyclopean-walled Mycenæ are well acquainted with the appearance of the great cavern known by tradition as the tomb of Agamemnon, and believed by some antiquaries to have been the treasury of Athens; between which and Newgrange comparisons have often been made: their resemblance, however, consists in the principle on which the dome is constructed."—*Wilde's Boyne.* Perhaps the most extraordinary features in this chamber are the carvings on the stones in every direction, on the basement, up in the roof, and in the recesses.* They consist of coils, spirals, lozenges, and one in particular in the western recess is ornamented with what was apparently intended for a fern. As in Dowth, the interior contains stone oval basins. That the remains of those who were buried in these gigantic mausoleums, as well as other valuables deposited with them, were plundered by the Danes about A.D. 860, is recorded in the 'Four Annals,' and it need not therefore excite any surprise in the visitor that nothing but the bare walls remain, though at the excavations carried on at Dowth in 1847 several articles were found, such as bones, pins, fibulæ, and a cinerary urn. On the opposite side of the river is Rosnaree, from whence the body of King Cormac was vainly endeavoured to be brought to Brugh-na-Boinne.

1 m. farther W., and nearer to

* The Celtic tomb of Locmariarker in Brittany exhibits ornamental carving similar to Newgrange.

Slane, is the tumulus of *Knowth* (the Cnodhba of the 'Four Annals'), an equally enormous mass, but to which there is no access as regards the interior.

62½ m. Dowth or Dubhadh is a conical hill of considerable size, on the western side of which a passage had long existed, that might have been possibly formed by the Danes when they rifled the tumuli of their contents. This was further opened and explored, and led to very gratifying discoveries. The entrance passage, which is by no means easy of access, is composed of 11 very large stones on the l. and 9 on the rt., set on end, and slightly inclined at top. It is 27 ft. long, and leads into a central chamber similar to the one at Newgrange. Notice the singular and beautiful carvings on the stones, consisting of spirals, concentric circles, and wheel crosses, together with straight lines like Oghain characters. In the centre of the chamber is a shallow stone basin measuring 5 ft. in diameter. Adjoining the chamber are 3 recesses, between 5 and 6 ft. deep, the southern one of which leads into another series of chambers and passages running southward. "Following the long southern gallery, we find its floor formed by a single stone, 10 ft. 6 in. long; and in the centre of this flag is a shallow oval excavation, capable of holding about a gallon, and apparently rubbed down with some rude tool."

Near the tumulus of Dowth is St. Bernard's Well and ruined ch., the latter containing a very singular figure built into its S. wall. There are also remains of a castle, a large military rath about 300 yards round, supposed to be the fort of Dun-na-Gedh, where Domhnall gave his celebrated feast; also a portion of a stone circle on the edge of a quarry overhanging the road. Dowth Castle is the estate of the late Lord Netterville, whose ancestor formed in the ground curious ramparts, baths, ponds, &c.

The valley of the Boyne is here extremely beautiful; the banks, which are in many places steep, are charmingly wooded and ornamented with fine residences, such as Townley Hall (B. T. Balfour, Esq.) and Oldbridge House (H. Coddington, Esq.).

At 64 m., the point where the Mattock flows into the Boyne, the traveller arrives at the battle-field, where that decisive contest took place in 1690 which proved so fatal to the crown of James II. He will observe that the Boyne here flows E. and W., and that the area of the valley is bordered by a steepish hill, up which the road to Drogheda is carried. In the centre of this area is the obelisk that marks the most important point in the field.

On looking down the river, notice 2 largish islands—Green and Yellow Island—close to the river-side. Higher up is the obelisk, from which the road, following the stream, takes a considerable curve, immediately under the beautiful woods of Townley Hall. At this point the Boyne doubles round upon itself and flows from the S., receiving the small brook called the Mattock, that joins it just beyond Townley Hall. A still smaller tributary emerges near the obelisk from a deep wooded ravine known as King William's Glen; and a 3rd glen is occupied by a rivulet which flows into the same side of the Boyne about 1 m. nearer to Drogheda. On the opposite or S. side the visitor will notice Oldbridge (immediately opposite the obelisk), and above it, rising up in a succession of slopes, the hill of Donore, the summit of which will be about 1 m. from the bank of the river. "To the rt. or E. the hill fines off towards Drogheda 1½ m. distant. Its western side abuts upon and is completely protected by the high precipitous banks of the Boyne, now covered by the plantations of the demesne of Farm. Immediately behind it, towards the S., the way lies open to Dublin along the seaward line."—*Wilde*. The tide comes up as far as the weir just above where the Mattock falls in, and here the Boyne is fordable with difficulty. Another and much shallower ford occurs at Yellow Island, passable at low water for a carriage and horses in summer time. Oldbridge was a village at the time of the battle. It is absolutely necessary that the visitor should make himself thoroughly acquainted with these details before he can understand the plan of the battle. James's army, having marched through Drogheda, took up a position on the northern face of Donore, the king himself passing the night in the little ch. "The Irish cannon were planted on 2 elevations commanding the fords, one a little to the S. of Oldbridge village, which was here intersected by narrow lanes; the other nearly opposite the Yellow Island." The English army, which arrived from Ardee on the 30th June, 1690, took up its position on the opposite slopes, with its right descending into the hollow of the King's Glen, and the left in the parallel ravine near Drogheda. Previous to the engagement an incident took place that gave great delight to the Irish army, viz. the wounding which, however, happened to be very slight of William as he was riding along the bank of the river reconnoitring. "The place where this happened was on the side of a small hillock by the water's edge, a little below the glen, and from which the stones have been taken to build the obelisk erected just beside it." Although the Irish army was protected by Drogheda on its rt., it was not so on the l., and, to take advantage of this, William despatched 10,000 men under the younger Schomberg to cross the ford near Slane, which they did before James could detach any force to meet them.

The 2nd passage of the river at Oldbridge was made at 10¼ A.M., the tide being out, by Schomberg, who, with the Blue Dutch Guards, the Enniskilleners, and the French Huguenots, emerged from the ravine opposite Grove Island, and dashed into the water, when the brave old general met his death in the encounter. "Without defensive armour he rode through the river and rallied the refugees, whom the fall of Caillemot had dismayed. 'Come on,' he cried to the French, pointing to the Popish squadrons; 'come on, gentlemen, there are your persecutors.' As he spoke a band of Irish horsemen rushed upon him and encircled him for a moment. When they retired he was on the ground. His friends raised him; but he was already a corpse. Almost at the same moment, Walker, Bishop of Derry, while exhorting the colonists of Ulster to play the men, was shot dead."—*Macaulay*.

"The 3rd passage was effected by the Danes and Germans at a shallow between the 2 principal islands, where the water must have been up to their armpits; while the l. wing, entirely composed of cavalry, passed or swam across opposite the eastern valley which intersects the hill of Tullyallen and effected a landing, apparently with little opposition, at a very deep and dangerous part of the river, nearly opposite one of the Irish batteries, and where the margin of the stream is wet and swampy. Here it was, however, that William himself, with his arm in a sling from the effects of his wound, plunged into the stream with Col. Woolsley, and passed with great difficulty, for his horse was bogged on the other side, and he was forced to alight till a gentleman helped him to get his horse out."—*Wilde*. In this area 26,000 men on the English side were engaged with 16,000 Irish, in addition to the 10,000 English who had crossed at Slane, and were occupied with the Irish l. wing. The result of the battle is well known: the Irish army falling back on Donore, and finally retreating to Duleek, where they passed the night, while King James himself fled to Dublin, which he reached about 10 o'clock that night.

It is to be hoped that the bitter animosities of party spirit which were, until very lately, so rampant on this subject, are becoming softened by time and the interchange of greater good will and forbearance. For more intimate details of the topography and incidents of the battle, the tourist is referred to Sir W. Wilde's exhaustive memoir on the Boyne, to which, as well as to the learned author's personal help and leadership, the writer of this notice is very greatly indebted.

From the battle-field the traveller, should he not wish to visit Mellifont now, soon rejoins the great N. road and arrives at

65 m. *Droghedа* (*Hotel*, Imperial), Rte. 2.

ROUTE 16.

FROM DROGHEDA TO NAVAN, KELLS, AND CAVAN, BY RAIL.

The branch rly. to Oldcastle, 36 m. in length, runs through as well-wooded and well-watered a district as any in Ireland, and for the antiquary a district richly stored with historic remains. It follows the S. bank of the Boyne, although, until the traveller arrives at Beauparc, the high grounds intervene and shut it out. The river is crossed at Navan, and the valley of the Blackwater ascended from hence.

4½ m. From *Duleek* Stat. a lane on rt. leads 1½ m. to the small hamlet and ruined ch. of Donore (Rte. 15), where James II. passed the night before his hopes were finally defeated at the battle of the Boyne. From Donore the Irish army " retreated in tolerable order towards Duleek, towards which place the left wing, already beaten above Rosnaree, had retired. Here with the Nanny water between them both parties halted for the night, with the exception of King James, who fled to Dublin, which he reached about 10 o'clock." — *Wilde*. A ch. was founded here in the 5th cent., by St. Kieran, a disciple of St. Patrick, and was called Duleek or Dam-liag, " because it was the first that was built with lime and mortar—and was so called from leac, a stone."—*Vallancey*. This ch. gave place to a priory for canons regular, founded in 1182 by Hugh De Lacy, who made it subject to that of Llanthony in Monmouthshire, and at the dissolution its possessions, which were large, were granted to Sir Gerald Moore, ancestor of the Drogheda family.

The ruins, of E. Eng. date, consist of a spacious nave 100 ft. in length by 20 ft. broad, lighted at the W. end by a 3-light lancet window, and terminated by a rather massive tower of 2 stages. Under the E. window are the armorial bearings of Sir John Bellew, 1587. Here is also the tombstone of an ecclesiastic. Adjoining the village is the demesne of the now extinct family of Earl of Thomond, entered by a castellated gateway that once led to the abbey. The Nanny, a small stream, is crossed by an old bridge, built by William Bathe of Athcarne and Genet his wife in 1587. On the banks of the same river, 2½ m. W., is the ancient seat of the de Bathe family,

Athcarne Castle (J. Gernon, Esq.), a large square Elizabethan building, defended at the angles by quadrangular towers, the whole of which was formerly surrounded by a fosse. 2 m. to the W. of Athcarne is Somerville, the beautiful seat of Lord Athlumney.

2½ m. rt. is Platten House (J. Gradwell, Esq.), built on the site of a castle of the time of Edward III., erected by Sir John D'Arcy (Lord Justice of Ireland).

Crossing the turnpike-road to Slane, the rly. arrives at 12 m. *Beauparc Stat.*, contiguous to Beauparc House, the seat of G. Lambart, Esq., situated on an elevation commanding an exquisite prospect. "Beyond the fall of Stackallan we pass through the most delicious scenery; on the rt. the modern mansion of Beauparc peeps through the never-ending green of tall pines, sycamores, oaks, and elms. On the l. the ivy-mantled walls of Castle Dexter (Rte. 15), raise themselves above the dark plantation, while the limestone rock, here twisted into a variety of contortions, breaks through the surface and relieves the eye, almost satiated with the endless variety both of colour and foliage." From Beauparc Stat. the pedestrian can reach Slane in 3½ m. From hence the rly. keeps nearly parallel with the road and the river to Navan. 13 m. l. is Dollardston House, and 15 m. rt. Ardmulchan House J. R. Taaffe, Esq., opposite whose residence are the ruins of Dunmore ch. and castle, and rt. the tower of Donaghmore (Rte. 15). Crossing the Boyne, the tourist arrives at

17 m. *Navan* (Hotel: Brady's), an ill-built dirty town, with a Pop. of some 4000, who have by no means appreciated its picturesque situation at the junction of the Blackwater with the Boyne, but "like those of most Irish towns through which a river runs, have turned their backs upon the stream, scarce a glimpse of which can be obtained from any of its narrow streets." With the exception of the parochial and county structures, such as ch., barracks, infirmary, and gaol, it has little to interest the tourist; though in the 16th cent. it was sufficiently important to have attracted a marauding expedition of the O'Neills and O'Donnells. Its ancient name was Nuachongbhail, and it was originally walled.

Many antiquities now in the Irish Academy were discovered in rly. cuttings adjacent to the river, besides a singular subterranean passage on the W. bank near Athlumney, dividing into 2 branches, which each ended in a rude circular beehived chamber. Navan is a good central position from whence to explore either section of the Boyne, which by means of a canal has been rendered partly navigable. The tourist can either drive or walk to Beauparc and Slane, or else descend the river and canal by boat.

Conveyances.—By rail to Drogheda, Kells, and Dublin.

Distances.—Slane, 8 m.; Drogheda, 17; Beauparc, 5; Bective, 6; Trim, 12; Athlumney, 1½; Donaghmore, 1½; Kells, 10.

Excursions.—

1. Trim and Bective (Rte. 15).
2. Slane and Newgrange.
3. Kells.
4. Duleek and Drogheda.

The tourist now quits the Boyne and follows the course of the *Blackwater* (anc. Abhuim-mor), a river rising from Lough Ramor in the S.E. corner of the county of Cavan, which, after flowing for 20 m. in a winding lazy stream, joins the Boyne at Navan, where they are nearly of the same size. The scenery of its banks is by no means as fine as that of the Boyne, but it is equally rich in early remains.

19¼ m. close to the line is *Liscarton Castle*, a noble-looking old fortress (partly inhabited), mainly consisting of 2 square towers connected together by a central hall, the whole of which forms a massive quadrangular building. It was held in 1633 by Sir William Talbot. Adjoining it is the ch., containing some exquisite E. and W. windows (Dec.) with beautiful tracery. "Upon the exterior face may be observed well-carved human heads projecting from the dripstone." On the opposite bank is *Rathaldron* (Capt. Donaldson), another specimen of the old quadrangular tower, to which a castellated mansion has been added. The entrance is through a very fine avenue of limes. Between this spot and Navan is the mutilated cross of *Nevinstown*, which from the researches by Mr. D. H. Smith appears to have been erected in memory of a knight of the Cusack family 1588. On l. of the line to the S. of Liscarton is Ardbraccan (Bp. of Meath).

[21½ m. rt., on the opposite bank of the river, is the ch. of *Donaghpatrick*, occupying the site of Domnachpadraig, the great ch. of St. Patrick, celebrated in the Book of Armagh for being 60 feet long—" pedibus ejus lx. pedum." This was the length prescribed by St. Patrick for this ch., " which the Prince Conall, the brother of the monarch Laoghaire, was to erect for him."—*Petrie*. The king even gave up his house for a site. Near the ch. is a specimen of the military rath, consisting of a mound rising out of as many as 4 successive embankments or circumvallations. Sir W. Wilde considers it to be the finest example of the kind in Ireland; but it is to be regretted that planting operations have to a great extent concealed it, and that at least one half of the lines of circumvallation have been levelled. A little further, on the same side of the river, we come to *Telton House*, occupying the gradually sloping bank of a hill which rises 292 ft. above the sea. The summit is crowned by a fort, Rath Dubh, which measures 321 paces in circumference and has openings N. and S. This was the site of the ancient palace of Tailtean, one of the 4 celebrated royal residences of Ireland, and for ages immemorial the locale of a great fair, established in the year of the world 3370, in remembrance of Tailte, " wife of the last king of the Firbolgs."—*Annals of the Four Masters*. Up to the time of Roderick O'Connor, the last king of Ireland, this fair was regularly held, when series of games, such as boxing, wrestling, chariot-races, and sham aquatic fights carried on in artificial lakes, were the order of the day. In addition to these attractions, it was the custom of all the lads and lasses who wished to try their luck to arrange themselves on either side of a high wall in which was a small opening, through which the female protruded her hand. If the swain admired it, the parties were married, an arrangement which, fortunately for both, only held good for a year and a day, when each was free to try their luck again. The proverb of a " Telton marriage" is not yet obsolete in Meath. Should the visitor not succeed in tracing the outworks of the fort or the site of the lakes to his satisfaction, he will at all events be rewarded by the magnificent view, embracing, W., Kells, the woods of Headford, and the ranges of the Cavan mountains in the distance; while E. he sees Liscarton, Rathaldron, Navan, the hills of Tara and Skreen, and the wide green plains of Meath, watered by the Boyne and Blackwater, together with their tributaries, the Moynalty and Silc.]

24 m. *Ballybeg* Stat., near which l. is Allenstown House (W. N. Waller, Esq.).

27 m. *Kells* (*Inn,* Hannon's), a rather pleasant little town, containing much that is interesting in the highest degree to the antiquary. Kells (anciently Ceanannus) was celebrated in early Christian ages as being the residence of St. Columb, to whom a grant was made by Dermot, the son of Fergus Kervaill, and who founded a monastery here in 550.

Although no traces of this at present exist, the visitor will find 3 remarkable remains: 1, The house of St. Columb; 2, The round tower; and 3, The crosses.

The saint's house is of the same class of high-roofed buildings as St. Kevin's Kitchen at Glendalough, and offers a remarkable example of the earliest cylindrical vaulting (Rte. 24. "It is of a simple oblong form, roofed with stone, and measures in height, from its base to the vertex of the gable, 38 ft.; and as the height of the roof and width of the side walls are nearly equal, the gables form very nearly equilateral triangles. The lower part of the building is arched semicircularly with stone, and has at the E. end, a small semicircular-headed window, about 15 ft. from the ground; and at the S. side there is a 2nd window, with a triangular or straight-lined head, measuring 1 ft. 9 in. in height. These windows splay considerably on the inside. The present doorway in the S. wall is not original or ancient; and the original doorway, which is now built up, was placed in the W. end, and at a height of 8 ft. from the ground. The apartment placed between the arched floor and the slanting roof is 6 ft. high, and appears to have been originally divided into 3 compartments of unequal size. In the largest, which is at the E. end, is a flat stone, 6 ft. long and 1 ft. thick, now called S. Columb's penitential bed."—*Petrie*. These buildings no doubt served the double purpose of habitation, together with rude arrangements for religious duties.

The Round Tower, frequently referred to in the Annals of Tigernach as the steeple or cloictheach of Kells, is a remarkably perfect specimen. It is 100 ft. high, has a door 10 ft. from the ground, and is lighted by 4 windows, which present all the varieties of form commonly found in Irish round towers, viz. round, square, and triangular-headed.

Of the *Crosses*, one, a little more than 11 ft. high, is close to the town; three are in the ch.-yard; while the Cross of Kells, par excellence, is in the market-place. The visitor to Monasterboice, near Drogheda, will at once recognise its similarity to the crosses there. The shaft, which is broken off at the top, is 8 ft. 9 in. high; the arms are 5 ft. 4 in. in width, and are connected by a wheel, perfect save a small portion where the top of the shaft should be. The cross is mounted on a broad base, having on its side a good sculpture of mounted horsemen in procession; also a "remarkable group of 5 fighting figures, 2 armed with spears and holding shields of a peculiar lunette shape." The shaft is divided into 4 compartments, representing military and ecclesiastical subjects, while a full-length figure occupies the centre of the arms. As an instance of the respect paid to these exquisite memorials, it may be mentioned that as lately as 1798 this cross formed part of the gallows of Kells. The ch. is modern, but the bell-tower, like the one at Athlone, stands apart. It consists of 3 stages, and contains some tablets built into the walls, and a black-letter inscription recording its rebuilding in 1578.

Only a small portion of a tower belonging to the walls remains, although it is known that Kells was strongly fortified and possessed a castle built by Walter de Lacy. The Annals of the Four Masters and those of Tigernach record many incidents in the history of Kells, in which the town and churches sustained grievous losses and damage at the hands of the native Irish, Norwegian hordes, and Danish robbers. It was devastated by fire, the sword, and pestilence many times; though the 2 greatest catastrophes were the destruction of the abbey in 1108 by Sitric and his Danes, and the subsequent burning of the town by Edward Bruce in 1315.

Kells was celebrated, not only for its ecclesiastical greatness and sanctity, but also for its advancement in literature, evidenced by the production of the illuminated Book of Kells, now in the Museum of the Royal Irish Academy, which, like its contemporary the Book of Ballymote, gives great insight into the national peculiarities of that period, and is a marvellous example of elaborate ornamentation. A fine view is obtained from the Hill of Lloyd, which is crowned with a column 100 ft. high, erected by 1st Earl of Bective.

About 6 m. W. of Kells are the moat and dun of Dinor, the former with a very large central mound and an outwork, like that at Newry. The dun is more ordinary, but there is a chain of 7 or 8 others on the green hills in the neighbourhood. About 3 m. to the W. is Lough Crew, the seat of J. L. Napier, Esq.

Kells is surrounded by many pleasant residences. The principal are *Headfort*, the seat of the Earl of Bective, adjoining the town, the woods and groves of which skirt and indeed occupy islands in the middle of the Blackwater; Oakley Park (G. Bomford, Esq.), Williamstown (W. S. Garnett, Esq.), Bloomesbury (R. Barnewall, Esq.), the Archdeaconry (Archd. Stopford).

Conveyances.—By rail to Drogheda and Dublin; rly. to Oldcastle; car to Baillieborough; car to Ballyjamesduff; car to Clonmellon.

Distances.—Navan, 10 m.; Telton, 5; Baillieborough, 14; Oldcastle, 14; Ballyjamesduff, 17; Virginia, 11; Athboy, 8½; Kingscourt, 14½; Trim, 16.

[An excursion may be made to Trim, through Athboy, passing 1½ m. rt. Cannonstown (W. Sadlier, Esq.), and 5½ m. rt. Johnsbrook (J. Tandy, Esq.), and Drewstown.

7½ m. on l. The ruined ch. or abbey of *Rathmore* contains a portion of a sepulchral cross and a monument erected to a member of the Plunket family 1531.

8½ m. *Athboy* (anc. Ath-brudhe-Tlachtga), "the Yellow Ford," an inconsiderable little town, situated on the Athboy stream, which falls into the Boyne. There is a very handsome R. C. chapel here, with a steeple 90 ft. high. To the E. of the town rises the hill of Ward, 390 ft., celebrated like Tailtean for being the site of the palace of Tlachtga, and the locale of a great fair, "when the fire of Tlachtga was ordained to be kindled on the 31st October, to summon the priests and augurs to consume the sacrifices offered to their gods."—*Crawford*.

11½ m. rt. is Clifton Lodge, the residence of the Earl of Darnley, who obtains the title of Athboy from this town. From hence the road approaches the valley of the Boyne to 16 m. Trim (Rte. 15).]

From Kells the rly. extends a few miles further to Oldcastle; but the tourist should take the road to Virginia, which crosses the Blackwater at Clavens Bridge 29 m., and thence keeps the l. bank.

30½ m. on the side of the river are the chapel and well of St. Kieran, with the "remains of 5 termon crosses in its vicinity, 4 of which are placed N., S., E., and W. of the river. The northern one was erected in a ford in the river, a very remarkable situation for one of these early Christian structures."—*Wilde*. This is accounted for by the story that St. Kieran erected these crosses with a great deal of trouble, and that St. Columb, who was then building at Kells, envied them so greatly that he determined to abstract one. The saint had got halfway across the river with the stone on his back when St. Kieran awoke and caught him. A struggle took place, in which St. Columb threw the base of the cross down in the bed of the river, where it has ever since remained. The ch. is a plain singular building of the 14th cent. or thereabouts, built on arches, so as to form a sort of crypt.

35½ m. the traveller arrives at the foot of Lough Ramor, from whence the Blackwater emerges, and follows the N. shore of the lough and under the slopes of Ballybrush (1631 ft.) to

38¼ *Virginia*, a neat pretty town, originally founded " in pursuance of the plan for colonizing Ulster in the reign of James I., when 250 acres were allotted for the site of a town, called Virginia, which was to have been made a borough, but was never incorporated."—*Lewis*. There is a modern Gothic ch., which replaced one partly blown down and partly burnt in 1832.

At Kilnaleck, a little to the N. of Mt. Nugent, a seam of anthracitic coal in the Lower Silurian beds was discovered by Mr. J. Kelly.

Lough Ramor, about 5 m. in length, is prettily wooded and varied with islands, planted by the Marquess of Headfort, who has an estate close to Virginia. The lake is said in the Annals of the Four Masters to have burst from a neighbouring height, called Sliabh Guaire, and it receives at Virginia the river Sele, which is to all intents and purposes identical with the Blackwater, although the latter only takes its name from the period of its rising from the lake. The original name of the river was Abhainn Sele, till St. Patrick cursed it and caused the water to become black, whence it took the name of Abhainn Ddhu or Blackwater.

Conveyances.—Car to Cavan; also to Drogheda and Virginia Road Stat.

Distances.—Cavan, 19 m.; Kells, 11; Ballyjamesduff, 6; Oldcastle, 7½; Mount Nugent, 11; Baillieborough, 7½.

The scenery has very much changed since the traveller left the flat pasture-lands of Meath, and he now finds himself gradually approaching high ground, although not exceeding 1000 ft.

45 m. New Inn [from whence a road on l. branches off to 3 m. a small town of the euphonious name of *Ballyjamesduff*, passing on the way a serpentine sheet of water called Lough Nadrageel.] The way lies over a dreary country, having on l. the conspicuous Cavan mountains Ardkilmore 767, and Slieve Glah 1057 ft.

At 51½ m. on rt. is the village of *Stradone*, with, adjoining it, Stradone House, the residence of R. Burrowes, Esq., from whence an uninteresting drive of 6 m. brings the tourist to

57½ m. the dirty little county town of *Cavan* (*Hotel:* Globe). Rte. 17.

ROUTE 17.

FROM MULLINGAR TO PORTADOWN THROUGH CAVAN AND ARMAGH.

A branch of the Midland Great Western Rly., which for some distance is also common to the Longford line (Rte. 18), conveys the traveller to Cavan, where a connection has lately been established with the North by means of the Clones branch of the Irish North-Western Company.

14 m. From *Float* Stat. it is 6½ m. rt. to Castle-Pollard (Rte. 18), through the village of Coole and the demesne of Turbotstown (J. A. Dease, Esq.). From hence the rly. pursues a northerly course through a very uninviting and dreary country, passing 18 m. l. Fernsborough and the ruined ch. of Abbeylara, in the tower of which is a grotesquely sculptured female figure.

20 m. *Ballywillan* Stat., close to

a small sheet of water on rt. called Lough Kinile, which is connected by a short stream with *Lough Sheelin.* This is one of the largest lakes in the county of Cavan, 4½ m. in length, and covering an area of 8000 Irish acres. On the E. shore is the small village of *Mount Nugent,* and on the S. of the lake is the ruined castle of Ross, beyond which the hills of Knocklaid form a very pleasing landscape.

[3½ m. l. of the stat. is the little town of *Granard* (*Inn:* Granard). It was burned by Bruce in 1315, but afterwards rose to importance in the reign of James I. Hard by is the Moat of Granard, a considerable artificial mound, believed to have been built by the Danes as a defensive post, and worth ascending for the sake of the view.

Some 3 or 4 m. to the N.W. is *Lough Gowna,* an irregularly-shaped lake, the shores of which in some places are steep and well wooded. On the island of Inchmore, at the S. end, is a ruined ch. The banks are adorned by pleasant residences—Derrycassan (Capt. Dopping-Hepenstal), Erne Head (H. Dopping, Esq.), Woodville (O. Lambert, Esq.), and Frankford. The river Erne issues from its N. end.]

From this point the country becomes still more boggy and dreary, though the monotony on the rt. is relieved by the picturesque elevations of the Cavan Hills, which rise conspicuously to the height of 760 ft., increasing at Slieve Glagh to 1050 ft. On the l. the line runs parallel with, though not very, near to, the river Erne.

In the neighbourhood of 31 m. *Crossdoney* Stat. are Lismore and Bingfield (J. Storey, Esq.).

36 m. *Cavan* (*Inn:* Globe). This dirty little town (Pop. 3209) will not induce the visitor to make a long stay, although it is situated in a very pleasing country, diversified by plenty of wood and water. It contains the usual county structures, such as gaol, infirmary, barracks, &c., and a pretty spired ch., which, though in the town, belongs to the parish of Urney. It once contained the castle of the O'Reilleys, and a monastery for the Dominican order, but they have long since disappeared. A sharp contest took place at Cavan in 1690 between a body of James II.'s troops and the redoubtable Enniskilleners under their gallant leader Wolseley; when the latter, who only numbered 1000, attacked the Duke of Berwick's reinforcements and utterly routed them. In the neighbourhood of Cavan is Farnham Castle, the beautiful residence of Lord Farnham.

[3 m. distant, on the road to Crossdoney, is the seat of the ancient bishopric of *Kilmore* (anc. Cill-mhor-na-mBreathnach), the first dignitary being one Andrew Macbrady, in 1454, although previous to that time prelates had been appointed who were styled Bishops of Breffni. In 1585 the see became Protestant, and was united in 1752 to Tuam, but, under the Church Temporalities Act, is now associated with Elphin and Ardagh. The cathedral, which has been restored, possesses no particular feature of interest, save a richly-sculptured Norm. doorway that was removed from the abbey of Trinity Island in Lough Oughter. Near the ch. is the Episcopal Palace. " The country immediately connected with Kilmore and Farnham exhibits a well-cultivated, and, at the same time, a pleasing rural character. The small lakes, which are thickly scattered over a surface of 76 square miles, by their labyrinthine windings give to that space the appearance of lake and island in alternate series. They are the principal feeders of the Erne, and are connected with each other by small rivers."—*Fraser.*]

Distances.—Kells, 31 m. ; Virginia,

20; Clones, 17; Newton Butler, 14; Kilmore, 3; Mullingar, 36; Belturbet, 11.

Conveyances.—Rail to Mullingar and Clones. Cars daily to Kells and Monaghan.

A rly. has been opened to Clones, where it joins the Dundalk and Enniskillen line. The high road passes through a pretty English country, well planted and well wooded.

[Rt. a road goes off to *Ballyhaise* 4 m., a small town, with a market place built on arches. Close to the town is Ballyhaise House (W. Humphreys, Esq.), the front of which is also curiously ornamented with arches.

10 m. at *Butler's Bridge*, the river Ballyhaise is crossed, near its junction with the Erne.

13 m. l. Clover Hill (Miss Saunderson), soon after which a road on l. turns off to 3 m. *Belturbet*, a neat town on the Erne (crossed by a bridge of 3 arches), a little distance from the expansion of that river into the Upper Lough Erne. By means of the waters of the lake, the inhabitants have communication as far as Belleek, 3 m. from Ballyshannon, in addition to the Ulster Canal that joins the Erne a few miles above the town. A good deal of business is carried on in corn and distilling. There are in "the ch-yard the remains of a fortification enclosing an extensive area." Also a portion of a round tower, built of limestone and red grit.

Belturbet was, like most of the towns in this neighbourhood, the scene of some sharp fighting in 1689, when the Enniskilleners, prior to the battle of Newton Butler, seized upon the town, which had been taken by the enemy, and, after dislodging them, fortified it for themselves.

Distances.—Enniskillen, 21 m.; Cavan, 10.

Conveyances.—Rail to Cavan.]

A little beyond Castle Saunderson, 46½ m. l. (E. J. Saunderson, Esq.), the road crosses the Ulster Canal, that connects Lough Erne with Lough Neagh, and runs parallel with it to 51 m. the picturesque town of Clones, described in Rte. 6, from whence the traveller can proceed by rail to Enniskillen or Dundalk.

57 m. *Smithborough*, an uninteresting little place, founded, as its name implies, by a Mr. Smith.

63 m. *Monaghan* (*Hotel:* Westenra Arms), a neat and thriving county town, but not offering sufficient interest to induce a prolonged visit (Pop. 3910). Of so modern a date is it, that on the settlement of Ulster, at the beginning of the 17th cent., when the Lord Deputy came hither to make arrangements respecting the forfeited lands, there was scarcely a house in which he and his train could be accommodated, and they were consequently obliged to pitch tents. The chief owner of the district is Lord Rossmore, whose beautiful seat of Rossmore is a little to the S. on the road to Newbliss. The principal square in the town is called the Diamond, and contains a linen-hall.

Conveyances.—Daily to Cootehill, to Enniskillen, to Omagh. By rail to Armagh, Portadown, and Clones.

Distances.—Armagh, 16 m.; Portadown, 26; Clones, 12; Cavan, 27; Newbliss, 10; Cootehill, 15; Emyvale, 7.

In the neighbourhood of Monaghan are Rossmore (Lord Rossmore), Ballybeck (J. Brownlow, Esq.), Brandrum (Major Coote), Mount Louise (R. Evatt, Esq.), Castle Shane (Hon. E. Lucas), Beechhill (W. Murray, Esq.).

From hence the rly. passes through an uninteresting hilly country to

68 m. *Glasslough*, a small town, the parish ch. of which has a tower 130 ft. high. Close to it is the fine estate of Castle Leslie (belonging

to the Leslie family), on the banks of a small lake.

Conveyances. — Car to Clogher, Aughnacloy, and Fivemile Town.

72 m. rt. *Tynan.* A portion of a stone cross, with bosses and line pattern, defaced by Cromwell, stands by the roadside near the ch.-yard. There is a smaller one over a well in the grounds of Tynan Abbey, the seat of Sir J. M. Stronge, Bart.

About 1 m. l. is *Caledon*, a thriving little market town, that has prospered under the auspices of the family of the Earl of Caledon, whose extensive park adjoins. It was formerly known by the name of Kennard, and was the head-quarters of Sir Phelim O'Neil, who in the 17th cent. successfully held the county of Tyrone for several years against the English.

79 m. *Armagh* (*Hotels:* Beresford Arms; Royal), a finely situated cathedral town, and the see of the Primate of all Ireland (Pop. 8969). "No city is so rich in historical associations, and yet has so little to show and so little to tell in the present day, as Armagh. St. Patrick's first ch. is now represented by the Bank of Ireland; the Provincial Bank comes close on St. Columb's; St. Bride's shares its honours with a paddock; St. Peter and St. Paul afford stabling and garden-produce to a modern *rus in urbe;* and St. Mary's is lost in a dwelling-house."—*Reeves.* There seems to be little doubt but that St. Patrick founded the early ch. in the 5th cent. on ground known as Druim saileeh, "the Ridge of Sallow," given to the saint by Daire, the chieftain of the district. The hill was called Rathdaire, and subsequently Ard-macha, after an Irish heroine of doubtful identity. Here, shortly after the foundation of the ch., was buried Lupita, the sister of St. Patrick.

The early history of the ch. embraces a long list of mishaps, long even for Irish religious establishments, which were particularly liable to misfortune. For 5 cents. or more it had to bear the repeated attacks of the Danes and other marauders, who, not content with plundering, burnt the city to the ground as often as it was rebuilt. The most complete ruin, however, was sustained at the hands of a native chieftain, O'Neil, in 1566, who reduced the cathedral to ashes. "Primate Loftus assailed the destroyer with the spiritual weapon of excommunication, and rejected his pretext, which was that he burned the cathedral to prevent the English troops from polluting its sanctuary by lodging within its walls. O'Neil was shortly after most inhumanly butchered in the Scottish camp, and his body thrown into a pit, where it lay inhumed for several days, until one William Piers disinterred it, and, severing the head, sent it 'pickled in a pipkin' to the Lord Deputy at Drogheda."—*Wright.*

Previous to the destruction by the Danes, Armagh was famous for its school of learning, the Alma Mater of many of the early scholars, viz. Aigilbert, Bishop of the Western Saxons, Gildas Albanus, and others. There is still a royal school here founded by Charles I.

Since the Reformation Armagh has been fortunate in its archbishops, the bulk of whom exercised their influence to benefit the metropolitan see. Of these the principal were Primates Ussher, Hoadley, and Robinson, who, after his translation from the bishopric of Kildare, was created Baron Rokeby. To the late primate Armagh owes the restorations of the cathedral, at a cost of 30,000*l.*, from his own private wealth; also the erection of the episcopal residence, the town library, and the observatory, which has contributed very largely to the annals of astronomical science.

The city is very finely situated on the slopes of a steep hill, the summit crowned by the venerable cathedral, while separated by valleys arise other hills, one of which is likewise adorned by the new R. C. cathedral. The visitor will mark with pleasure the substantial and orderly streets, the clean trottoir, the prettily wooded mall, and the general appearance of prosperity and good government. The geologist may discern many limestone shells in the flags.

The cathedral, which is in the centre of a close at the top of the hill, is a cruciform ch., consisting of nave with aisles, choir, and transepts, with a massive and rather low tower rising from the intersection. It had, previous to the recent alterations, a spire surmounting the tower, but this has been removed, and with the best effect. The tower, which is lighted with 2 windows on each side, should be ascended by the tourist for the sake of the extensive and beautiful view. The nave is separated from each aisle by 4 pointed arches with rounded and deeply moulded pillars, and is lighted by 5 Perp. windows, with 4 clerestory windows above. At the W. end is a lancet-headed 3-light, of good stained glass, there being also a Perp. stained window at the W. of each aisle. The roof is of timber, well carved, and ornamented with gilt bosses. The nave contains monuments to Dr. Sir T. Molyneux, by Roubilliac; to Dr. Stuart, late Primate, by Chantrey; an elaborate memorial to the 3 brothers Kelly; to Archdeacon Robinson; in the N. aisle to Dean Drelincourt, 1644, by Rysbrack. Notice also good moulding on the W. door, and an octagonal sculptured font; and a most beautiful monument has lately been put up to the late Primate, Lord J. Beresford. The N. transept is used as a robing-room, and contains a monument resplendent in colours to Lord Charlemont. The choir is separated by a sculptured and stone-panelled screen, is lighted by beautiful stained glass at the sides and E. end, and has a groined roof. The bells are remarkably sweet, and are enabled to be rung by one person. The whole cathedral is pleasing and grateful to the English eye, for every portion of it denotes a careful and zealous watch over it. The organ is good, and the choral service very well performed. The tourist should visit Primate Robinson's library, over the door of which is inscribed το της ψυχης ιατρειον, and also the observatory, which, with the astronomer's residence, is situated a short distance out of the town in prettily planted gardens. The scientific visitor will receive every attention either from the principal, Dr. T. Romney Robinson or the sub-astronomer, Mr. Rambaut. About 1½ m. from the town is the Palace (Right Rev. the Archbishop), a fine block of building erected by Primate Robinson, together with a private chapel, and an obelisk commanding views over beautiful grounds. A very conspicuous feature in Armagh is the R. C. cathedral, not yet finished, but which promises to be a magnificent building in Dec. style.

Of all the chs. and religious establishments that Armagh ever boasted, nothing remains, though the archæological visitor may visit the site of Emania, known as the Navan Fort, which occupies an area of 12 acres, a little distance from the city. It is said to have been the seat of the Ulster sovereignty for 600 years, during which period a series of kings reigned here prior to the year 332! In shape it is elliptical, embracing about 12 acres. "In the townland of Tray there is a mound to which tradition assigns the name of the King's Stables, and immediately adjacent was the palace of the Knights or Champions of the Curaidhe na Craubh Ruadh, or the Knights of the Red Branch."—*Doyle*. An interesting pamphlet has been written by the Rev. Dr. Reeves on the 'Ancient Churches of Armagh,' which the antiquary should consult.

Another early monument exists

on the banks of the Cullan Water on the road to Keady, in a mound that marks the tomb of Nial Caille, who, when his army was drawn up in battle array against the Danes, perished in an attempt to save one of his men who had fallen into the river.*

A little to the S. is Market Hill, with the Vicar's Cairn 840 ft. high. Adjoining the town is Gosford Castle, the seat of the Earl of Gosford.

The neighbourhoods of Armagh and Keady are celebrated for the production of brown and coloured linens, such as blouses, and hollands for window blinds, the tint of which is obtained by soaking the goods in solution of muriate of tin and catechu. After this operation they are glazed and finished by means of a "beetling" machine. This operation can be seen at Messrs. Kirk's factory in Keady, where 200 beetling machines are employed.

Conveyances.—By rail to Clones, Monaghan, Portadown, and Newry. Car to Keady and Castle Blayney.

Distances. — Monaghan, 16 m.; Portadown, 10; Richhill, 4; Keady, 7½; Moy, 7½; Blackwatertown, 5.

83 m. *Richhill*, another small town on rt. occupying high ground. In the demesne of Castle Dillon (Sir T. Molyneux, Bart.) adjoining is an obelisk erected by Sir Capel Molyneux to commemorate the Irish volunteers, 1782. From hence the line runs through an agricultural district to

89 m. Portadown (Rte. 3), where a junction is effected with the Ulster and the Dundalk rlys.

* The same legend, however, is current on the banks of the Nore, near Thomastown.

ROUTE 18.

FROM **MULLINGAR** TO **SLIGO**, THROUGH **LONGFORD**, **CARRICK-ON-SHANNON**, AND **BOYLE**.

A rly. extends from Mullingar to Longford, Carrick, Boyle, and Sligo, branching from the Midland Great Western at Mullingar (Rte. 14), and passing on l. the barracks and unionhouse.

2 m. l. is Levington Park (R. H. Levinge, Esq.), immediately after which the broad waters of *Lough Owel* (anc. Lough Uair) open out, the rly. running close alongside of it for the whole distance, 5 m. in length. The area of this lake occupies 2295 acres; and although the scenery around it is by no means striking, the wooded hills and numerous fine seats on its banks give it a pleasant and sheltered aspect. On the opposite side is *Portloman*, the residence of J. De Blaquiere, Esq., in whose grounds are slight remains of an abbey ch. 3¼ m. rt. are Ballynagall (T. J. Smyth, Esq.), and Knockdrin Castle, the seat of Sir Richard Levinge, Bart., M.P. for county Westmeath. At the upper end of the lake, on the W. side, is Mountmurray (H. Murray, Esq.), and close to the rly. l., Woodlands (E. Maxton, Esq.), and Clonhugh, a seat belonging to the Earl of Granard.

The angler can get good sport in Lough Owel, the trout running from 1 to 10 lb. The best season is about the time of the May-fly.

6½ m. Clonhugh Stat. 7½ m. close to *Multifarnham* Stat., amidst the trees on the l., is Wilson's Hospital, an establishment founded by the late Mr. Andrew Wilson, who bequeathed 4000*l*. a year for the education of Protestant orphans, and also for the maintenance of a certain number of old men. In the village are the partial ruins of *Multifarnham Abbey*, remarkable chiefly for its slender square steeple, 90 ft. in height. This house was founded for Conventual Franciscans in 1236 by William Delamere, and was notorious for having maintained its early splendour later than any other establishment; for "although formally dissolved by Henry VIII., those to whom it was granted did not dispossess the monks, who in 1622, even attempted the formation of a branch of their society at Mullingar."—*Lewis*. Many of the plans of the Civil War of 1641 were concocted here, for which the monks were driven away. They, however, returned again in 1823, and some Franciscans still dwell in the precincts of the ch.

[About 2 m. to the E. of Multifarnham is *Lough Derervaragh*, an irregularly-shaped lake about 6 m. in length. Its broadest expanse is in its northern portion, where it receives a considerable stream known as the Inny. Its banks are boggy and tame, but at the southern end the scenery improves wonderfully, becoming almost fine. The lake here is narrow, and is bounded on each side by steep hills—on the W. by Knockross 565 ft., and on the E. by Knockion 707, which rises sharply from the water. On the side of the latter hill is an old chapel and spring dedicated to St. Eyen, and an object of devout attention to the peasantry. The summit offers an extensive view from the comparatively flat nature of the country for many miles around. Indeed, it is asserted in Lewis's 'Top. Dict.' that the Atlantic and Irish Channel are both visible from it. A little to the N. of Knockion is Faughalstown or Falulty, where are the remains of a castle, the retreat of Mortimer Earl of March in the reign of Henry IV. The borders of the lake are studded with seats: on the W. Monintown, and Donore, the residence of Sir Percy Nugent, Bart.; and on the N. bank Coolure (Right Hon. Sir R. Pakenham).

2 m. to E. of the lake is *Castle Pollard* (*Inn*: Reilly's) a pleasant little agricultural town, in the immediate neighbourhood of the finely-wooded estates of Pakenham Hall (the Earl of Longford), and Kinturk (Major Urquhart, M.P.). [The antiquary will find at the village of Fore (anc. Fobhar-fechin), 2¼ m. on the road to Kells, the remains of an abbey founded by St. Fechin in 630, and rebuilt by De Lacy in the 13th cent. It was an important establishment, containing 3000 monks, and known locally as Ballylichen, "the Town of Books." The remains are, however, much more of a military than ecclesiastical character, and stand on a rock in the middle of a morass.

The village also contains portions of the ancient walls, a square tower used as a burial place of the Delvin family, and a defaced stone cross. The ch. of St. Fechin (who died of a great plague in 664) is remarkable for its doorway. "It is perfectly Cyclopean in character, constructed altogether of 6 stones, including the lintel. It has a plain architrave over it, which, however, is not continued along its sides, and above this there is a projecting tablet, in the centre of which is sculptured a plain cross within a circle."—*Petrie.*]

From Castle Pollard the tourist who is on his way to Cavan may rejoin the rly. at Float Stat. (Rte. 17). Castle Pollard is a good rendezvous for the angler, who will find plenty of large-sized trout in Lough Derevaragh.]

11 m., after crossing a lazy stream that connects the last-named lough with Lough Iron, the line reaches Cavan Junction (Rte. 17).

13 m. the rly. enters the county

of Longford ; l. 1 m. the village of Rathowen, near the small lake of Glen Lough. In the neighbourhood are Newpark (J. Auchmuty, Esq.), and Rockfield (M. Crawford, Esq.).

17 m. *Edgeworthstown*, though in itself only a neat, plain village, has acquired an interest that will never fade away on account of the social benefits that have accrued, not only to Ireland, but to the world at large, from the Edgeworth family. It has been established here ever since the year 1583, the first of the family who came to Ireland having been made Bishop of Down and Connor. Each generation of the Edgeworths was remarkable for their endeavours to improve the social condition of those around them, and none were more conspicuous in their efforts than the late Mr. Richard Edgeworth, who lived at the commencement of the present century, and was far ahead of his age in scientific knowledge and practice, as well as in his views on Irish education and questions of political economy. The charming novels of Miss Edgeworth, his daughter, have been read by all the world, and need no more than a passing allusion. Apart from these associations, Edgeworthstown House is a plain, comfortable mansion, with no particular architectural beauties about it. The ch. should be visited on account of its steeple, an ingenious contrivance of the late Mr. Edgeworth. It was formed of iron, covered with slates, and was cleverly hoisted into its position by means of windlasses—

"The chimney widened and grew higher, Became a steeple with a spire."

In the neighbourhood of Edgeworthstown are Colamber (— Blackall, Esq.), Whitehill House (H. Wilson Slator, Esq.), and *Lissard* (J. L. O'Ferrall, Esq.). At *Firmount*, which is a portion of this property, resided the Abbé Edgeworth, who attended Louis XVI. to the scaffold as his confessor.

Distances.—Longford, 8½ m.; Granard, 13; Ardagh, 5.

22 m., on l. about 3 m. is Ardagh Hill (650 ft.), from the summit of which there is a very fine view.

25½ m. *Longford* (*Hotel*: Longford), a tolerably flourishing inland little town, and the most important that the traveller will meet with in this route. It is the terminus of the Royal Canal, which is here supplied by the Camlin river. Being a corporate and county town, it contains the usual municipal buildings — such as gaol, court-house, barracks, and the like—together with a goodly number of stores and appliances for trade, which has been much encouraged by the Longford family. There are no remains of its castle or abbey, both of which were at one time important, a very large Dominican house, subsequently destroyed by fire, having been founded here in 1400 by O'Ferrol, Prince of Annaly. This family was all important here till the middle of the 17th cent., when the castle was taken, and all the garrison put to the sword. The tourist should visit the R. C. cathedral, which has a very lofty tower, and occupied 20 years in building.

Conveyances.— Car to Athlone daily, through Ballymahon; rail to Sligo and Mullingar.

Distances. — Edgeworthstown, 8½ m.; Lanesborough, 10; Carrick-on-Shannon, 22; Newtown Forbes, 3; Drumod, 11; Strokestown, 14; Athlone, 27; Mullingar, 25½; Dublin, 76.

The country, which hitherto has been little but a succession of bog, begins to improve soon after leaving Longford, and at 30 m. the village of *Newtown Forbes*, on l. of rly., is wooded and pretty. Extending to the banks of the Shannon, which the tourist now reaches, is Castle Forbes, a beautiful seat of the Earl of Granard, Lord Lieutenant of the county Leitrim, to whose ancestor, Sir Arthur Forbes, the estate was granted by James I. In 1641 the house sustained a severe siege at the hands of the insurgents, in which extremity it was gallantly defended by Sir Arthur's widow. The grounds extend for some distance along one of the expansions of the Shannon, known as Lough Forbes, one of those loughs so peculiar to it in the earlier portions of its course.

31 m. rt. a road is given off to the village of Drumlish, 4 m. Crossing the river Rinn, the rly. leaves on l. the village of

Rooky, at which point the traveller quits the county of Longford for that of Leitrim. Both counties are separated from Roscommon by the Shannon, here crossed by a swivel erected by the commissioners for the improvement of that river. Aughamore House is the residence of H. N. Lawder, Esq. [A road on l., crossing the bridge, runs to 1 m. *Strokestown*, passing the S. end of Lough Bofin, and subsequently of Lough Kilglass, both extensions of and connected with the Shannon, which twists about the country in an extraordinary manner.] From Roosky the road follows closely the E. bank of the Shannon, that here expands into Lough Bofin and Lough Boderg, which, from their indented and wooded shores, offer some very pretty scenery, all the more acceptable after the bare flats of Longford.

37 m. Drumod was at one period famous for its iron-works, established here to work the ore found in the parish.

39 m. l., on a wooded promontory dipping into the Shannon, is Derrycarne, the seat of W. Ormsby Gore, Esq., M.P. A sharp skirmish is recorded as having taken place at this spot where there is a ford, between the soldiers of James II. and William respectively.

[From Drumod it is 5 m. to *Mohill*, a small town situated near the head of Lough Rinn. A fine abbey of canons regular once existed here, but no traces are left except a small circular tower. In the neighbourhood are Rynn Castle, a seat of the Earl of Leitrim, Lakefield (D. Crofton, Esq.), Clooncahir (Sir Morgan Crofton, Bart.), and Drumod House (W. P. Jones, Esq.).]

43 m. l. is the little ch. of Annaduff, and

44 m. *Drumsna*, a village situated in the neighbourhood of lovely scenery. "In one direction are seen the windings of the Shannon through a fertile district, the projection of a wooded peninsula on its course, the heights of Sheebeg and Sheemore, with the more lofty mountains of Slievi-an-ieran in the distance; and in the other the luxuriant and varied swell of Teeraroon, the adjacent part of the county of Roscommon." The Shannon here makes a complete turn upon itself, running between the demesnes of Mount Campbell (W. A. Lawder, Esq.), and Charlestown, the seat of Sir Gilbert King, Bart. The road to Carrick, however, does not follow this serpentine course, but crosses the river twice within a mile, arriving at

45 m. *Jamestown*, a small market-town, incorporated by James I., which was the scene of a few skirmishes in 1689 between the Enniskilleners and the Irish under Sarsfield. The road passes under a castellated gateway, near which is Jamestown Lodge, the residence of Hugh O'Beirne, Esq.

47½ m. *Carrick-on-Shannon* (Inn, St. George's Arms), a small town, deriving its sole importance from being the county town of Leitrim, where all the assize business is held. It formerly sent 2 members to the Irish parliament, but the franchise was abolished at the time of the Union, when 15,000*l.* was awarded as compensation. The town has been much benefited by its situation on the Shannon, which by means of the Improvement Commission has been rendered navigable as far as Lough Allen.

Distances.—Leitrim, 3¼ m.; Boyle, 9½; Drumshambo, 7½; Longford, 22.

The principal proprietor in this neighbourhood is C. St. George, Esq., who resides at Hatley Manor, in the town.

Quitting Carrick, the traveller again crosses the Shannon for the last time, though in so doing he by no means loses sight of the chain of lakes, as the Boyle river, which now accompanies the road, is even more peculiar in its lough system than the Shannon. The Boyle water is in fact a succession of lakes, connected together by a short river.

[At 52 m. a road on rt. is given off to Leitrim and Drumshambo, crossing the Boyle at the E. end of Oakport Lough, and passing on l. the grounds of Oakport House (— Molloy, Esq.), while a little further on, near the ch. and glebe of Ardcarn, another road crosses at the end of Lough Key, and traverses the country at the N.E. of Lough Arrow, to Collooney and Sligo.]

At Ardcarn the tourist approaches the beautiful grounds of *Rockingham*, the seat of Viscount Lorton, which, for charming situation, united to all the improvements secured by modern landscape gardening, is equal to any place in Ireland. In front of the ruins of the mansion, which was unfortunately burnt down in April 1863,* spreads out Lough Key, the prettiest and most varied of all these northern lakelets, studded with islands and fringed with woods. On one are the ruins of a ch., and on another of a castle, formerly the stronghold of a chieftain named M'Dermott.

56 m. *Boyle* (anc. Buill) (*Hotel:*

* The restoration is being actively proceeded with.

Monson's) is in itself a dirty place, though redeemed by its very pretty situation on the river-side, and the unique ecclesiastic ruins hard by. The best part of the town is on the W. bank of the river, which is crossed by no less than 3 bridges, the principal one being balustraded, and of 3 arches of remarkably good span. The old residence of the Kingstown family is now used as a barrack. The ivy-clad abbey ruins, to which the attention of the archæologist will be at once directed, are situated on the N. of the town, by the side of the river, which here flows swiftly and deeply through a charmingly wooded glen, and is crossed by a good single-arched bridge. They are in the private grounds of the Misses Robertson, by whom admission is granted instantly. A Cistercian house was founded here by Maurice O'Dubhay in 1161, which in the same century had the honour of receiving the corpse of M'Dermot, King of Moylurg; but, like most abbeys, it suffered much harsh treatment, first in 1235 at the hands of the English forces under the Lords Justices Fitzgerald and M'William, and again from the soldiers of Cromwell, who, according to their usual practice, stabled their horses in it, and carved their names on the doors. From the road the visitor has a good view of the beautiful W. front, exhibiting the E. window at the end of the vista. It contains a single Early Pointed window with good moulding and dripstone, and is flanked by square buttresses. Like most of the abbeys of that period, Boyle was cruciform, with a central tower. The nave, which is 131 ft. long, is divided on the N. side by 3 Early Pointed arches. Notice the exquisite mouldings that form the corbels of the vaulting arches, and on the S. the 8 arches of pure Norm. character, with the curious distinction between the 4 westerly

Route 18.—Curlew Hills—Kesh Hills.

pillars, which are piers, while the remaining ones are columns. The sculpture on the capitals of the pier-arches is singular, and should be well studied. The arches on the other side have been apparently blocked. At the intersection of the tower are 3 exquisite segmental arches, though the chancel arch itself is Early Pointed. The N. transept, which has an aisle, is lighted by a 2 light Norm. window deeply splayed inwardly, and contains, as also does the S. transept, 2 Early Pointed arches leading into a recessed chapel, perhaps a sacristy. Underneath the courtyard, which is neatly and trimly kept—

"—— A flowry grene,
Full thick of grass, full soft and swete"—

is a subterranean passage, which communicates with the barrack in the town. The offices were very extensive, and are in tolerable preservation, especially as regards the kitchen and hospitium. In the porter's lodge the names of the soldiers of Cromwell are yet visible carved on the doors. The abbey contains the burial-place of the noble family of King, to whom it still belongs, and the antiquary will not fail to give credit to Capt. Robertson for having so diligently and zealously cleared the ruins from the accumulated rubbish of centuries.

The other remains in the neighbourhood of Boyle are the ch. of Asylyn, which stands on the banks of the river near Lough Key, and a cromlech "on the rt. side of the road leading to Lough Gara, the table-stone of which is 15 ft. long and 11 wide, and was formerly supported on 5 upright pillars."

Besides Rockingham, there are also the following residences in the neighbourhood of Boyle—Cootehall J. Burton, Esq., Mount Erris J. Duckworth, Esq., and Knockadoo.

Conveyances.—Car daily to Castlerea.

Distances.—Longford, 31 m.; Sligo, 23½; Tuam, 26; Frenchpark, 9; Castlerea, 17; Ballinafad, 4; Carrick, 9½; Leitrim, 11.

Very soon after leaving Boyle the road mounts in steep zigzags the *Curlew Hills*, which, though only 863 ft. in height, assume a certain importance from their sudden elevation. The views over Boyle, Lough Key, and, more to the rt., Lough Gara, are very beautiful, while from the summit an equally extensive view opens out over Ballinafad and Lough Arrow. Descending on the opposite side,

60 m. *Ballinafad* is prettily situated on the shores of *Lough Arrow*, a considerable lake about 5 m. in length, which, as far as a good many flourishing plantations go, is cheerful and smiling, though the bleak character of the country round detracts considerably from its beauty. The castle of Ballinafad is on the l. of the road, and consists of 3 circular towers with connecting walls. On the W. side of Lough Arrow the road passes the well-wooded demesne of Hollybrook (J. Frolliot, Esq.), while on the opposite shore are Kingsborough House, with 2 or 3 small ruins, ecclesiastical and military, the latter of which are dotted over the country in marvellous profusion. This district also abounds with raths, erroneously believed to be Danish.

Immediately on l. is a picturesque chain known as the *Kesh Hills*, consisting of 2 principal heights, Kesh Corrin (1183 ft.), and Carrowkesh (1062). From them there is a very fine view of the Ox Mountains, with the Sligo and Manor Hamilton Hills due N. On the W. face of Kesh Corrin, which is composed of tabular limestone, are the entrances to some extensive caves, said not to have been entirely explored. Here dwelt the harper Corran, to whom the Tuatha de Danaan gave this district as a reward for musical skill.

[67½ m., on l. 1 m. is Newpark House (Jemmett Duke, Esq.), and 3 m. beyond is *Ballymote* (anc. Baile-an-mhota), now little more than a village, but formerly of importance, owing to its fortress, which was built in 1300 by Richard de Burgo, Earl of Ulster, of such strength that it offered a serious impediment to the subjugation of Connaught. This castle, which is strengthened by towers at the angles, occupies an area of 150 square ft. There are also remains of a Franciscan monastery, with the mutilated figure of a pope over the entrance. The friars of this establishment were celebrated for their learning, and wrote the 'Book of Ballymote,' extant to this day. "It was written by different persons, but chiefly by Solomon O'Droma and Manus O'-Duigenan, and begins with an imperfect copy of the 'Leabhar Gabhála,' or Book of Invasions of Erin, followed by a series of ancient chronological, historical, and genealogical pieces, with pedigrees of Irish saints, &c."—*Prof. O'Currey.* The ch. of Ballymote has a very graceful tower and spire. A little beyond the town is Temple Lodge (Col. Perceval), on the banks of the lake of the same name; and in the grounds are the ruins of a house formerly belonging to the Knights Templars.]

Soon after passing the village of Drumfin, near which is Coopers Hill, the seat of C. W. O'Hara, Esq., M.P., the scenery begins to improve, and becomes very pretty at 71 m., near Cloonmahon (Mrs. Meredith), and *Markree Castle*, the splendid seat of the late E. J. Cooper, Esq., who contributed much to the advancement of astronomical science, and possessed some celebrated instruments for that purpose. The woods of this magnificent property extend for a long distance, and abound in charming glades, which are watered by the Unshin river and a number of small tributary brooks.

A little further on is the hamlet of Toberscanavan, close to a small lough; and at 73 m. the traveller arrives at

Collooney, as comfortable, well-built, and pretty a village as he will meet with in all Ireland. Two considerable rivers, the Owenmore and Owenbeg, unite their waters a little below Annaghmore, the seat of C. L'Estrange, Esq., and about 2¼ m. above Collooney, where a very large volume of water flowing over a ledge of rocks forms a picturesque cascade, and is available for some extensive corn-mills, which give a great air of business to the village. There is also a rather pretty ch. on some rising ground to the l.

[A road skirts the woods of Markree Castle, passing by Castle Dangan (T. Ormsby, Esq.) and the village of Ballintogher, to 10 m. Dromahaire (Rte. 8).]

Distances.—Ballysadare, 1½ m.; Dromahaire, 10.

The road now follows the river to 74½ m. Ballysadare (Rte. 22). Between these two villages a sharp skirmish took place between a body of French who landed at Killala in 1798, and a detachment of Limerick militia and some dragoons under Col. Vereker, who had unsuccessfully attacked the invaders. He was ultimately obliged to retreat with the loss of his artillery to Sligo.

Ballysadare, like Collooney, is a prosperous well-to-do place, dependent to a great extent on very valuable salmon-fisheries, which were the property of, and indeed owe their being to, the late Mr. Cooper of Markree, who placed a number of ladders by which the fish might ascend the falls. The river here falls into Ballysadare Bay over a considerable distance of shelving rock, forming the prettiest series of rapids possible.

On the opposite side of the river is a small ivy-grown abbey, founded by St. Fechin in the 7th cent., and which in its day was richly endowed. A good deal of business is done in the exportation of corn and flour; ships of 100 tons being enabled to come into the little harbour. From hence it is a pleasant drive to Sligo; Knocknarea, with its truncated summit on the l., and the Slish Mountains on the rt., forming constant changes of landscape.

79 m. Sligo (Rte. 8). (*Hotels*: Imperial, Victoria.)

ROUTE 19.

FROM **ATHLONE** TO **ROSCOMMON, CASTLEREAGH, BALLINA,** AND **BELMULLET.**

The Great Northern and Western Rly. runs at present from Athlone to Castlebar, a distance of 72 m.; passing through a very uninteresting and thinly inhabited country, although the first few miles are relieved by some charming views on the rt. of Lough Rea.

12 m. Knockcroghery (famous for its manufactory of tobacco-pipes) is the nearest station from whence to make an excursion to St. John's or Rindown Castle, about 5 m. to the S.E., occupying a promontory on the shore of Lough Rea. "Rin-duin," the point of the fort, is mentioned in the 'Annals of the Four Masters' as having existed in 1156, and is believed to have been an early stronghold of the Danish King Turgesius in the 9th cent. It was long in the possession of the O'Connors, from whom it was taken by the English in the 13th cent. As described in Weld's 'Survey of Roscommon,' this castle was built in the form of a P, the tail of the letter being occupied by a banqueting-hall, and the head by the keep, a massive tower, about 50 ft. in breadth, overgrown with ivy of extraordinary richness of growth. To the E. of the castle are the remains of a watch-tower, the whole being protected by a broad ditch, which formerly converted the peninsula into a promontory, and a wall 564 yds. long, with an arched gateway in the centre, and defensive towers at intervals. Near the castle are remains of a small early ch., of about the 13th cent. The pleasantest mode of visiting Rindown will be by water from Athlone, particularly as under the castle walls there is a snug little anchorage, known as Safe Harbour.

14½ m. Ballymurry.

18 m. *Roscommon* (anc. Rus-chomain) (*Hotels*: Victoria; Royal) is a neat-looking country town (Pop. 2731), with little beauty of situation to recommend it, but containing two remains of its former greatness—the Abbey and the Castle. The former, in the lower part of the town, consists of a ch. 137 ft. long, "with a northern transept, in which is an aisle separated by 4 pointed arches, resting on massive round pillars; over the principal entrance is a beautiful window, with an architrave decorated with pinnacles; the windows in the choir are lancet-shaped and much mutilated. Under an arch in the N. side of the choir is a tomb with a mutilated effigy, said to be that of O'Connor, and on the base are 4 warlike figures representing ancient Gallowglasses." This O'Connor, said to be interred here, was the founder of the priory and King of Connaught

in 13th cent. Seen from the railway the castle makes an imposing appearance on the side of the hill. The present building dates from 1268, and was the work of John D'Ufford, Justiciary of Ireland. It occupies a large quadrangular area, defended by a round tower at each angle, as well as by two similar ones projecting from the E. to protect the gateway. One only of these towers is roofed, and forms a lofty room, vaulted overhead, and said to have been a council-chamber. In the inner court is a rectangular building containing the state apartments. Roscommon Castle is, as far as extent goes, one of the finest in the kingdom, and, according to tradition, was in good preservation up to a later date than most fortresses. It is said to have been inhabited up to the battle of Aughrim, in the reign of William III., when the fugitive Irish escaping from that engagement set fire to it.

1½ m. to the N. E. of Roscommon are remains (though small) of the Abbey of Deerane, probably dependent on that of Roscommon; with the exception of a good window, they present nothing worthy of visit.

Conveyances.—Rail to Athlone and Castlebar.

Distances.—Castlereagh, 17 m.; Athlone, 18; Ballinasloe, 25.

24 m. at *Dunamon* the Suck river is crossed by a long causeway bridge, and again, a little below, at Castle Coote. On the opposite side of the water is Dunamon Castle (St. George Caulfield, Esq.). The line now follows the valley of the Suck, if such a sluggish stream can be said to have a valley, and, passing 31 m. l. the village of Ballymoe, arrives at

35 m. *Castlereagh*, an uninteresting town of about 1500 Inhab., rather prettily situated on the Suck, which is here adorned with some good timber belonging to the demesne of the late Lord Mount Sandford, and now the property of T. J. Sandford, Esq. The antiquary may visit the circular cemetery of Cruachan or Rathcroghan, "which is of a circular form, measuring 116 paces in diameter, and surrounded with a stone ditch greatly defaced. Within are small circular mounds, covering rude sepulchral chambers formed of stone, without cement of any kind, and containing unburnt bones. The monument of Dathi, with its pillar of red sandstone, is outside the enclosure, at a short distance to the E."—*Petrie*. To show the celebrity of this cemetery, the Connaught poet writes thus :—

"There is not at this place
A hill at Venach na Cruachna,
Which is not the grave of a king or royal prince,
Or of a woman or warlike poet."

Conveyances.—Rail to Athlone, Castlebar, and Westport. Cars daily to Ballina and Sligo.

Distances.—Boyle, 18 m.; Frenchpark, 8½; Claremorris, 22.

The remainder of this route is performed by a car, which traverses a dreary country, as far as Lough Cullin, when it begins to improve.

52 m. Kilkelly.

59 m. *Swineford*, a poor little place, in the neighbourhood of which is Brabazon Park, the seat of Major Brabazon. At 61 m. Cloongullaun bridge the traveller crosses the Moy (anc. Muaidh), one of the most important rivers in the N.W. of Ireland. It rises in the Ox mountains, in county Sligo, and, flowing southwards from thence, receives the waters of the Owenaher and the Owengarve, and for a considerable distance divides the counties of Mayo and Sligo. Near Swineford it flows due W. for a few miles, and then to the N., keeping a parallel course with Loughs Cullin and Conn. Soon the road diverges—that to the rt. direct to Ballina—[the other runs to Foxford, and then falls into the Westport road.

Route 19.—Ballina.

Foxford is a small town of some 1200 Inhab., in the neighbourhood of scenery far superior to any that the traveller has yet met with. The hills begin to close in, and on the N.W. attain the height of 1095 ft. in the range of the Sieve Gamph mountains. Foxford is a place of some antiquity, and was formerly the key to the district of Tyrawley, lying to the W. The Moy runs through the town, and is fordable at a point called Cromwell's Rock, where the Protector and his army are alleged to have crossed.] The remainder of the route follows the valley of the Moy, passing on rt. a few small loughs to

73 m. *Ballina* (anc. Bel-an-atha) *Htls*: Flynn's, tolerable ; Royal) Route 22, a busy, dirty place, some 5 m. distant from the mouth of the Moy. The only historical events connected with it are the attack and capture of the town by the French who in 1798 landed at Killala, under Gen. Humbert. On this occasion the Rev. S. Fortescue, the rector of the town and a volunteer, was shot by a party in ambuscade. The Moy is here developed into a broad stream, and separates Sligo from Mayo; the district on the rt. or Sligo side is called Ardnaree, and the communications maintained by a couple of handsome bridges. On the E. side is a large Roman Catholic chapel, worth a short inspection, together with the ruins of an ancient abbey, founded by St. Bolean, with a well-designed pointed doorway.

The situation of Ballina is good, and the views of Nephin and hills on the W. of Lough Conn are very fine ; but the town itself is not particularly attractive. The fishery is, however, of great importance. At the falls weirs have been built by Mr. Little at a cost of 1500*l*. "Boat and attendance 5s. a-day. All fish retailed at the weir or taken at the market price. The fish are small and plentiful, being mostly grilse, with an occasional salmon. A few good salmon are sometimes got in the spring."—*Angler's Register*.

Conveyances.—Car daily to Sligo; car to Westport; car to Belmullet, through Crossmolina and Bangor; to Castlereagh ; coach to Athenry.

Distances.—Foxford, 13 m. ; Sligo, 36; Dromore, 15; Westport, 23; Castlebar, 22; Pontoon, 11; Crossmolina, 7½ ; Belmullet, 49 ; Killala, 8; Roserk, 5.

Excursions.—
1. Killala, Roserk, and Moyne.
2. Pontoon.
3. Nephin.

The route followed by the public car to Belmullet traverses the dreary districts of Tyrawley and Erris. The best way for the tourist is to skirt the coast, by which means he may pay a visit to Roserk and Moyne Abbeys. From Ballina the road keeps the l. side of the Moy, passing through the demesne of Belleek Castle (F. Howley, Esq.) and Belleek Abbey (Col. Knox Gore).

5 m. in a dell overlooking the Moy are the ruins of Roserk or Rosserick Abbey (Ross-Searka, the promontory of Searka), founded for Franciscan friars by the sept of Joyce. It is somewhat similar to Clare Galway—a cruciform ch., with a lofty tower rising from the intersection of nave and transepts. Of a similar (Dec.) character is the Abbey of Moyne, 3 m. to the N., which has a length of 135 feet, some good Dec. windows, and a slender tower. "It lies in a sequestered pastoral district, on the banks of the bay, watered by a small rill, which, dipping into the granular limestone, rises again under the ch. and supplies the convent. From the top of the tower, the ascent to which is both easy and safe, a good view is obtained of the building, the surrounding country, the bay, diversified by the island of Bartragh, and the accompanying ledges of long low

white-crested sandhills."—*Fraser.* At the S. end of the island is Bartragh House (J. Kirkwood, Esq.).

9 m. *Killala*, an interesting little place, both as being the seat of a former bishopric, now consolidated with that of Tuam, and as the scene of the landing of the French under Gen. Humbert, in 1798. With two frigates, having on board 1100 men, this expedition sailed from Rochelle, with the intention of making a descent upon Donegal; but, in consequence of adverse winds, the General was forced to land in Kilcummin Bay, a little to the N. of Killala, and proceeded to Ballina, where the unfortunate death of Mr. Forester took place.

The see of Killala is very ancient, having been founded by St. Patrick in the 5th cent. The cathedral is a plain building of the 17th cent., with later alterations, occupying the site of a much earlier ch., erected by Gobhan, an eminent architect of the 6th cent. The round tower, which is placed on an insulated eminence, is of the same date, but was struck by lightning in 1800, and considerably damaged thereby. Of contemporaneous date, and built by the same individual, are the towers of Kilmacduagh and Antrim. Killala was at one time a brisk little seaport; but Ballina, with its superior advantages, has taken almost all the trade from it. The Owenmore is crossed by a fine bridge of 11 arches at Palmerstown, the property and former seat of the family of Palmer. The mansion was destroyed in the troubles of '98. On the rt. bank of the river is Castlereagh, the seat of E. Knox, Esq.

[1½ m. rt. are the ruined ch. of Rathfran and some earthen forts at Summerhill.

3 m. *Kilcummin*, containing the cell and burial-place of Cumin, or Cumean Fin, a saint who flourished in the 7th cent.]

18 m. *Ballycastle*, commands a splendid view of Downpatrick Head, which rises to the height of 126 ft. about 3 m. to the N. The singular rock of Doonbristy, standing detached from the land, testifies to the violence of the Atlantic waves along this coast. The geological composition of this coast is that of yellow sandstone, both at the Head and the opposite promontory of Benmore, between which is a narrow slip of lower limestone, affording at Pollnamuck many typical shells and carb. fishes. From Ballycastle to Belmullet the road lies through a country of wild desolate mountains, seldom rising above 1200 ft., but as dreary and untameable as anything in Ireland. It forms the district of Erris, lying to the N. of the barony of Tyrawley, and is very seldom visited. The coast scenery, however, will well repay any pedestrian tourist, with whom time is no object. From Ballycastle the traveller may return to Ballina through the valley of Ballinglen, about 16 m. A little way from the village the road crosses the Ballinglen, which falls into the Bay of Bunnatrahir, and then keeps close to the N. coast, at the base of Maumakeogh 1245 ft., and Glencolry 1155 ft., to Bealderrig Bay, from whence it runs inland to the S.W., leaving the finest part of the coast without any road at all, save footpaths to the coast-guard stations at Porturlin and Portacloy.

From Bealderrig Bay, where we enter upon a district of primary rocks, to Benwee Head, the coast offers a constant succession of grand scenes. "Moista Sound is 4 m. W. from Bealderrig. It is a chasm about a cable's length from one extremity to the other, so narrow that a boat's oars must be reefed in passing through it. It is formed by a gigantic trap-dyke; the trap rock has fallen out, leaving this chasm, the sides of which are absolutely vertical, the northern 350 ft. high, the other 450 ft., and on the southern side the cliff rises

350 ft. more, almost vertically, making 800 ft.; but when in the Sound the upper portion is variable. The Arch is about 8 m. from Bealderrig, and near the coast-guard station of Porturlin. It is 30 ft. in height, and may be rowed through in perfect safety at half-tide and in moderate weather. It is also a trap-dyke; here, however, the trap remains, excepting at the bottom, where, by its having fallen out, the arch is formed; the keystone, as it may be termed, being about 600 ft. high, reaching to the top of the cliff. From hence to the lofty and nearly isolated promontory of Doonvinallagh, 10 m. W. from Bealderrig, is one succession of magnificent cliffs, headlands, and bays. Near the northern extremity of the promontory, to the W. of the beautiful little harbour of Portacloy, is a cavern about 30 ft. high at the entrance, and wide enough for a boat to row in. It then expands into a spacious circular shape, with a lofty domical roof."—*Fraser.*

The Stags of Broadhaven, so conspicuous in all the coast views of Erris, and from the Donegal side, are 7 precipitous rocks, about 300 ft. high, 1½ m. to the N. of Benwee Head. This latter rises to 829 ft., and is well worth the ascent for the sake of the superb view over Achill, Blacksod Bay, and Ballycroy to the S., the Sligo and the Donegal coast to the N.E.; but the pedestrian must remember that there is no accommodation of any sort nearer than Belmullet, which is at least 8 miles distant across country. The road from Bealderrig to Belmullet passes through a very bleak and uninteresting district, which requires the most delightful weather to render it at all agreeable. At 35 m. it crosses the Glenamoy river as it enters an inlet of Broadhaven, and at 42 m. the isthmus that intervenes between Lough Carrowmore and Belmullet Sound.

Passing through Derrycorrib, a village at the foot of Glencastle Hill, and on the Glencastle river, the tourist reaches

49 m. *Belmullet*, 35 years ago a miserable collection of huts, and now a thriving little seaport. It is singularly placed on a strip of land 400 yards broad, intervening between Broadhaven on the N. and Blacksod Bay on the S.: a canal has been cut through it, so that vessels, which were formerly wind-bound for weeks in the neighbourhood of the Mullet promontory, can at once go through. There is a good market here; it being the emporium for the greater part of Erris and Ballycroy. Belmullet is the key of the peninsula of Mullet, which extends N. as far as Erris Head, and runs S., gradually tapering away to Blacksod Point, exactly opposite Slieve More, in Achill Island. Thus, while one side of the Mullet is exposed to the fiercest storms of the Atlantic, the other looks upon two landlocked havens, Broadhaven and Blacksod, each of which would contain in security all the navies of the world. From these advantages it was at one time proposed to make Belmullet a western terminus for a trunk railway.

There is not much of interest in the long peninsula of Mullet, inhabited localities being few and far between. Binghamstown is a collection of wretched hovels in the neighbourhood of Castle Bingham, a square castellated mansion belonging to the family of that name, and landlords of the greater part of this district. As may be imagined, trees are a rarity, everything being open to the fierce blasts of the W. The traveller who has not made special arrangements with the hotel-keeper at Ballina may return by the mail car through Bangor, or he may by chance catch a sailing vessel or "hooker" coasting down from Belmullet through Achill Sound to Westport or Galway.

ROUTE 20.

FROM GALWAY TO CLIFDEN, THROUGH OUGHTERARDE AND BALLYNAHINCH.

Galway (*Hotels:* Railway Hotel, at the terminus of the Midland Great Western Rly., attendance bad, and charges high ; Black's), besides being the rendezvous for all tourists bound to Connemara, contains within its precincts so much to interest that the traveller should make a point of staying here for 2 or 3 days. Very comfortable lodgings can be obtained at Miss Grogan's in Eyre Square. Independently of its being the principal town in the county, and indeed a county in itself, as well as the capital of Connaught, it enjoys considerable natural advantages, and has capabilities of becoming an important place, should improvement continue at the same rate at which it has been progressing for the last 10 years.

Under various names a town has been established here from the earliest times, and Ptolemy mentions a city called Nagnata, which is generally considered to be identical with Galway. This latter is derived, according to some, from a legend to the effect that a woman named Galva was drowned in the river hard by ; by others, from the Gallæci of Spain, with whom the town carried on an extensive trade ; and by others again, from the Gaels or merchants by whom it was occupied.

Its early history is that of repeated ravages by the Danes or by their Munster neighbours, who looked on the colony with jealous eyes; but after the invasion of Connaught by Henry II. walls began to be erected for the protection of the town, which caused a large influx of inhabitants, among whom were " a number of families, whose descendants are known to this day under the general appellation of 'the Tribes of Galway,' an expression first invented by Cromwell's forces, as a term of reproach against the natives of the town for their singular friendship and attachment to each other during the time of their unparalleled troubles and persecutions, but which the latter afterwards adopted as an honourable mark of distinction between themselves and their cruel oppressors."— *Hardiman's Hist*. There were 14 of these so-called tribes, the descendants of some of which, as Blake, Lynch, Joyce, D'Arcy, French, Martin, &c., are still found amongst the leading citizens who in those days carefully guarded themselves from any intercourse with the native Irish. In one of the bye-laws, of the date of 1518, it is enacted "that no man of this towne shall oste or receive into their housses at Christemas, Easter, nor no feaste elles, any of the Burkes, M'Williams, the Kellies, nor no cepte elles, without license of the mayor and councill, on payn to forfeit 5*l*., that neither O' nor Mac shalle strutte ne swaggere thro' the streetes of Gallway.'

The following singular inscription was formerly to be seen over the W. gate—

" From the ferocious O'Flahertics
Good Lord deliver us."

Owing to its excellent situation, Galway enjoyed for centuries the monopoly of the trade with Spain, from whence it received large quantities of wine, salt, &c., and caused so much personal intercourse that the town became impressed to a certain degree with Spanish features, both in the architecture of the streets as well as the dress and manners of the population: though it was nevertheless the habit of former writers to ascribe too much to the supposed Spanish origin of the town, overlooking the fact that it was inhabited by an essentially Anglo-Norman colony.

The 1st charter was granted by Edward III., and confirmed in successive reigns. Galway reached its highest point of opulence at the commencement of the Irish Rebellion in 1641, during which period it was remarkable for its loyalty to the King, and suffered a siege and such barbarous treatment at the hands of the Parliamentary army, that at the Restoration the town was almost wholly decayed.

"After the battle of Aughrim, Gen. de Ginkell, with 14,000 of William's army, laid siege to it; and, after holding out for some time, it surrendered on the 20th July 1691, on condition of a safe-conduct for the garrison to Limerick and a free pardon of the inhabitants, with preservation of their property and privileges."—*Lewis*.

Galway is *situated* on gently rising ground on the N. side and near the head of the bay. The greater portion of the town is built upon a tongue of land, bounded on the E. by Lough Athalia, an arm of the sea, and on the W. by the river which forms the outlet of Lough Corrib. The other and smaller part is on the opposite bank of the river and in the district known as Iar-Connaught, the connection being maintained by 1 wooden and 2 stone bridges. The *W. Bridge* is a very ancient structure of the date of 1342, and formerly possessed 2 tower gateways at the W. and centre; these, however, have long disappeared. The *upper Bridge*, leading from the Court-House, was erected in 1818. From a map (of which only 2 copies are extant) made in 1651, by the Marquis of Clanricarde, to ascertain the extent and value of the town, it appears that Galway was then entirely surrounded by walls, defended by 14 towers and entered by as many gates. A poetical description in Latin appended to this map informs us that—

"Bis urbis septem defendunt mœnia turres
   Intus, et ex duro est marmore quaque
     domus."

Since the middle of the last cent. the fortifications went fast to decay, and now nothing remains but a *fragment* near the quay, and a *massive archway* leading to *Spanish Place*. There is also a square *bastion* of great thickness in Francis-street, and a portion of wall with a round-headed blocked arch; but it is only of the date of William I., and was in a perfect state not many years ago. Within the last cent. the town has so much increased as to cover more than double the space formerly occupied within the walls. The streets, however, though containing several handsome buildings, are narrow, inconvenient, and dirty; nevertheless, the antiquary will find very much to interest him in the remarkable architectural features of the houses, which are foreign to a degree unknown in any other town in the kingdom. Yet too much has been written and said about the present appearance of Galway; for time and modern improvements have to a certain extent obliterated many of the ancient remains, which, with some exceptions, are not so patent to the general tourist as might be imagined from the glowing descriptions. The old houses require looking for, and the more time and care that the traveller bestows on the back streets, the more will he be rewarded. Many of the houses are built Spanish fashion, with a small court (patio in the centre, and an arched gateway leading into the street; but it requires some effort of imagination to identify these ill-kept and overcrowded dwellings with the gay residences of the Spanish merchants. The most striking specimen of domestic architecture is *Lynch's Mansion*, a large square building at the corner of Shop and Abbeygate-streets, having square-headed doorways and windows, with richly decorated mouldings and dripstones. There is also a portion of the cornice or projecting balustrade at the top of the house, the horizontal supporting pillars being terminated with grotesque heads. On the street face are richly ornamented medallions, containing the arms of the Lynches, with their crest—a lynx. Notice also the carved figure of a monkey and child, which commemorates the saving of an infant belonging to the family, by a favourite monkey, on an occasion when the house was burnt. The same anecdote is told of John 1st Earl of Kildare, whose crest, taken from this occurrence, consists of a monkey. This monument of a great and powerful family is now used as a chandler's shop. On the opposite side of the same street is another ancient house with windows of Saracenic character.

In *Lombard-street*, close to the ch., are a window and wall, on which is a stone bearing the legend of 2 cross bones and the inscription—

"Remember death. All is vanity of vanities"—1524—

In memory of the following occurrence. James Lynch Fitzstephen, the then Mayor of Galway, had been one of the most successful of the citizens in promoting commerce with Spain, which he had himself personally visited, having been received with every mark of hospitality. To make some return for all this kindness, he proposed and obtained permission from his Spanish host to take his only son back with him to Ireland, where the latter speedily became a favourite from his winning manners and beauty. The mayor had also an only son, unfortunately addicted to evil company, but who, he hoped, was likely to reform from the circumstance of his being attached to a Galway lady of good family. And so it might have proved, had he not jealously fancied that the lady looked too graciously upon the Spaniard. Roused to madness, he watched the latter out of the house, stabbed him, and then, stung with remorse, gave himself up to justice, to his father's unutterable dismay. Notwithstanding the entreaties of the townsfolk, with whom the youth was a favourite, the stern parent passed sentence of death, and actually hung him from the window with his own hand. It is generally believed, however, that the locality of this tragedy lay in another part of the city. The family of Lynch, one of the most celebrated in Galway annals, is said to have originally come from Linz in Austria, of which town one of them was governor during a siege. As a reward for his services, he received permission to take a lynx as a crest. The family came to Ireland in the 13th cent., and flourished till the middle of the 17th. In 1484 Pierce Lynch was made first Mayor under the charter of Richard III., while his son Stephen was appointed first Warden by Innocent VIII., and during the period of 169 years 84 members of this family were mayors.

In Lombard-street is a fine gateway belonging to the old Franciscan convent; and in Abbeygate-street is the mansion of the Joyces, with a finely sculptured doorway and the inscription—

"Nisi Dominus domum ædificaverit."—1649.

On a house in the adjoining street are the arms of Galway.

The ch. of *St. Nicholas* is a venerable cruciform building, " evidently the work of different periods, but remarkable for uniformity in the execution, and for order and plan in the general design." It consists of nave, with aisles, chancel, transepts, and central tower surmounted by a singular pyramidal belfry of much later date than the rest of the ch. The breadth across the transepts is 126 ft., and the total length 152 ft. The nave is separated from the aisles by 2 rows of good pointed arches, defaced, however, by a modern stone screen, which nearly blocks them up. The E. and W. windows (which are plain, of 5 lights) were formerly remarkable for the beautiful stained glass. The S. or Lynch's transept contains a small recess, in which is an altar of the Joyce family; 2 headless effigies and coats of arms of the Lynches, 1644; a richly-decorated side altar with finials; also the organ placed on a raised stone floor, the sides and front of which are sculptured. Underneath this lies Mayor Lynch, the hero of the tragedy mentioned above. The N. or French's transept is used as a vestry, and contains a slab to the family of Moriarty O'Tiernagh, 1580. In the N. aisle is an ancient confessional. The font rests on an antique base with sculptured sides. Externally the visitor should notice the beautiful pointed W. doorway, and the S. porch, which has a groined roof. Above it is the sexton's apartment, reached by a flight of steps. Close to the porch is the ruined chapel of St. Mary's, now blocked up, but exhibiting on its exterior some good carving.

Galway was formerly included within the diocese of Enachdone or Annaghdown (p. 181, united in 1324 to the Archbishopric of Tuam. The Irish clergy who were appointed gave rise to such dissensions that the ch. was made collegiate in 1484. During the reigns of Edward VI. and Elizabeth a change was made in the ecclesiastical conditions, and the ch. put under the charge of a protestant warden, an arrangement which held good until the recent death of the late Warden Daly. He had a jurisdiction distinct from that of the diocese, but Galway is now a portion of the see of Tuam.

The ancient collegiate establishment stood near the W. end of the ch., but is now let out into various tenements. Galway contains the usual buildings of a county town: 2 barracks, 1 known as the Shambles, near the W. bridge, and the other near William-street, where a gate formerly stood; a "tholsel" or exchange; a handsome modern *court-house* with a Doric front; and a gaol remarkable for being built without any timber. The *Roman Catholic parish chapel* is a large plain building in Middle-street, besides which are a chapel and nunnery established by Father Daly. Galway is the seat of a Roman Catholic diocese.

The best part of the town is *Eyre Square*, which contains some handsome residences, a bank, club-house, and the rly. stat. and hotel, all built of compact grey limestone. On the other side of the river is *Queen's College*, a fine Gothic building, with a spacious quadrangle, the architectural adornments of which are a feeble imitation of All Souls' College, Oxford. There are excellent museums adapted to the educational courses, and a good library, in which is a transcribed copy of the Galway records. The town can boast of several well-known scholars, as Lynch, the author of 'Cambrensis Eversus;' Flaherty, who wrote the 'Ogygia;' Kirwan, one of the most learned chemists of his day, and more recently Hardiman, the librarian of the college and author of the 'History of Galway.' The visitor who is interested in the education question should go and see the model school, a very well-managed institution on the national system. (Pop. 16,967.)

The *Harbour* has been much improved of late years, and has attracted a considerable share of public attention in consequence of the discussion about the Galway subsidy, in connection with the Atlantic Steam Company's contract to carry the mails to America. As a Transatlantic packet station there is no doubt that it possesses one advantage over other ports, viz. its proximity to America, it being only 1636 m. to St. John's, Newfoundland, 2165 to Halifax, 2385 to Boston, and 2700 to New York. The distance from Galway to St. John's is now frequently run in 5 days. The Bay of Galway consists of a long arm of the sea, protected at the entrance by the lofty cliffs of the islands of Aran, which in clear weather are visible at a distance of 29 m., and on the N. and S. by the coasts of Galway and Clare respectively. A legend in the annals of Ireland states that it was once a freshwater lake known as Lough Lurgan, one of the 3 principal lakes in Ireland, and was converted into a bay by the Atlantic breaking over and uniting with the water therein. There is no doubt that a submergence of the land, whether gradual or otherwise, has really been the cause of the formation of the bay.

"At *Barna*, probably 10 ft. below high-water mark, may be seen on the strand a turf bog of several feet in depth, in which are the stumps and roots of large trees and many branches of oak and birch intermixed. The same phenomena occur at the W. side of the island of Omey, which is far advanced into the Atlantic Ocean."—*Dutton's Survey.*

At the entrance of the harbour is *Mutton Island*, connected with the mainland by a ridge of sand at low water. There is a fixed light here 33 ft. above the sea. The holding-ground is good, but there is a want of shelter from westerly gales, a state of things which will be entirely obviated by the erection of the proposed breakwater, which is estimated to cost 150,000*l.* The spring tides rise in the bay from 12 to 15 ft. The American steamers, as long as they sailed, anchored outside Mutton Island. From Lough Corrib, which is only 3 m. distant, a river runs into the sea with such rapidity that it is only useful as a means of motive power, which is made available for working several flour-mills, but for the purposes of navigation a canal called after the Earl of Eglintoun was cut by Nimmo, a celebrated engineer of his day, to connect the lake with the harbour, and thus enable the small vessels plying inland to reach the sea.

There is ample accommodation for vessels in the floating dock, which is 5 acres in extent, and admits vessels of 14 ft. draught, and the tongue of land which separates the dock from the river is quayed to the distance of 1300 ft.

A large number of the population is employed in the salmon and herring fishery, and the *Claddagh*, the locality inhabited by the fishermen, should be visited by every tourist. It is an extraordinary assemblage of low thatched cottages, the denizens of which, in dress, habits and customs, are as different from those of the town which they adjoin as though they were 100 m. off. "The colony from time immemorial has been ruled by one of their own body, periodically elected, who is dignified with the title of Mayor, regulates the community according to their own peculiar laws and customs, and settles all their fishery disputes. His decisions are so decisive and so much respected, that the parties are seldom known to carry their differences before a legal tribunal or to trouble the civil magistrates."—*Hardiman's Hist.* They never allow strangers to reside within their precincts, and always intermarry with each other, the marriage not being thought *au règle* unless preceded by an elopement. They have several gala-days, such as the Feast of St. Patrick and the Nativity of St. John (June 24), at which time a procession is organised through the town, and a number of ceremonies gone through, not forgetting the indispensable bonfire. The dress of the women of the Claddagh is very peculiar, and imparts a singularly foreign aspect to the Galway streets and quays. It consists of a blue mantle, red body-gown and petticoat, a handkerchief bound round the head, and legs and feet *au naturel*. The traveller who is anxious to gain further particulars respecting this interesting community should consult Hardiman's 'History of Galway.'

Galway is one of the finest localities in Ireland for the salmon fisher, who will feel grateful for the systematic endeavours of Mr. Ashcroft to improve the fishery by breeding young salmon, and by establishing a fish-walk on the Cong river between Loughs Corrib and Mask.

Conveyances.—To Clifden, through Moycullen and Oughterarde; to Ennis, through Gort and Ardrahan. Rail to Dublin. Steamer once a fortnight to Westport and Liverpool.

Distances.—Clifden, 47 m.; Moycullen, 7; Oughterarde, 16½; Cong, 27 by water; Westport, 54; Headford, 17; Clare-Galway, 6½; Athenry, 12½; Gort, 21; Oranmore, 5; Barna, 3; Aran Islands, 29; Loughrea, 22.

Many nice residences are found in the neighbourhood of Galway, viz., Menlo Castle, the seat of Sir Thos. Blake; Furbo, A. Blake, Esq.; Barna, Nicholas Lynch, Esq.; Lenaboy, Capt. O'Hara; Ardfry Lord Wallscourt; Merview and Renmore, the seats of Pat. Lynch, Esq., and P. S. Joyce, Esq., both very prettily situated at the head of Lough Athalia.

Excursions.—
1. Barna.
2. Cong.
3. Clare-Galway (Rte. 21).
4. Moycullen.
5. Aran Islands.

[The pleasant coast-road may be taken that runs on the N. of Galway Bay, through 1 m. *Salthill*, the favourite suburb of the wealthy Galwegians, who are gradually creating a marine West-end. The geologist will find between this and Barna very much to interest him. Immediately to the rt. of the road the granite is seen cropping out and forming the high grounds to the N. almost as far as Oughterarde. On the opposite side of the bay are the cliffs of Clare, which present lower Silurian rocks flanking the conglomerate (beds never seen in England), succeeded by a valley of denudation in which the lower limestone shales are visible. From hence the cliffs rise to the W., with the upper limestones throwing off millstone grit and thin worthless coal-seams. The white low cliffs at the water's edge are of drift, of which a magnificent section is observable nearly opposite Barna House, at the projecting peninsula of Seaweed Point. Here and in the bays on each side are unique displays of drift cliffs, filled with fragments of rock of different formations, all exhibiting the peculiar groovings: on the shore, at the bottom of the cliffs, may be seen large blocks, some washed out of the cliff, and others still adherent to their bosses of clay. The geologist should on no account omit to carefully study these appearances, as the drift formation is here visible on a scale unknown in England. These drift promontories are in all probability the coast termination of the Eskers or ridges of sandy hill that extend across Ireland from Dublin, and separated the island into its first Milesian divisions of Leath Mogha on the S., and Leath Cuinn on the N.

3 m. *Barna House*, a well-wooded demesne facing the sea, and the residence of Nicholas Lynch, Esq. There are slight remains of a castle that formerly belonged to the O'Hallorans, from whom the Lynches acquired it by marriage. 6 m. *Furbough* or Furbo (A. Blake, Esq.), is another prettily-situated residence, affording pleasant contrast to the sterile rocks and highlands inland. Here the united streams of the Knock and Loughinch rivers are crossed.

9½ m. *Spiddle* (or Spital, from its being the site of an ancient hospitium, of which slight remains still exist) is a small village at the mouth of the Owenboliska river, a rather considerable stream rising in the dreary moorlands of Iar Connaught, a little to the S. of Oughterarde. The village is sometimes frequented by anglers. From hence a road is carried over the most desolate and barren hills to Moycullen 8½ m. (p. 175. Indeed, the whole of the district is very little different from that described by Molyneux in 1709. "I did not see all this way three living creatures, not one house or ditch, not one bit of corn, nor, I may say, one bit of land, for stones: in short, nothing appeared but stones and sea."

12 m. the Owenriff river is crossed near Cahir, where there is a lead-mine.

At *Minna* once stood the castle of Inveran, the locality, in 1549, of the murder of Walter Bourke; brother of "Iron Richard," the husband of Grace O'Malley.

19½ m. This road terminates at the coast of Cashla Bay, where, at the coast-guard stat., a boat may be obtained to cross the inlet. At 17½ m. a road on rt. runs for 3 m. to Derrynea Lodge. Here a fishing stat. has been established by a few gentlemen who preserve the Cashla river, a stream of some breadth, which rises in the moors to the N.,

swelling in its course into numerous loughs. The region to the W., which lies principally in the baronies of Kilcumin and Killanin, is seldom or never visited, and indeed holds out no inducement to the general tourist to do so, its principal features being moorlands of no great height, covered at different levels with small freshwater lakes, and frequently indented with the many bays which have obtained for this district the poetic name of Connemara, or Cuan-an-irmore, "the bay of the great waters." Detached from the coast are 2 considerable islands named Lettermore and Gorumna. Conspicuous in the S.W. are the

3 *islands of Aran*, or Aran-naneeuv ("the Islands of the Saints"), known 1000 years ago as "Insulæ in oceano occidentali positæ cognomento Arann," and still believed by many of the peasantry to be the nearest land to the far-famed island of O'Brazil or Hy Brisail, the blessed paradise of the pagan Irish. It is supposed even to be visible from the cliffs of Aran on particular and rare occasions—

"On the ocean that hollows the rocks where ye dwell
A shadowy land has appeared, as they tell;
Men thought it a region of sunshine and rest,
And they call'd it O'Brazil, the isle of the blest."
Griffin.

Passing over the tradition of Lough Lurgan (p. 168), "the earliest reference to its præ-Christian history is to be found in the accounts of the battle of Muireadh, in which the Firbolgs, having been defeated by the Tuatha-de-Dananns, were driven for refuge into Aran and other islands on the Irish coast, as well as into the western islands of Scotland."—*Haverty.* Christianity was introduced in the 6th cent. by St. Endeus, who obtained a grant of the islands from Ængus, the Christian King of Munster, and founded 10 religious establishments. Like Bardsey Island in

North Wales, Aranmore speedily obtained a world-wide renown for learning, piety, and asceticism, and "many hundreds of holy men from other parts of Ireland and foreign countries constantly resorted to it to study the Sacred Scriptures and to learn and practise the rigid austerities of a hermit's life;" in consequence of which the island was distinguished by the name of Arana Nauimh or Aran of the Saints. In 1651 the Marquis of Clanricarde fortified the castle of Ardkyn, which held out against the Parliamentary army for more than a year after the surrender of Galway, but on the occupation of the island the soldiers of Cromwell demolished the great ch. of St. Endeus to furnish materials for the repair of the fort.

The Aran islands lie across the entrance of Galway Bay, 29 m. from the harbour, and consist of 3 in number—Inishmore (the Great Island, 9 m. long and 1½ broad; Inishmaan Middle Island), 3 m. long and 1½ m. broad; and Inisheer South Island, 2½ m. long.

A yacht carrying the mails starts from Galway every second day, but the traveller must be prepared for emergencies; for, though he may reach the island frequently in 4 hrs., he may be detained 10 or even longer. The disembarkation is generally performed by means of the "currach, which is about 8 ft. long, with 1 square and 1 pointed end, capable of carrying 3 people. Such is the dexterity with which it is usually managed, that it will land from ships in distress through the roughest breakers."—*Arch. Camb.* Probably there is no district so replete with early remains as this, and the tourist who wishes to make himself more minutely acquainted with them should study Dr. Petrie's work on the Ancient Architecture of Ireland.

There are 2 villages on Aranmore—*Kilronan*, at which there is a decent inn, and *Killeany*, both on the shores of Killeany Bay, at the S.E. end of the island. The latter, now a wretched village, was once of great note, having obtained its name from St. Endeus or Eaney, the first Christian missionary. Close to the sea are the slight ruins of *Arkyne Castle* mentioned above. It is not more ancient than the time of Elizabeth. Ascending the hill, the visitor arrives at the *Round Tower*, of which, however, only the base remains, about 5 ft. high and 49 in circumference, though it was of very considerable height within the memory of man. Near this, and on the highest point of the eastern end of the island, is *Teampull Benain*, the ch. or oratory of St. Benan, an unique specimen of early Irish ch., and considered by Dr. Petrie to be of the 6th cent. Externally it is only 11 ft. broad and 15 ft. in length, and is remarkable for the great height of the gables, which was not less than 17 ft., and most probably formed of overlapping stones. The ch. stands N. and S., instead of the usual orientation. Close by are the remains of the hermitage, partly sunk in the rock; and of some cloghauns or stone-roofed dwellings, probably belonging to the monks of the ch.

On the S.W. coast of the island is *Dubh Caher* (Black Fort), a dun or fortress, with walls of enormous thickness, of very rude masonry, overlooking the cliffs. A chevaux-de-frise of sharp stones served as an extra means of defence on the land side, and in the interior are remains of cloghauns. Dr. O'Donovan considers that this fort was raised by the very earliest inhabitants of the country.

From hence a walk of about 2½ m. will bring the tourist to *Kilronan*, the principal village on the island, (where there is a decent inn, the Atlantic), either retracing his steps through Killeany or by keeping the

S. coast a little higher up to Dubh-Cathair (the Black City), a fortress constructed and defended in a similar manner to the last named. It is 2 m. over the hill from this spot to Kilronan. A walk of 2 m. to the N.W. will embrace a large number of interesting antiquities. About 1 m. on the rt. is *Teampull Chiarain*, which has a very beautiful E. window and some crosses. 1½ m. on the hill to l. is *Oghill Fort*, a large dun near the lighthouse, which, it may be mentioned here, shows a revolving light at the height of 406 ft. above the sea. In the neighbourhood of Cowragh are Teampull-an-Cheathrair-alainn (the ch. of the 4 Comely Saints), also a cromlech, and the ch. and Holy Well of St. Soorney.

4 m. from Kilronan, on the N. coast, are *Kilmurvey* and *Teampull Mic Duach*, a 6th cent. ch., consisting of nave and choir in beautiful preservation, exhibiting some very fine cyclopean masonry. "There are windows of extreme antiquity, with lintels formed of 2 leaning stones; and although the beautiful semicircular E. window is of a more recent date, there is a stone leaning against the E. gable, with a rudely-cut opening, which seems to have been the head of the more ancient window." There is also a remarkable narrow doorway, shaped like the entrance to an Egyptian tomb. Besides these remains there is Teampull Beg (the small ch.), together with the Holy Well and an *Aharla*, or monastic enclosure. On the S. coast, barely 1 m. distant, is the fortress of *Dun Ængus*, described by Dr. Petrie as "the most magnificent barbaric monument now extant in Europe." It is built on the very edge of a sheer precipice 300 ft. in height, and is in form of horseshoe shape, although some antiquaries incline to the belief that it was originally oval, and that it acquired its present form from the falling of the precipices. It consists of 3 enclosures, the wall which surrounds the innermost being the thickest: this enclosure measures 150 ft. from N. to S. Outside the second wall is the usual accompaniment of chevaux-de-frises, formed by sharp stones placed on end, seemingly to hinder the approach of an enemy. About the 1st cent. of the Christian era, 3 brothers, Ængus, Conchovar, and Mil, came from Scotland to Aran, and their names are still preserved in connection with buildings on the island—"the ancient fort on the great island, being called Dun Ængus; the great fort of the middle island, superior in strength and preservation to the former, bearing the name of Dun Connor or Conchovar; and the name of Mil being associated with the low strand of Port Murvey, formerly known as Muirveagh Mil, or the Sea-plain of Mil."—*Haverty*.

5½ m. *Dun Onaght* or Eoghanacht, on high ground to the l., is a circular Firbolgic fort measuring 92 ft. across. Like all the other duns in the island, the defences are maintained by 3 walls one inside the other. "Upon the inner side are 4 sets of steps leading towards the top, like those in Staigue Fort in the county of Kerry."

At the north-western extremity, 6 m. from Kilronan, is another interesting archæological group, consisting of the 7 churches, or at least what remains of them. There are only portions of a ch. known as *Teampull a Phoill*, or the ch. of the Hollow, and Teampull Brecain, the ch. of St. Brecain, who was the founder of the episcopal ch. of Ardbraccan, in the county of Meath, and grandson of the 1st Christian Prince of Thomond. At the opening of the grave by Dr. Petrie many years ago, a skull was found supposed to belong to the saint. The ch. has a chancel of rude masonry, and a more modern choir, with a lancet E. window. Traces of a monastic building, an engraved cross, and an inscribed stone were found by Mr. Wilde, who also discovered and put together a richly-sculptured cross in the neighbouring Aharla, or sacred enclosure. Overlooking the beach are the ruins of a strong square castle, known as Sean Caislean, the Old Castle. The *geological formation* of the whole island is that of carboniferous limestone, which presents much bold and grand sea fronts. "The soile is almost paved over with stones, see as in some places nothing is to be seene but large stones with wide openings between them, where cattle breake their legs."—*O'Flaherty*. At the beach of *Glenaghaun*, near the 7 churches, the strata are horizontal, singularly broken up by vertical fissures. Owing to the difficulty of walking on the huge limestone flags "the Aranites have adopted sandals, or pampooties, as they call them, of a very primitive kind. These, which all the children are taught to make at the age of 7, are formed of cowhide with the hair left on, cut away low at the sides, with only a little pointed piece in front, just sufficient to cover the ends of the toes."—*Arch. Cambr.* Traces of the drift are frequent in the shape of granitic boulders brought over from the high grounds of Connemara. There is a very conspicuous example near the ruins of Sean Caislean.

The middle island of Aran, or *Inishmaan*, is separated from the former by a strait about 1 m. across, known as Gregory's Sound. The principal archæological feature is *Dun Connor*, or Conchobhair, an oval fort on a steep cliff, surrounded by an external wall with a gateway, placed in a square fort. Close by is the ruined church of Teampull-saght-macree. Between 1 and 2 m. to the S. of Inishmaan, separated by the Foul Sound, is *Inisheer*, which contains a circular dun called Creggankeel; Furmina Castle, once a stronghold of the Clann Teige; and St. Gobnet's ruined ch. The population of the 3 Aran islands is upwards of 3000 souls, principally supported by fishing, although the pasturage, like on most limestone rocks, is of a very rich and sweet-flavoured description. The owners of the soil are the Misses Digby, who have done very much to ameliorate the condition of the people.

In 1857 the islands were visited by a detachment of the British Association, under the leadership of Sir W. Wilde, and the results of the visit were subsequently embodied in an interesting pamphlet, to which the writer of this notice is indebted.]

[A delightful excursion may be taken up the Lough Corrib to Cong, 27 m. A small steamer plies daily, and the time occupied in the journey is about 4 hrs. The river, which at the starting-point above the bridges is tolerably wide, soon narrows, and receives on rt., opposite the Distillery of Newcastle, an affluent known as Terryland river. Close by are the slight ruins of *Terryland*, or *Tirraleen Castle*, a residence of the De Burgos in the 13th cent. 2 m. rt. is *Menlough*, or *Menlo Castle* Sir Thos. Blake, an ivy-covered castellated mansion, very prettily situated on the bank of the river. About 1 m. distant from the village of Menlough, and close on the brink of the lake, are the marble-quarries of *Angliham*, which yield a very celebrated quality of stone. The marble is jet black, and susceptible of high polish. "It has been raised in solid blocks, often weighing upwards of 4 tons, and measuring from 18 to 20 ft. long," and the quarries are situated on the edge of that extraordinary plateau of the upper carboniferous limestone which surrounds Galway on the N. and E. sides.

From Menlough to the entrance of the lake the river narrows considerably, having on each side of it flat sedgy islands, the haunts of wild fowl. The other passages are scarcely navigable. After a course of about 4 m. the steamer enters *Lough Corrib* (anc. Lough Oirbse), one of the most extensive and peculiar of these freshwater seas for which Ireland is so remarkable. The length of the lake to Cong is about 20 m., and the greatest breadth 6 m., not including, however, the arm that runs up to Maume. It possesses 50 m. of shores, and occupies 30,000 Irish acres, with a considerable fall from the summit level to the sea, and a surface of 13 ft. 9 in. above high water. A survey was made by the Government with a view towards establishing a grand inland navigation from Galway, Lough Corrib, Lough Mask, and Lough Conn to Killala, and thereby saving the inconvenience and dangers of the coast route. The lake was deepened in some parts, and lofty piles of stones erected so as to mark the channel, but with the exception of these improvements, and the canal to connect the lake with the sea at Galway, the scheme became abortive—the navigation at present being limited to the steamer, and a few big barges which sail with the wind from Cong, carrying kelp, sand, &c. The direction in which Lough Corrib runs is N.W., and it is divided into 2 parts by a long narrow strait. Of these the northern is the largest, although, from the number of islands scattered about, it does not apparently present such a large expanse of water. Altogether, the islands are said to number 365, one for every day in the year, but the tourist will soon find out that this is a popular delusion applied to almost every lake and bay in the country. The depth is very variable, in some places upwards of 28 ft., although in winter this is always increased somewhat; while in other parts it is scarcely 3 ft.; long shoals of jagged rocks frequently appearing above the water.

On first emerging into the lake the traveller obtains directly ahead of him and to the N.W. a very lovely view of the Connaught hills, especially those in the neighbourhood of Maume. The shore on the rt. is flat and uninteresting, but on the l. is a continuous and gradually increasing chain of high ground, on the side of which the road to Oughterarde is carried, lined with pleasant woods and residences, amongst which is conspicuous a nunnery for the Sisters of Mercy, established by Father Daly.

A little to the N.E. is the isolated hill of Knocknaa, near Tuam, which, as the channel changes, shifts its position so much that the tourist is puzzled how to maintain his bearings. Numerous towers of castles or ruined churches stud the banks of the lake, the greater part of which will be found under their respective routes, as they are unable to be visited except by land. In the distance on the rt., about 1 m. up, are the towers of Clare-Galway castle and abbey (Rte. 21), while l. nearer the lake is the castle of Moycullen, otherwise called Hag's Castle, or Cuishla dda Cuilach. In about 4 m. the lake contracts, and the steamer enters the long and tortuous channel of Knock. On rt., close to the shore, are the ruins of Annaghdown Castle and ch., formerly the seat of the bishopric in which Galway was included; also the woods of Annaghdown House (— Blake, Esq.), and Woodpark House).

Half way up the strait is the ferry of Kilbeg or *Knock*, at which a pier has been erected for the convenience of the traffic to Headford, 3 m. distant (Rte. 21). Close by the landing-place are *Clydagh House*, the beautifully-wooded seat of F. Staunton Lynch, Esq., and the ruins of Cargen's Castle. A little farther on is *Anaghkeen Castle*; and nearly opposite on the other bank the tower of *Augh-na-nure Castle*, the old residence of the O'Flaherties close to Oughterarde. The lake now expands again, and presents some beautiful views towards Maume; the mountains being grouped together in a very peculiar manner. The big flat-topped hill is Benlavie, while the sharp escarpment to the rt. is that of Kilbride, which overhangs Lough Mask. The islands which form such an important item in the surface of this portion of the lake occupy about 1000 acres, 6 of them being inhabited. The steamer passes on the l. an island graced by a summer residence belonging to the Rev. J. D'Arcy, warden of Galway.

The island of *Inch-a-goill*, or Inisan-Ghoill Craibhthigh, "the island of the devout foreigner," should be visited by the antiquary for the sake of its interesting ecclesiastical ruins, and for this purpose a boat will have to be taken from Cong, distant about 3¼ m., as the steamer does not stop at the island. It contains the ruins of the small ch. of *Templepatrick*, considered to be of the age of, and indeed founded by, St. Patrick. It possesses a nave and chancel, although its total length is only 35½ ft. The doorway is of the simplest description, with inclined sides. A stone stands in the ch. on which is inscribed, according to Dr. Petrie—

LIE LUGNAEDON MACC LMENUEH;

in English, "the stone of Lugnaedon, son of Limeneuch."

The individual commemorated by this stone is supposed to have been a nephew of St. Patrick. The second ch., also ruined, is of much later date, of similar form and dimensions, though of more beautiful architecture. Almost opposite Inch-a-goill, on the eastern bank of the lake, is Ballycurin Castle and House (C. Lynch, Esq.. A little distance from this shore is the island of *Inishmicatreer*, on which an abbey formerly existed.

At the N.W. corner of the lake a narrow prolongation runs for some distance inland between the mountains terminating at Maume.

25 m. at the head of the lake are the pretty woods of Ashford (H. Guinness, Esq., and the village of Cong (p. 182).]

A car leaves daily for Oughterarde and Clifden from Bianconi's coach-office in Eyre Square. Passing over the river and canal and by the Queen's College, the traveller enters the district of Iar Connaught or Western Connaught, the head-quarters of the powerful clan of the O'Flaherties. This district extends for about 30 m., and is now comprised in the baronies of Moycullen and Ballynahinch. For several miles the road skirts the high grounds on the W. bank of Lough Corrib, passing many pretty wood-embowered villas, and amongst others a nunnery for Sisters of Mercy. Fine views are obtained of the hills at the head of the Lough, amongst which, on a clear day, the peak of Nephin, near Ballina, is very conspicuous. Far in the distance on the E. is Knocknaa, the Hill of the Fairies, in the direction of Tuam.

4¾ m. l. Woodstock House (F. Comyn, Esq.), well sheltered amidst thriving plantations; and further on is Kirkullen House (Capt. Hare.)

6¼ m. rt. is the small lake of *Ballycuirke*, beyond which is the lonely tower of *Hag's Castle*, or Cuishladda-Cuilach, a fortress of the O'Flaherties, who possessed nearly the whole of this territory.

In the time of Elizabeth the father of the then O'Flaherty was confined in this castle of Moycullen, and starved to death. 7¼ m. *Moycullen* is a neat village with the usual parochial institutions. The land in the immediate neighbourhood was the property of the late Lord Campbell, who did much towards its improvement; but very shortly the tourist enters upon the domain of Ballynahinch. A road on rt. runs up the side of the lake to 6¼ m. Knock Ferry, en route for Headford (p. 181), while one on the l. crosses the desolate hills to 8¼ m. Spiddle (p. 170 .

8 m. l. Danesfield House (G. Burke, Esq.); and bordering the road a little further on are Drimcong, Deerfield, and Knockbane, the residence of A. O'Flaherty, Esq. 9 m. on rt. below the road is Ross Lake, a long, narrow sheet of water, studded with prettily-wooded islets and patches of rock. *Ross House*, situated at the head of the lake, is the residence of Jas. Martin, Esq., whose family has been seated here since the time of Eliz. There are several ruins in the vicinity—as Oghery Castle on a small island and a ch. on the opposite side known as Templebegnanceve. At this point of the route the traveller enters the widely-spread domain of Ballynahinch (p. 179), through which he journeys for a distance of 26 m. The Law Life Insurance Company now hold this territory of the old Martin family, a territory so wild and extensive that it was the boast of Connaught that "the king's writ could not run in it." The traveller will, however, observe for himself during his journey that ₇⁄₁₀ of this property might well be spared, as regards its agricultural qualities. From hence the country begins to lose a great deal of the wood and timber which has hitherto sheltered it, and relieved it from its native wildness, which very soon begins to show itself in the wide melancholy moors between this and Oughterarde. On the l. they gradually rise to a considerable height, the highest point, Knockalee Hill, being 955 ft. Innumerable little streams, emerging from as many small lakes permeate their brown moors in every direction, the only signs of civilization being the long straight road that is visible for miles, and an occasional group of cottages on the hill-sides, of such a dubious colour that it is some time ere the eye becomes accustomed to the sight of them. Just after passing the lodge-gate of Ross the first beautiful peep occurs of the 12 Pins of Connemara, the highest points in the Western Highlands.

15 m. rt., near a spot where a stream is crossed by a natural bridge of limestone, are the ruins of *Aughnanure Castle* (the Field of the Yews), called otherwise the Castle of the O'Flaherties. The remains consist of a massive square tower surrounded by outworks and a banqueting-hall, the date of the whole being probably of the 16th cent. Notice in the latter the interlacing patterns of the windows. A small river washes the walls of the castle, which also commands a strong position over Lough Corrib. The O'Flaherties, to whom it belonged, were a powerful family who had held this country from time immemorial, and long struggled against the English Government, with which it was always at variance, as also with its neighbours the Galway colonists. In the reign of Elizabeth, however, government reduced it to obedience by fomenting discord amongst its members, and in 1569 Morough O'Flahertie was appointed governor of the county of Iar Connaught. The glories of the family establishment are enumerated in an ancient MS., as maintaining a physician, standard-bearer, brehon or judge, the keeper of the black bell, the master of the revels, the keeper of the bees, &c. The present representative is G. F. O'Flahertie, Esq , the owner of the neighbouring demesne of Lemonfield.

16½ m. *Oughterarde*, a straggling little town of a single broad street, situated picturesquely enough on the river Owenriff, which flows in a somewhat romantic channel into Lough Corrib. With the exception of its enormous Union House, it does not contain anything worth notice, but its proximity to the lake renders it a convenient station for fishing parties (*Hotel*, Murphy's). About ½ m. outside the town is an extremely pretty waterfall, in the bed of which, when the water is low, the geologist can see a good section of the carboniferous limestone.

Distances.—Galway, 16½ m.: Recess, 18; Maume, 12; Lough Bofin, 5¼; Flynns, 12.

[A road on rt. runs from Oughterarde along the side of Lough Corrib, passing 1 or 2 little hamlets, and skirting the base of Carn Seefin (1009 ft.), on the sides of which a copper-mine was established. At Cappanalaura, opposite the beautifully-wooded hill of Doon, a boat may be obtained, and the pedestrian may cross the arm of the lake, and follow the road on the N. bank to Maume.]

For almost the whole distance to Clifden the road is carried over a bleak moor, the geological character of which is mica rock, occasionally passing into talcose rock.

At 20 m. l. is Lough Agraffard, the first of the chain of lakes that accompany the road the whole way to the coast. It is succeeded by Lough Adrehid, and at 22½ m. by Lough Bofin, one of the largest of the whole chain. The scenery is peculiar, and, unless under a bright sun, depressing from the monotonous outline of the hills and the sombre colour of the peat and lake water. There is a solitary school-house at Glengoula. 25 m. Ardderry Lough, communicating with 27 m. Lough Shindilla, is one of the prettiest because the most wooded of the series. [A little before arriving at the E. end of this lake, which is the watershed of the rivers running into Lough Corrib and the Atlantic, a road on rt., at Butler's Lodge, turns over the moors to Maume (Rte. 21) 5 m., which speedily becomes interesting as it descends, from the views that open, over the arm of Lough Corrib and the island of Castlekirke.] The mountains on the rt. have now assumed a very different outline and character from those which have hitherto accompanied us. In fact, we have arrived at the great group of the Western Highlands, of which Bunnabeola, or the 12 Pins, is the centre; and the traveller now loses all sense of dreariness in the contemplation of the magnificent and rugged heights that constantly open out. The eastern portion of this range is mostly known as the Mamturk Mountains, and comprises, amongst others, the heights of Shanfolagh (2003 ft.) and Leckavrea (2012). Polypodium dryopteris grows abundantly on these hills. At the end of Lough Shindilla is a small shebeen-house, known as the Halfway House or Flynn's, where there is a change of horses. Miss Flynn, the daughter of a former occupant, was celebrated for her beauty, the praises of which were chanted repeatedly in the works of Inglis Barrow, and others. The family, however, have long left the neighbourhood. This is the highest point of the road, as is soon evident from the change of direction of the water's flow. [From hence a road runs direct to Kylemore 14 m., and it should be taken by the traveller who does not wish to go round by Clifden.]

Above 29½ m. l. Lough Ourid, rises the Ourid Hill, 1174 ft. From hence the road rapidly descends by the side of a mountain stream to 34½ m. *Recess* Inn, a comfortable and unpretending little hotel standing back from the road at the foot of Lissoughter, and an admirable station for investigating the beauties of Glen Inagh and the 12 Pins. *Garromin*, one of the most beautiful of these lakes, stretches before it, having on its opposite bank Glendalough, the thickly-wooded domain rented by the Duke of Richmond from the Law Life Insurance Company, but at present inhabited only by a caretaker. On an eminence opposite the hotel is Lissoughter Lodge (J. Bodkin, Esq.). The tourist should by all means ascend *Lissoughter*, which, though reaching the height of only 1314 ft., is so placed as to afford a better knowledge of the mountain scenery than almost any other hill. It is situated exactly at the end of a great transverse valley, of which it forms the key, the sides respectively being the Mamturk Mountains (Shanfolagh, &c.), and the 12 Pins, which are seen to great advantage. This valley is almost entirely filled up by the lakes of Derryclare and Lough Inagh, producing a magnificent scene seldom surpassed, although, from the lack of wood, invested with a severity peculiar to the Connemara scenery. On the side of the hill are marble-quarries, from which a valuable stone known as Connemara marble is extracted, and worked for the most part into ornamental articles. A road turns off near the Recess, which was commenced in the famine year, and intended to run the whole length of Glen Inagh to join the Kylemore road, but, like many other undertakings of that sad era, was never finished.

Derryclare, the first lake, communicates with Glendalough by a short stream called Bealnacarra, and also with Ballynahinch Lake by another. It is narrow, about 2½ m. long, and magnificently situated just at the foot of the 12 Pins. A little above it is *Lough Inagh*, even more beautiful, because occupying more fully the length of the valley for 3 m. The whole of the E. side is bounded by the lofty mountains of the Mamturk range, the most conspicuous points of which are, commencing from the S., Shanfolagh (2003 ft.), Maumeen (2076), Knock-na-hillion (1993), and Letter-breckaun (2193). In this valley are 2 oases of cultivation, Derryclare (Mr. Cunningham) and Coolnacarton, the demesne of Mr. Joyce.

Proceeding along the high road, the attention is altogether taken up by the 12 *Pins*—" bare, but glittering with the aërial brilliancy peculiar to their formation, their peaked summits rush together in elevations of from 2000 to 2500 ft., a splendid cloud-pointing assemblage. Connemara proper, though a mountainous, is not an upland country; the plain from which its greatest elevations rise is little more on an average than 100 ft. above the level of the Atlantic; so that its masses lose not a tittle of their real altitude, but, lifting themselves to their full height at a stretch, look over the plains with much greater majesty than many other mountains higher by 1000 ft. Benlettery and Derryclare stand foremost like an advanced guard to the group on the S., while in front, flank, and rear, open 4 principal glens, each one with his torrent, and 3 of them with their proper lakes; Glencoaghan, with the lower lake of Ballynahinch, looks southward on Roundstone and Birterbury; Glen Inagh, cradling its black waters under the tremendous precipice of Mamturk, down which the stream that feeds Lough Inagh falls 1200 ft., and opens the gorge of its prison upon the E.; Kylemore yawns N. and W. on Renvyle; and on the W. and S. the ravine whose torrent waters Clifden looks over the Atlantic."—*Bartlett*.

Bunnabeola, "the 12 most beautiful bens or Pins," the termination "la" signifying a superlative degree, is a grand irregular mass of slaty quartzite rocks, the peculiarity being not so much in the height as in the number of isolated points so nearly converging. The highest point, though not quite in the centre of the others, is Benbaun (2395 ft.), surrounded by Derryclare (2220), Benlettery (1904), Bengower (2184), Benbreen (2276), Bencollaghduff (2290), Bencorr (2336), Bencorrbeg (1908), Muckanaght (2153), Benglenisky (2710), Benbrach (1922), and a small supplementary summit known as the Key of the Pins. The beauty of their scarred and precipitous sides is still further enhanced by the colouring imparted to them from the various heaths and lichens. The tourist who wishes for a magnificent view cannot do better than ascend Ben-lettery (1904 ft.), which, though not quite so high as some of the others, is less surrounded by rival eminences. The view embraces Urrisbeg, Roundstone, and Birterbury Bays in the S., backed up in the distance by Galway Bay, while Cashel and Lettershanna mountains serve as a foreground; westward is Clifden and the whole country from Urrisbeg to Ardbear, Ballynakill Bay, the hill of Renvyle, with the islands of Bofin, Inishark, and many others; while further N. the sharp crags of Achill Head open out. E. are the ranges of the Mamturk Mountains, with the melancholy pass of Maumeen. The botanist will find among the sides of the 12 Pins a rich harvest: Arbutus uva-ursi, Lycopodium selago, Empetrum nigrum, Alchemilla alpina, Saxifraga umbrosa, Erica daboecia, S. oppositofolia, &c.

The road to Clifden crosses the Bealnacarra river, giving off on l., a by-road, which runs down to the sea at Birterbury Bay over a dreary moorland. The pedestrian who wishes to ascend either Cashel 1024 ft.) or Lettershanna should follow this road, but, if on his way to Roundstone, should carefully avoid it and keep straight on to

40 m. *Ballynahinch*, which stands a little off from and on the S. side of the lake of the same name.

[At Canal Bridge a road on l. leads to the house, and on to Derradia and Roundstone. The lake is irregular and picturesque, and contains in its western portion some wooded islands, on one of which stands the ancient castle, with only the keep, a square tower, remaining." The house, which was celebrated for being the residence of the Martins, who "reigned" for so many generations over this county, is a plain embattled building, pleasantly situated between the lake and the river. It is now the residence of Mr. Robinson, agent to the Law Life Insurance Company, who purchased the whole of this vast domain for 180,000*l*. when it came into the market. From all accounts, however, it would seem that the district has not derived that benefit which might be expected from such an undertaking. "Col. Martin, the representative of the family some 50 years ago, is said to have endeavoured to put the Prince Regent out of conceit with the famous Long Walk of Windsor, by saying that the avenue which led to his hall-door was 30 m. in length. The pleasantry was true to this extent, that the greater part of the distance of 40 m. from Galway to Ballynahinch lay within the Martin estates, while the road from the one to the other stopped short of the mansion, beyond which there was little else but rugged paths." It was on the fortunes of this amiable though ill-fated family that Lever has founded his novel of the 'Martins of Cro' Martin.' From Ballynahinch, where there is an inn, the road follows the l. bank of the Owenmore, a very pretty stream, and, what is more, an admirable sporting river, to 2 m. *Deraddia*, a fishing station, where there is also a comfortable little hotel kept by a Scotchman named Robertson, who is engaged in working the salmon fishery to a large extent, and sending the preserved contents to market. For this purpose he rents the fishery, paying 5½*d*. per lb. for all fish caught until June, and after that time 2*d*. per lb. The fish are cured here and packed in tin boxes. The river is crossed by a bridge of 3 arches at this point, to which the tide comes up. About 200 yds. from hence on the l. bank of the river are very slight remains of the abbey of Toombeola, of which nothing but a couple of gable walls and a doorway are left. A Dominican priory was founded here in 1427 by O'Flaherty, but was demolished in the reign of Elizabeth, and partly carried away to build some other castle.

About 2 m. further on is the little seaport of *Roundstone* (*Hotel*, Kelly's), that at one time was destined to fulfil a great purpose, no less than to be the starting-point from Ireland to America. For this end a good road was made to it, and a convenient pier built by Nimmo the engineer, who saw in the beautiful and capacious bay capabilities of no common order. But the course of events at Galway will most likely preclude the chance of Roundstone ever emerging from its obscurity. It is, however, a pleasant little place, and for fine coast-scenery, and bay studded with islands, few can compare with it. There is a monastery for brothers of the order of St. Francis, also a coast-guard station in the island of Inishlackan, and the remains of churches in Croaghnakeela Island some 6 m. out, formerly a deer-park belonging to the Martins.

About 2 m. further are more ch. ruins on St. Macdara's Island and Mason Island, the former consisting of a very primitive ch. only 15 ft. in length, and formerly possessing a high stone roof. The circular stone dwelling of the saint is adjoining, though greatly dilapidated. On the tongue of land adjoining is *Ard Castle*, a single tower with a staircase and interior passage at the top.

Immediately behind Roundstone rises Urrisbeg (987 ft.), which from its comparative isolation commands a remarkable view well worth the ascent. A remarkable trap-dyke runs from the summit to the sea. The botanist will find it to his account to make an excursion to Urrisbeg, if only to obtain a specimen of the Erica Mediterranea, a heath peculiar to Connemara, which grows luxuriantly for a space of 3 acres on the western declivity. It flowers in March and April. Another rare fern, Erica Mackaiana, grows on "a declivity of a hill by the road-side within 3 m. of Roundstone." From this spot a road follows the coast in a roundabout course to Clifden, and there is also a direct hilly road 11 m.] The former passes by Doohulla, where there is a lodge for anglers. A successful experiment has been carried on here by J. Knight Boswell, Esq., of stocking the river by means of artificial propagation.

From Ballynahinch the way lies under the 12 Pins and their outliers to 47 m. the romantic little town of *Clifden* (Rte. 22). *Hotels*: Hart's; Carr's; Mullarky's, a new hotel, is said to be good.

ROUTE 21.

FROM **GALWAY** TO **BALLINROBE** AND **WESTPORT**.

For the first 2 or 3 m. the road traverses a particularly desolate-looking district, which looks as if it was paved with stones—a huge table-land of carboniferous limestone, part of the same tract that strikes the tourist in his journey from Athenry by rail.

4 m. rt. is Killeen House (P.

Comyn, Esq.), in the grounds of which is the ruined tower of the same name. Border towers are very numerous over the whole of the W. of Galway and Mayo, and strongly impress upon us the insecure tenure of life and land in those days of hard hitting. Kiltullagh Castle is just such another tower about ¾m. to the rt., and there is a third on the l. near Rocklawn.

Adjoining Killeen is Rockwood.

From hence, passing some primitive mud-coloured Irish villages, worth notice from the extraordinary manner in which they are built and huddled together without any apparent plan, we arrive at

7 m. *Clare-Galway*, a small village on the Clare-Galway river, possessing a picturesque castle and a very beautiful abbey, erected in the 13th cent. for Franciscan friars by John De Cogan. It is a cruciform ch., consisting of nave, choir, and transepts, surmounted by a graceful tower of 3 stages, lighted by a small square window in each stage, though there is a Dec. window looking towards the E. The intersecting arches underneath the tower are very beautiful, as is the mutilated E. window of the choir, which is also lighted by 6 plain lancets on each side. It contains a Dec. altar-tomb of the date 1648. The nave has only S. wall standing, lighted by plain pointed windows, and having underneath 2 blocked arches, which probably served for altar-tombs. Of the N. wall there only remain 4 noble arches springing from rounded piers. A portion of the abbey is devoted to the use of a trumpery-looking little chapel. The castle, close to the road, is a massive square tower, lighted by a few loopholes, and is a good example of the better class of fortified mansions. It was erected by the family of De Burgo, and was garrisoned by the Marquis of Clanricarde in the war of 1641. 8 m. at Laghtgeorge a road diverges on rt. to Tuam. Crossing the Waterdale stream, on the banks of which lower down is another ruined tower (Liscananaun), we reach *Cregg Castle*, the wooded seat of F. Blake, Esq., formerly the residence of Kirwan, the chemist and philosopher, and the birthplace of his brother Dean Kirwan, equally celebrated as a theologian. A pretty river scene opens out as the road winds round the park and crosses the Cregg near some mills.

[¼ m. l., overlooking the low shores of Lough Corrib, are the ruined castle and ch. of *Annag'down*, which, though now desolate and neglected, was, as Enachdone, a celebrated ecclesiastical establishment (p. 167), being the seat of a bishopric, and containing a nunnery, an abbey, a monastery for Franciscans, and the college of St. Brendan.]

A little beyond Cregg is the Currabeg monastery. 18¼ m. l. are small remains of Cloghanower Castle, and very soon the extensive woods and park of Headford Castle come in sight. The house is a fine old Elizabethan building, and the residence of C. St. George, Esq., to whom as resident landlord the town and neighbourhood of Headford are greatly indebted.

20 m. *Headford (Inns:* Headford; Redington's), a neat little town, sheltered by the woods of the castle, and placed in a rather English-looking country. Although there is nothing in the town of interest, yet the tourist should by all means pay a visit to *Ross Abbey*, about 1½ m. distant, one of the most extensive and beautiful buildings in Ireland, built at the close of the 15th cent. by Lord Granard for Observantine Franciscans, and granted to the Earl of Clanricarde at the suppression of religious houses. Including the religious and domestic buildings, it covers a very large space of ground on the banks of the Black river, and overlooking a considerable tract of

bog. It is the cemetery of many good Connaught families, and probably contains more grinning and ghastly skulls than any catacomb, some of the tracery of the windows being filled up with thigh-bones and heads—a not uncommon way of disposing of these emblems of mortality in Irish abbeys. The ch. has a nave, choir, and S. transept, with a slender and graceful tower arising from the intersection. Attached to the nave are N. and S. aisles, and a chapel running parallel with the S. transept. The latter, together with the S. aisle, are separated from the nave by round-headed arches with octangular piers. Two round arches also divide the transept from the aisle, and 2 blocked ones from a chapel on the E. In the W. chapel of the S. aisle is a small monument of the O'Donnells, 1646. The nave is shut off from the choir by a broad-headed segmental arch. The latter part of the ch. is lighted on S. by 4 double-light trefoil windows; and on the S. side of the altar is a double-arched niche used as an ambry. The E. window is Dec., with very delicate tracery, and is worth notice, as is also the moulding of the W. door, close to which is the stoup for holy water. To the N. of the nave are the cloisters, which are in good preservation. The area is small, and surrounded by 10 beautiful pointed arches about 3 ft. high, the entrance of the passage within being under round-headed arches.

"By pointed aisle and shafted stalk,
The arcades of an alley'd walk,
To emulate in stone."

From the N. of the choir runs a long chapel lighted by E. Eng. windows, those on the N. side having ogee heads. A projecting building also on the N. of the choir was probably the abbot's residence, and beyond the N. transept is the kitchen, with ample fireplace and spout for carrying the water away; also a stone reservoir and pipe connecting it with the river, probably used as a fish vivarium. On the E. of the kitchen is the guesten-hall, in which there is an aperture communicating with the kitchen for the entrance of the viands. Probably there is no ruin in the kingdom showing the domestic arrangements to greater advantage than Ross, which on this account deserves to be attentively studied. The abbey is now the property of Mr. St. George, of Headford Castle.

Conveyances.—Car to Galway and Westport; car to Tuam.

Distances.—Galway, 20 m.; Ballinrobe, 14; Tuam, 12½; Shruel, 4; Cong, 10; Ross Abbey, 1½; Knock Ferry, 3½; Clydagh, 4.

[A very interesting détour may be made through Cong to Maume, and so on to Leenane or Clifden. 1½ m. rt., on the banks of the Black river, is Moyne Lodge (P. Ward, Esq.). In the grounds is Moyne Castle, a square tower, in the interior of which is a spiral staircase leading to a covered passage running round the building, and lighted by loopholes. On the high ground to the N. is Moyne ch. in ruins. The abbey buildings of Ross have an extremely beautiful effect when viewed from this side of the river.

5 m. is Glencorrib, the seat of Col. O. Higgins; and a little further on is Houndswood (E. Dawson, Esq.). The road, as it traverses very high ground, affords exquisite views of Lough Corrib and Lough Mask, with the giant ranges of the Maume mountains, and Benlevy in the distance, while more to the N. are Bohaun and the Partry mountains. In fact, a great portion of the wild Joyce's country is before the eyes, as regards its external boundaries.

7 m. the Cross, whence a road diverges to Ballinrobe. Garracloon Lodge is the residence of Dr. Veitch.

On rt. is Ballymacgibbon House.

10 m. *Cong* (*Hotel:* Burke's) is a quaint village situated in the

middle of a district teeming with natural curiosities, which in former times would have been considered as bordering on the supernatural. Cong is pleasantly situated on a rapid stream, that emerges from Lough Mask, and empties itself into Lough Corrib, after a course of about 4 m. The village is ¾ m. from the landing-pier on the latter lake, and near it on l. is Ashford House, the residence of H. Guiness, Esq., and on rt. Strandhill (Capt. Elwood). A new house is also being built by Sir W. Wilde at Gort-na-curra, the site of the ancient battle-field of Moytura.

The principal archæological remains are, 1. a stone cross in the centre of the street, with a very ancient Irish inscription in memory of Filaberd and Nicol O'Duffy, who were formerly abbots of Cong. 2. The abbey is remarkable for its beautiful Trans.-Norm. architecture, though as a whole it is not an imposing or an extensive building. Roderic O'Connor, the last native king of Ireland, spent the remaining 15 years of his life here in the strictest seclusion, dying in 1198, aged 82. His tombstone is shown by the guides, although, according to some, he was buried at Clonmacnoise. The visitor should notice the beautiful moulding of the entrance doorway, and also the W. front, which presents internally a Norm. blocked door with bead moulding, and on the exterior, 3 doors also blocked, one being plain roundheaded, and the others very rich Trans. from Norm. to E. Eng. There is a good 3-light window of remarkable length, and others deeply splayed and round-headed. The charnel-house is called the Stranger's Corner. Concerning this abbey Dr. Petrie says,—" I have found no authority to enable me to fix with precision the date of the re-erection of this noble monastery, or ascertain the name of its rebuilder; but the characteristics of its style are such as will leave no doubt of its being a work of the close of the 12th cent., while its magnificence indicates with no less certainty the pious bounty of the unhappy Roderic, who, in his later years, found refuge and, we may hope, tranquillity within its clo'stered walls." Adjoining the abbey is a neat villa, and part of the ancient fishing-house on the bank of the river, which runs swift and clear. The abbey of Cong was noted for its great riches and ornaments, of which fortunately the cross of Cong (now in the Royal Irish Academy) still remains as an example of exquisite chasing, showing to what a high pitch decorative art had attained. It is of pure gold, containing a large crystal in the centre. An account of it will be found at p. 11. Having examined the ruins, the visitor should explore the natural curiosities of Cong, chiefly caused by the vagaries of the river connecting Lough Mask with Lough Corrib. Although the distance is really 4 m., its apparent career is only ¾ m., as the remainder is hidden underground with but few tokens of its presence. The country to the N. of Cong, as far as Lough Mask, is a series of limestone plateaus of carboniferous, though, according to some geologists, of Silurian age. Whichever it may be, it is singularly perforated and undermined, and an approach to its subterranean beauties is permitted at the Pigeon Hole, about 1 m. distant from the village. In the centre of a field there is a marked depression, having on one side a perpendicular hole of some 60 ft. deep, and of a diameter barely that of the shaft of a coal-pit. The aspect of this aperture, covered as it is with ferns and dripping mosses, is very peculiar, and it requires a little resolution and a good deal of care to descend the slippery steps to the bottom, where we find a considerable increase of room, in consequence of the hollowing away of the rocks. When the tourist's eyes get fairly accustomed to the semi-darkness, he will perhaps be fortunate enough to detect in the river, which runs babbling by him, the blessed white trout which always frequent this same spot, and to catch which was an act of impiety too gross to be committed. In addition to the guide, he is accompanied down the hole by a woman carrying a bundle of straw, which she lights and allows to float down the stream. As she follows the windings of the cavern, every now and then disappearing behind the rocks, and then reappearing, waving the fitful torch above her head, the scene is at once mysterious and picturesque. Nearer Cong there are some more of these curious caverns: one of them is called "the Horse's Discovery," and contains stalactites. It is close to the old ch., which suffered so much injury from the depression of the ground, that a new one was obliged to be built. The tourist should engage the services of a guide, who rejoices in the name of Mick, and who has a legend for every spot, and a reason for everything. The river emerges for a few hundred yards close to some mills, where the water is plainly observed to bubble up and immediately run off in different directions, forming 2 separate streams. The canal is the last, and probably the greatest, curiosity, as an example, not to be matched in this kingdom, of a gigantic failure. During the frightful starvation crisis in Ireland, many hundreds were employed in this scheme, which was to connect the 2 lakes, and thus extend the inland navigation to Lough Conn and the Moy river at Ballina. As far as the relief given to the suffering peasants it was very good; but by some mistake in the engineering calculations, the canal was found, when finished, to be utterly incapable of holding water, from the porous and permeated character of the stone; and to this day it remains a huge useless blunder.

Conveyances. — Steamer daily to Galway.

Distances. — Headford, 10 m.; Maume, 13½; Ballinrobe, 7; Lough Mask Castle, 4. Galway by water, 27.

From Cong the road to Maume continues along the N. shore of Lough Corrib; passing on rt. 2 m. Rosshill, a seat of the Earl of Leitrim, on the banks of Lough Mask. In the grounds are inconsiderable ruins of the ch. or abbey of Rosshill; and adjoining is Benlevy Lodge (T. Blake, Esq.). Directly in front of the traveller the mountains rise with fine abruptness; on the rt. Benlevy, 1286 ft.; Bohaun and Loughnabricka, 1628; and to the l. the ranges of the Mamturk, in which Shanfolagh, 2003 ft., is most conspicuous. Towards Lough Mask the precipitous hill of Kilbride is seen. Benlevy mountain is a very good landmark for this district, in consequence of its peculiar square truncated summit, on which there is a clear lake. It is worth ascending, as by going more into the heart of the Joyce country the views over the lakes are a good deal shut out by the mountains immediately around them. At 8 m. the road crosses the Dooghta river, rising in Loughnabricka, and skirts the singular arm pushed by Lough Corrib into the very heart of the mountains. 21 m. l., on an island, are the conspicuous ruins of *Castle Kirke*, otherwise called Caislean-na-Circe, the Hen's Castle, of such extent as to cover nearly the whole of the island. According to a legend, very widely spread in this district, it was built in one night by a witch and her hen, which, together with the castle, she gave to the O'Flaherty, telling him that, if he was besieged, the hen would lay sufficient eggs to keep him from starving. The event soon happened, but O'Flaherty, forgetting the injunctions, slew the bird, and was immediately starved out. "Enough remains to exhibit its original plan, which was that of an Anglo-Norm. castle or keep, in the form of a parallelogram, with 3 projecting towers on its 2 longest sides; and the architectural features of the 13th cent. are also visible in some of its beautifully executed windows and doorways."—*Irish Pen. Mag.* It was really erected by the sons of Roderic, last king of Ireland, with the help of Richard de Burgo.

23¾ m. Maume Bridge (Rte. 22), where the traveller will find a pleasant little inn,* built, as well as the bridge, by Nimmo the engineer, to whom Connemara owes innumerable debts of gratitude. The situation is enchanting, at the base of the giant Loughnabricka, and right in front of Leckavrea and Shanvolagh; while 2 streams, the Bealnabrack and the Failmore, take away from the solitude and tempt the fisherman. Two other roads meet here—one from the Oughterarde and Clifden road 4½ m. (Rte. 20), and one from Leenane, running down the valley of the Joyce's river (Rte. 22).

Distances. — Cong, 13½ m.; Leenane, 8½; Halfway-house, 6¼.]

Continuing on his course from Headford, the traveller passes rt. Lisdonagh House. Far in the distance is Knocknaa Hill near Tuam, from its isolated position visible over a very large extent of country.

24 m. *Shrule*, a small town situated on the Blackwater, possessing the ruins of an abbey, a massive-towered castle, and the notoriety of as foul a massacre as was ever perpetrated in Christendom. In 1641 Sir Henry Bingham, with a number of Protestant gentry and 15 clergymen (among whom was the Bishop of Killala), arrived at Shrule from Castlebar (which he had been obliged to surrender from want of provisions), under promise of safe escort from Lord Mayo and the R. C. Bishop of Tuam. Notwithstanding this promise, they were handed over at Shrule Bridge to the keeping of a relation of Lord Mayo, one Edmund Burke, "a notorious rebel and bitter papist, the man who not long before, having taken the Bishop of Killala prisoner, wanted to fasten him to the Sow (a battering engine), with which he was attempting to beat down the walls of Castlebar, in order that the besieged in firing might shoot their own prelate."—*Otway*. The unfortunate Protestants were attacked by him in the most ferocious manner: some were shot, others were piked, others cast into the river; in all 65 were slaughtered. There is a very handsome R. C. chapel in Shrule.

In the neighbourhood of the town is Dalgan House, the beautiful seat of Baroness De Clifford. The Blackwater in its course from Shrule to Thorpe plays the same vagaries as the river at Cong, and has an underground course for some little distance.

28½ m. *Kilmaine*.

34 m. *Ballinrobe* (anc. Baile-anrodhba) (*Hotels:* Victoria; Ballinrobe), a town of some 3000 Inhab., in pleasant proximity to Lough Mask and on the river Robe, though in itself containing nothing of interest, save small remains of an abbey ch. and a fine R. C. chapel. It is, however, a good point from which to explore the beauties of *Lough Mask*, a noble sheet of water, 10 m. long by 4 broad, with 2 arms about 1 m. distant from each other stretching into Joyce's Country, the one extending for 4 m., the other for 3, and having its waters 36 ft. above the summer level of Lough Corrib. The eastern shore of the lough is comparatively tame, but the W. is bounded by the fine, though somewhat monotonous, range of the Partry mountains, the highest points of which are Toneysal, 1270 ft.; and

---

* The licence of the Maume Inn was taken away by the magistrates in Oct. 1863, to mark their sense of the insult offered by the owner, the Earl of Leitrim, to Royalty, in the person of the Lord Lieutenant, who was most inhospitably prevented taking up his night's quarters here as he intended.

Bohaun, 1294. 4½ m. from Ballinrobe, on the shores of the lake, is *Lough Mask Castle*, a solitary ruin of no great extent, but in a fine position. The island of Inishmaan, close to the shore, contains a ruined ch., originally built by St. Cormac in the 6th cent. and enlarged in the 12th. It has a good side doorway of quadrangular form, in which the weight of the lintel is taken off by a semicircular arch.

The geologist will find on the shores of this lake Upper Silurian strata, which are the equivalents of the May Hill deposits, and their passage upwards into Wenlock beds.

[6 m. l. is *Hollymount*, a small town, also on the Robe, containing a ch. with a cast-iron spire, and (at no great distance off) an Agricultural School. Adjoining the town are Hollymount Park (T. S. Lindsay, Esq.) and Bloomfield (Col. Rutledge).] From Ballinrobe the road gradually approaches Lough Mask, and at Keel Bridge crosses a narrow isthmus between it and *Lough Carra*, an irregularly shaped lake, about 6 m. long, though never more than 1 broad. On the opposite bank of Lough Mask, under the Slieve Partry Hills, is Toormakeady, a seat of the Bishop of Tuam. 42 m. at the head of the lake is *Partry*, a village that has attained an unenviable notoriety from the number and frequency of evictions unfortunately necessary or considered to be so by the landlord of the soil. Iron-works were once established here, but are no longer worked. The road now diverges, the direct and shortest route to Westport being to the l., but the antiquary will find it to his account in taking the other route, and thus visiting the ruins of *Ballintobber Abbey* (anc. Baile-an-Tobhair), which, though little known, are very beautiful, and well worth a purpose expedition. Careful inquiries should be made as to the direct locality, as they lie on a by-road to Ballyglass, and just opposite a public-house called "Lyons." It is a large cruciform ch., with nave, transepts, and choir, the latter still possessing its roof. The visitor will be struck with the immense height of the gable ends and with the intersection (where the tower once stood), which is marked by 4 splendid arches springing from sculptured imposts. The vaulted roof of the choir (which is divided into 3 bays) deserves particular attention. From each of them springs a vaulting arch right across to the opposite bay, as also one to the alternate angles, thus producing a singular intersection. Over the altar are 3 blocked windows of exquisite Norm. design, with double dog-tooth moulding, and over the middle light is another smaller Norm. window. On the S. side of the choir is an archway with 2 circular-headed arches, and on the N. is some moulding, apparently belonging to an altar-tomb. The nave is lighted by 8 Early Pointed windows, deeply splayed inwardly. In the transept are 2 chapels, the most northerly containing a stoup, the design of which is a misshapen head and face. The monastic buildings are at the end of the S. transept and adjoining the nave; and in what was probably a chapel to the S. of the choir is an elaborate altar-tomb, on the pediment of which are 5 singular figures representing ecclesiastics. The whole row was evidently filled by them, but the remainder have disappeared in the course of time. The visitor should also notice the doorway, an exquisite pointed arch resting on 4 receding columns. This fine abbey was founded in the 13th cent. by Cathal O'Connor, king of Connaught, for Canons Regular of the order of St. Augustine, and fortunately for the archæologist has but little history, as such generally entailed the complete destruction of all the finest features. A very dreary road leads from the abbey to the Triangle, following the course of the Ayle, which like the Cong river flows through a limestone table-land, and has at times a subterranean course. It rises near the village of Aughagower in an impetuous cavernous spring similar to that of the Shannon on Culkeagh mountain (p. 60), and of course is the subject of many a curious countryside story. If the geologist has time, he should follow the river up to its source, through this singular district. At all events, if the day is clear, he will be gratified with the distant views of Nephin over Lough Carra, and the Reek near Westport, which show to great advantage.

48 m. the Triangle, point of junction of the Castlebar and Ballinrobe roads.

A little further on l. is Ayle ch., and close by a mound surmounted by the shell of a ruin, known as McPhilbin's Castle.

[1½ m. l. is the village of Aughagower anc. Achadh-fabhair), which should be visited on account of its round tower, a venerable ivy-covered tower, of apparently 5 stages, of rude workmanship. It is lighted by 2 rude semicircular arched windows, and entered by a square doorway. The conical top is wanting. Close by is the ruin of a chapel with gable ends and high-ditched roof, lighted on E. by a very pretty 3-light window splayed inwardly. On the l. of the building is an oratory. Rejoining the high road, on l. is Mountbrown (J. Livingston, Esq.).

53 m. Westport (Rte. 22). *Hotel:* Imperial.

ROUTE 22.

FROM CLIFDEN TO LEENANE, WESTPORT, AND SLIGO.

Clifden (*Hotels:* Hart's, comfortable; Carr's. Mr. Hart is most ready to communicate to the tourist his large stock of local information about this district. After traversing the wild, heathery roads from Oughterarde and the Recess, Clifden, with its picturesque streets and escarped situation, is pleasant to look upon. It mainly consists of 2 streets, built at a considerable height, overlooking the harbour of Ardbear—one of those beautiful inlets which are at once the puzzle and the pride of Connemara, or Conmhaicné-mara, "the land of bays." It has no antiquities to boast of, being an entirely modern creation of the family of D'Arcy, who have been untiring in labouring for the good of the locality, both temporally and spiritually. Its buildings are a pretty ch. and schools, an Irish Mission House, an orphanage, and an enormous workhouse, the district of Clifden being one of those which suffered so fearfully in the famine year. The union comprises an area of 192,066 acres. But for the invalid and the searcher after the picturesque, Clifden will furnish much pleasure from the beauty of the coast and its proximity to the Twelve Pins, which are seen to the greatest perfection from every road leading from the town. A river descends from these mountains, forming a very pretty cascade close to the town, and falling into Ardbear. The road to Roundstone and Errislannin crosses an inlet of Ardbear, giving occasion to the driver to call attention to the fact of the traveller crossing the Atlantic in a car. On the l. the view is very pretty when the tide is up and fills the little bay, an island with a crucifix on it being in the middle and a monastery on the opposite shore. The country between Clifden and Roundstone (Rte. 20) is extremely dreary, as also all along the coast as far as Bunowen, the seat of Valentine Blake, Esq.; but by mounting the hill above it we get a good view of Slyne Head, on which is a lighthouse with one fixed and one revolving light. At Errislannin is the ruin of an old ch. The great lion of Clifden is Clifden Castle, formerly the residence of the D'Arcy family, and now of that of Eyre. Its situation is matchless, embosomed in woods overlooking the bay and opposite coast of Rusheen, beyond which stretches the blue Atlantic. At a distance, too, the towers look well, but the effect is spoilt by a nearer inspection. It is, moreover, badly and untidily kept. From the castle there is a charming walk down to the shore, and along the bay to Clifden, passing a Mission House and the villa of Lakeeragh. But little trade is carried on, save in fish. Enormous quantities of lobsters are annually sent away, so much so that there is great difficulty in procuring one in Clifden. A good deal of kelp is manufactured on the coast, and sent to Glasgow by Mr. Hart, who has a storehouse near Bunowen. The price varies from 2*l*. 2*s*. 6*d*. to 2*l*. 15*s*. per ton. The mouth of the harbour is almost closed by a reef of rocks, rendering the approach exceedingly dangerous to vessels.

Conveyances.—To Oughterarde and Galway, a car twice a day.

Distances.—Galway, 47 m.; Oughterarde, 31; Recess, 13½; Roundstone, 11; Bunowen, 8; Streamstown, 3; Kylemore, 13; Leenane, 21; Errislannin, 5; Ballynakill, 6.

Excursions.—
1. Kylemore and Killaries.
2. Bunowen.
3. Roundstone.
4. Twelve Pins.

From Clifden the road runs N. over high ground, the ascent of which is rewarded by a charming view on the l. of the bay or inlet of Streamstown, with the small island of Innishturk, and the larger one of Omey, at the entrance. On the S. side of the bay is the ruined ch. of Omey, and on the N. the castle of Doon—a fortress of the O'Flahertys, built upon a precipice with a trench round it. 3½ m. l. a road branches off to Claggin Bay. On the headland overlooking it is a Martello tower. The tourist will notice an increasing improvement in the appearance of land and houses all the way from Clifden. There is comparatively little waste bog, and it is evident that a very superior class of settlers have brought capital, industry, and patience to bear upon this hitherto neglected district.

6 m. at Ballynakill the road suddenly descends upon the bay and harbour of Ballynakill, a broad and beautiful fiord, which sends its arms in for a long distance and is sheltered on every side by hills. On the N. is the rocky mass of Rinvyle, rising almost directly from the shore, and on the E. the bay runs nearly to the foot of the outliers of Bunnabeola, or the Twelve Pins.

Off Claggin Head, about 3 m. from the shore, is *High Island*, or Ard-Oilean, uninhabited and difficult of access from its rocky sides. There are some curious remains here, consisting of a square of about 20 yards, at the corners of which were erected small houses, with walls 4 ft. high, and domical roofs, the covering being formed of one big stone. There is also a ch. 12 ft. long and 10 wide, with a stone altar. Many carved and sculptured stones are scattered about, as well as other graves—

probably of those who were not in orders. The house of St. Fechin, of which an illustration is given in Petrie's work, "is square in the interior, and measures 9 ft. by 7 ft. 6 in. in height. The doorway is 2 ft. 4 in. wide and 3 ft. 6 in. high. The material of this structure, which dates from the 7th cent., is of mica slate; and though its external appearance is very rude, its interior is constructed with admirable art. The doorway of the ch. is 2 ft. wide, and its horizontal lintel is inscribed with a cross. The E. window, the only one in the building, is semicircular-headed, and is but 1 ft. high and 6 in. wide. The chapel is surrounded by a wall, allowing a passage of 4 ft. between them, and from this a covered passage about 15 ft. long leads to a cell, which was probably the abbot's habitation. There is also a covered passage or gallery, 24 ft. long and 4 ft. 6 in. high, the use of which it is difficult to conjecture."—*Petrie.* From these facts, and from statements made by O'Flaherty, it was evidently an establishment for Eremitical or hermit-monks. In addition to the interest of these ruins, the visitor, should he be fortunate enough to have a calm day, will obtain grand views of the coast of Connemara.

Immediately opposite Ballynakill harbour is the large island of Inishbofin, containing a considerable population, mostly engaged in fishing, and probably in a little potheen-distilling. On the coast is some singular rock-scenery. Separated from it by the Stags of Bofin is the smaller island of Inishark. At the end of Ballynakill bay are a pretty ch. and lodge belonging to F. Graham, Esq.

8½ m. *Letterfrack*, a pleasant, well-to-do little colony, established some years ago by a Mr. Ellis, a Quaker, who built a neat village, with all the necessary stores, police-barrack, and schools for the establishment, besides draining and planting a very large portion of moorland.

Behind the village the beautiful mountain called Diamond Hill rises abruptly to the height of 1460 ft., forming one of the western groups of the Twelve Pins.

The road soon enters the lovely glen of *Kylemore*, one of the gems of Connemara, though possessing a somewhat melancholy character. On the N. the glen is bounded by Doaghrue (1717 ft.), the rocky shoulders of which are covered with green shrubs and underwood, giving it an English character not often to be found in Irish scenery. On the S. are the Twelve Pins—Adergoole (1577 ft.), Benbrack (1922), Muchanaght (2155), and Benbarron (2395), rising one over the other in grand groups. Indeed, from no place can the Bunnabeola chain be seen to greater advantage than from Kylemore, as in all the southern views such a vast amount of bog and flat coast intervenes that their noble height is lost, while here they gain from comparison with other mountains.

Before arriving at the Lough, which reposes placidly at the foot of the hills, we pass Adragoole, a well-planted settlement reclaimed from the barren wild by T. Eastwood, Esq.

The drive to the Hotel, which is on the N. bank, is exquisite, the road being carried under huge masses of rock, glittering in the sunlight with scales of mica, and festooned with creepers and ferns. Here is a comfortable inn, until lately kept by a clergyman of the name of Duncan —capital quarters for fishermen and mountain-climbers.

Excursions.—
1. Leenane.
2. Lough Inagh.
3. Salrock and Lough Fee.

From hence a road on rt. (one of those completed in the famine year by the Board of Works runs off to the S.E. to Lough Inagh. 1.5 m. crossing the little Owenduff river, we catch a glimpse to the l.

of Lough Fee, a long sheet of water encircled on every side by lofty hills (on the S. 1973 ft.), save where the stream emerges into the sea near the entrance to the Killary.

A road runs off to its N. bank, leading to the very pretty residence of Sir W. R. Wilde, who has pitched his solitary tent in one of the finest of Connemara glens; and from thence to Salrock, which the tourist had better visit from Leenane.

Passing over a dreary extent of moor, the next rise of the hill brings us directly in front of the Killary (anc. Caolshaile-luadh) — that wonderful fiord, which has scarce any parallel in the British Isles, and more resembles the coast scenery in Norway. It is an arm of the Atlantic, running inland to the very heart of the mountains for a distance of some 9 m. On each side steep and precipitous mountains descend to the water's edge, on the S. leaving barely room for the road. The mountain-scenery on the N. of the fiord is incomparably the finest, the enormous walls of Muilrea, the Giant of the West, and Bengorm, rising abruptly to the heights of 2688 and 2303 ft., while the excessive stillness of the land-locked water, in which the shadows of the hills are clearly reflected, make it difficult for the tourist to believe that it is the actual ocean which he beholds.

"A haven, beneath whose translucent floor
The tremulous stars sparkled unfathomably,
And around which the solid vapours hoar,
Based on the level waters, to the sky
Lifted their dreadful crags."
Shelley.

A short drive along the S. bank brings him to 21 m. *Leenane*, a solitary and welcome little hotel at the very edge of the water, not far from the head of the fiord, with lofty hills springing directly from the rear of the house, and a noble expanse of water in front. Many beautiful excursions can be made from hence:—

1. To Lough Fee, and thence to Salrock, 8 m. The best way is to take a boat from Leenane, and row the whole length of the Killary, turning abruptly round at the entrance, and then going up the Little Killary, at the head of which is *Salrock*, the exquisitely situated residence of the late Gen. Thompson. A more fairy-like picture can scarcely be conceived than is presented from the Pass of Salrock, looking over the Killary and the broad expanse of the Atlantic, dotted with occasional islands—the largest of which, Inishturk, lies some 11 m. out. The Pass of Salrock is said to have been formed by the struggles of St. Roc, who, having been chained by the Devil when he was asleep, made his way with an immense deal of friction through the mountain. From Salrock the visitor—having feasted his eyes with the beauties around—should return by a car sent by appointment from Leenane through the wild glen of Lough Fee. The whole of the mountains abound in rare and beautiful ferns and heaths, amongst which the white heath and Menzesia polyfolia are conspicuous.

8 m. beyond Salrock is Rinvyle House, the seat of the Blake family, finely placed on the edge of a lofty series of cliff-rocks. The ancient castle of the Blakes — a weather-beaten, massive tower — is about 1½ m. further on. The best way of visiting Rinvyle will be by water.

2. To Maume, 9 m. This is essentially a mountain-road, following the course of the glens that intervene between the Mamturk and Lugnabricka Mountains. Midway the tourist passes a very pretty waterfall, and the solitary graveyard of the Joyce sept—fit burial-place for a race of hill-giants. Thence we attain the watershed and descend the valley of the Bealnabrack river to Maume (Rte. 21).

In addition to these excursions, the angler will find plenty of sport in the waters of the Errive and in Lough Nafooey, which lies in the mountains between Leenane and Lough Mask. The geologist will find work enough in the constant variety of hills, which contain many minerals. The one at the back of the hotel, which is nearly 1800 ft., contains excellent specimens of jasper and mica.

3. [To *Delphi*. A boat must be taken to the little harbour of Bundorragha, where there are a small pier and a few cottages. From thence the course of a mountain-stream is followed up a narrow gorge, bounded on either side by Muilrea 2688 ft., and Bengorm 2303,— two of the finest mountains in the whole of the W. of Ireland. 1½ m., at the upper end of the little Fin Lough, are the woods and house of Delphi, formerly belonging to the Marquis of Sligo, and now to the Hon. D. Plunket. It may be safely said that, if Connemara contained no other beauty, Delphi alone would be worth the journey from London, for the sake of the mountain-scenery. 1 m. higher up is Lough Doo, a long sheet of water, from the banks of which the hills rise to between 2000 and 3000 ft. At the S. end is the pretty residence of Capt. Houston, who is the owner of an immense mountain property, and who possesses herds of horses, sheep, and "fat kine innumerable." From hence the road turns to rt. up the course of the Glenummera river, and, gradually ascending for many miles the wildest and most untamable mountain-slopes, crosses the watershed, and descends into Glenlawer. 8 m. at Sheffry the cliff scenery is on a grand scale. A little further on the Owenmore is crossed, and at 15 m. this road falls into the Westport high road. If the weather is fine, the tourist should by all means write for a car to Westport to meet him at Bundorragha, and take this route, which is very much finer than the usual one, though it must be confessed that the holes in the road require all the driver's attention and care.]

From Leenane the road winds round the head of the Killary, at the base of a lofty hill which rejoices in the name of the Devil's Mother.

At Ashlee are the residence of the Hon. D. Plunket, and a pretty Protestant ch. The Errive, whose stream we are now following, is an impetuous salmon-river, rising, under the name of the Owenmore Big river, in the chain of hills intervening between Lough Doo and Westport, where it is crossed by the road just mentioned.

28½ m. Errive Bridge, was the scene of a melancholy accident in 1860, when, the bridge having been carried away in a flood, an unfortunate lady was drowned in attempting to ford the stream in her car. As the road ascends the valley the vegetation becomes more scanty and the moorland more extensive. Crossing the watershed, we descend the valley of the Owenwee, and gain glorious views of the magical Clew Bay, which, if seen at sunset, forms, with its hundred islands, one of the most exquisite landscapes possible.

41 m. *Westport* (Rte. 21) (*Hotel*: Imperial) is one of the very prettiest towns that it is possible to visit in a long summer's day, and its beauty is enhanced by being approached for several miles each way through a high and rather bleak country. It is situated in a hollow, embosomed on every side in groves and woods, and watered by a small stream, which, after passing through the centre of the town and doing duty, both useful and ornamental, in Lord Sligo's Park, finds its level in Clew Bay, which, with all its magical scenery, is within a mile of the place. Westport consists of one long main street, with the stream in the middle, a broad promenade on each side, shaded by avenues of leafy lime-

trees, which give it somewhat the appearance of a Spanish Alameda. The foreign aspect is still further increased by the numbers of the Irish lasses, who, with petticoats tucked up, and bare legs, are constantly washing, wringing and beating the clothes at the water-side, to an *ad libitum* accompaniment of jokes and chatter. The town itself presents no object of interest save a statue to George Glendenning, a banker of Westport who managed to enrich himself and his native town, out of which he had never put foot during his long life. "'He was a rich man of this place,' replied the lad, 'and so they made him a startu.'"—*Sir F. Head.* The great charm of Westport is the park of the Marquis of Sligo, the gates of which are at the end of the street, and are ever open to all classes to wander about at their will and pleasure. In the centre of the park is the mansion, a handsome square building on a balustrated terrace, from the W. side of which is a delicious view of Clew Bay. A very pretty Protestant ch., used by the Westport inhabitants, stands embowered amongst the woods. Passing through the park we arrive at the port, which is perfect in all the arrangements, save, alas! the requisite of commerce. "There was a long, handsome pier (which no doubt remains at this present minute), and one solitary cutter alongside of it, which may or may not be there now. As for the warehouses, they are enormous, and might accommodate, I should think, not only the trade of Westport, but of Manchester too. There are huge streets of these houses, 10 stories high, with cranes, owners' houses, &c., marked Wine Stores, Flour Stores, Bonded Tobacco Warehouses, and so forth; dismal mausoleums as vast as pyramids—places where the dead trade of Westport lies buried."—*Thackeray.* It is to be hoped, however, that the extension of the rly.

from Athlone will be the signal for a renewal of bustle and trade, as Westport undoubtedly possesses many natural advantages over other ports. (Pop. 3819.)

Conveyances.—Rail to Castlebar, Athlone, and Dublin; car to Sligo daily, to Galway daily through Ballinrobe, to Athenry, to Newport, to Tuam.

Distances.—Newport, 8 m.; Achill Sound, 27; Murrisk, 6; Croagh Patrick, 8; Louisburgh, 12½; Clare Island, 16; Clifden, 41; Leenane, 20; Castlebar, 11; Pontoon Bridge, 22; Ballina, 33; Partry, 12; Ballintober, 10; Aughagower, 4; Ayle, 5; Ballinrobe, 19.

Westport is a central point for many excursions—

1. To Leenane, Lough Doo, and Delphi.
2. To Aughagower Round Tower, and Ballintobber Abbey (Rte. 21).
3. To Croagh Patrick and Murrisk Abbey.

[The road runs through the park and the port, emerging close on the S. side of *Clew Bay*, one of the most extraordinary and lovely of Irish islets. "The conical mountain on the l. is Croagh Patrick, or the Reek; it is clothed in the most magnificent violet colour, and a couple of round clouds were exploding as it were from the summit, that part of them towards the sea lighted up with the most delicate gold and rose colour. In the centre is the Clare Island, of which the edges were bright cobalt, while the middle was lighted up with a brilliant scarlet tinge. The islands in the bay looked like so many dolphins basking there."—*Thackeray.* The bay forms a noble expanse of sheltered water about 15 m. in length; the entrance being partially protected by the lofty cliffs of Clare Island, while the eastern extremity is studded with immense numbers of islands which, while they add to the picturesque beauty of the scene, add also to the difficulty of approach to the harbour.

These islands and channels are defended by a singular natural breakwater extending from Westport to the shore under the Reek. "This bar is a breakwater 1¼ m. long, on which are situated the islands of Dorcinch More and Dorcinch Beg. It slopes seaward, in some places, 1 in 30, and is formed of boulders. Though natural, it is perhaps one of the most remarkable hydraulic works that exist in Europe: its mass being greater than that of the breakwater at Plymouth or that of Cherbourg."—*Bald*. There are 6 navigable openings, the principal of which is marked by a lighthouse, erected by the Marquis of Sligo. Probably no bay in the kingdom is surrounded by such magnificent ranges of mountains. On the S. the rugged declivities of the Reek run down almost to the water's edge, while further seaward the coast is overhung, though at a greater distance, by Muilrea, Benbury, and the mountains of the Murrisk district. On the N. are the wild and lofty ranges of the Nephin Beg, ending in the precipices of Slieve More and Croghan in Achill Island. The precipitous cliffs of Clare Island form a fitting seaward termination to the beauties of this wonderful bay. The road passes by several pleasant seats to 6 m. *Murrisk*, an ancient abbey at the foot of Croagh Patrick, founded by the O'Malleys for Augustinian friars. It is of no great extent, being single-aisled, but has a beautiful Dec. E. window of 5 lights. On the N. of the chancel is a vaulted room, entered by a plain pointed doorway. The W. entrance, partially blocked up, is also by a pointed gateway. In the interior of the ch. is the tomb of the O'Malleys, part of a stone cross representing the Crucifixion, and a collection of the biggest thighbones that it is possible to conceive. From this point the ascent of the Reek anc. Cruach-phadraig, is always commenced. This extraordinary mountain rises with great abruptness for a height of 2510 ft., terminating in what is apparently a point, though there is really a small platform of about ½ an acre on the summit. On the S. side is a very steep precipice, known as Lug na Narrib, on the edge of which "St. Patrick stood bell in hand, and every time he rang it he flung it away from him, and it, instead of plunging down the Lug, was brought back to his hand by ministering spirits; and every time it thus hastily was rung, thousands of toads, adders, and noisome things, went down, tumbling neck and heels one after the other."—*Otway*. As may be imagined from its height and its isolation, the Reek affords most splendid panoramas of the W. of Ireland, extending northwards over Murrisk, Ballycroy, Achill, Erris, even to Slieve League on the coast of Donegal, and southward to the Leenane district and the 12 Pins; but to Irish minds, the mountain has a far higher interest, it being a sacred hill, devoted to patterns, on which occasions the numbers of "voteens" or pilgrims would be incredible to a stranger. Many hundreds may on these occasions be seen ascending the hill, stopping at the different stations to say their paters, and in some places to go round on their knees. This part of the performance is generally reserved for the summit of the mountain, the long station being 400 yards in circumference, and around this the devotees have to go 15 times, also on their knees, which before the termination are in a state of laceration. A very important adjunct to the whole affair is the whisky tent, a melancholy and suggestive feature of the occasion which requires such an excitement. Extraordinary as are the scenes of Irish life and character to be witnessed at these patterns, the tourist will probably enjoy his visit to Croagh Patrick far better in solitude and apart from these religious saturnalia. The botanist will find growing on this mountain Poa alpina, Melampyrum pratense, Pinguicula lusitanica, Saxifraga serratifolia.

At the foot of the westerly extension of hill, of which the Reek is the central cone, is Louisburgh, a large village with a fine view over Clare Island.]

4. To Newport and Achill. The road to Newport runs for the greater part of the distance within view of the Clew Bay, so as effectually to prevent any monotony. On the way the little river Rossow is crossed by a bridge of 2 arches, beneath one of which a whole family long kept house and home.

8 m. *Newport* (*Hotel:* Carr's), a small seaport at the mouth of the Newport river, looking better at a distance than is warranted by a nearer inspection. The N. bank of the river is embellished by the residence of Sir Richard O'Donnell, adding considerably to the beauty of the town. There is a good pier, where vessels of 200 tons can unload, but the trade of the port is very small.

Distances.—Castlebar, 11½ m.; Burrishoole, 2.

The road from Newport to Molrenny is nearly a straight line for about 10 m., and depends for its attractions very much on the weather that accompanies the tourist. If it be clear, there is a magnificent view seawards over the bay and the opposite mountains of Murrisk, while on the rt. inland is the equally fine range of the Nephin Beg hills, which run in a curving direction from N.E. to W. with remarkably bold outlines. The principal heights that are seen between Newport and the Sound are Buckoogh 1922 ft., Slieve Turk 1322, Nephin Beg 2012, Cushcamcurragh 2262, Knocknatintree 1646, and Knocklettaragh 1509. The streams issuing from these hills, and running into Clew Bay, are of no great importance, as the ascent is so immediate, but on the N. and W. slopes they have a longer course to Blacksod Bay, and are of considerably larger volume.

10 m. *Burrishoole*, at the entry of the Burrishoole river, gives its name to the whole district from Newport to Achill. Here are remains of a large monastery and ch. founded for Dominicans by Richard Bourke, Lord Mac William Oughter. It was a cruciform building, with a central slender tower, and has some good pointed arches, the whole building being of the 15th cent. Overlooking an arm of the sea is Carrighooley Castle, a square plain tower, formerly one of the fortresses of Grace O'Mealey, or Grana Uaile, the mountain Queen of the West, who lorded it over Mayo and the islands with a prompt fierce sway, that even in those days of lawlessness and rudeness commanded universal fear and respect. On the coast there are some singular caverns, believed to have been druidical chambers. To the rt. of the road, running up into the heart of the hills, is Lough Feoogh, the head of which lies between Buckoogh and Slieve Turk; and on its bank is the ruin of an iron-smelting furnace. At 18 m. Molrenny, a small "public" on the roadside overlooks a marvellously beautiful landscape. Very soon the road divides [on the rt. winding round the base of Knocknatintree and opening out on a landlocked inlet from Blacksod Bay. At the mouth of the Owenavrea river there is a 2nd division, the one on the l. taking a course near Annagh Sound and Tullaghan Bay to Creggranroe and Croy Lodge, both cultivated oases in this desert of the far West, which for untamed wildness surpasses anything in the kingdom, but is an Utopia for sportsmen according to the author of 'Wild Sports of the West.' The district of Ballycroy embraces all the Ne-

phin Beg range from Burrishoole to Erris, and contains in this enormous area scarce half a dozen inhabited houses. "Along the seashore there is some cultivation; but inland, townless, roadless, treeless, one wide waste of bog covers all. But it is not to be supposed this is like the great flat flow bogs in the centre of the island, such as the Bog of Allen. No; the Bog of Erris, as well as those of Connemara, covers mountains, hills, champaigns, and vales: nature's universal brown vesture, it fits all; and that is what makes the reclamation of these wastes hopeful."— *C. Otway.* On the seashore below Cregganroe is *Duna Castle*, an ancient stronghold of Grace O'Mealey's (Grana Uaile). It is a massive square tower, with wonderfully strong masonry, though it could not withstand the heat of a large fire which had been accidentally kindled, causing the ruin to become ten times more a ruin. The main road, that parted company at the Owenavrea, runs more inland through a monotonous district to Derrycorrib, where it joins the route to Belmullet (Rte. 19.).

The route to Achill now enters the peninsula of Curraun, which, by the little inlet from Blacksod Bay just mentioned, is very nearly made an island. The whole of it is occupied by the mountain of Knockletteragh 1509 ft., and the road winds round the northern side to *Achill Sound*, a narrow strait of about ½ m., which communicates between Clew and Blacksod Bays, affording a most valuable cut for vessels coasting up or down, that would otherwise have to round the dangerous cliffs of Croghan and Slievemore in Achill. On the landside is an establishment for preserving fish and provisions, and on the Achill side is a convenient little store and inn, where the tourist may procure a car. A small toll is charged at the ferry. The traveller must bear in mind that in all probability the inn at the Sound will be the only place where he can procure a conveyance, and the only place but one where he can put up; this other being at the Settlement at Doogurth; so that he must make his arrangements accordingly. If he makes a hasty run over the island, he had better keep the car at the Saltpans to take him back to Westport; or he may possibly catch one of the coasting hookers running down the Sound from Belmullet, which, if the wind be fair, will land him at Westport in the course of 3 or 4 hours. "The *Island of Achill* (Pop. 5776), the largest off the Irish coast, is 16 m. in length and 7 in breadth, forming a shore-line about 80 m. in circumference, and comprising 46,000 acres. The western side is mostly a precipitous range of cliffs, but the eastern is in every part well sheltered. Achill Head, a bold promontory, is situated on the S.W. extremity of the island, and at the N. end is Saddle Head, at the entrance of Blacksod Bay. Between this and the smaller island of Achill Beg is a channel called Achill Hole, where vessels drawing 10 or 12 ft. of water may rest in safety in all weathers. A very powerful tide runs in the Sound at the northern entrance called the Bull's Mouth."—*Lewis.*

The general aspect of the island is one unvaried mass of dark heather, covering the broad undulating moors that stretch from the high ranges at the W. end of the district. A main road traverses the island, passing l. the residence of W. Pike, Esq., whose gardens, reclaimed from the bare mountain, are worth a visit. A little further on is Bunahurra, the residence of the Rev. J. Henry, the Roman Catholic priest, occupying a position that commands the most magnificent coast and mountain views, extending over Ballycroy, Blacksod Bay, the Nepihu ranges, and the high grounds of Curraun. The road soon gains the highest level, and the tourist is charmed with an equally fine view westward of the mighty mass of Slievemore, the cloud-capped summit of Croghan, and to the S. the precipitous ridges of Minnaun. On rt. a road runs for about 3 m. to the N. coast, where, sheltered under the steep rocks of Slievemore, is the Protestant colony of Doogurth, commonly known as the Settlement, 10 m. from the sound. It is a cheerful-looking square of plain white houses, in the centre of which stand the ch. and the clergyman's residence. In the square are an inn (not of the best), residences for the various officials, a printing establishment, 3 schools, an orphan home, and dispensary. This missionary establishment was set on foot by the Rev. E. Nangle, to whose self-denial and labours many have borne testimony, as also to his uncompromising battles with the Roman Catholics; as carried on in the 'Achill Herald,' some may think a little too warmly. It is not the province of a Handbook to enter into religious discussions, but it may not be out of place to warn every tourist in the west of Ireland that he must be prepared for extreme statements, whether from Protestants or Roman Catholics, and for a lack of religious charity which each party would do well to discard. The ascent of Slievemore which overhangs the colony at a height of 2217 ft., may be undertaken here, but if the tourist wishes to see Croghan, he had better reserve himself. Slievemore is an extraordinary cone of quartzose rocks rising abruptly from the sea, and, with its dark rifted sides occasionally relieved by shining masses of mica, presents a study for the painter at once grand and remarkable, especially at sunset, when its apex is often encircled by rose-coloured clouds. Proceeding onwards, we come to the village of Keel, a singular collection of wigwams peculiar to Achill. There is a beautiful strand here, bounded on the E. by the cliffs of Minnaun 1530 ft.; a path runs along the cliffs to Dooega, another Achill village, at an altitude and of a character sufficient to try the nervous climber. The little heaps of yellow-red earth all around are coloured with ochre, which is dug out with the bog iron ore in considerable quantities in this neighbourhood. We next come to Dooega, and further on to Keem, 14 m. from the Sound, both miserable hamlets of round houses built without gable-ends. It would seem that the aborigines of the island still hold their court here. Towering above Keem is the stupendous mass of Slieve Croghan, which, together with the cliffs of Mohir in Co. Clare and Slieve League in Donegal, is considered the finest cliff scenery in Great Britain.

The Croghan, 2222 ft. in height, is a long range of mountain running along the N.W. coast of Achill, and cutting off the promontory of Saddle Head, which is to a certain extent an offshoot from it. But its grand and peculiar feature is that at the very highest point it would seem as if the rest of the mountain had been suddenly cut away, leaving a vast and tremendous precipice descending down to the water for nearly 1950 ft. "Here we came upon a precipice nearly 2000 ft. high that went down almost plumb; and then there was an inclined plane covered with the débris of the upper stratifications; and then again, 200 yards further on rt., there were cliffs about 300 ft. high, against which the waves washed. Here we sat, the cloud just festooning, as it were, a raised-up curtain over our heads, and all below was serene; and from the lowest edges of the precipice at this point there extended a pretty little vale in which was a tarn, so clear that it might have been taken for a mermaid's looking-glass."—*C. O.*

The view seawards is of course boundless, the nearest land being

America, unless we believe in the enchanted land of Hy Brisail (p. 170), in which the dwellers on the W. coast have such a belief. Looking S. is the small isolated rock of the Billies, and northwards towards Mullet are numerous islands, of which the principal are *Inishkeen* and *Inishgloria*, where, according to some, the dead are subject to such extraordinary and preserving influences, that their nails and their hair grow as in life, "so that their descendants to the 10th generation can come, and with pious care pare the one and clip the other:"—

"Cernere Inisgloria est Pelago, quod prospicit Irnis
Insula avos, atavos solo post fata sepultos,
Illæsos servare suas vegetisque vigere
Unguibus atque comis, hominum caro nulla
putrescit."
 Sir Wm. O'Kelly.

Further out are the Black Rocks, on which is a lighthouse.

[On the return, before recrossing the ferry, the traveller may diverge to the S. of the island, where at Kildamnat, close to the water's edge, is another square tower, formerly one of Grana Uaile's fortresses. From thence a visit may be paid to the primitive village of Dhuega, lying underneath the cliffs of Minmann; or else the narrow strait may be crossed which separates Achill from Achill Beg, an inhabited isle of considerable extent. Within the last 2 or 3 years Achill has become more valuable in consequence of its mineral treasures being worked. Mr. Peel of Curraun has obtained considerable supplies of rich bog iron-ore, as well as of steatite soap-stone, of which material there are large supplies in the coast between Kildamnat and Dhuega.]

5. To Clare Island, a pleasant water excursion for those who are not disconcerted by the breezes of the Atlantic. It is about 4 m. in length, and comprises an area of 3900 acres, the coast being for the most part defended by lofty cliffs. It contains very slight remains of an abbey founded for Carmelite friars in 1224. It has a rather singular window of 2 lights, trefoil-headed, with sculptured spandrils. For many years the skull of Grace O'Malley was shown here, decorated with ribbons. The castle of this Queen of the Isles is a square massive tower similar to that at Duna. Clare Island was the home and headquarters of this Amazon, who lived in the reign of Elizabeth, to whom she once paid a visit. So far, however, from paying homage to the queen, Grace O'Malley conducted herself in so rude a manner as fairly to nonplus her Majesty, who offered to make her visitor a countess—an honour declined by Grana Uaile, who informed the queen that she considered herself equal to her Majesty in every respect. Her first husband was O'Flaherty, Prince of Connemara, and the owner of the castle in Lough Corrib, which, being nearly lost to the Joyces through him, was saved by Grana's intrepidity, and so acquired the name of the Hen's Castle (p. 184). Her second husband was William Bourke McWilliam Oughter. "The marriage was to last for one year, and if at the end of that period either said to the other 'I dismiss you,' the union was dissolved. It is said that during that year Grana took care to put her own creatures into garrison in all McWilliam's coastward castles that were valuable to her, and then one fine day, as the lord of Mayo was coming up to the castle of Carig-a-hooly, Grace spied him, and cried out the dissolving words, 'I dismiss you.'"

A car leaves Westport every morning for Sligo, though the tourist may go as far as Castlebar by rail. With the exception of distant views of the Croaghmoyle and Nephin ranges, the way is uninteresting. Passing Greenhill — Stafford, Esq., and Spencer Park J. Larminie, Esq., we arrive at

52 m. *Castlebar* (*Hotels:* Daly's; Armstrong's), principally celebrated for its capture in 1798 by the French, who had landed at Killala Bay (Rte. 19) under Gen. Humbert, and made themselves masters of the town, which they evacuated on the approach of the Marquis of Cornwallis. This little episode was known by the name of the Castlebar Races. It is a good-looking place, with all the buildings necessary to a small country town, viz. gaol, court-house, and barracks, in addition to a shady and well-timbered mall, which is certainly a very pleasant adjunct. The Lawn is the residence of the Earl of Lucan, who has done more than any landlord in the country to improve the agriculture of this district, of which he owns about 30,000 acres. The country around Castlebar is not inviting, although the mountains, some 5 m. to the N., rise to a considerable height, Knockmore to 1259 ft., and Spinkanilen 1290 ft., being the only barriers that separate Castlebar from the conical mass of Nephin 2646 ft., one of the most lofty and conspicuous hills in the W., which give such characteristic features to the scenery of Lough Conn.

Conveyances.—To Athenry daily; to Westport; to Ballina and Sligo; by rail to Castlereagh and Athlone.

Distances.—Pontoon Bridge, 11 m.; Newport, 11½; Westport, 11; Ballina, 22; Crossmolina, 19; Balla, 8; Castlereagh, 37.

[The antiquarian may pay a visit from Castlebar to Balla, a village about 8 m. to the S.E. on the road to Hollymount. Here is a round tower about 50 ft. in height, and the remains of a ch. built by St. Mochun in the 7th cent. He also caused 2 wells to be formed, which he enclosed with walls, from whence the town took its name : " Unde oppidum novum nomen Balla et etiam Mochun cognomen Ballensis accepit."

In the neighbourhood of Balla are Attavalley (Sir R. Blosse, Bt.), and Broomhill. A little to the S. is the district known as the Plains of *Mayo*, and in the village of the same name are slight ruins of an abbey, which was the locale of an university very celebrated in the 7th cent., and founded by St. Colman, who for that purpose resigned his cell of Lindisfarne in Northumberland. There are one or two ancient fortified mansions in the neighbourhood.]

Following up the Castlebar river, is 56 m. Turlough, in which parish is another round tower. The bleak and boggy scenery begins to improve, especially as we near the long ranges of the Croaghmoyle Hills and the *Loughs Conn* and *Cullen* at Pontoon Bridge. The former is a very fine sheet of water 15 m. long, interspersed with beautiful islands, and overhung by mountains, especially on the W. bank, which is almost entirely occupied by the mighty mass of Nephin. Lough Cullen is sometimes called Lower Lough Conn, and is connected by a short stream, across which the road is carried by a bold single-arched bridge known as the Pontoon. The view looking up and down from this bridge is of a very remarkable and beautiful character. " An extraordinary phenomenon is visible here in the alternate ebbing and flowing of these lakes; the water is sometimes seen rushing with great force through the channel into Lough Cullen, while at others it runs with equal force into Lough Conn. The shores of both lakes being composed in many places of a fine red sand, the line of high water mark can be distinctly traced several miles above the water, and then in the space of an hour it rises to the higher level in one lake, while it is low in the other."—*Lewis*. An hotel was built on the Castlebar side of the Pontoon by Lord Bingham, but it is now shut up. Near the bridge is a singular rocking-stone close to the lake.

[A road branches off along the

W. side of the lough under Nephin, to the little town of

Crossmolina, situated on the line of road between Ballina and Erris. Previous to reaching it, we pass on rt. the peninsula of Errew, on which, overlooking the water, are remains of an abbey with a good E. window. The Deel runs through Crossmolina, and on its banks is the modernised mansion of Deel Castle, occupying the site of an ancient fortress.

Conveyances.—To Ballina; to Bangor and Belmullet; the road to the latter places being carried over one of the wildest hill commons that even the dreary barony of Tyrawley can show.]

Crossing the Pontoon Bridge rt. is a road to Foxford (Rte. 19). From hence we skirt the S.E. corner of the lake, obtaining magnificent mountain views of Nephin, on which, by the way, the botanist will find Pinguicula lusitanica. Soon approaching the valley of the Moy, we arrive at

74 m. *Ballina* (*Hotels:* Flynn's; Imperial), together with the northern coast of Killala and Downpatrick, described in Rte. 19.

The road now runs over monotonous high ground for many miles, crossing the Easky river, a considerable stream, the mountain valley of which is strewn with granite boulders, to 89 m. Dromore, a very pretty village on the wooded banks of a rushing stream that descends from the Slieve Gamph Mountains, at the foot of which the road runs nearly the whole way to Ballysadare. They are of picturesque outline and considerable height, averaging 1600 ft. Woodhill is the residence of L. Jones, Esq.; and Seaview of — Jones, Esq.

Suddenly the sea bursts upon the sight, and, with occasional interruptions, forms a welcome feature in the landscape all the way to Sligo.

In the distance, on the l., is Aughris Head, and the ruins of the old castle of Ardnaglass, a stronghold of the M'Swynes. This parish of *Skreen*, the ch. of which stands prettily amongst the trees, is said to have been at one time so important as to have contained 7 churches.

The beautiful woods of Tanrego (W. Knox, Esq.), and Dromore Ch., occupy the banks of Ballysadare Bay, which here forms a very charming inlet, bounded on the N.E. by the truncated cone of Knocknarea.

106 m. Ballysadare (Rte. 18).

110 m. Sligo (*Hotels:* Imperial; Victoria) (Rtes. 8-18).

ROUTE 23.

FROM **DUBLIN TO WEXFORD, THROUGH WICKLOW, ARKLOW, AND ENNISCORTHY.**

This route is performed by rail to Enniscorthy, and thence by coach. The Dublin, Wicklow, and Wexford line was in 1856 united to that of the Dublin and Kingstown Co., and although at present only extending to Enniscorthy, a distance of 36 m., is intended to be carried on to Wexford. The tourist may take his choice of proceeding by 2 rlys. as far as Bray. The Kingstown and Bray line is described in Rte. 24.

Quitting the Harcourt-str. Stat., a plain, massive, Doric building, approached by a flight of steps and a colonnade, we pass through the suburbs of Rathmines and Milltown, near which stat., 2 m., the Dodder, a bright active stream running from the Dublin mountains, is crossed; thence passing Windy Harbour and leaving on rt. Rathfarnham, we arrive at, 3 m., *Dundrum*, another suburb much resorted to as a residence by the worthy citizens. To l. of the stat. is *Mount Anville*, the seat of William Dargan, Esq., to whose active enterprise and patriotism almost every portion of Ireland can bear testimony, although his greatest improvements have been effected in Bray and the county Wicklow generally. The house and grounds, with its conservatory and look-out tower, are well worth seeing; the former contains statues of the Queen and Prince Consort, presented by her Majesty to Mr. Dargan after her visit.

We now get near sight on the rt. of the beautiful ranges of mountains, and can appreciate the advantages which the Dublin inhabitant possesses in being able to emerge almost out of the streets of a great town into the heart of bold hill scenery. Immediately on the rt. the most conspicuous object is the Three Rock Mountain, 1763 ft. (on which the Pinguicula Lusitanica is to be found), the advanced guard of granite hills that extend from hence to Naas, in the co. of Kildare. It is worth while to make an excursion to the summit, leaving the rly. at 5¼ m., Stillorgan, from which point the distance is not great, though the collar-work is heavy. The views over Dublin Bay, the Hill of Howth, and the ranges inland, are at once exquisite and peculiar. At the foot of the hill, near Step-aside, is the ruined tower of Kilgobbin, which, whether from its name or otherwise, is popularly attributed to Gobhan Saer, and was supposed to have contained marvellous treasures at its foundations. The neighbourhood to the l. of the railway is crowded with villas and residences; amongst which are Newtown Park and Stillorgan, the seat of H. Guinness, Esq. (the latter containing some remarkably fine limetrees); the same may be said of Foxrock and Cabinteely, a village situated at the western foot of Killiney Hill, which, with the high ground running down from Kingstown and Dalkey, intercepts the view of the sea for the present. The line has been traversing, between this last range and the Three Rocks, a hill valley sometimes called the Vale of Dundrum; and at *Carrickmines*, 7 m., it enters that of Shangannagh, emerging on the coast at Bray. Near the stat. are some antiquarian remains; on the rt. the ruins of the little ch. of Tully (said by Ledwich to have been built by the Ostmen), with a cross in the burying-ground; and on the l., in the grounds of *Glendruid*, is a cromlech, consisting of a large tablestone, 14 ft. long by 12 broad, supported by 6 uprights.

At the village of Kilternan, near Golden Ball, 2 m. to rt., is a second cromlech, the covering stone of which measures 23 ft. 6 in. by 17 in breadth, and also rests on 6 supporters.

The little ch. of Kilternan presents an ancient side-wall and W. gable, with a blocked squareheaded doorway, the present one being on the S. side. "This alteration was made probably at the time of the re-erection of the E. end, the style of which indicates a period not earlier than the close of the 13th cent., about which time the custom of placing the doorway in the W. end appears to have ceased."—*Wakeman*.

9½ m., at Shankhill stat., a junction is formed with the Kingstown and Dalkey line, and a very picturesque view is obtained of Kil-

Route 23.—Wicklow.

liney Hill, its quarries, and its villas, with a broad expanse of sea on the l., while on the rt. are fresh summits and peaks — the Two Rock Mountain, 1699 ft., on the W., and the Sugarloaf, 1659 ft., just appearing on the S. Immediately to the rt. of the rly. is a rather low hill surmounted by a tower, serving both as a shot-tower and an outlet for the smoke of the lead-mines of Ballycorus. Behind this ridge is the Scalp, leading from Enniskerry to Dublin, described in Rte. 24.

The parish of *Rathmichael*, in which Shankhill is situated, was once of considerable importance, and was claimed by the Vicars Choral of the cathedral of Dublin as their perquisite. There are slight ruins of the ch.

About ¼ m. on rt. of stat. is another cromlech in good preservation, together with a few remains of Puck's Castle and a round tower, though of this last only about 2 ft. exist.

On rt. of the junction are Shanganah Castle (Capt. Hayman), and the ruins of Kilturk ch.

The line now runs along the coast to

12 m. *Bray*, described in Rte. 24. (*Hotels*: Breslin's, International, both first rate; Quin's, good.)

For the remainder of the distance to Wicklow the rly. closely hugs the coast—so closely that in many places it tunnels through projecting headlands or is carried at great heights over cliffs, gullies, and ravines, at the bottom of which the waves may be seen leaping up with terrible fury. Indeed it is difficult to find anywhere more romantically placed or bolder executed works. Gliding out of the stat. at Bray, we round Bray Head by a succession of short tunnels, and on emerging on the other side obtain beautiful views on rt. of the Sugarloaf (Great and Little), with the charming seat of Kilruddery (Earl of Meath) at the foot of the latter. (Rte. 24.) A little before arriving at Greystones, 17 m., we pass on the rt. the ruins of the ch. and Castle of Rathdown. Greystones is a pleasant little bathing-place, about 1½ m. from Delgany, which, with the Glen of the Downs, had better be visited by road from Bray.

Near Kilcoole stat., 20 m., are Ballygannon and the village of Kilcoole 1 m. to rt., and Woodstock House (Col. Tottenham). 22 m., at Newcastle, the hills recede, and leave a considerable tract of level alluvial ground. 25¼ m. Killoughter stat. is 3 m. from Ashford and the neighbourhood of the Devil's Glen.

From this point it is nearly 3 m. to *Wicklow* (anc. Cill-mantain) (*Hotels*: Railway; Fitzwilliam), which, with the quaint-looking town stretching in a semicircle round the bay, the tower of Black Castle, and the distant promontories of Wicklow Head, makes up a very charming landscape.

It is said to have derived its name from its position at the outlet of a long narrow creek, called the Murragh, that runs N. nearly as far as Killoughter, and receives the waters of the Vartry; also to have been called Wigginge Lough, "The Lake of Ships," from its being one of the earliest maritime stations of the Danes. A castle was begun by Maurice Fitzgerald in the 12th, and finished by Fitzwilliam in the 14th cent. Portions of the tower still remain on a promontory at the end of the town. The ch. possesses a copper cupola and a good Norm. doorway, that has been transplanted from an older building.

The town itself is not particularly clean or inviting, but there are some fine walks in the neighbourhood along the cliffs to Bride's and Wicklow Heads, on each of which is a fixed lighthouse.

Conveyances.—Rly. to Dublin and Enniscorthy; car to Shillelagh.

Distances.—Dublin, 28 m.; Rathdrum, 8; Ashford, 4½; Gorey, 25; Arklow, 15; Avoca, 10; Bray, 16.

K 3

Excursions.—
1. Rathdrum and Vale of Avoca.
2. Ashford and Devil's Glen.
3. Wicklow Head.

The rly. now turns inland to the S.W., and ascends towards the mountains, passing the village of Glenealy, where the scenery is picturesque and varied with extensive woods.

On rt. are Glencarrig (Rev. G. Drought), Ballyfree (Rev. H. Tombe), and Hollywood (G. Tombe, Esq.), situate at the wooded base of Carrick Mountain, 1252 ft.; and on l. is a wooded defile known as the Deputy's Pass, from the fact of the army of Sir William Fitzwilliam, the Lord-Deputy, having marched through it in 1595.

36 m. Rathdrum (Rte. 24).

[The road from Wicklow to Arklow is not remarkable in any way; generally speaking it is prettily diversified with hill and dale, keeping inland so as seldom to obtain views of the sea, though frequently of the mountains which keep company on the rt. At 32 m. is Ballymoney House (— Revel, Esq.), and a little farther on, occupying an elevated position, is Westaston, the seat of T. Acton, Esq. At the former spot the road divides; the one keeping closer to the coast, and the other making a slight détour inland, and crossing at Kilboy Bridge the Potters' River, a small stream that runs down through the Deputy's Pass. On its bank, between the 2 roads, is the ruined keep of Danganstown Castle. The character of the coast will be seen to have changed a good deal, for, instead of the steep and rugged cliffs of Wicklow Head, we have now low sandy dunes, interrupted solely by the promontory of Mizen Head. The hills to the rt. and the distant woods to the W. of Arklow plainly show the course of the "sweet vale of Avoca," the mouth of which we cross by a long narrow bridge, and enter the little port of

43 m. *Arklow* (Rte. 24) (*Inn:* Kinsela's), a busy fishing and shipping town, on the side of a hill overlooking the sea. Under the name of Arclogh it was included under those grants of territory for which Henry II. caused service to be done at Wexford, and possessed a castle and a monastery, which have both disappeared save a fragment of the tower of the former. This is the shipping port for the copper and lead-mines in the valley of the Avoca, the material being brought down by a tramroad. In consequence of this trade, Arklow is a rendezvous for a large number of coasters waiting to take the ore to Swansea. The beautiful scenery in the neighbourhood of Shelton and Wooden Bridge is described in the Wicklow tour (Rte. 24).]

Distances.—Wicklow, 15 m.; Gorey, 10; Shelton, 2½; Wooden Bridge, 4.

Continuing by rail from Arklow, the traveller arrives at

Gorey, a small town of one street ¾ m. in length, associated with Ferns as the seat of a bishopric. A little to the N. of the town is Ramsfort, the residence of the family of Ram, which was burned down by the insurgents in the troubles of 1798.

3 m. to the S.E. is Courtown House (Earl of Courtown), in the sheltered valley of the Owenavorragh at its entrance into the sea. The evergreens in the park are especially worthy of notice. "Among them is one which has assumed more the habit of the bush than the tree. Its outline is domical; the stem, at 3 ft. from the ground, is 16 ft. in circumference, but above this it divides into numerous ramifications; the branches extend over an area whose periphery is 210 ft."—*Fraser.*

To the S. of Courtown is the mount of Ardamine, a singular earthen spherical mound standing on an artificial platform. It was probably sepulchral, as the ch. and graveyard of Ardamine are adjoining. The geologist may examine the Lower Silurian rocks in this neighbourhood, the equivalents of the Bala and Caradoc beds of Wales.

Distances.—From Wexford, 25 m.; Ferns, 10½; Newtown Barry, 19; Enniscorthy, 18.

[The direct coach-road to Wexford runs due S. over high ground, descending into the valley of the Owenavorragh river, and passing Ballywalter House (J. Pounden, Esq.), 58 m. the villages of Ballycanew, Killenagh, and Wells House, the prettily-wooded seat of R. Doyne, Esq. When the road again ascends the high ground, the traveller gains distant views on rt. of Vinegar Hill, near Enniscorthy, and the range of Mount Leinster in the far west.

76 m. is the pretty village of Castlebridge, with its neat little ch. and extensive flour-mills; soon after which the long wooden bridge is crossed to 79 m. Wexford.]

The rly. passes Camolin, a decayed village at the head of the valley of the Bann, a tributary of the Slaney. To the N. at the base of Slieveboy, 1385 ft., is the extensive demesne of Camolin Park, formerly the seat of the Earl of Valentia, but now out of repair.

Keeping on rt. some considerable woods, known as Kilbora, Coolpuck, and Coolroe Woods, we arrive at

63½ m. Ferns, a poor, miserable town, yet claiming some importance as being the seat of a bishopric, united with that of Ossory and Leighlin.

In the year 598 Brandubh King of Leinster made a grant to St. Edan, who forthwith built a monastery, in which he was himself interred. Time after time did the city suffer from the incursions of the Danes. John Earl of Morton, who built the castle, offered the bishopric to Giraldus Cambrensis, who, however, refused it. The cathedral is a modern Perp. building with a square embattled tower, built on the site of an old ch. which was supposed to have been the original ch. of St. Edan. There are remains of the monastery for Augustinians founded in the 12th cent. by Dermod M'Murough, consisting of some E. Eng. windows and "a tower of 2 stages, of which the lower is quadrangular and the upper polygonal, and covered with moss and ivy, which give it a circular form; within is a geometrical staircase leading to the top of the square tower."

The castle was a quadrangular fortress overlooking the town. One of the round towers that flanked the corners is still in good preservation, and contains a chapel with a groined roof. The Episcopal Palace dates from the last cent., and is the centre of a pleasant demesne adjoining the cathedral. It was built by Thomas Ram in 1630, "who, being of very advanced age, placed this inscription above the porch—

'This house Ram built for his succeeding brothers:
Thus sheep bear wool, not for themselves, but others.'"

[An extremely pretty excursion can be made to the valley of the Slaney and the town of Newtown Barry, 9 m. From the high ground between Ferns and the Slaney the tourist gains splendid views of Mount Leinster, 2610 ft., Black Stairs, 2409, and White Mountain, 1259—a noble and romantic range that intervenes from N. to S. between the valleys of the Slaney and the Barrow (Rte. 28). 4½ m. the Enniscorthy road is joined on the l. or E. bank of the Slaney, just between Clobemon Hall (M. De Renzy, Esq.) and Ballyrankin (Rev. J. Devereux,.

A little higher up is the village of Clobemon, with its mill and cotton factory.

Here the river is crossed, and the road continues on the W. bank to

9 m. *Newtown Barry* (*Hotel:* Gillis's), a neat and well-built town, in a very fine position overlooking the Slaney, and at the feet of Greenogo and Black Rock Mountains, both shoulders of Mount Leinster. The

Slaney is crossed by a bridge of 7 arches, as is also the Clody, a small stream that here divides Carlow from Wexford. Newtown Barry has a very good agricultural trade, and possesses several flour-mills. The ch.-spire rises prettily from a wooded grove, and the whole town is surrounded by ornamental residences: Woodfield (R. Hall Dare, Esq.), the grounds of which are beautifully laid out, and extend for some distance on each bank of the Slaney; Rainsford Lodge (S. Ram, Esq.); and Ravenswood.

Newtown Barry is a convenient point from whence to ascend Mount Leinster, as the road to Borris passes through the defile of Corrabut Gap between it and Kilbrammish. Take the road to the S. that turns off here, and follow it to a spot called Ninestones, from whence the ascent is steep, but direct. Ninestones is 7½ m. from the town.

Distances.—Ferns, 9 m.; Borris, 14; Clonegall, 5; Enniscorthy, 12.

Excursion.—

Mount Leinster.]

The line now follows the valley of the Barrow, and strikes upon the Slaney near Scarawalsh Bridge, 67 m., a road from which is carried on both sides of the river. On the E. bank is Killabeg (S. Davis, Esq.), Solsborough (Rev. S. Richards), and Greenmount (T. Waring, Esq.).

72 m. *Enniscorthy* (*Hotel:* Nuzam's) is one of the prettiest little towns in the kingdom, the largest portion of it being on a steep hill on the rt. bank of the Slaney, which here becomes a deep and navigable stream, and is crossed by a bridge of 6 arches. From the stream above the bridge dividing its channel the prefix Ennis (Ynys island) was probably obtained, and the latter half of the name is said to have been derived from "Corthoe, the capital of the Coriondi." The things to be seen are a ch. in better taste than most in Ireland, a single tower of the old Franciscan monastery, and the picturesque ivy-covered square keep, flanked by drum towers, of the castle built by Raymond le Gros. It has, however, been modernized, and is inhabited by a caretaker. Overlooking the E. bank is Vinegar Hill, an eminence only 384 ft. in height, but worth ascending, partly for the very fine view over the valley of the Slaney, the Leinster range, and the district towards the coast, and partly from the association of the battle of Vinegar Hill, on the 29th May, 1798, when the insurgents, in number upwards of 10,000 men, were attacked by Gen. Lake and completely routed. The rebels had a few days previously succeeded in plundering and very nearly destroying Enniscorthy, many of the loyal inhabitants having been captured, led to the camp, and put to death. A great deal of trade is carried on here, coal being brought up the river from Wexford into the interior, and corn and butter sent back.

In the neighbourhood of the town, on the Borris road, are Verona (G. F. Newbery, Esq.), Daphney Castle (T. Davies, Esq.), Monart (Counsellor Cookman), and Killoughrum (T. Buckley, Esq,); the latter in the midst of a thick and extensive plantation known as Killoughrum Forest.

Conveyances.—Cars daily to Waterford, to Wexford; rail to Dublin.

Excursions.—
1. Newtown Barry.
2. Vinegar Hill.
3. Ferns.

Distances.—Gorey, 18 m.: Wexford, 13½; Newtown Barry, 12; Ferns, 8; Ballywilliam, 14, [to which latter place it is an uninteresting drive, relieved during the latter portion by fine views of Mount Leinster and Blackstairs.]

The road from Enniscorthy to Wexford is full of great beauty, in which the chief elements are a noble river with lofty wooded banks, rich pastures, and pleasant country-houses.

On the opposite or W. bank, a little below the confluence of the Urrin, is the site of St. John's House for Augustine Friars. On the rt. bank, Borodale (D. Beatty, Esq.) and Bormount (V. Bartolucci, Esq. ; on the l. bank Rochfort (Mrs. Callaghan), and Edermine, the charming seat of Sir J. Power, Bart.

Here the road gradually draws off from the river, and, as it ascends higher ground, commands even more beautiful views. 77 m., rt. bank, are Mackmine (J. Richards, Esq.); and below, Bellevue (A. Cliffe, Esq.) and Brookhill (T. Bell, Esq.), opposite to which on rt. is Kyle House (P. Harvey, Esq.).

[At Kyle Cross Roads, 80 m., a road on l. leads to Castlebridge (p. 203); passing St. Edmond's (Capt. Irvine) and Artramon (G. Le Hunte, Esq.), 2 fine estates on the N. shore of the estuary, together with the ruined ch. and keep of Artramon Castle. By this road, however, the tourist loses a beautiful landscape, as he descends to the wooden bridge over the Slaney, which narrows at this point, swelling out on the l. in a broad estuary, and on the rt. in a quiet reach with high rocky banks fringed with brushwood. A ruined tower commands the bridge on the N., and there are also slight traces of one on the S., said to have been the first fortress erected by the Anglo-Normans in Ireland. Looking up the river are Killowen P. Walker, Esq.) and Ardcandrisk (Hon. Mrs. Morgan on opposite banks, and on the l. bounding the N. shore is Saunders Court (Earl of Arran).

Crossing the bridge, where a toll has to be paid, the road divides; on the rt. to Enniscorthy by the rt. bank and on the l. to]

85½ m. *Wexford* (Rte. 28, (*Hotel*: White's, tolerable . Pop. 11,673. At a distance Wexford is a pleasant-looking place, owing to its situation on the side of a hill, the summit of which is plentifully garnished with wood and overlooks the estuary of the Slaney and Wexford Haven. But the streets are inconvenient, and narrow to such a degree that it is a matter of arrangement to prevent 2 vehicles meeting each other in the principal thoroughfares ; indeed, the tourist when ensconced in his hotel is rather startled to find himself with an Asmodeus-like view of the interiors of the opposite houses. Wexford is, however, a quaint and ancient little place, and a day may be spent to advantage. It was an early and important maritime settlement of the Danes, and from its secure harbour and its proximity to England was naturally one of the earliest landing-places of the Anglo-Norman invaders. Here Strongbow resided and celebrated the marriage of his sister Basilica with Raymond le Gros; and here, in modern times, were the head-quarters of the rebels in '98, who kept it for nearly a month in their possession, and put to death 91 of the inhabitants. Wexford was a walled town, and possessed an unusually early charter, granted by Adomar de Valence in 1318. Of these walls, "5 of the towers, 3 square and 2 round, are still in a sufficient state of preservation to show that the walls were 22 ft. high, and were supported on the inside by a rampart of earth 24 ft. thick."

At the W. end of the town, where the W. gate stood, are the ruins of St. Peter and St. Paul, usually called Selsker ch. This abbey was founded at the close of the 12th cent. by the Roches, Lords of Fermoy, and seems to have partaken a good deal of the defensive character : but of late years so much modern building has taken place here, that it has almost destroyed the main features of the ruins. Connected with the ancient tower is the modern E. Eng. ch. of St. Selsker, on the site of the spot where the first treaty ever signed by the English and Irish was ratified in 1169. There is a singular legend that Cromwell took away the peal of bells from this ch., and shipped them off to a ch. in Liverpool; in return for which, freedom of the town and exemption from port dues were granted to Wexford merchants.

Nearly in the centre of the town are the scanty ruins of St. Mary's.

As regards religious edifices, the Roman Catholics carry off the palm in Wexford, and the tourist should not omit to visit St. Peter's ch., an elaborate and really beautiful Dec. building with a very lofty spire and a remarkably good rose-window. This ch. is attached to St. Peter's College on Summer Hill, overlooking the town, which, with its square central tower, is a conspicuous object. As a county-town, Wexford possesses the institutions usually found, but none of them are worth seeing, except the gaol at the W. end, a fine castellated building.

One of its most singular features is the wooden bridge built by Lemuel Cox, the American bridge architect; as it stands at present it consists of 2 causeways projecting from the opposite banks, 650 and 188 ft. long respectively, the roadway between being 733 ft. The state of the bridge-flooring, however, is such, that the traveller who crosses it by coach, and sees the boards tilt up as it passes, becomes very uncertain as to the probability of getting safe to the other side: so bad is it indeed that the Wexford citizens are bestirring themselves to build a new one. "The harbour is of an oblong shape, formed by the estuary of the Slaney, extending 8 m. from N. to S. or parallel with the coast, and 4 m. wide, comprising an area of 14,000 acres. It is admirably situated for commerce from its proximity to England and being at the entrance of the Irish Channel; but these advantages are not available in consequence of a bar at the mouth, having only 18 ft. water at high tides. The quays extend 1000 yards in length, and there is a dockyard and patent slip."— *Thom's 'Directory.'*

Conveyances. — Coaches to Enniscorthy and Waterford.

Excursions.—
1. Forth Mountains.
2. Lady's Island.
3. Enniscorthy.
4. Taghmon. (Rte. 28.)

Distances.—Dublin, 79 m.; Gorey, 26; Arklow, 36; Enniscorthy, 13½; Forth Mountains, 5; New Ross, 22; Duncannon, 23; Ballywilliam, 28.

[An excursion into the barony of Forth, which extends S. to the seacoast, is replete with interest, partly from the number of fortified houses and towers, of which there are said to be nearly 60 in an area of 40,000 acres, and partly from the fact that the barony is inhabited by the descendants of a Welsh colony, somewhat in the same way as the districts of Castlemartin and Gower on the opposite Pembrokeshire coast are inhabited by Flemings. Indeed, it would be more correctly stated that the Wexford colonists were descended from old residents in Wales, rather than Welshmen, as there is no doubt but that the Norman, English, and Flemish families who had gained possessions in South Wales, were the adventurers who pushed their fortunes and settled in Ireland. Many names belonging to the Principality, such as Carew, Roche, Scurlock, Barry, &c., are naturalized in Ireland. The present inhabitants of Forth and Bargy are said to be peculiar in their dialect, habits, and folk-lore.

Quitting Wexford by the S. road and leaving the Forth Mountains to the rt., the tourist reaches, 4 m., Johnstown Castle (Sir T. Esmonde, Bart.), a beautiful castellated residence built of Carlow granite and incorporated with a tower of the old fortress. The grounds are very ornamental and well laid out.

6½ m. Rathmacknee (Capt. Armstrong), near which, in remarkably good preservation, is the ancient fortalice of the same name. About 4 m. to the S. is another castellated residence, that of Bargy, formerly the property of the ill-fated Bagenal Harvey, and now of his descendant John Harvey, Esq. It is situated at the head of Tacumshin Lake, a pill that runs inland for some little distance. The coast in this neighbourhood was notorious for the number of wrecks that annually took place, before it was lighted as well as it now is. The Saltee Islands enjoyed a particularly bad reputation amongst sailors, as there are a number of banks and half-tide rocks extending from thence to the Tuskar, but they are now protected by a light-ship showing a fixed double light. Between Bargy and Rathmacknee is the ruined ch. of Mayglass, which possesses some semicircular-headed arches.

13 m., at the head of Lady's Island Lake, are the ruins of the same name, erected in 1237 by Rodolph de Lamporte or Lambert, and consisting—1, of a keep, entered by an arched gateway and connected by side walls with the water on either side; 2, a tower adjoining appears to have been built at a later date, as it is of limestone, whereas the former one is of granite; 3, of an Augustinian monastery, which, being dedicated to the Virgin, probably gave the name to the island.

On the coast to the E. is Ballytrent House (J. Talbot, Esq.), in whose grounds is a remarkably perfect rath, consisting of 2 concentric enclosures, the outer one being 649 yards in circumference. Some distance out at sea is the famous Tuskar Rock, on which a lighthouse was established in 1815. "It consists of 21 Argand lamps acting on reflectors, having 7 lamps, presenting one light every 2 minutes, while one seven of the 21 presents a deep red light every 6 minutes—the term of the revolution. The lights are 105 ft. from the base, and the vane from highwater mark is 134 ft." The district to the W. between Wexford and Duncannon is described in Rte. 28.]

ROUTE 24.

FROM DUBLIN TO RATHDRUM AND ARKLOW.—TOUR THROUGH WICKLOW.

A tour through Wicklow is the great delight of all Dublin residents, who are, indeed, fortunate in having almost at their own doors a succession of changing scenery, in which mountain, sea, wood, and river, are blended together in delicious landscapes, from the quietly beautiful to the strikingly romantic, furnishing an environ that no other city in the world can boast.

The direct line from Dublin to Bray is described in Rte. 23, and the rly. from Kingstown to Dublin in Rte. 1. It will therefore be sufficient if we commence this route from Kingstown. The rly., which up to this point has closely hugged the seashore, now runs inland for a short distance, cutting off the promontory of Dalkey 8 m., and passing on l. Bullock's Castle, a tall, square keep, with Irish stepped battlements, flanked by a square turret at one angle, and surrounded by a bawn. A little distance from Sorrento Point, on which is a terrace of fashionable residences, is *Dalkey Island*, separated from the mainland by a sound 900 yards long and 300 wide. Upon it is a small ruined ch., originally founded for Benedictines. Dalkey, however, does not found its claims to distinction upon this, but upon certain farcical proceedings periodically enacted at the close of the last century, when it was called the Kingdom of Dalkey, and was the seat of a singular mock ceremonial, where the so-called King held his Court amidst much noisy rejoicing and festivity. He was dignified with the title of "His facetious Majesty Stephen the First, King of Dalkey, Emperor of Muglins, Prince of the Holy Island of Magee, Elector of Lambay and Ireland's Eye, Defender of his own Faith and Respecter of all others, Sovereign of the Illustrious Order of the Lobster and Periwinkle." Such an absurd burlesque would scarcely be worth the chronicling, had not the spirit of the times, together with the social status of the actors, infused into it a large amount of politics, so much so as to cause the daily papers to devote a regular column to the doings of "the Kingdom of Dalkey."

Conspicuous on the rt. are the granite-quarries of Dalkey and *Killiney* Hill, which rises in bold outline to the height of 480 ft. The former of these were worked from 1817 to 1857, and supplied most of the stone used in the formation of Kingstown Harbour. "In general character the Killiney and Dalkey granite is rather quartzose, of pale, clear-gray colour, and is traversed by numerous veins of eurite. These frequently assume the magnitude of thick dykes, one of which to the N. of the rock called Black Castle, on the shore of Killiney Bay, measures 40 yds. across. On the southern flank of Roche's Hill, close to the garden wall of Killiney Park, is a remarkable granite dyke traversing the mica slate." — *Geological Survey*. This last-named mica schist is, in fact, Lower Silurian slate altered from the contact with the granite, which feature can be observed in many places along the shore of Killiney Hill. The hill itself is private property, but the owner permits visitors access to enjoy the glorious panorama from the summit. The botanist will find on its slopes Asplenium maximum, Galium erectum, G. saxatile, and Crithmum maritimum or the samphire-plant.

Near the martello tower stands "The Druid's Judgment Seat," formed of rough granite blocks, "which bear many indications of having been re-arranged at no very distant period." Mr. Wakeman considers it to be an archæological forgery, founded on a veritable early remain.

The antiquary should also visit Killiney ch., one of those ancient and primitive buildings so characteristic of early Irish architecture. It is about the same date as the ch. at Glendalough (p. 216), and consists of a nave measuring 12½ ft. in breadth, and a chancel only 9½ ft. The doorway is in the west gable, and is square-headed, with slightly inclined sides. Notice the primitive form of cross sculptured on the soffit of the lintel. The height of the circular choir arch is 6½ ft. The E. window is square-headed, with inwardly inclined splays. "The comparatively modern addition on the northern side of the nave, which appears to have been erected as a kind of aisle, is connected with the ancient ch. by several openings broken through the N. side wall. The pointed doorway offers a striking contrast to that in the W. gable; and its eastern window differs from that in the chancel, being larger, and chamfered on the exterior."— *Wakeman*. At the summit of Killiney is an obelisk, marking the spot where a Duke of Dorset was thrown and killed when hunting.

The visitor can, if he prefers, descend on the other side of the hill to Mount Druid, and, after seeing the cromlech, catch a train on the Harcourt Road line.

13¼ m. *Bray*, the Brighton of Dublin, and the sunniest and gayest of watering-places. *Hotels*: the Royal Breslin, facing the sea, and the International, both first class. It is only within the last few years that Bray has emerged from the primitive quiet of the fishing village into the full-blown gaiety which it now exhibits —a change partly owing to the exquisite scenery of which it is the portal, and partly to the earnest spirit with which Mr. Dargan devoted himself to improving and beautifying a locality which his far-seeing eye told him was so admirably adapted for it. In one respect, too, he was fortunate, for, as the ground was new, there was little or no portion of ancient Bray to be pulled down; so that to all intents and purposes we may consider it essentially a place of to-day. The station is close to the sea, between the two large hotels of Breslin and the International, both of them establishments of great size, and some pretensions to architectural beauty. The situation of the town is very charming, occupying a broadish basin, and surrounded on all sides by hills, save on that which is bounded by the sea. On the N. are Killiney and Two Rocks; on the W. the mountains at the back of Enniskerry; more to the S. are the Sugarloaves, with the lofty range of Douce, which, as seen from Bray Head, rises directly from the town. From all these hills wooded shoulders are thrown out, softening their stern features, and insensibly merging into the well-kept grounds and parks of the many residences in the neighbourhood. Bray itself contains little to interest the tourist, save a very pretty old ch. with a tower at the W. end, as almost all the other buildings are modern. From the general loveliness of the place, its accessibility to Kingstown and Dublin, and its genial and even temperature, it is much sought after as a place of residence; and in consequence many fine terraces and streets have risen up with wonderful rapidity. The neighbourhood, however, is not so soon exhausted as the town, and affords a constant succession of pleasant drives and excursions.

1. To Bray Head. The southern road towards Delgany should be taken, passing l. Newcourt; 1 m. the suburb of Newtown Vevay; and soon after on l. the entrance to Bray Head (G. Putland, Esq.). 2 m. rt. is Kilruddery, a very charming Elizabethan residence of the Earl of Meath, who permits visitors to inspect it on Mondays and Tuesdays. In the interior is a fine hall, wainscoted with oak, with a carved oak ceiling. This leads to several beautiful apartments, of which the drawing-room is particularly worthy of notice. Kilruddery was built after designs by Morrison, the architect of Shelton. The gardens are worth seeing, and the views from the grounds, which slope up towards the Little Sugarloaf, are exquisite. Opposite Kilruddery Gate is a road leading up to the Bray Head, 655 ft., a fine breezy headland, commanding a noble panorama of the Wicklow Hills and the sea. Should the pedestrian wish it, he may extend his ramble to the S., rejoining the turnpike at Windgate; but the pleasantest way homewards is to get on to what is called the Railway Walk, which offers some fine scenery of the ravines and gullies across which the line is carried. The ramble to Windgate, and back by the Head, will be 6 m. The geologist will find at the foot of the Head numbers of specimens of the Oldhamia antiqua; this, together with Howth, being the only known locality in Ireland.

2. The Glen of the Downs is described in the continuation of the route p. 212.

3. To the Scalp (p. 219), through Enniskerry, returning by Old Connaught, the beautiful seat of P. Riall, Esq. (now vacant), which, from its situation, is a conspicuous object in all Bray views.

4. The Dargle and Powerscourt are the great lions of the district, and the picnic rendezvous, *par excellence*, of every Dublin holiday-maker. The road turns off from the one to Dublin, and runs through Little Bray, following upwards the valley of the Bray river, locally called the Valley of Diamonds; it is set off with many a pretty villa, and begirdled with woods, over which the distant hills show their summits. More extensive views are obtained from Lord Herbert's new road, which falls into the main road at the pretty new ch. of Kilbride. On the N. side of the Cookstown stream is St. Valery, the picturesque residence of the late Judge Crampton, the grounds of which are worth a visit. At Fassaroe is a well-preserved cross, with a sculptured representation of Our Saviour. A little further, on l., is the entrance to the Dargle, the road to Enniskerry keeping straight on by the Cookstown river. By this entrance, however, pedestrians only are admitted, cars having to keep along the road and wait for their occupants at the second gate. The walks on the northern bank, through which the visitor is allowed to ramble, belong to the Powerscourt demesne; and those on the opposite side to Charleville, the property of Lord Monck. The Dargle, about which so much has been said and written, is a deep, thickly-wooded glen, at the bottom of which flows the Dargle river, an impetuous mountain-stream; and in truth it well deserves admiration, for a more lovely dingle it is difficult to conceive. Nevertheless it is a question whether it would have been the theme of so much admiration were it not for its easy accessibility and its proximity to Dublin; for, while confessing its charms, there are yet many glens containing finer or more romantic scenery. The chief points of rendezvous are the Lover's Leap, "a huge rock, projecting far from the glen's side, and overlooking rt. and l. the still depths of the ravine. Shadowing, and bending away in a densely-wooded slope, the opposite side of the glen rises grandly upwards; while 300 ft. down below us steals the ever-present river towards the sea, the blue line of whose distant horizon rules the topmost branches of the trees away on our l."—*Powell.* There are also the Moss House and the View Rock, from whence a good distant view is gained of Powerscourt, backed up by the lofty ranges of Kippure. Having exhausted the beauties of the Dargle, the tourist emerges from the second, or furthest gate, into the turnpike-road, between Dublin and Rathdrum. If a short excursion only is intended, he can turn to the rt. to Enniskerry, and retrace his way back to Bray by the N. bank of the Cookstown stream; but, if bent on seeing the waterfall, he should follow the road to the l., running between the woods of Powerscourt and the grounds of *Tinnahinch* (Lady Louisa Grattan), a plain house, surrounded by dense woods, which founds its reputation on having been the residence and favourite retreat of Henry Grattan, to whom it was presented by the Irish Parliament. There is an exquisite view at Tinnahinch Bridge, where the Dargle is again crossed, and where the road ascends, having on l. Bushy Park (Rt. Hon. Judge Keogh) and Ballyorney (Maj. Kenny); and on rt. Charleville, the seat of Lord Monck. At the S. end of these demesnes is the Glebe House, $4\frac{1}{2}$ m., where a road on rt. turns off to enter Lord Powerscourt's deer-park, a large enclosure of some 800 acres, "of which the greater part is under young plantations; enough, however,

of the old trees remain to carry back the imagination to what this place was some years ago, when venerable oaks were scattered along the sides of the glen, and when herds of deer bounded over the fern-covered surface, or stood motionless on the cliffs when danger was in the wind."— *Fraser*.

It is a charming excursion through the deer-park to the waterfall, where the Dargle is precipitated over a rock 300 ft. in height, immediately under the N.E. side of the Douce Mountain. It is certainly a very fine fall, though, like every other, dependent for scenic effect on the volume of water in the river. From hence an ascent may be made to the summit of the Douce, 2384 ft., which, with its compeers and neighbours, War Hill, 2250 ft., and Kippure, 2475 ft., are amongst the loftiest of this northern chain of Wicklow mountains. The views, seawards and landwards, are wonderfully fine, the latter embracing range after range in Wicklow, and even in Waterford.

Powerscourt waterfall is usually the limit of a Bray excursion, but if the traveller has time he may, with advantage, follow from the deer-park the road up the Glencree to Loughbray 5 m. from the point where the Dargle is crossed at Valclusa). Here are two mountain tarns, Upper and Lower Lough Bray, occupying deep basins just under the summit of Kippure, being 1453 ft. and 1225 ft. respectively above the level of the sea. Amongst the plants that have their habitat here are, Isoetes lacustris, Poa pratensis, and Listera cordata. On the N. bank of the latter lake, which is much the largest, is a picturesque old English cottage, built for the late Sir Philip Crampton by the Duke of Northumberland: very near which spot the road falls into the Great Military Road, and, winding round the head of the glen at Glencree Barracks, runs down on the opposite side to Enniskerry, passing at the back of the grounds of *Powerscourt* (Lord Powerscourt). To see the grounds and house an order is necessary, to be obtained from the agent at Enniskerry. The mansion is a plain building, chiefly remarkable for its size and the unsurpassable beauty of its situation. The principal interest internally is the large saloon, in which George IV. partook of a banquet in 1821. The whole of the demesne occupies 26,000 acres, being the largest and most varied estate of any in this part of the kingdom. The botanist will find in the neighbourhood of Powerscourt and Dargle — Polypodium phlegopteris, Aspidium dumetosum and on Douce Mt.), Trichomanes brevisetum, Hymenophyllum Tunbridgense, Carex pendula, C. strigosa (Dargle), Festuca calamaria (Dargle), Poa pratensis, Circæa lutetiana, Arenaria trinervis, Viola palustris; and in Glencree, Cnicus pratensis, Hymenophyllum Wilsoni. If the tourist intends seeing the waterfall after the house, he should leave the park by a gate opposite Tinnahinch; but if he is returning to Bray, by a fine Grecian gateway very near the little town of *Enniskerry* (*Hotel:* Shirley's), famous for its situation in the centre of a district teeming with beauty. Nearly opposite the park-gates is a very pretty Protestant ch., the spire of which is sheathed with copper. For the pedestrian who wishes to extend his rambles with greater ease, or for the angler, Enniskerry is more convenient than Bray.

An omnibus runs daily between the two places. The pedestrian should not omit to ascend the Great Sugarloaf, which is perfectly easy, though steep, and commands a finer panoramic view than any mountain in the district, embracing in clear weather the hills of Wales.

The whole of the neighbourhood of Bray abounds in pretty villas and seats. In addition to those already mentioned are, near the Dublin road, Wilfort C. Toole, Esq., Moatfield

(D. Mackay, Esq.). Old Connaught House, Palermo (Miss Hutchinson), Cork Abbey (Col. Verner), Ravenswell, Mount Eden, Jubilee Hall, &c.

Conveyances.—Rail to Dublin and Wicklow; omnibus to Enniskerry three times a day.

Distances.—Dublin, 12 m.; Killiney, 4; Kingstown, 7; Shankill, 2½; the Scalp, 5; Kilternan, 6; the Dargle, 3; Tinnahinch, 3½; Powerscourt, 4; Enniskerry, 3; Glencree, 9; Waterfall, 7; Roundwood, 12½; Glendalough and seven churches, 19; Annamoe, 15; Lough Bray, 10; Delgany, 5; Bray Head, 1½; Glen of the Downs, 5; Devil's Glen, 10; Newtown Mount Kennedy, 9; Rathdrum, 24; Wicklow, 16.

Three roads leave Bray for the S.; the one nearest the coast runs direct to Wicklow parallel with the rly. (Rte. 23). The middle one should be followed by the tourist to Newtown Mount Kennedy.

2 l. is *Hollybrook*, the seat of Sir George Hodson, and a favourite showplace for visitors to Bray. The house is of Tudor style, and in very good taste. It replaced an older mansion, dating from the 17th century, a fact to which may be attributed the age and luxuriance of the shrubs and evergreens, particularly the ilex and arbutus. Hollybrook was once the residence of Robin Adair, so famous in Irish song. On the opposite side of the road is Wingfield (H. Darby, Esq.). The scenery is wonderfully picturesque, as the road passes a defile between the Great and Little Sugarloaf, two of the most conspicuous and characteristic eminences in Wicklow, the former 1659 ft., and the latter 1120 ft. Although steep and very conelike in summit, they are perfectly accessible, and afford a view well worth the trouble of ascent. The Hymenophyllum Wilsoni and the pretty Potentilla argentea grow on their sides. At Kilmurry, it is said, but on no authority, that General Wolfe was born.

At the 5 m. the tourist enters a very charming scene at the *Glen of the Downs*, a deep woodland ravine of a good mile in length, the banks of which on either side rise to the height of some 800 ft. At the entrance is Glenview, the residence of W. Lindsay, Esq.; and running parallel with it on the l. is Bellevue, the beautiful park of the La Touche family. A very extensive view is obtained from a little temple erected on the top of the bank. At the S. entrance of the glen [a road on l. leads to Delgany (*Hotel:* Fitzsimon's), from whence the traveller may return to Bray by rail].

9 m. *Newtown Mount Kennedy* (*Hotel:* Newell's) is a small town, remarkable only for the charming scenery and for the number of handsome residences in its neighbourhood —Mount Kennedy House (R. G. Cuninghame, Esq.); Tinnapark (J. Clarke, Esq.); Glendarragh (T. Barton, Esq.); Altidore (late Rev. L. Hepenstall), in the grounds of which are some well-arranged cascades; Woodstock House (Col. Tottenham).

Conveyances. — Cars to Delgany station.

Distances. — Rathdrum, 15 m.; Devil's Glen, 8; Glen of the Downs, 4; Kilcoole village, 2—station, 3.

The next point of interest is at 12 m. the prettily wooded glen of Dunran, where there is some good rock-landscape.

15 m. *Ashford* (*Hotel:* Ashford) is a pleasant spot for a short stay, and the centre of some of the prettiest scenery in Wicklow. It is situated on the bank of the Vartry river, which, after flowing through the Devil's Glen, has but a short course prior to its entering the Murrough of Wicklow. 1 m. from Ashford to the E. is Newrath Bridge (*Hotel:* Hunter's, good), adjoining which is Rosanna House, the seat of D. Tighe, Esq., a former member of whose family lives in the recollection of the lovers of Irish

poetry as the authoress of 'Psyche' (Rte. 26). The grounds and house of Broomfield (F. Wakefield, Esq.) are worth a visit. But the excursion *par excellence* of Ashford is the Devil's Glen, a very fine and romantic defile of nearly 2 m. in length, through which the Vartry flows. It is of a different nature from that of the Dargle, the chief characteristic of which is wood; while here rock scenery predominates. Cars are not allowed to drive up, but have to wait on the road some little distance from the head of the glen. Bordering the ravine on either side are Glenmore Castle, the seat of F. Synge, Esq., and Ballycurry House (C. Tottenham, Esq., M.P.); and immediately at the entrance, adjoining the bridge of Nun's Cross, is the Protestant ch. The botanist will find in the glen Asplenium ceterach. Between Roundwood and the head of the glen are the newly constructed reservoirs of the Dublin Waterworks, from whence the waters of the Vartry are made to supply the necessities of the Dublin population. Here is a storage reservoir of 400 acres, or five times that of the ill-fated reservoir of Sheffield. When filled, this basin will hold 2,482,810,483 gallons of water, being a supply of 12,000,000 gallons daily for 200 days. The embankment is 1600 feet long by 500 wide, the material being puddled earth faced with granite.

Distances. — Rathdrum, 10 m.; Devil's Glen, 1; Newrath Bridge, 1; Rathnew, 2¼; Wicklow, 4¼; Newtown Mount Kennedy, 6; Glendalough, 9½; Annamoe, 6; Roundwood, 12.

The visitor has choice of two roads, — one, through Ballinalea to Glenealy (Rte. 23,, a picturesque and prettily-wooded route; the other, on the N. side of Carrick Mount, 1252 ft., is more hilly and desolate, until within 2 or 3 miles of

Rathdrum (a poor Inn), perched in the most romantic way, like many a Tyrolese village, on the steep banks of the Annamoe, which runs through a very beautifully wooded ravine. Neither the town itself nor the accommodation offers sufficient inducement for the traveller to stay here; and he will only bait his horse or change his car previous to his excursion to Glendalough or Arklow, to which latter place he may, if he choose, proceed by the rly. (Rte. 23), running between Bray and Enniscorthy, but by this means he will lose half the beauty of the route.

Conveyances.— Rail to Wooden Bridge, Arklow, Enniscorthy, and Dublin.

Distances. — Ashford, 10 m.; Wooden Bridge, 8; Wicklow, 8; Arklow, 12; Meeting of the Waters, 3; Drumgoff, 7; Laragh, 7; Seven Churches, 8; Roundwood, 12; Annamoe, 9½; Devil's Glen, 11; Bray, 25.

The road to Wooden Bridge and Arklow now follows the high ground on the rt. bank of the Annamoe, into the lovely valley of which the traveller gets frequent peeps. Passing Avondale (— Edwards, Esq.) and Kingston House, the magnificent situation of Castle Howard (R. Brooke, Esq.) is the principal object of attention, together with the exquisite view of the Vale of Avoca and the Meeting of the Waters, described in Moore's well-known stanzas.

"The meeting" is at the confluence of the Avonmore and Avonbeg, which here unite in their course to the sea at Arklow. When seen from above the vale is charming, though it must be confessed that tourists often feel a certain amount of disappointment in it, a necessary result when any place or thing has been exaggerated; and were it not for the immortality conferred on Avoca by Ireland's poet, it would have simply ranked as one out of the hundreds of pretty valleys in this district. Moreover the soft charm about it is rather dispelled by the new rly. from Rathdrum to Gorey, and by the fact that the vale has become the scene of very considerable mining operations. "The metalliferous clayslate district occupies but a small space, being very narrow in breadth, and not more than 10 m. long from Croghan-Kinshela on the S. to W. Acton on the N. At various depths occur beds of what is known as soft ground, containing one or more layers of copper pyrites, varying in thickness, and sometimes acquiring a breadth of several fathoms. Five of such beds are met with, one in Connoree, two in the old or upper mine of Cronbane, one in the new mine, and one in Tigroney."—*Kane*. These 3 mines are on the E. side of the Avoca, and on the W. are those of Ballymurtagh, which have yielded a great deal of copper. Associated with the copper lodes are beds of bisulphuret of iron, which for many years was an actual impediment and detriment to the work; but owing to an exorbitant tariff placed on the article of sulphur by the Neapolitan Government, the iron pyrites became very valuable as an article from which to extract the pure sulphur. "The copper-ore at Ballymurtagh contains at least 30 per cent. of sulphur-ore; and the greater part of the pyrites workings in the same mine contain about 2½ per cent. of copper." The presence of the sulphur is abundantly manifested in the yellow colour of the soil and of the stream. Neither is it unpicturesque; but at one spot near Ballymurtagh, where an immense cliff stands boldly overhanging the road, it produces effects of great beauty from the rich colouring of the metallic stains on the face of the rock.

30 m. at *Newbridge* is a very pretty new ch. Continuing down the vale, and passing l. Ballyarthur House (Col. Bayley), the tourist arrives at a second and far more beautiful meeting of the waters at 33 m. Woodenbridge, where there is a comfortable little hotel.

The valleys of the Aughrim and the Gold Mines rivers here fall into that of the Avoca, which turns to the S.E. to join the sea at Arklow.

[A branch rly. runs up the Aughrim valley, which contains some good scenery in the vicinity of Aughrim bridge and Rodenagh bridge, where the two streams of the Ow and Derry join to form the Aughrim. At the head of the valley of the Derry and surrounded by hills is *Tinnahely*, a neat little town belonging to Lord Fitzwilliam, whose seat of Coolattin is about 3 m. to the S. Adjoining it, and indeed forming part of the property, is the wood of Shillelagh, famous for having given its name to the pet weapon of the Irishman, whose talent for head-breaking would at once be destroyed were he deprived of his shillelagh. As the greater portion of the wood was cut down about 1693 to supply the ironworks of that period, only a few plantations are left. Except for the scenery, Tinnahely offers no inducement for a visit.

The stream of the Gold Mines has but a short course from the sides of Croghan Kinsheela, a mountain that at one time obtained a large degree of notoriety from the discovery of gold in such quantities that it was believed to be a perfect El Dorado. "It occurred in massive lumps, and in small pieces down to the minutest grain; the gold was found accompanied by other metallic substances dispersed through a kind of stratum, composed of clay, sand, gravel, and fragments of rock, and covered by soil which sometimes attained a very considerable depth in the bed and banks of the stream. The total quantity of gold collected by the Government workings, in about 2 years, was 945 oz., which was sold for 3675*l.*; but the cost of the workings and of various trials made in search of the original deposit of the gold exceeded the return, and the operations, having been interrupted, were not again resumed by Government. It has been calculated that at least 10,000*l.* was paid to the country people for gold collected before Government took possession; the gold was associated with magnetic iron-stone, iron pyrites, brown and red hæmatite, manganese, and fragments of tin-stone in crystals, together with quartz."—*Kane.*

Distances from Wooden Bridge :— Tinnahely, 12 m. ; Aughrim, 4½ ; Rathdrum, 8; Arklow, 4, the road to which place is replete with beauties of wood and river, passing between the demesnes of rt. Glenart Castle, the seat of the Earl of Carysfort, and l. Shelton Abbey, a beautiful Gothic mansion of the Earl of Wicklow, built from designs by Morrison, "meant to convey to the spectator the idea of an ancient abbey, changed after the Reformation, into a baronial residence." In the interior are a beautiful hall and saloon, leading into the cloister gallery, by which the chief apartments are approached. There are some good paintings and a fine library, the greater portion of which was collected by Lord Chancellor West. Visitors are allowed to inspect the grounds. Passing rt. Ballyraine H. Hodgson, Esq.) and Lambertown, the tourist arrives at 37 m. Arklow (Rte. 23*j.*).]

The tourist who prefers a wild mountain route instead of the sheltered river valleys, may take a circuitous course from Rathdrum to the Seven Churches by the Great Military Road, joining it at Drumgoff Barracks, 7 m. This fine work was completed with a view to opening up the fastnesses of the Wicklow Mts. during the troublous times of the rebellion, and thus enabling large bodies of military and police to move quickly through the district. It commences in the hilly country some 4 m. N. of Tinnahely, and runs due N. to the Barracks of Aghavannagh, Drumgoff, Laragh, and Glencree, keeping for the whole distance a solitary mountain course, at the height of 1600 or 1700 ft. above the sea, and but seldom descending to any of the valleys. From Glencree it continues over the Killakee Hills (passing Killakee House, the residence of Mrs. White, from whence one of the finest possible views is obtained over the Dublin plain), and finally ends at Rathfarnham. From Drumgoff a road runs W. to Dunlavin : this is a good route from which to ascend Lugnaquilla, which towers on the l. to the height of 3039 ft. ; the view extends a marvellous distance, especially on the S. into Wexford, Waterford, and Cork.

The return from Rathdrum to Dublin should be through the western portion of the co. of Wicklow, following upwards the stream of the Avonmore ; the road runs through thick groves of wood, at a considerable height above the river, to 3 m. Clara Bridge, an extremely pretty village at the bottom of the Vale of Avonmore, on the sides of which rise Trooperstown Hill, 1408 ft., on rt., and Kirikee, 1559 ft., on l. Nearly at the head of the vale, at the entrance of the grounds of Derrybawn (Mrs. Bookey), the great military road is joined, 1 m. from which, at Laragh, a road on l. turns sharply off to 8 m. Jordan's Hotel, a very comfortable and romantic resting-place in the immediate vicinity of the Seven Churches and the Vale of Glendalough.

Two valleys fall in at this point from the N.E.—the Vale of Glendasan, a river which has a course of about 3 m. from Lough Nahanagan, and the Vale of Glendalough, the upper portion of which is watered by a small stream, the Glencalo, that descends from its rocky fastnesses in the Table Mt. to fall into the upper and lower lakes ; the scenery of the upper lake is of a very grand character. On the N., Camaderry, 2296 ft., and on the S. Lugduff, 2176 ft., rise in fine escarpments from the brink of the water, approaching so closely together at the head as scarce to leave a passage for the mountain torrent that feeds the lake. The lower lake is much smaller, and the valley is much more open; but the presence of the round tower and the deserted ruins gives it an aspect of weird melancholy quite indescribable—an aspect very much enhanced if the clouds are lowering over the head of the lake,

——" whose gloomy shore
Skylark never warbles o'er."

and throwing dark shadows over the pass. Before exploring any of the ravines and glens in the neighbourhood, the visitor will of course bestow his attention first of all on the ecclesiastical ruins of the valley.

The foundation of the city of Glendalough may be ascribed to St. Kevin, who as early as the 6th cent. founded a ch. on the S. bank of the upper lake, from which he subsequently removed to the opening of the valley. Even in the 12th cent. the city is described as having lain waste for 40 years, and being a veritable den of robbers, "spelunca latronum." The objects of interest may be divided into 3 groups, according to their situation.

Immediately at the back of the hotel is an enclosure containing the ruins of the cathedral, Our Lady's ch., St. Kevin's House or Kitchen, and the Round Tower. 1. The enclosure is entered by a magnificent though terribly dilapidated gateway, which Dr. Petrie compares to the Roman-built Newport gate at Lincoln. In form it was a square, having external and internal arches, from between which rose a tower. Enough of it remains to show the undressed blocks of mica slate and the chiselled granite blocks of the arches and pilasters. 2. The cathedral is considered to have been erected about the commencement of the 7th cent., probably by Gobhan Saer, the great architect of that day; the original ch. was 55 ft. long, but the chancel appears to be of later date. It is entered by a square-headed doorway, in which the weight upon the lintel is taken off by a semicircular arch. The masonry of the chancel is much less massive than that in the body of the ch., and moreover is not bonded like that of the nave, thus showing its more modern erection. The E. window is remarkable for its ornamented character, possessing a chevron moulding and a sculptured frieze running on either side from the spring of the arch. It is worth notice that the stone of which this E. window is built is a sort of oolite not found anywhere in the district.

3. The ch. of Our Lady is believed to have been the first erected in the lower part of the valley or the city of Glendalough by St. Kevin, "qui ibi duxit vitam eremiticam," and was buried here. It possesses a remarkable doorway, of a style resembling Greek architecture. It is 6 ft. high, 2 ft. 6 in. wide at the top and 3 ft. at the bottom, being formed of 7 stones of the thickness of the wall; the lintel is ornamented on its soffit with a cross, "salticr wise," somewhat after the fashion of Killiney (p. 208).

4. The Round Tower, which stands at one corner of the enclosure, close to the cathedral, is about 110 ft., and is deficient in the conical cap. It has a semicircular-headed doorway without any ornament, and "is constructed of blocks of granite, chiselled, though the wall of the tower generally is formed of rubble masonry of the mica slate of the adjacent mountains; and in this circumstance it resembles the doorways of several chs. in the valley." Its probable date is the 7th cent.

5. The most interesting feature in the enclosure is the cell of St. Kevin. The tourist who has visited Kells (Rte. 16) will at once recognise the great similarity between St. Columb's house and St. Kevin's, although the latter has been to all intents and pur-

poses changed into a ch. by the subsequent addition of a chancel and bell turret, neither of which in all probability belonged to the original building; this chancel has been destroyed, but it will be perceived on close examination that the walls of the adjoining sacristy are not bonded into those of the main building. " It will be observed also that the chancel-arch is of subsequent formation ; for its semicircular head is not formed on the principle of the arch, but by the cutting away of the horizontally laid stones of the original wall, in which operation a portion of the original window placed in this wall was destroyed, and the remaining portion of the aperture built up with solid masonry."—*Petrie*. Divested of these additions, we find that St. Kevin's house is an oblong building with a very high-pitched stone roof, an arched room below, and a small croft between. A stringcourse runs at the base of the roof, and is carried along the base of the end wall. It was entered by a door on the W. side, and lighted by 2 plain windows in the E. end, one above the other, and one in the S. wall; the door, which is now blocked up, was square-headed, with the weight taken off the lintel by a semicircular arch as in the cathedral door. Rising from the W. gable is the addition of a small round-towered belfry, 9 ft. high, with a conical roof and 4 quadrangular apertures facing the cardinal points. The entrance is from the croft.

The sacristy was apparently similar to the chancel, being stone-roof'd and ornamented with a rude stringcourse similar to that of the main building.

It is considered by Dr. Petrie that these additions took place not long after the death of St. Kevin, whose name was held in such reverence that naturally enough it was sought to convert his residence into a ch.

The remaining chs. are all at some little distance off; they are—6. Trinity ch., near the road leading from Laragh to Glendalough. In the chancel wall is a semicircular-headed window, the arch cut out of a single stone— also a triangular-headed window; the chancel arch is semicircular, and springs from jambs " which have an inclination corresponding with the doorways and windows." A round tower was formerly attached to this ch. 7. On the opposite bank of the river, near Derrybawn, are the ruins of St. Saviour's, or the Monastery, which possess more interesting details than any of the others. The chancel contains a stone seat at the E. end, and 3 niches in the S. wall, which probably served for piscina or ambry. The piers only of the chancel arching are left, and, before the ch. became so dilapidated, must have shown some very interesting and beautiful sculpture. It consisted of 3 " receding piers with semicolumns," and the capitals and bases should be carefully studied for the sake of the fantastic sculptures of human heads and animals—a not uncommon decoration of the 12th cent. of Irish architecture.* Dr. Ledwich, whatever his authority may be worth, considered that all this ornamentation was of Danish origin; but Dr. Petrie holds that we are to look for the prototypes in the debased architecture of Greece and Rome. Similar sculpture and beauty of detail existed in the Priest's House, of which however there is now scarcely any vestige.

8. The ch. of Reefert, situated on the S. bank of the upper lake, was the " clara cella " first founded by St. Kevin before he moved to the lower part of the valley. It contains a square-headed doorway of chiselled blocks of granite, and near the ch. stood a sepulchral cross, marking the spot of the cemetery of the Kings, where the celebrated King O'Toole

* Similar examples are found at Clonmacnoise.

[*Ireland.*] L

is said to be buried. Still further, near the cliff of Lugduff, are—10. the very scanty remains of the ch. of Teampul na Skellig.

It is a charming woodland walk along the S. bank of the lakes, and at the foot of Derrybawn Mountain, where the Osmunda regalis flourishes. At the back of the inn, which is situated just between the 2 lakes, the tourist should ascend Lugduff brook for a short distance to see the Pollanass waterfall: and having visited Reefert and Teampul na Skellig, should cross the Causeway and take boat on the upper lake to St. Kevin's Bed. "This wonder-working couch is a small cave in the face of a rock, capable of containing 3 persons at most, hanging perpendicularly over the lake; the approach is by a narrow path along the steep side of the mountain, at every step of which the slightest false trip would precipitate the pedestrian into the lake below. After passing the Rubicon of the Lady's Leap, the landing-place immediately above the cave is soon reached without difficulty; but the visitor must descend with caution, his face turned to the rock down which he climbs, while the guide directs which way he is to turn, and where to plant his foot, until at last he reaches the mouth of the sainted bed."— *Otway.* Here it was that St. Kevin, to escape from the

"Eyes of most unholy blue"

of Cathleen, who loved him not wisely but too well, fixed his hermit's couch, fearing an interruption :—

"'Here at least,' he calmly said,
'Woman ne'er shall find my bed.'
Ah! the good saint little knew
What that wily sex can do."
MOORE.

But she traced him out, and St. Kevin woke one morning from his sleep to find her watching his countenance. He rose, and with a sudden impulse of madness hurled poor Kathleen into the lake :—

"Down gazed he frenzied on the tide.
Cathleen! how comes he lonely?
Why has she left her Kevin's side,
That lived for Kevin only?"
GERALD GRIFFIN.

Should the tourist have time, he should make an excursion up the Glendasan valley, and past the Lugganamon lead-mines (which are 3 m. distant from the 7 chs.), to the summit level at Wicklow Gap, 1569 ft., from whence he will obtain very fine mountain views. The road from this point continues to Blessington and the plains of Kildare.

Distances of the Hotel—from Bray, 19 m.; Roundwood, 6; Annamoe, 3½; Laragh, 1; Rathdrum, 8; Luggelaw, 11; Wicklow Gap, 4½; Devil's Glen, 8; Sally Gap, 13.

On the return, the road is retraced and followed to Laragh. Passing l. Laragh House (G. Booth, Esq.), and winding up a steep and long hill, the village of Annamoe is reached, adjoining which is Glendalough, the seat of T. Barton, Esq. Between 3 and 4 m. to the rt., and visible from the road, is the entrance of the Devil's Glen. The tourist should visit the reservoir of the waterworks lately formed for the supply of the city of Dublin (p. 213).

Roundwood (*Hotel:* Murphy's), a prettily situated village on the banks of the Vartry. This is a favourite place with many, the quarters being comfortable, and the situation central for Glendalough, the Devil's Glen, and Luggelaw. It is moreover a good fishing station. In the neighbourhood are Roundwood Lodge and Roundwood Park (T. Gower, Esq.).

From Roundwood 3 routes are available :—1. A direct road to Bray, running through Calary, skirting the deer-park of Powerscourt, and crossing the Dargle at Tinnahinch Bridge (p. 210).

2. A bleak mountain road to the E. of this last, which steers clear of Powerscourt and Enniskerry, and winds round the Great Sugarloaf,

falling into the Bray road near Hollybrook.

3. A more circuitous route, by turning off to the l. at Anna Carter Bridge, and following the road to Luggelaw. From Sally Gap, where the military road is joined, it is 5 m. to Glencree. The pedestrian should not leave Roundwood without visiting Lough Dan, which he may do either by proceeding to the Old Bridge, and thence walking up the Annamoe river; or else by turning off from the Luggelaw road near the Police-station, and following the Annamoe down. Lough Dan is a rather long sheet of water, 685 ft. above the sea, situated in a hollow between the mountains of Knocknacloghole and Slieve-Buckh; it is fed by the Annamoe and Inchavore rivers, the former of which discharges itself at the lower end of the lake, near the desmesne of Lake View. Although a characteristic mountain lake, it does not possess the stern and more romantic beauties of Lough Tay, which is some 2 m. to the N., and occupies a circular corrie nearly at the head of the glen of the Annamoe. The cliff scenery here is very fine, and agreeably contrasts with the woods and grounds of Luggelaw, a romantic retreat as far away from the busy hum of men as any hermit could wish. "A monstrous face of regular formation is distinctly traced in the outline of the rock, looking gloomily and angrily on the lake below. The eyebrows, broad and dilating, are marked by moss and heath, and the prominent cheeks and deep-sunk eyes, perfectly formed by the clefts in the rock."—*Wright.* Carex axillaris, Orobanche major, are to be found near the waterside, and char is an inhabitant of this lake as well as that of Glendalough.

It is said by the way that St. Kevin dwelt at a cell at Luggelaw, until driven away by the importunities of Kathleen.

From Lough Tay and Luggelaw the road keeps along the bank of the Annamoe, and on the S.W. side of Douce and War Hill, to join the military road at Sally Gap. At the height of 1700 ft. is the watershed of the Annamoe and the Liffey, the source of which last is but a very short distance from the Gap. From this point the military road runs at an average elevation of 1700 ft. past Lough Bray to Glencree.

The route from Enniskerry to Dublin is carried on the W. flank of Shankhill Mountain, through a wild and singular ravine known as the *Scalp*, which appears to have been rent by some tremendous shock, leaving only just room for the formation of the highway. Huge masses of granite are tossed about and piled up in picturesque confusion, affording a strong contrast to the other glens which the tourist has visited. A little further on a cromlech may be visited at Mount Venus, which is 19 ft. in length and 11 in breadth. The table-stone, like that of Howth, has been dismounted.

Passing through the village of Rathfarnham (Rte. 1) the tourist soon reaches Dublin.

ROUTE 25.

FROM DUBLIN TO CORK, BY THE GREAT SOUTHERN AND WESTERN RAILWAY.

Rather more than half of Ireland is traversed by the tourist in about 7 hrs by this line, which in its appointments and general management ranks amongst the first in the kingdom. It was commenced in 1844, under the engineering superintendence of Sir John McNeil, and was opened for the whole distance to Cork, 165 m., in 1849. The country through which it runs exhibits a very fair specimen of Irish scenery, being for the most part a vast expanse of rich grazing land, relieved by groups of mountains, and occasionally a genuine bog, as dreary and melancholy as only an Irish bog can be. The stat. at Kingsbridge, at the S.W. end of Dublin, is a fine, though somewhat florid Corinthian building, consisting of a central front, flanked on each side by wings surmounted by clock towers. The interior is graceful and convenient, and covers an area of 2½ acres. Gliding out of the stat. the traveller catches a glimpse on the rt. of the Phœnix Park with its conspicuous Wellington obelisk, and on the l. of the Royal Hospital of Kilmainham, and passes rapidly through the locomotive establishment at *Inchicore*, where the cleanly and even tasty appearance of the buildings and offices will attract attention.

2 m. rt. 1 m. is the village of Chapelizod, bordering on the Phœnix (Rte. 1), and 4½ m. l. the round tower of *Clondalkin*, nearly 1 m. from the stat.; but as this forms a favourite excursion from Dublin it has been described in Rte. 1. 7 m. Lucan stat.; the village of the same name (Rte. 14) being 1½ m. on rt. and nearly midway between this and the Midland Great Western Rly., by which the visitor may return to Dublin after inspecting Lucan and Leixlip.

2 m. l. of the stat., crossing the Grand Canal, is Castle Bagot (the seat of J. Bagot, Esq.). As the train gains the open country, the beautiful ranges of the Dublin mountains are very conspicuous on the l., and for the whole distance to Kildare form a most charming background to the landscape. They may be considered as the frontier belt which guards the lovely county of Wicklow.

10. *Hazelhatch* stat. 1½ m. rt. is *Celbridge*, where dwelt Esther Vanhomrigh, the ill-starred Vanessa of Swift. Celbridge Abbey (C. Langdale, Esq.), the place of her residence, was originally built by Dr. Morley, Bp. of Clonfert. On the same side of the Liffey is St. Wolstans (R. Cane, Esq.), with its ancient gateway, and on the opposite bank is Castleton, the magnificent seat of T. Conolly, Esq., M.P., conspicuous from its obelisk (Rte. 14).

[2 m. l. of the stat. is the village of *Newcastle*, formerly a royal borough of James I. The ch. has a good E. window. 4 m. *Rathcoole*, very prettily situated at the foot of Slieve Thoul, which rises to the height of 1308 ft. About 4 m. to the E. are the inconsiderable ruins of Kiltcel Castle and ch.]

Before arriving at 13 m. *Straffan* stat., the line passes l. *Lyons Castle*, a beautiful seat of Lord Cloncurry. The house, which consists of a centre range, flanked by semicircular colonnades, is placed in a wooded park at the foot of Lyons Hill, 631 ft. The interior contains a fine gallery of sculpture. Between Lyons and Rathcoole to S.E. is *Athgor*, in the grounds of which is the old keep of Colmanstown castle. *Straffan* is a pretty village on the l. or N. bank of the river, which here approaches pretty close to the rly. In the neighbourhood are Straffan House (H. Barton, Esq.), and Killadoon (the Earl of Leitrim). 2 m. l. of the stat. is *Oughterarde*, where (on the summit of a steep eminence) are ruins of a small ch., the crypt being used for a burial-place of the Ponsonbys of Bishop's Court; also the stump of a round tower with a circular-headed doorway 10 ft. from the ground.

18 m., near *Sallins* Stat., the line crosses the *Grand Canal*. This

work, which, when commenced in 1765, was justly considered as the finest work of the day, was set on foot to supply inland navigation to the towns and districts between Dublin and the Shannon, and is carried from the metropolis to a spot called Shannon Harbour, near Banagher (Rte. 34). The main line, together with 4 branches and an extension to the Suck, at Ballinasloe, is 161 m., 'the summit level, 279 ft. above the sea, being at Robertstown, 26 m. from Dublin. The annual tonnage of merchandize carried on the canal is 300,000 tons, producing toll to the amount of 20,000l. a year."—*Thom's Directory.* Beyond Sallins a branch is given off to Naas. [5 m. rt. the Liffey is crossed by a bridge of 6 arches at *Clane* ("Cluain," a retreat', where a Franciscan abbey, a portion of which still remains, was founded by Sir Gerald Fitzmaurice in the 13th centy. A little further on is the Roman Catholic college of *Clongowes Wood*, a fine quadrangular building, flanked by 4 towers at the angles.]

On l. of Sallins stat. 1½ m. is Palmerstown House, the seat of Lord Naas; also Punchestown, famous for its steeplechases. [From Sallins a car runs daily to Dunlavin, passing through 3 m. *Naas*, pronounced *Nace*, which gives a title to the family of Mayo, and is a busy little assize town of 3000 Inhab., though not so brisk as in the days of coaching, when it lay in the high road for Waterford and Limerick. (*Hotels*: Royal; M'Evoy's.) It is said to have been one of the oldest towns in Ireland, and the royal residence of the kings of Leinster, and was in a flourishing state up to the time of the Pale, possessing a castle and 3 or 4 abbeys and monasteries. Of these nothing now remains, the only antiquity in the town being a rath where the states of Leinster held their assemblies. The Rectory is built on the site of the castle. "1 m. on the Limerick road is Jigginstone House, a spacious brick mansion, commenced by the unfortunate Earl of Strafford, but never finished, the walls of which and the vaulted cellars, from the excellent quality of the bricks and cement, are still in a very perfect state."—*Lewis.* After all, the chief attraction of Naas is the splendid range of hills which approach near enough to tempt the pedestrian to a ramble into North Wicklow and the source of the Liffey].

In the neighbourhood are Forenaghts (Dean Burgh) and Oldtown House (T. De Burgh, Esq.).

Excursions.—
1. Blessington.
2. Phoul-a-phooka.

[The lover of the picturesque should not omit to visit the waterfall of Phoul-a-phooka on the Liffey, which is 2 m. beyond the little town of Ballymore Eustace, and 5½ to the S. of Blessington. It is a succession of magnificent cataracts, by which the Liffey descends from the hills to the valley, of 150 ft. in height.

— " Whilst the broad river,
Foaming and hurrying o'er its rugged path,
Fell into that immeasurable void,
Scattering its waters to the passing winds."

The middle fall is the finest: at its base is the basin or pool, which has given its name to the fall, in conjunction with the Phooka, the Puck of Irish legend. "The great object of the Phooka is to obtain a rider, and then he is in all his most malignant glory. Headlong he dashes through brier and brake, through flood and fell, over mountain, valley, moor, or river indiscriminately; up or down precipice is alike to him, provided he gratifies the malevolence that seems to inspire him. As the 'Tinna Geolane,' or Will-o'-the-wisp, he lives but to betray; like the Hanoverian 'Tucklold,' he deludes the night wanderer into a bog and leads him to his destruction in a quagmire or pit."—*Hall.* A single-arched bridge crosses the stream at the Falls, from which, as well as from Lord Miltown's grounds, the best views are to be obtained.]

Distances.—Sallins, 3 m.; Blessington, 8; Newbridge, 11; Phoul-a-phooka, 9.

[The Liffey is crossed at a prettily-wooded spot, bordered by the demesnes of Harristown (J. La Touche, Esq.), Newberry (H. M'Clintock, Esq.), on the N. bank, and Sallymount (C. Roberts, Esq.) on the S. 2 m. rt. is *Kilcullen*, a queer rambling village, "which tumbles down one hill and struggles up another" on either side the river, here crossed by an ancient bridge. The antiquary will find an attraction, 2 m. to the S., in *Kilcullen Old Town*, which, previous to the building of the new town in 1319, was a strong city fortified by walls and entered by 7 gates. There are some scanty remains of the abbey founded for monks of the Strict Observance in the 15th centy.; also part of a round tower and the shaft of a cross, divided into compartments and sculptured with figures. A little to the W. is a very large circular fort, known as Don Ailline.

From the Liffey, at Sallymount, it is 5 m. to Dunlavin.]

The Grand Canal, or rather the branch to Naas, is crossed a second time after leaving Sallins, as is also the Liffey (which for the next few miles keeps to the l. of the line), by a timber bridge, 270 ft. long.

25½ m. *Newbridge* stat. The frequent presence on the platform of bearded and moustached warriors betokens the proximity to the cavalry barracks, which are about the most extensive in Ireland, and accommodate a large number of men and horses. [Kilcullen, 5 m., may be more conveniently visited from here than from Sallins, and by keeping on the rt. bank of the Liffey, the antiquary may inspect the ruins of the Priory of Great Connell, or Old Conal, founded in 1202 by Meyler Fitzhenry, who stocked it with friars drafted from Llanthony Abbey. A part of the E. gable and some mutilated tombs still remain. In its prosperous times, the priors of this abbey ranked as Lords of Parliament, and enjoyed many privileges unknown to abbeys of poorer means.] Soon after leaving Newbridge, the line skirts the *Curragh of Kildare*, and the traveller may obtain occasional peeps of the block-huts of the encampment. "The Curragh is a magnificent undulating down, 6 m. long and 2 broad; it lies in a direction from N.E. to S.W., having the town of Kildare at its western extremity, and crossed by the great road from Dublin to Limerick; and is in fact an extensive sheepwalk of above 6000 acres, forming a more beautiful lawn than the hand of art ever made. Nothing can exceed the extreme softness and elasticity of the turf, which is of a verdure that charms the eye, and is still further set off by the gentle inequality of the surface; the soil is a fine dry loam on a substratum of limestone." —*Lewis.* Geologically speaking, this fine loam is nothing but drift, about 200 ft. in thickness.

There are but few early remains in it—and these only of an ancient road running nearly parallel with the high road, and a chain of small raths. It has been the scene of many an encampment prior to the permanent establishment that occupies it at present: in 1646 by forces under General Preston; in 1783, by volunteers; and in 1804, by 30,000 insurgents. At present several regiments are constantly quartered here, and the camp presents the same civilised means and appliances that exist at Aldershott. We must not pass the Curragh without alluding to its races, which both from its peculiarly springy turf, and the opportunities afforded to spectators, have long held the first rank in the estimation of Irish sportsmen. They are held four times a year—in April, June, September, and October.

30 m. *Kildare* (Rte. 26), Kildare, "the ch. of the oaks," an important junction, whence the line to Carlow, Kilkenny, and Waterford is given off.

The town (*Hotel*: Railway) has a venerable age, and contains sufficient to interest the antiquary. As early as the 5th centy. St. Bridget founded a monastery, of which Black Hugh, king of Leinster, who had donned the Augustine habit, was abbot. The history of Kildare from its commencement to the close of the 18th centy. is nothing but a series of raids, fires, and devastations, "usque ad nauseam," principally at the hands of Danes and native Irish. The bishopric, now united with the archbishopric of Dublin, dates from the time of St. Bridget, and was always somewhat needy, owing to the alienation of estates at various times. The diocese includes the county of Dublin and the greater part of Kildare, King's and Queen's Counties. The town itself is small and poor, and, were it not for the interesting cluster of antiquities, would not be worth even a passing visit.

These are tolerably close to the stat., and consist of the abbey, the choir of which is used as a parochial ch., and the Round Tower. The former was cruciform in shape, consisting of nave, choir, and transepts, with a tower springing from the intersection — but of this only the S. and part of the W. wall remains. The nave is lighted by Early Pointed windows; and in the choir is the vault of the earls of Kildare. Adjoining the ch. is a stone cell known as the "Fire-House," where the sacred fire—

"The bright lamp that shone in Kildare's holy fane"—

lighted by St. Bridget the foundress, is said to have burnt without intermission from the 5th centy. to the 13th, when it was extinguished by Henry de Londres, Archbishop of Dublin. It was subsequently relighted, and continued so until the general suppression of monasteries :—

"Apud Kildariam occurrit Ignis Sanctæ Brigidæ, quem inextinguibilem vocant; non quod extingui non possit, sed quod tam solicite moniales et sanctæ mulieres ignem, suppetente materia, fovent et nutriunt, ut a tempore virginis per tot annorum curricula semper mansit inextinctus."—*Giraldus Camb.*

The round tower adjoins the ch., and is remarkable for its great height of 130 ft., the summit being crowned with a modern and very inapposite battlement. The chief interest lies in the doorway, which is 14 ft. from the ground, and consists of 3 concentric arches, adorned with very beautiful chevron or zigzag mouldings, and a diagonal panelling on the inner arch. From this unusual feature, the age of this tower has been set down as of the Anglo Norm. time; but Dr. Petrie contends that from the legends of Giraldus Cambrensis and others, this tower was considered to be of great age in the 12th centy., and while allowing the mouldings to be of Norman character, he only sees in this fact a proof that these ornaments are of considerably anterior date—at all events in Ireland—to what they are usually considered. A number of bracteate coins, or laminar pieces of silver struck only on one side, were found under the floor. As Sperlingrius and others ascribe these coins to the 12th centy., this was held to be a proof of the later erection of the tower; but on the other hand Dr. Petrie proves that minted money was used in Ireland from a very remote period—even at the time of the introduction of Christianity.

The visitor who is sufficiently interested in the discussion will find it at length in Petrie's work on the 'Round Towers,' p. 208.

Near the tower is the castle, erected by De Vesci in the 13th centy.

In the ch. are the sculptured shaft of a mutilated cross, with some interesting monuments of knights and ecclesiastics.

To the S. of the town are scanty remains of an abbey, founded in the 13th centy. by De Vesci for the order of Grey Friars.

From its open situation upon a ridge of hills, Kildare commands a widespread prospect, embracing on the W. a portion of the great central limestone plain of Ireland, in the direction of Monasterevan and Portarlington; while to the N. are the *Red Hills* — a small chain, about 7 m. long, of old red sandstone intervening between Kildare and Rathangan. The most conspicuous points are Hill of Allen, in the N.E., 676 ft.; Dunmurry Hill, 769; and the Grange, on which is the Chair of Kildare, 744. But the geological structure of the Chair itself consists of a narrow bed of limestone associated with a protrusion of lower Silurian shales and grits, with porphyritic greenstone, from 400 to 1000 ft. thick; the beds very much tilted and disturbed, and having suffered much from denudation prior to the deposition of the lower carb. limestone. Many Silurian fossils have been found here, viz., some from the limestone of the Chair, and others from the red slates of Dunmurry Hill — orthoceras, ilænus, phacops, some gasteropodous shells, and corals.

Distances: — Monasterevan, 6½ m.; Rathangan, 6; the Chair, 4; the Camp, 3.

Leaving on l. the line to Carlow and Kilkenny, we arrive at (36½ m.) *Monasterevan* (*Hôtel*: Drogheda Arms), a small town of one street, lying on the banks of the Barrow, which at this point makes a wide sweep from the S. to the W. towards Portarlington. The rlwy. crosses the Grand Canal and also the river by a fine viaduct 500 ft. long, constructed of thin bars of malleable iron. A monastery, founded on the ruins of a still more ancient house, was established by Dermod O'Dempsey, king of Ophaley, in the 12th centy. Upon the site of it now stands Moore Abbey, the Gothic residence of the Marquis of Drogheda, whose beautiful woods extend for some distance on the banks of the island-covered Barrow.

The entrance-hall is said to have been the room in which Loftus, Viscount Ely, held a court of Chancery in 1641.

The ch. of Monasterevan is a fine old building, with a square tower, a rather unusual feature in Irish modern churches, which almost always have spires.

Distances.—Portarlington, 5 m.; Ballybrittas, 4.

Still through the flat plain the line runs westward, keeping parallel with the canal and Barrow to 41½ m. *Portarlington*, the point of junction for the Athlone branch. (*Hotel*: Portarlington Arms). The town, with its graceful spired ch., is some little distance to the rt. It formerly possessed the singular appellation of Cootletoodra, from which reproach it was rescued by becoming the property of Lord Arlington, temp. Charles II.. Until of late years there were a number of descendants, resident in the town, of French and Flemish refugees, who settled here at the beginning of the 16th centy. It is neat and well-built, and contains 2 churches—the one generally called the French ch., from its having been originally appropriated for the use of the refugees. The Barrow here separates Queen's from King's County. Amongst the residences in the neighbourhood of Portarlington are Barrowbank House (W. Humphreys, Esq.), Lawnsdown (J. Scott, Esq.), Woodbrook House (E. Chetwood, Esq.), and about 5 m. to the S. Emo, the splendid domain of the Earl of Portarlington, who takes his title from this town. The interior of the mansion is worth seeing, and is remarkable for its beautiful fittings and decorations.

The antiquary should visit *Lea Castle* 2 m. to the E., situated between the river and the canal. In consequence of its central position, and its contiguity to the Pale, Lea was early defended by a strong fortress erected by De Vesci in 1260, which underwent much rough treatment between the English lords and the Irish chiefs. "It was built in the usual style of the military architecture of the times, consisting of a quadrangular building of 3 stories, flanked by round bastions, of which but 1 now remains. The outer entrance, which is still in good preservation, consisted of a gate defended by a portcullis, the whole surrounded by a tower. In the rear was the inner ballium, in which was a tennis-court and tilt-yard."— *Wakeman*. The last inhabitant of Lea was a noted horse-stealer of the name of Dempsey, who converted the vaults underground into stables, and carried on a flourishing trade.

Some 4 m. to the S. of Lea on the road from Monasterevan to Maryborough is *Ballybrittas*, a small village, the locale of a battle in Elizabeth's reign between the Earl of Essex's army and the Irish under O'Dempsey. The latter were victorious, and cut off so many feathers from the English helmets, that the spot was afterwards called "the Pass of the Plumes."

Spire Hill is conspicuous near Portarlington, from an obelisk erected by Viscount Carlow to give employment to the poor during a season of scarcity.

Distances.—Athlone, 39 m.; Maryborough, 8½; Lea, 2; Mountmellick, 7½; Emo, 5; Monasterevan, 5.

Excursions.—
1. Lea.
2. Monasterevan.
3. Emo.

Conveyances. — Rail to Dublin, Cork, and Athlone. Car daily to

[*Mountmellick*, a small but busy town, nearly surrounded by the river Owenas, whence its name Moun-cha-Meelick, "the green island." Quakers have settled here, and, as they usually do, have contributed principally to the prosperity of the place. Near it are Knightstown (Maj. Carden), Garryhinch House (R. Warburton, Esq.), and Killeen.]

[The branch line to Athlone, connecting the Great Southern with the Midland Great Western, passes for the greater part of its course through a very bare and desolate district, a good portion of it being included in the famous Bog of Allen. A few words respecting the Irish bogs will not be out of place. Mr. Moore divides them into red, brown, black, and mountain bog, the difference of colour and consistence depending chiefly on the locality, according as the substances vary in degrees of moisture, temperature, and altitude. Red and brown bog are least valuable for fuel, and are supposed to have been formed on the sites of extensive lakes or wet morasses, as he infers from the small quantity of wood found in it. Sphagnum constitutes a considerable portion of the substance of the peat, and the roots and branches of the phanerogamic plants form a kind of framework, and bear up the cryptogamic species. The black bog contains most woody matter, and is believed to have been formed on the site of ancient forests.

9 m. *Geashill* Stat. The little town of that name lies about 2½m. to rt. and has some remains of a castle of the O'Dempseys, who formerly held all this territory. Geashill Castle is the seat of T. Trench, Esq.

16 m. *Tullamore* (Pop. 4797) (*Hotel*: Charleville Arms) is an oasis in the desert, in the shape of a well-built thriving country town, containing the usual civil and municipal buildings, such as gaol, court-house, &c.

There is not much to see in the neighbourhood save the very pretty park of the Earl of Charleville, which unites all the essentials for landscape gardening, in wood, ornamental water, and a stream

L 3

running through a glen. There are several small castles, or rather fortified houses, in the district round Tullamore, showing that, however unprolific the country, the early settlers thought it worth defending.

The Grand Canal passes through the town, and a trip may be taken by it to the former capital of King's County, *Phillipstown*, 9 m. distant, and in a still more boggy situation than Tullamore. It was formerly the centre of the district of Offaley, and of course possessed a castle, erected in the 16th centy. by Sir William Brabazon, Lord Chief Justice of Ireland.

Excursions.—
1. Phillipstown.
2. Rahin.
3. Tullamore Park.

Distances.—Kilbeggan, 7 m.; Phillipstown, 9; Clara, 8.

5½ m. is the Abbey of Rahin, partly used as the parish ch. It was founded in the 6th centy. by St. Carthach or Mochuda, afterwards Bp. of Lismore, and is remarkable for its archæological details. The visitor should notice the chancel archway, which consists of 3 rectangular piers on each side, rounded at their angles into semi-columns, and adorned with capitals elaborately sculptured with human heads. The original E. window is gone, but lighting a chamber between the chancel and the roof is a remarkably beautiful round window, with ornaments in low relief. The antiquary should compare the decorations of the capitals with those at Timahoe. There are also ruins of 2 other chs., one of them containing a doorway with inclined jambs (indicative of early Irish architecture), and an arch adorned with the characteristic moulding so like Norman.

24m. *Clara* is on the banks of the Barrow, and surrounded by several nice estates, as Clara House (A. Cox, Esq.), Woodfield (J. Fuller, Esq.), Ballyboughlin, and Belview. The soft and pulpy nature of the red bog was curiously exemplified in 1821 at a spot 2 m. to the N., when a bog burst its bounds, and flowed for 1½ m. down the valley, covering 150 acres. A branch rly. runs in here from Streamstown, a station on the Midland Great Western.

Passing m. rt. Hall House and Castle Daly, the line soon arrives at 39 m. *Athlone* (Rte. 14). *Hotel:* Bergin's.]

On leaving Portarlington the traveller will observe that the extensive plain through which the line has passed has given place to a ridge of hills on either side—that on the l. commencing near Lea Castle, and running nearly due S. These are the Rocky Hills, the highest point of which is Cullenagh (1045 ft.), broadly separating the valleys of the Barrow and the Nore. On the rt. are the Slieve Bloom mountains—a very important chain, occupying the area between Maryborough, Parsonstown, and Roscrea. The highest points are Ridge of Capard, 1677 ft. ; Slieve Bloom, 1691 ft. ; and Ard Erin, 1733 ft. At the foot of the former is Ballyfin, the beautiful Italian mansion and grounds of Sir Chas. Coote, Bart., who purchased it from the family of Pole, the original possessors.

Following the broad valley thus indicated, the train arrives at 50¼ m. *Maryborough* (*Hotel:* Fallen's), the capital of Queen's County, which although boasting a corporation of the time of Elizabeth, looks unusually modern (Pop. 2935). It is neat and well built, and has some remarkably spacious buildings, such as the Lunatic Asylum, the joint property of Westmeath, Longford, King's and Queen's Counties, erected at an expense of 24,000*l*. The objects of antiquity embrace only a bastion of the old castle; but the Rock of Dunamase, 3½ m. on the road to Stradbally, is worth a visit.

The summit of this rock, 200 ft. high, is entirely covered with the ruins of a castle, at one time the property of Strongbow Earl of Pembroke, who acquired it by marriage with the daughter of Dermod McMurrough, King of Leinster. Its chief points are a watch-tower defending the S.W. and most accessible side; an outer and an inner court; the whole being surrounded by thick walls, which were fortified at intervals with towers. It was eventually destroyed by Cromwell, and a small tump on the E. is still known as Cromwell's Lines.

[From the rock it is 2¼ m. to *Stradbally*, a pleasant little town on the Bauteogue, a tributary of the Nore. It is bounded on either side by the parks of Stradbally (R. Cosby, Esq., Brockley (J. Young, Esq.), and Ballykileavan (A. Walsh, Esq.).

The visitor may thence pursue his journey to Athy (Rte. 26), 8 m. distant, or else may return to Maryborough by a detour to the S., so as to visit the Round Tower of *Timahoe*, containing some unusual and interesting features. It derives its name Teach-Mochoe from St. Mochoe, who flourished in the 6th centy. About 30 ft. only remain, fortunately, however, possessing a very beautiful doorway, "formed of a hard silicious sandstone, and consisting of 2 divisions, separated from each other by a deep reveal, and presenting each a double compound recessed arch, resting on plain shafts, with flat capitals.'—*Petrie*. Notice particularly the manner in which the floor rises to each arch by steps, and then study the decorations of each. The capitals of the outer arch have human heads, as have also the bases, with the addition of an hourglass. The soffit of the arch has a pellet and bead moulding. The second or middle arch is also decorated with human heads, and on the soffit with a diagonal panelling of chevron moulding. The heads on the W. and E. capitals differ in the way in which the hair is dressed.

Respecting the antiquity of these decorations, Dr. Petrie remarks: "Of these capitals decorated with human heads we have examples as old as the 6th centy. in the Syriac MSS. of the Gospels. They are used in the earliest examples of Romanesque architecture in the German chs., of which a beautiful example, remarkable for its similarity in design to some of those at Timahoe, is found at St. Ottmar's chapel at Nürnberg, assigned to the 10th centy." The archæologist will recognize the similarity of the capitals to those at Rahin.]

Conveyances from Maryborough.— Rail to Dublin and Cork; car to Abbeyleix and Durrow.

Excursions.—
1. Rock of Dunamase.
2. Timahoe.
3. Athy.

*Distances.—*Stradbally, 6 m.; Abbeyleix, 9; Timahoe, 7; Dunamase, 3½; Mountrath, 9½.

60 m. *Mountrath* stat., the town being 2¼ m. to rt., and situated on the Mountrath river, a tributary of the Nore. 2 m. to the S. is *Castleton*, on the Nore, which obtained its name from a fortress garrisoned by Sir Oliver Norris, son-in-law of the Earl of Ormond, to curb the power of the Fitzpatricks. In the neighbourhood are Westfield Farm (J. Price, Esq., and Moorfield House (R. Senior, Esq.).

Passing the planted hill of Knockahaw, which forms part of the estate of Lisduff (Rt. Hon. J. Fitzpatrick), the line reaches

67 m. *Ballybrophy*, from whence a branch of 22 m. leads off to Roscrea, Parsonstown and Nenagh (Rte. 27). Near the stat. is Ballybrophy House.

As the train glides on through the open plain we come in sight of the Devil's Bit (1572), a singular chain of mountains rising some 3 or 4 miles to the W. of Templemore, and exhibiting a very marked gap at the summit. This is accounted for by the fact that the Prince of Darkness, in a fit of hunger and fatigue, took a bite at the mountain, and, not finding it to his taste, spat it out again some miles to the E., where it formed the rock called nowadays the Rock of Cashel.

79 m. *Templemore* (*Hotels:* Queen's Arms; Commercial), supposed to have originated, as its name implies, with the Knights Templars. It is a pleasant town, and has thriven well under the auspices of the Carden family, whose residence, the Priory (Sir John Carden), is hard by. In the grounds is a gable end of the old monastic ch., entered by a round-headed doorway and lighted by a Gothic 2-light window; also the remains of a square keep of the ancient Templar fortress. The mansion is modern, and the grounds are very prettily ornamented by a fine sheet of water, and backed up in the distance by the picturesque range of the Devil's Bit.

In the neighbourhood of the town are Belleville, Woodville (D. Webb, Esq.), Lloydsborough (J. Lloyd, Esq.), and, under the range of the Devil's Bit, Barnane, the residence of John Carden, Esq.

Conveyances. — To Dublin and Cork by rail.

Distances. — Nenagh, 20 m.; Thurles, 8; Borrisoleigh, 6; Devil's Bit, 4½.

[*Borrisoleigh*, or Two-mile Borris, is a small town, with a ruined castle and fort; considering, however, the immense number of ruins in the county, it will scarcely repay a visit. Fishmoyne is the residence of another branch of the Carden family.]

81 m. l. *Loughmore*, close to the rly., is the old castellated mansion of the Purcells, consisting of 2 massive square towers, connected by an intermediate dwelling of the time of James I., which, together with the N. tower, would seem to have been an addition to the remainder. As the tourist journeys on through the great limestone plain he obtains beautiful distant views, if the weather be clear, of Slieve-na-man and the Commeragh Mountains in the W.

A little further, on the same side of the line, is Brittas Castle, the modern Norm. mansion of Col. Knox; soon after which he arrives at

87 m. *Thurles* (*Hotel:* Boyton's), sacred to every Roman Catholic as the seat of the Archbishopric, and the spot where the famous Synod was held. It is of no modern extraction, but was famous as early as the 10th centy. for a great battle between the Danes and the Irish. (Pop. 4866). As the town increased and prospered, a castle was erected some time about the 12th centy., the keep of which, a fine old tower, guards the bridge across the Suir. Another fortress, ascribed to the Templars, and part of an old monastery, existed in the town; though, as regards ruins, it is mentioned that within the last 40 or 50 years there were the ruins of 7 castles in this single parish. Thurles abounds in colleges and schools, maintained by the agency of the Roman Catholics. The cathedral is a very handsome building, and has a good organ.

Conveyances. — Car to Clonmel daily. To Kilkenny, through Urlingford, daily.

Distances.—Cashel, 12 m.; Urlingford, 11; Holycross Abbey, 3½.

[It is a charming drive to Holycross, the road being just sufficiently elevated to command a view over a prettily wooded country, with a background on the S.E. of the Slievenaman and Waterford mountains, and on the N.W. of the Devil's Bit range. Crossing the rly. a second time, we approach the Suir as it runs lazily through its sedgy banks and arrive at Holycross, the most venerable abbey in the S., and perhaps in all Ireland.

It is beautifully situated amidst a

thick grove of wood on the banks of the river, which kept the worthy monks well supplied with their favourite diet. "This place was distinguished as the site of a Cistercian monastery, founded in honour of the Holy cross, of which a portion is said to have been preserved here by Donogh Carbragh O'Brien, King of Limerick, who in 1182, endowed it with lands constituting an earldom, and conferring the title of Earls of Holy Cross upon its abbots, who were barons of Parliament and usually vicars-general of the Cistercian order in Ireland."—*Lewis.*

The abbey however was really founded by Donald O'Brien, the father of Donogh Carbragh.

The ruins are very extensive, and abound in elaborate detail of such exquisite feature as to deserve very careful attention. The plan of the ch. was cruciform, consisting of nave with aisles, choir, transepts, chapels, and a tower springing from the junction of the choir with nave.

The nave is separated from the N. aisle by round-headed, and from the S. by pointed arches, and is lighted by an exquisite 6-light window. The N. aisle is divided in two by a round arch, crowned by a sculptured head, and is continued to the very end of the nave. The S. aisle has a beautiful window (close to the S. transept) blocked up save in the upper mullions. The N. transept is the gem of the ch.; attached to it are two chapels on the E., and an aisle on the W. running parallel with the nave. One of these chapels possesses a delicately groined roof and a 3-light window of different design to the one in the second chapel; but the chief interest lies in a short passage which runs between, supported by a double row of pointed arches with twisted pillars. The roof of this little sanctum is also elaborately groined as though the resources of the architect had been taxed to the utmost in decorating it. It has been supposed that this passage was used for the temporary resting-place of the bodies of the monks previous to burial. Leading from the N. transept is a stone staircase and a deeply recessed doorway entering a room full of mouldings.

The S. transept is also divided off into two chapels, each of which contains a piscina and groined roof, although they have not the mortuary passage. The windows here again differ from each other in design, constituting one of the most singular features of the abbey. "The choir arch is not placed as usual beneath the tower, but 30 ft. in advance of it, thus making the choir of greater length by 14 ft. than the nave, which is but 58 ft. long, the entire length of the ch. being 130 ft. This peculiarity appears, however, to be an afterthought and not the design of the original architect, which was evidently to limit as usual the length of the choir to the arch in front of the tower, and the second arch is unquestionably of more modern construction."—*P.*

The roof of the steeple tower is also groined and supported by graceful pointed arches. The choir is lighted like the W. end by a 6-light window, the tracery of which should be particularly noticed. It contains an elaborate Perp. monument of the Countess of Desmond. This was usually considered to have been erected to Donagh Cabragh O'Brien, but the style of the tomb which is about the close of the 14th century, or Trans. Perp., at once forbids the supposition; and the arms between the crockets of the arches are those of the houses of Ormond and Desmond. This fact too will reconcile the anachronism of the erection of the abbey by the aforesaid Donald in 1182, whereas the whole style of the abbey is a couple of hundred years later. Coupling this with the position of the tomb, viz., on the rt. of the high altar, the place assigned to the builder, it would be reasonably assumed that Holy Cross was rebuilt in the time of, and very probably by, the same person to whom the tomb was erected. A staircase leads from the N. transept on the roof, and is protected by a stone balustrade. On this side of the ch. were the offices and abbot's residence. The tower may be ascended by means of this staircase. A large grass-covered court adjoins the N. aisle, and was entered from without by a gateway and also from the N. aisle by a Norm. arch, now blocked.

The visitor will also notice on a wall outside the abbey precincts an inscription and coat of arms. 2½ m. S. of Holycross is the wooded eminence of Killough, and at the foot of it the old tower of Killough Castle.

Adjoining the abbey are Holycross House, and, on the opposite bank of the Suir, Graiguenoe House (O. Clarke, Esq.).] Before arriving at Goold's-Cross stat. the line passes the vicinity of a perfect cluster of castles — Milltown, Clonyharp, Graigue, and Clogher—all within a mile of each other. "The district of Upper Ossory, which the line now intersects, appears to have been encompassed with a continuous circuit of these castles, each communicating with and commanding those next it, so as to form a chain of defence round the territory."—*Wakeman.*

95 m. *Goold's-Cross* stat., from whence it is a drive of 5 m. to *Cashel,* [passing 1½ m. Longfield House, the residence of Chas. Bianconi, Esq., to whose patient energy and foresight Ireland is more indebted socially than to any living being. A short sketch of the wonderful manner in which this one man opened up seven-tenths of the country to civilization and commerce will be found in Introd., page xliv.

2½ m. a very pretty landscape opens out at *Ardmayle,* where the Suir is crossed. On the l. are the ruins of the castellated residence of the Butlers. It afterwards passed into the hands of the Cootes, the last proprietor having been hanged by Cromwell on the capture of the castle.

On l. is Ardmayle House (R. Price, Esq.). As the road mounts the high ground, the singular Rock of Cashel, "the outpouring of the Devil," as far as the rock is concerned, though the very casket of sanctity as far as regards the buildings on it, appear conspicuously in the foreground.

Cashel itself (*Hotel :* Corcoran's) is a dirty town grouped at the foot and at one side of the Rock, which rises steeply and even precipitously to the height of about 300 ft. (Pop. 4374.) The objects of interest are many and deeply interesting— they embrace : 1. the ecclesiastical buildings on the Rock; 2. Hore Abbey below it; and 3. the Dominican Abbey in the town. The city of Cashel, as it is called by a charter of Charles I., dates from the early kings of Munster and the arrival of St. Declan, who in the time of St. Patrick founded a ch. here. It was an important stronghold in those days, and was fortified by Brian Boroimhe, although it was not until the 12th centy. that Cormac McCarthy, king of Desmond, built the chapel now known by his name. Henry II. in his Irish invasion received here the homage of Donald O'Brien, king of Limerick, the builder of the cathedral. Edward Bruce also held a parliament on the Rock. The cathedral, however, was burnt in 1495 by the famous Earl of Kildare, who had a grudge against the Archbishop, and defended his conduct before the king on the ground that he would not have set fire to it if he had known the Archbishop was *not* inside the building. The seeming candour of this answer procured from the king his appointment to be Lord Lieutenant of Ireland. Having gained admission into the enclosure at the top of the Rock, the first object of interest is the cathedral, which has no western door, but is entered on the S. by a pointed doorway and porch with groined arches. The ch. is cruciform, with nave, transepts, choir, and a belfry, supported by beautiful Early Pointed arches, the clustered pillars of which are all dissimilar. Notice the sculpture on the capitals of the pillars, both at the entrance and also of a small doorway on W. The nave is unusually short, but contains some interesting tombs, one of which is ornamented with curious stucco-work, and another (date 1574) with a good trefoil canopy. The S. transept is lighted by an E. E. 3-light window, similar to that in the N., but with the addition of a rose window, which has a depression of the middle arch. The heads of these lights have been filled up.

There is a series of sculptures in the N. transept, representing on one side 6 of the apostles, St. Catherine and John the Baptist, St. Michael and St. Patrick, with shields of the Butler and Hacket families; on the other St. Bridget, the remaining 5 apostles, and the 4 evangelists typified by beasts.

On the E. of the transept is a chapel with a 2-light window under one dripstone, and a portion of the original altar in the centre. In another chapel is the sarcophagus of King Cormac, A.D. 908, and above it is a crucifixion, which was discovered amidst the rubbish of the well.

The chancel is lighted by a large E. window and some lancets. There are some singular apertures between the heads of these windows, differing in pattern on the N. and S. sides, while all of them are quatrefoiled on the outside.

Having examined the ground-floor of the cathedral we enter through a very graceful pointed arch into Cormac's Chapel, at once the best preserved and most curious structure in the country; combining the richest Norm. decoration with the high stone roof. Amongst the peculiarities of this structure, are the absence of an original entrance doorway on the W. side (the present one being obviously of later date); and its having both a northern and southern entrance: but the most remarkable is a square tower at each side of the termination of the nave at the junction with the chancel, which thus gives the ch. a cruciform plan. These towers are of unequal height—that on the S. side, which wants its roof, being about 55 ft. in height; while the other, including its pyramidal roof is but 50 ft. The S. tower is ornamented with 8 projecting belts or bands, the lowest being but 3 ft. from the ground, and a projecting parapet, apparently of later erection. The northern tower is similarly ornamented with bands, but exhibits only 6 instead of 8. The walls of the body of the ch. are decorated with blank arcades of semicircular arches, arranged in 2 stories; resembling very much the churches sculptured on the marble fonts in Winchester Cathedral and in the neighbouring one of East Meon; and the lowest of these arcades is carried round the S. tower.—*Petrie.* On this same S. side is a very beautiful blocked doorway. It is circular headed, containing 5 mouldings of the richest Norm. style, and showing on the lintel the sculpture of an animal. "The N. doorway, which was obviously the grand entrance, is of greater size, and is considerably richer in its decorations. It has 5 separate columns and one double column, supporting a very elaborate arch moulding, and containing in the tympanum the sculpture of a centaur shooting at a lion, as if to rescue a smaller animal under the lion's feet." There are also 2 smaller doors, the S. with an ornamented architrave, and the N. with a chevron moulding.

Internally the chapel is divided into chancel and naves, separated by a magnificent chancel arch, which causes a singular effect from its not being quite in the centre. The roof is composed of semicircular arches "resting on square ribs, which spring from a series of massive semicolumns set at equal distances against the walls. The bases of these semicolumns are on a level with the capitals of the choir arch, the abacus of which is continued as a string-course round the building. The walls of both nave and chancel, beneath the string-course, are ornamented with a row of semicircular arches, slightly recessed and enriched with chevron, billet, and other ornaments and mouldings."—*Wakeman.* There is this difference, that in the choir the arches spring from columns, but in the nave from square pilasters. These wall arcades are all decorated on their faces or soffits with zigzag mouldings, and the choir arch has one of its mouldings composed of heads.

The columns are twisted in the quadrangular recess which serves for the altar, and which projects externally so as to create a third division. There are also 3 heads under the string-course occupying the blanks between the arches of the arcades. The archæologist should carefully study the divers ornaments and heads which cover the capitals both of the doorway and the arcades.

There are two features which should not be omitted: 1. That the chapel is not parallel with the cathedral, and that therefore its orientation differs; 2. That above the nave and chancel, between the vaulted roof and the high stone roof, are apartments or crofts - that of the chancel being 6 ft. lower than the one over the nave. This latter contains a singular fireplace, with flues passing through the thickness of the wall. The croft at the E. end of the chancel is lighted by an unusual holed window.

The visitor will now ascend the staircase from the belfry to the transepts in the thickness of the wall—the one in the N. leading to the round tower by a passage lighted by quatrefoiled windows. Here we arrive at the defensive portion of this ecclesiastic fortress, which could only be entered from the ch.; but the doors in the staircase were protected by holes for the purpose of throwing molten lead. The most ancient portion of the building is to be found in some offices above the W. end. Underneath is the cellar, surmounted by the refectory, and above that again is the dormitory. The round tower, at the E. angle of N. transept, built of freestone, is about 90 ft. high, and 56 ft. round, and is remarkable for the angular headed apertures formed of a single stone in the upper story.

In the cemetery adjoining the cathedral is the Cross of Cashel raised on a rude pedestal, and sculptured on one side with an effigy of St. Patrick. Nor will the visitor leave the Rock of Cashel without drinking in the exquisite view that opens out in every quarter, embracing to the S. the rich scenes of the golden vale of Tipperary (more beautiful in its natural than its social features) backed up by the lofty ranges of the Galtee mountains, and more to the W. by Slieve-na-man and the Clonmel hills. Northward is the country around Thurles and Holy Cross, with the valley of the Suir and the Devil's Bit mountains in the distance. W. the dark masses of the Slieve Phelim mountains, between Cashel and Limerick; while underneath lies the town grouped around the Rock, the ruins of Hore Abbey, and many a tower and ruined ch.

II.—Of a similar date to the Cathedral on the Rock are the last-named ruins of Grey or Hore Abbey, founded for Cistercians in 1272 by David MacCawell, Arch. of Cashel, and endowed with the revenues of the Benedictines, whom he had expelled from the Rock.

It is a cross ch. of lancet style, with some later innovations. The nave is long, consisting of 5 bays and a deep respond, and possesses aisles, though the piers are singularly plain, being perfectly square, relieved only by a chamfer, and without any capital or impost mouldings. It is lighted by a clerestory with quatrefoil windows. As at Holycross, a wall cuts the nave in two, though for what reason it is difficult to determine.

The choir is short, and possesses a piscina and some remains of arcades. It is lighted by a triple lancet window, with insertions in the 2 side ones, the upper portion having been blocked up. The roof of the intersection is groined, though not with any elaborate detail. On either side of the choir were two chapels; only the arches leading to them exist on the S. side; but on the N. are remains of the chapel, containing a piscina, and some traces of vaulting. To the N. of this is another chapel, roofed with a pointed barrel vault, and further on a rectangular building, probably the chapter house. "Two late windows are inserted at the E. end one above another, showing that there must have been once an upper floor, while two vaulting shafts, one at each angle, and running the whole length, prove that this was not originally the case. These innovations seem to suggest that at the later period portions were converted into a castle."—*C. West.*

III.—The Dominican Priory is another fine old ruin situated amidst a nest of back streets in the town. It has a beautiful E. window of the 13th centy., which may be seen to better advantage from the garden of the Hotel than from any other spot.

Hacket's Abbey, a Franciscan Monastery, is occupied by the modern Roman Catholic ch.

Conveyances from Cashel.—Car to Goold's Cross.

Distances. — Tipperary, 12 m.; Goold's-Cross, 5; Holy-Cross, 8½; Fethard, 10.]

At 99¾ m. Dundrum Stat., the line passes through some very fine and thick woods, enclosed in the demesne of Dundrum (Visct. Hawarden), a handsome Grecian mansion on the l. of the line.

The traveller will have finished nearly two-thirds of his southward journey by the time he arrives at

107 m. *Limerick* Junction, the "Swindon" of Ireland, as far as bustle goes, though not in luxury and elegance. Nevertheless, the hungry "voyageur" may obtain an excellent dinner in the quarter of an hour allowed for refreshments. As the Waterford and Limerick line effects a junction here, all the trains to Dublin, Cork, Waterford, and Limerick start together, producing at stated times a busy scene.

Distances.—Dublin, 107 m.; Cork, 58; Mallow, 37; Limerick, 22; Waterford, 55; Tipperary, 3; Clonmel, 28.

As the train continues its southerly course, the most conspicuous object is the *Galty* range, which embraces some of the highest mountains in the S. of Ireland. In front, the long hill of Slieve-na-muck, 1215 ft., extends nearly E. and W., cut off by the Vale of Aherlow from the main ridge which rises very steeply, with deep clefts and gullies which are well seen from the rly. They extend as far as Clonmel, and their highest points are Galtymore 3015 ft., and Galtybeg, 2703 ft. The former is, indeed, the highest eminence between Lugnaquilla in County Wicklow, and the Killarney mountains in Kerry. They are formed geologically of old red sandstone, rising from the valleys of mountain limestone (R. 30).

To the rt. of the Stat. is Ballykisteen House, a well-planted and handsome seat of Lord Stanley.

Passing on l. Moorsfort House (C. Moore, Esq.), we arrive at 117 m. *Knocklong*, in the vicinity of which are several ancient remains. On the hill adjoining the Stat. on l. is the shell of a castle erected by the family of Hurley. From its position on Knocklong Hill a remarkably fine view is obtained.

[A charming excursion may be made to Galbally, 6 m. from the stat., towards the Galtee mountains. *Galbally* is a finely-situated village on the Aherlow, a tributary of the Suir, mentioned before as cutting off Slieve-na-muck from the Galtees. This valley, being the only pass into Tipperary from the N. parts of Cork, was a constant bone of contention between rival chieftains, although the O'Briens and Fitzgeralds held it "vi et armis" for more than 300 years. Very near the village is *Moor Abbey*, the remains of a Franciscan abbey, founded in the 13th centy. by Donagh Carbragh O'Brien. It is of E. E. date, and is conspicuous for the lofty tower rising from the body of the ch. Following the course of the Aherlow are some demesnes finely situated at the foot of the mountains, viz. Riversdale (H. Massy, Esq.) and Castlereagh.]

3 m. to the rt. is *Hospital*, formerly a locality of the Knights-Templars, which afterwards passed by gift of Queen Eliz. to Sir Valentine Brown, who erected a fortress called Kenmare. The hospital has passed away and the castle very nearly so, but in the ch. there is a figure of a knight in a niche of the chancel. A little to the E. is *Emly*, so far important that it was the seat of a bishopric prior to its incorporation with Cashel in 1568. The see was one of the oldest in the county, having been founded by St. Ailbe, or Alibeus, in the 6th centy. Even before this it is mentioned by Ptolemy as "Imlagh," one of the 3 powerful towns in Ireland. In these modern days it has been principally remarkable for being the locale of a number of faction fights between two parties calling themselves respectively "The Three-year" and "The Four-year Olds."

Tipperary may, in the matter of buildings, be said to be the land of decay; and nowhere will this be more forcibly brought before the traveller than at

Kilmallock (anc. Cill Mocheallog) (*Inn*: Sullivan's), 124 m., where nearly a whole town is marked with the desolation of nakedness. Although Kilmallock, or the "ch. by St. Molach," is known to have existed, and to have been important, at an early date, it is not until the reign of Edw. III. that we find it received a charter, at which time it was surrounded entirely by fortifications and entered by 4 gates—St. John's, Water-gate, Ivy, and Blossoms-gate respectively. It would be tedious to recount all the sieges that the city underwent. It is sufficient to state that it was by order of Cromwell that the fortifications were destroyed, from which date the place went to ruin.

Kilmallock possesses sundry features over and above the usual defensive remains, as it was the residence of many of the nobility and gentry who held their town houses within its walls, and it is this peculiarity which imparts to the whole place such an aspect of fallen greatness. A few of these houses, dating from the time of James or Elizabeth, still remain.

"The plans are nearly all the same: they present 2 or more gable ends to the street, and are divided into 3 stories. The entrances, by spacious portals with semicircular arches, open into small halls, which communicate with broad passages that probably contained the stairs, whence there are doorways leading to the principal apartments.

The windows, of a square form and small in proportion to the size of the room, are divided into compartments by one or more uprights, and sometimes by a cross of stone."—*Weld*.

The 2 mansions that still remain belonged to the Earl of Buckinghamshire and the family of Godsall. Two of the 4 gateways still exist, although one is used as a dwelling-house instead of a gateway, and through them pass the roads to Limerick and Charleville. The latter, formerly known as the Blossoms-gate, and a small portion of the walls, may be traced connecting the 2 on the S. side of the town. The ch. of Sts. Peter and Paul stands within the walls, and is partly used as a parish ch. It consists of nave and S. transept in ruins, and a choir still used for service. The former is separated from an aisle by plain pointed arches springing from square pillars. The choir is lighted by a 5-light lancet window. This ch. differs from most Irish abbey chs. in the arrangement of the tower, which does not rise from the intersection, but is placed at the W. of the N. aisle, and is moreover round and of 2 stories, and lighted by narrow pointed windows. It is one of the old Round Towers, the upper portion being of later date, probably repaired when the ch. was built. In the body of the ch. are monuments of the Fitzgerald, Vernon, and Kelly families, who flourished principally in the 17th centy.

A small river runs round Kilmallock on the N. and W. sides, and on its bank stand the ruins of the Dominican priory, one of the finest in Munster, founded in the close of the 13th centy. by Gilbert, Lord of Offaley. A lofty square tower, supported by extremely narrow arches, rises from the centre of the ch., which is cruciform, and possesses very good details of Trans. E. Eng. style. "A great part of the cloister still remains; but it was never of an ornamental character, the ambulacrum having been formed out of timber."

The choir is lighted by a really magnificent 5-light E.E. window of delicate and graceful design. It contains a canopied mural monument, in which the moulding of the heads of the columns should be noticed. In addition to the E. window, the choir has 6 Early Pointed windows on the S. side. The nave, of which the S. wall is destroyed, is lighted by a quatrefoil window inserted in a pointed arch. To the N. of the nave are the domestic offices. The S. trans. had a window with tracery (now blocked up) similar to Holycross. It also contains a mural monument, the shafts of which are ornamented with heads.

The choir contains the broken tomb of the White Knights, "a title assumed by a branch of the Fitzgeralds, or, as they are frequently called, the Geraldins, and, according to Camden, originating from the grey hairs of the founder of that line."—*C. Croker*.

The fortunes of the Desmond family, who owned more land and possessed more influence in Munster than any family before or after them, are interwoven with the whole history of Kilmallock, and indeed with that of the S. of Ireland, and have been the subject of many a tale from the wonderful address and courage, the hair-breadth escapes, and the romantic career of many of its members. Adjoining the town are Ashhill Towers, the residence of E. Eyre Evans, Esq.; Mount Coote (C. Coote, Esq.), and Ardvullen House (Rev. J. Gabbett), and about 4 m. distant, near Kilfinnan, is Chanadfay Castle, the ancient seat of the Oliver family, but now of Lord Ashtown. Sir Eyre Coote, the conqueror of Hyder Ali, was a native of Kilmallock; and General Lord Blakeney who added Minorca to the British possessions) was born at

Mount Blakeney, about 2 m. on the Charleville road.

Conveyances.—Car daily to Limerick. Car to Bruff and Kilfinane.

Distances.—Bruree, 4 m.; Bruff, 6; Charleville, 5.

[The antiquary should make a visit from Kilmallock to Lough Gur, 10 m.; passing through, 6 m., *Bruff*, another of the principal towns of the Geraldines. It is situated on the banks of a river with the poetical name of the Morning Star, and possesses a good E. Eng. ch. with an octagonal spire. In the neighbourhood are Camus (F. Bevan, Esq.), Baggotstown House (J. Bouchier, Esq.), and Kilballyowen (W. O'Grady, Esq.).

10 m. *Lough Gur*, a pretty lake, bounded by undulating shores, where, according to Irish belief, the last of the Desmonds is doomed to hold his court under its waters, from which he emerges at daybreak on the morning of every 7th year fully armed. This has to be repeated until the silver shoes of his steed are worn out. A similar legend is told at Killarney of the O'Donoghue. Lough Gur is about 5 m. round, and, as it was the centre of the Desmonds' district, was guarded by 2 castles. One of them, a massive square tower, stands upon an island connected with the main land by a causeway. But by far the most interesting objects of Lough Gur are a number of early remains and circles, of which 100 are known to have existed within the memory of man. On the W. side are 3 stone circles, and near a ruined ch. on the shore is "Edward and Grace's Bed," an assemblage of rocks which had once formed a chamber, covered over with large flags. It was however destroyed by treasure seekers after the death of an old woman who used to dwell in it.

Near this is a cromlech, resting on 4 supports; also Carrigalla Fort and 2 singular circular forts of very rude and large masonry. Many other of these primitive remains can also be traced in the neighbourhood of the lake. The geologist should examine the limestone hill of Carrig-na-Nahin or Mass Rock, which is full of chasms.]

129 m. at *Charleville* a direct line diverges to Limerick, saving in the journey from Cork a distance of 19 m. In comparison with some other towns in this county, Charleville (*Inn:* Copley's) is modern, having been founded by the Earl of Ossory in 1621, and named out of compliment to the king; it having been called before "by the heathenish name of Rathgogan." The Duke of Berwick dined here in 1690, and, as a delicate return for hospitality, ordered his men to burn it at his departure.

Close to the town is Sanders Park, the seat of the Sanders family.

[5 m. to the S.E. is *Ardpatrick*, with a few remains of an ancient monastery, said to have been founded by St. Patrick. There are also the stump of a round tower and a quadrangular well, lined with stone. Sunville is the old residence of the Godsall family, who possessed one of the mansions in Kilmallock. About 2 m. to the E. of Ardpatrick is *Kilfinane*, famed for the big rath outside the town.

It is "130 ft. high, 50 ft. in diameter at the base, and 20 ft. at the summit, encircled by 7 earthen ramparts about 20 ft. apart, gradually diminishing in height from the inner to the outermost, which is 10 ft. high and 2000 ft. in circumference."—*Wakeman.*

As the rly. continues its course southward, a considerable range of mountains approach very closely on the l., being in fact an outlying continuation of the Galtees, "which are here succeeded by a lower chain, generally known as the Castle Oliver Mountains, that form the striking boundary of the plain as far as the village of Kilfinane, whence its southerly limits are continued by the Ballyhoura hills to Mallow."—*Fraser.* Following down the valley of the Awbeg, and passing l. Velvetstown House, we arrive at 137½ m. Buttevant, at one time famed for ecclesiastic and now for its military occupants.

The river Awbeg, which by the way is known for its fine trout, is celebrated by Spenser under the name of the Mullah or Mole :—

"Mulla, the daughter of Old Mole so bright,
 The nymph which of that watercourse has charge,
That, springing out of Mole, doth run downright
To Buttevant, where spreading forth at large
It giveth name unto that ancient city
Wich Kil-ne-mullah cleeped is of old,
Whose cragged ruines breed great ruth and pity
To travellers, which it from afar behold."
   Spenser.

"This parish was anciently called Bothon, and is said to have derived its present name from the exclamation 'Boutez en avant' (Push forward), used by David de Barry, its proprietor, to animate his men in a contest with the M'Carthys, which was subsequently adopted as the family motto of the Earls of Barrymore, who derived their title of Viscount from this place."—*Lewis.*

The town contains many interesting remains, of which the chief is the Franciscan abbey, founded, or as some say restored only, by David Oge Barry at the close of the 13th century. It consists of a nave and choir, the central tower having fallen about the year 1818. The W. end is entered by a pointed doorway, and is lighted by 2-light windows, with the upper portions blocked up. In the nave are some good Dec. canopied monuments and a very singular one with short twisted columns and small pointed arches on the N. wall close to where the choir arch once stood. Of this, however, there is only one column left. The choir is lighted on the S. by a series of Early Pointed windows, deeply splayed internally. The middle one has some delicate tracery. The E. window of 3 lights is of unusual pattern.

Attached to the S. of the nave is a beautiful chapel to the Virgin Mary, containing tombs of the Barrys, Fitzgeralds, and Butlers. "The chancel being built on a steep bank of the Awbeg, is raised to the level of the nave by 3 crypts or vaults, the middle of which is supported by a single pillar, so constructed as to resemble 4, with fanciful and well-wrought capitals." *Croker.* A portion of adjoining tower erected by one of the Desmonds for the protection of the abbey is incorporated with the modern Roman Catholic chapel, a handsome cruciform building with a square tower rising from the centre.

Buttevant castle is now modernized, and a residence of Lord Doneraile. It was originally called John's Castle, and formed a corner building at an angle of the wall. The view down the Awbeg, including the spire of the ch., which is within the grounds, is very charming, and the tourist should not omit to stroll as far as the bridge, nearly opposite which are some ruins of the old abbey of Ballybeg.

There is also in the town a square tower, that formerly belonged to a castle of the Lombards.

The modern buildings of Buttevant are the barracks, which will scarcely interest the visitor.]

Distances.—Mallow, 7½ m.; Doneraile, 4½; Kilcolman, 6; Liscarroll. 7.

[Following the course of the Awbeg, which eventually falls into the Blackwater, we arrive at *Doneraile*, a small pretty town redolent of association with Edmund Spenser, who had a paternal estate in the neighbourhood, which was purchased from his son by Sir William St. Leger, President of Munster in the reign of Charles I. In Lord Doneraile's demesne, adjoining the town, the timber is very fine, and the ilex is especially worthy of notice.

Kilcolman, the residence of the poet, is about 3 m. to the N. of Doneraile, a little to the l. of the road to Charleville. It consists of a single ivy-covered tower, on the margin of a small lake, and, it must be confessed, overlooking an extremely dreary tract of country.

To the N. of Kilcolman is Ballnivonear, the seat of J. Barry, Esq.; and immediately behind are the Caroline and Carker mountains, 1188 ft.

Close to Doneraile are—Doneraile House (Lord Doneraile), Kilbrack, and Creagh Castle (G. Brasier Creagh, Esq.), in the grounds of which is the ancient tower of Creagh.]

A car runs from Doneraile to Mallow.

[7 m. to W. of Buttevant are the ruins of Liscarroll Castle, built in all probability soon after the Norman invasion. It is a massive square building, 240 ft. in length, flanked by 2 square and 4 round towers of great strength.]

A charming landscape opens out as the line approaches, 145 m., *Mallow* (*Hotel:* Queen's Arms), a pretty English-looking town, seated on the banks of the Blackwater, beautifully wooded and besprinkled with many a pleasant villa. Mallow was once fashionable, attracting visitors partly by its scenery and more by its spa; but the usual caprice which attends watering-places has long since robbed it of its hypochondriacs and valetudinarians. The castle is situated near the E. end of the town and on the bank of the river. It is the modern Elizabethan residence of Sir D. Norreys, and in the grounds is the square tower of the old fortress. The streets have houses with projecting bay windows which give a quaint and old-fashioned look to the place.

The residences in the immediate neighbourhood are numerous, and include, in addition to the castle—Bearforest, (J. A. Shiel, Esq.), Ballyellis (K. Brasier, Esq.), Rockforest (Sir J. Cotter, Bart.), Ballygarrett (W. Creagh, Esq.).

Two important junctions occur at this stat.; on the l. to Fermoy, and on the rt. to Killarney and Tralee. (Rte. 31.)

The fishing on the Blackwater is notoriously good, although after a flood the river becomes very dirty, and takes a long time to clear. The flies are large and gaudy.

Conveyances. — Rail to Dublin, Cork, Fermoy, Killarney. Car to Killarney and Tralee, through Castle Island; car to Doneraile.

Distances.—Cork, 11 m.; Blarney, 5; Kanturk, 12; Fermoy, 17; Dromaneen, 5.

Excursions.

1. Fermoy, Mitchelstown.
2. Dromaneen.
3. Abbey Morne and Blarney.
4. Buttevant and Doneraile.

From hence the line passes down the valley of the Clydagh, leaving on rt. Dromore House (A. Newman, Esq.).

149½ m. on l. is *Abbey Morne*, once a preceptory of the Knights Templars, and a walled town temp. Edw. III. There is nothing very remarkable in the ch., which appears to have been defended by strong bastions. On the opposite side of the river is Castle Bassett, a tower belonging to a fortress built by the Bassetts. Soon the stream of the Martin shows itself, becoming more picturesque and wooded as we approach

160 m. *Blarney*, where it falls into the river of the same name amidst very charming scenery.

Blarney Castle is nearly 1½ m. from the stat., and the most convenient way of visiting it is to take a car direct from Cork. It was built in the 15th centy. by the McCarthys, who were themselves descended from the kings of Munster, and it underwent much rough treatment and many vicissitudes, not the least singular of which is its being annually visited by thousands, attracted not so much by the charming scenery in which it is placed as the reputation it has gained for flattery and soft speeches. As regards the former, who has not heard of

> "The groves of Blarney
> That look so charming
> Down by the purling
> Of sweet silent streams"?

The main feature of Blarney Castle is a square tower with a battlement and machicolations; and below the parapet is a stone, which, when kissed, endows the performer with wonderful powers of speech. The difficulty and even danger of reaching this stone is so great that another Blarney stone has been substituted on the tower, which, if the visitor believes the guides, confers equal power.

> "There is a stone there
> That whoever kisses
> Oh! he never misses
> To grow eloquent.
> 'Tis he may clamber
> To my lady's chamber,
> Or become a member
> Of Parliament."

Having exhausted the castle and wandered in the groves, so well adapted

> "To speculation
> And conversation
> In sweet solitude,"

the visitor may inspect the caves, which were used by the former proprietors as a ready-made dungeon; though, occurring as they do in a limestone formation, they need not be invested with any supernatural legends. The tourist will find at Blarney a neat little inn, Turkish baths, and several Irish guides, who display a strong affection for "backshish."

A rapid run of nearly 6 m. brings the rail to the outskirts of Cork where the locomotive depôt is situated, and thence through a very long limestone tunnel into the centre of the southern metropolis.

Hotels: Imperial, first-rate; Victoria, pretty good.

ROUTE 26.

FROM **DUBLIN** TO **CARLOW, KILKENNY,** AND **WATERFORD, BY RAIL.**

From Dublin to Kilkenny the tourist travels by the Great Southern and Western Rly. as far as Kildare (30 m.) (Rte. 25), the Carlow line at this point branching to the S. and running down the valley of the Barrow.

36 m. l. the old tower and modern demesne of Kildangan Castle (Moore O'Ferrall, Esq.), while about 2 m. on l. are Monasterevan and the woods of Moore Abbey, the noble seat of the Marquess of Drogheda (p. 224). The general features of the country through which we are now passing are low, wet, and boggy, the land lying very little above the level of the Barrow. Passing rt. Bert Hall (late Lord Downes) and Kilberry, the towers of

45 m. *Athy* soon come in sight (*Hotel:* Leinster Arms). It was in early times a place of importance as a neutral ground between the territories of Leix and Caellun, which as a matter of course were always at desperate feud, and struggled hard with each other for possession of Athy or Ath-legar, "the ford towards the west." Subsequent to the English invasion the Lords Justices regarded it with equal jealousy, from its being on the frontier of the Kildare Marches, and a castle, now called White's Castle, was accordingly erected for its defence by Fitzgerald Earl of Kildare, at the commencement of the 14th cent. It is a massive rectangular and embattled building, flanked at each corner by a small square turret, and overlooks the bridge that crosses

the Barrow. This bridge bears the curious name of Crom-a-boo, from the ancient war-cry of the Fitzgeralds, and is in itself worth notice. A little distance to the N. of the town by the river-side is another square fortress, called Woodstock Castle, which, although usually ascribed to the Earl of Pembroke, is considered, with more probability, to have been built in the 13th cent. by an Earl of Kildare, who received the manor of Woodstock by marriage with the daughter of O'Moore of Leix. It is remarkable for the thickness of its walls, its square mullioned windows, and a round-headed gateway adjoining the tower. Formerly a monastery existed for Crouched Friars and another for Dominicans, both established in the 13th cent. There are also the remains of Preston's Gate leading into the town. Athy is a well-built little place, and is, jointly with Naas, the assize town of Co. Kildare. Its situation in the middle of a rich plain, together with facilities of water and land carriage, commands for it a large agricultural business.

A branch of the Grand Canal from Monasterevan here joins the Barrow, forming the commencement of the Barrow navigation, by which water communication is maintained between Athy, Carlow, Bagenalstown, Borris, New Ross, and the sea.

Excursions.—
1. Kilberry.
2. Moat of Ardscull.

[1. From Athy to Kilberry, 3 m. to the N., between the rly. and the river, and near. Lord Downes' seat at Bert. On this spot 2 strong castles and an abbey formerly stood, of the latter of which there are slight ruins; and on the other side of the river is *Rheban Castle* (Righ-ban), "the House of the King," one of the fortresses of Richard de St. Michael (the same who founded the monastery for Crouched Friars in Athy). But it is probable that he only enlarged or rebuilt it, as not only the name appears to be of an early date, but it is even mentioned by Ptolemy as an inland town of some note.

2. The Moat of Ardscull, 3½ m. on the road to Kilcullen, is a high mound (now planted), supposed to have been raised to commemorate a desperate battle in the 3rd cent. between the men of S. Leinster and those of Munster. About 2 m. to the E., by a cross-road, is another historical spot, the *Rath of Mullaghmast* (Mullach-Mastean), "the Hill of Decapitation." It was formerly known as "the Carmen," where, on 16 conical mounds, as many of the elders of the province of Leinster held their councils; but it derived its other name "in consequence of the act of some English adventurers in the 16th cent., who, being resisted in their encroachments by some of the Irish chieftains, invited the latter to a conference on New Year's Day, fell upon them unawares, and slew them."—*Lewis.* In consequence of the anathematization of Carmen the place of assembly was removed to the rath at Naas. Visible in the W. is the tower of Inch Castle, one of King John's fortresses, which was the locale of a severe engagement in 1642 between the armies of Ormond and Mountgarrett.]

*Conveyances.—*Rail to Dublin and Kilkenny. Car to Baltinglass. Car to Ballitore.

*Distances.—*Stradbally, 8 m.; Carlow, 11; Timahoe Round Tower, 10 (Rte. 25); Ardscull, 3½.

48 m. on the W. bank of the Barrow is Kilmoroney House (Rev. F. S. Trench).

51 m. *Mageney* Stat., [3½ m. on rt. is Kilkea, an interesting modernised Anglo-Norm. castle, originally built by De Lacy in 1180, and subsequently rebuilt by one of the Fitzgeralds. It was again added to by Mr. Caulfield, who held it for a time

previous to its reverting to the hands of its ancient possessors, the family of Kildare. The interior contains an oak staircase and some basso-relievos on subjects connected with the Kildare family.

A little to the N.E., on the road to Ballitore, is Moone Abbey (F. Carroll, Esq.), where another castle is incorporated with the dwelling-house; and Timolin, celebrated for its monastery, founded in the 7th cent. by St. Moling. From hence it is 1¼ m. to the little Quaker town of Ballitore].

3 m. rt. *Castle Dermot*, according to some, obtained its name from St. Diermot, who founded a monastery in 500, though others believe it to have been the residence of the Dermots Kings of Leinster. However that may be, it is certain that there are some fine remains :—

1. A round tower, slender and tall, adjoining a more modern ch., and said to have been erected in the 9th cent. by the Abbot Carpreus.

2. The remains of the Franciscan monastery founded at the beginning of the 14th cent. by Thomas, Lord of Offaley. This must have been a fine Dec. building. It was cruciform, the W. end lighted by 2 lancet windows, and the N. transept being occupied by the chapel of the Virgin. Here is a 4-light window, having the crown of the arch filled with a large cinquefoil, and the spandrils ornamented with trefoil.

3. Of contemporary date with the round tower are several sculptured crosses, of which the only one standing exhibits a representation of the Crucifixion in the centre, and some figures on each arm.

4. A Norm. arch with dogtooth mouldings, all that is left of a ch. built by the early English settlers.

Crossing the Lea, where we enter Co. Carlow, and passing l. Oak Park, the ornamental demesne of H. Bruen, Esq., M.P., the line arrives at

56 m. *Carlow* (anc. Ceithiorlach) [*Ireland*.]

(*Hotel*: Club-house; tolerable), brisk and cheerful-looking, containing all the usual accompaniments of a county and assize town, such as court-house, gaol, lunatic asylum, infirmary, and the like. (Pop. 8341). The former is built with a Doric portico after the model of the Parthenon at Athens, and has an effective-looking front. The Protestant Ch. is remarkable for its lofty spire, although it is surpassed by the R. Cath. Cathedral, which has a lantern tower 151 ft. high springing from a western front overloaded with florid ornamentation. In the interior is a good monument to the memory of Bp. Doyle by Hogan, an Irish sculptor, whose studio is at Rome. The subject represents the effigy of the Bishop, with prostrate Ireland weeping by his side. Adjoining the ch. is a college for R. C. students, a handsome building, consisting of a centre and 2 wings, in a shady and pleasant park overlooking the river Barrow, which—

"Though deep, yet clear; though gentle, yet not dull;
Strong without rage; without o'erflowing full"—

flows merrily through the town, and past the ruins of Carlow Castle, access to which is obtained through the kitchen-garden of a grocer close to the bridge. It is ascribed to King John, and must have formerly been a very massive building : it was apparently rectangular, with drum towers at each corner; now only the W. face of wall with the flanking towers remain, a state of decay partly owing to the effects of time and hard usage, it having sustained 3 sieges, one at the hand of Sir E. Poynings in 1494, another by the insurgents in 1641, and lastly by the Republican army under Ireton. Nor was this all, for in 1814 a speculative physician fixed upon the old fortress as an useful site for a lunatic asylum, and, applying gun-

M

Conveyances.—By rail to Kilkenny and Dublin. Car to Tullow.

Distances.—Kilkenny, 25 m.; Athy, 11; Castle Comer, 13; Killeshin, 3.

[An excursion to this latter place should not be omitted by the ecclesiologist, who will find in the old ch. a most unique specimen of carving. The road from Carlow crosses the Wellington Bridge, connecting it with the populous suburb of Grague. Very soon after leaving the Barrow the road begins to rise as it approaches the ridge of limestone hills which begirdle the great Leinster coal-field, the most important coal-basin in Ireland. At Killeshin it pierces this girdle, at a spot known as the "Cut of Killeshin," where for nearly a mile it is carried through a pass varying from 10 to 40 ft. in depth, and only a few feet wide. The date of Killeshin Ch. is in all probability considerably anterior to the Norm. invasion, although the Norm. decorations so plentifully lavished would appear to make it of that particular era, but we have already seen at the round towers of Kildare and Timahoe (Rte. 25) that this style is frequently found in Ireland very much earlier than the Norm. era. "The 4 concentric arches which form the doorway of Killeshin display a great variety of ornamental detail, consisting of chevron work, animals, &c. A pediment surrounds the external arch, and a window on the S. side wall is canopied by a broad band ascending and converging in straight lines."—*Wakeman.* Round the abacus an Irish inscription formerly extended, but this has been nearly obliterated by time, and the zealous efforts of a resident who, we are credibly informed, devoted a good deal of labour towards destroying it. The visitor should particularly notice the heads on the capitals, which, in the arrangement of the hair, resemble those at Timahoe. There is also a very ancient font in the graveyard, of a bulbous form, with the base cut into an octagon.

Continuing towards Castlecomer, the road at length attains the summit of the table-land that forms the Leinster coal-field. The average height of the E. side is about 1000 ft., and the highest point is a little to the S. of this at Clogrenan, from whence the views over the Wicklow Mountains are extremely fine, Lugnaquilla occupying a prominent place in the centre. The valley of the Barrow consists of the calp or middle limestone measures resting on the granite without any old red or silurian intervening. Overlying the limestone, at a height of about 250 ft. above the sea, are the coal-measures, which form, therefore, the greater portion of this ridge of hills. Their geology is explained more at length in Introd. (p. xxvi), although it may be briefly stated here that the general section of the Castlecomer fields shows a series of 6 beds of coal, altogether occupying a thickness of 1850 ft.

The most interesting colliery for the fossil collector is Bilboa, about 2 m. W. of Cloghrenan. Here, in addition to many typical coal-ferns and sigillaria, have been found two new crustacea related to the Limulus, or King crab, and named Bellinurus regius and B. arcuatus.

11 m. Castlecomer is a small colliery town, situated on the river Dinin, and on the W. side of the basin; and contains nothing of interest, except a new Roman Catholic chapel of good design.]

The remainder of the line to Kilkenny belongs to the Irish South Eastern Co., but is worked by the Great Southern and Western Co., who receive 5000*l.* per annum for so doing. Crossing the Burreen river, we still follow the valley of the "goodly Barow," in view of the hills of the Castlecomer coal-basin, and of the demesne of Clogrenan (H. Rochfort, Esq.), while to the S.E. glimpses are caught of that noble range of mountains between Bagenalstown and Enniscorthy, in which Mounts Leinster and Blackstairs are the most prominent points.

60 m. Milford stat. In the village by the banks of the river is a perfect colony of flour-mills, which, together with Milford House, belong to J. Alexander, Esq.

64 m. on rt. 1 m. is *Leighlin-bridge* (anc. Lleith-ghlionn), divided into 2 portions by the Barrow, which is crossed by a bridge of 9 arches, built by Maurice Jakis, a canon of Kildare, and in his day a famous bridge-architect, by whom those at Kilcullen and St. Wulstan's were erected. For the protection of the monastery which then existed, the fortress of Black Castle was built on the E. bank of the river by John de Claville, in the 12th cent.

From the remains still left it would have appeared to have been constructed in the usual Anglo-Norman style of a quadrangle. The tower at one of the angles and a portion of surrounding wall are yet visible. An old building at the S. end of the W. wall is supposed to have formed part of the monastery, which, by the way, after the Dissolution was converted into a fort.

Stewart Lodge is the residence of the family of Stewart, the proprietors of the town.

[The village of *Old Leighlin*, 1½ m. W., was the seat of a flourishing monastery in the 7th cent., containing, at the time of the rule of St. Laserius, no less than 1500 souls. It is now a portion of the diocese of Ossory and Ferns, which is the smallest in the province of Dublin.

The cathedral is a very plain building, consisting of nave and choir, the latter rebuilt by Bishop Saunders in 1527. In the interior are some monuments of the time of the 16th cent.]

66 m. *Bagenalstown*, with its graceful spire looks very pretty as we approach it, but the town contains nothing whatever to interest the visitor, being, in fact, quite a modern place. It is rather an important junction of the Irish South-Eastern and the Wexford lines. The latter rly. is only at present completed to Ballywilliam, 5 m. from New Ross, and it is extremely doubtful whether it will ever get farther, until the monetary prospects of the company are a little brighter.

2 m. W. are the ruins of Ballymoon Castle, the walls of which form a large quadrangle formerly surrounded by a moat. On the N. and S. are 2 square towers of great strength, the average thickness of the walls being not less than 8 ft. It is probably one of the earliest Anglo-Norman fortresses. [To Ballywilliam the line runs down the vale of the Barrow, passing on rt. the ruins of Ballyloughan, a fortress of the Kavanaghs, whose district we are now entering. In form it is a square, entered by a pointed gateway flanked by drum towers on either side.

8 m. *Borris*, an extremely pretty village, shaded by the woods of Borris House, the beautiful residence of Arthur Kavanagh, Esq., the lineal representative of the MacMurroughs, the ancient line of the Kings of Leinster, "Donald Kavanagh having been a natural son of MacMurrough, last King of Leinster, whose name and authority he subsequently assumed." The neighbourhood is very picturesque, and embraces fine views of Mount Leinster and Blackstairs, which lie close to the rly. on the left.

21 m. Ballywilliam, the present terminus of the line Rte. 28. From hence to New Ross it is 5 m.]

From Bagenalstown the Kilkenny

M 2

line turns off to the S.W., crossing the Barrow, and passing rt. Shankill Castle (J. Aylward. Esq.). Good views of Mt. Leinster, Blackstairs, and Mt. Brandon accompany us on the l.

74 m. Gowran stat. Adjoining the village 1 m. rt. is Gowran Castle, a seat of Lord Clifden.

At 78 m. a junction is effected with the Waterford line, and the 2 rlys. enter side by side the remarkable old city of *Kilkenny* (anc. Cill-chain-nigh) (Rte. 27) (*Hotels*: Club-house, good; Imperial), which, in interesting remains, associations, and situation, is surpassed by very few cities in the kingdom. (Pop, 14,174).

In the 12th cent. Strongbow made it his head-quarters, although he was temporarily dispossessed of it by Donald O'Brien, King of Thomond; but towards the end of the cent. the former was succeeded by William le Mareschal, who built the castle, and established a government over one portion of the town, the other part (still called Irishtown) being under the control of the Bishop of Ossory. Gilbert de Clare, Earl of Gloucester, by marriage with Le Mareschal's daughter, obtained the co. of Kilkenny, which passed again by marriage to Hugh le Spencer, from whom it was purchased by James Butler, 3rd Earl of Ormonde. Thus it was that the great family of Ormonde became possessed of Kilkenny.

Several Parliaments have been held here at different times—the first in 1294, the last in 1536; and it played a notorious part in the parliamentary war, when the garrison, having suffered terribly from the plague, was obliged to surrender the city to Cromwell.

Its situation is charming—

"The stubborne Newre, whose waters gray,
 By fair Kilkenny and Rosseponte boord,"

runs through the town from N. to S., dividing it into 2 unequal portions, of which the W. contains the castle and all the principal streets.

The cathedral is in Irishtown, which is separated from the main portion by a little stream called the Breagh. Two bridges cross the Nore —the one with a handsome balustrade is called St. John's Bridge, and from it is obtained a very beautiful view of the river front of the castle. Green Bridge connects Irishtown with the opposite bank.

The castle occupies an elevated site overlooking the Nore, and though originally built by Strongbow, and added to by Le Mareschal, has since then been so repeatedly altered and added to, that only 2 or 3 of the original towers are left. The latest improvements by the present Marquis have in effect amounted to a rebuilding, and as it now stands it is a fine baronial building, forming two sides of a quadrangle. The grounds are well laid out, but are limited in space. The interior contains some splendid suites of rooms, a picture-gallery full of family portraits of the Butlers, the original picture of the family of Charles I., by Vandyke, and some interesting tapestry, the manufacture of which was introduced into Kilkenny in the 16th cent. by Piers Earl of Ormond. For this purpose he brought several workmen from Flanders; but further than supplying the wants of the castle, nothing of any permanence was done.

The present building is from the designs of Mr. Robertson, of Kilkenny. There is a very pleasant walk along the banks of the Nore immediately under the castle.

The cathedral of St. Canice, in Irishtown, is the gem of Kilkenny antiquities. Although not situated in the best part of the town, it is on such high ground, and so shaded by trees, as to be in no way influenced by it; and, with the exception of Armagh, there is no cathedral in Ireland so well kept. Nor is this all, for the close proximity of a lofty round tower imparts the effect of additional antiquity to the whole building, and involuntarily carries back the mind to the early ecclesiastical days of the 6th and 7th centuries.

The date of St. Canice, however, is precisely fixed at 1180, the foundations having been laid in that year by Felix O'Dullarny, Bishop of Ossory. He built the choir, the remainder of the ch. not being completed till 100 years after. Subsequently Bishop Ledrel beautified it, and added a magnificent stained glass E. window, which was not likely to escape the sacrilegious attention of Cromwell's soldiers.

Bishop Pococke, in the last cent., restored the cathedral to something like its pristine beauty, replacing the monuments as they were formerly, and filling a window over the w. door with some of the stained glass from the old E. window. It is said that the Pope's Nuncio thought so highly of it that he offered 700*l.* for it; but this, though a large sum for those days, when ecclesiology was in abeyance, was refused.

It is a cruciform ch., from the centre of which arises a very low and massive tower. Its length from E. to W. is 226 ft., and the breadth of the transepts 123 ft. Externally the most noticeable things are the tower, the battlement with which the walls of the clerestory and the transepts are finished, and the quatrefoil windows by which the former is lighted. Notice also the S. porch, and a remarkably beautiful w. door, with 2 trefoil-headed compartments, the crown of the arch being occupied by a quatrefoil. Immediately above it are 3 singular quatrefoil windows at the base of the E. window.

Internally, the nave is separated from the side aisles by 5 clustered columns supporting pointed arches on each side.

"The tower, which is 37 ft. square, is sustained by 4 massive columns, and its floor is supported by groins springing from the columns as from a single point, spreading out in many strings or beads until they all meet in the centre, forming a very strong and beautiful arch." This arch was built by Bishop Hacket, in the 15th cent. The transepts are lighted by E. E. windows, and both of them have chapels attached. The N. trans. is the parish ch., and contains the chair of St. Kieran, who is said to have preceded St. Patrick by 30 years. There is also a fine E. Eng. W. window, beneath which, and over the door, is a double trefoil-headed recess under a pointed arch.

The worst part of the cathedral is the choir, which is disfigured by a trashy cornice.

Amongst the tombs are that of Bishop David; Bishop Walsh, assassinated by one James Dollond, who stabbed the prelate in the heart with a skein; Bishop Pococke, whose pride was ever to adorn the cathedral and to do good to the town; Peter Butler, Earl of Ormonde, and Margaret his wife, temp. 1539; and John Grace, Baron of Courtstown, 1568.

Adjoining the S. transept is the round tower, 108 ft. high, and 47 in circumference at the base. The entrance faces the S., and is about 8 ft. from the ground. It has some features unlike the general arrangement of the round towers, one of which is the width of the windows.

There are 5 square openings, placed obliquely between the door and summit, in addition to 6 windows at the summit, the number usually being limited to 4. "The circumference at top is exactly filled by an arch which, to the eye beneath, presents the appearance of a large millstone." The antiquary who wishes to study St. Canice more fully should consult the exhaustive treatise on it by the Rev. Dr. Graves and Mr. Prim.

Not far from the cathedral stands the ruins of the Franciscan monastery, part of which is used as a brewery, the other part as a tennis-court. It still possesses a very delicate 7-light window, and a graceful tower resting on groined arches.

Before leaving Irishtown the visitor should inspect the Dominican or Black Abbey, which is now used as a R. Catholic chapel. This also is a Dec. building, cruciform, with a central tower, finished off with graduated battlements. The E. window is of 5 lights, of remarkably beautiful design, as are also the windows of the choir on the N. side.

The parish ch. of St. John, on the E. bank of the Nore, was formerly the hospital of St. John, and founded by William Earl of Pembroke in 1220. Agreeably to the law of mutations which appears to govern Kilkenny ecclesiastical ruins, St. John's was turned into a barrack before being again appropriated to its rightful use. It was noted for the extreme number and beauty of its windows, which obtained for it the name of the Lantern of Ireland. Some of these windows are blocked, though their mouldings are visible externally. The choir is still in ruins. Notice the machicolations under the battlements of the tower, an unusual feature in Irish chs.

St. Mary's ch. should be visited for the sake of the monument to Sir Richard Shee, temp. 1608, with its 10 sculptured figures at the base. There is also one to his brother, Elias Shee, of whom Holinshed wrote that he was "a pleasant-conceited companion, full of mirth, without gall."

For modern ecclesiastical buildings the tourist should inspect the new R. Catholic chapel, which, with its noble tower of gray limestone, is a most conspicuous feature in all views of the city. It is by far the finest and best designed building of the kind in Ireland, being a cruciform ch. with a lofty apse. All the details are worked out with a taste which the architects of R. Catholic chapels seldom show in this country.

The house in which the Confederate Catholics held a parliament in 1642, and where the old oak table and chair of the Speaker were for a long time preserved, is now unfortunately pulled down.

The Court-house, which has a singular cupola like a lighthouse, is still called "Grace's Old Castle," from its standing on the site of an old castle built by Grace, or Le Gras, whose tomb is in the cathedral.

Kilkenny bears an honourable name in the annals of education, the institutions for which are numerous and good. First and foremost is the college originally founded by Pierce Butler, Earl of Ormonde, and subsequently made a royal college by King James. Swift, Congreve, and Farquhar received their education here, and it has always taken rank amongst the most celebrated grammar-schools of Ireland.

The Roman Catholic College, near the Clonmel road, is a modern Gothic building, and is dedicated to St. Kyran.

In addition to these, there are gaol, infirmary, lunatic asylum, almshouses, and the usual buildings belonging to a county town. Owing to the neighbouring geological formation being composed almost entirely of carboniferous limestone, Kilkenny has been spoken of as paved with marble. Additional advantages are perpetuated in the old couplet—

"Fire without smoke, air without fog,
 Water without mud, land without bog."

The former excellency is to be attributed to the general use of the anthracite or stone coal, which emits very little smoke, and is raised from the Castlecomer coal-field (p. 242), though, notwithstanding its virtues, Kilkenny coal is not so much patronized as that from Newport in S. Wales. Taking it altogether, it is undeniable that Kilkenny is one of the pleasantest cities in the kingdom, and will well repay a lengthened acquaintance.

Conveyances.—Rail to Dublin and Waterford. Daily cars to Castlecomer, Durrow, Thurles, Urlingford, Callan, Ballyragget.

Excursions.—
1. Dunmore and Freshford.
2. Jerpoint and Thomastown.
3. Callan, Kells, and Kilree.

Distances.—Dublin, 81 m.; Carlow, 25; Thomastown, 11; Waterford, 31; Dunmore. 2½; Callan, 10; Gowran, 7; Urlingford, 18; Bennett's Bridge, 6; Freshford, 9.

The banks of the Nore are very pleasant and picturesque, particularly to the N. of the town in the direction of *Dunmore*, where there is a cave in the limestone that is worth a visit. It is of no great length, but expands into a large chamber known by the name of the Market Cross. A very accurate description is given by Banim, in his novel "Crohore of the Billhook." Near the cave is Dunmore House, one of the Marquis of Ormonde's seats. About a mile higher up the Nore is Threecastles House (J. Bull, Esq.), where the Dinin river flows in, and a little to the N. is Jenkinstown Park, the seat of G. L. Bryan, Esq., and the Goodwood of Ireland, as far as racing is concerned, the Jenkinstown meeting being considered the most select of Irish fixtures.

4 m. from Kilkenny, nearly insulated by the Nore, is Inchmore Castle, a massive square keep with a bartizan-tower attached to a large gable mansion of the time of James I. It was erected by Robert Grace, Baron of Courtown.

The following residences are in the neighbourhood of Kilkenny, viz., Kilcreen E. Smithwick, Esq.), Castle Blunden Sir J. Blunden, Bart.), Bennett-town House W. Blunden, Esq., Newtown J. Greene, Esq., Castle Bamford.

[10 m. from Kilkenny is Callan, formerly a walled town of considerable importance, though now the only traces that it possesses are in the ruins of the Friary, founded in the 15th cent. by Sir Jas. Butler. It is a long aisled ch. of Dec. style, with a tower rising from the centre. The choir is now occupied by the parish ch. The founder is supposed to have been interred near the E. window of the aisle. The remains of the castle also overlook the King's River. Close to the town is West Court; and between Kilkenny and Callan are Desart (The Earl of Desart) and Farmley (W. Flood, Esq.). Some 7 m. to the W. of Kilkenny is the village of Tullaroan, once the centre and most important part of the property of the family of Grace, who were descended from "Le Gros," the brother-in-law of Strongbow, and who owned a district of 80,000 acres known as "Grace's Country." From Callan the road may be taken to Jerpoint, passing midway the village of Kells, another ancient walled town, erected by one of Strongbow's followers. Here are the ruins of an extensive priory founded in the 12th cent. by Sir Geoffrey de Monte Morisco, and peopled by him with monks from Bodmin. "It was comprehended within a large oblong square, divided into 2 courts separated by a strong wall. The southern or Burghers' court is 400 ft. square, and was apparently never occupied by buildings. In each of the northern angles, and in the centre of the N. and W. curtains, is a strong tower in good preservation, fitted up with fireplaces, closets, and narrow staircases. A branch of the King's River, together with a high wall flanked by a strong tower, divides this court from the other, which contains the church, cloister, and monastic attachments. Every necessary adjunct to a monastery seems to have been placed here, including what probably many houses did not possess within their walls, a mill. The church was rather an irregular building, and consisted of a choir, nave, and N. transept, besides a Lady chapel; which last appears, from the remains of some windows, to have been the most lately erected portion of the priory." The whole style of the buildings at Kells appears to partake considerably more of the military and defensive than of the ecclesiastical fashion.

Nearly 3 m. S. of Kells is the Round Tower of Kilree, about 96 ft. in height, though it has lost its cap. Adjoining it is a stone cross made out of a single block of freestone, said to have been erected in memory of Neill Callan, King of Ireland, who perished in his endeavour to save one of his followers while drowning. The river was afterwards called King's River. The same tradition is current in co. Armagh, where there is a mound erected for the same reason.]

For the first 3 m. on our way to Waterford we run parallel with the Irish S. Eastern, obtaining an excellent view of the town, and passing rt. the lunatic asylum, Larchfield, Archersgrove (J. Reid, Esq.), Inch House (J. H. Knaresborough, Esq.), and l. Lyrath House (Sir J. Cuffe, Bart.).

At Lavistown, 2 m. the lines diverge, the one to Waterford, trending to the S., and following the valley of the Nore to

6 m. Bennett's Bridge. Here the Duke of Ormonde held a review in 1704, which attracted such hosts of visitors that an innkeeper is said to have made as much by his beds as paid his rent for 7 years.

[About 2½ m. on l., and halfway between Bennett's Bridge and Dungarvon, is the round tower of Tullo-herin, which has an entrance 12 ft. from the ground, and was lighted by 8 windows at the summit, part of which, with the cap, is deficient.

The ruins of a large ch. are adjacent, and it is a singular fact that while this latter is built of limestone, the tower was built of silicious breccia.]

From hence the rly. runs over rather high ground, which now and then offers pleasant views of the pastoral vale of the Nore to rt. as it flows through a succession of well-wooded demesnes. On rt. bank, Annamult; on the King's River, Johnswell; and Mount Juliet, the seat of the Earl of Carrick.

On the l. bank are the grounds of Ballyhinch (W. Fitzgerald, Esq.), between which and the rly. are ruins of a fortress called Legan Castle, the ancient residence of the last Abbot of Jerpoint.

11 m. *Thomastown* (*Inns*: Cullen's; Trully's) is a small town of about 1900 inhab., of note only as being the nearest place to Jerpoint Abbey, and the beautiful scenery in the neighbourhood. It derives its name from Thomas Fitz Anthony Walsh, one of the early English proprietors, who built a castle, and enclosed the town with walls. From that period it rapidly increased, and from its position on the Nore, which up to a late date was navigable to this point, became an important emporium for Kilkenny and the neighbouring country. The river, however, silted up, and as no steps were ever taken to deepen or clear the bed, the navigation point is now Innistiogue, and Thomastown has consequently become a petty village.

It contains several relics of its former greatness, viz., square towers at each end of the bridge that crosses the Nore, and part of an aisle of the Dominican Abbey, of the foundation of which history is silent, although it is probably of the date of the 13th cent. It may also be mentioned that the R.C. chapel contains the old high altar that once belonged to Jerpoint. About ½ m. below the town, and on the opposite side of the river, is the ruin of Grenan Castle, by which name Thomastown was called previous to the arrival of Fitz Anthony Walsh.

The great attraction of this neighbourhood is *Jerpoint Abbey*, founded in 1180 by Donogh O'Donoghoe, King of Ossory, for Cistercian monks. It speedily attained a high reputation, and became the burial place of the royal founder and subsequent bishops, flourishing until the Dissolution, when it came into the hands of the family of Ormonde, together with 6500 acres of land.

The ruins are situated about 1½ m. from Thomastown, between the rly. and the rt. bank of the river, and as seen from the line afford an exquisite foreground to a very charming bit of landscape. They are those of a cruciform ch. of the date of transition from Norman to E.E., traces of both of which styles are very distinct, though the former predominates.

It consisted of nave, choir, and transepts, with a square tower rising from the intersection, which, from the shortness of the choir, places it very much nearer the E. than the W. end.

"The tower, though of considerable antiquity, is evidently of later date than the transition period, and was probably added contemporaneously with the decorated window in the E. end of the choir."—*Wakeman.*

The battlements of the tower are deserving of study "as being identical with many found in the N. of Italy, but very unlike anything either in England or Scotland. They give a foreign look to the whole building, which is very striking."—*Fergusson.*

Internally the tower is supported on arches, those facing the transepts and nave being pointed, while the one leading to the choir is circular-headed. Of the nave, the S. wall is wanting. On the north side is an aisle separated from the body of the nave by 6 pointed arches, between each of which is a clerestory window, with semicircular heads. Of a similar character is the W. window (the E. being of later date). It consists of 3 lights with semicircular heads, each divided by a mullion, and surmounted with a continuous weathermoulding. "The only entrance to the body of the ch. from the exterior appears to have been a small doorway in the wall of the nave, and this is defended by a bartizan similar to those found upon castles of the 12th cent."

The stone roof of the choir is in good preservation, and there are still several interesting monuments, and in particular the tomb of Donogh (Mac Gillapatrick), the royal founder. The figures are those of a male and female, in the costume of the 12th cent., the former holding a crucifix in his right hand. On the base are figures of the Apostles, with long beards, and at the foot are 2 crowned figures, besides a kneeling angel. Here is also the tomb of an abbot with his crozier, at the lower end of which a serpent is gnawing. There are also other tombs of ecclesiastics, more or less mutilated, after the fashion of Irish abbey ruins, which have not even the negative advantages of being left to the ravages of time alone. It is, however, greatly to the credit of the Kilkenny Archæological Society that they have taken steps towards the preservation of Jerpoint.

Besides the estates before mentioned, there are 2 handsome seats 2 m. N. of Thomastown—Kilfane and Kilmury, the former belonging to Sir J. Power, Bart., and the latter to H. Butler, Esq.

Conveyances.—Rail to Kilkenny and Waterford. Car to New Ross.

Distances.—Kilkenny, 11 m.; Jerpoint, 1½; Innistiogue, 6; New Ross, 16; Woodstock, 7; Waterford, 20.

[If time is not an object, the traveller should make a détour to New Ross, following the course of the Nore, which continues to justify its reputation of being the most quietly beautiful river in the S.

Passing on l. bank the Court and

Brownsbarn House (Capt. Blackburne); and rt. bank, Coolmore (P. Connellan, Esq.) and Ballyduff (R. Langrishe, Esq.), we arrive at 6 m. *Innistiogue* (anc. Inis-teoc), a charmingly-situated little town overlooking the Nore, which is crossed by a bridge of 10 arches, ornamented on one side with Ionic pilasters. The town is built in the form of a square, which being planted with limetrees give it a peculiarly fresh and pretty appearance. Innistiogue was once a loyal borough, and famed for its religious establishments. It also possessed a large Augustinian monastery. All that is now left of it are 2 towers, one of them incorporated with the parish ch.; the other is square at the base and octagonal in the upper stages.

This is a good point from which to ascend *Brandon Hill*, a conical eminence 1694 feet in height, that intervenes between the valley of the Nore and that of the Barrow.

The view from the summit into these 2 valleys is very lovely, overlooking St. Mullins and Graigue-na-Managh (Rte. 28), while to the E. the view is bounded by the superior heights of Mount Leinster and Blackstairs. The great lion of Innistiogue is Woodstock, the seat of Rt. Hon. W. F. Tighe (Lieutenant of the co. Kilkenny), the grounds of which abound with the most beautiful views. The demesne stretches for a considerable distance along the Nore, and is laid out with every diversity of landscape that wood and water can bestow. The house contains a valuable library and some good paintings, while in the grounds are several cottage-ornées, placed in situations that command the most charming bits. At the back rises a wooded hill to the height of 900 ft., the summit crowned with an ornamental tower.

To Woodstock succeeds Bromsford, opposite to which is the ruin of Clonamery castle.

At 10 m. on rt. bank is Newgrove House, and on l. Ballinabarney (J. Bolger, Esq.), Rathsnagadan, and Russellstown House.

At 14 m. Ringwood (Mrs. Chapman) the Barrow—

"The goodly Barow, which doth hoor
Great heaps of salmons in his deep bosome,
All which, long sundred, doe at last accord
To ioyne in one, ere to the sea they come;
So, flowing all from one, all one at last
become."—*Spenser*,—

joins its waters with the Nore, and they flow together in a noble stream, backed by high wooded banks, to 16 m. New Ross (Rte. 28).]

From Thomastown the line passes close to Jerpoint Abbey, where the valley of the Nore is crossed. Close to the Abbey is Jerpoint House (P. Hunt, Esq.), and 2 m. to the W., Flood Hall.

15 m. Ballyhale Stat., 1 m. from which on rt. is Knoctopher village and House, the latter the residence of Rev. Sir H. Langrishe, Bart.

The charming river and valley scenery now gives place to dreary high ground, the line passing at the base of the Booley range of hills to 23 m. Mullinavat. If the weather be clear, however, there are beautiful distant views on rt. of Slieve-na-man and the Commeragh Hills. At Mullinavat a small stream, called the Black Water, runs S. to join the Suir, and of this valley the rly. takes advantage.

26 m. Kilmacow Stat. At Dunkitt the Waterford and Limerick line is joined.

31 m. Waterford (Rtes. 28, 30).

Hotels: Adelphi, Dobbyn's, Cummins'.

ROUTE 27.

FROM KILKENNY TO ATHENRY, THROUGH PARSONSTOWN AND LOUGHREA.

A car leaves Kilkenny for Urlingford, by a pretty road on the rt. bank of the Nore, passing rt. the Mount Eagle Distillery, where the Dinan river flows in from the district of Castle Comer (Rte. 26).

At 9 m. the village of *Freshford*, the antiquary should visit the ch., originally built by St. Lachtin in the 7th cent., but rebuilt about the commencement of the 12th, as is proved by two Irish inscriptions over the inner arch of the entrance doorway; the one running thus—

"A prayer for NIAM daughter of Core, and for MATHGAMAIN O'CHIARMEIC, by whom was made this church."

The other—

"A prayer for GILLE MOCHOLMOC O'CENCAIN, who made it."

"It is to be regretted that neither our annals nor genealogical books preserve the names of any of the persons recorded in this inscription, so that it is impossible to determine exactly the period at which they flourished; but it is obvious, from the surnames applied to the three individuals concerned, that they could not have lived earlier than the 11th cent., when the use of hereditary surnames was generally established in Ireland."—*Petrie*. Notice the magnificent Norman decoration of the receding arches, in which the bead and chevron mouldings are conspicuous: on either side of the spring of the outer arch are 2 singular sculptures—one of a man on horseback; the other of two figures standing up. A very peculiar feature is the sculpture of lions' heads on the soffits of the outer arch immediately over the imposts. The ancient name of Freshford was Achadh ur, "Waterfield." To the N. of the town is Lodgepark House (W. Warren, Esq.); on the S. is Upper Court.

Passing l. Woodsgift (Sir R. St. George, Bart.), Balief (H. St. George, Esq.), and Wilton House, we come to

18 m. *Urlingford*, an uninteresting town, offering nothing but a pretty panoramic view from the racecourse. In the neighbourhood of 21 m. Johnstown, once celebrated for its spa, are Violet Hill and Foulkscourt (C. Hely, Esq.).

From here a road runs nearly due N. through a hilly country to

31 m. *Rathdowney*, near which place are several ruined keeps, viz. Coolkerry on the Erkina stream; Kilbreedy on the N.E.; Clonburren on the S.W.; none of them being of any importance. 33 m. the village of Donaghmore, and 53 m. Borris station on the Great Southern and Western Rly. (Rte. 25), from whence a convenient branch-line runs to Roscrea, Parsonstown, and Nenagh. Keeping on l. Ballybrophy and Ballymeelish, is 38 m. *Borris*, distinguished by the addition of Ossory from the Borris near Kilkenny, which is properly Borris-Idrone. This was once a place of importance, from being the great pass into Munster, for the protection of which a castle, now in ruins, was erected by the Fitzpatricks. On rt. are Charleville (H. White, Esq.), Kilmartin, Mount Butler (Lady Carden), Derryvale, Racket Hall (Mrs. Bridge), Birchgrove (J. S. Birch, Esq.), and Monaincha (G. Birch, Esq.), all in the neighbourhood of

45 m. *Roscrea* (*Hotel:* Brown's), in former times the locale of a large monastery for Augustines, founded by St. Cronan, and the seat of a diocese, which, however, in the 12th cent. was united to that of Killaloe. St. Cronan was celebrated for his sanctity and learning, and many mi-

racles were attributed to his prayers; in one case, the fury of the Ossorians, who were marching against his countrymen, was checked at his intercession; at another time, "he suspended the sword of King Fingin of Munster, which was raised to destroy the people of Meath;" and he eventually died in the fulness of years and good works, as abbot or bishop of Roscrea, in the 7th cent. The points of interest in the town are—1. the ch., which preserves the doorway of the ancient abbey, having niches on either side, and an image of St. Cronan very much mutilated. In the ch.-yard is a cross, and a monumental stone in the wall, on which is sculptured a rude representation of the Crucifixion; this is known as the shrine of St. Cronan. 2. The round tower is in remarkably good preservation, and is very similar to that of Devenish Island in Lough Erne (Rte. 6). The doorway has a circular head, is 15 ft. from the ground, and possesses a groove and pivot-hole, evidently showing that it was provided with double doors; a fact which goes to prove the argument that the round towers were used as places of defence and security. (Petrie on 'Round Towers,' p. 369.) It is ornamented with a plain flat architrave; over the doorway is a triangular-headed aperture. The summit, which is about 80 ft. from the ground, is covered with a dome roof of wood. 3. The old Franciscan friary, founded in 1490, by Mulrany-na-Feasoige O'Carrol and Bribiana his wife, is incorporated with the Roman Catholic chapel, which, by the way, contains a good altarpiece of the Crucifixion.

Besides these ecclesiastical ruins are some interesting structures, viz.: a circular tower belonging to the castle built by King John, and a lofty square keep of the fortress of the Ormondes, which has been made use of in part as a barrack and storeroom. Roscrea was at one time the residence of St. Canice, "who wrote here a copy of the 4 Gospels called Glas Kennic, or 'the Chain of Canice,' which, till the time of Archbishop Usher, was preserved in this place. There was also a curious copy written by Darima, a scholar, the son of Œngus, the son of Carthin, which was also kept there in an ornamented box, and was probably the MS. in the possession of Sir William Betham, Ulster King-at-Arms."—*Lewis*.

The town is prettily situated on a small river flowing into the Brosna, and is surrounded by undulating hills; there are many nice seats in the neighbourhood, some of which have been mentioned. Amongst others are — Ballystanley (H. Scroope, Esq.), Inane House (F. Jackson, Esq.), Mount Heaton, Hillsborough (H. Buckley, Esq.), Glenalbert (A. Maxwell, Esq.), Golden Grove (J. Hutchinson, Esq.), and Dungar (Mrs. Evans). In the grounds of Corville House (H. Prittie, Esq.), 1 m. S.E., are slight remains of the abbey of Corbally; and in those of Monanicha are also remains of Inchanameo Abbey, a Culdee establishment, which flourished in the time of St. Columba.

Conveyances.—Rail to Borris, Parsonstown, and Nenagh.

Distances.—Borris, 10 m.; Parsonstown, 11; Nenagh, 20; Moneygall, 9; Cloghjordan, 12.

The line now keeps the valley of the Little Brosna river, leaving on l. the villages of Brosna and Shinrone, and on rt. the grounds of Gloster (Col. Lloyd).

52 m. rt. Sharavogue (Col. Hon. J. Westenra) and Rathmore (E. Synge, Esq.), and l. Ballincor House (F. H. Toone, Esq.).

56 m. *Birr* or *Parsonstown* (*Hotel:* Dooley's), the former name being obtained from the ancient abbey of Biorra, founded here by St. Brendan; and the latter from the family of the Parsons, to whom, in the time of James I., the town and neighbourhood were assigned. They built a castle, which has been modernised,

and is now the residence of the Earl of Rosse, to whose labours the science of astronomy is so much indebted. The great objects of interest are the Earl's famous telescopes, to visit which permission is granted to the tourist.

The chief difficulty of the proper combination of metals most useful for specula, as to their whiteness, porosity, and hardness, was solved by Lord Rosse, who found that one of copper (126 parts) with tin (58 parts) was the best. He also successfully cast specula, by an improvement in the shape of the mould, which, instead of being of solid cast-iron, " was made by binding together tightly layers of hoop-iron, and turning the required shape on them edgeways." The speculum of the large telescope is 6 ft., weighs 3 tons, and required 16 weeks to anneal. As regards the machinery by which it is worked, " the tube is 56 ft. long, and is made of deal 1 inch thick. The focal length of the speculum is 52 ft. The tube is fixed to mason-work in the ground, by a large universal hinge, which allows it to turn in all directions. At each side of it, at 12 ft. distance, a wall is built, which is 72 ft. long, 48 ft. high on the outer side, and 56 on the inner; the walls are thus 24 ft. apart, and lie exactly in the meridian line. When directed to the S. the tube may be lowered till it becomes almost horizontal, but when pointed to the N. it only falls until it is parallel with the earth's axis, pointing then to the pole of the heavens; a lower position would be useless, for as all celestial objects circumscribe that point, they will come into view above and about it." —*Shiels.*

The town is well built and regularly laid out, and, as will be seen at a glance, is under the surveillance of a careful resident landlord; the streets converge to Duke Square, in which there is a Doric pillar in memory of the Duke of Cumberland and his victory at Culloden (Pop. 5101).

The ch. is of Early Pointed style with a spire 100 ft. in height; but this is eclipsed by the Roman Cath. Cathedral, a fine Perp. building. In the neighbourhood of Parsonstown are the Castle, Syngfield (E. Synge, Esq.), Chesterfield (Col. Manners), &c.

The country round is not remarkable for beauty; the town itself is situated on the little river Camcor, a tributary of the Brosna, and in the centre of Ireland, so much so that Sir William Petty, in his 'Survey of Ireland,' calls it "Umbilicus Hiberniae." If the tourist has time he may make an excursion towards Nenagh, and ascend the hill of Knochshegoona about 6 m. S.W. Although of no height, 700 ft., it commands a wide view over the surrounding plains and the ranges of the Slieve Bloom Mountains.

Excursions.—
1. Seir-kyran.
2. Roscrea.
3. Portumna and Loragh.
4. Banagher.

[6 m. to the E. is Seirkyran, which was in old days an important ecclesiastical establishment, dedicated to St. Kyran. In addition to several ruins, there is a round tower about 20 ft. high, surmounted by a conical cap, at the base of which are several loopholes. The ch. has a figure of St. Kyran on the western gable, and on the eastern one of those singular nude figures occasionally found. The parish is said to derive its prefix from Seir, "a heel," in consequence of its shape. Clereen is the seat of R. Smith, Esq.]

Conveyances.—Rail to Roscrea; car to Athlone, through Ferbane; daily to Ballybrophy, to Ballinasloe, to Banagher.

Distances.—Borris, 18 m.; Roscrea, 11; Borrisokane, 12; Banagher, 8; Portumna, 15; Loughrea, 35; Frankford, 10.

Passing l. Woodfield and Dovegrove House (J. Johnstone, Esq.), the road runs N.W. over a dreary portion of

King's County to the valley of the Shannon, which is crossed at 64 m. Banagher (Rte. 34). 66½ m. Near the rt. bank of the river at Shannon View (H. Moore, Esq.) the geologist will perceive one of those singular Eskers or drift ridges which run through the centre of the great limestone plain of Ireland.

71 m. Eyrecourt is a small uninteresting town adjoining the estate of the family of Eyre. Either of 2 roads may be followed from Eyrecourt to Loughrea; the upper one passing Frenchpark, Belview (W. Lawrence, Esq.), Ballymore Castle (T. Seymour, Esq.), and the village of Kiltormer; the lower one runs through Killimor, crossing at Hearnesbrook a considerable tributary of the Shannon.

Leaving on l. Ballydoogan House (T. Burke, Esq.), the traveller soon enters

91 m. *Loughrea* (*Hotels:* Carroll's, Lynch's), a Galway town of some note and beauty, situated on the northern bank of Lough Rea, a lake of between 2 and 3 m. in circumference, on which a large number of crannoges or ancient stockaded islands have lately been discovered. In the centre of the town are some remains of an E. Eng. monastery founded by Sir Richard de Burgh for Carmelite monks; also of the old fortress built by the same individual, and once the residence of the Clanricarde family. There are, moreover, a couple of ruined towers, about 1 m. to the N. The scenery between Loughrea and Athenry is of that peculiar rocky and desolate character which belongs to Galway, although the monotony is somewhat relieved by the distant views of Slieve Aughty to the S., on the confines of Clare and Galway. Passing St. Cleran's (Major Burke), Dunsandle (Lord Dunsandle), and Moyode Castle (B. Persse, Esq.), the tourist reaches the Midland Great Western Railway at Athenry (Rte. 11).

ROUTE 28.

FROM **WEXFORD** TO **CORK**, THROUGH **WATERFORD, DUNGARVAN,** AND **YOUGHAL.**

The road from Wexford to New Ross does not present any very remarkable features. It leaves the embouchure of the Slaney, and the Enniscorthy road, altogether to the rt.; and at 4½ m. [gives off a branch to 3½ m. the village of *Taghmon* (Theagh Munno, "the House of Munno") from a monastery founded by St. Munno in the 6th cent., of which very few traces now remain. Here are, however, a square tower, a portion of the old castle of the Talbot family, and a rude cross in the ch.-yard. Taghmon is situated near the N.W. foot of the Forth Mts., a conspicuous feature in South Wexford landscape, although only 776 ft. high. In the neighbourhood, and on the road to Foulkesmill, are Rahcenduff (Capt. Beattie), Horetown (S. Goff, Esq.), and Hillburn (T. Hawkshaw, Esq.)].

[8 m. rt. a road branches off to Enniscorthy, and a little farther on, also on rt., is Camaross Hill, a singular granite hillock, 598 ft., an outlier of a low range of hills that intervene between this district and New Ross. The road runs near a similar though rather more lofty eminence at Carrickburn, and then crosses this range, descending on the other side directly upon

22 m. *New Ross* (*Hotels:* Ross; Bridge), a busy, foreign-looking little town of about 5000 Inhab., with narrow streets running up the side of the hill and along the banks of the

Barrow, which is here a noble and stately stream, crossed by one of the long wooden bridges so common in the S.E. of Ireland. Very shortly after the invasion, Ross was founded by Isabella daughter of Strongbow, and became of great importance, the circuit of its walls being upwards of a mile, and boasting a garrison of 363 crossbow men, 1200 long-bow archers, 3000 pikemen, and 104 horsemen. A castle was built: and "so anxious were the townspeople to accomplish their undertaking, that not only did the whole of the male population work at it by turns in companies, but many of the young women also aided in it, to commemorate which a strong tower or gate, called Maiden Tower, was erected eastward in the town, for a prison exclusively for persons guilty of offences against females."—*Lewis.* In the Parliamentary war, Ross was garrisoned for the Royalists by the Duke of Ormonde; but on the approach of Cromwell, it surrendered immediately. The bridge of Rosseponte was broken down by the Irish at this time, and a ferry was used until Lemuel Cox, who constructed the bridges at Waterford, Wexford, Youghal, and Londonderry, built the present one, which is 508 ft. long, and has a drawbridge to allow of the navigation. Ross formerly had 5 gates; of these, one called Bishop's Gate is still standing: it is to the N. of the town, and possesses a good pointed archway. One went by the name of Three-bullet Gate, from the circumstance of 3 cannon-balls, fired by Cromwell, lodging in it. There are also some walls and good pointed windows of the old Conventual ch., founded in the 13th cent. On the site of a portion of it the modern ch. of St. Mary has been erected. The interior contains some mural monuments to the family of Tottenham, while in the ruins are the tombs of Peter Butler 1599, and Rose M'Room. Ross has a fine position as a port, and a considerable trade in grain and coal; but it is dependent on the port of Waterford, which has had the best of it in the race for superiority.

Although it is not the pleasantest of towns to stay at, it is a good central point for excursions up or down the Barrow and Nore, which unite their streams about 2 m. to the N. The Nore should be ascended by boat to Woodstock and Inistiogue. (Rte. 26.)]

[An excursion may be made up the Barrow, to St. Mullins and Graiguemanagh. For the first mile the road winds up a terrace overlooking the broad reaches of the river, and passing on rt. the ancient keep of Mountgarrett Castle. Descending the hill on the other side, having on l. Rosemount (E. Byrne, Esq.), and rt. Woodville (E. Tottenham, Esq.), it follows the l. bank of the Barrow —the road on the rt. bank leading to Inistiogue, and by a more direct route to Graiguemanagh. Near the site of MacMurrogh's castle the traveller turns off to Ballywilliam (Rte. 26), the present terminus of the Irish South-Eastern Rly.

At 6¼ m., where the Pollmounty stream falls into the Barrow, the scenery becomes very picturesque, as the Barrow flows between Mt. Brandon on l. and the range of Blackstairs and Mt. Leinster on rt. The wooded banks on each side of the river attain a height of 300 ft. or thereabouts.

8½ m. *St. Mullins,* a village placed in a most charming situation at the mouth of a rivulet that flows from Glynn.

St. Mullins (from St. Moling, Bishop of Ferns, who founded a monastery here) was of ancient ecclesiastical importance, and even now contains traces of "5 small structures in the ch.-yard, extending from E. to W., with 2 walls, once forming part of a 6th, and the western walls of a 7th, outside the enclosure: at the E. of the largest are remains of a stone cross and a small roofless building, with steps descending into it."

The tide flows as far as St. Mullins—from whence the towing-path should be followed for the remainder of the excursion. The same character of scenery, viz. high wooded banks running up towards the mountains continues nearly the whole distance; and about halfway on the opposite side are the ruins of Galway fortress.

Graiguemanagh, 13 m., is connected by a bridge with the suburb of Tinnahinch, in the co. of Carlow, the main part of the town being in Kilkenny. A portion of the old abbey founded by the Earl of Pembroke in the 13th cent. is incorporated with a R. C. chapel. Extending some distance down the river are the grounds of Brandon Dale (D. Burtchaell, Esq.).

Distance.—6 m. from Borris.

On the return from Graiguemanagh to Ross, the tourist should follow the direct road on the W. side of the Barrow; and from it may easily ascend Mount Brandon, 1694 ft., one of the most graceful little hills in the S. of Ireland, and one from which the home views are particularly charming—the more extensive prospect to the E. being cut off by Mt. Leinster and Blackstairs.]

[Second excursion down the bank of the Barrow to Dunbrody, 9½ m., passing Oaklands (R. Tyndall, Esq.), Stokestown (T. Deane, Esq.), and Landscape (J. Usher, Esq.) on the l. bank; with Annagh's House (W. Sweetman, Esq.), and Castle on the opposite shore. With the exception of the conical hill of Slieve Killter, 887 ft., on the l., the country is comparatively level, and very different from the deep ravines and dells of the upper part of the Barrow, near St. Mullins.

Passing in succession Killowenn (J. Glascott, Esq), Pilltown, and Kilmannoch House (G. Houghton, Esq.), the tourist crosses a small pill that joins the estuary of the Barrow, opposite Cheek Point, where the waters of the Suir fall in, and arrives at 9½ m. *Dunbrody* Abbey, the largest and most beautiful ruin in the co. of Wexford. It dates from the 12th cent., when it was founded by Hervæus de Montemarisco, or Hervey de Montmorency, marshal of Henry II., and seneschal of the lands obtained by Strongbow, who, with a rare consistency, gave up all his property with the exception of the lands belonging to the abbey, of which he was first abbot. It is a cruciform church, consisting of nave, aisles, choir, transepts; with a low and massive tower rising from the intersection. The great E. window, which in Grose's time was singularly perfect, is a 3-light E. Eng. lancet window, deeply splayed inwardly and surmounted by three smaller ones above. The nave is separated from the aisles by rows of Early Pointed arches, between which are trefoil-headed clerestory windows. The piers of the arches are square, and the arches themselves have particularly good mouldings arising from corbels a little below the spring of the arch. Grose mentions the splendour of the W. door, which was adorned with "filigree open work cut in the stone."

Close to the abbey, is Dunbrody Castle, a building of the time of Henry II., incorporated with a modern house. After examining Dunbrody, it will be better for the tourist to proceed further S., past Arthurstown, a seat of Lord Templemore's, to Duncannon (p. 259), where the packet may be taken up the river to Waterford.]

Conveyances.—From New Ross to Enniscorthy; car to Thomastown; coach to Waterford and Wexford; steamer daily to Waterford.

Distances.—Wexford, 22 m.; Waterford, 15; Dunbrody, 9½; Ballywilliam, 5; Woodstock, 8; Inistiogue, 9; St. Mullins, 8½; Tinnehinch, 13.

Excursions.—
1. Dunbrody and Duncannon.
2. St. Mullins.
3. Inistiogue.
4. Wexford.

The road to Waterford crosses the Barrow by the long wooden bridge to Rosbercon, a pretty suburb, possessing a few ruins of an old ch. or abbey, comprising a tower resting on 4 pointed arches and the side wall of the aisle; and then turns to the l. along the rt. bank of the river, passing on l. Annagh's House W. Sweetman, Esq.), in whose grounds are the remains of a fortress. The scenery is picturesque near this point, a terrace road running close to the river, which is ornamented on the opposite bank with the well-wooded demesnes of Stokestown and Landscape. At the village of Glenmore the traveller ascends a long and steep pitch, commanding from the top a magnificent view of Brandon, Mount Leinster, and the Blackstairs. Not much can be said of the scenery for the rest of the journey, the country being bleak and hilly, with but little to relieve the eye until the descent commences into the fertile valley of the Suir, and past many neat villas to Ferrybank, from which another long wooden bridge brings us in the centre of

37 m. *Waterford* (anc. Port-lairge) Rte. 26. (*Hotels*: Adelphi, very good; Dobbyn's, tolerable; Cummin's, bad,—a city, a county, the seat of a diocese, and one of the most ancient towns in the kingdom; its history dating back from 853, when the Danes founded a colony under their leader Sitricus. They kept their position not only in Waterford, but through a good portion of the S.W. of Ireland, until the latter part of the 12th cent., when the advanced guard of Strongbow, under Hervey de Montmorency and Raymond Le Gros overthrew them. Here Dermot M'Murrough, King of Leinster, gave his daughter Eva to Strongbow in marriage, when Henry II. landed to take possession of his new kingdom. Subsequently, John Earl of Morton, when Lord Chief Governor of Ireland, established a mint, a privilege which the city enjoyed until the time of Edward IV. To detail all the sieges and reverses which it underwent would be to write the history of a great part of Ireland; for from its position as a port, and its proximity to England, scarcely anything important took place that did not directly or indirectly affect Waterford. It sustained a siege of 12 days at the hands of Perkin Warbeck and the Earl of Desmond; and again, in 1641, by Cromwell, who was obliged to retire. In the next year, however, the city capitulated to Ireton.

The situation of Waterford is admirably adapted for a shipping port, its long quays stretching for more than a mile along the S. bank of the Suir, which rolls in a broad stream in a direction N.W. to S.E.

——" The gentle Shure, that making way
By sweet Clonmell, adornes rich Waterford."

A small portion only of the city is on the N. bank, including the rly. terminus of the Kilkenny and Limerick lines; and below the bridge the high grounds that overlook the river are adorned with pleasant countryhouses and gardens. The connection between the suburb of Ferrybank and Waterford is maintained by a wooden bridge, 832 ft. long, supported on piers of stone and oak. Like Wexford, this was the work of Lemuel Cox, the Boston architect, who not only built it substantially, but still more strangely, for a considerably less sum than the estimate. The particulars of the building are set forth on a tablet in the middle of the bridge; though the inscription is not altogether free from orthographical error. The view from the bridge is worth a few minutes' notice—from the picturesque escarpment of the banks in the immediate neighbourhood, the pretty hills on the one side, and the gradually ascending tiers of houses on the other, with a long perspective of quay and river.

With the exception, however, of this quay, and the Mall that runs out of it at right angles at the southern end, there is not a single good street in Waterford, which, it must be confessed, has, generally speaking, an ancient and fishlike smell, mixed up with odours of butter and pigs. The visitor will not wonder at this, when he observes that Waterford is the nearest and most crowded port of export for Irish produce into England, particularly at the time of the sailings of the Bristol packets, when it would seem impossible to stow away the immense droves of cattle that throng the quays, and certainly do not add to the cleanliness of the streets. "The harbour of Waterford is formed by the channel of the Suir, from the city to its confluence with the Barrow; and from thence by the joint estuary of these rivers to the sea, a distance of 15m.; the entrance 2½m. wide, which is well lighted by a bright fixed light on Hook Tower, 139 ft. above the sea, by a red light on Dunmore pier, and 2 leading lights at Duncannon. Vessels of 800 tons can discharge at the quays, which are described by the Tidal Harbour Commissioners as the finest range in the United Kingdom. The income of the port, arising from tonnage, ballast, anchorage, quayage dues, and pilotage, amounted in 1843 to 6948*l*. On the Kilkenny side of the river there is a shipbuilding yard, with patent slip, graving bank, and dock. The exports are almost wholly agricultural; the value of the principal articles exported in 1835 was, bacon and pork, 523,983*l*.; butter, 475,884*l*,; grain, 229,775*l*.; flour and meal, 404,263*l*.; cattle, sheep, and pigs, 137,098*l*."—*Thom's Directory*. Notwithstanding its extreme age, it is surprising how few antiquarian remains are left: of the walls and fortifications which surrounded it, and enclosed an area of 15 acres, there are only a tower, close to the Tramore rly. station, and the circular tower which stands at the corner of the Mall or Quay, and which we are told by an inscription was built by Reginald the Dane in 1003; held as a fortification by Strongbow in 1171; re-edified in 1819, and now appropriated as a police lock-up. It is mentioned as a curious feature in the social history of Waterford that there were "in addition to the regular fortifications of the city, several private fortresses called by the names of their respective proprietors, and supposed to have been not less than 20 in number. In Colbeck Castle, from which that street took its name, was the Chamber of Green Cloth or Chamber of Waterford, sometimes used by the Mayor as a place of confinement for refractory citizens. The palace in which King John resided during his stay at Waterford occupied the site on which the Widows' Apartments are built, and on the erection of which the vaults of that ancient structure were discovered."—*Lewis*.

There were also a Franciscan monastery, on the site of which was established the Hospital of the Holy Ghost; and a Dominican priory, the tower and belfry of which are still in existence.

The cathedral is a large plain building, with a lofty spire, and replaced (with the old materials) in 1773 the ancient ch., built by the Ostmen of Waterford, in 1096. With the exception of one or two monuments it contains but little of interest; adjoining it are an extremely comfortable-looking Bishop's Palace and Deanery.

The R. C. Cathedral in Baron-strand Str. has a fine though dingy front, and is said to have been built for 20,000l., all of which was defrayed by pence taken at the door.

The neighbourhood of Waterford is plentifully studded with seats, particularly on the banks of the river. Facing the city are Rockshire (R. Morris, Esq.), River View, Belmont, Barron Court (Sir Henry Barron), Killaspey (A. Sherlock, Esq., Rockland, close to the ch., and Newpark (G. Bloomfield, Esq.).

Conveyances.—Rly.' to Kilkenny, Limerick, and Tramore; steamers daily to Milford (with the mails), twice a week to Bristol, once a week to Glasgow, weekly to Plymouth, twice a week to London, three times to Liverpool, daily to Duncannon, daily to New Ross. Car daily to Borris, daily to Enniscorthy, daily to Gooldscross, daily to Dungarvan and Lismore, daily to Youghal, daily to Maryboro', daily to Wexford.

Distances.—Wexford, 37 m; New Ross, 15; Duncannon, 10½; Dunbrody, 7; Passage, 8; Thomastown and Jerpoint, 20; Clonmel, 28; Carrick, 14; Portlaw, 10; Dungarvan, 29; Kilmacthomas, 15; Tramore, 7.

Excursions to New Ross by steamer, Dunbrody, Dungannon by steamer, Tramore and Dunmore.

[The sail to Passage and Duncannon is beautiful; the river as far as Check Point being bounded by high wooded banks, from which in frequent succession pretty villas peep out. On the l. side Newpark (G. Bloomfield, Esq., Larkfield, Snowhouse, Springfield, Belview, Suirview (Mrs. Brownrigg), and Snow Hill (N. Power, Esq.; on the rt. Belmont (W. Fitzgerald, Esq., Blenheim, Ballycanvon, Woodland P. Power, Esq.), and Faithlegg (N. Power, Esq.

About 2 m. down is the Little Island, on which is an uninhabited castle; and at 6 m. Check Point, where the Barrow mixes its waters with those of the Suir, which may now be said to become an estuary. At the head of a small pill on the opposite shore the ruins of Dunbrody Abbey (p. 256) are plainly visible in their desolate grandeur. The river widens from Check Point to 8½m. Passage, from whence there is a ferry to Ballyhack and Arthurstown, where the cliffs begin to show themselves. At Ballyhack the tourist can get a car and visit Dunbrody. Passing Dunbrody, the seat of Lord Templemore, the steamer soon arrives at

10½ m. Duncannon, a pleasant village, trying hard to aspire to the dignity of a watering-place. From the reign of Henry II. a fort has existed here, for the purpose of watching the approaches to the harbour. It has been garrisoned since the time of the Spanish Armada, and occupies the projecting cliff to the W. of the village. "The fortifications, including the glacis, occupy about 3 statute acres, and are adapted for mounting 40 pieces of cannon. It contains accommodation for 10 officers and 160 men."—*Fraser*.

From Duncannon the road continues to skirt the coast until it reaches the villages of Slade and Churchtown, 2 villages at the end of the singular promontory of Hook Head, which juts out to the S. in a narrow strip, barely ¾ m. wide. At the extreme point is a fixed light, at no great height above the sea. The whole of this district is full of interest. The point of Bag-an-brun was the locale of the landing of Strongbow and his adventurous band on the 23rd of August, 1171, the commencement of that career of conquest by which the English obtained such an ascendancy in Ireland. The geology of Hook Point consists of coarse sandstones and conglomerates, overlaid by carboniferous limestone, remarkable for the variety and beauty of the corals found in it—such as Astreopora, Michelina, and Zaphrentis: also for the crinoids, of which Actinocrinus, Platycrinus, Poteriocrinus, and Rhodocrinus are the most beautiful forms. — *Harkness.* Should the tourist have time, he may proceed inland on the road to Wexford, turning off to the rt. at Curraghmore to *Tintern Abbey,* the seat of J. Colclough, Esq. William Marshall, Earl of Pembroke, being shipwrecked on this coast in 1200, founded this abbey, which he peopled from, and named after, the more celebrated establishment in Monmouthshire. Unfortunately the mansion was formed out of the chancel, so that little but the tower remains to identify it. The ch. at Tintern contains a monument to the Colclough family, temp. Henry VIII., who, from holding estates that once belonged to the Church, are ever more under the "curse of fire and water."

The sandy estuary of Bannow Bay appears to have been the boundary of the district occupied by the English settlers. It was then called the Pill, according to Holinshede, who writes that "Weisforde, with the territorie baied and perclosed within the river called the Pill, was so quite estranged from Irishrie, as if a traveller of the Irish had pitcht his foote within the Pill and spoken Irish, the Weisfordians would command him foorthwith to turne the other end of his toong and speake English, or els bringe his trouchman with him." The ravages committed by sand are exemplified in the old town of Bannow, of which no traces can be seen, a ruined ch. being all that is left, though we know that it was of some note as late as Charles I.'s reign.

At the mouth of the Corrock is *Clonmines,* where in the time of the Danes an ancient town existed of sufficient importance to possess a mint. Close to the river are the tower and walls of the Dominican monastery, founded by the Kavanaghs in the 14th cent.; and of the Black Castle, built by the family of Sutton. There is also a picturesque chapel with 2 turrets, said to have been raised in memory of his mother by a cowherd, and still called the Cowboy's Chapel. From Clonmines there is a road to Wexford direct, or *viâ* Taghmon, up the vale of the Corrock, passing Rosegarland (F. Leigh, Esq.) and Coolcliffe House (Sir W. Cox).]

[The great attraction to the citizens of Waterford is Tramore, whither they betake themselves for sea-bathing by a short railway of 7 m. It leaves Waterford at the S. of the town, and pursues a most uninteresting route through sand-hills to *Tramore* (the Great Hotel), a pleasantly situated little wateringplace, and a remarkably fine sea. It is placed on a hill at the N.W. corner of Tramore Bay; a fine open bay, though terribly exposed to the southerly gales. The cliffs on the W. from Tramore to Great Newtown Head are bold and precipitous, but eastward is a long extent of narrow strand, which shuts off from the sea a large lagoon, known as the Back Strand. The only outlet of this immense body of water is at the E. boundary of the bay, where the cliffs again rise boldly, terminating at Brownstown Head. A scheme has been set on foot by Mr. Malcolmson, the good genius of Waterford, for the purpose of draining and reclaiming the Back Strand, a plan which ought to yield a very handsome profit eventually.

The pillars scattered along the coast and on the promontories are landmarks. The tourist who remains at Tramore may excurse to Dunmore (easier visited from Waterford), a picturesque little bathing village, with some interesting caves in the cliffs. The geologist will find in the neighbourhood of Tramore Lower Silurian rocks of Bala and Caradoc age.]

A coach leaves Waterford daily for Dungarvan and Youghal.

For the first few miles the road is uninteresting, all views of the river on the rt., and the sea on the l., being cut off by intervening high ground, although the course of the Suir is plainly marked as far as Clonmel. At 41 m. the grounds of Whitfield (W. Christmas, Esq.) on l., and Mount Congreve (J. Congreve, Esq.) on rt., offer a pretty bit of landscape, and soon the traveller gains distant views of the Commeragh Mountains, part of the great southern range that forms the backbone of Waterford.

52 m. *Kilmacthomas*, an exposed and bleak-looking little village, situated on either side the banks of the Mahon, which, taking its rise on the S. slopes of Knockanaffrin, 2336 ft., runs noisily down to the sea. [At Bonmahon, a bathing village some 5 m. to the S., on the opposite side of the stream, are the copper-mines of Knockmahon, which, as regards amount of produce, are the 2nd mines in Ireland, yielding in 1858 4700 tons of ore, of the value of 42,500l.] The mountain pedestrian may make a very pleasant excursion from Kilmacthomas to Lake Coomshingawn, or Coomshenane, a deep tarn nearly surrounded by a wall of rock—one of the most romantic spots in the country. The stream that issues from it is utilised at the factory at Portlaw. It lies about 6 m. to the N., amongst the Commeragh Mountains, at a height of 2500 ft. "The precipitous sides of these mountains present a remarkable appearance as seen from the land, exhibiting, from their bold projections and deep-receding cavities, vast masses of light and shadow."—*Fraser*.

From Kilmacthomas, this same range of hills, under the name of the Monavullagh Mountains, trends to the S.W., overlooking Stradbally and Dungarvan, the road to the latter place winding at their base, passing on rt. Commeragh House, and on l. Saralville. From the steep hill above the Dalligan river a very lovely distant view is gained of Dungarvan, with its bay, and Helvick Head in the distance.

63 m. rt. Cloncoskoran, the seat of Sir N. Humble, in whose grounds there is a singular gap or pass in the wooded range behind. From hence it is 3 m. to

Dungarvan (*Hotel*, Devonshire Arms, very bad), a seaport containing very little of interest and an immense deal of dirt (Pop. 5886). It was a place of greater importance in early times, and had the honour of several charters from various sovereigns. It was saved the fate of bombardment by Cromwell, who was so flattered by a woman drinking his health at the entrance of the town, that he spared it. A portion of the keep of the castle, founded by King John, still exists; but the most interesting remains are at Abbeyside, a district on the opposite shore of the harbour, which is connected with Dungarvan by a causeway and one-arched bridge, crossing the Corrigan. The Abbeyside ruins consist of a keep of a fortress, erected by the M'Graths, who were also the founders of the Augustine monastery, now incorporated with a R. C. chapel. A very graceful tower, with some E. Eng. arches, remain in *statu quo*. There is a pretty view from the ch.-yard, of the estuary and the opposite town. Dungarvan is mainly the property of the Duke of Devonshire, who has effected many improvements, though scavengering cannot be enumerated among them. Should the tourist be spending an afternoon here, he may walk out 4 m. to Helvick Head, the S. boundary of the harbour, where, if the weather is at all rough, there is sure to be a fine sea.

Distances.—Stradbally, 8 m.; Bonmahon, 12½; Kilmacthomas, 11; Waterford, 29; Helvick, 7; Clonmel, 25; Colligan, 4; Ardmore, 14; Youghal, 18.

Conveyances.—Coach daily to Waterford, daily to Youghal, daily to Lismore; [car daily to Clonmel, by a picturesque route over the high grounds between the Monavullagh and the Knockmeile-down Mountains. For the first few miles the road winds by the side of the glen of the Colligan, a charming ravine, bordered on each side by thick woods of birch and fir.

About 4 m. up is Colligan, the seat of J. Gallwey, Esq., overlooking the glen and the distant bay of Dungarvan, and backed up by ranges of mountains.

A still more charming view is gained on the descent into the valley of the Nier, a rapid and impetuous stream, rising on the slopes of Knockanaffrin, near the source of the Mahon. As we descend this valley we pass Ballymacarbry, a seat of Lord Stradbrooke, and the residence of his agent, A. Coates, Esq.; and a little further on Ballymakee (Capt. Mulcahy).

From this point the Nier dashes off to the l., to fall into the Suir, the road climbing a long hill, and eventually descending into the richly cultivated vale of the Suir. The main points of scenic interest in this valley are the noble peaks of the Galty mountains on the l., with their peculiar ravines and gullies (Rte. 30), and the rounded boss of Slievenaman right over Clonmel. At 25 m. the Suir is crossed by a handsome stone bridge, and the traveller enters Clonmel (Rte. 30). *Hotels:* Hearne's, comfortable; Cantwell's.]

From Dungarvan to Youghal the road is hilly. At Killongford Bridge, C8½ m., it crosses the mouth of the river Brickey, and ascends a low range of hills that run in a S.E. direction from the Blackwater, near Lismore, to the Suir. At the 11th m. from Dungarvan a *détour* should be made to the l. for 3 m. to *Ardmore*, to visit its interesting remains.

They consist of a round tower, cathedral, church, oratory, and well—nearly all bearing the name of the patron saint and early missionary St. Declan, who was the son of a noble family in the county of Waterford, and commenced his Christianising labours about the 5th cent. Of all the buildings, the oratory is the most ancient, and probably of the same date as St. Declan—a rude primitive little hut of 13 ft. long by 8 ft. broad, the door of which (now blocked up by accumulations of earth) has its lintel formed of a single stone. The side walls project a little beyond the roof. It is lighted by an E. window with a single-piece circular head. There was also a monastery founded by Declan, which appears to have arrived at considerable importance in learned and ecclesiastical matters, its heads usually ranking as bishops.

The *Cathedral* consists of a choir, probably the earliest portion of the building, which is separated from a nave of later date by a remarkably beautiful pointed arch with capitals sculptured in the form of lotus-buds. This portion was entered from the S. by a doorway, now built up, and presents in the N. wall a course of masonry of rude and Cyclopean character, probably of the same date as the oratory. The nave is of the 11th cent., called by Mr. Hayman " of the Hiberno-Romanesque style." It was entered by a doorway on the S. (now blocked) and one on the N., containing a good round-headed arch, within which a later pointed door has been inserted. The N. wall of the nave contains not only the 2 available windows, but also decorations of arcades of very early Norman (Saxon?) date. The chief beauty of design, however, is lavished on the W. gate, " which presents a series of sculptured niches of elaborate execution. About 6 ft. from the ground are 2 large semicircular compartments, enclosed in a moulded string-course. In that to the N. are 3 arched niches, the central one containing a sculpture representing the Tree of Life, with the serpent coiled round the trunk, and

Adam and Eve standing on either side. The right-hand niche of this compartment commemorates the conversion of the Pagan Prince of the Deisi, who, with his spear couched and resting on his shoulder, bows himself before the Christian missionary. The left-hand niche contains an ox. At the top of the S. compartment is the Judgment of Solomon, and below it are 6 niches, in the square niche to the extreme left being the Virgin and Child, and in the remaining 4 the Magi with their Offerings."—*Hayman*. The interior of the cathedral contains a trefoil-headed canopy, a sepulchral arch, and a couple of Ogham stones discovered in 1854-5, one of which commemorates the fact that "Lughudh died in the sea on a day he was a-fishing, and is entombed in the grave's sanctuary;" the other marks the burial-place of "Amada."

The round tower is remarkably perfect, and is 97 ft. in height, with a conical cap somewhat thrown out of the perpendicular by lightning. The door is 13 ft. from the ground, and has a bead decoration round the edges. The tower is divided by string-courses into 5 stories, all of which may be viewed from the interior by means of a ladder which gives access to the door. "The lower stories are lighted by splaying spike-holes, some having square, some having circular heads; and, as the visitor ascends, he meets grotesque corbels at intervals, staring at him from the concave walls. The highest story has 4 tapered windows, facing the cardinal points. The stone lintels remain over the opes where the beam of the bell rested, which, tradition says, was of so deep and powerful a tone that it was heard at Glean-Mhor, or the Great Glen, 8 m. distant."—*Hayman*.

From excavations made at the base of this tower by a number of antiquaries, when two skeletons were discovered, Mr. Windele deduced that the round towers were used principally for sepulchral purposes—a conclusion which is argued against by Mr. Petrie in his volume on the Round Towers, p. 81.

St. Declan's Well stands on a rather precipitous rock, overhanging the sea. Over the 2 doorways are rudely sculptured effigies of the Crucifixion. The festival of St. Declan is held on the 24th July, when numbers of devotees attend and perform the penance of crawling under St. Declan's stone.

Close to the well is *Teampull Deiscart* (Church of the South), supposed to have been erected in the 13th cent. by Moel-ettrim O'Dhuibe Rathra, Bishop of Ardmore. The remains consist of a W. gable and S. wall, with a doorway in the latter possessing "the keystone of the flat arch, on its bend, apparently inverted—a matter which has given rise to much speculation; but the result of a keen scrutiny will show that it was so cut to the depth of a few inches only, and that then it is constructed as usual to meet the laws of gravitation."

From Ardmore the pedestrian may walk past Whiting Bay and Woodbine Hill, an ancient seat of the Roche family, to the Ferry. The carriage-road takes a longer round, rejoining the Dungarvan road at Kinsalebeg, and passing Pilltown, where slight remains of a castle of the Walshes exist. It is said that a small pill on which the village is situated was at a very remote date the ancient course of the Blackwater, which emptied itself into Whiting Bay instead of that of Youghal. We now cross the wooden bridge, built of Memel fir, in 1829, by Nimmo, the engineer, at a cost of 22,000*l*. It is 1787 ft. long, and is supported on 57 piers, each pier being of 30 ft. span. To connect the bridge with the shore there is a causeway 1500 ft. in length, having traversed which

the tourist enters the county of Cork, and 84 m. the thriving seaport of
Youghal (anc. Eochaill) (Rte. 29) (*Hotel:* Devonshire Arms); a pretty and interesting town situated on the side of a hill, partly wooded and partly rocky, overlooking the mouth of the Blackwater, which, immediately after passing the bridge, swells out into a lagoon of considerable size, though shallow depth, with flat shores on either side. Between the town and the ferry it becomes very much narrower, but immediately widens again, while the character of its banks change to rocky and precipitous headlands.

The town (Pop. 6514) consists of a main street over 1 m. in length, with branches to the water's side; and thrives, as is perceptible at a glance, by its coasting-vessels and trade. The tourist will, first of all, visit the ch. of St. Mary, a beautiful collegiate building, lately restored to its former magnificence from the ruins in which it lay for so many years. As long ago as 1681 it is described by Dyneley "as being in use, though much out of repaire. It was anciently a collegiate church, and at this time sayd to be the fairest parish church of the province." This establishment was founded in 1464 by the Earl of Desmond, and consisted of a warden, 8 fellows, and 8 singing-men; and the building, as it stood prior to the restoration, was of remarkably beautiful Dec. architecture.

Externally the ch. consists of a nave with side aisles, a chancel with battlemented wall—to which a sacristy, now taken away, was once attached—2 transepts, with a tower, the wall of which is 8 ft. in thickness. A round tower stood at the W. end, and on the S. of the ch. a mortuary chapel extended for some distance. There is a good Early Eng. W. door, with circular shafts and clustered mouldings. On entering this door is a round-headed arch leading to the round tower. The nave is separated from the side aisles by 5 Early pointed arches on each side. Notice in the N. transept a singular obtuse-angled arch, separating a little chapel from the middle aisle; a carved-oak pulpit; a restored monument to Hartford, Mayor, 1618; a double piscina; a monument to the Uniacke family, 1632; Tobin's floor monument, 1517; Llewellyn, Mayor of Youghal, 1628; also a round-arched Norman tomb. The N. aisle contains a curious wooden cradle, in which the sword of the corporation used to repose; also the Early Eng. tomb and recumbent figure of the Earl of Desmond, the founder of the ch.; and an octagonal font of black marble. On the N. side of the chancel is the door of the sacristy, and on the S. is one leading into the college. It is lighted by a good 6-light E. window of stained glass, contains an altar-tomb to Thomas Fleming, and sedilia on the S.W. Observe also above the windows the apertures for reverberation. In the S. transept, otherwise called the Lady Chapel, are the tombs of Richard Bennett and the Earl of Cork.

The ch.-yard is surrounded by the town-walls of Youghal, flanked by the Earl of Cork's ugly round towers and 5 pieces of his artillery. The visitor should ascend the tower for the sake of the view, which, though not extensive, is very pretty — embracing on the N. the wooden bridge over the Blackwater, the wooded hills above, and, in the extreme distance, the summits of Slievenaman and the Knockmeiledown Hills. On the E. is Ferry Point, with its ch., while immediately underneath lies the town with its ruined abbeys and populous streets in close juxtaposition.

To the N. of the ch. is the house of Sir Walter Raleigh, who, in 1588-89, was chief magistrate of Youghal, where he was in the habit of entertaining the poet Spenser. It is now the property of S. W. Pine, Esq., who allows visitors to inspect the grounds. It is a perfect Elizabethan gabled house, with some of the rooms wainscoted and decorated with carved oak, and is said to contain a subterraneous passage from the dining-room to the ch. In the garden is Raleigh's yew-tree, where the knight, under the influence of his beloved tobacco, was in the habit of poring over his favourite 'Faerie Queen.' This garden is also celebrated as being the receptacle of the first potato planted in Ireland. To the N. of the town is the Dominican Friary, founded in 1268 by Thomas Fitzgerald, surnamed the Ape. The remains consist of the W. gable with its doorway and a 3-light window, and a portion of the arch connecting the nave with the aisle. There are also some traces of the St. John's House of Benedictines, founded in the 14th cent., and converted in the reign of Charles II. into a storehouse for keeping ammunition. The E. wall of the chapel possesses a pointed doorway, with ornamented spandrils, and a few square-headed windows.

Conveyances from Youghal.—Rail to Cork; a steamer in the summer season to Cappoquin. Car to Waterford and Dungarvan.

Distances.—Ardmore, by the ferry, 5¼ m.; Dungarvan, 18; Cappoquin, 16; Lismore, 20; Strancally, 10; Rhincrew, 2½; Middleton, 15; Cork, 21.

Excursions.—
1. Cappoquin and the Blackwater.
2. Castlemartyr.
3. Ardmore.

The remainder of the route from Youghal to Cork is traversed by rly., and does not contain anything of remarkable interest.

91 m. *Killeagh*, a small town, adjoins the grounds of Aladoe, where the family of Brooke have lived for 600 consecutive years—an unusual tenure, which the peasantry have recognised by terming it "The Maiden Estate," in allusion to its never having been forfeited. The grounds, which extend for a considerable distance up the romantic glen of the Dusoin, are celebrated for their beauty and the extent of the views.

A little to the l. of Mogeely Stat., 94 m., is the town and demesne of *Castlemartyr*, the former once a place of considerable importance, as commanding the country between Cork and Youghal, and the latter the beautiful seat of the Earl of Shannon. Within the grounds are 2 ruined chs., and the remains of the castle of Imokilly, which underwent at different times much severe treatment, and was eventually taken after a longish siege by Lord Inchiquin in 1645. Passing Brookdale House, we arrive at

99 m. *Middleton*, a neat and pretty town of one long street (*Inn:* Buckley's), chiefly remarkable for its distilleries — one establishment alone, that of Messrs. Murphy, producing 400,000 gallons of whisky annually. With this exception there is nothing to see. 1 m. to the S. is *Ballinacurra*, a small port at the mouth of the Owencurra river, from whence the tourist may run up to Cork by steamer, which starts twice a-day. In the neighbourhood of Middleton, near the rly., are Cahermore (Viscount Middleton), in the grounds of which are the ruins of a castle; Roxborough; Killeagh; Broomfield (D. Humphries, Esq.); Ballyedmond (J. Courtney, Esq.); and Bally-na-Glashy (H. Wilson. Esq.).

103 m., passing Carrigtuohill Stat., near which a number of subterranean chambers were discovered in 1835, the rly. traverses one of the innumerable mazes of Lough Mahon, and soon joins the Queenstown Rly., continuing along the bank of the Lee to Cork Rte. 37. *Hotels:* Imperial, very excellent; Victoria, pretty good.

ROUTE 29.

FROM YOUGHAL TO CAHIR, THROUGH LISMORE AND FERMOY.

By this route the tourist follows the vale of the Blackwater, which, more than any other river in Ireland, abounds in scenery of a high order, with many interesting ruins and remains. During the summer a steamer leaves Youghal to make the excursion up the river about 3 times a week, but, as the navigation extends only to Cappoquin, the rest of the journey has to be performed by road and rail. Inquiries should be made at Cork as to the times of sailing, which are somewhat uncertain. The Blackwater, spoken of by the poet Spenser as

"Swift Awniduffe, which by the Englishman Is callde Blackewater"—

has a course of nearly 80 m., taking its rise in the mountain of Slieve-logher, on the borders of counties Cork and Kerry, and flowing thence nearly due E. past Mallow, Fermoy, Lismore, and Cappoquin, at which point it turns S. to enter the sea at the bay of Youghal.

On leaving the pier at Youghal, the steamer approaches the Ferry Point, where, in 1645, Lord Castlehaven made a vain attempt to bombard the town; from thence passes through the long wooden bridge built by Nimmo (Rte. 28); and at once enters the narrows of the river, which are flanked on the l., near the confluence of the Towing with the Blackwater, by the wooded hill of *Rhincrew* (Rinn-cru—Point of Blood). On the summit are the dilapidated ruins of the fortress of the same name, formerly a preceptory of the Knights-Templars, and founded by Raymond Le Gros in the 12th cent. They appear to have consisted of an irregular quadrangle, containing chapel, cloisters, refectory, kitchen, and dormitories; the refectory stands at right angles to the chapel, possesses a portion of vaulted roof, and is lighted by 7 narrow, deeply-splayed windows. At the N. end of the refectory is the kitchen, and above it are the walls of the dormitories. On the opposite bank is Ardsallagh House (J. Ronayne, Esq.), and at the junction of the Glendine river on l. 4 m. Temple Michael ch. and castle — a square keep, with a round flanking tower on the N.E. On the N. bank of the Glendine is Ballynatray, the beautiful seat of the Hon. C. M. Smyth. Close to the bank of the Blackwater, and, in fact, joined to the mainland by a causeway, are the ruins of the abbey of Molana, founded in the 6th cent. by St. Molanfide for Augustinians. To commemorate this fact a statue of the saint in his Augustinian robes was erected by a late owner of Ballynatray in the quadrangle of the abbey—the same lady depositing a funeral urn in memory of Raymond Le Gros, who, according to the authority of the Carew MSS., was buried here in 1186.

On the S. bank of the Glendine is Cherrymount (Lady Thackwell), and on the opposite side of the Blackwater is Loughtane (S. Allin, Esq.), a former seat of the Bluetts, temp. Henry VIII. The river here slightly widens, and a small pill runs in from Clashmore, the property of the Earl of Huntingdon, who obtained it by marriage into the family of Power.

7 m. l. are the ruins of *Strancal'y Castle*, "Strath-na-Cailligho," "The Hags' Holm"—finely placed on a rock overlooking the river. In this rock is a cave or chamber, popularly known as the "Murdering Hole," concerning which a legend is current that one of the lords of the castle was in the habit of making his guests merry with wine, and then despatching them in this cave for the sake of adding their possessions to his own.

Passing the ferry of Cooneen, we leave on l. Strancally New Castle (G. W. Lloyd, Esq.), very prettily situated, together with Headborough House — Smythe, Esq.), at the junction of the Bride with the Blackwater. The former is a fine castellated building, from a design by Mr. Payne of Cork.

12 m. Villierstown, a small village, where the Earl of Grandison vainly tried to establish the linen manufacture.

Higher up, on rt., is Dromana Forest and House (the seat of Lord Stuart de Decies). In the grounds are the remains of an old fortress of the Desmonds, in which was born "Catherine, the old Countess of Desmond, who, at the age of 140 years, presented herself at the English Court to petition James I. for her jointure, of which the attainder of the last Earl of Desmond had deprived her. The cherry was first domesticated in this country at Affane, near Dromana, having been brought from the Canary Isles by Sir Walter Raleigh; and the Countess's death is attributed to have taken place in consequence of a fall from a high branch of a favourite cherry-tree."—*Haynau*. As the course of the river is ascended, the tourist approaches the hills which have been looming in the distance, and are very beautifully grouped. The highest point is Knock-meile-down (Cnoc-maol-dun,—bare, brown hill), 2069 ft., the summit of the lofty chain of hills between Lismore and Clonmel.

At 15 m. Affane was born Valentine Greatorex, celebrated for his so-called miraculous power of curing diseases by stroking the hand of the individual. He lived in the 17th cent. Affane House is the seat of S. Power, Esq. On opposite bank is Tourin (Sir Richard Musgrave, Bart.). Higher up, near the ruin of Normisland Castle, the navigation partly ceases in consequence of the shallowness of the river.

17 m. *Cappoquin* (*Hotel*: Power's) is a charmingly placed town at the bend of the Blackwater, where it turns to the S. The castle, of which there are no remains, was besieged and taken by Lord Castlehaven in 1645. The river is crossed by a stone bridge, which replaced a singular timber viaduct built by the Earl of Cork. Overlooking the town are the pretty grounds of Cappoquin House (Sir John Keane). It is an interesting excursion from here to the monastery of Mount Melleray, a convent of Trappists, on the slopes of the mountains about 4 m. to the N. It is a large quadrangular building, the sides of the square occupied by refectories, kitchens, dormitories, and chapel. The whole of the district was extremely bleak and wild, but the labours of the brethren have very much improved its external appearance. From Cappoquin are 2 charming roads, one on each side the river, to

21 m. *Lismore* (*Hotel*: Devonshire Arms). The foundation of the bishopric is ascribed to St. Carthagh, in the 7th cent., whose establishment soon attracted not only many learned and pious men, but others of less peaceful tendencies, such as the Danes and Ossorians, who repeatedly burnt the town until the erection of a castle by John Earl of Morton in the 12th cent. This fortress

was the residence of the bishops of the diocese until it was granted by Neil Magrath to Sir Walter Raleigh, who sold it to the Earl of Cork, from whom it eventually came by marriage to the present owner, the Duke of Devonshire. Lismore is placed at a considerable height above the river, which is crossed by a stone bridge of remarkably good span. On the brink of the water is the castle, a lofty and extensive pile of building; the greater part is the work of the 2nd Earl of Cork. "The first doorway is called the Riding-house, from its being originally built to accommodate 2 horsemen who mounted guard, and for whose reception there were 2 spaces, which are still visible under the archway." Over the gateway are the arms of the Earl of Cork, with the motto "God's providence is our inheritance." The interior of the castle is beautifully fitted up, and has within the last few years been decorated by the hands of Mr. Crace. The entrance saloon and the dining-room are both splendid apartments, although the drawing-room carries off the palm, from the exquisite view from the windows. The castle is still in process of remodelling. One of the windows is called King James's window, from the circumstance of his entering the room, and starting back in a fright at suddenly seeing the great depth at which the river flowed below, an appearance which is due to the great difference of level between the N. and the S. fronts. The view from the upper rooms up and down the Blackwater is one of the most beautiful in the S. of Ireland, and embraces the heights of Knockmeledown and the town of Cappoquin. The cathedral ch. of St. Carthagh, which possesses an extremely graceful white limestone spire, was restored and almost re-edified by the Earl of Cork in 1663, and has since had many additions; the choir contains some stained glass, and a monument to the family of Magrath, 1548. "This building was held in such veneration by the Irish that, in 1173, Raymond le Gros found, when wasting the Decies country, that the easiest mode of extracting a heavy black-mail lay in the threat of burning down the cathedral." The ecclesiastical annals of Lismore do not include anything of note, either in the roll of bishops or the history of the diocese; but the parish can boast of being the birthplace of two celebrated men—Robert Boyle the philosopher, and Congreve the poet. To the E. of the town is a rath, which gave the name of Lis Mor (Great Fort). The neighbourhood of Lismore is richly adorned with well-wooded seats and plantations, the principal of which are Salterbridge (R. Chearnley, Esq.), Bellevue, Ballyrafter, Ballyinn (— Kane, Esq.), Glencairn Abbey (G. P. Bushe, Esq.), Fortwilliam, and Ballysaggartmore, the elaborate Gothic residence of A. Usher, Esq.

Conveyances.—Coach to Waterford, through Dungarvan.

Distances.—Youghal, 21 m.; Cappoquin, 4; Mallow, 33; Fermoy, 16; Tallow, 4; [the latter a village to the S.W. on the Bride, which is navigable up to this point.

Close to the village is the castle of Lisfinny, a strong, square tower of 3 stories, once the residence of the Desmonds, but now incorporated with the modern house of Major Croker. From the battlements is a charming view of the valley of the Bride.

Between Tallow and Rathcormack is Britway, which contains an interesting old ch.; the doorway has a flat architrave, carried along the sweep of the arch till it terminates in a curious figure in the keystone.

About 4 m. W. of Tallow is the lofty square tower of Conna on a high limestone rock overlooking the Bride.]

Route 29.—Fermoy.

From Lismore the road continues along the N. or l. bank of the Blackwater, passing Ballysaggartmore and Flower Hill (B. Drew, Esq.), to 27 m. Ballyduff. On the opposite bank are Glencairn, Fortwilliam, Ballygally, and Glenbeg. At Ballyduff the river is crossed. A little further, 29 m. rt., is the ruin of Macollop Castle, and 33 m. on the same side Kilmurry (T. Grant, Esq.).

37 m. Fermoy (*Hotel:* Queen's Arms) has grown up to its present importance entirely within the last 60 or 70 years. At that time there were only a few cabins; but a Mr. Anderson built an hotel and some good houses, and finally entered into an arrangement for the erection of some barracks with the Government, which was anxious to form a central military depôt; as such it has answered the purpose, and is now one of the largest stations in Ireland. The barracks are on the N. side of the river, and are divided into two establishments, called the E. and W. barracks, to accommodate nearly 3000 men. Those on the W. were for some time used as the Union House. The greater part of the town is on the S. bank of the Blackwater, which is crossed by a bridge of 13 arches. It is spacious and well built, having been carefully laid out by Mr. Anderson, who benefited the district by roadmaking and establishing mail-coaches, somewhat after the fashion of Mr. Bianconi. He also built a large military school, now called the College. Although Fermoy is a modern town, there are several antiquities in the neighbourhood. The scenery, moreover, is extremely pretty, the river-banks being of the same elevated character as in the rest of its course, and ornamented with many an overhanging plantation and pretty villa. Close to the town are the well-planted grounds of Fermoy House. 1 m. to the E. are the ruined towers of Carrigabrick and Liclash Castles, on the S. and N. banks respectively.

Conveyances.— Rail to Mallow; car to Mitchelstown.

Distances.—Mallow, 17 m.; Mitchelstown, 10; the Caves, 16; Cahir, 27; Lismore, 16; Cappoquin, 20; Rathcormack, 4½; Kilworth, 3.

Excursions.—
1. Mallow.
2. Lismore.
3. Glanworth.
4. Mitchelstown and Caves.

[The journey from Fermoy to Mallow is usually performed by the rly., which, by keeping on high ground, does not allow many of the beauties of the Blackwater to be visible. To the N. the high ranges of the Knockmeiledown have disappeared, but on the S. is a new chain of hills, known as the Nagles Mountains, of which the heights of Knock-naskagh, 1406 ft., and Corran, 1345 ft., are most conspicuous. Quitting Fermoy by the road, the tourist passes Castle Hyde (J. Hyde, Esq.), Cregg Castle (T. Hyde, Esq.), and Templemore, on the N. bank, and Cregg O'Lympry on the S. The scenery is particularly pretty at Ballyhooly, where a road is given off rt. to Castlerock, and l. to Mallow (crossing the river) and Cork.

Near Ballyhooly are the seats of Convamore (Earl of Listowel), Renny (F. Blackburne, Esq., and Woodville (R. Gibbings, Esq.).

At 19 m. Castletownroche Station the line crosses the Awbeg (Spenser's Mulla, p. 237) at its confluence with the Blackwater. The village lies nearly 1½ m. rt., and is picturesquely situated on the Awbeg, which runs between precipitous banks. Incorporated with Castle Widenham is the old keep of the fortress of the Roches, which was defended in 1649 by Lady Roche for many days against Cromwell's army. The ch. is remarkable for an octagonal spire: "the lower stage is pierced with a window on every face, the copings of which form a zigzag ornament continued all round."

Close to the village is Glananore, and higher up the Awbeg are Bally-walter (R. Welsted, Esq., Rockvale, and Annsgrove (R. Annesley, Esq.). Near the station are the remains of the abbey of Bridgetown, founded in the reign of King John by Fitzhugh Roche. On l. Clifford (C. Tisdale, Esq.) and Caringunna Castle (H. Foot, Esq.), near the village of Killawillin, where the Blackwater is again spanned by a bridge.

Passing Carrig House (W. Franks, Esq.), Rockforest (Sir J. Cotter), Ballygarrett (W. Creagh, Esq.), the traveller reaches 17 m. Mallow (*Hotel:* Queen's Arms). Rte. 25.]

The first point between Fermoy and Mitchelstown is 3 m. *Kilworth*, a village at the foot of the Kilworth Mountains, and equidistant from the streams of the Funshion and the Douglas, both tributaries of the Blackwater.

[Two excursions can be made from here:—1. on the l. to Glanworth, 5 m., following the valley of the Funshion, and passing Glenwood, the ruins of Ballyhindon Castle, and Ballyclogh House, the Elizabethan seat of Capt. Barry.

Glanworth is worth a visit, not only from its picturesque position, but on account of the castle, formerly a residence of the Roche family. The remains consist of a square keep and an addition of later date, in which were the state apartments. They are defended by a quadrilateral curtain wall flanked by round towers.

A little to the N. of the village are the remains of the Dominican abbey, an E. Eng. ch. founded in the 13th cent. by the Roches. A tower rises from the junction of the nave and chancel, resting on 4 graceful arches. From Glanworth the tourist may return direct to Fermoy 5 m., without revisiting Kilworth.

The 2nd excursion is through the romantic glen of the Araglin, a stream which rises at the foot of the Knockmeiledown hills, and falls into the Douglas some distance below Kilworth. It is particularly picturesque at Castle Cooke, the residence of W. Cooke Collis, Esq.]

Adjoining Kilworth are Mary Ville (L. Corban, Esq.), Moore Park (Earl of Mountcashel), Ballynacarriga, and Rushmount (A. Geran, Esq.). The road now ascends, crossing the Kilworth hills at an elevation of 750 ft. On the l., near the highest point, is the solitary and ruined tower of Caherdrinney.

47 m. *Mitchelstown* (*Hotel:* Kingston Arms) is a very neat, pretty little place in an elevated valley between the Kilworth and Galty Mountains, which rise immediately above the town in splendid abruptness. The great attraction is the castle, a fine modern castellated building, and the family seat of the Earls of Kingstown. Visitors are admitted on application to view the house and the grounds, which are very delightful, and which from their elevation command extensive views. A castle was erected here by the White Knight, whose heiress Margaret Fitzgerald married Sir William Fenton. His daughter again brought the property by marriage into the possession of Sir John King, created Baron Kingstown by Charles II. The present building was from designs by Mr. Pain, and cost 100,000*l.*; the principal entrance being flanked by 2 square towers, one of which is called the White Knight's Tower; the entrance hall is 80 ft. in length, and adorned with a fine groined roof. Indeed the whole arrangements both externally and internally combine to make Mitchelstown one of the finest residences in Ireland.

Close to the park is the town, in which the noticeable features are a Perp. ch. with octagonal spire, a handsome Roman Catholic chapel, and Kingstown College, an asylum founded by Lord Kingstown for decayed gentlefolk.

Distances—The Caves, 6 m.; Cahir, 17; Fermoy, 10.

The road to Cahir lies at the foot of the Galty Mountains, which present on their southern face a very much finer aspect than on the northern side. Galtymore, 3015 ft., and Galtybeg, are the most lofty points of this magnificent range. The Funshion is crossed at Killcheny, and again at Brackbaun, not far from which point is a public-house, where the visitor to the caves should stop, procure guides, and change dresses. The opening of the Mitchelstown Caves, so called because they happened to be on part of the Mitchelstown estate, is situated about 60 ft. above the level of the road. As is commonly the case with caverns of any size, they occur in the carboniferous or mountain limestone, and are remarkable for their extent and the beauty of the stalactites; they are divided into the new and old cave, the former being the one usually visited. "A narrow passage of about 4 ft. in height and 33 in length, and sloping at an angle of about 30° with the horizon, terminates in an almost vertical precipice, 15 ft. in depth, down which the visitor passes by a ladder. Advancing forward, the floor resumes its original angle of inclination, which it maintains for the distance of about 28 ft. It now becomes nearly horizontal, and continues so for 242 ft., until the opening into the lower middle cave is reached. This is one of very considerable magnitude. In shape its ground-plan resembles a bottle with cylindric neck and globular bottom, the vertical section of its wider end being that of a dome or hemisphere. From the southern extremity of this chamber a passage of 60 ft. in length leads to the upper middle cave, the most remarkable part of the entire cavern, from the magnitude, beauty, and fantastic appearance of its sparry productions."—*Apjohn*. The stalactites and the stalagmites are the principal beauties; and of these there are every variety, from the slender column of spar to broad sheets, like drapery, so thin as to be transparent. The principal features are the Drum, the Pyramid, the Table, the River, the Organ, the Garret Cave, the Kingstown Gallery, the Land Cave; all of which are duly pointed out by the guides. The visitor cannot see the whole series under 2 or 3 hours, and will have to undergo a considerable amount of rough walking, squeezing, and slipping. The road to Cahir is very fine, being on a descent, from which noble views are gained of the valleys of the Suir and the parallel ranges of the Knockmealdowns. On the slopes of these latter hills is the village of Clogheen, on the road from Mitchelstown to Ardfinan, and near it is Shanbally Castle, the seat of Lord Lismore.

64 m. **Cahir** (*Hotel:* Glengall Arms). Rte. 30.

ROUTE 30.

From **LIMERICK** to **WATERFORD**.

This route is performed by the Limerick and Waterford Rly., an important line of 77 m. in length, which not only connects 2 of the principal southern ports, but, until the construction of the direct Cork and

Limerick Rly., was the only means of transit between the 2 latter places. Leaving the town by the joint station, the line gives off the Foynes, Ennis, and Killaloe branches, and runs S.W., passing through an open and picturesque country, affording fine distant views on the l. of the Killaloe Hills, Mount Keeper, and the hills running up towards Nenagh.

4½ m. Killonan Stat.; and 8 m. Boher: the latter being the station for Caherconlish, a little town about 2 m. to rt.

On l. are the scanty ruins of Butler's Castle, formerly an old residence of the Bourke family; and on the slopes of the distant hills may be seen the woods of Glenstall, the beautiful seat of Sir M. Barrington.

11 m. Dromkeen, between which and Pallas, 14 m. on rt., is Linfield House (Rev. M. Apjohn).

Near Pallas, the Slievefelim mountains to the N. are conspicuous features, occupying an area E. and W. between Thurles and Limerick. Slieve Callan, the highest point, is 1523 ft.; Mauherslieve, or Mother Mountain, 1783; and the geological composition of the range is for the most part Lower Silurian, though "the outer slopes of the mountains, and some of the lesser elevations overlooking the low country, are formed of old red sandstone, which rests uncomformably upon the Silurian; and where the slope of the ground is gentle, frequently runs upwards over the lower rock to elevations of 1200 and even 1400 ft." — *Geol. Survey.*

In the neighbourhood of Pallas, carboniferous limestone is the prevailing stratum, although there are numerous instances of trap rock; and in a wood close to Linfield House a fine façade of basaltic columns may be seen.

3 m. l. of Pallas is Castlegard.

18 m. *Oola* Stat. On a hill on l. is Oola Castle, one of those square fortified mansions erected by English settlers, probably in the time of Elizabeth. It was destroyed by Gen. Sarsfield, who surprised it by a night attack, and blew it up, together with a quantity of ammunition brought hither by William III. On rt. of line is Castle Lloyd (H. Lloyd, Esq.), and, 2 m. distant, Derk (H. Considine, Esq.).

22 m. Limerick Junction (Rte. 25), where passengers bound for Dublin and Cork diverge N. and S. Not far from the station is Ballykisteen, the Irish residence of Lord Stanley.

The traveller is now in *Tipperary*, and soon approaches, 5 m., the capital of a county as fertile and prolific as any kingdom might wish to possess, though, alas! to a great extent vitiated by the agrarian acts for which Tipperary has become so infamous in the social history of Ireland, a notoriety unfortunately not limited to this county only. Indeed there can be no greater proof of the richness and consequent value of land in this district than the fact that it fetches a higher price in the market than any lands in the neighbouring counties, notwithstanding the insecurity of life that so often threatens the resident landlord. Although a modern built town (*Hotel:* Dobbyns), Tipperary (Tiprarac, "the well of the plains") dates from the time of King John, who built a castle here. Henry III. also founded a monastery for Augustinians; and it is to be presumed that society in those days was better ordered, as we find a grant made by Edward II. to the "bailiffs and good men of Tipperary of murage for 3 years." An arched gateway is all that is left of the abbey, and is, indeed, the only remains of antiquity in the town.

It is pleasantly built and laid out, and the situation at the foot of the glorious Galty range is very charming. In the near vicinity of the town are Sadlier's Wells, Roesboro',

Greenane (R. Mansergh, Esq.), and Scalaheen (W. Sadleir, Esq.).

Conveyances :—Rail to Limerick and Waterford; car daily to Limerick.

Distances :—Limerick, 25 m.; Waterford, 52; Limerick Junction, 2; Cahir, 14½; Cashel, 12; Galbally, 9½; Athassel, 9. [The ruins of Athassel (anc. Ath-an-tuisil) are beautifully placed about 1½ m. below the village of the same name, on the banks of the Suir, which here assumes the proportions of a considerable stream.

The road from Tipperary turns off near the demesne of Thomastown Castle, the residence of Viscount Chabot, and formerly of the Earl of Llandaff. The Abbey of Athassel was founded at the close of the 12th cent. by Will. Burke, or De Burgo, and was a large and magnificent E. Eng. building, the choir, which overlooks the river, being 44 ft. in length, and lighted by a series of lancet windows. The visitor should notice in particular the deeply-recessed and rounded doorway, above which is a blocked pointed arch, with delicate shafts, the whole being enclosed by a triangular or straight-sided pointed arch. In the interior are the tomb and effigy of the founder, who died within the walls.]

29¼ m. Bansha Stat. On rt. are Bansha Wood, the Castle O. Ryan, Esq., and on l. Lismacore, the seat of H. Baker, Esq. Crossing the Aherlow, and leaving on l. Kilmoyler F. O'Meagher, Esq.), the line enters the long vale of the "goodly Shure," by the side of which it completes the remainder of the journey to Waterford. At this point we approach very near the base of the *Galty Mountains*, where the Aherlow valley joins that of the Suir.

This large and important group occupies an area which may be broadly defined by the boundary points of Cahir, Tipperary, Kilmallock, Kildorrery, and Mitchelstown; although the western portion, known as the Ballyhoura hills, overlooking Buttevant, are somewhat divided from the main group by a depression between Mitchelstown and Galbally. Here the Aherlow rises, taking a northerly course as far as the last-named town, and then turning to the W. The true Galty range is not only lofty, but peculiarly conspicuous and picturesque from its sudden elevation from the plains of Tipperary, and for the bold escarpments and precipitous gullies on every side, but more particularly on the S., which faces the Knockmeledown Mountains, and overlooks Mitchelstown. The summit of Galtymore, 3015 ft., is plainly visible from any of the Killarney hills, and is one of the 3 highest points in the S. of Ireland. The whole of the Galty range is composed of old red sandstone, which rises up from under the limestone of Mitchelstown Valley. Here old red beds rest on Lower Silurian rocks, as may be seen on the S. side of the range, in the remarkable excavation, Pigeon Rock Glen, "where, at the upper end of the Coolatinny stream, the Lower Silurian in the bed of the rock for about ½ m. is covered on either side by beds of old red, that appear one above another in the sides of the glen, uniting above in consequence of the rise of ground, and below in consequence of their own dip becoming greater than that of the slope of the hill."—*Geological Survey.* The botanist will find on Galtymore Carex rigida, Saxifraga hirta, and Ranunculus hirsutus.

The rly. now turns to the S. to

38 m. *Cahir* (*Hotel:* Glengall Arms), a thriving town of some 3500 Inhab., in the midst of charming scenery and well-kept estates. From its situation in a rich corn country, Cahir is a great place for flour-mills, an immense lot of wheat being annually sent to Waterford.

The principal object of interest in the town, which, by the way, is unusually clean and well kept, is the Castle, which stands on an island in the Suir. Although modernised to a great extent, it was originally built in 1142, by Connor, King of Thomond. Notwithstanding its age, there is but little history attached to it, except that it underwent a short siege by Lord Inchiquin, and 2 or 3 years later by Cromwell.

"It is of considerable extent, but irregular outline, consequent upon its adaptation to the form and broken surface of its insular site, and consists of a great square keep, surrounded by extensive outworks, forming an outer and inner vallum, with a small courtyard between the two, these outworks being flanked by 7 towers, 4 of which are circular, and 3 of larger size square. The ancient and proper name of the town is Cahir-duna-iascaigh, or the 'circular stone fortress of the fish-abounding dun or' fort,' a name which appears to be tautological, and which can only be accounted for by the supposition that an earthen dun or fort had originally occupied the site on which a cahir or stone fort was erected subsequently. Examples of names formed in this way, of words having nearly synonymous meanings, are very numerous in Ireland, as Caislean-dun-more, the castle of the great fort, and as the Irish name of Cahir Castle itself, which, after the erection of the present building, was called Caisleau-na-caherach-duna-iascaigh, an appellation in which 3 distinct Irish names for military works of different classes and ages are combined."— *Penny Journ.*

At present this castle, which, fortunately for English tongues, has not kept its Irish name, is used as a depôt for the Tipperary militia.

The tourist should visit the demesne of Cahir House, which stretches for about 2 m. alongside of the Suir, and is one of the best laid-out and most beautiful estates in the county. "The Cottage" is a favourite resort for its picturesque and secluded locality. This fine estate was long the property of the Earls of Glengall, but was unfortunately brought into the Encumbered Estate Court, and changed hands like many another noble Irish property. In the neighbourhood of Cahir are also Cahir Abbey (R. Grubb, Esq.), Loughlohery (W. Quin, Esq.), Ballydavid (G. Baker, Esq.), and Rochestown (S. Barton, Esq.).

Conveyances.— Rail to Limerick and Waterford; car to Cappoquin.

Distances.— Waterford, 39 m.; Clonmel, 11; Tipperary, 14½; Mitchelstown, 18; the Caves, 7; Ardfinane, 5; Cashel, 11.

[Mitchelstown caves may be visited from here (Rte. 29), as well as *Ardfinane*, "the hill of St. Finian," the leper, who founded here a monastery in the 7th cent. The interest of Ardfinane, however, is due not to this, but to a castle built by King John when Earl of Morton. It is a large, rambling ruin, of quadrangular shape, and flanked by square towers at the corners, two of which are in very good preservation. Its position on a steep, precipitous rock overlooking the Suir, and with a background of the distant ranges of the Galty and Knockmeiledown Hills, has a fine effect. The castle is said to have been granted after its erection to the Knights Templars, and was considered one of the strongest Irish fortresses until its destruction by Cromwell, who planted his cannon on the opposite hill. The Suir is crossed by a remarkably long bridge of 14 arches, carrying the road from Clonmel to Cork. The tourist may, instead of returning to Cahir, proceed at once to Clonmel, 8 m.] From Cahir the rly. takes another sweep to the S., and passing l. Loughlohery House, and Woodruff House

(W. Perry, Esq.), gradually reapproaches the valley of the Suir.

49 m. *Clonmel* (*Hotel:* Hearne's, comfortable; Cantwell's) is decidedly the cleanest and most business-like inland town in the S. of Ireland, and is, moreover, graced with extremely pretty outskirts, diversified with wood and water. The exportation of grain is the principal business, although at different times efforts have been made to establish cotton and woollen manufactures—the latter as far back as 1667, when 500 Walloons were brought over from Canterbury by the Duke of Ormonde, the then Lord-Lieutenant. Clonmel was a fortified town, and bravely resisted a long siege at the hands of Cromwell, although the garrison was eventually obliged to yield. The remains of the walls surround the churchyard, and are strengthened at intervals by square towers. The west gate, the only one left out of the four, has been kept in good repair, and stands at the entrance of the main street. St. Mary's is an interesting ch., and is overshadowed by a thick grove of trees, which, together with the old town walls, gives an additional appearance of age. The church itself, however, has been much modernised, though still possessing some singular features. At the N.E. corner is an octagonal steeple, rising from a square base, and at the other is a square tower, where the sexton resides. The body consists of nave and aisles, the former lighted by clerestory windows and surmounted externally by battlements. The E. window is of very good design, and is filled with stained glass. There are ruins of 2 other churches—St. Nicholas in the S., and St. Stephen in the W. end of the town.

The Suir is here a broad and rapid stream, and separates the counties of Waterford and Tipperary—Clonmel being almost wholly in the latter county, and part of it being on an island formed by the division of the river.

From the abundant supply of waterpower, there are numbers of flour-mills and warehouses, the contents of which are sent down by barges to Carrick and Waterford. The valley of the Suir at this spot is very beautiful, Clonmel being sheltered on the S. by the Commeragh mountains, which separate it from the vale of the Nier, and merge into the broad and lofty group that runs towards Dungarvan. To the N.W. of the town is Slieve-na-man, a conical and rather isolated hill, 2362 ft. in height. The immediate outskirts and banks are wooded and pretty, affording very pleasant walks,—as "the Wilderness, which, for solemn gloom and wild grandeur, might convey no inadequate idea of that in which the Baptist preached; the road of Heywood, a charming sylvan walk; the Green, commanding a delightful prospect of the river; and Fairy Hill road, the fashionable promenade."—*Hall.* The latter is situated on the rt. bank of the river, about ½ m. below the town. There are, also, an unusual number of handsome residences in the neighbourhood. To the W., proceeding up the valley of the Suir, are Marlfield (J. Bagwell, Esq., M.P.), the grounds of which are very picturesque; Oaklands (Col. Phipps): Coole; Knocklofty, the seat of the Earl of Donaghmore; and Kilmanahan Castle (T. Watson, Esq.) To the N. are Haywood (J. Mulcahy, Esq.); Glenconner (P. Gough, Esq.). On the E. or Carrick side, Powerstown (G. Grene, Esq.); Castle Anner (Rev. H. Mandeville); Newtown Anner (R. Osborne, Esq., M.P.).

The tourist, who is now enabled to visit almost every part of Ireland by rail or car with such comfort and speed, should not forget that Clonmel was the starting-point of the first public car to Cahir, by Mr. Bianconi, of Longfield, in 1815. He was then in humble circumstances, and it is impossible to speak in too high terms of his perseverance and foresight, and of the debt of gratitude which Ireland owes him. (*Introd.*, p. xliv.)

Conveyances.—Rail to Waterford and Limerick; car daily to Dungarvan; daily to Fethard, to Goold's Cross, to Thurles.

Distances.—Fethard, 8½ m.; Ardfinane, 8; Cahir, 11; Cashel, 14; Knocklofty, 5; Gurteen, 5½; Carrick, 14; Dungarvan, 25.

[It is a pretty drive to the curious old town of Fethard, which still preserves a good portion of its walls and gateways, and an Early Dec. ch., with a fine tower and E. window.

The importance of Fethard (anc. Frodh-ard) may be gathered from the fact of its being governed " by a sovereign, 12 chief burgesses, portreeve, and an indefinite number of freemen, assisted by a recorder, town-clerk, serjeant-at-mace, and other officers." The road from Clonmel crosses the river Moyle or Moile, and passes Lakefield, the residence of W. Pennefather, Esq. If the tourist has time he should return by another road along the banks of the Clashanly, which are ornamented with the woods of Grove House (T. Barton, Esq.) and Kiltinan Castle (R. Cooke, Esq.), very finely placed on a precipitous rock overlooking the river. Opposite is the huge mass of *Slieve-na-man*, or, more properly Sliebh-na-mhan-Fionn-na-Heirin, "the mountain of the fair women of Ireland," on the summit of which Fin MacCoul, wishing to take a wife, and puzzled as to his choice, seated himself, while all who chose ran a race from the bottom to the top, the winner to secure the honour of his hand—an honour obtained by Graine, daughter of Cormac, King of Ireland, who proved herself not only the fleetest but the longest-winded.

Slieve-na-man is also celebrated by Ossian as the hunting-ground of the Finian chiefs :—

"One day Fin and Oscar
Followed the chase in Sliebh-na-mhan-Fionn
With three thousand Fenian chiefs,
Ere the sun looked out from his circle."

Geologically speaking, this block of mountain consists of old red sandstone, although on its eastern slope some clay-slates appear (associated with some igneous rocks), believed to be of Lower Silurian era. At its N.E. termination is the village of Nine Mile House, and a little beyond it Killamery, where, in a quarry 300 yards from the ch., the fossil-collector may find Cyclopteris Hibernia.]

From Clonmel the line runs still E., nearly following the course of the Suir, and the very picturesque valley formed on the N. by Slieve-na-man and on the S. by the wooded outliers of the Commeragh mountains, which descend almost to the banks of the stream.

6 m. rt., near the village of Kilsheela, is Gurteen, the beautiful seat of J. Power, Esq. The woods here are very extensive, and numerous little ravines and dells, each with its characteristic rivulet, are continually opening up charming bits of landscape. A considerable slate-quarry has been worked at Glen Patrick.

58 m. Ballydine (Capt. Power), and further on Coolnamuck (J. Sadleir, Esq.), remarkable for the growth of native wood in the grounds. At this point the Suir becomes tidal, and enters

63 m. *Carrick* (*Hotel:* Besborough Arms), a small, straggling town, which, apart from the beauty of its situation, need not detain the tourist. The only object of interest is the castle of the Butlers on the rt. or Waterford side of the river, which is crossed by a long bridge connecting Waterford with Tipperary; a small portion of the town is also in Kilkenny. As at Clonmel, the Suir divides and becomes of considerable breadth, being navigable for barges of large tonnage. In the neighbourhood of the town are

Tinvane and Mount Richard, and 2 m. to the N. the demesne of Cregg (T. Lawler, Esq.).

From Carrick the valley of the Suir becomes broader and more open, the Commeragh Mountains, which have so long bounded the landscape to the S., falling back towards Dungarvan. On L. at Piltown, are the estates of Belline, and Besborough House, the latter the residence of the Earl of Besborough, and the former of his agent. At 67 m. Fiddown the Suir is crossed by a remarkably long bridge, resting sideway on a large island in the middle of the stream. This is the only means of connection between the rly. and

Portlaw, 3 m. to the S., a busy little manufacturing town, where the Malcolmsons, the merchant-princes of Waterford, have a large factory, employing 1000 hands. Close to the village is the residence of W. Malcolmson, Esq.; and about 1½ m. to the W. is Curraghmore, the seat of the Marquis of Waterford. It is more than 4000 acres in extent, and is remarkable for the beauty of the grounds and timber, in which the Scotch firs are pre-eminent. The scenery of the Suir near Fiddown is very beautiful. The banks rise to a considerable height, and are finely wooded at Mount Bolton, on the rt. of the stream. From hence there is nothing worth seeing for the remainder of the journey. At Dunkitt the Blackwater is crossed, and a junction formed with the Kilkenny line, shortly after which we reach the gloomy terminus of

Waterford. *Hotels:* Adelphi, very good; Dobbyn's, pretty good; Cummin's, bad. (Rtes. 26, 28.)

ROUTE 31.

FROM MALLOW TO KILLARNEY AND TRALEE.

The opening of the Great Southern and Western branch from Mallow was a real boon to the tourist, whom a run of 2½ hours places at once in the heart of the most lovely and far-famed scenery in Ireland, the lakes and mountains of Killarney.

For a great portion of the distance the line passes through an uninviting country, in which extensive stony uplands, watered by broad open streams, are the general features, occasionally diversified by wooded slopes and ravines. But as soon as the distant outlines of the Killarney Hills break upon the eye, all else is forgotten in watching the fantastic outlines and purple hues of these magnificent ranges.

Crossing the clear stream of the Blackwater we leave the main line to follow up its picturesque valley for several miles.

At 1 m. the little river Clyda is crossed, having on l. of rly. Dromore House (A. Newman, Esq.), and on rt. Clyda, Woodfort (N. Ware, Esq.), and Dromaneen, the grounds of these last skirting the banks of the Blackwater. On the opposite side of the river are Summerville (R. Bolster, Esq.) and Longueville (R. Longfield, Esq., both occupying commanding situations.

2 m. l. is the prettily wooded knoll of Gazabo Hill, crowned with a

turret, which is said to have been erected by a former proprietor of Woodfort to protect his estate.

At the further end of the demesne of *Dromaneen* is the old castle rising from a steep escarped rock overhanging the Blackwater, with its square mullioned windows and gable ends. The ruins are less those of a castle than of a fortified house of the date of Elizabeth or James I., about whose time Dromaneen belonged to the family of the O'Callaghans.

7 m. l. Mount Hillary (1287) is an outlying portion of the Bochra Mountains, a dreary and uncultivated range intervening between the valley of the Blackwater and that of the Lee near Macroom. The road from Kanturk to Cork crosses them at a height of about 1000 ft. Near the junction of the Glen River with the Blackwater is, 9½ m., Kanturk Stat., distant 3¼ m. rt. from

Kanturk (*Inn:* Tierney Arms), a pretty little town, situated on the banks of 2 streams, the Duallua and the Allua, each of which is crossed by bridges of 5 or 6 arches. The former river gives name to the barony of Duhallow. Kanturk became a place of some importance in the days of Elizabeth, owing to the building, by MacDonagh Carthy, of an immense castle (still called McDonagh's Folly), of such proportions and vast strength, that the jealousy of the English Government was roused and a veto placed on any further proceedings. "It occupies the 4 sides of a quadrangle 120 ft. in length by 80 ft. in breadth, being 3 stories high, and flanked at each angle by a square tower of 4 stories, having 3 windows in each story in the central portion; the groins, mouldings, beltings, and other ornamental parts, are of hewn stone. The battlements, if ever carried up, have fallen down, and the additional story mentioned by Smith in his 'History of Cork' is only apparent on one side, where it forms the underground or cellar floor."—*Lewis.* The castle stands about ½ m. to the S. of the town.

The R. C. Chapel in the town is worth visiting for its entrance gateway and font, both the work of a native artist.

[5½ m. to E. of Kanturk, passing on the way Rathmaher, Assolas, and Ballygiblin (Sir H. Becher, Bart.), are the village of Cecilstown, and Lohort C istle (Earl of Egmont), a fine baronial residence, approached by a long straight avenue.

Near Newmarket, which lies to N. Kanturk, are Newmarket House (R. Aldworth, Esq.), and the Priory, once the residence of John Philpot Curran, whose convivial proceedings with the chosen wits and talent of that day have been described by Lever under the designation of 'The Monks of the Screw.'

Newmarket is placed at the foot of a very dreary and barren range of hills which, with but few breaks, may be said to extend northwards to the banks of the Shannon, and westwards to the coast. From Charleville to Listowell, and from Newmarket to Tralee, the whole district is occupied by this wild and bleak region, each range taking a different name. Those near Newmarket are the Use Mountains, while to the N.W. they are called Mullagharcirk, and still westward the Clanruddery and Flesk Mountains. Woe betide the pedestrian who gets benighted here, "for there is not, between Mr. Aldworth's seat at Newmarket and the Knight of Glin's on the banks of the Shannon, a distance of 34 m., a single house worthy of the name of a gentleman's residence."—*Fraser.*]

Close to Kanturk Stat. is the village of Banteer, and 1½ m. to E. Clonmeen, a residence of the O'Callaghans.

Still following the Blackwater, and leaving on rt. Rosnalee (W. Leader, Esq.), Dromagh Castle (N. Leader,

Esq.', Keale, Rathroe (D. M'Carthy, Esq.), and Flintfield, we arrive at
20 m. Millstreet. A little before arriving at the stat. on l., on the banks of the river Finnow, is *Drishane Castle* (the residence of Col. Wallis', a castellated building flanked by a square tower at each end and incorporated with the old fortress, the ivy-covered tower of which rises from the modern portion. Drishane was built by Dermot M'Carthy in 1436.

The most attractive point about Millstreet (*Hotel:* Wallis Arms) is its situation in an open wooded valley on the Finnow, surrounded by mountains, which at Cahirbarnagh to the S.W. attain a height of 2239 ft. In fact they are the advanced outposts of the Killarney group, that has for some time past been looming in the distance. The scenery of Millstreet is enhanced by the woods of Drishane, Altamont Rev. G. Morgan), Coomlogane M'Carthy O'Leary, Esq.', and Mount Leader, the residence of the Leader family, at the foot of Mount Clare.

Near the mountains, on the road from Millstreet to Macroom, are the ruins of Kilmeedy Castle, which commanded the descent into the valley from the Muskerry Hills. After passing Shinnagh Stat. 26 m., where the river Awnaskirtaun is crossed and the Blackwater turns off to the N., the interest of the landscape is all concentrated on the l., when the noble Cahirbarnagh 2239 ft., and the still more conspicuous range of the Paps 2268 ft., herald the approach to the finest scenery in the kingdom. To the Paps, which are easily recognizable by 2 conical eminences separated by a deep ravine, succeed Crohane 2162 ft., and Mangerton 2379 ft., one of the principal lions of Killarney. Immediately to the S. this range of mountains is separated only by the lofty highland valley of the Flesk from a fresh range known as the Derrynasaggart Mountains, which spread over a large area, and in fact extend with more or less interruption all the distance to Gougane Barra and the source of the Lee.

33 m. Headfort Stat., passing which the line runs parallel with the Flesk River, that leaps from rock to rock with impetuous torrent. A very fine mountain road runs S. from Headfort to Macroom.

Soon a sudden turn of the valley brings us in sight of Flesk Castle, the seat of D. Coltsman, Esq., crowning a wooded knoll, round the base of which sweeps the river. It commands one of the most enchanting views over the lake and mountains that it is possible to conceive.

41 m. *Killarney* Stat. Here the train, though by no means near its journey's end, usually disembogues 9-10ths of its passengers, the greater part of them eager for the Lake beauties which nature has scattered so prodigally over this favoured region: a region so charming, that no amount of journeying to reach it can be considered too great or too wearisome. The Killarney district is well supplied with hotel accommodation, and amongst the 3 or 4 principal establishments the visitor will scarcely go wrong whichever he chooses. The Railway is a magnificent and first-class house adjoining the stat., but this, though convenient in some respects, has, to the generality of visitors, the disadvantage of being nearly a mile from the Lake, the view of which is almost entirely cut off by the woods of Lord Kenmare's demesne. Next in rank is the Royal Victoria Hotel, about 1½ m. from the town, and situated in its own grounds sloping down to the N. shore of the Lake; the accommodation here is first-class in every way, and the situation overlooking the whole of the Lower Lake, and the splendid panorama of mountains from Mangerton to the Reeks is superb; moreover, it is the most central for excursions to the Gap of Dunloe and that neighbour-

Route 31.—Mallow to Tralee. IRELAND.

hood. The Lake Hotel is also excellent, overlooking the eastern bank or Castle-Lough Bay, and also 1½ m. from the town on the Kenmare road. There are also 2 good hotels, Sullivan's and the Mucross, 3 m. S. of Killarney at Mucross. It will be advisable for the tourist to locate himself outside the town for one reason, and that is, to avoid the beggars. All Irish towns are pestered with beggars to a degree that is disgraceful to the local authorities; but the nuisance is felt with tenfold force in Killarney, which seems to be the head-quarters of everything that is bold and repulsive in Irish mendicancy. No sooner does the visitor put foot outside the hotel or station precincts than he is driven wild by touters, guides, and hordes of beggars, and should he be weak enough to stop and listen to any one of them, he need not expect to be left alone any more while he is in the town. Indeed, with the exception of a few shops containing local curiosities, such as ornaments made out of arbutus trees and such like, there is very little to detain him; for, notwithstanding the enormous number of visitors who annually resort here, it has a wretched decayed look about it, with scarcely a single good street. "Along the 3 main streets are numerous arches, down every one of which runs an alley, intersected by other alleys, and swarming with people. A stream or gutter runs commonly down these alleys, in which the pigs and children are seen paddling about, while the men and women loll at their doors or windows to enjoy the detestable prospect."—*Thackeray.* It must be allowed, however, that since the author of the 'Irish Sketch-Book' passed through Killarney, it has considerably improved in cleanliness. The only building in Killarney worth inspection is the R. C. Cathedral, a very elaborate Gothic building after the design of Pugin. It contains some beautiful interior decorations by Mr. M'Carthy.

Before describing the scenery of this neighbourhood, it is as well to touch upon the guides, a necessary concomitant to every tourist according to the notions of the hotel-keepers and the natives themselves. As most visitors are tied to time and are anxious to see as much of the district as they can, a guide cannot well be dispensed with, and even should the visitor wish to do so, it is not easy to make the guide dispense with the visitor. At every corner and every point a new cicerone starts up, and so beleaguers the unfortunate pedestrian, that he wishes he had taken one at first, if only to keep off the others. In justice to the guides, it is but fair to add that they are generally intelligent, good-humoured, always talkative, ready to protect their charge from being bothered by others, and useful in carrying any overcoats or superfluities. If the visitor is staying at an hotel, he should consult the landlord, who will provide him with an accredited guide at a fixed tariff; but if he takes one of the irregular guides, he should take care to make his bargain with him before starting. The hotels also provide ponies and boats for lake excursions at a fixed price, which the visitor can see before starting, and thus calculate beforehand the expense of his excursions. He should also take the precaution to have plenty of small change about him, for, putting aside the beggars, to give to whom were as unpardonable and unnecessary as to cast pearls before swine, he will find that the Killarney natives are wonderfully ingenious in extracting small sums—from the generously inclined, because they urge such good reasons for charity—from the closely inclined, to get rid of their importunities. First there is the purveyor of box-wood, arbutus-wood, and bog-oak ornaments, who lies in wait along the frequented roads, and offers for sale pretty knicknacks at only double their value. 2ndly there is the peculiar tribe of mountain-dew women, who, when you least expect interruption, whether at the tops of the mountains, or in the wildest glens, follow in droves of half a dozen at a time, carrying with them small jars of goats' milk and a bottle of whisky, strongly recommended by them as a specific against mountain air. From the first comer the visitor sips, but, his heart failing at the sight of so many others, he is glad to compound at the expense of a shilling or two of small change. Associated with this class are idle fellows with a cracked bugle or an old cannon, or failing that amount of property, with their own powerful screech with which to awake the echoes for "his Hanner, worthy gintleman," to hear. Many of these ragged hangers-on are very amusing for a time, but they become a desperate nuisance when from half a dozen to a dozen persist in accompanying you the whole length of your walk, taking off from the grandeur and solemnity of the scenery by their clamour and determination to make themselves heard. It is really a question which the lords of the manor would do well to entertain, as to the propriety of keeping these gentry in due bounds, and thus preventing so many visitors leaving Killarney with a full determination never to come there again.

Whichever hotel the visitor may select for his stay, it will add very much to his pleasure if he thoroughly studies the physical geography of the neighbourhood before commencing his excursions.

The Lake of Killarney may be described as a large irregular sheet of water lying in a basin at the northerly base of a very high range of mountains.

In the journey from Millstreet it will be remembered that a range of mountains running nearly E. and W. commences with Cahirbarnagh (p. 279), and joins on to the Paps. Then comes the highland valley of the Flesk, causing a deflection of the range a little to the S.W. in Croghane and Mangerton. At this latter, or more correctly at the Tore Mountain, which may be said to belong to it, the easterly group of Killarney comes to an end, being divided from the western group by what is called the Middle Lakes. The westerly group rises precipitously from the opposite side of this narrow strip of water, and runs for many miles nearly due E. and W., forming the finest and most lofty mountains in the kingdom. The mass immediately overhanging Killarney are called the Tomies and the Purple Mountain. These are imaginarily separated on the W. by the Gap of Dunloe from the Alpine chain of McGillicuddy's Reeks, commonly known as the Reeks, the centre of which is Carrantuohill shooting upwards to the height of 3414 ft. These 2 groups of the Reeks and Mangerton are those with which, broadly speaking, the Killarney tourist has to do at present; but it must not be imagined that they are isolated or detached chains of mountains; for on the contrary, they extend on the W. as far as the sea-coast, and similarly to Kenmare on the S.

In a basin then between these groups lies the Lake of Killarney, the first and by far the largest portion bounded on the W. by the Toomies and the Glena or Purple Mountain; on the S. by Tore Mountain, on the N. by gently swelling hills, of no great height (between 400 and 500 ft.), and on the E. by the undulating and wooded slopes that fringe the base of Mangerton. Like most highland lakes, the chief grandeur of Killarney is at its head; for just at the point of separation between Tore and the Glena Mountain runs a narrow prolongation, a river in fact, called the Long Range, which, gliding round the Eagle's Nest, expands into the Upper Lake, embedded in the very heart of the mountains. This portion is fed by a stream which rises from the Dark Valley, or Cummeenduff, one of the most sublime glens skirting the southern base of the Reeks, and dividing them from the remainder of the Kenmare group.

If the tourist will study these broad outlines and take the following objects of bearing, viz. the Victoria Hotel for the N., Tore Mountain for the S., the Tomies to the W., and the Lake Hotel, or Ross Castle, to the E., he will not be so liable to be puzzled, when he gets on to the Lake, as to his whereabouts.

The *Lower Lake*, otherwise called Lough Leane, comprises 5000 acres of surface, and is 5 m. in length to $2\frac{1}{2}$ in average breadth. Its longest axis is from S.E. to N.W., which portion is the broadest as well as the most free from islands. The number of islands is one of the most characteristic features of the Lower Lake, there being upwards of 30, embracing a total area of 52 acres, varying in size from 21 acres (Innisfallen Island) to a mere rock of 9 perches.

In addition to these islands, the greater number of which are congregated on the eastern side of the Lake, there is also the peninsula of Ross, generally called Ross Island, jutting out from the E. bank between Kenmare grounds and the mouth of the Flesk. The bay between Ross Island and Muckross is called Castlelough. The Upper Lake is on the same level with and separated from the *Middle* or *Muckross Lake* by a narrow peninsula extending from the mainland at Muckross nearly across to Dinish Island on the extreme S.W. side, the connection between this latter island and Muckross being maintained by Brickeen Bridge, so that the waters of the 2 lakes are only connected at Brickeen, and that portion of the Long Reach which winds round Dinish, called the Meeting of the Waters.

The islands in Middle Lake, therefore, are 4, of which Brickeen and Dinish Island are 19 and 34 acres respectively.

From the S.W. corner of the Lower Lake, joining this narrow outlet at Dinish with the Middle Lake, there is a tortuous stream, known as the Long Range, of about $2\frac{1}{4}$ m. in length, which connects both Lower and Middle with the *Upper Lake*, the most beautiful, though the smallest, of all. It is 5 ft. higher in level than the others, about $2\frac{1}{2}$ m. in length, $\frac{3}{4}$ in breadth, with a surface of 430 acres, and contains 8 islands of 6 acres altogether. It is nearly separated from the rest of the Lake by the Purple Mountain, which projects between the two, the Upper Lake thus occupying a basin at the foot of the Cummeenduff, or Black Valley. It is fed by the Cummeenduff River, by the Owenreagh, a stream that flows into the same glen from the S.W., and also by a small stream from the S. flowing past the Police Barracks, and forming the Derrycunihy cascades. The Middle Lake receives the waters of the Mangerton group, flowing in at the Owengarriff River, while the Lower Lake is supplied by the small Muckross River, the Flesk running in on the E. shore, and the Deenagh close to Killarney town. There are also 2 or 3 little mountain streams on the W. shore.

It will thus be seen that the lakes form a great reservoir for the waters of this important group of mountains, discharging them into the Atlantic by the river Laune, which emerging from the N.W. of the Lower Lake finally empties itself into the sea at Castlemaine.

The next point which the tourist will have to settle will depend on the time which he has to spare for seeing Killarney, which will of course be influenced by many circumstances, such as weather, or the visitor's capability of fatigue, &c.

Should only one day be available, a good deal may be seen in that one day; although only in the most cursory manner. In this case, an early start by car to the foot of Mangerton is recommended (if the morning is clear). The car should wait at the foot and take the visitor to Muckross and the Tore Waterfall. Having completed this, another car should be engaged for the Gap of Dunloe, and an arrangement made that a boat should meet the tourist at Lord Brandon's cottage on the Upper Lake, and bring him back to the hotel.

For 2 days.— Mangerton, Tore, Muckross, and a drive to the Police Barrack on the Kenmare road will suffice for the 1st day; while the 2nd may be employed in the Gap, taking on the way Aghadoe and the castle of Dunloe, and visiting on the return water excursion, Glena, Innisfallen, Ross, and O'Sullivan's Cascade. A third day may be devoted either to a row round the lakes, or the ascent of Carrantuohill and the Reeks.

It need scarcely be observed that these rides, drives, walks, and water excursions may be spun out and diversified *ad infinitum*.

Excursion 1.— To Gap of Dunloe, and hence by water. Leaving the town at the western side and passing the R. C. Cathedral, a private road (open only to pedestrians) leads through a portion of the demesne of Lord Kenmare, emerging near the grounds of the Victoria Hotel 1¼ m., the view from which over the Lake and opposite mountains would be in itself sufficient attraction, even were it not increased by the accommodations offered, first-class in every way. His Royal Highness the Prince of Wales stopped here during his visit to Killarney. A little further on a lane turns off to the rt. and breasts the upland for about ¾ of m. to

Aghadoe (anc. Achadh-da-eo, celebrated for its ch. and round tower, once the seat of a bishopric, and stated in the Annals of Innisfallen to have been the burial-place of a son of O'Donoghue. This singular building consists of 2 portions of different dates: the nave being considered by many antiquaries to be as old as the 8th cent., while the choir was an addition of the 13th. The latter, which contains some tombs, is lighted at the E. end by a double-light lancet window splayed inwardly. The nave was lit by round-headed windows, and is entered by a magnificent Romanesque door in the W. wall, which even now in its decay shows many traces of exquisite architecture. It consists of 4 recessed arches, the 3 outer ones springing from pillars about 3 ft. high, and ornamented with chevron, bead, and tooth mouldings, continued under the crown of the arch. Notwithstanding the apparent Norm. age of these mouldings and decorations, Dr. Petrie has shown in his work on the 'Round Towers of Ireland' (p. 260) that the use of such ornaments in Ireland was of an age considerably anterior to the importation of Norm. architecture into the country. The round tower stands a little distance from the N.W. angle of the ch., and is in fact incorporated with the wall of the enclosure. The height of what little is left is about 12 ft., and its circumference is 52 ft., the masonry of which it is composed being remarkably regular. On the opposite side of the town is a massive round tower belonging to the castle of Aghadoe of rude materials and workmanship, and evidently of early date, although history mentions it not. There are traces of earthworks all round it.

Even if the visitor does not care for archæology, the view from Aghadoe will be sufficient recompense. That to the N. is bleak and desolate, but on the S. it beggars description, embracing the whole panorama of

Killarney lakes, mountains, woods, and islands, with their glorious lights and shades—such a panorama as once seen, never leaves the memory.

2½ m. rt. a road is given off to Milltown and Castlemaine 10 m., and occupying the angle of junction is *Aghadoe House*, the very charming Italian mansion of Lord Headley, the owner of nearly all the land to the N. of the lake. Further on l. is Grenagh House (D. Shiel, Esq.), and at 5 m. the Laune is crossed at Beaufort Bridge. A beautiful spot is this, and a paradise for salmon fishers, who can have fine sport from the pools underneath the bridge, while the trout fisher will find ample employment in the still backwaters at the side of the stream underneath the shady fringe of wood. A road on N. bank continues to Killorglin 7 m.

Passing the grounds of Beaufort House (Rev. Fitzgerald Day), the tourist should diverge to the l. to visit *Dunloe Castle*, originally a mountain stronghold of O'Sullivan Mor, and now the modernised residence of D. Mahony, Esq. Some of the most exquisite views of the Lake, looking westward, are to be obtained from the grounds.

In a field adjoining the high road, near the entrance to the Gap, is the celebrated cave of Dunloe, discovered in 1838, which must be regarded "as an ancient Irish library lately disinterred and restored to the light. The books are the large impost stones which form the roof. Their angles contain the writing."—*Hall*. This writing consists of Ogham characters, the age and reading of which has long been a disputed point amongst antiquarians. "The conclusion to which Prof. Graves has arrived, as regards the age of the Ogham writing, is that it does not belong to the period antecedent to the introduction of the Latin language and Christianity into Ireland, in short, that it is an invention of the early monkish period.

That the alphabet is not a very ancient one is sufficiently manifested by the arrangement of the letters. The five vowels, a o u e i, are formed into a group arranged in that order, thus manifesting the art of the grammarian in distinguishing vowels from consonants, and again in dividing the vowels into 2 classes of broad and slender. A comparison of the Ogham alphabet with the Persepolitan and Phœnician alphabets, manifests that the pretended relationship between it and them has no existence." The alphabet consists of series of scores or short lines branching off in different portions from a centre line called the Fleasg, which may be likened to a stem, the scores attached to which are the branches. The relative position of these scores to the main line constitute the difference of the letter. Generally speaking the corner angle of the stone is made use of as a Fleasg or medial line, though in the Ogham stone on Slieve Callane (Rte. 33) the Fleasg is in the centre.

The visitor soon enters the *Gap of Dunloe*, which for savage grandeur is equal to anything in Great Britain, though on a much smaller scale than Llanberis. "The road now mounts up the hill by the side of the Loe, the ravine now becoming more wild and sombre, the hill sides more precipitous and frowning; while as you gain each successive step of tableland, the little dusky ravine expands itself at the levels into dark and gloomy tarns which add wonderfully to the effect." When fairly within the entrance, the car pulls up at a cottage, where dwells the representative and granddaughter of the fair Kate Kearney. Unfortunately the beauty has not descended with the name to the dispenser of mountain dew, of which the tourist is expected to partake; being the first instalment of successive troops of attendant Hebes, who pertinaciously follow everybody up to the top of the Gap, utterly destroying the charm of the solitary grandeur by their ceaseless gabble and importunities for money. At one place a cannon is fired off, producing a really fine echo.

About the 9th m. the Loe is crossed as it issues from a savage-looking tarn, rightly called the Black Lake, and here the car returns, leaving the tourist to walk up to the head of the Gap and down again to the head of the lake on the other side. A magnificent pass it is, guarded on each side by the precipitous crags of the Tomies (2413 ft.) and the Purple Mountain (2739 ft.) on one side, and the Reeks on the other, the summit of the former group being frequently visible. One singular feature of the Gap of Dunloe is the comparatively large population that is scattered through it. Although at a distance appearing as though far removed from man's haunts, the eye soon detects the little sad-coloured cabins with their plot of potato or rye ground perched here and there amongst the rocks and streams. Just before arriving at the head of the Gap, there is a fine view looking back to the N., but the moment the summit is reached, the panorama is glorious —one which should be drunk in silently and at leisure. If the lights are good, the effect is perfectly magical in the transition from the dark gloom of the Gap to the bright-some Lake lying at one's feet in still repose.

The lake is of course the chief point of attraction, although the eye catches only the Upper Lake, with a portion of the Long Range and the river that feeds it, flowing from the rt. through the wonderful Cummeenduff, a savage Alpine glen that runs up into the heart of the Reeks for some 4 m., terminated by a semicircular cwm, from which the precipitous mountains rise sheer up on all sides but one. Should the Black Valley be overcast by lowering clouds, while the Lake is in sunshine, an effect is produced quite unsurpassable for contrast. At the head of the valley is a series of small tarns which give birth to the river. Soon after beginning the descent of the zigzag road to the head of the lake there is a singular logan or balancing stone on the side of the hill to the l. Arrived at the bottom, the tourist follows the stream of the Gearhameen from the Black Valley and arrives at a bridge, the gate of which is kept locked, until a silver key is applied to the janitor. From the Black Lake in the Gap of Dunloe to Lord Brandon's cottage, at which the tourist has now arrived, it is 5 m., that is, providing the road has been followed all the way instead of the short cut down the mountain. This is practicable, yet, although it appears to be plain sailing, it requires care, especially on the flat near the river, where the bogs are very awkward, and more particularly after wet weather. The boat should be waiting here by appointment, and now the tourist is in the hands of another class of Killarney guides, good-humoured, intelligent fellows, with a story for every rock, and a fable for every island. Their ingenuity in finding out impossible likenesses for each stone or stump is only equalled by the bold audacity with which they swear to the truth of the legend with which they have invested it. The principal islands in the Upper Lake are Eagle, Juniper, Ronayne's, and Arbutus Islands: the latter pre-eminently conspicuous for the indigenous arbutus (*Arbutus unedo*), the great peculiarity and glory of Killarney. "This is the only shrub peculiar to Killarney; it is also found at Glengarriff, and in other parts of the barony of Bear. It prevails to a great extent throughout the Killarney woods; in sheltered places attaining to a great size: and by its foliage and fruit adds much to their interest and variety."—*Fraser*. There is something peculiarly weird and wild in the twisted boles and gnarled stems of this tree, covering the island with an interlacement of wood down to the water's edge; and Mackay, in his 'Flora Hibernia,' mentions a tree near O'Sullivan's Cascade which he measured and found to be 9½ ft. in girth. The brilliant red berries are in perfection about October and November, and add an additional glow of colour to the scene. Not only on the islands, but from the water's edge along the banks (of the whole of the Upper Lake in particular), rises mass after mass of foliage, so dense as scarcely to allow the scars and peaks of the mountains to appear. As the altitude becomes greater, the vegetation thins and the character of tree is smaller and less dense; till at length the mountain soars far above, as though it rejoiced to have escaped the close companionship of the forest below. It is this wonderful succession of vegetable beauty, varying in its colours from the brightest green to russet brown, and contrasting with the gleaming scars, each one of which is tufted with its miniature tree-garden, that gives Killarney such a magic about its scenery, and confers such superiority over all other British lakes.

Another scenic advantage that the Upper Lake possesses is in its solitude and absence of habitations; indeed, the only trace of man, save Lord Brandon's cottage, is the large castellated police barrack that overlooks the Lake from the Kenmare road. We now arrive at the outlet of the Upper Lake, which is so narrow and hidden by the little bays and jutting promontories, that it is difficult to foretell from which side it may emerge; an opportunity not lost by the boatmen, who cunningly lay on their oars and offer a small bet that the visitor will not be able to guess it. The narrow passage is close under the W. bank, and is called Colman's Eye, soon after which is Colman's Leap. "This Colman, once upon a time, was lord of the Upper Lake, and instead of following the example of his namesake, who, as a saint and peacemaker, assisted St. Patrick in converting Ireland to Christianity, spent most of his time in quarreling with the O'Donoghue, and in provoking him to single combat. Being in a minority at one of these diversions, it appeared to him a prudential course to fly, and, closely pursued by his adversary, took this celebrated jump over the river, where the guides show you his footprints on the rock."—*Little Tour*.

And now the tourist enters the Long Range (2¼ m.), replete and overflowing with delicious beauty, such as is described by Shelley—

"Where the embow'ring trees recede and leave
A little space of green expanse, the cove
Is closed by meeting banks, whose yellow flowers
For ever gaze on their own drooping eyes
Reflected in the crystal calm: the wave
Of the boat's motion marred their pensive task
Which nought but vagrant bird or wanton wind
Or falling spear-grass, or their own decay,
Had e'er disturbed before." ALASTOR.

The banks on either side are covered with arbutus, and fringed along the water-side with the lofty *Osmunda regalis*, while a sudden turn of the river often brings in view the stately form of the red deer (*Cervus elaphus*), which still holds covert in the woods and forests of Killarney, the only other habitat in the kingdom being the mountains of Erris, in the Co. Mayo. Indeed, a staghunt is still a great event at Killarney, although it is but seldom that such an exciting incident occurs, the last occasion being on the visit of Her Majesty to Mr. Herbert, at Muckross.

About half way down the range one of the most striking scenes in Killarney district occurs, as the river winds round the foot of the *Eagle's Nest*, a gigantic precipice of about

1200 ft., presenting a bold front so beautifully draped with wood and vegetation that it is like a vast mass of green wall. At the summit of this cliff the Eagle still builds its nest, and various stories are told by the boatmen of bold attempts to capture them. Here, if the boatmen possess a bugle, is the place to try the sweet echoes, and here, in former days, it was the practice to fire cannon, the reverberations of which are described by those who have heard them as something peculiarly wonderful. But in consequence of a frightful accident that happened in one of these fusillades, the practice is forbidden.

Onward drifts the boat with the current. until it comes to the end of the Long Range, where the channel contracts, the banks become lined with overarching trees, and the tourist sees a-head of him the Old Weir Bridge, through the arches of which the water rushes with a rather fearful rapidity. But if he expects to land, he is mistaken, for with an admonition to sit quiet and keep up his pluck, the boatmen make preparations for shooting the rapids, which they do with admirable coolness and nerve. Indeed, so used are they to this difficult passage, that they can steer through it by night equally as well as by day, and all chance of danger is in reality very small, provided the passenger does as he is told. Once in still water, however. it is, indeed, a lovely spot. This is the Meeting of the Waters, where the Long Range is deflected by Dinish Island, the stream to the l. going off to the Lower Lake, and that to the rt. to Muckross, or Middle Lake.

The visitor will scarcely have time in this excursion to visit Muckross Lake, but he should not neglect to do so, for it is most charmingly-sheltered, almost entirely cut off on the N. from the Lower Lake, save by the 2 narrow passages of Dinish and Bric-keen, and surrounded on the E. shore by the groves and grounds of Muckross. On the S., too, rises that wonderful landscape mountain, the Tore, 1764 ft., which with its tiers of wood passing from thick groves to the slender bushes that catch footing in the crevices of the summit, is one of the most striking and picturesque features in all Killarney; it is moreover, such a changing feature that it is not always easy to recognise it.

The tourist may, if he prefers, land on the Kenmare road, and walk or drive back to Killarney, visiting the waterfall and the Abbey (p. 289. Emerging from the Long Range on the W. bank of Dinish Island (on which there is a very picturesque cottage embowered in trees), or from the Middle Lake by Brickeen Bridge, we now enter the Lower Lake at its narrowest portion, and row into the Bay of *Glena*, where the lofty *Glena*, a portion of the Purple Mountain, casts deep shadows over this quiet nook, the clear water of which reflects the green forests which so densely cover the face of the hill—

"From Dinis' green isle to Glena's wooded shore."

Lord Kenmare has a cottage ornée on the bank, a perfect little gem as regards situation, and he has, moreover, with a kind thoughtfulness, built a similar one for the use of tourists. Here all necessaries are provided for cooking a dinner; and for a picnic party bent on combining lovely scenery with their creature comforts, there is not a more beautiful place in this world. You can catch your salmon in the Bay of Glena, and have it broiled directly afterwards on arbutus skewers, and appreciate the difference between salmon fresh caught and salmon that has been lying for hours on the fishmonger's slab.

From Glena it will be as well to coast round the wooded face of the Tomies for about 2 m., and land at

O'Sullivan's Cascade. There is, however, a very fine fall called the Minister's Beck, soon after turning the corner of the promontory. The adventurous who do not mind a sharp struggle up-hill, through an almost primæval forest and over boggy ground, will be repaid, but the way is not by any means fit for ladies or for the delicate. "Sullivan's Cascade consists of 3 distinct falls; the uppermost, passing over a ridge of rock, falls about 20 feet perpendicularly into a natural basin underneath; thence making its way between 2 hanging rocks, the stream hastens down a 2nd precipice into a similar receptacle, from which, concealed from the view, it rolls over into the lowest chamber of the fall. Beneath a projecting rock, overhanging the lowest basin, is a grotto, from which the view of the cascade is peculiarly beautiful, appearing as a continued flight of 3 unequally elevated, foaming stages."
— *Wright*.

From this waterfall it is a short mile across to the exquisite island of *Innisfallen* (anc. Inis-faithlen), the gem of Killarney, "in which is found hill and dell — wood as gloomy as the ancient Druidical forests, thick with giant ashes and enormous hollies — glades sunny and cheerful, with the beautiful underwood bounding them — bowers and thickets — rocks and old ruins — light and shadow — everything that nature can supply, without a single touch from the hand of art, save the crumbling ruins, and all in a space of 21 acres, makes Innisfallen justly the pride of the worthy denizens of Killarney."

"Sweet Innisfallen, long shall dwell,
 In memory's dream, that sunny smile,
Which o'er thee on that evening fell
 When first I saw thy fairy isle."
                             MOORE.

Close to the landing-place are the ruins of an abbey founded at the close of the 6th cent. by St. Finhian Lothar (the Lesser), and adjoining these ruins is a chapel or oratory, with a Romanesque doorway, decorated with tooth-moulding. In this remote and sheltered spot was compiled the Annals of Innisfallen, "a composition usually attributed to the early part of the 13th century, though there is very good reason to believe that they were commenced at least 2 cent. before this period."
— *Prof. O'Currey*.

Strange to say, there is no copy in Ireland, and only one in the Bodleian Library at Oxford, which possesses 57 leaves.

"These annals contained a short account of the history of the world in general, and very little of Ireland till the year 430, when the author professedly begins a chronicle of Ireland thus: — 'Lasgairé Mac Neil regnavit annis xxiv,' and thenceforward it contains a short history of Ireland to 1318.

"These 3 manuscript chronicles, the Saltair of Cashel, Tighernach, and Innisfallen, are written in Irish characters and in the Irish language, intermixed with Latin. They were formerly collected, with many other valuable MSS. relating to Ireland, by Sir J. Ware, and came first to the Earl of Clarendon, and then to the Duke of Chandos." — *O'Connor*.

The visitor who has no interest in the annals will find plenty in rambling about this charming island, and taking in the opposite views of the Tomies and Torc on the S., the Slieve-mish mountains overlooking Tralee and Castlemaine on the W., and Ross Castle, with the Kenmare woods, on the E., and will return to Killarney after a day of such varied scenery as seldom falls to his lot.

2. Excursion to Muckross, Ross, Mangerton, Torc, and Lough Looscannagh.

This is essentially a land excursion, and keeps all the way along the eastern side of the lake. Immediately on leaving the town on rt. are the woods and mansion of Kenmare House, the residence of the Earl of Kenmare, the principal landlord of the neighbourhood. The house itself is plain, but the gardens are worth visiting, and the grounds, from many points, offer most enchanting views of the lake. The demesne extends from near the Victoria Hotel on the N. to Ross Peninsula inclusive on the S. The little river Deenagh divides it into 2 portions, in one of which is Knockrier Hill, a hillock generally ascended for the sake of the view.

The peninsula of Ross is 158 acres in extent, and is connected with the mainland by a causeway, which in the high level of winter is flooded, so as really to make it what it is generally called, Ross Island. On this neck of land is *Ross Castle*, a fortress of about the 15th cent., consisting of a graceful tower or keep—

"Where ivy clasps the fissured stones
With its entwining arms,"

surrounded by outworks, flanked by small circular towers at the angles.

The interior contains apartments from which exquisite lake views are obtained; indeed, it is to its situation more than its intrinsic interest that Ross owes its celebrity. Although its founder is unknown, there is every reason to believe that it was the residence of O'Donoghue, the Lord of the Lower Lake, or rather of O'Donoghue More, one of the 3 families into which the main branch was divided.

It played no inconsiderable part in the civil war of 1641, when it surrendered to Ludlow, "who was attended in the expedition by Lord Broghil and Sir Hardress Waller, and was the last place that held out in Munster against the English parliament. At the end of the siege the son of the Lord Muskerry who held the castle, and Sir Daniel O'Brien were delivered up as hostages for the performance of the treaty; in consequence of which about 5000 Irish,

[*Ireland.*]

horse and foot, laid down their arms and delivered up their horses."

The remainder of the peninsula of Ross, which is generally the place of embarkation for Killarney visitors, is prettily laid out and planted. A copper-mine was opened at one time, and promised to be productive, until the water got in and drowned it. The visitor should not omit to try the echoes under the castle, if the guides or any of the party happen to have a bugle.

From the entrance to Kenmare House the well-sheltered road continues due S., crossing 1 m. the Flesk at a pretty reach in the river. On the l. is Danesfort (S. Horsley, Esq.), and rt. the Lake Hotel.

2½ m. is the hamlet of Cloghreen, and on rt. the exquisite grounds of *Muckross* Abbey, the seat of Capt. Herbert.

The visitor who has rowed round the Middle Lake will have seen a great portion of the beauties of this charming place, which as far as landscape goes has no equal in the kingdom.

A very handsome Elizabethan building has been built of late years to supersede the old house, from designs by Mr. Burns. The attraction of Muckross, in addition to its scenery, is the *Abbey*, the entrance to which is at the further gate, near the village and hotels.

The foundation of Muckross or Irrelagh is ascribed to McCarthy, Prince of Desmond, one of the most powerful of the clans who held property near the Lake, and the representative of the kings of Munster. The date of the building is stated by Archdale to be 1440, and by the Four Masters to be of the 12th cent. It was, however, re-edified or restored in the 16th cent., as we learn from a Latin inscription on a stone in the wall of the choir. The plan of the ch. is that of nave and choir, between which is a low square tower. On the S. side of the nave is a trans.,

o

and on the N. the cloisters, with the conventual offices, consisting of refectory with vaulted apartment underneath, dormitory with cellar, and Abbot's house. There is also a small sacristy attached to the choir. The tower is supported by 4 narrow pointed arches, and contained one bell, which has long since disappeared. There is a pointed doorway at the W. end, and an exquisite 4-light eastern window.

"The chancel is in imitation of the style of the end of the 13th cent., the nave and transept in that of the 14th, and the central tower in that of the 15th."—*Gent. Mag.*

The chief beauty of Muckross is the cloisters, which are remarkably perfect. A small door leads from the N. trans. to them. They consist of a series of graceful arches ranged round the sides of a quadrangle about 50 ft. square, and lighting a vaulted ambulatory. On the S. and E. sides these arches are circular-headed, while the remainder are pointed. The buttresses are carried sloping from the ground, as at Adare, without any uprights. The interior of the square is almost filled up by a gigantic yew-tree, with a girth of 13 ft., which spreads branches throughout the whole area of the cloisters. At the angles of the ambulatory are staircases, mounting to the conventual apartments, viz., the kitchen, refectory with its large fireplace and arched recess for sideboard, and the dormitories.

In the centre of the choir is the modern tomb of the family of McCarthy More. The care which is bestowed on the abbey and precincts is a pleasant contrast to the neglect generally observable in Irish abbey ruins, where in nine cases out of ten the mouldering relics of humanity are left bleaching in the open air.

Close to the hotel a road turns off on the l. to *Mangerton*, which rears its huge mass to the height of 2756 ft. It is not by any means a picturesque mountain, being rounded and monotonous in outline; but it is a favourite ascent with Killarney visitors, on account of the magnificent view gained from the summit, and its easy accessibility, a fair road winding up almost to the top, so that ladies can ride up. When the visitor gains a plateau at about a third of the height he finds, as usual, the ad libitum accompaniment of mountain-dew girls, buglers, and idle guides, who from their elevated resting-places can spy every traveller. The pedestrian need not imagine, therefore, that he can dodge them by leaving the road, for they are sure to cut him off somewhere. At the steepest point, ¾ of the way up, it will be observed that Mangerton, although so regular in outline from below, is abruptly divided into two great depressions, the one to the W. being a crater-like hollow, from which the mountain rises steeply on every side, the hollow being occupied by a considerable tarn known as the Devil's Punchbowl, from which issues one of the streams that contribute to form Torc waterfall.

An old hag has her station at a little well at the mouth of the Bowl, who, true to the creed of the natives, endeavours to levy a toll on the credulous visitor.

From hence a very steep "breather" lands the visitor on the summit of Mangerton, when he will perceive that the eastern boundary wall of the Punchbowl is very narrow, and separates it from a much more precipitous and magnificent cwm or corrie, known as Glenacappul, or the Horses' Glen, as fine a bit of scenery as any in the district. A chain of 3 small tarns, Lough Erhogh, Lough Managh, and Lough Garagarry, are almost entirely hemmed in by the precipitous cliffs of the mountains around, the hill which immediately adjoins, and in fact forms part of Mangerton, being called Stoompa.

A little more to the E., situated in a basin at the junction of the bases of Mangerton and Crohane (2102 ft.), is the large deep lake of Lough *Guitane*, where the fisher is sure of good sport. The trout grow to a great size, one weighing 50 lbs. having been captured in this lake. It is, however, not easy to fish without a boat.

The view from Mangerton is superb, embracing in the E. Crohane, the Paps, Cahirbarnagh, and all that extensive country lying between Millstreet, Mallow, and Tipperary, with the blue range of the Galtees in the far distance. Northward, and to the W. is Tralee, with the Slieve-mish mountains in the neighbourhood of Dingle and Ventry, while a faint white line in the horizon marks the north estuary of the Shannon as it flows past Tarbert and Kilrush. Due west are the Tore, the Purple mountains, and the Reeks, with Castlemaine Haven and the Laune running at their feet: to the S. is an immense sea of hills occupying the district towards Kenmare. The Bays of Kenmare and Bantry are prominent objects in this view—a view which never can be blotted out from the memory. At the foot lie the Lakes of Killarney in all their beauty, with the thick woods and groves encircling their shores. It ought to be mentioned that views, much superior to Mangerton, can be obtained from the Purple Mt.

3½ a road on rt. turns off to Kenmare, being in fact the old road running between Tore and Mangerton, never used now except by pedestrians. It is a fine walk up the Owengarriff River (on which is the Tore waterfall to Galway's Ford, 5 m., from whence a short cross-road leads to Galway's Bridge, on the new road, some little distance below the Police Barracks.

About ⅔ of the distance there is a very pretty fall, called Cores Cascade, occurring on the river Crinnagh, at the entrance of the Eskramucky glen.

4¼ m. The visitor should turn up the ravine of the Owengarriff, and follow the well-kept walks to the *Tore Waterfall*. It is a fine fall of 60 ft., although, like most others, it requires a large volume of water to give it due effect. The steep rocky sides of the glen are thickly planted, and it is at all times a very charming and picturesque spot.

From Tore the road runs by the side of the lake. It is beautifully shaded by woods, and as the altitude becomes increased the views over the Upper Lake in particular defy all description. At the base of Cromaglan mountain an additional effect is obtained by a tunnel through which the road is carried.

10 m. Galway's Bridge, where the old road to Kenmare may be joined. A little above the bridge the Galway and the Ullauns streams unite, and in their steep course downwards to the lake form a broken and majestic fall, known as Derrycunihy cascade. In fact, the whole course of this mountain river may be said to be a continuous cascade, and the effect is wonderfully increased by the foliage that so thickly borders it.

Further on, we arrive at the Mulgrave *Police Barrack*, a lonely castellated house, which seems put there for no other purpose than for the constabulary to enjoy the view, so strangely out of place does it appear.

12½ m. *Looscaunagh Lough* is a wild and rather dreary-looking sheet of water on the table-land at the summit of the hill; and there is a road-side inn, generally considered the terminus of this excursion. From hence it is 7 m. to Kenmare. A new road of about 2 m. in length has been made by Mr. Preston White through his property, near the upper lake, which enables the tourist to drive all round the lake, and obtain some of the most unique views in the district.

The ascent of *Carrantuohill* 3414 ft., the highest ground in Ireland, is

o 2

undertaken comparatively rarely from Killarney, as the distance is long, and the ground very trying. Moreover, the liability to mist and clouds is even greater here than in most mountain districts, and after a long and wearisome journey, the tourist has to retrace his steps without gaining his point.

As regards lake views, it is not nearly so good as Mangerton; but the character and features of the Reeks is so entirely different—so precipitous and riven with gullies, that it is worth the toil of an excursion to investigate them.

The distance by the nearest way is 15 m. from Killarney. There are 2 or 3 ways of proceeding; one by the Cummeenduff, or Black Valley; also the Gap of Dunloe, at the entrance of which a bridle-road turns off to the rt., crossing the Loe, and passing a hamlet near Cullenagh, where a guide should be obtained; but the most usual way is to proceed on the Killorglin road as far as Churchtown, and turn up to the hills, following the course of a largish stream called the Gaddagh (accent on the last syllable), the scenery at the head of which is magnificently grand.

The river emerges from 2 lakes, Lough Gouragh and Lough Callee, between which is the Hag's Glen, at the very base of Carrantuohill, which frowns upon it, as though forbidding further approach. To the rt. is the mountain of Knockbrinnea (Knock a Brian hu, "The Hill of the Sheep Raddle,") 2782 ft., from the sides of which project the Hag's Teeth, singular rocks, resembling the buttress of some mouldering edifice. For about ¼ m. the path continues up the steep, through rocks, stones, long grass, moss, and shingle. Whenever a steady footing is obtained for a moment, you are induced to turn and enjoy the scenery; but from the deep retreat in which the pathway is embosomed, the view is greatly contracted, and altogether interrupted towards the W.

The way to the highest peak lies along the summit of a ridge, something like the red ridge (clawdd-coch) of Snowdon, the top of which is a narrow convex, and covered with grass so short and slippery that it can hardly be walked over in dry weather unless in stocking-feet.

The summits of the Reeks are composed of a species of shingle, which after heavy falls of snow loosens and unbinds, gliding down the mountain's breast in the thaw. For this reason naturalists say, "the height of the Reeks may have been sensibly diminished in the lapse of time."—*Wright.*

The principal magnificence of the view from Carrantuohill is in the seacoast stretching from the Shannon round by Dingle, Castlemaine, Valentia, Kenmare, and Bantry, to Cape Clear.

As regards the Lakes of Killarney, they are to a great extent hidden; but a fine view is obtained of Lough Curraghmore (Rte. 35), together with an immense number of small tarns. The tourist may descend, with care, into the Black Valley, but this will depend on his arrangements, for unless he has a boat ordered for him at the head of the Upper Lake, he will find himself in no mood for the walk to Killarney after his mountain travels.

The following is the comparative heights of Carrantuohill with a few other British mountains:—

Carrantuohill	3414
Snowdon	3571
Inglehoro'	2361
Ben Nevis	4368
Ben Lomond	3197
Cader Idris	2914
Slieve-Donard	2796
Nephin	2646
Lugnaquilla	3039

Distances from Killarney.—Mallow, 41 m.; Tralee, 24; Millstreet, 21; Aghadoe, 2½; Dunloe, 7; Beaufort Bridge, 5; Miltown, 11; Killorglin, 12; Head of the Dunloe

Gap, 11; Lord Brandon's cottage, 11; Glena, 4; O'Sullivan's Cascade, 4; Innisfallen, 2; Ross Castle, 1½; Muckross, 3; Tore Waterfall, 4½; Mangerton Summit, 7; Police Barrack, 9¼; Eskrainucky Glen, 7; Lough Looscaunagh, 12; Kenmare, 19; Cahirciveen, 37; Valentia, 40; Glengarriff, 36.

The geology of the Killarney district is by no means intricate, the entire district belonging to the eras of the Old Red Sandstone and the Limestone. The low ground to the E. of Killarney is composed of carboniferous limestone, which is also observed at the peninsula of Ross, and the various islands of the Lower Lake, such as Innisfallen, Rabbit Island, &c.

"On Innisfallen we have beds which from their flagginess and continuous chert beds, and being interstratified with dark grey shales, may possibly belong to the base of the Lower Limestone, just above the lower shales. The general dip is either to the N. or S., at angles varying from 20° to 80°, and frequently they are vertical. From the amazing contortion to which these beds have been subjected, a thickness of 100 ft. of them would be sufficient to form the island. Along the W. shores of Ross Island and the opposite coast of Ross Bay, we find beds of dark grey flaggy limestone, dipping to the S., and in many instances reversed and inverted in sharp curves. At the N.W. point of the island is a spot called O'Donohue's Library, where the alternate layers of chert and limestone weathering out unequally give the broken fragments of the rock an appearance not unlike that of a lot of large books tumbled about."—*Geol. Survey.*

This plain of limestone is continued to the W., occupying the synclinal axis between the Slieve-Mish Tralee; and the Reek chain of mountains. Both these ranges, like all the mountains in this district, are Old Red, which have been upheaved by forces acting from below, and afterwards acted upon from above by denudation.

The chain of which Mangerton is a portion is also Old Red, like the Purple Mountains, Toomies, and the Reeks, principally composed of green and red grits and shales, the lower being green and coarsely arenaceous, known as Glengarriff grits, while the upper strata are characterized by a purple hue.

"The Mangerton range is traversed by a great anticlinal curve, one side dipping to the S. towards Kenmare, and the other to the N., towards Muceross and Lough Guitane. The upper beds, known as the yellow sandstones, do not occur often. They may be seen at the entrance to the Gap of Dunloe, and (probably) at O'Sullivan's Cascades. In the Gap of Dunloe, at the S. of the Black Lake, a great fault is observable, having a strike of W.N W. across the valley, and causing a downthrow on the N.E. side. By this fault the lower Glengarriff grits appear in juxtaposition with the purple upper beds."

The thickness of the Old Red in this district is very great. "The precipice on the N.E. flank of Carrantuoghal, from the summit of the mountain to Lough Callee, exposes beds to the thickness of 2318 ft., and this mostly in the purple subdivisions of the group. On the S. side of Cummeendufl' Glen a section is obtained of 5525 ft., through part of the Glengarriff grit series with the purple beds; while Mr. O'Kelly determines the thickness of one section over the mountain to the W. of the Blackwater at not less than 8000 ft." Taking, therefore, the yellow sandstones, we arrive at a thickness of something like 12,000 ft. With the exception of a few imperfect and rare plant impressions, the labours of the fossil collectors have proved unrewarded.

We must not, however, omit to mention that igneous rocks occur to the S. of Lough Guitane, in a hill called Bennavonmore, in the form of felstone of a columnar structure, and of felstone ash in the glen of the Cappagh river, and the north slopes of the hill between Stoompa and Eskduff. Taking into consideration the interstratification of the ashes with the sandstones, it is most likely that the intrusion occurred in the Old Red sandstone era.

Perhaps the most interesting feature in Killarney geology is that of the Glacial era, known as drift. From Cahirbarnagh to Killarney, all along the north base of the Paps, Croghane, and Mangerton, is observable a steep slope of drift and boulder deposit, and it is particularly well seen near the spot where the rly. joins the Flesk, which has cut its course through this drift. At Killarney itself it disappears, but reappears again on each side of the Gap of Dunloe, and runs W. all the way to Killorglin.

Of course, with such a formidable range of mountain precipices, there are plenty of glacial groovings and evidences of glaciers. The best and most accessible are in the Gap of Dunloe, about 1 m. from the north entrance. "It consists of 3 lunette-shaped mounds of local boulder drift, sand, and gravel, arranged in a rude, concentric form, one beyond the other, across the mouth of the Gap, the 2 entire mounds measuring fully 1 m. in length by 100 yards in width. The S.E. termination of the 2 outer moraines rests on the flank of the Purple Mt., at an elevation of about 400 ft. The inner mound is only 650 yds. in length by 150 in width, and it is cut through in its central part by the Loe, the road to Killarney also passing through the cutting. On the E. side of the Gap entrance, and at the base of Toomies rock, the drift is arranged in massive mounds. These have been steeply escarped at an angle of fully 30° to the W. The two last deposits left by the glacier, as the local climate became warmer, may now be seen on the N. flanks of Tomies, and at the N. end of the Black Lake, the former at an elevation of 800 ft., and the latter 512 ft., or 178 ft. above the waters of the Lake." — *Geol. Survey.*

There can be no doubt that the Lake of Killarney was once much more extensive than it is now, and that there has been a good deal of local elevation; and as a proof, the geologist may visit some limestone rocks in the pasture-land of the S. part of Cahernane demesne, very much waterworn, and in fact perfectly eaten away at the base.

Of plants and ferns there is more abundance than there is of fossils. Of ferns the following are found:—

Polypodium dryopteris .. Torc Mountain.
Aspidium thelypteris ... Muckross Demesne.
A. Felix-mas............Mangerton.
Asplenium viride ......Torc Mountain.
A. adiantum nigrum ...On the limestone rocks at Muckross.
A. filix fœmina.........Muckross.
Scolopendrium vulgare..
Pteris aquilina ....
Trichomanes brevisetum. Torc Waterfall.
Hymenophyllum Wilsoni Killarney.
Osmunda regalis ....
Ophioglossum vulgatum.
Lycopodium alpinum ...Mangerton.
Equisetum variegatum ..Muckross.
Thalictrum minus .....Gap of Dunloe Isle.
Nymphæa alba ....Reeks.
Draba incana ....Torc, Mangerton,
Saxifraga geum.........Torc.
S. elegans ....Dunloe.
S. hirsuta ....On Carrantuohill.
S. serratifolia...........Dunloe.
S. hirta ....Carrantuohill.
Rubia peregrina ....Muckross.
Lobelia Dortmanna .....Lakes.
Solidago cambrica ......Mangerton.
Hieracium molle........Reeks.
H. sabaudum ... .Ross Island.
Apargia taraxaci ....Reeks.
Erica cinerea...........Muckross.
Arbutus unedo ....Islands in Lake.
Orobanche minor ....Muckross Abbey.
Melampyrum prat......Mangerton.
Scutellina galericuense ..Lower Lake.
S. minor ....lata ...
Oxyria reniformis.......Reeks.
Paris quadrifolia ......Ross.
Rhyncospora fusca......From Upper Lake.
Carex rigida............Carrantuohill.

Dicranum flagellare	In woods at Glenflesk, very rare.
D. fulvellum	Reeks.
Hypnum micans	Woods nr. Killarney.
H. crassinervium	Muckross.
H. confertum	Tore Waterfall.
Hygrophila irrigua	Do.
Jungermannia Lyellii	Woods nr. Killarney.
J. sphærocarpa	Tore Waterfall.
J. scutata	Do.
J. Woodsii	Mangerton.

The fishing in Killarney Lakes ought to be first-rate, but it is not, as regards angling, the usual method being cross-fishing, by which a good many salmon are secured. For the angler the rivers are the best sport. The Flesk is very good for trout, and when there is plenty of water, for salmon; but it is far surpassed by the Laune, where both salmon and trout fishing are remarkably good.

There is also good trout-fishing in Lough Guitane, but it will require a boat, which would have to be sent from Killarney. The *almo ferox* is plentiful in this last lake.

It would, perhaps, be scarcely fair to dismiss Killarney without referring to its legends, although to recount them in detail would be foreign to the purpose of a handbook; and moreover, the visitor will hear plenty of them from the boatmen and guides, who will spin yarns in proportion to the willingness or credulity of their listeners. The O'Donoghue is, of course, the staple hero. "Every rock of unusual form is forced into an illustration of his story. The guides will point out to the tourist O'Donoghue's house, prison, stable, library, pigeon-house, table, cellar, honeycomb, pulpit, and his broom; while scores of the peasantry may be encountered who have as firm a belief in the existence of the spirit chieftain as they have in their own; and there are persons of education who do not hesitate to express their opinion as to the truth of his periodical appearance."—*Hall*.

This appearance happens every May morning at sunrise, when the O'Donoghue emerges from the water armed cap-à-pie, and mounted on his favourite white steed, and rides over the territorial waters on which he once held sway. Fortunate is that person who catches a glimpse of him, for good luck is sure to follow him.

"For when the last April sun grows dim,
    Thy Naiads prepare his steed for him
        Who dwells, bright lake, in thee.
Of all the proud steeds that ever bore
Young plumed chiefs on sea or shore,
        White steed, most joy to thee,
Who still, with the young first glance of spring,
From under that glorious lake dost bring
    My love, my chief to me."

MOORE.

The remainder of the route from Killarney to Tralee does not require much description. The line runs through a dreary boggy country, which offers a wonderful contrast to the beauties that the tourist has just left—a noticeable feature, by the way, in the best Irish scenery, which, like an oasis in the desert, is always approached through a melancholy and ugly country.

Near Farranfore stat., 52 m. the river Manin is crossed in its course towards Castlemaine. Very near its source is the little town of Castle Island, at the foot of the Clanruddery mountains. There are slight remains of the old fortress, but scarcely of sufficient interest to warrant a divergence thither.

63 m. Tralee (Rte. 32). (*Hotel:* Blennerhasset Arms, bad.)

ROUTE 32.

FROM **LIMERICK** TO **TRALEE.**

Three routes lie open to the tourist:—

1. By steamer every second day, from Limerick down the Lower Shan-

nou, calling at Beigh, Foynes, Glin, Tarbert, and Kilrush.

2. By rail to Foynes; and from thence by steamer to Tarbert.

3. By mail car all the way to Tralee.

It will be sufficient to point out the various places passed by the steamer in its course, which cannot be visited except they lie near the landing-places.

Gliding past the quays of Limerick and leaving in the distance the tower of the cathedral, the steamer enters the Pool, which is bordered by numerous pretty villas. Soon the river bends, having on rt. the towers of Coreen Castle, and to l. 3¼ m. the demesnes of Tervoe (Hon. W. Monsell, M.P.), and Cooperhill (J. C. Cooper, Esq.), behind which rise, from its eminence, the ruins of Carrigagunnell Castle.

5 m. rt. are the keeps of Castle Donnell, Cratlockeel, and Cratloe, backed up by the woods of Cratloe, at the foot of which runs the Ennis rly.; and fine views are gained of the Clare hills, that lie between this district and Killaloe.

10 m. passing sundry islands which are grouped about the widening stream, is on rt. Bunratty Castle, situated a little distance up the Bunratty river. This together with the foregoing ruins are noticed in Rte. 33. On the l. shore is the mouth of the Maigue, a considerable stream that rises in the S. of the county, and flows past Croom and Adare. A long shoal now intervenes in the tideway, breaking up the channel into N. and S.

13 m. l. is the little pier of Ringmoylan, the port, if it may be called so, for Pallaskenry, which lies 2 m. to the S. Farther still on l. are the demesnes of Castletown (Rev. W. Waller), and Bushy Park, the latter near the station of

16 m. *Beagh*, the landing-place for travellers to Askeaton (p. 299). Close to the quay are remains of the ancient castle of Beagh; the parish of Iverus, in which it is situated, deriving its name from a Danish adventurer who built a ch. here. The whole district abounds with raths.

From the quay it is 4½ m. to Askeaton. Nearly opposite is the broad embouchure of the Fergus, which runs up to Castle Clare (Rte. 33), and is the means of supplying from that county immense stores of grain and provisions. There are at this point considerable islands and sand-banks, which do not by any means add to the security of the navigation. Passing l. the mouth of the little river Deel, we arrive at 24 m. Foynes, the snug little harbour and terminus of the Limerick and Foynes Rly., sheltered from the N. by Foynes Island. On the N. bank of the Shannon, which is here nearly 2 m. in breadth, are the village of Killadysert and the demesne of *Cahircon* (— Kelly, Esq.), one of the finest residences on the Lower Shannon.

2. The Foynes and Limerick Rly. leaves the general station in company with the other lines, soon turns off to the S., and runs through an uninteresting district to

7¼ m. *Patrick's Well*, the junction of the direct Cork and Limerick Rly., which runs through Bruree and Croom to Charleville, there joining the Great Southern and Western (Rte. 25).

[About halfway between Patrick's Well and Limerick, to the N. of the line, is the village of

Mungret, where the antiquary will find several ecclesiastical ruins. A monastery for Augustines was founded here by St. Patrick, and, notwithstanding repeated destruction by the Danes, was always re-edified, and continued to flourish until the Dissolution, containing, according to the Saltair of Cashel, an establishment of 1500 monks. The ruins are those of the walls of the nave and choir, which was lighted by a Pointed E. window, and of a square embattled tower. Besides this abbey, there are remains of 2 chs. and of a castle a little to the N.]

In the neighbourhood of St. Patrick's Well are Faha (T. Russell, Esq., Elm Park (Lord Clarina), Spring Lodge, to the rt. of the rly., and Attyflin (D. Westropp, Esq.), Fortetna, and Green Mount (F. Green, Esq.) to the l.

[The direct Cork line runs due S. to 6 m. Croom, passing on l. the tower of Ballinveala, and on rt. that of Fanningstown. Croom is rather prettily situated on the Maigue, which is here crossed by a bridge of 6 arches, and is a town of some antiquity, appearing to have derived its name from its connexion with the Kildare family, and their motto " Crom-a-boo." The castle, which is now modernised and the residence of Col. Dickson, M.P., was built by one of the Earls of Kildare.

1 m. W. of the town (across country) are the ch. and round tower of Dysart, the latter very similar to that of Rattoo, co. Kerry (Rte. 33). It is divided into stories, with a window for each. Notice the window with a semicircular head externally. " while its internal construction preserves the quadrangular form by a lintel which rests on the jambs."—*Petrie*. The adjacent ch. is of the same date as the tower.

2¼ m. E. on the Comnoge, a tributary of the Maigue, is the ruined Abbey of Monasternenagh or Manister, founded by O'Brien, King of Munster, in 1151, to commemorate the defeat of the Danes at the adjoining fortress of Rathmore, and was both in extent and political importance one of the first in the kingdom.

It most probably was a cruciform building, although now only the nave is left, with side aisles and the choir, which was separated from the nave by a screen. The latter was lighted by a good 3-light Early Eng. window, and was remarkable for possessing above the roofs a chamber or croft of the same dimensions as the choir, and approached by a private staircase from the altar through the wall of the N. aisle.

In the neighbourhood of Croom are Caherass House (Sir D. Roche, Bart.), Croom House (H. Lyons, Esq.), and Islandmore (R. Maxwell, Esq.

The line now follows up the valley of the Maigue, passing 8 m. Clunygrove and Glen Bevan, to

13 m. *Bruree*, which possesses remains of a strong " triple " fortress of the De Lacy, enclosed by a rampart wall more than 120 yds. round. There is also close to the ch. a castellated building erected by the Knights Templars, in the 12th cent. Bruree House is the residence of Captain Shelton.

18 m. Charleville. Rte. 25.]

The next station on the Foynes line is 11 m. Adare, the woods and ruins of which are very prettily seen from the rly., and which doubtless gave the name of " Ath-Dara," the Ford of Oaks. The history of Adare is intimately associated with the great family of Fitzgerald, Earls of Kildare, who founded the 3 Abbeys and erected the castle. The whole of the estate reverted to the Crown on the rebellion of Thomas Fitzgerald, otherwise Silken Thomas. The castle subsequently sustained some sieges at the hands alternately of the Desmonds and the English, and was ultimately dismantled by Cromwell. The ruins are situated on the banks of the Maigue, and, together with the long narrow bridge of 14 arches, are a very picturesque item in the scene.

Adare is particularly rich in ecclesiastical remains, and as fortunate in owning in the Earl of Dunraven, a proprietor of the soil who is not only resident and interested in the locality, but a zealous and earnest antiquary, bent on the due preservation of these beautiful ruins. Adare Manor has been of late years rebuilt in very good taste of limestone from the estate, and

o 3

is now one of the handsomest residences in Ireland. The abbeys are three:—

1. The Trinitarian Abbey, founded 1230, is an Early Eng. building, consisting of nave and choir, now used as a Roman Catholic chapel, and surmounted by an embattled tower. It is situated near the entrance of the park, and has been restored with great care. There is some excellent stained glass in the interior. Notice also the schools, which are in keeping with the rest of the ch., together with a very beautiful cross and well.

2. The Augustinian Abbey (date 1306), near the bridge, has been in like manner converted to the uses of the parochial ch., and contains on the N. side, in addition to the nave, choir, and tower, the cloisters which have been restored by the late Earl of Dunraven, who built a mausoleum close by. The refectory has been happily appropriated for a schoolhouse.

3. By far the most beautiful ruin is that of the Franciscan Abbey (date 1464), within the grounds of the Manor, though on the opposite side of the river. This also has a nave, choir, and S. transept, with a very graceful tower rising from the intersection; and attached to the transept are chapels and oratories. The nave contains 3 crocketed niches and an Early Pointed 3-light W. window. The S. trans. is a little to the W. of the intersection, and has on the E. 2 beautiful little chapels, also with niches. A door on the N. side leads to the cloisters, which are in good preservation, together with the refectory and domestic offices. The interior of the choir has some elaborately worked niches and sedilia and an exquisite 4-light window.

There are 2 ruined churches in the ch.-yard; one the *Old Parish Ch.*, the other a chapel of 14th cent.

The ruins of the Castle are most extensive, consisting of an inner ward surrounded by a moat, and enclosed by a spacious quadrangle. The keep or central tower (which may be ascended) is defended by a gateway connected with the tower by a semicircular flanking wall on one side. It is thus placed in connexion with the E. side of the inner court.

The grounds of the demesne are charmingly wooded, and the river Maigue flowing through them affords excellent salmon and trout fishing. Admission to the park is obtained by ticket from the inn. An antiquarian work on the ecclesiastical remains of Adare has been undertaken by the noble owner.

Continuing his course by the rail, the traveller passes l. Clonsire House (W. Power, Esq.), and rt. Hollywood (G. Hewston, Esq.). 3 m. rt. is Curragh Chase, the magnificent seat of Sir Vere de Vere, Bart., situated in a very large park, embellished with a lake and much wood.

17 m. *Rathkeale* Stat. The town of Rathkeale, nearly 2 m. to the S., is a long straggling place on the river Deel, though the second largest town in co. Limerick, and contains some ecclesiastical ruins. The Earl of Desmond built a castle, which was repaired in the reign of Elizabeth by Sir Walter Raleigh, and has since been rendered habitable. There are also remains of an Early Eng. priory, founded by one Gilbert Harvey in the 13th cent., and consisting of side walls, gable, and tower. In the neighbourhood of the town are Rathkeale Abbey (G. Leech, Esq.), Castle Matrix, Beechmount (T. Lloyd, Esq.), Ballywilliam (D. Maunsell, Esq.), and Mount Browne (J. Browne, Esq.) [the last on the road to Ballingarry, which lies 5 m. to the S.E.

Here is another Franciscan monastery in ruins, though with the exception of the tower there is little worth seeing; also a castellated building in the town, known as the Parson's Castle; and the ruins of two others, Lissamoota and Woodstock, in the neighbourhood. The country near Ballingarry becomes a little more hilly and striking, rising at Knockfearina to nearly 1000 ft. A conical heap now occupies the site of what is said to have been an ancient temple.]

[7 m. to the S.W. on the direct road to Abbeyfeale and Listowel, is the town of

Newcastle (anc. Nua) (*Inns;* Victoria; Courtenay Arms), on the river Arra, a small tributary of the Deel. After the death of the great Earl of Desmond, the property was granted by Elizabeth to the Courtenay family, in whose hands it still remains. Of the castle, there are still several round and square towers, together with the banqueting hall. Close to the town are Ringwood and Castle View (Rev. R. Rodwell).

Conveyances.—To Abbeyfeale and to Rathkeale, daily.]

The line now makes a sudden bend to the N.W., passing rt. Nantinan Ch. and House, and crossing the Deel, arrives at

21 m. *Askeaton* (anc. Eas-Geph-tine), another town of the Fitz-geralds, who, according to their wont, defended it by a strong castle, and adorned it with a magnificent abbey for Conventual Franciscans in 1420, in which James Fitzgerald, 15th Earl of Desmond and High Treasurer of Ireland, was buried in 1558. The scenery of the Deel, which runs through the demesne of Inchirourke More, a little above the line, is rendered broken and romantic by a waterfall and salmon leap; but below this the Deel becomes tidal, allowing small coasters to approach. Overlooking the river from a rock of limestone, are the ruins of the Desmonds' Castle, of which the great hall with its windows are in fair preservation, together with a large arched vault beneath. The parish ch. was a commandery of the Knights Templars, and still shows a portion of the ancient building of the date of the 13th cent.,

in the ruins of the S. transept, which was separated from the nave by 2 Early Pointed arches, now blocked up. At the E. end rose 2 towers, square at the base and octangular above. The Franciscan or Rock Abbey is on the E. bank of the river, a little to the N. of the town. It was a magnificent cruciform ch., of later date than most that the tourist has visited in this part of Ireland. The cloisters are remarkably perfect, and are enclosed on each side by 12 Pointed arches, supported by cylindrical columns with richly foliaged capitals. The line now approaches the coasts and inlets of the Shannon, and arrives at the terminus of

26 m. *Foynes*, where the traveller embarks on board the steamer and sails out into the channel of

" The spacious Shenan spreading like a sea,"

the banks of which are prettily wooded, although of not sufficient height to be called bold. The geologist may be glad to know that good coal-plants and shells have been found in the coal-shales near Foynes (*Introd.* p. xxvii.). Soon after leaving Foynes, the tourist passes on l. the grounds of Mount Trenchard (Hon. S. Rice). The next stoppage is at Glin, adjoining which is the Castle, the seat of the Knight of Glin, whose family has held it in succession for between 600 and 700 years. The old Castle of Glin was celebrated for its siege by Sir George Carew, during the rebellion of the Earl of Desmond in the reign of Elizabeth, in which, after a fierce hand-to-hand fight, the Knight of Glin and his gallant band were destroyed. A full account of this affair will be found in 'Pacata Hibernia, or, Ireland Appeased and Reduced, under the Government of Sir George Carew, some time Lord President of Munster.'

35 m. *Tarbert*, with its wooded headland, its lighthouse, and battery, is one of the prettiest portions of the

river. The channel, defended by the Tarbert Battery on the S. and Kilkerin Battery on the N., is known as Tarbert Reach, immediately past which is a considerable estuary running up on the N. to Clonderalaw Bay.

Tarbert (*Hotel:* Gallagher's) is a quiet little town about 1 m. from the landing-place, the road running by the woods of Tarbert House (J. Paterson, Esq.).

As all the routes from Limerick converge here, the mail road must now be described. Quitting the city through the S.W. suburbs, the road runs straight for 3 m. Mungret Cross Roads, where the traveller will find a little to the l. the castle and ecclesiastical ruins (p. 296). Passing rt. Tervoe House (Hon. W. Monsell), and l. Elm Park (Lord Clarina), the isolated towers of *Carrig a Gunnel* (the "Rock of the Candle") Castle are seen about 1½ m. to the rt. It was built upon a basaltic rock 500 ft. above the Shannon, by O'Brien, Prince of Thomond, in the 14th cent. But, though it changed hands several times, it does not appear to have played any important part until the Revolution, when it was blown up by order of General Ginckel; "84 barrels of powder being employed on account of its great strength." Saxifraga tridactylites will be found growing on the ruins.

At 6½ m. the Maigue is crossed by a drawbridge, and the ruins of 2 castles are visible. On rt. Court Castle, and on l. that of Cullan, 10 m. A road is given off to Pallaskenry, 2 m.

Further on l. the tower of Derreen Castle is perceived, with Castle Grey and the fine estate of Curragh Chase. 14 m. l. Bally England House, and 16 m. *Askeaton*.

The next point of interest is at 23 m. Shanagolden, a little to the S. of which is the ruin of Shanid Castle, one of the Desmonds' strongest fortresses, from which they derived their war-cry of Shanid-a-boo. Between Shanagolden and Foynes is Knockpatrick Hill, 574 ft., commanding a very extensive view of the Shannon and the whole plain up to Limerick, together with the hills of Clare and Ennis on the opposite bank. On the slope of the hill is a ch., said to have been built by St. Patrick, whose chair and well are shown in an adjoining field.

31 m. *Glin*, from whence the road runs pretty close to the river, passing Glin Castle, Westwood, Fort Shannon, and Ballydonohoe (T. Fitzgerald, Esq.), to 35 m. Tarbert.

[From Tarbert a run of 8 or 9 m. will bring the tourist to Kilrush (*Hotel:* Vandeleur Arms), a small seaport on the Clare coast, chiefly remarkable for containing an excellent harbour, frequently used by ships in distress. As it is the only port in co. Clare really on the seaboard, it possesses a fair share of trade, which in the summer time is considerably improved by the numbers of tourists and families bound for the bathing-place of Kilkee, which is 8½ m. distant. To the S.E. of the town is Kilrush House, the residence of the proprietor of the soil, Colonel Vandeleur. The antiquary should not omit to take a boat from Kilrush and visit the ecclesiastical remains on Scattery Island (anc. Inis-cathaig), where the holy St. Senanus founded an establishment. Like St. Kevin, he sought a remote spot, where he vowed female foot ne'er should tread —not so remote, however, but that he was found out by St. Cannera, a female saint who wished to set up her tent with him, but who met with a stern refusal :—

"The lady's prayer Senanus spurned;
The winds blew fresh, the bark returned;
But legends hint, that had the maid
Till morning's light delayed
And given the saint one rosy smile,
She ne'er had left his holy isle."

According to the Life of St. Senanus, which may be found in the 'Acta

Sanctorum Hiberniæ,' his refusal was couched as follows ;—

> "Cui Præsul: Qui fœminis
> Commune est cum monachis?
> Nec te nec ullam aliam
> Admittemus in insulam."

The remains are those of a couple of churches of the rudest and most primitive form, and the oratory of St. Senanus, "which measures 18 ft. by 12. The doorway, which occupies an unusual position in the S. side, is 6 ft. in height, 1 ft. 10 in. wide at the top, and 2 ft. 4 in. at the bottom. The E. window splays externally, and in this respect is probably unique in Ireland."—*Wakeman*. The round tower is 22 ft. in circumference, and 120 ft. in height, and possesses a doorway on a level with the ground, another unusual feature. It was struck by lightning, which caused a great rent from the summit. St. Senanus is the same who built the ch. on Inishcalthra, in Lough Derg (Rte. 34).

Kilkee (*Hotel:* Moore's), the fashionable bathing-place for the S.W. of Ireland, is situated on a snug little stream retreating from that terrible line of coast rocks which form Malbay, and rightly so called, for if a vessel happen to be entangled there, the only chances of saving the ship are on the northern side of the intermediate small inlets of Dunbeg and Liscannor. For about 20 m., that is, from Loophead to Dunbeg. "the shore presents on a magnificent scale the ruins of Nature in the numerous and endlessly varied caverns, chasms, bays, and island-rocks, into which the ceaseless roarings of the Atlantic waves have broken this bold rocky coast."—*Fraser*. Moore's Bay, at the head of which Kilkee is situated, is sheltered to a great extent by the ledge of the Duggerna Rocks; but a short walk only is necessary to convince the tourist of the splendid cliff scenery and the gigantic force of the Atlantic waves. To the N. he may wander to Ballard Bay, 4 m., where the cliffs increase in height, and contain many fine caves in their recesses; while to the S. it is a magnificent walk to Castle Point, crowned with the ruined tower of Doonlicha Castle. The most prominent features of this part of the coast are Grean's Rock and Bishop's Island, an immensely bold, escarped rock, called in Irish Oilean-an-Easpoig-gortaigh (the Island of the Hungry Bishop), a name that well signifies the barren and savage aspect and the difficulty of reaching it. There is on it, however, a fine specimen of Bee-hive oratory and a house. "The exterior face of the wall, at four different heights, recedes to the depth of about 1 ft.; a peculiarity not found in any other structure of the kind, and probably introduced with the view of lessening the weight of the dome-shaped roof, which was formed, not on the principle of the arch, but, as usual, by the gradual approximation of the stones as the wall ascended."—*Wakeman*.

For more distant excursions the traveller should visit Loop Head, 16 m. to the S.W., the road to which runs about midway between the Shannon and the Atlantic, leaving to the l. the village and bay of Carrigaholt, and passing through the hamlets of Cross and Kilbaha.

From the lighthouse at Loop Head is a magnificent view of the estuary of the Shannon to the E.; Kerry Head, Brandon Mount, and the hills of Dingle Promontory to the S., backed up by the lofty summits of M'Gillicuddy's Reeks; and to the N. the mountains of Connemara and the 12 Pins, with the islands of Aran standing out to sea. It is probably as fine and wild a panorama as can be seen anywhere in the three kingdoms. The cliff scenery on this portion of the coast is also very remarkable. Immediately round the Head is an isolated rock, known as Dermot and Grania's Rock; and at Ross (nearly 3 m. higher up) are some of the natural bridges which are such wonderful features of this coast. The following are the dimensions of the arch : " The span is 72 ft.; height from the water, 49 ft.; thickness of the arch at the crown, composed of rock, and covered with earth and verdure, 19 ft.; width of the sheet of rock underneath the arch, 45 ft.; and width of the grassy walk on top, 30 ft. The other bridge is 45 ft. span; the thickness above the arch, 9 ft.; and the width, 30 ft."—*Mrs. Knott.*

The geological explanation of these is very simple. All this line of cliffs consists of carbonaceous slates, which, being soft, are less able to resist the force of the waves and atmospheric elements. In the case of the bridges, some of the lower beds, eaten away by the water, have fallen in; and the upper ones, dipping both to sea and inland at low angles, have formed the natural arch.

A little higher up, near the ruins of Cloghan-sauvaun Castle, there is a fine "blow," or "puffing-hole," and cave.

The pedestrian who has time at his disposal, and does not wish to travel S., cannot do better than make an excursion up the coast past Ballard and Dunbeg to Miltown Malbay (Rte. 33) and the cliffs of Mohir.]

Tarbert is 11 m. from Listowel, and the road is about as dreary and monotonous as any road can be. The ground is very high, and there is little cultivation or wood to please the eye until the river Geale is passed, when a long descent opens out a pretty view of the valley of the Feale, to

6 m. *Listowel* (*Hotel:* Listowel Arms), a small country town on the banks of the Feale, which is a noble salmon and trout stream, though rather late in the season. There is nothing to see save a couple of ivy-covered towers of the old castle, which was the last that held out against Elizabeth in the Desmond insurrection.

Conveyances.—Car to Tarbert and Tralee.

Distances.—Tarbert, 11 m.; Tralee, 17; Abbeyfeale, 10; Ballybunion, 9.

Excursion.

Ballybunion.

[A road runs along the banks of the Feale to the S.E. to Abbeyfeale, in itself a small uninteresting town, but situated in the heart of a very wild district, at the foot of the Mullaghcirke Mountains.]

A more pleasant excursion can be made from Listowel to the little bathing-place of Ballybunion, 9 m. distant, the road thereto crossing the Galey, a tributary of the Feale. The coast at Ballybunion is famous for its caves. "The cliffs immediately contiguous to the bay extend in numerous intricate passages, through which a boat may pass for a considerable distance parallel with the coast, without entering the open sea." The largest, known as Neptune's Hall, or the Pigeon Cave, is from 70 to 80 ft. in height. The visitor should ramble up the coast to Doon, where are some detached rocks and natural arches. The coast was well defended in days of yore, as in this short walk the ruins of no less than 3 castles are visible.

[Some 7 m. to the S., near the village of Ballyduff, is the ch. and round tower of Rattoo. The latter is 92 ft. in height, and 48 ft. in circumference at its base, which is placed on a terrace or platform, connected with a causeway, that extends in a line opposite its doorway. This is semicircular-headed, the arch being formed by 3 stones, and ornamented with a flat band. The interior of the tower is divided into 6 stories, the uppermost of which contains windows facing the cardinal points.]

Adjoining Listowel is Ballinaddery (J. Todd, Esq.). The road to Tralee is carried over rather high ground skirting the Stack and Clanruddery Mountains, which, though of no great height, are wild and desolate in appearance. Save a pretty glen through which the road runs, there is not much of interest until within 3 or 4 m. of Tralee, where the view of the Slieve Mish and Dingle Mountains, with the sharp peaks of the Reeks rising over them to the l., is extremely fine, and quite repays a dull drive.

21 m. Tralee (*Inn*: Blennerhasset Arms, not good) is the largest seaport not only in Kerry, but in the S.W. of Ireland, and exhibits a considerable degree of bustle and animation. The port of Blennerville is about 1 m. distant, and is connected with the town by a ship canal, as the Tralee river is remarkably shallow. Tralee is an ancient place, and has been identified with the history and times of the Desmond family; indeed the grave of *the Desmond par excellence* is to be seen about 8 m. to the E. of the town, and a little to the N. of the demesne of Maglass, on the road to Castle Island. Notwithstanding these associations it possesses few or no antiquarian remains. Adjoining the town, which contains the usual accompaniments of an assize town, are the grounds of Sir Edward Denny, which are liberally thrown open to the inhabitants. (Pop. 10,309.)

The archæologist should visit the ancient ch. of Ratass, which possesses a very characteristic square-headed doorway of Cyclopean masonry. The ch. is built of old red sandstone, a singular fact when we observe that the neighbourhood consists of limestone.

Conveyances.—Car to Limerick; also to Tarbert; rail to Killarney and Dublin.

Distances.—Killarney, 22 m.; Tarbert, 21; Castle Island, 11; Miltown, 12; Killorglin, 17; Castlemaine, 10; Dingle, 27; Limerick, 56; Listowel, 17; Ardfert, 5.

Excursions.
1. Ardfert.
2. Dingle.
3. Killarney.

4. Cahirconree.
5. Ratass.

[Tralee and Castlemaine are the northern and southern entrances respectively into the Promontory of Dingle, one of those extraordinary prolongations of land which are so common on the S. and S.W. coasts of Ireland from Tralee to Dunmore Head, and from Brandon to Ventry. The whole of the promontory is occupied by a backbone of mountains, which attain very considerable heights, and slope precipitously down to the seaboard. The best way of seeing the promontory will be by making the circuit, or as near a circuit as the roads will permit. The route skirts the S. shore of the bay of Tralee, close at the foot of Cahir Conree and Bautregaum, which rise abruptly to the heights of 2713 and 2784 ft. A little tarn under the rugged escarpments of the former mountain gives birth to the Derrymore stream, which is crossed at 5 m. 8 m. at the Finglas river, which rises in Caherbla, 1926 ft., a direct road is given off to Dingle, joining the S. road at Anascaul. 13 m. at Castle Gregory, a little triangular-shaped town at the foot of Beenoskee, 2715 ft., a sandy promontory is thrown out to the N. of 4 m. in length, that divides the bays of Tralee and Brandon. The termination of this peninsula, however, is rugged and dangerous, and is, moreover, guarded by a series of rocky islands, known as the Seven Hogs. Brandon Mount, with its magnificent cliffs, is now the principal object in the landscape, rising to the great height of 3126 ft.; it also stretches out N. and S., so as almost entirely to fill up the remaining portion of the promontory. On the sea side particularly the precipices are tremendous, and descend with such sudden escarpments as to forbid the approach of any road, which is therefore necessarily defective towards the S.W., crossing over to Dingle by a fine mountain-pass between Brandon and Connor Mountains. As the road emerges from the defile, the tourist gains exquisite views of Dingle Bay and the opposite mountains of Iveragh. Both Brandon Mount and Connor Hill are admirable localities for the botanist, many beautiful ferns and plants finding a habitation in their savage cliffs; amongst others Trichomanes radicans, Poa alpina, Oxyria reniformis, Sibthorpia Europæa, Saussurea alpina, Pyrethrum maritimum, Saxifraga affinis, S. cæspitosa, S. argentea, and S. geum.]

27 m. Dingle (*Inn*: clean and comfortable) is one of the most westerly towns in Ireland, and probably one of the most wretched, but it is finely situated at the foot of Ballysitteragh, 2050 ft., and at the head of Dingle harbour, a snug, sheltered bay, on the W. shore of which are the grounds and mansion of Burnham, the seat of Lord Ventry, a narrow neck of land, of about 1 m. in breadth, separating the harbour of Dingle from that of Ventry, which is considerably larger, though much more exposed to S.W. gales. This neck of land is said by tradition to have been the very last piece of ground occupied by the Danes in Ireland. The village is situated at the N. of the harbour, near the termination of a smooth strand. At *Fahan*, a village a little to the W. of Ventry, is the most remarkable collection of Beehive ancient houses in Ireland. The distance between Dingle and the opposite coast is so small that a good deal of intercourse is carried on between this district and that of Iveragh, in which Cahirciveen is situated (Rte. 35); and the tourist who is bound for Valentia and Waterville cannot do better than sail across, always provided that the weather is settled and the wind fair. To the W. of Ventry the promontory is terminated by Eagle Mountain, 1695 ft., a fine abrupt hill, ending seaward at Dunmore Head.

The most peculiar features of the district are met with in the Blasket Islands, that lie off the land, and are frightfully ironbound. In the Great Blasket the cliff of Slieve Donagh, on the N. side, rises steeply from the water to a height of 967 ft. higher than the cliffs of Mohir. Further out is Tearaght Island, a lofty rock of 600 ft., also rising out of the water in a similar manner to the Skellig (Rte. 35); and to the N. of the Blasket is Inishtooskert, where are to be seen the ruins of St. Brendan's oratory.

The Dingle promontory has been called the key to the geological structure of the S. of Ireland. It contains—1, Upper Silurians; 2, Tilestones, with Pentamerus Knightii; 3, Glengariff grits; 4, Dingle beds, which latter are really a subordinate division of the Old Red, consisting of red slates and sandstones with thick beds of conglomerate intermixed with pebbles of Sil. limestone and fragments of jasper and hornstone. Above these are red sandstones passing conformably into yellow sandstone and carboniferous shales. The geologist will find good Sil. fossils at Ferritor's Cove, and some fine sections between Sibyl Head and the Slieve Mish Mountains, and again from Brandon Head to Bull's Head.

Various legends are in existence with respect to the former colonisation of the Dingle promontory by the Spanish; and 3 m. to the N.W. of Ventry is Ferritor's Cove, where, in 1579, Sanders, the Pope's Nuncio, and 80 Spaniards, landed and built a fort, which was afterwards garrisoned by a party of 700 men. They were, however, attacked and massacred by the Lord Deputy and Sir Walter Raleigh. Several ancient encampments are to be seen at Smerwick, which is on the W. coast of Smerwick Harbour, a fine sheltered bay, bounded on the W. by the headland of the Three Sisters, and on the E. by the rising ground of Brandon Mountain.

In this neighbourhood is the finest range of *sea cliffs* in Munster, the chief elevations being Sibyl Head, the Three Sisters, Bally David Head, and Brandon Head, varying in height from 700 to 1000 ft. "The neighbourhood of Smerwick Harbour abounds with the remains of stone fortresses and circular stone houses, together with ancient oratories exhibiting only an imperfect development of the Roman mode of construction, being built of uncemented stones admirably fitted to each other, and their lateral walls converging from the base to the apex in curved lines."—*Petrie*. The antiquary should look out for the oratory of Gallerus, one of the most singular of these early remains. It measures 43 ft. in length, by 10 ft. in breadth; while its height to the apex of the roof is 16 ft., the roof being formed by the gradual approximation of the side walls from the base upwards. It is entered by a square-headed doorway in the W. gable. In the graveyard is an inscribed pillar-stone, with an imperfect inscription in the Byzantine character, of the 4th or 5th cent.

At Kilmalkedar, 1 m. distant, is another pillar-stone, in which the inscription is perfect; and also a very interesting little ch. of 11th or 12th cent.

At Temple Geal, 3 m. N.W. of Dingle, are some remains of the oratory of St. Monachan, together with a pillar-stone inscribed with Ogham characters.

The return from Dingle by the S. road is finer than on the N., owing partly to the greater abruptness of the hills and the magnificent views of the opposite coast. In the neighbourhood of the village of Anascaul, on the river Owenascaul, there are several forts. At Inch the road enters the sandy flats of the Castlemaine river, and keeps along the N. side of Castlemaine harbour to the town of Castlemaine (Rte. 35).

The following excursions can be recommended from Dingle:—

1. To the Cliffs at Sibyl Head, which are very fine, and can easily be visited by taking a car to Ferritor's Cove. Directions for a pedestrian: Turn off to the rt. after passing the mill at Milltown, and proceed by Gallerus and across the sands at the end of Smerwick Harbour. Return by the regular road as far as the ruined castle on the top of the hill above Ventry; then turn to the l. and keep along an old road which leads into the main road again halfway between Ventry and Dingle. The distance will be about 20 m.

2. To Brandon Head.—Take a car to Coosavaddig (9 m.), from whence it is a steep climb of 3 or 4 m. to the top of the Head.

3. Brandon Mountain.—The ascent can be made either from the W. or Ballybrack side, or from the Cloghane or E. side. The former is the easiest; but the finest view is obtained by the latter route, passing through a wild glen with precipices on every side. It will be advisable to take a guide for this route.

4. Take a car to Glenfahan (8 m.), then walk round Slea Head to Dunquin, and from thence back to Dingle by the regular road. There is a splendid view from the top of the hill between Dunquin and Ventry. Distance from Glenfahan about 12m.

5. The Coumanare Lakes.—Ascend Connor Hill (4 m.) and strike off to the rt., keeping in a N.E. direction for about 1 m., when the lakes become visible. It may be mentioned that a number of arrow-heads have been found on Connor Hill. Tradition speaks of a great battle.

6. To the Blasquets by sea.—The boatmen are exorbitant in their charges.

7. The Cliffs of Esk, on the opposite side of Dingle Harbour—*C. T.*

[Another excursion may be made

to Ardfert, 5 m., the seat of W. Crosbie, Esq. Here are some of the finest remains in the co. of Kerry. The see of Ardfert is united with that of Limerick. The cathedral consists of a nave and choir of E. E. date. The nave contains 4 circular-headed arches, together with 3 arches supported by square pillars leading into a chapel. The choir is lighted by a beautiful 3-light window of great height, and also, on the S. side, by a series of 9 trefoil-headed windows. On either side the altar are niches, one of them containing an effigy, supposed to be that of St. Brandon, the patron saint. To the N.W. of the ch. is the burying-place of the Countess of Kerry, and now of the Crosbie family. A round tower, 120 ft. in height, formerly adjoined the W. front, but it fell in 1771. A portion of the cathedral has been incorporated with the parochial church. Close to the cathedral are the ruins of an interesting chapel of 12th cent. Very little remains of Ardfert Castle, which was finally destroyed in 1641 during the wars of that period. Ardfert Abbey is the seat of the Crosbie family, who have been settled here since the reign of Elizabeth. Within the grounds are the ruins of the Franciscan Abbey, founded in the 13th cent. by Thomas, Lord of Kerry. They consist of a nave and choir, with a tower on the W., a chapel on the S., and the refectory and cloisters on the N. The choir is lighted by 9 windows on the S., and also by a 5-light E. window of beautiful design. It contains 5 monumental recesses underneath the windows. The S. chapel is separated from the nave by 3 pointed arches with round piers: on one is an inscription to the effect that Donald Fitz Bohen completed the chapel in 1453. The window of the chapel is particularly good. Some few miles to the N.W. of Ardfert is Ballyheigue, the seat of Major Crosbie.]

ROUTE 33.

FROM LIMERICK TO BOYLE, THROUGH ENNIS AND TUAM.

Limerick, anc. Luimneach (*Hotel:* Cruse's, good), combines the associations of one of Ireland's historical cities with the improvements of modern towns, and may be said to be almost the neatest and best built of any place in the kingdom. (Pop. 44,408.) Like most of the Irish seaports it was originally inhabited in great force by the Danes, who were expelled by Brian Boroimhe when he assumed the sovereignty over Munster and Thomond, Limerick thus becoming the royal city of the Munster kings. After passing through the usual stages of intestinal native war, its next important epoch was marked by the erection of a strong fortress by King John, who committed the care of it to the charge of William de Burgh; and from that time, with a few intervals of check, it steadily gained in importance until the reign of Elizabeth, when it was made the "centre of civil and military administration." But the great episode in the history of Limerick took place during the wars of William and James, when the events occurred which fastened on it the name of the "City of the Violated Treaty." After the fall of Athlone and Galway, Tyrconnel, the Lord Lieutenant, still held Limerick as the last stronghold that King James possessed, the city having been previously unsuccessfully assaulted by the English in 1690. A fit of apoplexy carried off Tyrconnel, when the government, both civil and military, fell into the hands of D'Usson and Sarsfield. Ginkell, the English commander, endeavoured to take the town by an attack on the fort which overlooked and protected the Thomond Bridge. "In a short time the fort was stormed. The soldiers who had garrisoned it fled in confusion to the city. The Town Major, a French officer, who commanded at the Thomond Gate, afraid that the pursuers would enter with the fugitives, ordered that part of the bridge which was nearest to the city to be drawn up. Many of the Irish went headlong into the stream and perished there. Others cried for quarter, and held up their handkerchiefs in token of submission. But the conquerors were mad with rage, their cruelty could not be immediately restrained, and no prisoners were made till the heaps of corpses rose above the parapet. The garrison of the fort had consisted of about 800 men. Of these only 120 escaped into Limerick."—*Macaulay.*

The result of this capture was the fall of James's power in Limerick, and indeed in Ireland, and the signing of the famous treaty on the stone near the bridge on 3rd Oct. 1691, the 9th article of which provided that the Roman Catholics should enjoy the same privileges of their religion as they enjoyed in the reign of Charles II., and that William and Mary would endeavour to ensure them immunity from disturbance on account of their religion. This article, however, was never carried into effect. The city has ever since been a station for a large quantity of troops, and is at the present day one of the most bustling and pleasant garrison towns.

It is situated in a broad plain, watered by the Shannon, and backed up in the distance by the hills of Clare and Killaloe. The river, which soon becomes an estuary, rolls in a magnificent and broad stream through the heart of the town, and sends off a considerable branch called the Abbey River.

The junction of this with the main channel encloses what is known as the King's Island, on the southern portion of which is built the English Town, united to the mainland by 3 bridges, and containing the most ancient buildings. In contradistinction is the Irish Town, which lies to the S. of it, and more in the direction of the rly. station. These 2 districts comprised the fortified old town. Up to Edward II.'s time only the English Town had been defended by walls, but these were subsequently extended so as to include Irish Town, which was entered by St. John's Gate.

Newton Pery, the district between this and the river, was then bare, but, having come into the possession of the Pery family, it was speedily built upon, and is now equal to any city in Ireland for the breadth and cleanliness of its streets. Of these the principal is George Street, a handsome thoroughfare of nearly a mile in length, giving off others on each side at right angles, and adorned with a statue of O'Connell at the end of it. There is also to the N. a monument to the memory of Lord Montcagle.

The Shannon is crossed by 3 bridges, of which the Thomond Bridge, rebuilt in 1839, claims priority from its ancient associations. It connects English Town with the Co. Clare, the entrance from which, through Thomond Gate, was protected by the fort mentioned above, and King John's Castle. On the N., or Clare side, the stone is still to be seen on which was signed the treaty of 1691. Wellesley Bridge connects Newtown Pery with the road from Limerick to Ennis. It is a fine modern bridge of 5 elliptic arches, with an open balustrade, and having a swivel on the city side, so that the Shannon navigation might not be interfered with. Athlunkard Bridge, also consisting of 5 arches, can scarcely be said to be in the city; it connects the N.E. suburbs with the Killaloe road. Besides these 3, there are some minor bridges crossing the Abbey stream.

New Bridge continues the main street into English Town; and Baels (pronounced Bawls) Bridge, connects English and Irish Towns, at the spot where the Lock Mills Canal, cutting off a long reach of the Shannon, falls in. This bridge replaced in 1831 an older one called the Tide Bridge in maps of the time of Elizabeth, and which was washed away by an unusually high tide in 1775, together with several houses that projected over the water. The origin of the name is supposed by some to be "Bald" Bridge, being so called in Latin documents (pons calvus) because it had no battlements; others think it was Boyle's Bridge, as forming part of the grant made to Boyle, Earl of Shannon.

The 2 principal objects of interest are the castle and cathedral, both close together in the English Town. The former still retains the massive gateway and strong drum towers which characterised the fortresses of the early English settlers; but its venerable appearance is marred by the addition of the modern roofs and buildings of the barracks into which the interior has been converted.

The cathedral is still under process of restoration, but fortunately, is under judicious hands, and is not modernised like the castle. Although said to have been originally built by Donald O'Brien, King of Limerick, in the 12th cent., it has been so often added to and altered, that little, if any, of the old edifice is in existence.

The plan of the ch. is not cruciform but 3-aisled, with a fine tower rising directly from the W. end. A battlement runs along the aisles externally, and the angles of the tower are finished off with Irish stepped turrets. Internally the arrangement is singular. The aisles are subdivided both lengthways and crossways, so as to form a series of chapels. Immediately on the rt. of the entrance porch is one containing the tombs of the Earls of Limerick, and adorned with some good stained glass and an illuminated ceiling. A chapel in the N. aisle contains the organ,* and an early mural inscription under some trefoil-headed arches. In the chancel, which is lighted by an E. E. window with stained glass, is an elaborate marble monument of different colours to the Earl of Thomond, which we are told in the epitaph suffered great defacement in the rebellion, and was subsequently restored by the Earl of Limerick. On S. side of the altar is an ambry lighted by a circular painted window. The nave is divided from the side aisles by 3 plain Early Pointed arches, and there is a triforium with plain round-headed arches. The tower should be ascended for the sake of the view, which is very charming, embracing a wide expanse of the Shannon, and the plain through which it flows, the hills in the neighbourhood of Castle Clare, Mount Keeper and the Killaloe hills; while the foreground is occupied with the antique-looking English Town, the modern city, and the busy harbour. A pretty story is told about the bells, viz. that they were made by an Italian, and of such exceeding sweetness that he was very proud of them, and sold them to a convent. In course of time troubles came upon the religious house, so that it was broken up, and the bells carried off to distant lands. The Italian, whose fortunes shared in the general wreck, was driven from his home, and became a wanderer. Chance brought him to the Shannon and to Limerick, when the first sound that greeted him as he sailed up the river was from his own bells, the pride and joy of his heart. Such pleasure was too great for the heartbroken exile, who was found by the boatmen dead ere they got to the landing-place. The visitor should not omit to ramble through

* The service on Sunday is choral, and remarkably well done.

the foreign-looking streets of English Town, although it must be confessed that the inhabitants thereof are neither so attractive nor orderly as in the other districts. The other objects of interest in Limerick are of a civil and military character: the latter embracing 4 large barracks; the former, the Exchange, County Courthouse, a Merchants' Quay, gaol, and the infirmary founded by the Barrington family in 1829. The tourist should visit the new R. C. *Cathedral*, and the ch. of the Redemptorists, designed by P. C. Hardwick. From its noble situation on the Shannon, Limerick has long commanded a prosperous trade, and should, from its proximity to the Atlantic and consequently to America, have been one of the principal American ports. Cork and Galway, however, are keen competitors for the latter honour. "The harbour extends about 1600 yards in length and 150 in breadth, with from 2 to 9 ft. at low water, and 19 at spring tides; which latter enables vessels of 600 tons to moor at the quays. The quayage and wharfage extend 1600 yards, and cost 18,000*l*. The commerce of the port has considerably increased, and will be greatly benefited by the floating docks, constructed at an expense of 54,000*l*.; in 1826 there was scarcely a vessel belonging to it, there are now 105 of 13,000 tons. In 1835 the exports were 726,000*l*., in 1842 upwards of 1,200,000*l*.'—*Thoms*.

The linen trade has been of late years established here by an enterprising firm, Messrs. Russell, whose factory is on the Clare side of Wellesley Bridge. The other excellences of Limerick are—fishhooks of beautiful finish and temper; gloves, the leather of which is so fine that a pair will pass through a wedding-ring, or may be packed up in a walnut-shell;* and lace, for which

* Cork is the real seat of the manufacture of the so-called Limerick gloves.

indeed the town has been as famous as Honiton or Valenciennes. The principal establishment is that of Messrs. Forrest at the corner of Glentworth Street, where several hundred females are constantly employed. The lace factories are not open to public inspection, and the visitor will regret it the less as no machinery whatever is employed, all the work being done by hand on frames or patterns. Some of the varieties, especially that known as Guipure, are extremely beautiful, and often fetch very high prices. Last, but not least, Limerick is famous for the beauty of its women, a reputation not undeserved, as may be seen even by a casual stroll through the city.

Conveyances.—Rail to Ennis; to Waterford; to Cork direct, also by Limerick Junction; to Killaloe; to Foynes. Steamer to Liverpool weekly. Car daily to Bruff; to Ennis; to Killaloe; to Kilmallock; to Scariff; to Tipperary; to Tulla; to Tralee.

Distances.—Castle Connell, 10 m.; Killaloe, 17; Bunratty, 12; Ennis, 25; Clare Castle, 23; Adare, 11; Askeaton, 21; Rathkeale, 17; Foynes, 26; Kilrush, 43; Tipperary, 25; Charleville, 26; Mungret Abbey, 3.

Excursions.—
1. Killaloe and Castle Connell.
2. Bunratty.
3. Carrig-a-gunnell.
4. Tarbert.
5. Adare.

Quitting the terminus, which serves for all the 5 rlys. that leave Limerick, the line to Ennis soon branches off to the l., and passing over the canal winds completely round one half the town, crossing the Shannon by a long low bridge just above the spot where the Abbey River is given off. A little to the rt. is St. Thomas's Island and Quinsboro' House. The line thence runs N.W., and gradually approaches the ranges in the neighbourhood of Six Mile Bridge, and keeping the noble estuary of the Shannon well in view on the l.

Near *Cratloe* Stat., on rt., is Cratloe Wood, and nearer to the river the remains of three castles or fortified mansions, viz. Cratloe, Cratloe-keel, and Castle Donnell. 2 m. from the station, at the mouth of the Bunratty River, is the fine old fortress of *Bunratty*, once the residence of the Earls of Thomond, and now a police barrack. Thackeray in his 'Irish Sketch-book' spins an irresistible 3 volume novel (in 2 pages) respecting this fortress, commencing with the description—" It is a huge square tower, with 4 smaller ones at each angle; you mount to the entrance by a steep flight of steps, being commanded all the way by the crossbows of 2 of the Lord De Clare's retainers, the points of whose weapons may be seen lying upon the ledge of the little narrow meurtrière on each side of the gate. A venerable seneschal, with the keys of the office, presently opens the little back postern, and you are admitted to the great hall, a noble chamber, *pardi!* some 70 ft. in length and 30 high. 'Tis hung round with 1000 trophies of war and chase," &c. A modern house has been built in the demesne by T. Studdert, Esq. The anchorage at the mouth of the Bunratty is so safe that American vessels for Limerick always discharged their cargo here.

13 m. *Six Mile Bridge* Stat. and *Newmarket Fergus*, the town being about 1 m. l. of the stat. To the N. of it is *Dromoland Castle*, the very handsome seat and extensive domain of Lord Inchiquin, and between it and the rly. are some large earthworks.

At 20 m. *Ardsollus*, the line crosses the river of the same name, which on rt. flows past the little town of

Quin (anc. Cuinche), celebrated for possessing one of the best preserved abbeys in Ireland. It is of Dec. date, having been built at the commencement of the 15th cent. by one MacCann Dall Macnamara, Lord of Glencoillan. It consists of a nave and chancel, surmounted by a graceful tower rising at the junction of the two, and built upon the gable ends. There is also a chapel to the S. of the choir, containing the sculptured figure of a saint. In the choir is the high altar, and the monument of the family of Macnamara of Ranee, also a representation of the Crucifixion in stucco. Amongst those buried here is Macnamara, the duellist (who obtained the soubriquet of "Fireball), together with another gentleman, who fell in a quarrel with him. Two lovers also, who were drowned in the adjoining river, were interred here in the same grave; from which, as in the Border ballads, a brier and an elder-tree have grown intertwined. The visitor will notice the signs of the dead person's calling on many of the tombstones. "The cloister is of the usual form, with couplets of pillars, but is particular in having buttresses round it by way of ornament. There are apartments on 3 sides of it, the refectory, dormitory, and another room to the N. of the chancel, with a vaulted room under them all."

An unusual number of ruined castles lie within a reasonable distance of Quin: such as Ballymarkahan, Corbally, and Dangan, the latter a quadrangular tower, flanked by round towers at the angles, said to be the oldest fortress in Munster. There are also some pleasant seats in the neighbourhood, viz., Moyriesk (J. F. Vesey Fitzgerald, Esq.); Knappogue, "Kiss on the Hill," the restored residence of Lord Dunboyne; Cullane, which originally belonged to Steele, the friend of O'Connell; Dangan House, and Lough O'Connell, on the banks of a considerable sheet of water which rejoices in the name of Callannyhuda.

5 m. from Quin, and about 2 from

Tulla, is the "Toomeens," an exceedingly curious bit of river scenery, in which the stream, flowing through the estates of Kiltarnan (J. Molony, Esq.), and that of T. O'Callaghan, Esq., of Maryfort, passes through a series of limestone arches, with occasional apertures like very steep railway cuttings.

23 m. *Clare Castle.* Here we have the *Fergus,* a broad river that flows into the Shannon, and is navigable as far as Clare, from which a very large amount of grain is shipped in the course of the year. On an island in the bed of the river is the ruin of the castle, connected by a bridge with either side of the bank. Although Clare possesses such manifest advantages, yet it has been passed in the race for precedence by

Ennis (*Hotels:* Carmody's; Brennan's), a queer little town, with narrow streets, or rather lanes, filled with a bustling, foreign-looking people. (Pop. 7175.) Its modern attractions are a very good classic Courthouse, built of grey marble, and a column erected to the memory of Daniel O'Connell, the Great Liberator. In the interior of the Court-house is a statue to the memory of Sir Michael O'Loughlin, one of the county magnates. The antiquities are more interesting. Ennis, under the name of Iniscluan ruadha, was famous for its seat of learning and its Franciscan monastery, founded by the family of O'Brien, who were princes of Thomond. The latter is now incorporated with the ch., and presents a curious mixture of modern building with ivy-covered gables. A fine 5-light Early Pointed window still exists at the E. end, and in the interior of the ch. is the Abbot's chair, "which, with the altar, is highly sculptured with figures in relief."

About 1 m. from Ennis, close to the rly., is

Clare Abbey, founded for Augustinians at the end of the 12th cent., by Donald O'Brien, King of Limerick. It is like all the others, a very graceful cruciform ch., with a lofty tower, that from the nature of its situation is visible from a great distance.

[3 m. to S. of the town is a third ruined abbey, that of Killone, which has the attraction of an extremely pretty situation on the banks of Killone Lough. This was founded at the same time as Clare by a daughter of O'Brien, who "excelled all the women in Munster for piety, almsdeeds, and hospitality." On the road to it from Ennis is Cahircalla House, Beech-park (Marcus Keane, Esq.), Edenvale (R. Stacpoole, Esq.), a very romantic spot, and Newhall (Major Armstrong-Macdonnell).]

Distances. — Limerick, 25 m.; Castle Clare, 2; Gort, 19; Lough Cooter, 15; Miltown Malbay, 20; Kilfenora, 17; Dysert, 2.

Conveyances.—Rail to Limerick. Car to Gort and Galway; car to Miltown Malbay.

Excursions.—
1. Miltown Malbay.
2. Kilfenora.
3. Dysert and Corrofin.

[Ennis is the best starting-point for *Miltown Malbay,* 20 m., a little village on the coast, which has of late years become a fashionable watering-place, especially for the Galway and Limerick residents. The Atlantic is a tolerable hotel. The village itself is poor and wretched, but the scenery of the cliffs of Clare will make amends for many shortcomings in the way of accommodation. About half way from Ennis the road approaches the ranges of the Clare Mountains, which, although not in reality very lofty, are a fine relief to the otherwise monotonous landscape. Slieve Callane rises to the height of 1282 ft., and presents the appearance of a flat-topped hill with terraced sides. This hill, together with the whole of this district, consists geologically of the upper limestone measures, "while the coal-measures, consisting of softer but tougher materials, form higher land, which ends in a continuous and rather steep escarpment. On examining the position of the rocks near these escarpments, it is at once evident that the limestone rises up to the surface from beneath the coal-measures, and that the beds of the latter end abruptly at the escarpment. It is clear that this abrupt termination of so great a thickness of beds can only be due to the fact that the former continuation of these beds has been cut off and removed by the action of denudation."

On the S.E. side of Slieve Callane is a cromlech, "consisting of 3 immense stones; 2 of them pitched on end, and the 3rd laid incumbent on these. The latter measures 12 ft. in length by 4 in breadth; the others are each 10 ft. in length, 8 broad, and 1 thick; 2 more lie extended on the ground, closing when erect, the extremities of the crypt, which the whole structure formed when complete."—*Windele*. This cromlech is celebrated for containing an Ogham inscription, first discovered in 1784.

About 2 m. l. of the road at Handcross is Lough Doo, a solitary sheet of water surrounded by hills. The principal attraction at Miltown Malbay is the scenery of the coast, which is very fine, although, as the name of Malbay implies, it has proved very dangerous to shipping. The geologist should ramble along the rocks to the S. A little below Kilmurry the river Annageragh flows into the sea through the lagoon of Lough Donnell, which is defended from the tide by a bed of shingle 29 ft. high. To the N. of Spanish Point, near the old ruin of Freagh Castle, is a very remarkable Blowing or Puffing Hole.

7 m. to the N. of Miltown Malbay is Lehinch, from whence a road diverges inland for 2 m. to

Ennistymon, a prettily-situated little town on the Inagh river, which, below the bridge, falls over a ledge of rocks in a cascade. On the N. bank is Ennistymon House, the residence of Col. Macnamara. Continuing over an expanse of sandy dunes, and crossing the Inagh near the ruined tower of Dough, the tourist arrives at Liscannor, at the head of Liscannor Bay, where there is another square tower, formerly the residence of the O'Connors.

Soon after passing 11 m. rt. Birchfield (G. O'Brien, Esq.) the road reaches the promontory of Hag's Head, the commencement of the famous *Cliffs of Moher*, which run for 5 m. with a sheer precipice wall of 600 ft. Although not nearly as high as the cliffs of Croghan in Achill, or Slieve League in Donegal, which is nearly 2000 ft., the cliffs of Moher form some of the most sublime objects of the western coast, and when seen in rough weather, with the huge waves of the Atlantic dashing in showers of spray over them, are a sight never to be forgotten. The view is magnificently extensive, embracing the whole of the coast from the Loop Head in the S., to Black Head in the Bay of Galway, while the 3 Aran Islands are conspicuous in the N.W. A very good road runs the whole length of the cliffs, in addition to which Mr. O'Brien of Birchfield has erected a tavern and hotel for the accommodation of the tourist. At Doolin, should the visitor not elect to follow the road up to Black Head, he may return to Ennis through

Kilfenora (anc. Cill-fronnabrach), which was formerly a place of importance, and is even now the seat of a bishopric united to that of Killaloe. In the ch., which has a massive square tower, is a monumental effigy, supposed to be that of the founder, St. Fachnan. Kilfenora was celebrated for the number of its crosses, of which 2 only now remain.

5 m. from Kilfenora the traveller approaches the Fergus, a little before it falls into the Inchiquin Lough. At this spot are various remains of anti-

quity; the stump of a round tower about 10 ft. high; the tower of the old castle, which is said to have once been the residence of the Deans of Kilfenora; the ruins of a ch. and stone cross fixed on a rock by the road-side, "consisting of a shaft with two arms curving upwards, on each of which near the top is a head carved in relief, and in the centre 2 hands clasped; this was erected in memory of the reconciliation of 2 persons who had been long in violent enmity."

The old castle of Inchiquin, formerly the residence of the O'Quins, of whom the present Earl of Dunraven is the representative, and which gives a title to the family of O'Brien, is on the northern shore of Lough Inchiquin, an extremely pretty little lake flanked on the W. by a range of wooded hills. On the same side are Adelphi W. Fitzgerald, Esq.) and Clifden House E. Burton, Esq.).

8 m. *Corrofin*, a small decayed market town on the Fergus, midway between the Lakes of Inchiquin and Atedaun. About 1 m. to the N.E., on the road to Gort, is the square fortress of Ballyportry, in better preservation than most of the Clare castles. Near Toonagh House are the ruins of Ballygriffy Castle, and to the S. is *Dysart*, the old ch. of which should be visited on account of a very beautiful Norman doorway. There is also a round tower about 30 ft. high, with a door 20 ft. from the ground. The ruined castle was formerly the residence of the O'Deas.

17 m. Ennis.]

The road from Ennis to Gort is very dreary, passing through a wide open limestone country, interspersed with low craggy hills and sandy loughs. A rly. has just been commenced to connect Ennis with Athenry, and thus bring it nearer to Dublin.

31 m. rt Incheronan Lough, and on l. Ballyline House Augustus Butler, Esq.). Dromore is another rather large lough to the l., prettily wooded on the N. by the demesne of Dromore (T. Crowe, Esq.).

33 m. Crusheen.

There is a pretty bit of English scenery at 37 m., where the road passes the estates of Bunnahow (W. Butler, Esq.) and Cregg (A. Harnett, Esq.), affording, with its wood and pleasantly shaded trout-stream, an agreeable variation from the monotonous expanse all around.

39¼ m. is the gateway of Lough Cooter Castle (Hon. G. S. Gough), through the grounds of which the coach is frequently driven, by the permission of its owner. It is a pretty modern castellated house, most charmingly situated on the W. shore of Lough Cooter, the largest lake in the S. of Galway. The views between the wooded islands, most of which are tenanted by a ruined ch. or castle, are lovely. The river between the lake and Gort has a portion of its course underground.

43 m. *Gort* (*Inn*: Royal Mail), a neat, clean-looking little town, of one square, or rather triangle, with 3 or 4 streets leading out of it. There is nothing to see in it, and the traveller will be disposed to agree with the author of the 'Irish Sketch-book,' who remarks "that it seemed to bore itself considerably, had nothing to do, and no society." But in the days when the cavalry barracks were tenanted, Gort was considerably livelier than it is now.

[The antiquary should visit Kilmacduagh, 3 m. from Gort to the S.W. Here St. Colman, son of Duach, founded a see, over which he himself presided, in the 7th cent. In 1602, however, it was held together with that of Clonfert, and eventually became merged into Killaloe. The ch. was built for St. Colman by his kinsman Guaine Aidhne, King of Connaught, and is remarkable for a Cyclopean doorway (now closed up), "6 ft. 6 in. in height, and in width 2 ft. 2 in. at the top, and 3 ft. 2 in. at the bottom. The lintel-stone, which extends the entire thickness of the wall, is 5 ft. 8 in. long, 1 ft. 9 in. high, and 3 ft. wide."

This doorway was closed up with rubble masonry in the 14th or 15th cent., when the ch. was rebuilt and considerably enlarged, and a new doorway in the Pointed style placed, as was usual in that age, in the S. wall.

The round tower, which is remarkable for leaning out of the perpendicular some 17 ft., is considered to be of the same age as the ch., viz. the commencement of the 7th cent., and is stated by the traditions of the country to have been the work of Gobhan Saer, the architect of Antrim and Glendalough towers.

The doorway is 26 ft. from the ground, and is semicircular-headed, the arch being formed by cuttings in the horizontal stones.]

The drive from Gort to Oranmore is across such a bleak and desolate country that the traveller will involuntarily long for the railway and its happy powers of shortening uninteresting distances. The whole of the district is of the shallow-soiled limestone rock for which Galway is so famous; stones everywhere, in the walls, the roads, the hills, the plains, and the fields; all one unmitigated sheet of grey monotony, only relieved by the distant hills of Clare. At 45 m. l. the scenery is a little improved by the demesnes of Coole (W. Gregory, Esq.) and Rabeen (S. Lopdell, Esq.).

50 m. Ardrahan, some 8 m. to the W. of which, between Kinvarra and Black Head, are the ruins of the Cistercian Abbey of Corcomroe, which contain interesting details of the beginning of the 13th cent. The tourist should notice the ornamentation and human heads sculptured on the capitals of the arches, similar to those found at St. Saviour's Ch., Glendalough.

54½ m. Kilcolgan, to the l. of which is Tyrone House, the beautiful seat of Christopher St. George, Esq., the owner of immense property in Galway and Mayo. On the N. the grounds run along the shore of Kilcolgan River, a small arm of the Atlantic, which on this part of the coast pushes in an immense number of little creeks and bays.

A little further on is Clarin Bridge, to rt. of which is Kilcornan (Sir T. Redington).

At 59 m. *Oranmore* (Rte. 14), an arm of Galway Bay breaks prettily into the scene. On l. is the old castle of Oranmore, a massive square tower by the water's edge. This fortress was in 1641 placed by the Earl of Clanricarde under the command of Capt. Willoughby, who surrendered it to the Catholic forces.

The traveller northward will here leave the coach which goes to Galway, and betake himself not unwillingly to the Midland Great Western Rly., which passes through equally dreary scenery to

Athenry, Ath-na-Riogh (Rte. 14) (*Hotel :* Railway), from whence a branch line is given off to Tuam. The rly. passes rt. and l. the demesnes of Castle Ellen (W. P. Lambert, Esq.), Belleville (Major Mahon), and Bingarra House (A. Clarke, Esq.).

On rt. is *Monivea*, a small town, almost entirely surrounded by the grounds of Monivea Castle, the residence of Robert French, Esq.

9 m. *Ballyglunin* Stat., adjoining Ballyglunin House (M. Blake, Esq.), through the grounds of which flows a small stream, called the Abbert river.

[2 m. to the rt. are the remains of *Abbey Knockmoy* (anc. Croc-Muaidhe), so celebrated for its frescoes. In 1189 Cathol O'Connor, surnamed Crorre-Dearg, or the Red Hand, King of Connaught, obtained a victory over the English forces under Almeric St. Lawrence, and to commemorate it founded the abbey of

Cnoc Muaidhe, or the Hill of Slaughter. The nave is short and plain, but the chief interest is in the choir, where are the tomb of the founder and the frescoes. "Over the tomb of Cathol is represented the taking down of our Saviour from the cross. Nearer to the altar, and on a large compartment of the wall, are 2 designs. The upper represents 6 figures clothed in rich and flowing robes; the one in the middle is said to be Roderic O'Connor, monarch of Ireland; on either side the princes, his vassals; one holds a hawk on his thumb, the other a sword. Below this is a man sitting with what appears to be a roll of paper in his hand. To his right is a young man fixed to a tree, and transfixed with arrows, and 2 archers are in the act of shooting more at him. It is said that the youth represents Mac Murrough, son of the King of Leinster, who betrayed Ireland to the English, and that Roderick O Connor condemned the youth to this fate in revenge for his father's treason."— *Otway*. The costumes of the kings belong to the 12th cent., and these frescoes are considered, by competent antiquarians, to have been the work of the 14th cent. These singular paintings are fast disappearing, and it is only owing to the stone vaulting of the roof that they have been preserved so long.]

[To the rt. of rly., on either bank of the Abbert river, are Moyne (M. Browne, Esq.) and Abbert (J. Blakeney, Esq.)

Near *Newtown Bellew*, 10 m. rt., is a small lake, *Lough Lasarac*, or the illuminated lake, the waters of which are said to be illuminated by phosphoric light, once every 70 years. It is therefore in high reputation with the peasants, as those who wash in it have no chance of dying for that year.

13 m. *Mount Bellew*, a rather pretty little town near the banks of the Shiven, which ere long falls into the Suck. Mount Bellew is the residence of the family of Bellew.

From hence the traveller may proceed to Roscommon, through Mount Talbot and Athleague.]

After leaving Ballyglunin Stat., the round hill of Knocknaa becomes visible on the W., and soon afterwards the towers and buildings of

15½ m. *Tuam* (*Hotel:* Daly's, very bad), a place of considerable antiquity, was originally a religious establishment, founded in the 6th cent. by St. Jarlath, and from that time to this has ever maintained a high station in the ecclesiastical polity of Ireland. At one time it was the seat of a Protestant archbishop, but of late years it has been altered to a bishopric, the see comprising with Tuam the diocese of Achonry. It is also the head-quarters of the R. C. Archbishop, Dr. McHale, with whose edicts all readers of Irish politics are familiar. The town itself is small and not particularly interesting, with the exception of one or two objects of antiquity which no tourist should omit. They are the cathedral and the cross. The former, which is also the parish ch., is a small, unimpressive building, though a large amount of defect is covered by the W. door, as magnificent a specimen of ancient Norman work as any building in Great Britain can boast. It is built of red sandstone, altogether foreign to that district. The date of this doorway, which formed part of the chancel of the old ch., is somewhere between 1128, when O'Hoisin became abbot, and 1150, when he was made archbishop. Of the ancient ch. nothing but the chancel remains, "its E. end being perforated by 3 circularheaded windows, ornamented with zigzag and other mouldings both externally and internally, and connected with each other by stringcourse mouldings, in which the external one is enriched with paterae. But the great feature of the chancel is its

P 2

triumphal arch, erroneously supposed to have been a doorway, composed externally of 6 semicircular concentric and recessed arches. The shafts of the columns, which, with the exception of the outermost at each side, are semicircular, are unornamented, but their capitals, which are rectangular, on a semicircular torus, are very richly sculptured, chiefly with a variety of interlaced traceries, and in 2 instances, those of the jambs, with grotesque human heads. The arch mouldings consist of the nebule, diamond frette, and varieties of the chevron, the execution of which is remarkable for its beauty."—*Petrie.* Preparations have already been begun for rebuilding the cathedral, when this masterpiece of architecture will be restored to its former position. The cost of restoration of the ch. is estimated at 10,000*l.*

The cross of Tuam, also of sandstone, once broken into 3 pieces, and the property of 3 different owners, is now happily re-united and re-erected. The base contains inscriptions in memory of O'Hoisin, the abbot, and Turlough O'Connor, King of Connaught. In proportion to the plainness of the Protestant cathedral the Roman Catholic ch. is elaborate. It is a fine cruciform Perp. building, though unsatisfactory from its excessively florid ornamentation. " The walls are strengthened with panelled buttresses of several stages, terminating in richly crocketed pinnacles rising above the parapet, which is enriched with open tracery." The interior of the cathedral, though very expensively decorated, has no solemnity or impressive effect about it.

Excursions.—
1. Knockmoy.
2. Headford and Ross Abbey.

Conveyances.—Rail to Athenry. Car to Headford.

Distances. — Athenry, 15½ m.; Knockmoy, 11; Dunmore, 9; Headford, 13, [the road to which place runs at the base of Knock-naa, "the Hill of Fairies," which, from the flatness of the country round, is seen for a very long distance, being a conspicuous object even from Lough Corrib. At the foot is Castle Hacket, the seat of D. Kirwan, Esq.].

At 24½ m. rt. *Dunmore* the monotony of the country is somewhat relieved by the Slieve Dart Hills, which run between this, Ballyhaunis, and Castlereagh. Dunmore need not detain the tourist, for the only interest that attaches to it arises from the circumstance that Trollope has here laid the scene of his novel 'The Kellys of Castle Kelly.'

At *Castlereagh* (Rte. 19) the traveller may either avail himself of the rly. to Roscommon, or else continue his journey over a very bleak and desolate country to *Frenchpark*, a little village protected by the woods of Lord De Freyne's park.

[From hence a road runs E. to *Elphin* (anc. Ailphima), the seat of a diocese united with those of Kilmore and Ardagh. It is a prettily situated town, with a plain modernised cathedral used as a parish ch.

From Frenchpark a hilly road, relieved occasionally by a distant view of Lough Gara on the l., runs to

Boyle (Hotel: Monson's) (Rte. 18).]

ROUTE 34.

THE SHANNON, FROM ATHLONE TO LIMERICK.

This route, about the most beautiful in the inland portion of Ireland, requires a little arrangement in its performance, so as to take advantage of the steamer, which starts every 2nd morning about 11 o'clock, returning from Killaloe on the following day. A few words on the physical geography of the Shannon will not be out of place here. Its source in Legmonshena Mountain, co. Leitrim, is described in Rte. 6, as also various portions of its upper course as far as Lough Ree and Athlone. It possesses 234 miles of continuous navigation, and washes the shores of 10 counties, viz. Leitrim, Roscommon, Longford, Westmeath, King's County, Galway, Tipperary, Clare, Limerick, and Kerry. "From Killaloe in the co. of Clare, to its source, the river assumes a great variety of character. In some places it stretches out into seas or lakes, two of which — Lough Derg and Lough Rea — are each above 20 m. long. The falls and rapids, which on the whole line amount to an elevation of 147 ft., are overcome by lateral canals and locks." "Rising in one coal formation, emptying itself through another, and washing the banks of our most fertile counties, it delivers into the sea the rain collected from an area embracing 3613 square miles of country N. of Killaloe. In all the geographical characters of its basin we find the conditions for great evaporation fulfilled. The country whose waters it receives is flat — its streams sluggish — the soil upon its banks either deep and retentive clays or extensive bog. Expanding into numerous lakes of considerable size, often overflowing the lowlands on its banks, it may be considered as almost in the condition of presenting a true water-evaporating surface."—*Kane.*

Quitting Athlone with its noble bridge and fortifications, nothing claims attention for the first few miles, except where the stream divides and encloses the flat surface of Long Island, at the end of which is a pile of stones in the river, marking the division between the counties of Westmeath, Roscommon, and King's County; but at

9 m. is one of the most interesting and holy places in all Ireland—the 7 churches of *Clonmacnois*—" Cluain Mac Nois, Retreat of the Sons of the Noble"—a name gained by the celebrity in former ages of its monastic establishments, its gatherings of learned and pious men, and the shelter that it afforded to everything that was holy and good in the days of dark ignorance and superstition. In 548 an abbey was founded by St. Kieran on ground given by Dermod MacCervail, King of Ireland, and continued to flourish under a succession of prelates, notwithstanding the incursions of the Anglo-Normans, who more than once destroyed and laid waste the town and ecclesiastical buildings. The ruins consist of: 1. The churches. 2. The Round Towers. 3. The Crosses.

(*a.*) The Dahmliag Mor, or Great Ch., is recorded by the Four Masters as having been built in 909 by Flann, a King of Ireland, and Colman Conaillech, Abbot of Clonmachnois. It was, however, subsequently re-edified in the 13th or 14th cent. by Tomultach McDermott, chief of Moyhurg: it is now called Teampul McDermott. The chief points of interest about this ch. are—the great western doorway, of which Petrie says, "But though the ch. was thus re-edified, we still find in the sandstone capitals of its great W. doorway remains of a more ancient ch., as their style and material, which are different from those of every other ornamented portion of the building, sufficiently show; and that such capitals belonged to the doorway of the original ch. I see no reason to doubt." The N. doorway, built by Dean Odo, is of later date, and presents an elaborate Perp. ornamentation. Over the arch are 3 effigies – St. Patrick in his pontificals in the centre, with St. Francis and St. Dominick on either side; on a higher row their portraits are repeated; and on the pillars is the inscription—

"Dōus Odo Decanus Cluanni me fieri fecit."

(*b.*) Teampul Finghin, or Fineen's Ch., supposed to have been erected about the 13th cent. by Fineen Mac Carthy More, presents little but its chancel and a round tower attached to the S.E. junction with the nave. The chancel-arch, which remains, formerly possessed 3 concentric arches; the inner one has fallen away, and its place is supplied by a plain arch. Notice the chevron moulding on the second arch, the Egyptian-looking heads of the capitals, and "the bulbous characters of the bases of the columns." The chancel is lighted by a small circular-headed window, and possesses an ornamented piscina.

(*c.*) Teampul Connor, founded in the 10th cent. by Cathol, the son of Connor, is used as a parish ch.; its sole antiquity is a circular-headed doorway of that period.

In addition to these, there is a small ch. or oratory of St. Kieran, who also possesses here a stone, a well, and a cellar. This last is just to the S. of Teampul McDermott, and has a small octangular belfry.

2. The Round Towers are two :—

(*a.*) The largest, or O'Rourke's, is roofless, and stands on an elevation at the W. side of the ch.-yard. It is composed partly of the grey limestone with which this district abounds, and is entered by a door 15 ft. from the ground. Dr. Petrie considers it to have been erected about 908 (coeval with the Dahmliag Mor), though he considers "that it was indeed repaired at a period long subsequent to its erection, there is abundant evidence in the masonry of the building itself, the upper portion being of coarse-jointed masonry of limestone; while the greater part of it below is of close-jointed ashlar sandstone; and besides, it is quite obvious that the tower when such restoration was made was reduced considerably in its original height, as proportioned to its circumference." From its situation, this tower is a very conspicuous feature. "It was high enough to take cognizance of the coming enemy, let him come from what point he might; it commanded the ancient causeway that was laid down, at a considerable expense, across the great bog on the Connaught side of the Shannon; it looked up and down the river, and commanded the tortuous and sweeping reaches of the stream, as it unfolded itself like an uncoiling serpent along the surrounding bogs and marshes; it commanded the line of the Aisgir Riadha; could hold communication with the holy places of Clonfert; and from the top of its pillared height send its beacon light towards the sacred isles and anchorite retreats of Lough Rea; it was large and roomy enough to contain all the officiating priests of Clonmacnois, with their pixes, vestments, and books; and though the pagan Dane or the wild Munsterman might rush on in rapid inroad, yet the solitary watcher on the tower was ready to give warning, and collect within the protecting pillar all holy men and things, until the tyranny was overpast."—*Otway.*

(*b.*) McCarthy's tower, attached to the chancel of the ch., is more perfect; it is 7 ft. in diameter within and 55 ft. high, with a conical cross on the summit. The door of this tower is level with the ground—an unusual feature.

3. In front of the W. door of Teampul McDermott, and coeval with

it, is the great cross, formed by a single stone, 15 ft. high and elaborately carved. In the lowest compartment of the W. front of the shaft is an Irish inscription :—

"A prayer for Flann, son of Maelsechlainn."

And on the reverse side :—

"A prayer for Coleman, who made this Cross on the king Flann."

This settles the question of the date and the building of the cross. The sculptures on the W. side are intended to relate to the original foundation of Clonmacnois by St. Kieran, while the opposite side commemorates scenes in the life of our Saviour, from which it obtained the name given it in the Annals of Tigernach, of the Cros na Screaptra—or Cross of the Scriptures. St. Kieran is represented with a hammer in one hand and a mallet in the other.

In addition to the Crosses, there are a number of inscribed tombstones, some of them of the age of 10th cent. —such as the one to MaelFinnia (abbot, 992), Blaimac (abbot, 896), Flannchadh (abbot, 1003), Suibhne MacMaelhumai (one of the three Irishmen who visited Alfred the Great, 891), Coirpe Cromm (bishop, 899, and many others. The whole place is crowded with gravestones, showing the preference given to Clonmacnois as a place of interment. The festival of St. Kieran is held on the 9th of September, when immense numbers of people from the most remote parts of the country attend it, and, after performing their stations, end the day in the usual fashion of drunkenness.

We must not forget to mention the episcopal palace and castle of the O Melaghlins, which stands with bastions overlooking the river to the S.W. of the cemetery, and defended by a dry fosse. It is now, however, a heap of ruins. "Some parts lie in masses larger than human habitations in the form; others are rolled in immense heaps in the vallum; a curtain-wall, at least 10 ft. thick, lies at an angle of 45°, reclining upon about ¼ ft. of its thickness."— *Otway.*

Some distance to the N.E. are the remains of the nunnery built by Devorgilla, daughter of O'Melaghlin, connected, it is said, with the ch. by a subterranean passage; the road between the two, and carried on to the E., is known as the Pilgrims' Road.

The geologist will notice before leaving Clonmacnois the singular gravel ridges or hills forming the "Aisgir Riadha," known as "Eskers," which intersect Ireland from E. to W. They here cross the Shannon, causing the river to be deflected and form a bend. In fact, the 7 chs. are situated on a great mass of drift.

Distances.—By water from Athlone, 9 m.; by land, 13. Shannonbridge, 4 by land; 5 by water.

14 m. *Shannonbridge* is a small town at the confluence of the Suck with the Shannon, dividing Galway from Roscommon, which is crossed by a bridge of 18 arches, resting on a small island. The Connaught end of it is defended by a tête du pont and an artillery barrack. At 19½ m. we arrive off Shannon Harbour (for an account of which with its "Hotel," see 'Jack Hinton'), which, ere the days of railway communication, was of some importance as the point of junction between the Shannon navigation and that of the Grand Canal, which may, in one sense, be said to cross the Shannon, as it sends off a branch of 15 m. to Ballinasloe; the distance from this point to the Liffey at Dublin is 80 m. Here also the river Brosna flows in, running near Lough Owel (Mullingar), and flowing past Clara and Ferbane. Bordering its N. bank is the demesne of Moystown House (formerly the seat of the L'Estrange family, and near it are the ruins of Lisclooney Castle.

24 m. *Banagher* (Rte. 27) (*Hotel:* Harp), celebrated for its fairs and its old bridge, which is supposed to have stood for over 400 years. But as it showed signs of incapability, and some of the projecting buttresses were extremely inconvenient, a canal with a swing bridge was cut on the Galway side. Both sides of the river are strongly defended by barracks and batteries; and on the opposite bank is another of the Esker gravel ridges. In the neighbourhood of Banagher are Castle Garden, Claremount (J. Armstrong, Esq.), near which is the keep of Garry Castle, and Castle Iver (J. F. Armstrong, Esq.).

Conveyances.—Daily to Parsonstown.

Distances.—Athlone, 24 m.; Parsonstown, 8; Portumna, by water, 13; Shannon Harbour, 4½; Cloghan, 5; Clonfert, 5.

[An excursion may be made to Clonfert, 5 m. to the N.W. (Cluainfearth, the retired spot), where St. Brendan founded in the 6th cent. a ch. famous for its 7 altars. It subsequently became the seat of a diocese, and is now united with Killaloe, Kilmacduagh, and Kilfenora. The cathedral, which is also parish ch., does not contain very much of interest.]

Below Banagher the Shannon begins to divide, and becomes very tortuous and uncertain. Near Esker Bridge, on rt. are Shannon View, and Shannon Grove (Hubert Moore, Esq.); and further W., Lismore Castle, and the village of Eyrecourt, adjoining which is the fine seat of the family of Eyre.

28½ m. near the junction of the Little Brosna is *Meelick* (anc. Miline), where an abbey for conventual friars was founded in the 12th cent. by O'Madden, chief of the county. The remains stand on the Galway side, on a plot of ground which, in winter, is frequently an island.

Commanding Meelick, on the opposite bank, is a martello tower, and on an island a little above are the Keelogue batteries. The navigation in this portion of the river is so devious, that a canal has been cut from above the batteries, rejoining the Shannon at the mouth of the Little Brosna. Passing on rt. Harding Grove, and l. Ballymaccgan House, the tower of Portland Castle, and Portland House (T. Stoney, Esq.), the voyager arrives at

37 m. *Portumna* (*Inn:* Taylor's), which, though in itself situated on rather flat ground, yet commands fine views of Lough Derg and the Slieve Baughta hills on the W. The most noticeable objects are the wooden bridge over the Shannon, built by Lemuel Cox, the American architect of Derry, Waterford, and New Ross bridges. Its total length is 766 ft., the middle part resting on an island in the stream.

There are no traces left of De Burgos' ancient castle; but there are some of the Dominican abbey founded about the 13th cent., consisting of a few arches and an E. window. It was originally a cruciform building with a lofty tower long since fallen. The modern castle of the Earl of Clanricarde, the owner of the town, was burnt down in 1826, and has not been rebuilt. Portumna is a neat little place, and carries on a good business in grain. Adjoining, in addition to the Earl of Clanricarde's domain, are Palmerstown (W. Palmer, Esq.), Fairy Hill (C. Cooper, Esq.), Wellmount (Capt. M'Donagh), Oakley Park; and on the opposite side of the river, Belleisle, the seat of Lord Avonmore, on whose grounds are the keeps of 2 castles.

[The archæologist should visit the ruins of the Abbey of Loragh, which is a short distance to the E. It is a long pile of building, the E. gable of which is destroyed, though the W. gable, containing a good window, is in fine preservat'on. It was lighted at the sides by Early Pointed windows, nearly all of them built up;

which might have been adopted as a means of defence during Cromwell's visit to Loragh. The date of the building is about the 13th cent., although the original foundation is ascribed to St. Ruan, in the 6th cent. There are ruins of other buildings in the vicinity.]

The tourist is now fairly launched on the broad expanse of the Shannon, known as Lough Derg, which extends as far as Killaloe, and in fact occupies all the remainder of the route as far as the navigation is concerned. The scenery on the E. shore is generally tame and uninteresting; but that on the W. is of a high order, embracing a lofty range of mountains rising from the water's edge.

Lough Derg (which the tourist must not confound with Lough Derg in Donegal co.) is an expansion of the Shannon of about 25 m. in length and from 2 to 3 m. in breadth, running in a direction from N.E. to S.S.W. "It has been observed that in wet weather the level of the water in Lough Derg often rises 2 or 3 in. in 24 hours, and has been known to rise 12 inches. As the area of the Lough is 30,000 statute acres, this extent of water weighs 3,000,000 tons for each inch; and hence as much as 36,000,000 tons have accumulated in a single day and night. The average difference between summer and winter level of the Shannon at Killaloe, where, narrowing from Lough Derg, it resumes the river form, is about 6ft., but the total of the rises of the water during the year are found to be 11 ft. The rising of the waters occupied an average of 77 days; in falling to the summer level they occupied 107 days. The quantity of water thus accumulated in the great natural reservoir of the Lough was 532,551,696 cubic yards, or 403,116,600 tons, which is discharged in 107 days at the rate of 155,926 tons per hour. By this, a force continuing day and night of 177 horse-power per foot of fall may be obtained." — *Industrial Resources of Ireland.*

Quitting the little bay in which Portumna is situated, and gliding between the wooded point of Rinmaher, rt., and the headland of Derrymacegan, l., we pass l. Slevoir House (— Synge, Esq.), and enter a considerable expanse—the Upper Lough; a range of hills, the Slieve Baughta, occupies all the country on the W., commencing indeed to the S. of Loughrea, and embracing the district between Killaloe on the S. and Gort on the W.; the most lofty points are the Scalp, 1074 ft., and Knockeven, 1243 ft.

On rt., situated at the foot of one of the wooded spurs of Slieveanore, is the little town of *Woodford*, from whence a small river runs into the Shannon at Rossmore. Iron-ore was at one time extensively worked in this neighbourhood; and, its very frequent concomitant, a chalybeate well, used to attract a good many people. On the road to Newtown Daly is Marble Hill, the beautiful seat of Sir T. Burke, Bart., M.P. A number of ruined keeps stud the banks of Lough Derg at various intervals; there is one very near the head of the lake on the W. shore; a second, called Cloondagavoe, on Cregg Point, rt.; and a third on l., in the grounds of Drominagh (Capt. Tuthill. At this point the Lough narrows, and is studded with several small islands; but it widens again opposite the demesnes of Kilgarvan, Mota, Brookfield, and Belleview. Nearly halfway, the steamer passes the island of Illanmore, the largest in the lake. On the N.E. side are remains of a ch. The mainland on the E. abounds not only with ruined chs., but also castles, of which there are 5 or 6. Although possessing no peculiarly interesting features in themselves, they show the store that the early settlers set upon this region.

Nearly opposite Illanmore on l. are Castle Cambie, with the remains

P 3

of Kilbarron Abbey ch. Then comes Annagh Lodge, with the adjoining castles of Cashlaunteigeboght and Tullaun. Below these are Annagh Castle, Springmount, Ballycolliton, Johnston House, Prior Park, Woodpark, and Prospect House. In the little bay of Dromineer are the ruins of Dromineer Castle, Hazel Point Cottage, and Shannonvale; while on the opposite shore are the harbour of Williamstown, and Meelick House. At this point the direction of the Lough changes more to the W., and the most beautiful part of the scenery opens up in the Bay of Scariff.

On the northern shore is the little village of *Mount Shannon*, nestling at the foot of Knockeven, 1242 ft., and adjoining the village are the prettily wooded grounds of Woodpark (Philip Reade, Esq.). The antiquary should land at Mount Shannon for the purpose of visiting Inniscalthra (Innis-Calthair, or Holy Island), so remarkable for its chs. and round tower. In the 7th cent. St. Caimin visited it, and established a monastery which became famed for its sanctity and learning—St. Caimin himself having written a commentary on the Psalms. His ch. or chs. experienced the usual fate of destruction from the Danes; but were more or less re-edified by Brian Boroimhe, King of Munster, in 1027. The principal ch. is considered by Dr. Petrie to present in its ruined nave the original features of St. Caimin's plan, while the chancel is the work of Brian; the nave is internally 30 ft. in length by 21 ft. in breadth, the chancel being a square of 15 ft. "These measurements, however, appear to be those of the original ch. of St. Caimin, erected in the 7th cent., as it seems obvious, from the character of the masonry and of some of the features in the nave, that the latter, though unquestionably remodelled, was never entirely destroyed." Notice in the nave the windows, one being semicircular-headed, with an architrave such as belongs to many of the round towers; another is square-headed with inclined sides; and there is a triangular window formed of 3 stones, "unique in form of Irish architecture." The W. doorway must have been remarkably fine, though unfortunately there is very little left. It consisted of 3 concentric semicircular arches, ornamented with chevron mouldings in hollow lines, but carved in relief. The piers, which are rectangular and rounded at their angles, have human heads at the capitals.

The chancel-arch has also 3 receding and concentric arches, but of a totally different style; they are simply "of square-edged ribwork, and the ornamental sculpture is confined to the piers, which are rounded into semicolumns."

The round tower, of date of about the 10th cent., was celebrated as being the residence of an anchorite (inclusorius) of the name of St. Cosgrath "the Miserable." Its height is about 80 ft., and its upper story is wanting.

At the head of the bay is Scariff, a very charmingly situated little town, at the junction of 2 important roads: 1. From Woodford and Mount Shannon to Killaloe; 2. to Tulla and the co. Clare. The range of hills which have been accompanying us for so many miles, here experience a check, but rise again almost immediately to the S. between Scariff and Killaloe; the result is a pretty mountain valley through which flows the river Graney, rising in a considerable tarn called Lough Graney, and, when near Scariff, passing through Lough O'Grady, from whence it emerges as the Scariff river. Advantage has been taken of this valley to form a line of road to the little town of Tulla.

Opposite Mount Shannon, the main course of the river runs nearly due S. down to Killaloe, narrowing very considerably between Aughinish Point and Castlelough. The hills speedily rise again, but now on both sides of the channel. Below Castlelough on l. are the ch. and the ruins of the castle; succeeded by Towerlough Castle and Derry Castle, the latter in the grounds of F. Spaight, Esq. On the rt. are the ch. and schoolhouse of Tinarana, above which rise the heights of Croughnagower and Glengalliagh, 1726 feet; and speedily the steamer rounds a long reach in the river, and comes in sight of the picturesque town of

52 m. *Killaloe* (*Hotel*: Royal, tolerable', the Utopia of Irish anglers, who have in the broad weirs and rapids of the Shannon one of the finest opportunities for sport in all the kingdom. " Owing to the water, 'flies are very large and gaudy. They can be obtained at Limerick, also at Mrs. Blacker's, Dean-street, Soho." It is charmingly situated at the foot of the Slieve Bernagh mountains, which rise to the height of 1746 ft., and close along the bank of the river, that rushes. " brawling loud music," under the 19 arches of a long and narrow bridge.

The tourist should not fail to visit the venerable old cathedral, occupying the site of a ch. founded in the 6th cent. by St. Lua or Molua (Killda-Lua, Church of St. Lua). He was the first bishop, and was succeeded by St. Flannan, son of Theodorick, King of Munster, who bestowed many benefactions on the ch., which speedily attained great celebrity, and became the burial-place of Muircheartach O'Brien, King of Ireland, 1120. It is a fine cruciform ch. of the 12th cent., with a central tower arising from the intersection of the nave, choir, and transepts. The choir is used as the parish ch. Its re-erection is attributed to Donell More O Brien, King of Limerick, who died in 1194: but the gem of the whole building is a magnificent blocked Romanesque doorway of considerably earlier date, that is said by tradition to have been the entrance to Muircheartach's tomb. It consists of 5 concentric arches with singular mouldings and sculpture. Notice particularly the figures on the 2nd arch from the inside.

The W. end is lighted by very narrow early lancet windows, deeply splayed within. Within the precincts of the ch.yard is a second singular building—a stone-roofed ch.— said to have been built by St. Molua or St. Flannan. Internally it is 29 ft. 4 in. long by 18 ft. broad. It is lighted by a semicircular-headed window in the W. gable, and by a triangular or straightheaded one in the E. It is entered by a remarkable doorway, the capital of which " on the N. side presents a rude imitation of the Ionic scroll, while that on the S. presents 2 figures of animals representing lambs; while the architrave exhibits none of the ornaments considered as characteristic of Norm. architecture." Dr. Petrie considers that the erection of this ch. is to be attributed to St. Flannan; while the one built by St. Molua is to be found on an island in the river.

The navigation from Killaloe to Limerick is carried on by a canal, so as to avoid the rapids of Killaloe and Castle Connell. " The minimum discharge of the Shannon at Killaloe has been estimated by Mr. Mullvany, in the driest summer, so low as 100,000 cubic feet of water per minute."—*Kane.*

Conveyances.— Steamer to Athlone; rail to Limerick.

Distances.—Scariff, by water, 11 m.; Holy Island, 12; Limerick, 17; Castle Connell, 7½; Nenagh, 12; [to which place a road runs round the southern base of the Arra hills, and immediately fronting the range of the Silver-mine Mts., which culminate in the lofty summit of Mt. Keeper, 2278 ft.

Nenagh is a small garrison town situated on a stream that runs down from the Silver-mines Mts. into Lough Derg. It does not contain much of interest, save the circular keep of the Castle of the Butlers, usually known as " Nenagh Round," and one of the largest and most important Norman keeps in the kingdom.]

Conveyance.—Rail to Parsonstown, Dublin, and Limerick.

The remainder of this route is performed by rail, passing 3 m. Bird Hill Station.

7½ m. at *Castle Connell* the tourist should stop to view the rapids; where "the Shannon pours that immense body of water, which, above the rapids, is 40 ft. deep and 300 yds. wide, through and above a congregation of huge stones and rocks which extend nearly ½ m., and offers not only an unusual scene, but a spectacle approaching much nearer to the sublime than any moderate-sized stream can offer even in its highest cascade. None of the Welsh waterfalls nor the Griesbach in Switzerland can compare for a moment in grandeur and effect with the rapids of the Shannon."—*Inglis.* The river on either side is lined with pretty grounds and residences; on the l. bank the principal are Castleview, Woodlands, the Hermitage (Lord Massey), and New Gardens; and on the right are Waterpark and Doonass House (Sir Hugh Massy, Bart.). In the neighbourhood of the Annacotty station are Mount Shannon (Earl of Clare), Mulkear, and Thornfield (Gen. Bourke); soon after which the rly. crosses a small river called the Slievemohean, and at Killonan station joins the Waterford and Limerick line.

17 m. *Limerick* (Rte. 33) (*Hotel:* Cruse's).

ROUTE 35.

FROM KILLARNEY TO VALENTIA AND KENMARE.

A car leaves Killarney every morning at 8, taking the high road along the upper shore of the lake, which passes Aghadoe, and crosses the Laune at Beaufort bridge. The tourist will find this portion minutely detailed in Rte. 31. At the bridge there are 2 roads to Killorglin; the one on the N. bank of the Laune is the prettiest; but the car follows the other, winding round the grounds of Beaufort House, where it abruptly leaves the road to the Gap of Dunloe.

Near Cullenagh House (K. Mahoney, Esq.), and close to the roadside, is the circular fort of Labballow. The country traversed by this road is wide, open, and bleak; although on the l. the landscape is relieved by the noble ranges of the Reeks and their secondary ranges, which rise up in a grand sweep from the undulating morasses in the foreground.

8 m. *Churchtown* (Sir R. Blennerhasset, Bart.). Close by is the ch., where the McGillicuddys are buried, and a little to the S. is the tower of Castle Core, where they lived. This is the best point from which to ascend the Reeks. At Banecloon the Gaddagh is crossed near its junction with the Laune, on the opposite bank of which is the ruin of Ballymalis Castle.

At 12 m. the Cottoners river is crossed, and a broad road running parallel with the Laune leads into

Killorglin, a mean-looking town, though prettily placed, overlooking the valley of the Laune, which is crossed by a long bridge leading to Miltown and Castlemaine. Here is still the shell of a castle formerly belonging to the Knights-Templars; but on their dissolution it reverted to its former owners the Fitzgeralds, who lost it again in the Rebellion. Killorglin will not delay the tourist long, unless he be an angler.

Conveyances.— Car to Killarney; car to Cahirciveen; car to Tralee, through Milltown and Castlemaine.

Distances. — Killarney, 13 m.; Lough Carra, 7; Milltown, 5. [To the latter place the road follows the rt. bank of the Laune, which very soon enters a sandy estuary conjointly with the Maine. There are several circular forts in this neighbourhood, one of which close to the road, 1 m., is called Farrenmacwilliam. Thence crossing a shoulder of high ground, we descend into

Milltown and the valley of the Maine. Adjoining the town is Kilcoleman, the beautifully wooded Elizabethan seat of Sir W. Godfrey, Bart., in whose grounds are the remains of Kilcoleman or Killeagh Abbey, founded for Augustinians in the reign of Henry III., by Geoffrey de Maurisous, and now consisting of some portion of the walls and an E. window.

A little distance from Kilcoleman is Fort Agnes, in the grounds of which is a large circular fort. The Maine is crossed at 7 m. *Castlemaine* "by a bridge supposed to be coeval with the Thomond Bridge at Limerick. The ancient castle stood over it, and projected considerably on the E. side; the buttresses of the arch by which it was supported are remaining, and the stone socket on which the pivot of the castle-gate turned is still to be seen."

Castlemaine formerly had a good deal of trade from its position as a port; but the Maine having silted up, and a formidable bar having formed at the entrance of the haven, all commerce has nearly deserted it. *Persicus maritimus*, a rare plant, may be found on the shores of Castlemaine Bay.] Climbing the steep hill of Killorglin, the road is hilly and elevated until a shoulder of high ground is crossed, and a rapid descent made to 19 m. Carra Bridge, where the river Carra rushes down, a perfect specimen of a Highland stream, from *Lough Carra*. About 1 m. from the bridge is the lower end of the lake, which runs for about 3½ m. in an irregular curve into the heart of the mountain district, offering very great temptation to the pedestrian who is fond of fine hill scenery. The lake is narrow, but its banks are in many places well fringed with native wood, which appears to have been much more abundant in times gone by than it is now. Carex filiformis has its abode there. There is magnificent trout and salmon fishing here, and comfortable accommodation in the house of a farmer named Breen, who keeps a lodging-house. The road to the head of the lake winds close to the shore for one-third of the distance, and is then cut off from it by a hill of nearly 1000 ft. in height. It soon rejoins the river higher up at Lickeen and Blackstones, two beautifully situated fishing lodges. At this point the Carra-beg flows in, taking its rise from Lough Acoose, at the foot of Derryfanga, 1170 ft.

Still higher, we strike the cross-mountain road from Waterville to Killorglin. The Carra-beg itself is formed by a number of small streams taking their rise from Coomenagh, 2535 ft., and is well worth exploring, from the magnificent mountain views of the Reeks. Indeed, it is a very good point from whence to ascend these latter points, as the tourist thereby gains an entirely different set of views to those from the other side. The tourist should stay for a time at Breen's, and, with the help of the Ordnance map, visit the recesses of these ranges of hills, which are known to few.

21 m. we arrive at *Glenbay*, or Glenbehy, a charming little spot at the foot of a thickly-wooded knoll, round which the river Behy winds. The Headley Arms is a comfortable inn, generally filled by anglers in search of salmon fishing, and occasionally some bathers. Both the Behy and the Carra flow into Dingle Bay at the point of junction with the Castlemaine Haven.

Following up the glen of the Behy, we have more fine mountain scenery, particularly near the summit, where on the l. a magnificent amphitheatre of hills unfolds itself. The highest point about the centre is Coomacarrea, 2542 ft. (at the foot of which are a couple of large tarns), flanked on the l. by Meenteog, 2350 ft, and on the rt. by Been Hill, 2189 ft.; the eminence on the extreme rt., under which the road runs, is Drung Hill, 2104 ft., on the top of which a pattern is held. Soon after passing a cottage, where horses are changed, a very splendid view bursts on the sight—as the road surmounts the shoulder of the hill and suddenly drops upon Dingle Bay, alongside of which a fine terrace is carried for some miles at a great elevation. Parallel with us on the opposite coast are the fine ranges which extend from Tralee to Ventry—viz., Cahir-couree, 2796 ft.; Benoskee, 2715; Brandon, 3127; and Mt. Eagle, 1695, with the different inlets up which lie Annascaull, Dingle, and Ventry—while the end of the promontory is finished off with the rocky islands of the Blaskets. The view to the l. is entirely cut off by the steep hills overhanging the road, until the coast trends a little to the S. at the picturesque village of Kells or Hollymount, with its cheerful-looking coastguard station. Here the mountains close in on either side, the road cutting off the view of the sea; and we descend the open valley of the Ferta. There is a pretty bit of scenery at Carhan Bridge, with the wooded knoll of Hill Grove right in front, and the river on the rt. Close to the bank is the ivy-covered ruin of Carhan, a cottage where Daniel O'Connell first saw the light.

38 m. *Cahirciveen* (*Inn*, Fitzgerald's), a miserable little town on the side of a hill overlooking the Valentia river and harbour. There is nothing to see in it, but the antiquary should cross the river and visit the ruins of Ballycarbery Castle, a little to the N. of which is a singular stone fort, in good preservation, not unlike the Staigue fort (p. 329). *Cahirciveen* is situated rather finely at the foot of those bluff mountains which have kept company with the tourist all the way from Killarney. The hill overlooking the town is Bentee, 1245 ft.

Conveyances. — Car to Killarney daily.

Distances.—Killarney, 38 m.; Killorglin, 25; Glenbehy, 17; Valentia, 3; Waterville, 12; Inny Bridge, 9½. [The ferry to Valentia Island is 3 m. from the town, and the distance across to Knightstown is nearly ½ m. There is a comfortable hotel, from whence the tourist can visit the neighbourhood.

The island of *Valentia* is about 5½ m. long, by 2 broad, and is separated from the mainland by a circuitous passage, very narrow at the N. and S. entrances, but swelling out in the interval, so as to afford a secure harbourage. Generally speaking the surface is bold and rocky, rising at Ceokaun Mount, the most northerly point, to 880 ft.; and at Bray Head, on the S., to 792 ft. Between these two points, however, the land sinks to 200 or 300 ft. The finest scenery, and, indeed, nearly all that is worth seeing is towards the N. of the island. At Knightstown the principal thing is the slateworks, where the processes of cutting and polishing the slabs may be constantly seen. Forming part of the office is the room (almost historically celebrated) in which were conducted the operations of the Atlantic Telegraph—operations which the inhabitants of Valentia fondly hope will ere long be revived, to the benefit of the trade and business which the establishment of the Telegraph brought to this district. As may be seen any day in the papers, Valentia is still an important telegraph-stat. for meteorological reports. Proceeding by a very capital road on the N. coast, we arrive at

Route 35.—Valentia—Waterville.

Glanleam, the only seat on the island, and the residence of the Knight of Kerry, the owner of the soil, and according to all accounts, a landlord who lives firmly seated in the affections of his tenants. It is prettily situated on a cliff overlooking the harbour and underneath the road, here covered with foliage and brushwood. About ½ m. ahead of it is the lighthouse of Fort Point, guarding the narrow entrance between the 2 islands of Valentia and Beghinish. This latter islet is an awkward impediment to the navigation, being situated exactly midway between Fort Point and Doulas Head, a precipitous cliff of 400 ft. in height, offering a sorry welcome to any unfortunate vessel unable to make the harbour on a stormy night. A storm here is a grand sight, for even in calm weather the Atlantic rolls in gigantic waves, that are said to be of greater volume at Valentia than any other place in the kingdom. The visitor should follow the road to the slate-quarries, and thence ascend Ceokaun, which seaward presents a lofty cliff, but towards the town is a bluff grassy slope. There is a fine view from the summit of the whole of the island, of Doulas Head, part of the Dingle Mountains, and the Blasket Point to the N. To the S. is Bolas Head in the distance; while inland there is a broad and extensive sweep of hills running down from Cahirciveen to Waterville. The *Cliffs of Brey Head* at the W. end of the island are nearly 800 ft. high, and well worth visiting. For boat excursions the tourist may visit Ballycarbery Castle or the shores of Lough Kay, where there is a fine cave. The road from the ferry-house, where a car may be obtained, runs between the channel and the foot of the mountains, giving off a road to the rt. to Portmagee, opposite the southern end of Valentia.] Hence it turns inland, and at 47¼ m. crosses the Inny river, a fine trout and salmon stream, that rises in the hills between the coast and Lough Carra, and falls into Ballinskelligs Bay, an open though ironbound bay, with a noble white strand, the terror of all vessels that may have drifted into this neighbourhood, as there is no holding ground for them.

50 m. *Waterville*, is a little village, most romantically situated close to the side of Ballinskelligs Bay, and on a narrow neck of land that separates the sea from Lough Curraun or Lough Leane. On the banks of the lake is the Hartopp Arms, a very comfortable hotel, where the visitor, be he fisherman, artist, or pedestrian, may with comfort and pleasure bide a while. Lough Curraun, next to Killarney the finest southern lake in Ireland, extends into the heart of the mountains for about 3 m., and is connected with the sea by a short stream. In fact, were it not on a higher level, it might be taken for a large lagoon. The head of the lake, which is fed by the Cummeragh River, is embosomed in mountains, and is surrounded by scenery of no mean order. Boats can be had for viewing the lake or for fishing; the expense of the latter item is for a boat and man 5s. per day. If possible, the fisherman should obtain the services of Jim Bradley, who knows the lake thoroughly. The short connecting river is preserved by Mr. Butler, whose house is adjoining the village, but leave for fishing can be had for asking. There are several islands in the lake, one of which, the Church Island, contains the ruins of an ancient ch. and of the house of St. Finian Cam, of the date of the 6th cent. It is nearly circular externally, but quadrangular inside, with a rude doorway on the N. side.

The coast scenery in this neighbourhood is fine. Ballinskelligs Bay is almost circular, the 2 seaward promontories being, on the E.

the Hog's Head, with the rocky island of Scariff a little further out; and on the W. Bolus Head, from the cliffs of which rises Bolus Mt., 1350 ft. in height. [But the most singular features of the coast are 3 little islands, some distance out at sea, known respectively as the Lemon Rock, the Little Skellig, and the Great Skellig. The latter (the farthest out), although little more than a single cliff, is the object of veneration to crowds of devotees, who annually perform their difficult pilgrimage to the ruined abbey of St. Finian and the station of St. Michael. "The penance consists in passing, or rather squeezing, first through a circular aperture in the rock, some feet in length, called 'The Needle's Eye;' and then, by creeping up the smooth surface of a sloping stone, to reach a little platform about 1 yard in width, the sides of which slope down to the ocean below. From the further side another slanting rock or inclined plane ascends, in which small indentations are made for the hands and feet. The ascent of this flag is so difficult and frightful that it is called 'The Stone of Pain.' In accomplishing this passage the courage of the faithful is deeply tried; the least slip will carry the pilgrim back to the narrow platform, whence the acquired momentum of the descent may contribute to hurry the victim of credulity down the sides of the rocks into the depths of the ocean. After the performance of the station on the sublime pinnacle of St. Michael's Pillar, only one service remains to be accomplished by the faithful worshipper at this shrine of the ocean. A narrow stone, 2 ft. in breadth, and about 10 in length, projects at right angles from the highest pinnacles of the rock; and at its extremity, called 'The Spindle,' a cross is rudely graven, which the pilgrim is required, as the criterion of his belief, to reach, and repeat over it a Pater Noster. When the pillar is recovered again the pilgrimage is passed. The mode of reaching the point of imminent danger, on which the cross is raised, is by sitting astride upon the spindle, and cautiously edging forward to the cross, and, without attempting to turn round, edging back again with equal care."—*Wright*.

On the summit of this lone island, 714 ft. above the sea, are the ruins of the monastery, which we are told was so desolated in 812 by the Danes, that the unfortunate monks were starved in their cells.

In this present day the appearance of the Skellig is welcomed by thousands of sailors, for it is the seat of 2 noble fixed lighthouses, the one 372 ft., and the other 173 ft. above high-water, the light of both being visible for 25 m.

A singular little rock to the S. of the Great Skellig is called the Washerwoman's Rock. Although the Skelligs may be visited from Waterville, the usual way is to make the excursion from Valentia, as the boats of the latter place are more available.] [A fine mountain excursion may be taken from Waterville to Lough Carra, 24 m., although one that requires settled weather. The road runs by the W. shore of Lough Currane, and passes to the l. of Lough Derriana, eventually crossing the Inny not far from its source, and then cutting through a broad range of mountains to the valley of the Carra (p. 325).]

Excursions.—
1. Valentia.
2. Lough Curraune.
3. Lough Carra.
4. Derrynane.

Distances from Waterville.—Valentia, 11 m.; Cahirciveen, 12; Sneem, 20; Staigue Fort, 13; Kenmare, 36.

It is a magnificent drive along the coast from Waterville to Sneem. About 1 m. from the former place is the ruined ch. of Templenakilla, and on the rt. of the road a very perfect circular earthen fort.

The views are fine over Ballinskellig, the Hog's Head, and Bolus Head; while on the l. the mountains rise directly from the road to a height of 1600 ft. At 5 m. from Waterville there is a very beautiful view of Derrynane Abbey, the residence of D. O'Connell, Esq., the grandson of the great Liberator; from this point a new feature in the landscape appears, in the rocky headlands and ranges on the opposite side of Kenmare Bay. At *Caherdaniel*, 7 m., is a small stone fort on rt. of road. We now cut off the projecting promontory of the Lamb's Head, and descend to the pretty village of Cove. [A little beyond West Cove (E. O'Sullivan, Esq., 11 m.), a road to l. runs up into the hills for about 2 m. to *Staigue Fort*, one of the most wonderful antiquarian remains in Ireland. The best way for the tourist to visit it is to walk, directing the car-driver to go forward, and pick him up again at a spot some 4 m. further, where a cross mountain-road from the fort comes in. "It is an enclosure, nearly circular, 114 ft. in diameter from out to out: and in the clear 88 ft. from E. to W.; and 87 ft. from N. to S. The stones are put together without any description of mortar or cement; the wall is 13 ft. thick at the bottom, and 5 ft. 2 in. broad at top at the highest part, where some of the old coping-stones still remain. It has one square doorway in the S.S.W. side 5 ft. 9 in. high, with sloping sides. In the substance of this massive wall, and opening inwards, are 2 small chambers; the one on the W. side is 12 ft. long, by 4 ft. 7 in. wide, and 6 ft. 6 in. high. The northern chamber is not so long, but higher. They formed a part of the original plan, and were not, like other apertures in some similar structures, filled up gateways. Around the interior of the wall are arranged 10 sets of stairs, the highest reaching very nearly to the full height of the wall, and the secondary flight being about half that much. Each step is 2 ft. wide, and the lower flights project within the circle of the higher. They lead to narrow platforms, on which its warders or defenders stood. Although larger forts of this kind are known in Ireland, nothing so perfect in the construction of the staircases encircling the interior is to be found, with the exception of Dunmohr, in the middle island of Aran. A date of 2000 years cannot be considered too old for this monument, which is still in a state of great preservation, and only to be equalled by those in Aran, which, however, do not evince so much care in their design and construction. What may have been the original Irish name of 'Staigue Fort,' which is quite a modern appellation, has not yet been determined." — *Wilde*.

The short cut from the Fort to the road over the hills should not be attempted without a guide, as the ground is boggy and difficult.] The road now keeps tolerably near the coast—obtaining fine landscapes of the opposite hills on rt., and still finer ones on l. Where the old and new roads join, there is a beautiful view looking up the cwm towards Coomcallee (2134 ft.), a sharp, precipitous mountain, with a tarn at the foot. The summits of the numerous hills belonging to this group lying between the coast and Killarney, peer one above the other in wild confusion, and form a picturesque entrance to 20 m. *Sneem*, a poor little town, or rather village, near the mouth of the Sneem river, and embosomed amidst rocks and mountains. There is a small inn, clean and moderate, where the tourist may put up for a night. It is a fine mountain-road from hence to Killarney, crossing the Blackwater, and joining the Kenmare road. About 2 m. from the village is a wooded oasis of gentlemen's residences, viz., Holly Wood (F. Hyde, Esq.), Parknasilla (now held by Dean Graves), Derryquin Castle (F. C. Bland, Esq.), Reenaferrara (Capt. Hartley).

2 m. from *Sneem* is the small *Island of Garinish*, belonging to the Earl of Dunraven, the views from which combine a variety of outline with a picturesque beauty of detail scarcely to be met with on the W. coast of Ireland.

At 28 m. the road crosses the Blackwater, which runs in a deep ravine under the one-arched bridge, foaming and rushing as though it were still a highland stream, instead of falling into the sea. With its dense woods on either side and its festoons of ivy this is a spot of rare beauty.

[A road on the l. leads to a fishing-lodge some distance up the river. It is worth following the Blackwater to its source, which is extremely fine, in a deep amphitheatre of mountains, called "The Pocket." Steep escarpments surround it on all sides save the one from which the stream escapes. The cliffs on the W. of the Pocket are formed by Beown Mt. (2468 ft.), and on the N. by Mullaghnathin (2539). These summits form the watershed between the Blackwater and the Carra.] Leave for fishing the river can be obtained from Mr. Mahoney, or by stopping at the Blackwater inn, Old Dromore.

On the opposite side of the river are the woods and grounds of Cappindeush or Dromore Castle, the beautiful seat of R. Mahoney, Esq., who kindly allows the tourist to drive through his demesne. It is a modern castellated residence, commanding charming views of the bay and river of Kenmare, and contains the keep of the ancient castle.

Leaving on rt. Dunkerron Castle (J. Taylor, Esq.), the traveller enters

36 m. *Kenmare* (*Hotel:* Lansdowne Arms, tolerable). This prettily situated little town dates from 1670, the time of its foundation by Sir William Petty, the ancestor of the Lansdowne family. "Scarcely any village built by an enterprising band of New Englanders, far from the dwellings of their countrymen, was more completely out of the pale of civilisation than Kenmare. Between Petty's settlement and the nearest English habitation, the journey by land was of 2 days, through a wild and dangerous country. Yet the place prospered : 42 houses were erected ; the population amounted to 180 ; the cattle were numerous ; the supply of herrings, pilchards, mackerel, and salmon was plentiful, and would have been still more plentiful had not the beach been, in the finest part of the year, covered by multitudes of seals. An attempt was made with great success to set up iron-works. The neighbourhood of Kenmare was then richly wooded, and Petty found it a gainful speculation to send ore thither."—*Macaulay.*

In 1688 the success of the little colony attracted the jealous and greedy eyes of the natives, who, regarding the inhabitants as heretics, set to work to plunder and injure them in every way. For a time they held out, and were enabled to keep their own; but at length, being besieged by a regular army of 3000 men, the colony was forced to capitulate, and embark in a vessel for Bristol.

It is charmingly situated at the very head of Kenmare Bay, where the Roughty river empties its waters. The town itself does not contain any object of interest, save the Suspension Bridge which crosses the Sound on the road to Glengarriff. The tourist will soon find out, from the pertinacity of the girls who offer it for sale, that lace-work is an article of manufacture here as well as at Limerick.

The rides and drives in the neighbourhood of Kenmare are remarkably varied and beautiful, and the following are recommended :—

1. To Dromore, then up the Blackwater to Lough Brin, from thence along the valley of the Owenreagh, and by the new road home.
2. To Headfort by Kilgarvan and the valley of the Flesk. The rock scenery in this vale, especially at Fileadown or the Demon's Cliff, is very fine.
3. To Glengarriff by the "Priest's Leap."
4. Along Kenmare Bay to the Lakes of Clonee, Inchiquin, and Glenmore, and thence to the harbour of Kilmichaeloge.

Conveyances.—Car to Sneem daily, and, in the season, car to Glengarriff and Bantry; also to Killarney.

Distances. — Killarney, 19 m.; Glengarriff, 17; Macroom, 29; Bantry, 27; Sneem, 16; Waterville, 36.

The road to Killarney follows up the course of the Finnihy river, and gradually ascends from the valley into the mountains, offering very fine views, looking to the S., of the Caha and Slieve-Miskish Mts., in the proximity of Bearhaven, between the bays of Kenmare and Bantry.

At the 6th m. a pass in the mountains is entered, and the Sneem road is joined. Hence it is carried along the valley of the Owenreagh to 8 m. Looseaunagh Lough. This is one of the finest routes in the S. of Ireland —especially when, after passing the Lough, the view of the Lakes of Killarney bursts upon the sight.

The remainder of this route is given in p. 291.

ROUTE 36.

FROM CORK TO KENMARE, VIÂ BANDON, BANTRY, AND GLENGARRIFF.

A portion of this route is performed by the Cork and Bandon Rly., opened in 1851, the terminus of which is in the S. portion of the city, adjoining the Exchange. Passing on l. the Union House and several pleasant suburban villas, the first object of interest is the Chetwynd Viaduct, consisting of 4 arches of 121 ft. span.

6½ m. Waterfall Station, a little beyond which on rt. are the walls of the abbey of Ballymacadane, an Augustinian abbey of the 15th century, founded by Cormac McCarthy. The line now passes through a tunnel, and arrives at Ballinhassig stat. The village is about 1 m. to the W. The road from the station passes at the back of Mount Mary, over a very fine arch which spans the glen. Ballinaboy House is the seat of J. Molony, Esq. Crossing the Owenboy river, which flows into the sea near Carrigaline and Crosshaven (Rte. 37), the traveller next arrives at Crossbarry, where there is a junction with the Kinsale branch, 11 m. in length, which has the merit of being one of the cheapest lines in the kingdom, it only having cost 6000l. a mile.

24 m. *Kinsale* (*Hotel:* Royal George; a new one is now building by the Railway Co.) is both quaint and striking in its appearance, the houses rising in tiers on the side of the Compass Hill, overlooking the windings of the Bandon river. On the same side, but fronting the town, are the villages of Scilly and Cove, which are a good deal frequented in the bathing season. The harbour is defended by Charles Fort, a little below Cove, and the Old Fort, occupying a promontory round which the river makes a great bend. The latter, however, otherwise called Castle-ni-park, is no longer kept up; it is hexagonal in shape, and the towers and intrenchments are in tolerable condition. Kinsale does not contain much of antiquarian interest, save the ch., a fine old cruciform building, said to have been erected by St. Multosia in the 14th century. It contains a venerable tower at the W. end, with the upper stage of smaller dimensions, and a small broach spire; a N. transept with a 5-light window; a S.

trans. in ruins. The doorway of the tower is evidently of later date. In the interior are some monuments to the families of Southwell and Perceval, temp. Charles I. It must not, however, be inferred that the town is modern, for, on the contrary, it is one of the oldest in Ireland, and is alluded to in ancient MSS. as Cean Taile, "the headland in the sea." In the 14th century it came into the possession of the powerful family of Courcy, who built a castle and made it a walled town, and ever since that period Kinsale knew very little peace, but came in for an unusual number of hard blows, principally at the hands of the Spaniards in 1601. They seized and held it for some days against the English army under Lord Mountjoy and Sir J. Carew, who, when they called on the Spanish commander to surrender the town, received for answer that "it was held for Christ and the King of Spain." Kinsale suffered again during the Parliamentary war, in which it declared in favour of Cromwell. There is a very charming walk at the back of the ch. and round Compass Hill, from which the visitor gains beautiful views of the Forts and the Bandon river, with a ruined ch. and castle on the opposite bank. From the security of the harbour and the speed with which vessels could gain the open sea, Kinsale has been extensively used as a rendezvous for squadrons of the navy and homeward or outward bound vessels. It is lighted by a fixed light at Charles Fort, off which there is rather an awkward bar; also by a fixed light on the Old Head of Kinsale, 294 ft. above high water, and visible for 23 nautical miles. It is a pleasant excursion from the town to the Head, a promontory anxiously looked for by the homeward-bound voyager from America, who sights the Old Head of Kinsale before any other British land. The best though longest way is by the village of Ballinspittle, where there is a remarkably perfect fort with treble ramparts and intrenchments. It is, however, considerably nearer to cross the ferry. The Danes are said to have received their first defeat from the Irish at this spot. Passing Garrettstown (A. Forster, Esq.), the road emerges upon Courtmacsherry Bay, and enters the peninsula at Lispatrick. The geologist will find Posidonia lateralis in the slates of this district. The Signal Tower is placed on a strip of land, where the interval between the rocks on either side becomes very contracted; the little bay on each side is known as Holeopen Bay, and on the W. side of it are the ruins of the old castle, built by the De Courcys in the 12th century. The Head itself, though only 256 ft. above the sea, presents magnificent coast views, the chief points to the W. being the Seven Heads and the Galley Head. The distance from the town to the lighthouse by the nearest road is 5 m., and by Ballinspittle 9 m.; to Bandon, 13 (by road); Cork, 24; Inishannon 8; Carrigaline, 13.

1½ m. from Brinny stat., and near the grounds of Beechmount is a remarkably large Cashel Fort occupying an eminence of 600 ft.

At 18 m. Inishannon stat., the rly. crosses Bandon river, a little above the point where the Brinny falls in. A very lovely view it is, the course of the river being marked by charming wooded creeks and residences.

On the N. side of the Bandon is Domdaniel House (Rev. R. Clarke), in the grounds of which are the ruins of the castle, built by Barry Oge in 1476. On the S. bank are Belmont and Cor Castle (J. Corker, Esq.), commanding views of the valley of the Brinny, the confluence of which with the Bandon is thought by many to exceed in beauty the Vale of Avoca.

[1½ m. down the river is the little town of Inishannon, which, though once an important walled and castellated place, has little to recommend it now but its beautiful situation. Still further down towards Kinsale are the beautiful grounds of Shippool (W. Herrick, Esq.), extending for a considerable distance along the river-side; the ruins of Poulnalong Castle, an old fortress of the McCarthys; and Rock Castle, in the grounds of which are slight remains of Carriganass Castle.] Skirting the demesne of Woodlands, and passing rt. the tower of Kilbeg Castle, the train arrives at its terminus at

20 m. *Bandon* (*Inns*: Devonshire Arms; French's), next to Cork the busiest and most important town in the county. It is pleasantly situated on the rt. bank of the Bandon river, in a broad open valley bounded on the N. by the Clara Hills. With the exception of the handsome modern ch. and a modern R. C. chapel, the town itself contains very little that is interesting to the tourist, except the Earl of Bandon's Park of Castle Bernard that stretches along the banks of the river to the W. The Bandon is navigable only to Inishannon, which may therefore be considered as its port; but a great deal of business is carried on in distilling, the principal establishment being that of Messrs. Allman, one of the largest in the S. of Ireland.

Conveyances.—Rail to Cork; car to Bantry and Dunmanway; in the season daily to Glengarriff and Kenmare; daily to Skibbereen; daily to Clonakilty.

A rly. is in course of construction to Skibbereen.

Distances.—Cork, 20; Inishannon, 3; Dunmanway, 17; Clonakilty, 14; Timoleague, 8; Bantry, 37; Skibbereen, 34; Rosscarbery, 22½.

Excursions.—
1. Inishannon.
2. Timoleague.
3. Enniskeen and Kinneith.

The direct route from Bandon to Bantry is through Dunmanway, the road to which keeps the N. or l. bank of the river, skirting the grounds of Castle Bernard and Laragh House.

26 m. on S. side is Kilcolman (W. Lamb, Esq., and on the N. the Glebe House of Morragh and Palace Ann (A. Beamish, Esq., a curious old-fashioned residence of the 17th cent.

29 m. are the villages of Enniskeen and Ballyneen.

[3 m. to rt., on the old mountain road to Macroom, over the Clara Hills, is the Round Tower of Kinneith or Kinnergh, 75 ft. high and 65 in circumference. The chief peculiarity about it is that for the first 15 ft. it is of hexagonal shape, and circular for the remainder of its height.]

31½ m., at the confluence of the Blackwater with the Bandon, the road passes several pleasant seats, that make a contrast to the monotonous character of the scenery. On l. Kilcaskan Castle (O'Neill Daunt, Esq.); and on rt. Fort Robert (once the residence of the late Feargus O'Connor), Laurel Hill, Carrigmore, and Manch House (D. O'Connor, Esq.).

[33 m. l. a road to Clonakilty crosses the Bandon, soon passing the ruins of *Ballynacarrig Castle* (the Hamlet by the Rock), a fortress built by the McCarthys to command the pass. "It is a lofty square pile of building, the walls of which are 6 ft. in thickness; a spiral stone staircase leads to the battlements. The upper apartment is lighted by circular arched windows, with mouldings enriched with curious devices and various scriptural emblems, among which is our Saviour on the cross between 2 thieves. There are also the initials 'R.M.—C.C., 1585,' commemorating Randal McCarthy and his wife

Catherine Collins. Below this apartment is a lofty vaulted hall, which from the brackets and small windows still remaining is supposed to have been originally divided into 3 different stories."—*Lewis*.]

The country, which has been hitherto undulating, becomes wilder and more mountainous at *Dunmanway* (*Inn:* Wagner's), 37 m. which is on the slopes of the shoulders thrown out to the S. by the Sheehy Mountains. The Bandon here makes a turn from the N., Dunmanway itself being situated on an affluent formed by 2 streams dignified with the names of The Brewery and the Dirty River. Immediately at the back of the town is Gunery Hill and Yew-tree Rock, 1032 ft., the Bandon taking its rise in the elevated moors between the latter and the Sheehy Hills. There are 2 roads from Dunmanway to Bantry, and it is hard to say which is most hilly and dreary; the one usually taken is to the S., following up the stream of the Brewery, and then crossing the hills to 45 m. the village of Drimoleague, soon after which the Ilen, which joins the sea near Skibbereen, is crossed. If the traveller takes the N. road, he will pass the ruins of Castle Donovan, a solitary and rude fortress-tower of the O'Donovan family.

57 m. Bantry. [If the tourist is not tied to time, he will find a more interesting though considerably longer route to Bantry, by coasting it to Timoleague, Clonakilty, and Skibbereen. A pleasant road runs S. from Bandon up the little valley of the Bridewell, giving off rt. at Old Chapel, 1 m., a direct road to Clonakilty. Mayfield on rt. is the seat of T. Poole, Esq.]

At the mouth of the Arjideen river, 8 m., is *Timoleague* ('Ty-Mologua, "The House of St. Mologua"), celebrated for its Franciscan Abbey, founded in the commencement of the 14th cent. by the McCarthys. It consists of a nave, choir, and S. transept, with a singular light square tower rising between the 2 former to a height of 68 ft. This tower, together with the library and dormitories, was an addition of the Bishop of Ross in the 16th century.

On the S. of the nave and the W. of the transept is a graceful open arcade, "supported by 7 irregular arches resting on cylindrical and square pillars without capitals."

The nave is lighted by pointed, square-headed, and ogee windows; the E. window and the one in the transept are of 3 lights (E. Eng.), while the W. window is of 2 lights.

To the E. of the transept are the remains of an oratory; there are also portions of the domestic offices. The situation of the abbey is charming, as the sea washes its very walls, running up an inlet from the bay of Courtmacsherry. A convenient circumstance was this for the friars, who were thus enabled to receive at their doors many a cargo of Spanish wine. Adjoining the village are Timoleague House and Ummera. 2½ m. to the S.E. is the pretty village of Courtmacsherry, principally inhabited by fishermen, on the S. side of the inlet.

To the N. of the road between Timoleague and Clonakilty is the ch. of Kilmaloda, which has been well restored by Mr. Bence Jones, a gentleman residing near Clonakilty.

14 m. *Clonakilty* (*Inn:* Donovan's; bad) will not detain the tourist long. It is rather pleasantly situated at the head of an inlet of the sea, which, however, is very detrimental to the trade of the town, owing to its tendency to silt up, and thus prevent any but small vessels from approaching the harbour.

The Earl of Shannon built a Linen Hall and tried to establish a trade, but it did not answer. The archæologist will find a good many ruins in the neighbourhood, although none of them are of importance or offer any very interesting features. They consist of a ch. on the island of

Inchdoney, a castle at Arundel on the E. coast of the inlet; also at Dunnycove, Dunowen, and Dundeady on Galley Head. The last 3 are about 8 m. to the S. of Clonakilty. There is also a stone circle 1 m. N. of the town.

Conveyances.—Car to Bandon.
Distances.—Bandon, 14 m.; Timoleague, 6; Rosscarbery, 8½; Galley Head, 9; Skibbereen, 20.

The scenery improves considerably in the neighbourhood of

22½ m. *Rosscarbery,* the termination of Carbery being added to distinguish it from Ross in co. Waterford. It is a charmingly situated little town at the head of a pill running up from Rosscarbery Bay, part of which is crossed by a long causeway road from the E. shore. Looking N. are the woods of Cahermore (T. Hungerford, Esq.) In the 6th cent. St. Faughnan, otherwise called Mongach, or "the hairy," founded a monastery and religious school, the nucleus of the present diocese of Ross, associated in jurisdiction with Cloyne and Cork. The cathedral (also the parish ch.) is a Perp. cruciform building, with an octagonal spire rising from the tower. There is a circular-headed S. doorway, and a W. window of 3 lights, and the nave is separated from the choir by a screen. At the W. end, in the interior, is a circular-headed arch, the crown of which is ornamented with a head.

To the S. of the cathedral are the remains of St. Faughnan's ch., of which very little is left but the walls of the choir.

1 m. to the E. is Templefaughtna, the ruins of an old establishment of the Knights Templars. It is a pretty walk to the Bay of Rosscarbery, the shores of which are adorned by the grounds of Creggane (R. Starkie, Esq.) and Castle Freke (the beautiful estate of Lord Carbery). On the W. coast of the inlet is Downeen (Rev. J. Smyth), a modern residence, together with the tower of the old castle.

Adjoining the town on the upper road to Leap is Derry, the seat of H. Townsend, Esq. The lower one crosses the Roury river, passing J. Roury House, and Coppinger's Court, a ruined mansion of that family, who flourished in the time of Elizabeth.

The head of another estuary is crossed at

27 m. *Leap,* a picturesque village, where the Leap river flows through a deep ravine that, in the days of bad roads and facility of getting into debt, provoked the saying, "To live beyond the Leap was to live beyond the Law." Both these reproaches are now remedied, and the Leap is spanned by a good bridge. On the opposite bank of the estuary of Glandore are Brade House (T. Swanton, Esq.) and Myross (S. Townsend, Esq.), the woods of which add much to the beauty of the scene. Lower down is the village of Unionhall, from whence there is a ferry to the opposite village of Glandore.

[About 7 m. to the S. of Leap is Castle Haven, another of these numerous inlets, along the W. shores of which are the village and woods of Castle Townsend (Rev. M. Townsend). The views from the bay and cliffs are extremely fine, commanding Toe Head and the whole line of coast from Galley Head to Cape Clear.] Passing a series of freshwater ponds, called the Shepperton Lakes, and well stocked with trout, the traveller reaches

33 m. *Skibbereen* (*Inns:* Commercial; Becher's Arms) is a town of some importance in this district, as it is the largest in the S.W. corner of Ireland, and does a fair business in grain and agricultural produce, though to English cars it is principally associated with distress, this locality having suffered to a fearful extent in the famine year. It is situated some distance up the Ilen, which is navigable for small vessels to the town, and for larger ones as far as

Old Court, some 3 m. down. The town itself does not contain much worth seeing, though the Roman Catholic chapel is a pretentious Grecian building. [A very pretty trip can be made along the E. bank of the Ilen to the little port of Baltimore, passing Old Court and Creagh (Sir H. Becher, Bart.), off which is the island of Inchbeg.

8 m. *Baltimore* is finely situated on the E. coast of the Bay of the same name, which is sheltered on the W. by the island of Sherkin : a rock overlooking the pier is crowned with the ruins of the castle. From its accessibility and its convenience as a harbour of refuge, it was always the resort of a number of foreign fishermen, so much so that Edward VI. had it in contemplation to build a fort and make them pay tribute. The 2 great events of the town were its surrender to the Spaniards by Sir Fireen O'Driscoll in 1662, and its subsequent capture by the Algerines, who carried off 200 prisoners to Algiers. The principal interest lies in the pound, approached by a steep flight of steps, up and down which the wretched animal has to be conveyed.

The whole of this coast is indented and irregular in the highest degree, and offers to the pedestrian some fine cliff scenery. On the return to Skibbereen a détour to the E. should be made to visit Lough Hyne, a sort of cul-de-sac of the sea, which can only enter in by a very narrow passage, just wide enough for a boat, causing at high water an extraordinary commotion. In the centre of the Lough is an islet with a ruined tower on it; and on the W. bank is a cottage ornée,. built by Sir H. Becher. The scenery at the head, underneath the cliff and head of Knockomagh, is particularly romantic.]

Conveyance.—Car to Bandon.

Distances.—Bandon, 34 m. ; Cork, 54; Rosscarbery, 11½; Clonakilty, 20; Baltimore, 8 ; Bantry, by Drimoleague, 20 ; Dunmanway, 16 ; Ballydehob, 10 ; Roaring Water, 7 ; Skull, 14 ; Lough Hyne, 4.

Excursions.—
1. Skull.
2. Leap.
3. Lough Hyne.
4. Baltimore.

The usual route followed to Bantry pursues the valley of the Ilen, passing l. Hollybrook, the seat of J. Becher, Esq., and Mount Music. At Drimoleague it joins the direct road from Bandon.

[The traveller, with whom time is no object, and does not mind roughing it a bit, should continue round the coast by the Crookhaven road, that leaves Skibbereen along the rt. bank of the Ilen, parting company with it at Newcourt (L. Fleming, Esq.) To the rt. of the road a wild range of hills comprise the district of West Carbery, forming a sort of backbone to the long, jutting promontory, which, with many others, characterise this S.W. coast. The scenery is romantic at Roaring Water, 7 m., where a mountain river rushes impetuously through a deep glen, into the bay of the same name. A second inlet runs up to Ballydehob, 10 m., in the neighbourhood of which copper-mines have been worked.

The Bay of Roaring Water is of considerable extent, and contains some rather large islands—the most important, and the farthest out at sea, being familiar to every schoolboy under the name of Cape Clear.

Clear Island is nearly 2 m. in length by ¾ m. in breadth, and contains a coastguard station, a lighthouse which shows a revolving light, and a telegraph which effects a saving of some six hours in the transmission of American news.]

14 m. *Skull* (*Inn:* Prince of Wales) is a little village at the head of Skull Harbour, at the foot of Mount Gabriel, which rises to the height of 1339 ft. The parish is of enormous

size, and externally is wild and desolate. Copper, however, has been largely found and extensively worked, principally at Cappagh, overlooking the coast between Ballydehob and Skull, and also at Horse Island. There is another mine immediately opposite Skull, near the ruined Castle of Ardentenant, a fortress of the sept of Mahony.

Close to the village is Ardmanagh House. The Ultima Thule of civilization will be found at 26 m. *Crookhaven*, a considerable village partly on the mainland and partly on a long peninsula adjoining it, the intervening water forming the haven.

The ch. was built by the Bishop of Cork, in 1701, for the accommodation of the sailors visiting the port, of which, in times of war especially, there used to be considerable numbers. The promontories at the termination of this district are Brow Head, Mizen Head, and Three Castles. The tourist, however, can cut across from Crookhaven and coast up Dunmanus Bay to Dunmanus, where there is another ruined keep of the Mahonys, and again a third higher up at Dunbeacon. On the opposite shores, which are bold and picturesque, are the pretty sequestered residences of Evanson's Cove R. Evanson, Esq., and Donovan's Cove T. O'Donovan, Esq.). Near the village of Carrig Boy, at the head of the Bay of Dunmanus, are Blair's Cove and Ardogeena (R. T. Evanson, Esq.

Bantry (Hotels: Vickary's; Lannin's, has attained an historical notoriety from its position at the head of Bantry Bay, a position which the French have twice singled out as the most fit for their schemes of invasion. The first occasion was in 1689, when a French fleet was engaged by Admiral Herbert, in which the former appear to have had somewhat the best of it; and the second was in 1796, when a fleet with 15,000 men appeared in the Bay, with the intention of landing. Fortunately, however, a severe storm dispersed it b. fore the mischief was done. It is a small and poor town, "in a small valley encircled by lofty mountains, which, attracting the clouds in their passage over the Atlantic, involve it in almost continuous rain." Adjoining the town is Bantry House, the seat of the Earl of Bantry; and opposite it is Whiddy Island, once a forest, but now converted into farms. It is defended by 3 redoubts, and contains near the northern one the ruins of a fortress of the O'Sullivans. There are also fine views of the opposite coast of Bearhaven, to which, if the weather is fine, it is the best plan to proceed by water, as thus there is a saving of 13 m.

Conveyances.—Coach daily in the season to Glengarriff, Kenmare, and Killarney; daily to Dunmanway and Bandon.

Distances.—Cork, 57 m.; Bandon, 37; Dunmanway, 20; Skibbereen, by Drimoleague, 20; Crookhaven, 22; Skull, 15; Castleton Bearhaven (by water), about 20; Glengarriff, 10; Kenmare, 27; Gougane Barra, 16; Macroom, 34.

Excursions.—
1. Pass of Keimaneigh.
2. Gougane Barra.
3. Crookhaven.
4. Glengarriff.

The chief beauty of the southern route to Killarney may be said to commence at Bantry, the road following the N.E. bend of the bay, passing l. Newtown House, and soon afterwards crossing the Mealagh, which, in its fall over a ledge of rocks, produces a charming little cascade. On l. is Dunnamark House, and on rt., up the valley of the Mealagh, Drombrow and Inchiclogh. 60½ m., at Ballylickey House (A. Hutchins, Esq. the Owvane is crossed, and the road falls in from Gougane Barra and the Pass of Keimaneigh Rte. 37. On the bank of the Owvane, at Carrignoss, is a ruined tower, built by O'Sullivan, and defended against the forces of Elizabeth. At 61¼ m. the Coomhola is crossed. This is a very considerable stream, running from the mountains parallel with the Owvane, and rising about 7 m. to the N. in Lough Nambrackderg, a beautiful mountain tarn, surrounded on all sides by the lofty precipices of Kinkeen, 1666 ft., similar to, only on a smaller scale than Gougane Barra. The recesses of these hills can be explored by following the road up the valley of the Coomhola. A little further on are the beautiful grounds of Ardnagashel (S. Hutchins, Esq.), and soon the attention of the traveller is entirely occupied by the exquisite views of

Glengarriff, "The Rough Glen," 67 m., the brightest and most beautiful spot in Co. Cork. Glengarriff is the name of a harbour which runs in with a singularly indented coast outline from the N.W. head of Bantry Bay. The great charm of the place is the beautiful framework of mountains in which the picture is set, and the foreground of woods that surround the eastern portion of the harbour and the course of the Glengarriff. "Were such a bay lying upon English shores, it would be a world's wonder. Perhaps if it were on the Mediterranean or the Baltic, English travellers would flock to it by hundreds. Why not come and see it in Ireland? The best view of this exquisite scene— the charm of a soft climate enhancing every other—is obtained from the height of the hilly road leading to Killarney, and at the foot of which is a pretty cottage, preferred as a residence for many years by Lord Bantry to the stately mansion at Bantry. This cottage is placed on an island formed by a mountain stream, the approach to which is by a bridge made from the mainmast of a French ship of the line, one of the invading fleet of 1796." —*Thackeray.*

Roche's Royal Hotel, and Eccles' Hotel, are both tolerable; the latter rather the best; and the tourist cannot do better than stay a day or two to explore the beauties of the neighbourhood. Writers and travellers of all classes have united in singing the praises of this delightful bay, which is in truth a perfect Paradise, the only drawback to which is, that it puts one out of conceit with the rest of the country.

The view from the hotel of the almost landlocked bay, with its many islands, the grounds and woods of Glengarriff Castle (R. H. White, Esq.) on the l., and the coast towards Bearhaven on the rt., is in itself an inducement that very few hotels can offer. The principal objects of interest are the grounds of Glengarriff, together with the adjoining property of George P. White, Esq., through which run charming walks and drives; Cromwell's Bridge, on the old Bearhaven road, a ruinous old bridge said to have been built by Cromwell at an hour's notice; the ascent of Cobdhuv, 1244 ft., at the back of Glengarriff Castle; and an exploration of the Caher Mountains, a most picturesque range that intervenes between Bantry and Kenmare Bays. The Glengarriff river rises amidst a number of small tarns on the E. side of the Eagle's Nest, 2005 ft. They are all full of trout, and the angler will obtain good sport, particularly in the Bantry Lake, a rather large tarn, under Crossterry Mountain, 1130 ft., sending off a tributary to the Glengarriff. The geologist will find some splendid sections at the head of Bantry Bay of the Glengarriff grits (or upper cornstones), overlaid by the Dingle beds and red sandstones of the conglomerate series, passing up from them into the carboniferous slates.

[An excursion should also be made to Castleton Bearhaven, 22 m., in which the tourist will obtain many beautiful mountain and sea views.

The road keeps the W. coast of the bay, skirting the foot of the Caher ranges to 12 m. Adrigoole Harbour, a picturesque little inlet situated at the base of Hungry Hill, the highest point of the Caher mountains, 2251 ft. "It is from the precipitous acclivities of Hungry Hill that the Adrigoole stream is thrown over a ledge of rocks 700 ft. in height, and which is the finest mountain cataract in the kingdom: particularly after rains, when the river is swollen, the effect is sublime. From its breadth and elevation, the fall can often be distinguished at Bantry, a distance of 11 miles."—*Fraser.* The ranges of the Caher mountains now give place to the Slieve Miskish, the slopes of which run down to the end of the promontory of Dursey Head.

22 m. *Castleton Barharen* (*Inn*: Harrington's, comfortable) has grown to its present importance principally since the discovery of the Bearhaven copper-mines at Allihies.

Opposite the town, and separated by the Bear Haven, is Bear Island, a rocky island of some 6 m. in length, which is still nominally kept up in a state of defence by the Government. There are several redoubts, looked after by a sergeant and a few men under him.

A road runs from Castletown right across the promontory, passing Dunboy Castle (H. Puxley, Esq.), to the mines, which are 7 m. distant. "In the space of 3 or 4 m. are several veins, most of which run E. and W., and dip to the N. Some of them were found on trial unproductive, and were abandoned: but 2 veins, one called the Mountain, being situated 450 ft. above the level of the sea, and the other the Camniche vein, which runs N.E., have furnished the principal workings. Of the former the yield is about 200 tons a month, of about 10 per cent. produce. The Camniche vein has been very productive: the ore is cleaner than in the Mountain vein, and the breadth of the lode is from 1 to 12 ft."—*Kane.*

About 1000 people are employed at these mines, which are worked by 5 steam-engines, and the produce of which is shipped to Swansea. The tourist can either return to Glengarriff by the same road, or else cut across the promontory, and reach Kenmare by a road along the S. side of Kenmare Bay by Kilmichelogue Harbour. If time permit this route is well worth following. The views about Kilmichelogue and Derreen are most lovely.] The drive from Glengarriff to Kenmare is very fine. The road winds up the valley of the Glengarriff for a little distance, passing Glengarriff Lodge, and then strikes up into the mountains, crossing immediately under Turner's Rock, 1393 ft., by a tunnel. It then crosses the Sheen river, and descends its valley, passing altogether through 3 tunnels, 45 ft., 84 ft., and 600 ft. in length. The views, both amongst the mountains and on the descent, are of the most beautiful description.

The Kenmare river is crossed by a suspension bridge of 410 ft. in length, and the tourist arrives at

84 m. *Kenmare* (*Hotel:* Lansdowne Arms), Rte. 35, in which the remainder of the route to Killarney is described.

ROUTE 37.

FROM CORK TO BANTRY, VIÂ MACROOM.

Cork is one of the most inconsistent cities in Ireland,—a mixture of noble streets and broad quays, with the very dirtiest of ill-paved lanes, the whole being set off by a charming frame of scenery that compensates. for many a defect. *Hotels:* Imperial, first-class; Victoria, pretty good. Good lodgings at Tanner's, confectioner, Grand Parade. Pop. 80,121.

The earliest notices of the city date from the times of St. Nessan and St. Finbar, who flourished about the 6th cent. Then the Danes, after repeatedly plundering it, took a fancy to settling down here themselves, and carried on a somewhat flourishing commerce until the Anglo-Norm. invasion. At that time the ruling power was in the hands of Dermot McCarthy, Prince of Desmond, who promptly made submission to Henry II. on his arrival in 1172, and did him homage. Cork took an active part in the disturbed history of the middle ages, at which time it was described by Camden as "a little trading town of great resort, but so beset by rebellious neighbours as to require as constant a watch as if continually besieged." Its most noticeable event was the siege by William III.'s army under Marlborough and the Duke of Wurtemburg, when the garrison surrendered after holding out 5 days.

Cork is well situated on the Lee—

"The spreading Lee, that, like an island fayre,
Encloseth Corke with his divided floode"—
FAERY QUEENE—

as it emerges from a wooded and romantic valley upon a considerable extent of flat alluvial ground, in its course over which it divides. The island thus formed commences about 1 m. above the town, is enclosed by the N. and S. channels of the river, and contains the greater portion of the city.

The N. or principal channel is crossed by the Northgate and St. Patrick's Bridges: the latter, which connects the principal thoroughfares of the town, is a fine limestone bridge of 3 elliptic arches, surmounted by a balustrade. Crossing the S. channel are Clarke's, Southgate, Parliament, and Anglesey Bridges. The banks of both channels are lined with quays, which are more extensive in Cork than any other city except Dublin. The streets offer remarkable contrasts: some of them, as the Mall and the Grand Parade, are broad and well built, while the generality are irregular, narrow, and unclean. The city is badly off for public ground, although it possesses a flat melancholy-looking park running parallel with the Lee, and offering very little inducement for a promenade, save the pretty view of the opposite bank. There is, however, near the W. entrance of the town, and between the 2 banks of the river, a very charming walk called the Mardyke, of about a mile in length, well sheltered by trees, which form a natural arch overhead, and which, when the lamps are lit at night, present an agreeable and foreign appearance. But the suburbs of Cork are so pleasant that the want of a good park is not much felt. In the unprepossessing S.W. district of the town was the old cathedral of St. Finbar, small and very unlike what a cathedral should be. With the exception of the tower, which was believed to have formed part of the old ch., it was a modern Doric building, with a stumpy spire of white limestone. The mode in which the funds were raised for its erection is singular, viz. by levying a tax on all the coal imported for 5 years. Near it is the episcopal palace and a cemetery, in which, according to the Litany of St. Ængus Killideus, written in the 9th cent., 17 bishops and 700 holy people lie interred with St. Nessan and St. Bar. A new cathedral is just approaching completion, from designs by Mr. Burgess, who, having but a small sum of money at his disposal, has been at present obliged to dispense with the towers. The arrangement in the ch. is that of nave, aisles, and transept, together with an apsidal choir and ambulatory, and will when finished have an exceedingly good effect.

St. Anne's Shandon Ch. is remarkable for its extraordinary many-storied tower 120 ft. high, faced on 2 sides with red stone, and on the others with limestone.

There is a very pretty Dec. Presbyterian ch. on the N. side of the river, near the rly. stat.; also a R. C. chapel, with a singular cupola, the corners of which are supported by statues; and a Perp. chapel in good taste, opposite George's Quay.

The Queen's College is charmingly situated at the W. of the town on an elevation overlooking the Lee, and is a really fine Tudor building, characterized by Lord Macaulay "as worthy to stand in the High street of Oxford." It is built of carboniferous limestone, and occupies 3 sides of a triangle, having the lecture-rooms on the W., the residences on the E., and the hall and library on the N. This, in common with Belfast and Galway, is one of the Queen's Colleges founded under an act passed in 1845, and consists of a president, vice-president, and 20 professors. From the opening in 1849 up to 1860, 536 students had matriculated.

The Court-house, situate in George's st., possesses a remarkably beautiful portico, "worthy of Palladio," consisting of 8 columns supporting an entablature and cornice, with a group representing Justice between Law and Mercy.

Among the remaining public buildings are the Mansion House near the Mardyke, the Cork Institution, Library, Club-house, the Lunatic Asylum; on the N. side of the Lee the Barracks, Custom-house, &c. Attached to the Imperial Hotel are the City Rooms, to which all visitors staying at the hotel are admitted.

Cork has always held a high position in her contributors to the fine arts and literature, amongst whom may be mentioned Sheridan Knowles, Dr. Maginn, Haynes Bayley, Crofton Croker, and Hogan the sculptor. A very large trade is carried on, chiefly in provisions, grain, and butter, which are exported to Bristo and the Welsh ports, principally in return for coal. In the year 1859 a total of 4410 vessels entered and cleared out from the port, the value of the exports in butter alone being upwards of 101,000*l*. The portion of the harbour from the city to Passage has been considerably deepened, so that vessels of 600 tons can unload at the quay, where there is a depth of 7 ft. of water at low tide.

Conveyances. — By rail per Gt. Southern and West Rly. to Dublin; rail to Youghal and Queenstown; rail to Passage; rail to Bandon and Kinsale. (The stations of the 2 former lines are near each other on the N. side of the river above Penrose Quay, the 2 latter on the S. side.) Car to Dungarvan daily. Steamers to Queenstown several times a day; also to Aghada, Crosshaven, and Ballinacurra; to Bristol and London twice a week; to Cardiff and Newport alternate weeks; to Waterford, Liverpool, and Glasgow weekly; to London weekly.

Distances.—Dublin, 166 m.; Waterford, 113 by rail; Limerick, 62; Youghal, 21; Queenstown, 10; Blackrock, 2; Passage, 6; Middleton, 6; Blarney, 5; Mallow, 20; Macroom, 23; Gougane Barra, 41; Kinsale, 24; Bandon, 20; Bristol, 262; Liverpool, 283; Plymouth, 275.

The tourist has plenty of choice of excursions offering from Cork. 1. To Blarney (Rte. 25,: to Youghal (Rte. 28,; to Queenstown by river, returning by rail. Steamers leave the moorings at St. Patrick's Bridge 9 or 10 times a day, doing the distance in about an hour, and calling at Passage. As far as Blackrock the river runs in a straight course, passing on l. the Great Southern and Western Rly. terminus, and the steam-packet offices on Penrose Quay. The high banks on this side, at the foot of which run the Glanmire road and the Youghal Rly., are charmingly wooded, and ornamented with pleasant villas, the most important betwen Cork and Glanmire being Tivoli (M. Cagney, Esq.), Fort William, Lotamore (Lieut.-Col. Beamish), Lota House (G. A. Wood, Esq.).

On the S. side the elevation is not so great, nor are the banks so close to the water, a large flat area intervening, dignified by the name of the Park. The Cork and Passage line is a conspicuous feature here. The principal residences are Clifton (J. Murphy, Esq.), Sans Souci, Temple Hill (W. J. Hoare, Esq.), and Dundanion (lately occupied by Sir Thomas Deane.)

3 m. l. the Glashaboy river enters the Lee, amidst pretty groves and parks running up to the suburban villages of Glanmire and Riverstown. Nearly opposite this embouchure is *Blackrock Castle*, a very prominent feature in all the river views. It is a modern castellated building, placed at the end of a jutting promontory, and consists of a circular battlemented tower with a smaller turret, in which a light is burnt for the convenience of shipping. In the old castle, which was destroyed by fire in 1727, courts of Admiralty were held to preserve the rights of the Corporation. On l. again are the woods of Dunkettle (J. Morris, Esq.), North Esk, and Inchera House, the latter situated on the Little Island, a considerable tract separated from the mainland by a narrow tidal stream; while overlooking all these places is the Mathew Tower, a round tower erected by Mr. Connor to the memory of Father Mathew, of temperance celebrity. It is well worth making a pedestrian excursion from Cork through Glanmire for the sake of the noble panorama of the Queenstown river.

As the Lee turns round the corner at Blackrock the shores sweep away on either side, enclosing a magnificent sheet of water known as Lough Mahon. On l., at the S. bank of Little Island, there is a beautiful pass up one of the branches, separating it from Foaty Island, the extremity of which is crossed by the Queenstown Rly.

6 m. rt. Passage West, a pretty village embosomed in woods, and a considerable place of call both for tourists and others bound up and down the river. It is busy and prosperous, and boasts a large private dock and timber-yard, the property of Mr. Brown—

"The town of Passage is both large and spacious,
  And situate upon the say;
'Tis nate and dacent, and quite adjacent
  To come from Cork on a summer's day.
There you may slip and take a dip in
  Forenint the shipping that at anchor ride,
Or in a wherry cross o'er the ferry
  To Carrigaloe on the other side."
      LOVER'S IRISH LYRICS.

Passing the Turkish Baths and the water establishment of Carrigmahon, the next point of interest is

8 m. rt. *Monkstown*, situated amongst thick woods at the mouth of one of the small pills that run into the main estuary. Its principal object of interest is the castle, a quadrangular building flanked by square towers, built in 1636 at the cost of a groat. "Mrs. Anastasia Archdeckan, while her husband was absent in a foreign land, determined to afford him an agreeable surprise by presenting him, on his return, with a castle of her own erection. Having engaged workmen, she made an agreement with them that they should purchase food and clothing solely from herself. The thrifty lady then laid in a good store of these necessaries, charging the workmen a commission on the sales. When the edifice was completed, on balancing her amount of

receipts and expenditure, she found that the latter exceeded the former by 4 pence."—*Cody.* Probably this is the first example on record of truck practice on a large scale.

The steamer now rounds the point, and enters the magnificent harbour of Queenstown, in former days known as the Cove of Cork. "The harbour of Cork, pre-eminent for its capacity and safety, is situate 11 m. below the city; it is 3 m. long, 2 broad, completely landlocked, and capable of sheltering the whole British navy. Its entrance is by a channel 2 m. long and 1 broad, defended by batteries on each side, and by others in the interior."—*Thom.* The channel just mentioned is between Rock's Point and Ram's Head, both headlands being guarded by a fort, on the former that of Carlisle, and on the latter that of Camden.

10 m. *Queenstown (Hotel:* Queen's, an excellent establishment) extends for some considerable distance along the N. coast of the harbour, and, from the improvements that have taken place within the last few years, is likely to rank high amongst the southern watering-places. To the W. of the town a splendid promenade is furnished by the quay erected in 1848 by Lord Middleton. The great charm of Queenstown is the noble scenery of the harbour, with its islands of Hawlbowline and Spike, and the constant succession of shipping that is provided by the arrivals and departures of the American steamers and emigrant-ships. It is also a celebrated locality for regattas. Immediately opposite the town are—Hawlbowline Island, depôt for ordnance and victualling stores; Rocky Island, on which there are a magazine and barracks; and Spike Island, which contains the Westmoreland Fort and the convict prison, numbering about 800 inmates, who are chiefly employed in the fortifications. The forts at the entrance to the channel until lately have been only nominally kept up, but are now being restored to their original defensive state.

A little to the N. of Ram's Head is the fishing village of Crosshaven at the mouth of the Owenboy, which runs inland in a considerable stream as far as *Carrigaline,* picturesquely situated on high ground overlooking the river. The ancient fortress had the reputation during the whole of Elizabeth's reign of being impregnable. The ch. is a fine Perp. building, with a pinnacled tower and an octagonal spire rising from it. It contains the monument and leaden effigy of Lady Newenham, who died 1754. In the neighbourhood of the village are Kilmoney Abbey (M. Roberts, Esq.), and Mount Rivers (Capt. Roberts); and between it and Crosshaven, on the N. bank, is Coolmore (Rev. E. H. Newenham, and on the S. Aghamarta (Standish O'Grady, Esq., and Hoddersfield. In the grounds of the former is the ruined castle of Aghamarta, a fortress of the Earls of Desmond, overlooking a reach of the river in which Sir Francis Drake once took shelter when hard pressed by some Spanish vessels.

On the eastern promontory (opposite to Queenstown are the villages of Whitegate and Aghada, adjoining which are Careystown (W. Hickson, Esq., Hadwill Lodge (Rev. R. Austin, Aghada House (Sir J. Thackwell, Rostellan Castle formerly a seat of the Lords of Thomond), in the grounds of which is a cromlech within high-water mark. To the S., near Roche's Point, familiar to the readers of telegrams from America, are Trabolgan (Lord Fermoy), and Roche's Mount (Miss Roche. [Aghada is the nearest place from whence to visit the ancient cathedral town of

Cloyne, 6 m. distant, which is associated with Cork in its bishopric. The cathedral, also used as the parish ch., is a plain cruciform building, dating from about the commencement of the 14th cent. In the interior are monuments to Bishops Warburton and Woodward, and one to the memory of a Miss Adams with an inscription from the pen of Mrs. Piozzi. In the ch. are remains of a stone house, which tradition says was built by St. Colman, the founder of the abbey, in the 7th cent.

The most interesting building in Cloyne is the round tower adjoining the W. door of the cathedral. The entire height is 102 ft., though from this amount 10 ft. must be deducted for its modern castellated top, which was added after a considerable rent had been produced by lightning, and for the protection of the cathedral bell, which hung in the upper stage. The tower is remarkably cylindrical, and divided into 5 stages or floors. The door is about 13 ft. from the ground.]

[From Aghada the steamers continue their course up a wooded and picturesque creek of the river to Ballinacurra (Rte. 28), from whence the tourist can walk or procure a car to Middleton 1 m., and return to Cork by rly.*].

The road from Cork to Macroom leaves the western portion of the town, keeping on l. the college and gaol, and on rt. the Mardyke wall, Shanakiel House (F. R. Leahy, Esq.), the Lunatic Asylum, and Mount Desert (Nich. Dunscombe, Esq.), on the high bank overlooking the Lee.

4 m., at the junction of the Blarney river, is the restored castle of Carrigrohane, which, after serving as the feudal fortress of the McCarthies, and subsequently of the Barretts, was the head-quarters of Capt. Cope and daring band of brigands. From this point a road is given off to Macroom along the S. bank of the Lee, passing through Ballincollig.

At Carrigrohane the river is

* The line between Cork and Macroom has just been opened.

crossed just below the bend, where there is the deep pool of Poul-an-Iffrin, fabled to be guarded by a gigantic snake. On the opposite side of the Aunbeg or Blarney river are Rosanna (Capt. Webb), Kitsborough, and Leemont (S. Coppinger, Esq.) at the foot of a picturesque wooded hill.

The road now keeps close to the river, having on the opposite bank the artillery barracks and the gunpowder mills of Ballincollig, to 7 m. l. Inishcarra Ch., founded by S. Senan, situated at the confluence of the Bride, soon after which is the Glebe House, and 8½ m. rt. Ardrum, the beautiful seat of Sir G. Colthurst, Bart.

The scenery at Inishcarra, and from thence to Ardrum, is some of the most delightful that is to be found on the Lee. The square keep of Castle Inch is on the opposite bank; and further on are the remains of the ch. of Inishleena, or Inishluinga, founded by the same holy man that built Inishcarra. The road now quits the Lee for a space, and runs up the valley of the Dripsey river to 13 m. the village of Dripsey. The antiquary will find in this locality an Ogham stone near St. Olave's Well.

The tourist is now fairly in the district of Muskerry, whose mountains, giving birth to the Lee and many smaller southern streams, appear to the W. Running parallel, but at some distance to the S. of the road hitherto traversed from Cork, are the Clara Hills, separating the valley of the Lee from that of the Bandon. In the neighbourhood of Inchigeelah, however, they gradually trend to the N., and unite with the main ranges of Muskerry.

15 m. Coachford village, and on l. Riversdale, and Leemount House (T. H. Broderick, Esq.). The road then crosses the Glashagariff stream, and passes rt. Oakgrove, to Carrigadrohid, where the Lee is spanned by a bridge. In the middle

of the river is a rock crowned with the ruin of Carrigadrohid Castle, and a most picturesque appearance it has, reminding the tourist of some of the castles of the Rhine or Moselle. "Its site is said to have been chosen by the lovely Una O'Carroll, to gratify whose caprice her lover Diarmid M'Carthy raised the castle in a marvellously brief time on the cliff she had chosen, where they both lived happily after their nuptials." Carrigadrohid was besieged in 1650 by Lord Broghill, who had captured the Bishop of Ross at Macroom, and promised him a pardon on the condition of his persuading the garrison to give in. The bishop consented; but, on being brought before the walls, fervently exhorted them to hold out, for which patriotic act he was then and there hung. Indeed, it was only by stratagem that the English got hold of it at all, viz. by drawing some heavy timber up, which the garrison took for cannon, and so surrendered. There is an entrance to the castle from the bridge which, by the way, was built by Cromwell's order; hence the name Rock of the Bridge. On the opposite side of the stream are Killinandrish (J. Hassett, Esq., and Nettleville (R. Nettles, Esq.).

The Lee now winds to the S., and the road cuts off a great round, passing through Glencaum, one of the most romantic and striking glens in the district.

At 22 m. a small river called the Laney joins the Sullane, and near the confluence is the solitary tower of Mashanaglass Castle, built by Owen MacSwiney, otherwise called "Hoggy of Mashanaglass."

23 m. Macroom.

The 2nd route on the S. bank of the Lee passes through Ballincollig, the powder-mills of which lie at a safe distance between the village and the river. A little distance to the S. is Ballincollig Castle, surrounded by a "bawn." This was a fortress of the Barretts, temp. Edward III. Passing Lisheen House (R. Donovan, Esq.), and crossing the Bride, is the village of Ovens, in the neighbourhood of which are a number of remarkable caves, but little known and seldom visited.

[At Elm Park a détour of a mile should be made to the l. to visit the abbey ruins of *Kilcrea*, very prettily situated at the end of an avenue of trees on the banks of the Bride, towards which the Clara Hills gradually slope down. It is a Franciscan Friary of the 15th century, founded by Cormac McCarthy Laidin, Lord of Muskerry, and consists of nave, choir, and transepts, with a tower 80 ft. high rising from the junction of the 2 former. Separated from the nave by 3 pointed arches is a side aisle, which was divided in the same manner from the transept. There is very little ornamental detail, the mullions of the windows having been destroyed, according to tradition, by Cromwell and his soldiers. The interior contains the vault of the McCarthys of Muskerry; also in the S. trans. the tomb of Herlihy, Bishop of Ross, one of the 3 Irish bishops who attended the Council of Trent. A little to the W. of the abbey is the keep of Kilcrea Castle, where the McCarthys held their rule. The traces of the bawn and outworks are still visible.]

The road now passes Fanan Lodge, Rye Court (Capt. Rye), near which are the keep of Castlemore Castle, Crookstown, Kilcondry, and Lissardagh (W. Baldwin, Esq.), and leaving Warren's Court Sir A. Warren, Bart. to the l., striking on the Lee a little below the confluence of the Sullane.

21 m. Coolcour House (W. Browne, Esq. .

23 m. *Macroom (Hotel:* Queen's Arms) is prettily situated in the valley of the Sullane, an affluent of the Lee, which rises some 10 m. to

the W. in the Derrynasaggart Mountains, a range that intervenes between this district and the Paps of Killarney. The town itself possesses no very great object of interest except the castle, a quadrangular keep, said to have been erected in the reign of King John. It has now been modernized, and is the residence of the Hon. W. Hedges. It was the scene of several sieges in the 17th cent., when it was burnt down no less than 4 times. During one of these struggles it was garrisoned by the Bishop of Ross, the same who was hanged by Lord Broghill before the walls of Carrigadrohid. Admiral Penn, the father of the Pennsylvanian hero, is said to have been born within Macroom Castle. The R. C. chapel, from its situation on an eminence to the S. of the town, is a conspicuous feature. Amongst the seats in the neighbourhood are Mount Hedges (Col. Hon. W. Hedges), Rockborough (H. Browne, Esq.), Raleigh House (E. J. Leahy, Esq.), Ashgrove (T. Leader, Esq.), and Codrum (A. Orpen, Esq.), all in the valley of the Sullane, and near the road to Killarney.

Distances. — Killarney, by Kenmare, 50 m.; Cork, 23; Bantry, 34; Keimaneigh, 18; Inchageelah, 9; Gougane Barra, 19; Kenmare, 31; Carrigaphuca, 3.

Excursions. —
1. Inchageelah.
2. Carrigaphuca.
3. Dripsey.
4. Kilcrea.

[The direct road from Macroom to Killarney follows up the valley of the Sullane, keeping the Boggeragh Mountains to the rt., and passing 3 m. near the confluence of the Finnow, the square keep of Carrigaphuca Castle, another of the many fortresses of the McCarthys. At 13 m. the village of Ballyvourney, the road strikes right into the heart of the Derrynasaggart Mountains, about 1500 ft. in height, and then descends somewhat into the valley of the Flesk, which it crosses at Poulgorm Bridge. From this point the tourist keeps company with the Flesk, which, as seen in Rte. 31, leaves the hills through a gap between the Paps and Croghan.] The remainder of the distance from Macroom to Bantry 34 m. is through some of the finest and wildest scenery in the S. of Ireland, and care should be taken that the car and horse be good, as there is little chance of a relay anywhere on the road, which leaves the valley of the Sullane, and rejoins the Lee at Toom Bridge, from whence a visit can be paid to the tower of Dundareirke Castle. The Lee has quite a different character here from what it has lower down, as it flows for a considerable distance through a morass, the effect of which is to divert its stream and form a number of sedgy islets.

A little before arriving at 32 m. the village of Inchageelah, is on l. the tower of Carrynacurra, or Castle Masters, rising upon a finely escarped cliff above the river. It belonged in the times of the "troubles of '41" to the O'Learys, a sept only second to the McCarthys, to whom, indeed, they were subject. Inchageelah (*Inn*: Brophy's; a good locality for the angler) is situated near the E. end of Lough Allua, a winding enlargement of the Lee, of about 3 m. in length, along the northern shore of which the Bantry road keeps to the village of Bealnageary. At the W. end of Lough Allua is a mountain with the sad though poetic name of Coolnegreenane, "the mountain unknown to the sunbeam." To the S. of Lough Allua are the Sheehy Hills, 1796 ft., which intervene between the valley of the Lee and the Bandon at Dunmanway.

½ m. from Bealnageary, where the small and picturesque stream of the Bunsheelin flows in, the Lee is crossed by the 1st bridge on its course, and the mountains which encircle the mystic lake of Gougane Barra begin to show their precipitous and gully-riven sides. At 41 m. rt. a short road leads to the lake from whence the Lee has its source. Gougane Barra, "the Gurgling Head," is a small and deep tarn, almost entirely surrounded by mural precipices, save on the E. side, where a narrow outlet permits the infant Lee to emerge.

The cliffs on either side rise directly from the banks of the lake, casting deep shadows over its waters, and adding greatly to the solemnity with which the locality is invested from its association with the holy St. Finbar, who built on the island an oratory still held in great veneration. The origin of his retreat here was as follows: "St. Patrick, after banishing the reptiles out of the country, overlooked one hideous monster, a winged dragon, which desolated the adjacent country, and power was conferred on a holy man, named Fineen Bar, to drown the monster in Gougane Lake, on condition of erecting a ch. where its waters met the tide; and the saint, having exterminated the monster, fulfilled the agreement by founding the present cathedral of Cork." The buildings on the island are rude and primitive, and consist of some cells, together with a portion of the chapel and oratory, the former being about 36 ft. long by 14 broad. On a causeway at the S. of the lake is a small cemetery, held in great repute from its close companionship with the remains of the saint. Immediately above Gougane Barra the mountains rise up to a height of 1700 or 1800 ft., the principal summits being Conicar, 1886 ft., and Foilastookeen, on the S.; Nadan-viller, "the Eagle's Nest," on the W.; from any one of which is a magnificent view of the Killarney Mountains to the N., Bantry Bay and Glengarriff to the S.W., with the sterner features of the Pass of Keimaneigh and the lake close at hand. Turning suddenly to the S., the road enters a magnificent gap in the Sheehy Mountains, known as the Pass of Keimaneigh, "the Path of the Deer"—

"Where the severed rocks resemble fragments of a frozen sea,
And the wild deer flee"—M'CARTHY—

one of the finest and most savage of the ravines in the S. of Ireland. It is about 1 m. in length, and is bounded on each side by precipitous walls of rock, in the rifts and crevices of which ferns, heaths, and wild flowers find a congenial home. The London Pride is peculiarly abundant and fine in this locality.

At the head of the pass, between Conicar rt. and Doughill l., is the watershed of the streams running N. to the valley of the Lee, and those, like the Owvane, which flow to the sea at Bantry Bay.

Down this valley it is a rapid descent, during which many beautiful views of the bay open out. At Ballylickey, where the Owvane enters the sea, the Glengarriff road is joined, and from thence it is 3¼ m. to Bantry (Rte. 36).

INDEX.

INDEX.

ABBEYFEALE.

A.

Abbeyfeale, 302.
Abbeylara, 147.
Abbey Knockmoy, 314.
Abbey Morne, 161, 238.
Abbeyside, 261.
Achill Head, 195.
—— I., 195.
—— Sound, 195.
Adare, 297; abbeys, 298.
Adragoole, 189.
Adrigoole, Waterf., 339.
Affane, 267.
Aghada, 343.
Aghadoe, 283.
Aghamarta C., 343.
Agriculture of Ireland, xxxvi.
Ahadoe, 265.
Aherlow, 273.
Allihies Mines, 339.
Anagarry, 90.
Anaghmore, 64.
Anascaul, 305.
Angitham, 173.
Anglo-Norman remains, lii.
Annaduff, 155.
Annaghdown, 181.
Annalong, 41.
Annamoe, 213, 218.
Antiquities, xlvi; table of, liii.
Antrim, 104.
Aragtin R., 270.
Aran I., 91, 170.
Ard C., 180.
Ardbo, 104.
Ards H., 97.
Ardanaine, 202.
Ardara, 93.
Ardee, 30.
Ardfert, 306.
Ardfinane, 274.
Ardglass, 43.
Ardmayle, 270.
Ardmore, 262.
Arringlass C., 169.
Artknown, 51.
Ardpatrick, 336.

[Ireland.]

BALDANGAN.

Ardrahan, 314.
Ardsollus, 310.
Arklow, 202.
Arkyne, C., 171.
Armagh, history and situation, 150; cathedral, antiquities, 151; manufacture, 152.
Armer's Hole, 41.
Armoy, 113.
Arrigal Mount, 89.
Artane, 19.
Artramon C., 205.
Ashford, 212.
Ashlee, 191.
Askeaton, 299.
Asselyn, 157.
Assey C., 136.
Athassel, 273.
Athboy, 146.
Athcarne C., 142.
Athclare, 30.
Athenry, 128, 314.
Athgor, 220.
Athlone, 124; siege, 124; barracks, railway bridge, 125.
—— to Limerick, 317.
—— to Roscommon, 158.
Athlumney C., 136.
Athy, 239.
Avoca, 202.
Avonmore, 215.
Auburn, 126.
Audley, C., 44.
Aughagower, 187.
Aughnanure C., 176.
Aughrim, 127.
—— R., 214.
Awbeg R., 269.
Ayle R., 187.

B.

Bagenalstown, 243.
Baily Lighthouse, 20.
Balbriggan, 24.
Baldangan C., 24.

BALLYLICKEY.

Baldoyle, 19.
Balla, 198.
Ballina, 161.
Ballinacurra, 265.
Ballinafad, 157.
Ballinamallard, 62.
Ballinasloe, 126.
Ballincollig, 345.
Ballinderry, 124.
Ballindrait, 86.
Ballinglen, 162.
Ballinhassig, 331.
Ballinrobe, 185.
Ballinspittle, 332.
Ballintobber A., 186.
Ballintogher, 158.
Ballintoy, 110.
Ballintra, 77.
Ballitore, 241.
Ballybay, 55.
Ballybeg, 144.
Ballyboley, 80.
Ballybogan, 131.
Ballybrittas, 225.
Ballybrophy, 227.
Ballybunion, 302.
Ballycanew, 203.
Ballycarbery, 326.
Ballycarry, 117.
Ballycastle, 111, 162.
Ballyconnell, 98.
Ballycorus, 201.
Ballycroy, 194.
Ballycuirke, lake, 175.
Ballydehob, 336.
Ballyduff, 269, 302.
Ballygalley Head, 115.
Ballygannon, 201.
Ballygarth, 25.
Ballygawley, 61.
Ballyglunin, 314.
Ballyhale, 252.
Ballyhalse, 149.
Ballyhinch, 248.
Ballyhooly, 269.
Ballyjamesduff, 147.
Ballykeeran, 126.
Ballykelly, 99.
Ballylickey, 347.

B

BALLYLIFFIN.

Ballyliffin, 69.
Ballyloughan C., 243.
Ballymahon, 126.
Ballymena, 102.
Ballymoe, 160.
Ballymoney, 102.
Ballymoon C., 243.
Ballymore Eustace, 221.
Ballymote, 158.
Ballymurry, 159.
Ballymurtagh, 214.
Ballynacarrig C., 333.
Ballynahatna, 31.
Ballynahinch, 46, 179.
Ballynakill, 188.
Ballynatray, 266.
Ballyneen, 333.
Ballyportry C., 313.
Ballysadare, 158.
Ballyshannon, 76.
Ballytrent, 207.
Ballyvourney, 346.
Ballyvoy, 114.
Ballywillan, 147.
Ballywilliam, 255.
Balrothery, 24.
Baltimore, 316.
Banagher, 100, 320.
Banbridge, 35.
Bandon, 331.
Bancecloon, 324.
Bangor, 54.
Bann R., 35, 102, 203.
Bannow, 260.
Bansha, 273.
Banteer, 278.
Bantry, 337.
Bargy, 207.
Barna, 170.
Barnageera, 24.
Barnesmore Gap, 79.
Baronstown, 137.
Barrow R., 224, 242, 250.
Bautregarm Mount, 303.
Beagh, 296.
Bealderrig, 162.
Bealnabrack R., 190.
Bealnageary, 346.
Bear I., 339.
Dearhaven coppermines, 339.
Beaufort Br., 284.
Beauparc, 143.
Bective, 134.
Beechmount, 332.
Belcoo, 61.
Belfast, 47; trade, harbour, bridges, buildings, 48; churches, flax-mills, steamers, 49.
—— to Donaghadee, 47.
Bellarena, 101.
Belleek, 59.
Belmullet, 163.
Beltany, 86.
Beltoy, 116.

BURTON.

Beltrim C., 65.
Belturbet, 149.
Ben-aghlan Mount, 60.
Benbulben, 74.
Benburb C., 64.
Bengorm Mount, 190.
Benlevy Mount, 184.
Benlettery Mount, 178.
Bennett's Bridge, 248.
Benyevenagh, 101.
Beragh, 63.
Betaghstown, 25.
Bilboa, 242.
Binghamstown, 163.
Birchfield, 312.
Birr, 252.
Bishop's I., 301.
Blackrock C., 342.
Blackwater R., 64, 143, 185, 238, 266, 330.
Blackwatertown, 64.
Blanchardstown, 119.
Blarney, 238.
Blasket I., 304.
Bloody Bridge, 41.
Bog of Allen, 225.
Bober, 272.
Bonamargy A., 111.
Bonet R., 61, 73.
Borris, 243.
B. in Ossory, 251.
Borrisoleigh, 228.
Bovevagh, 100.
Boyle, 156.
Boyne R., 130.
—— battle of, 141.
Brandon Hill, 250, 256.
—— Mount, 303.
Bray, 209.
Brey Head, 327.
Brinny, 332.
Brittas C., 228.
Britway, 268.
Broadstone, 102.
Brookeborough, 57.
Bromsford, 250.
Brosna, 252.
Brown's Bay, 116.
Bruce's Cast., 112.
Bruckless, 82.
Bruff, 236.
Brugh-na-boinne, 138.
Bruree, 297.
Bryansford, 42.
Bullock's C., 207.
Bunahurra, 195.
Buncrana, 69.
Bundoran, 75.
Bunduff Bridge, 75.
Bunlin Br., 95.
Bunnabeola, 178.
Bunratty, 310.
Burial I., 53.
Burrishoole, 194.
Burton Port, 91.

CARTON.

Bushmills, 107.
Butler's Bridge, 149.
Butler's C., 272.
Butler's Lodge, 177.
Buttevant, 237.

C.

Cabinteely, 200.
Caherconlish, 272.
Caherdaniel, 329.
Cahir, 273.
Cahirbarnagh, 279.
Cahirciveen, 326.
Caledon, 150.
Callan, 247.
Camaross Hill, 254.
Camolin, 203.
Cannistown, 136.
Cappanalaura, 177.
Cappoquin, 267.
Carberry, 129.
Carhan, 326.
Carlingford, 39; castle and oysters, 39.
—— Mount, 40.
Carlow, 241.
Carncastle, 115.
Carn Cochy, 35.
Carndonagh, 69.
Carndoo, 116.
Carney, 74.
Carngaver H., 52.
Carnlough, 115.
Carnowry Gap, 101.
Carra Bridge, 325.
Carrabeg, 325.
Carrantuohill, 291.
Carrick, 83.
—— Hill, 130.
Carrickabraby C., 69.
Carrickarede, 110.
Carrickbroad river, 32.
Carrickburn, 254.
Carrickfergus, 117.
Carrickhugh, 99.
Carrickmacross, 55.
Carrickmines, 200.
Carrickmore, 63.
Carrick-on-Shannon, 155.
Carrick-on-Suir, 276.
Carrig-a-drohid C., 345.
Carrig-a-gunnel C., 300.
Carrigaline, 343.
Carriganoss, 337.
Carrigans, 65.
Carrig-a-phuca C., 346.
Carrigboy, 337.
Carrighooley, 194.
Carrigmahon, 342.
Carrig-na-Nahin, 236.
Carrigrohane C., 344.
Carrigtuohill, 265.
Carrowkeel, 70.
Carton, 122.

INDEX. 351

CASHEL.

Cashel, history, 230; cathedral, 231; Grey Abbey, 232; Priory, 233.
Cashla B., 170.
Castles, lii.
Castlebar, 198.
Castlebasset, 238.
Castlebellingham, 30.
Castle Bernard, 333.
Castleblayney, 55.
Castlebridge, 203.
Castle Caulfield, 63.
Castlecomer, 242.
Castle Connell, 324.
Castle Coole, 57.
Castle Coote, 160.
Castle Dawson, 103.
Castlederg, 65.
Castledermot, 241.
Castledexter, 137.
Castle Dillon, 152.
Castle Donovan, 334.
Castlefinn, 80.
Castle Gregory, 303.
Castle Howard, 213.
Castle Inch, 344.
Castle Island, 295.
Castleknock, 119.
Castlemaine, 325.
Castlemartyr, 265.
Castle Masters, 346.
Castle Oliver Mountains, 256.
Castle Pollard, 153.
Castlereagh, 50, 160.
Castleton, 227.
Castleton Bearhaven, 339.
Castletown H., 31, 120.
Castletown, 124.
Castletown Roche, 269.
Castletownsend, 335.
Castlewellan, 42.
Castle Widenham, 269.
Castleyard, 272.
Cavan, 148.
Cave Hill, 49.
Ceaun Gubba, 116.
Cecilstown, 278.
Celbridge, 121, 220.
Chair of Kildare, 224.
Chapel Izod, 16, 220.
Charlemont, 64.
Charleville, 236.
Cheek Point, 259.
Churches, Irish, li.
Church Hill, 59.
Church I., 73, 327.
Churchtown, 259, 324.
Claelagh river, 60.
Clady 80; Bridge, 99.
Clady Church, 135.
Clandeboye, 54.
Clane, 221.
Clanruddery Mountains, 302.
Clara, 226.
—— Bridge, 215.

COPPINGER'S.

Clare A., 311.
—— C., 311.
Claregalway, 181.
Clare Island, 192, 197.
Clashmore, 267.
Classylaun, 75.
Claven's Bridge, 146.
Clear I., 336.
Clew B., 192.
Clifden, 187.
—— to Sligo, 187.
Cliffony, 75.
Clobemon, 203.
Clogh-a-Stucan, 114.
Clogheen, 271.
Clogher, 62.
Clogher Head, 30.
Cloghreen, 289.
Cloghrenan, 242.
Clonakilty, 334.
Clonard, 131.
Clones, 56.
Cloncoskoran, 261.
Cloncurry, 122.
Clondalkin, 17, 220.
Clonfert, 320.
Clongowes, 221.
Clonmacnois, 317; seven churches, 317; round towers, 318; crosses, inscribed stones, castle, geology, 319.
Cloumel, 275.
Clonmines, 260.
Clonsilla, 119.
Clontarf, 17.
Clough, 43.
Cloughmore, 40.
Cloyne, 343.
Clydagh H., 174.
Coachford, 344.
Colebrooke, 57.
Coleraine, 101.
—— to Belfast, 106.
Colin Glen, 50.
Colligan, 262.
Collooney, 158.
Comber, 51.
Commeragh Mountains, 261.
Cong, 182; archæological remains, caverns, 183; canal, 184.
Confey C., 120.
Conna, 268.
Connemara, 170.
Connor Mnts., 304.
Convoy, 86.
Cookstown, 103.
Coolmore, 77.
Coolnamuck, 276.
Coolnegreenane, 346.
Coomhola R., 338.
Coothill, 55.
Copper Mines, 214.
Coppinger's Court, 335.

DEERANE.

Corcomroe Abbey, 314.
Cores Cascade, 291.
Cork, 339; history, situation, description, cathedrals, 340; buildings, trade, excursions, 341.
—— to Kenmare, 331.
—— to Bantry, 339.
Corrigan Head, 83.
Corrofin, 313.
Cottage Isl., 73.
Courtmacsherry, 334.
Courtown H., 202.
Cove, 329.
Craigmore, 33.
Cratloe, 310.
Creeslough, 97.
Cregg, 312.
—— C., 181.
Cregganroe, 194.
Crevelea, 73.
Croagh Patrick, 192.
Croghan, 131, 160, 196.
Croghan Kinshela, 214.
Crom Castle, 56.
Cromlechs, xlvi.
Cromwell's Bridge, 338.
Crookhaven, 337.
Croom, 297.
Crossbarry, 331.
Crossdoney, 148.
Crosses, lii.
Crossgar, 46.
Crosshaven, 343.
Crosshill, 111.
Crossmaglen, 53.
Crossmolina, 199.
Crown Bridge, 34.
Croy Lodge, 194.
Crumlin, 16.
Crusheen, 313.
Cuilcagh, 60.
Culdaff, 70.
Culloville, 55.
Culmore, 99.
Cultra, 54.
Cummeenduff, 282, 285.
Curlew Hills, 157.
Curragh, 227.
Curragh Chase, 298.
Curraghmore, 277.
Curraun, 115, 195.
Cushendall, 114.
Cushendun, 114.

D.

Dalkey I., 208.
Dane's Cast., 35.
Dangan C., 134, 312.
Danganstown C., 202.
Dargle, 210.
Dartrey, 55.
Deel R., 86, 199, 296.
Deerane, 160.

r 2

DELGANY.

Delgany, 201, 212.
Delphi, 191.
Deputy's Pass, 202.
Deraddla, 179.
Derricunihy cascade, 291.
Derry, 65.
Derrybawn, 215.
Derrycarne, 155.
Derryclare, 178.
Derrycorrib, 163.
Derryloran, 104.
Derrynasaggart Mountains, 279, 346.
Derrynane, 329.
Derryveagh, 88.
Devenish I., 58.
Devil's Bit, 227.
Devil's Glen, 213.
Dhuega, 197.
Diamond Hill, 189.
Dingle, 304.
—— Bay, 325.
—— Promontory, 303.
Dinish I., 287.
Doagh, 95.
Dodder R., 200.
Doe C., 97.
Donabate, 23.
Donaghadee, 54.
Donaghmore, 63, 80, 137.
Donaghpatrick, 144.
Donegal, 78; castle and abbey, 78.
Doneraile, 237.
Donnybrook, 16.
Donore, 132, 140.
Doocharry Br., 91.
Dooega, 196.
Doogurth, 196.
Doohulla, 180.
Doolin, 312.
Doon, 188, 302.
—— Point, 112.
Douce Mount, 211.
Down Hill, 101.
Downpatrick, 45.
—— Rath of, 46.
Dowth, 140.
Drimnagh C., 16.
Drimoleague, 334.
Dripsey, 344.
Drishane C., 279.
Drogheda, town and harbour, 25; commerce, walls and gates, abbeys, 26; history, excursions, 27.
—— to Cavan, 142.
Dromahaire, 73.
Dromana, 267.
Dromaneen, 278.
Dromiskin, 30.
Dromkeen, 272.
Dromore, 37, 62, 199, 330.
Drowes river, 75.
Druib Mor, 37.

DUNGLOW.

Drumbanagher, 34.
Drumbo, 50.
Drumcliff, 74.
Drumlish, 155.
Drumman Bridge, 87.
Drumnasole, 114.
Drummail, 114.
Drumod, 155.
Drumsisk, 40.
Drumsna, 155.
Dubh Cabir, 171.
—— Cathair, 172.
DUBLIN: situation, 3; hotels, street conveyances, 4; bridges, 4, 5; quays, 5; docks, canals, railway stations, Bank of Ireland, 6; Post-office, Custom-house, Exchange, 7; Four Courts, Castle, 8; Trinity College, 9; Library and Museum, 10; Roman Catholic University, statues, 10; Royal Dublin Society, Royal Irish Academy, Museum of Irish Industry, Irish National Gallery, St. Patrick's Library, Christ Church Cathedral, 11; St. Patrick's Cathedral, 12; churches, R. C. chapels, 14; Phœnix Park, 14; Zoological Gardens, Rotunda, other Institutions, 15; suburbs, 16; conveyances, history, 18.
—— to Arklow, 207.
—— to Carlow, 239.
—— to Cork, 219.
—— to Dundalk, 19.
—— to Wexford, 199.
Duff river, 75.
Duleek, 142.
Duna, 195.
Dunally, 69.
Dunamon, 160.
Dunamase, 226.
Dunass Head, 69.
Dunbrody, 256.
Duncannon, 259.
Duncarbry, 75.
Dun Connor, 173.
Duncrue, 118.
Dundalk, 30.
—— to Belfast, 30.
—— to Galway, 119.
—— to Sligo, 54.
Dundarave, 107.
Dundareirke C., 346.
Dundonald, 51.
Dundrum, 43, 200, 233.
Dunfanaghy, 97.
Dungannon, 63.
Dungarvan, 261.
Dungiven, 100.
Dunglow, 91.

FARRENMACWILLIAM.

Dunkincely, 82.
Dunkitt, 250, 277.
Dunleer, 30.
Dunlewy, 89.
Dunloe, 284.
Dunloy, 102.
Dunluce, 107.
Dunmanway, 334.
Dunmoe, 137.
Dunmore, 143, 247, 260, 316.
Dunmurry, 38.
Dun-na-gedh, 140.
Dun-Ængus, 172.
Dun-Onaght, 172.
Dunran Glen, 212.
Dunree Head, 69.
Dunseverick, 110.
Dunsink Observatory, 17.
Dusoin Glen, 265.
Dysart, 297.
Dysert, 313.

E.

Eagle's Nest, 286.
Easky R., 199.
Eden, 117.
Edenderry, 129.
—— to Drogheda, 129.
Edgeworthstown, 154.
Eglinton, 99.
Elphin, 316.
Ely Lodge, 59.
Emania, 151.
Emly, 234.
Emo, 224.
Enfield, 122.
Ennis, 311.
Enniscorthy, 204.
Enniskeen, 333.
Enniskerry, 211.
Enniskillen, 57.
—— to Derby, 61.
—— to Killybegs, 80.
Ennistymon, 312.
Erne R., 57, 76.
Errew, 199.
Erris, 162.
Errislannin, 189.
Errive R., 191.
Esk Valley, 79.
Eyrecourt, 254.

F.

Fahan, 304.
Fairhead, 111, 113.
Fairy Water Bridge, 64.
Falcarragh, 98.
Fanet Head, 95.
Farranfore, 295.
Farrenmacwilliam, 325.

INDEX.

FASSAROE.

Fassaroe, 210.
Faughalstown, 153.
Faughart, 31.
Feltrim, 22.
Fennor, 138.
Fergus R., 296, 311.
Fermoy, 269.
Ferns, 203.
Fernsborough, 147.
Fernslock, 122.
Ferritor's Cove, 304.
Ferrybank, 257.
Fethard, 276.
Fiddown, 277.
Finglas, 17.
Finn R., 65.
—— Valley, 80.
Finn's Fingerstone, 41.
Fintona, 62.
Fintown, 80.
Fintragh, 83.
Firmount, 154.
Five Mile Town, 62.
Flax, cultivation of, xxxiv.
Flesk C., 279.
Florence Court, 50.
Flynn's, 177.
Fore, 153.
Forth barony and mountains, 206, 254.
Fort Stewart, 94.
Foxford, 161.
Foyle R., 65.
Foynes, 196, 299.
Frenchpark, 316.
Freshford, 251.
Furbo, 170.

G.

Galbally, 234.
Galty Mountains, 233, 273.
Gallerus' Orat., 305.
Galway, history, 164; situation and description, 165; antiquities, church of St. Nicholas, 166; buildings, harbour, 167; fishery, 168; suburbs, 169.
—— to Clifden, 164.
—— to Westport, 180.
Galway's Ford, 291.
Gap of Dunloe, 284.
Garbally, 127.
Garnish, 330.
Garrison, 59, 76.
Garromin, 177.
Garron Tower, 114.
Gasabo Hill, 277.
Greshill, 225.
Geology of Ireland, xxiv.
Giant's Causeway, 108.
—— Ring, 51.
Gifford, 35.

GREENCASTLE.

Glanleam, 327.
Glanworth, 270.
Glanmire, 342.
Glasnevin, 17.
Glassan, 126.
Glasslough, 149.
Glen of the Downs, 212.
Glena, 287.
Glen-a-Cappul, 290.
Glenaghaun, 173.
Glenalla Mountains, 83.
Glenariff, 114.
Glenarm, 115.
Glenbay, 325.
Glencaum, 345.
Glencar, 74.
Glencastle, 163.
Glencolumb, 84.
Glendalough, domain of, 177.
—— vale of, 215.
—— city, its founder, 216; cathedral, church of Our Lady, Round Tower, St. Kevin's Cell, 216; Trinity church, the monastery, church of Reefert, 217.
Glendasan, 215.
Glendowan, 88.
Glendruid, 200.
Glendun R., 114.
Glenealy, 202.
Glenfarn, 61.
Glengard Head, 69.
Glengariff, 338.
Glengeask, 93.
Glen Lough, 96.
Glenmore, 257.
Glenoe, 116.
Glensheskin R., 111.
Glenties, 92.
Glin C., 299.
Glossary of Irish words, lxix.
Glyde R., 30.
Glynn, 116.
Gobbins, 116.
Gobhan's C., 111, 113.
Gold Mines, 214.
—— R., 214.
Goold's Cross, 230.
Goragh Wood, 33.
Gorey, 202.
Gormanstown, 25.
Gort, 313.
Gortin, 65.
Gorumna Island, 170.
Gougane Barra, 347.
Gowran, 244.
Grace Hill, 102.
Gragtic, 242.
Graiguenamagh, 256.
Granard, 148.
Grand Canal, 220.
Grange, 76.
Great Connell Priory, 222.
Greencastle, 41, 70, 106.

INISHBOFIN.

Greenore, 40.
Grenan C., 248.
Grey Abbey, 52, 232.
Greystones, 201.
Grianan, 68.
Groomsport, 54.
Guns I., 44.
Gurteen, 276.
Gweebarra R., 91.
Gweedore, 89.

H.

Hag's Castle, 175.
—— Glen, 292.
Handcross, 312.
Hare I., 126.
Hawlbowline I., 343.
Hazelhatch, 220.
Hazelwood, 72.
Headford, 181.
—— C., 181.
Headfort, 146, 279.
Hearnesbrook, 254.
Hen's Castle, 184.
High I., 188.
Hill, Lord George, his improvements at Gweedore, 89.
Hill of Down, 122.
Hillsborough, 37.
Hilltown, 41.
Hollybrook, 212.
Hollymount, 186.
Hollywood, 51.
Holycross, 228.
Holyhead to Kingstown and Dublin, 2.
Hook Pt., 259.
Hospital, 274.
Horse's Discovery, 184.
Howth, 19; Harbour, Abbey, Castle, 20.
—— Hill, 21.
Hy Brisail, 197.

I.

Iar Connaught, 170, 175.
Illanmore, I., 321.
Inokilly C., 265.
Inch C., 46, 249.
Inchageela, 346.
Inch-a-goill, 175.
Inchicore, 220.
Inchmore, 247.
Inchiquin, 313.
Industrial resources of Ireland, xxxiv.
Inishannon, 333.
Inishark, 189.
Inishbofin, 189.

INISHCARRA.

Inishcarra, 344.
Inisheer, 173.
Inishfallen, 288.
Inishgloria, 197.
Inishkeel, 92.
Inishleena, 344.
Inishmaan, 173, 186.
Inishmacsaint, 76.
Inishmurray, 75.
Inishowen, 68.
Inishtrahull, 69.
Iniskeen, 55, 197.
Inniscalthra, 322.
Innistiogue, 250.
Inver, 82.
Ireland's Eye, 21.
Isl. Magee, 117.

J.

Jamestown, 155.
Jenkinstown, 247.
Jerpoint, 249.
Johnstown, 206, 251.
Jonesborough, 32.

K.

Kanturk, 278.
Keady, 152.
Keel, 196.
Keem, 196.
Keeper Mountain, 323.
Keimaneigh, 347.
Kells, 144, 247, 326.
Kempe Stones, 51.
Kenbane, 111.
Kenmare, 330.
Kesh, 81.
Kesh Corrin, 157.
Kilbarrock, 19.
Kilbarron C., 77.
Kilberry, 240.
Kilbride, 175.
Kilbroney, 41.
Kilcar, 83.
Kilcarn, 136.
Kilclief C., 44.
Kilcock, 122.
Kilcoleman, 325.
Kilcolgan, 314.
Kilcolman, 238.
Kilcommodon, 127.
Kilconnell, 127.
Kilcoole, 201.
Kilcrea, 345.
Kilcullen, 222.
Kilcummin, 162.
Kildare, 223.
Kildaunat, 197.
Kilfenora, 312.
Kilfinane, 236.
Kilgobbin, 200.

KILSHEELA.

Kilkea, 240.
Kilkee, 301.
Kilkeel, 41.
Kitkelly, 160.
Kilkenny, history, castle, cathedral, 244; monastery, 245; abbey, churches, colleges, 246.
—— to Athenry, 251.
Killadysert, 296.
Killakee, 215.
Killala, 162.
Killaloe, 323.
Killamery, 276.
Killan, 129.
Killarney, hotels, 279; beggars, guides, 280; the Lake, 281; lake islands, 282; excursions, 283-292; geology of the district, 293; botany, 294; fishing, legends, 295.
—— to Kenmare, 324.
Killary, 190.
Killasnet, 75.
Killawillin, 270.
Killeagh, 265.
Killeany, 171.
Killeary, 32.
Killeen, 181.
Killenagh, 203.
Killeshin, 242.
Killester, 19.
Killimor, 254.
Killiney, 208.
Killonan, 272.
Killone, 311.
Killough, 43.
Killoughter, 201.
Killorglin, 324.
Killucan, 122.
Killuspugbrone, 72.
Killybegs, 82.
Killydonnell, 94.
Killygordon, 80.
Killyleagh, 47.
Killyon, 132.
Kilmacduagh, 313.
Kilmacow, 250.
Kilmacrenan, 87.
Kilmacthomas, 261.
Kilmaine, 185.
Kilmalkedar, 305.
Kilmallock, 234.
Kilmaloda, 334.
Kilmore, 148.
Kilmurry, 212.
Kilmurvey, 172.
Kilnaleck, 147.
Kilnasaggart, 32.
Kilree, 248.
Kilronan, 171.
Kilroot, 117.
Kilruddery, 209.
Kilrush, 300.
Kilsheela, 276.

LINFIELD.

Kilteel, 220.
Kilternan, 200.
Kiltinan, 276.
Kiltormer, 254.
Kilturk, 201.
Kilworth, 270.
Kingstown, 2.
Kinlough, 76.
Kinnafad, 130.
Kinneith, 333.
Kinsale, 331.
——, Head of, 332.
Kinsalebeg, 263.
Kippure Mountain, 211.
Kircubbin, 53.
Kish Light, 2.
Knightstown, 326.
Knock, 51, 174.
Knockalla Mountains, 95.
Knockcroghery, 159.
Knockfearina, 299.
Knocklayd, 111.
Knocklong, 234.
Knockmahon mines, 261.
Knocknaa, 315, 316.
Knocknarea, Glen of, 72.
Knocknucean, 25.
Knoctopher, 250.
Knowth, 140.
Kyle Cross Roads, 205.
Kylemore, 189.

L.

Labbalow, 324.
Ladies' I., 207.
Lagan R., 30, 48.
Laghtgeorge, 181.
Laghy, 78.
Lakes of Killarney, 281.
Lambay I., 23.
Landestown C., 23.
Laracor, 134.
Laragh, 124, 218.
Larne, 115.
Laurencetown, 35.
Layton, 25.
Laune R., 284, 324.
Lea C., 226.
Leacht Con, 73.
Leap, 335.
Lee R., 344.
Leenane, 190.
Legmonshena, 61.
Lehinch, 312.
Leighlin Br., 243.
Leinster Br., 131.
Leixlip, 120.
Letterfrack, 189.
Letterkenny, 86.
Lettermore I., 170.
Liffey R., 4, 120, 221, 222.
Lifford, 85.
Linfield, 272.

INDEX. 355

LIMERICK.

Limerick, history, 306; situation, bridges, 307; castle, cathedral, 308; harbour, trade, 309.
—— to Boyle, 306.
—— to Tralee, 295.
—— to Waterford, 271.
—— Junct. 233.
Lisbellaw, 57.
Lisburn, 36.
Liscannor, 312.
Liscarroll, 238.
Liscarton, 143.
Lisfinny, 268.
Lismany, 127.
Lismore, 267.
Lisnacarrick, 81.
Lisnaskea, 56.
Lissadell, 74.
Lissoy, 126.
Lissoughter, 178.
Listowel, 302.
Lohort, 278.
Londonderry, 65: siege, 66: walls, cathedral, bridge, 67; trade, antiquities, 68.
—— to Belfast, 99.
—— to Gweedore, 93.
Longfield, 230.
Longford, 154.
Long Range, 286.
Loop Head, 301.
Loragh, 320.
Lough Agibbon, 87.
—— Agraffard, 177.
—— Allua, 346.
—— Altan, 89, 98.
—— Anure, 91.
—— Arrow, 157.
—— Beg, 103.
—— Birroge, 92.
—— Boderg, 155.
—— Bofin, 155, 177.
—— Bray, 211.
—— brickland, 35.
—— Carra, 186, 325.
—— Conn, 198.
—— Coomshingawn, 261.
—— Cooter, 313.
—— Corrib, 174.
—— Cullen, 198.
—— Curraun, 327.
—— Dan, 219.
—— Deel, 86.
—— Derevaragh, 153.
—— Derg, 81, 317, 321.
—— Doo, 113, 191, 312.
—— Doon, 92.
—— Dunlewy, 89.
—— Easke, 79.
—— Ennell, 121.
—— Erne, 36, 57.
—— Fee, 190.
—— Feeogh, 174.
—— Fern, 87.

MAIDEN.

Lough Finn, 80.
—— Forbes, 155.
—— Foyle, 99
—— Gara, 157.
—— Gartan, 87.
—— Gill, 72.
—— Glen, 89, 96, 154.
—— Glenade, 76.
—— Gowna, 148.
—— Guitane, 291, 295.
—— Gur, 236.
—— Hyne, 336.
—— Inagh, 178.
—— Key, 156.
—— Kilglass, 155.
—— Kiltooris, 92.
—— Lasarac, 315.
—— Looscaunagh, 291.
—— Macnean, 60.
—— Mask, 185.
—— —— Cast., 186.
—— Melvin, 76.
—— more C., 228.
—— Mourne, 79, 116.
—— Muckna, 55.
—— Nafooey, 191.
—— Nambrackderg, 338.
—— Neagh, 105.
—— Owel, 152.
—— Ramor, 147.
—— Rea, 126, 254, 317.
—— rea, 254.
—— ry, 104.
—— Salt, 96.
—— Sheelin, 148.
—— Shinny, 24.
—— Strangford, 52.
—— Swilly, 69, 86.
—— Veagh, 88.
Louisburgh, 194.
Louth, 31.
Lowtherstown Road, 62.
Lucan, 119.
Lugduff, 215.
Luggelaw, 219.
Lugnaquilla, 215.
Lurgan, 36.
Lurgan Green, 30.
Lurganboy, 61, 76.
Lusk, 24.
Lyons C., 220.

M.

MacGilligan Mountain, 101.
MacPhilbin's C., 187.
Macroom, 345.
Mageney, 240.
Magharafelt, 103.
Maghera, 103.
Magheramorne, 117.
Maguire's Br., 57.
Maiden Rocks, 115.
Maiden Tower, 255.

MOUNT.

Maigue R., 296.
Main R., 102.
Malahide, 22; castle, 22; Abbey, 23.
Malin, 69; Head, 69.
Mallnmore, 84.
Mallow, 238, 269.
—— to Killarney, 277.
Mamturk Mountains, 177.
Mangerton, 290.
Manister, 297.
Manor Cunningham, 86.
—— Hamilton, 61.
Marble Arch, 61.
Markree, 158.
Maryborough, 226.
Mashanaglass C., 345.
Mathew Tower, 342.
Maume, 185.
Mayglass, 207.
Maynooth, 121.
Mayo Plains, 198.
Mealagh Falls, 337.
Meelick, 320.
Meigh, 33.
Melliont, 27.
Menlough, 173.
Middleton, 265.
Milford, 87, 95, 243.
Military road, 215.
Millstreet, 279.
Milltown C., 30, 325.
—— Malbay, 311.
Minerals of Ireland, xxxviii.
Minna, 170.
Minnaun, 196.
Mitchelstown, 270.
—— caves, 271.
Moat of Ardscull, 240.
Moate, 124.
Mogeely, 265.
Mohill, 155.
Moher Cliffs, 312.
Moira, 36.
Moista Sound, 162.
Molana Abbey, 266.
Molrenny, 194.
Monaghan, 149.
Monasterboice, 28.
Monasterevan, 224.
Monasteroris, 130.
Monavullagh Mount, 261.
Monea C., 59.
Moneymore, 103.
Monivea, 314.
Monkstown, 3, 342.
Moone, 242.
Moor A., 234.
Moross C., 95.
Montgevlin C., 65.
Mount Anville, 200.
Mount Bellew, 315.
Mount Charles, 82.
Mountgarrett C., 255.
Mount Hillary, 278.

INDEX.

MOUNT.
Mount Leinster, 204.
Mount Melleray, 267.
Mountmellick, 225.
Mountnorris, 34.
Mount Nugent, 148.
Mountrath, 227.
Mount Pleasant, 32.
Mount Shannon, 322.
Mount Stewart, 52.
Mourne R., 65.
Moville, 70.
Moy, 64, 160.
Moycullen, 175.
Moyne C., 182.
—— A., 161.
Moyry, 32.
Moyvalley, 122.
Muckross A., 289.
Muff, 70, 99.
Muilrea, 190.
Mule's Leap, 131.
Mulgrave Barrack, 291.
Mullaghmast, 240.
Mullaghmore, 75.
Mullet, 163.
Mullinavat, 250.
Mullingar, 123.
—— to Portadown, 147.
—— to Sligo, 152.
Mulroy, 95.
Multifarnham, 152.
Mungret, 296.
Murlough B., 113.
Murrisk, 193.
Muskerry, 344.
Mutton Isl., 168.
Mylerstown C., 129.
Myrath, 98.

N.
Naas, 221.
Nagles Mount, 269.
Naran, 92.
Narrow-water C., 38.
Navan, 143.
Nenagh, 323.
Nephin, 193, 198.
Nevinstown, 144.
Newbliss, 56.
Newbridge, 120, 214, 222.
Newcastle, 41, 220, 299.
Newgrange, 139.
New Inn, 147.
Newmarket, 278.
Newmarket Fergus, 310.
Newport, 194.
New Ross, 254.
Newrath Bridge, 212.
Newry, 33.
—— to Belfast, 38.
Newry Canal, 34.
Newton Pery, 307.
Newton Trim, 133.

PORTACLOY.
Newtownards, 52.
Newtownbarry, 203.
Newtownbellew, 315.
Newtownbreda, 50.
Newtownbutler, 56.
Newtowncuningham, 93.
Newtown Forbes, 154.
Newtowngore, 73.
Newtownlimavaddy, 99.
Newtownmountkennedy, 212.
Newtownstewart, 64.
Nier R., 262.
Nine-mile-house, 276.
Ninestones, 204.
Nore R., 247.
Nun's Cross, 213.

O.
Oghill Fort, 172.
Oldbridge, 141.
Old Connaught, 210.
Olderfleet C., 116.
Old Leighlin, 243.
Omagh, 62.
Omeath, 38.
Oola, 272.
Oranmore, 128, 314.
Oratories, xlix.
Oughterarde, 176, 220.
Ovens, 345.
Owencarrow R., 88.
Owenduff R., 189.
Owenea R., 92.
Owengarriff R., 291.
Owentocker R., 93.
Owvane R., 337.

P.
Pallas, 272.
Pallaskenry, 296.
Palmerstown, 16.
Paps, 279.
Parsonstown, 252.
Partry, 186.
Passage, 259.
Passage West, 342.
Patrick's Well, 296.
Pettigoe, 81.
Phillipstown, 226.
Phoul-a-phooca, 221.
Physical geography of Ireland, ix.
Pigeon-holes, 74.
Pilltown, 263, 277.
Places of interest, lviii.
Platten H., 143.
Pleaskin, 110.
Pocket, 330.
Pomeroy, 63.
Pontoon, 198.
Portacloy, 163.

RINDOWN.
Portadown, 36.
Portaferry, 53.
Portarlington, 224.
Porthcoon, 108.
Portlaw, 277.
Portmagee, 327.
Portmarnock, 22.
Portnaspania, 110.
Portnoffer, 109.
Portora, 58.
Portraine, 23.
Portrush, 106.
Portstewart, 106.
Portumna, 320.
Poul-an-iffrin, 344.
Powerscourt, 211.
Poyntz Pass, 35.
Pullins, 77.
Puncheston, 221.

Q.
Queenstown, 343.
Quin, 310.

R.
Raghly, 74.
Raheny, 19.
Rahin, 226.
Rakenny, 56.
Ram I., 105.
Ramsfort, 202.
Randalstown, 102.
Raphoe, 86.
Ratass, 303.
Rathaldron, 144.
Rathcoole, 220.
Rathcormack, 268.
Rathdowney, 251.
Rathdrum, 213.
Rathfarnham, 16, 200.
Rathfran, 162.
Rathkeale, 298.
Rathlin I., 112.
Rathmacknee, 206.
Rathmelton, 93.
Rathmichael, 201.
Rathmines, 16, 200.
Rathmore, 146.
Rathmullan, 94.
Rathowen, 154.
Rattoo, 302.
Ravensdale, 32.
Recess, 177.
Red Bay, 114.
Red Hills, 224.
Red Lion, 61.
Reeks, 293.
Rheban C., 240.
Rhincrew, 266.
Richhill, 152.
Rindown C., 159.

INDEX. 357

RINGMOYLAN.

Ringmoylan, 296.
Rinn R., 155.
Rinvyle, 190.
Riverstown, 342.
Roaring Water, 336.
Roche's Point, 343.
Rockcorry, 55.
Rockingham, 156.
Rock of Doon, 87.
Rocky Hills, 226.
Rocky I., 343.
Roe R., 99.
Roosky, 155.
Rosapenna, 96.
Rosbercon, 257.
Roscommon, 159.
Roscrea, 251.
Roserk A., 161.
Ross C., 289.
—— A., 181.
—— H., 176, 301.
—— Lake, 176.
Rosscarbery, 335.
Rosses, 90.
Rossow R., 194.
Rostrevor, 40.
Roundstone, 180.
Round Towers, origin and uses of, 1.
Round Towers—
—— Aghadoe, 283.
—— Antrim, 104.
—— Aranmore, 171.
—— Ardmore, 263.
—— Clondalkin, 220.
—— Clonmachnois, 318.
—— Dysart, 297.
—— Glendalough, 216.
—— Kells, 145.
—— Kildare, 223.
—— Kilree, 248.
—— Kinneath, 333.
—— Lusk, 24.
—— Monasterboice, 28.
—— Mount Shannon, 322.
—— Rattoo, 302.
—— Roscrea, 252.
—— Swords, 23.
—— Taghadoe, 122.
—— Timahoe, 227.
—— Tory Island, 93.
—— Tullaherin, 248.
—— Turlough, 198.
Round Town, 16.
Roundwood, 218.
Rush, 24.
Rutland I., 91.
Rye Water, 121.

S.

St. Bernard's Well, 140.
St. Doulough's, 22.
Saintfield, 47.

[Ireland.]

SLIEVE.

St. Edmonsbury, 120.
St. Fintan's Church, 21.
St. John's, 43
St. John's Point, 82.
St. Johnstown, 65.
St. Kevin's Bed, 218.
St. Kieran's Well, 146.
St. Macdara's Church, 180.
St. Mullins, 255.
St. Valery, 210.
St. Wulstan's, 120.
Sallagh Braes, 115.
Sallins, 220.
Sally Gap, 219.
Salrock, 190.
Saltees, 207.
Salthill, 3, 169.
Salthole, 117.
Saul, 46.
Scalp, 219.
Scariff, 322.
Scarva, 35.
Scattery I., 300.
Scurloughstown, 134.
Sean Caislean, 173.
Seir Kyran, 253.
Sele R., 147.
Seven Churches, 215, 317.
Seven Hogs, 303.
Shanagolden, 300.
Shane's C., 102.
Shanid C., 300.
Shankhill, 200.
Shannon R., 124, 155, 296, 307, 317, 321; source, 61.
—— Bridge, 319.
—— View, 254.
Sheehy Mountains, 346.
Sheep I., 110.
Sheephaven, 96.
Sheffry, 191.
Shepperton Lakes, 335.
Shelton A., 215.
Shillelagh, 214.
Shimna R., 42.
Shinnagh, 279.
Shinrone, 252.
Shrule, 185.
Silvermine Mountains, 323.
Sion Mills, 65.
Six Mile Bridge, 310.
Six Mile Cross, 63.
Six Mile Water, 105.
Skeleton tours, lxiv.
Skellig Rock, 328.
Skerries, 24.
Skibbereen, 335.
Skreen, 199
—— Hill, 136.
Skull, 336.
Slade, 259.
Slane, 117.
Slaney R., 203.
Slaughterford Bridge, 117.
Slieve Bán, 40.

TEAMPULL.

Slieve Baughta, 321.
Slieve Bernagh, 323.
Slieve Bloom, 226.
Slieve Callane, 311.
Slieve Croob, 47.
Slieve Daeane, 73.
Slieve Donard, 42.
Slievefellm, 272.
Slieveguaven, 41.
Slieve Gullion, 32.
Slieve League, 83.
Slievemore, 196.
Slieve-na-griddle, 46.
Slieve-na-man, 276.
Slieve Russell, 63.
Slieve Snaght, 69, 91.
Sligo, 70; abbey, 71.
—— to Strabane, 70.
Slish Mountain, 73.
Slyne Head, 188.
Smerwick, 304.
Smithborough, 149.
Sneem, 329.
Sperrin Mountains, 100.
Spiddle, 170.
Spike I., 343.
Spire Hill, 225.
Stack Mountains, 302.
Staigue Fort, 329.
Stags, 163.
Stillorgan, 200.
Strabane, 65.
—— to Killybegs, 85.
Stradbally, 227.
Stradone, 147.
Straffan, 220.
Straneally, 267.
Strangford, 44.
Stranorlar, 80.
Streamstown, 124.
Strokestown, 155.
Struel, 46.
Suck R., 160.
Suir R., 274.
Sullivan's Case., 288.
Summerhill, 162.
Sunville, 236.
Sutton, 19.
Swanlinbar, 60.
Swineford, 160.
Swords, 23.
Sydenham, 51.

T.

Taghadoe, 122.
Taghmon, 254.
Tallow, 268.
Tanderagee, 35.
Tanrego, 199.
Tara Hill, 135.
Tarbert, 299.
Taylor, Jeremy, 37.
Teampull Benain, 171.

6

TEAMPULL.

Teampull Brecain, 172.
Teampull Chiarain, 172.
Teampull Deiscart, 263.
Teampull Mic Duach, 172.
Teampull Pholll, 172.
Teelin R., 83.
Telton, 144.
Templecarne, 81.
Templecoran, 117.
Templecrone, 91.
Templefaughtna, 335.
Templegeal, 305.
Temple Lodge, 158.
Temple Michael, 266.
Templemore, 228.
Templenakilla, 328.
Templepatrick, 175.
Termonfeckin, 29.
Termon M'Grath C., 81.
Thomastown, 248.
Three Rocks, 200.
Three Sisters, 304.
Thurles, 228.
Ticroghan, 131.
Timahoe, 227.
Timoleague, 334.
Tinarana, 323.
Tinnahely, 214.
Tinnahinch, 210.
Tintern A., 260.
Tipperary, 272.
Tirraleen, 173.
Toberscanavan, 158.
Tolka R., 19.
Tollymore, 42.
Toome, 103.
Toombeola A., 180.
Torc waterfall, 291.
Tormore, 85.
Tory I., 98.
Tralee, 303.
Tramore, 260.

VALLEY.

Travelling view, xl.
Tray, 151.
Trew, 64.
Trillick, 62.
Trim, 132.
Trimlestown, 132.
Trostran Mount, 114.
Trubley C., 134.
Trumery, 36.
Tuam, 315; cathedral, 315; cross, 316.
Tulla, 322.
Tullaghan, 75.
Tullamore, 225.
Tullaroan, 247.
Tulloherin, 248.
Tully C., 59.
—— Church, 200.
Tumuli, xlvi.
Turlough, 198.
Tuskar R., 207.
Twelve Pins, 178.
Tynan, 150.
Tyrawley, 162.
Tyrone coalfield, 63.
Tyrone H., 314.

U.

Upton C., 105.
Urlingford, 251.
Urris Hills, 69.
Urrisbeg, 180.
Use Mountains, 278.

V.

Vale of Avoca, 213.
Valentia, 326.
Valley of Diamonds, 210.

YOUGHAL.

Vartry, 212, 218.
Ventry, 304.
Victoria Bridge, 65.
Villierstown, 267.
Vinegar Hill, 204.
Virginia, 147.

W.

Waringstown, 36.
Warrenpoint, 38.
Waterfall, 331.
Waterfoot, 14.
Waterford, history and situation, 257; harbour, trade, remains, cathedral, 258; neighbourhood, conveyances, 259.
Waterville, 327.
Westport, 191.
Wexford, 205.
—— to Cork, 254.
White Abbey, 106.
—— Head, 111.
—— River, 30.
—— Rocks, 107.
Whitegate, 343.
Wicklow, 201.
—— tour through, 207.
Wooden Bridge, 214.
Woodford, 321.
Woodlands, 119.
Woodlawn, 127.
Woodstock, 250.

Y.

Yellow river, 130.
Youghal, 264.
—— to Cahir, 266.

THE END.

LONDON: PRINTED BY W. CLOWES AND SONS, STAMFORD STREET,
AND CHARING CROSS.

www.ingramcontent.com/pod-product-compliance
Lightning Source LLC
Chambersburg PA
CBHW020542300426
44111CB00008B/767